THE FABER BOOK OF FOOD

THE FABER BOOK OF

FOOD

EDITED BY
Claire Clifton and Colin Spencer

faber and faber
LONDON · BOSTON

First published in 1993
by Faber and Faber Limited
3 Queen Square London WC1N 3AU
This paperback edition first published in 1996

Photoset by Wilmaset Ltd, Wirral
Printed in England by Clays Ltd, St Ives plc

A CIP record for this book is available from the British Library.

ISBN 0–571–17887–1

2 4 6 8 10 9 7 5 3 1

Contents

Acknowledgements

❦

We would like to express our gratitude for the initial enthusiasm of Roger Osborne and for the patience of our editor, Tracey Scoffield, and to thank all the friends who loaned us books and made suggestions, particularly Martina Nicolls, Barbara Machin, Nina Gatward, Merlin Holland, Jean Stern and James Farrent. Our thanks too to Maureen Howard for hoovering around the books on the floor and Anne Cox for heroic typing.

For permission to reprint copyright material the publishers gratefully acknowledge the following:

Diane Ackerman and Chapmans Publishers Limited for two extracts from *A Natural History of the Senses*; Harold Acton and Artellus for two extracts from *Memoirs of an Aesthete*; Martin Amis and Peters Fraser & Dunlop for an extract from *London Fields*; three extracts from *The Art Of Eating in France* and *The Art of Using Leftovers: Paris, 1850–1900* by Jean Paul Aron in Robert Forster and Orest Ranum, eds., *Food and Drink in History: Selections from The Annales, Economies, Societies, Civilisations*, The Johns Hopkins University Press, Baltimore/London, 1979; J. G. Ballard and Victor Gollancz Limited for an extract from *Empire of the Sun*; *Plain Southern Eating: From the Reminiscences of A. L. Tommie Bass, Herbalist*, edited by John K. Crellin, copyright 1988 Duke University Press, Durham, reprinted with permission of the publishers; Georgina Battiscombe for an extract from *English Picnics*; an extract from *The Glass of Fashion* by Cecil Beaton by permission of his Literary Trustees; Sybille Bedford for an extract from *Jigsaw*; the Estate of Sir John Betjeman for the poem 'How to Get On in Society' from *Collected Poems*; André Deutsch for one extract from *Last Letters* quoted by Olivier Blanc; Lesley Blanch for five extracts from *The Wilder Shores of Love*; The Estate of Caryl Brahams – Ned Sherrin for an extract from *No Bed for Bacon* by Caryl Brahams and S. J. Simon; Charlotte Du Cann for two extracts from *Offal and the New Brutalism*; the Estate of Truman Capote for an extract from *A Christmas Memory*; F. T. Cheng for an extract from *The Musings of a Chinese Gourmet*; the Estate of Colette and

Farrar, Straus & Giroux for an extract from *Letters from Colette*, selected and translated by Robert Phelps; Susan Cooper and the editors Michael Sissons and Philip French for an extract from *The Age of Austerity*; Bruce Cost for an extract from *Ginger East and West*, first published in the *Journal of Gastronomy*; Jeni Couzyn for a poem 'Preparation of Human Pie' from *Life By Drowning: Selected Poems* (Bloodaxe Books, 1985); Graham Payn and Little Brown & Company for five extracts from *The Noël Coward Diaries*, edited by Graham Payn and Sheridan Morley, and a poem from *Not Yet the Dodo*; the Estates of Robert Croft-Cooke and Noel Barber for one extract from *Cities*; Jill Norman and the Elizabeth David Estate for two extracts from *Summer Cooking* and *An Omelette and a Glass of Wine*; Bernard Darwin for an extract from *Receipts And Relishes*, 1950; Alan Davidson for two extracts from *A Kipper with my Tea*; Stephen Dobyns and David Higham Associates for the poem 'Spiritual Chickens' from *Cemetery Nights*; Professor Mary Douglas for two extracts from *In the Active Voice* and one extract from *Implicit Meanings*; J. M. Dent & Sons for an extract from *Siren Land* and an extract from *Alone* by Norman Douglas; Pimlico Press and the Estates of J. C. Drummond and Anne Wilbraham for extracts from *The Englishman's Food*; Ian Duhig and Bloodaxe Books Limited for a poem from *The Bradford Count*; Alexander Dumas for an extract from *Adventures in the Caucausus* translated by A. E. Murch, 1962; Lawrence Durrell and Faber & Faber for an extract from *Bitter Lemons* and an extract from *Reflections on a Marine Venus*; Sheil Land Associates and Alice Thomas Ellis for three extracts from *The 27th Kingdom*, 1982, and two extracts from *The Sin Eater*, 1977; the Estate of George Ewart Evans for an extract from *Ask the Fellows Who Cut the Hay*; *Consuming Passions* by Peter Farb and George Armelagos, Copyright © 1980 by the Estate of Peter Farb, reprinted by permission of Houghton, Mifflin Company, all rights reserved; the Estate of Etheland Fearon and Little Brown for an extract from *Most Happy Husbandman*; Jeannette Ferrary for 'Navettes for Mrs Fisher' first published in the *Journal of Gastronomy*; M. F. K. Fisher for four extracts from *An Alphabet for Gourmets*; the Estate of Theodora Fitzgibbon and David Higham Associates for two extracts from *With Love*; the Estate of C. S. Forester and Peters Fraser & Dunlop for two extracts from *The African Queen*; the Estate of E. M. Forster for an extract from 'We Shall Eat And Drink Again'; John Fuller and Secker & Warburg for the poems 'Black Pudding' and 'Sorrel'; Charles Neilson Gattey for two extracts from *Foie Gras and Trumpets*; Susan George and Penguin Books for an extract from *How the Other Half Dies*; the Estate of André Gide and Martin Secker & Warburg for two extracts from *Fruits of the Earth*; John and Rumer Godden for two extracts from *Two under the Indian Sun*; HarperCollins Publishers and The Estate of W. H. Auden for an extract from *Italian Journey* by J. W. Goethe; Amanda Goodfellow for an extract from *A Household Legacy*; John Murray for three extracts from *Princes of the Black Bone* by Peter Goullart; Patience Gray and Prospect Books for an extract from *Honey From A Weed*; Germaine Greer and Picador for an extract from *The Mad Woman's Underclothes* and an extract from *Sex And Food*; the Joyce Grenfell Estate and Macmillan London for two extracts from *In Pleasant Places*; Barbara Griggs for an extract from *The Food Factor*; Francine du Plessix Grey for an extract from *The Best*; the Estate of Jane Grigson and David Higham Associates for an extract from *Good Things* and an extract from *Exotic Fruits and Vegetables*; Marvin Harris for an extract from *Cannibals and Kings*; the Estate of Dorothy Hartley and Little Brown for an extract from *Food In England*; A & C Black Publishers for an extract from *Kitchen Front Recipes and Hints* by Ambrose Heath; the Estate of Ernest Hemingway for an extract from *Islands in the Stream*; Andrew Higgins for two extracts from an article in the *Independent on Sunday*; Kazuo Ishiguro and Rogers, Coleridge & White for an extract from 'A Family Supper'; Madhur Jaffrey for two extracts from *A Taste of India*; the Estate of Lady Jekyll for an extract from *Kitchen Essays*; Andrew Johnson for an extract from *Factory Farming*; Mireille Johnston for an extract from *Educating a Palate is Educating a Soul*; an excerpt from *I Married Adventure* by Osa Johnson, Copyright 1940 by Osa Johnson, Copyright renewed © 1968 by Mrs Belle Leighty, reprinted by permission of HarperCollins Publishers; Erica Jong for one poem from *Half-Lives* and one poem from *Fruits and Vegetables*; Molly Keane for an extract from *Nursery Cooking* and an extract from *Good Behaviour*; Garrison Keillor for an extract from *Leaving Home* and an extract from *Lake Wobegon Days*; Collins Harvill, an imprint of HarperCollins Publishers Limited for two extracts from *The Leopard* by Giuseppe di Lampedusa; André Launay for an extract from *Caviar and After*, 1966; James Laver for an extract from *Eating Out – An Historical Dissertation*, 1947; From *Kangaroo* by D. H. Lawrence, Copyright 1923 by Thomas Seltzer, renewed © 1951 by Frieda Lawrence, used by permission of Viking Penguin, a division of Penguin Books USA; Jane Legge for the poem 'Eating Meat and Eating People'; an extract from *Blue Highways* by William Least-Heat Moon, reprinted by permission of Martin Secker & Warburg; the Society of Authors as the literary representative of the Estate of Rosamond Lehmann for an extract from *Invitation to the Waltz*; Claude Lévi-Strauss and Jonathan Cape for an extract from *The Origin of Table Manners* translated by John and Doreen Weightman; Paul Levy and Chatto & Windus for two extracts from *Out to Lunch*; Hsiang Ju Lin and Tsuifeng Lin for extracts from *Chinese Gastronomy*; Penelope Lively, André Deutsch and Penguin Books for an extract from *Moon Tiger*; Norman Longmate and Arrow Books for three extracts from *How We Lived Then*; George Macbeth for the poem 'An Ode to English Food'; A. M. Heath for three extracts from *The Egg and I* by Betty Macdonald; Giles MacDonough and Sheil Land Associates for an extract from *A Palate in Revolution*; Sheila MacLeod and Virago for an extract from *The Art of Starvation*; Leaf for Life for one extract from *All Grass is Flesh* by Carol Martin, published by Milton Ash Editions, 1990; the Estate of Vicomte de Mauduit for six extracts from *They Can't Ration These*; Cal McCrystal for an extract from *The Greying of John Major*; Cyra McFadden for an extract from *The Serial*; Jonathan Meades and HarperCollins Publishers for three extracts from *Peter Knows what Dick Likes*; George Melly and Weidenfeld & Nicolson for an extract from *Rum Bum and Concertina*; two extracts from *Sinkin' Spells, Hot Flashes, Fits and Cravin's* by Ernest Matthew Mickler, Copyright © 1988, reprinted by permission of Ten Speed Press, Berkeley, California; the Estate of Nancy Mitford and Peters Fraser & Dunlop for three extracts from *Talent to Annoy*, an extract from her Paris column in the *Sunday Times*, an extract from *The Blessing*, two extracts from *The Pursuit of Love*, three extracts from *The Water Beetle* and an extract from *Love In A Cold Climate*; Jonathan Cape and Random Century Group for 'Ode to the Tomato' by Pablo Neruda, translated by Nathaniel Tarn; Eric Newby for two extracts from *A Short Walk in the Hindu Kush*; Lord Norwich for eight extracts from *Lady Diana Cooper*; Edna O'Brien for an extract from *In The Hours of Darkness*; Flannery O'Connor and Faber & Faber for an extract from *Everything that Rises Must Converge*; Raymond Olivier and Peter Owen Publishers for an extract from *The Art Of Eating In France*; the Estate of the late Sonia Brownell Orwell and Martin Secker & Warburg for an extract from *The Road To Wigan Pier* by George Orwell; the Estate of Arnold Palmer for an extract from *Movable Feasts*, by permission of Oxford University Press; Viking and Penguin, London and Delacorte & Dell, New York, for an extract from *Looking for Rachel Wallace* by Robert B. Parker; the Estate of William Plomer and Jonathan Cape for a poem from *Collected Poems* by William Plomer; Jonathan Raban for an extract from *Living on Capital*; Gwen Raverat and Faber & Faber for three extracts from *Period Piece*; the Estate of Marjorie K. Rawlings and Scribners for eight extracts from *Cross Creek*; J.-F. Revel for an extract from *Culture and Cuisine*, translated by Helen R. Lane; Gillian Riley for five extracts from *The Fruit, Herbs and Vegetables of Italy* by Giacomo Castelvetro; Claudia Roden for two extracts from *A Book of Middle Eastern Food* and *Cooking in Israel: A Changing Mosaic*, Oxford Symposium, 1981 (National and Regional Styles of Cookery); Elizabeth Romer for two extracts from *The Tuscan Year*; Jeremy Trevathan for Jeremy Round's poem and extract from *The Independent Cook*; George Augustus Sala and Chatto & Windus for an extract from *The Thorough Good Cook*; the Estate of Siegfried Sassoon and Faber & Faber for an extract from *Memoirs of a Fox-Hunting Man*; C. W. Schwabe for an extract from *Unmentionable Cuisine*; the Estate of William B. Seabrook for an extract from *Jungle Ways*; Mary Taylor Semeti for two extracts from *Sicilian Food*; the Society of Authors on behalf of the Bernard Shaw Estate for a postcard on the 'Vegetarian Diet'; the Estate of Sacheverell Sitwell and David Higham Associates for three extracts from *Truffle Hunt*; the Estate of Osbert Sitwell and David Higham Associates for an extract from *Laughter in the Next Room*; the Estate of Edith Sitwell and David Higham Associates for a poem from *Façade*; William Heinemann for an extract from *I Capture The Castle* by Dodie Smith; *The Collected Poems* of Stevie Smith, Copyright © 1972 by Stevie Smith, reprinted by permission of New Directions and James

MacGibbon; Raymond Sokolov for one extract from *The Jewish American Kitchen*; Johns Hopkins University Press for an extract from *The Semiotics of Food in the Bible* by Jean Soler; Alexander Solzhenitsyn for an extract from *One Day in the Life of Ivan Denisovich*; the Estates of Constance Spry and Rosemary Hume for four extracts from *The Constance Spry Cookery Book*; G. B. Stern for an extract from *The Epicure's Companion*; Random House for two extracts from *Table Topics* by Julian Street (1959); Michael Symons for two extracts from *One Continuous Picnic*; *Dylan Thomas: Collected Stories*, Copyright © 1984 by The Trustees for the Copyrights of Dylan Thomas, reprinted by permission of David Higham Associates and New Directions Publishing; Alice B. Toklas for four extracts from *The Alice B. Toklas Cookbook*; Penguin Books for three extracts from *Anna Karenina* by Leo Tolstoy, translated by Rosemary Edmonds, 1954; Andrew Tyler for two extracts from the *Independent*; Anne Tyler for an extract from *The Accidental Tourist*; Camden Press for three extracts from *The Memoirs of Elisabeth Vigée-Le Brun*, translated by Sian Evans; Isabelle Vischer for two extracts from *Now to The Banquet*; Margaret Visser for an extract from *Much Depends on Dinner*; the Estate of Evelyn Waugh for two extracts from *Remote People* and an extract from *Labels*; Fay Weldon and Sheil Land Associates for an extract from 'Weekend'; Eudora Welty and Virago Press for an extract from *Introduction to the Jackson Cookbook*; the Estate of Rebecca West and Macmillan London for three extracts from *The Fountain Overflows*; the Estate of Patrick White and Jonathan Cape for two extracts from *Riders In The Chariot*; Elsie de Wolf for three extracts from *Recipes for Successful Dining*; six excerpts from *The Bed-Book of Eating and Drinking* by Richardson Wright, Copyright © 1943 by Richardson Wright, reprinted by permission of HarperCollins Publishers; Theodore Zeldin for three extracts from *The French*.

Faber and Faber Limited apologize for any errors or omissions in the above list and would be grateful to be notified of any corrections that should be incorporated in the next edition or reprint of this volume.

Introduction

❦

This book is about all kinds of food. It is a celebration not just of gastronomic pleasures but also of the world that lies behind them. It is about not just surfeit but the paucity of food too. We have tried to include as many different ways of living and eating, cooking and thinking about food as we could find. Chronologically the excerpts begin with a toothache remedy of 3000 BC and they end in the present with a journalist's harrowing description of a slaughterhouse in Surrey. They are taken from novels, memoirs and diaries; travel and recipe books; lectures, essays, letters and poems; works on anthropology and philosophy; histories, surveys and children's books; newspapers and books of etiquette. There is even a Shavian postcard. The pleasures of the table are of course here, even gastronomic excess, but also there are culinary disasters and disappointments, while often the extracts depict rivalry and snobbery, pretension and generosity, as well as simple delights and strange food in faraway places.

With a net flung so wide there are bound to be writers included whom we do not readily connect with food. All the more fascinating, we felt, to know what Plato thought about cooking, Adam Smith about meat eating, Mozart on a hungry Dominican or Joyce Grenfell on dining at Windsor Castle. We wanted to broaden the experience, to present as wide a picture as space allowed: St Louis sharing his food with the poor on the Crusades, Goethe in Sicily, Louis XV on a 'picnic' at Compiègne, sixteenth-century Muscovy and pre-war Tibet.

We bring all of ourselves to a meal, not only the hungry body but our cultural traditions. We carry with us to the table the history of our land, its past and present ecology. Upon our plates there are links with colonial expansion and the Columbian exchange. The aroma of spices can conjure up the silk route of China, and the cup that cheers, the conquest of India. Anyone writing about food also brings to it the same complex heritage.

Food is, at its most basic, survival. We grow ill and weak if we do not sustain ourselves with enough nourishment. The spectre of infirmity lurks in the shadow of our appetite, and in these pages we do not ignore starvation brought about by war, rationing and imprisonment.

The book begins with the pleasures and disasters of childhood eating. Some of the food seems like dire punishment inflicted upon the helpless: the rabbit served as 'a black veined leg sitting humped in a thin cornflour sauce' recalled by Molly Keane; 'the hairy brawn and knobbly porridge' of Harold Acton's Lawnwood crammer; and the purgatory of *lutefisk* that 'tasted of soap and gave off an odour that would gag a goat', despised Advent food of Garrison Keillor's childhood. The foods recalled as especially wondrous and delicious are, for the most part, those discovered by the children themselves. It is somewhat astonishing that the simple act of eating should accrue such complex forms of social domination. Table settings can seem to a child, as Germaine Greer suggests, to be an altar laid with sterile surgical instruments. But it is in this way and many others – the taboos and austerities enforced on childhood – that we signal the significance of food in our lives.

Even the simplest meal can be so much more than its parts, a wealth of pleasures so indelible that it can be recalled, even after decades, as fresh as if it happened yesterday. Why, when we forget so much else, should this be so? Appetite surely sharpens the senses, refines the sensual appreciation of sight, smell and taste. Even indeed of hearing – an example being potato crisps which, as Diane Ackerman points out, are too large to fit into the mouth, so that part of the pleasure of eating them is hearing the starch granules twang and crackle as they are bitten into.

Hunger, too, an extreme form of appetite, will endow such food with a succulence and zest that a satiated person might not discover. And because hunger is such a driving force we have a constant and perpetual fear, for the most part suppressed and kept under control, that food will either vanish completely or will shrink to mere scraps that can barely sustain.

No wonder we feel ecstatic at the sight of simple fruits, coming upon them as Nana did the strawberries in the rain, or recognize that singular 'sweetness of distant places' which Jane Grigson always smelled at Fauchon's in Paris. Though simple pleasures to some can seem mundane or bizarre to others – John Major's preference for hamburgers, for example, or John Fuller's 'whole black quoit of black pudding'. Such pleasures are determined by a whole regiment of influences, not least those determined by where we were born, which are examined in the section on national styles.

It was always so: Tacitus notes that the Germans 'satisfied their hunger without any elaborate cuisine or appetisers'; Michael Symons sees the Australian pavlova as a 'fantasy with all the froth and bubble of a Busby Berkeley movie'; Virginia Woolf's Mrs Ramsay thinks: 'A whole French family could live on what an English cook throws away.'

The British have a fervent preoccupation with the picnic, and it is on the water where some of the most haphazard yet enjoyable meals were eaten, from the *African Queen* to Jerome K. Jerome's rowing boat. But picnics like every other meal are staged with great variety. We could not resist including the sad story told by Madame de Sévigné of the suicide of the king's chef Vatel. Happier occasions in these pages include a Balmoral shooting party with Edward VII, Tolstoy's haymakers' dinner, and picnics from Mexico and Cyprus.

Modes of behaviour grow more complicated with ascent up the social scale. As the meal became grander so the formal details of behaviour, dress and custom grew more precise and ornate. Ambassadors visiting foreign courts had to learn highly involved procedures. We are fortunate to have a glimpse of Muscovy in the sixteenth century from Sigmund von Herberstein, as well as one of China from Marco Polo. Did he really see the magic flying flagons of wine and milk that whizzed around the table to refill empty cups? Or was that the medieval view of the mysterious orient?

Travellers who had met or even gazed on kings, emperors, khans and princes never omitted to mention it; a touch of royalty invested their works with a special glamour for their readers. Jean de Joinville was impressed at what Saint Louis, King of France, gave away to the poor. Froissart was shocked by the table manners of the four great Kings of Ireland. The Comtesse de Boigne thought the Prince Regent's Pavilion in Brighton was 'a masterpiece of bad taste', but was more complimentary about the food and noted that the Prince Regent 'took especial pride in showing off his kitchens'. The first cookery books were written by cooks with royal, or at the very least noble, connections, a tradition that continued for centuries. Gabriel Tschumi, who began his long career in the British royal kitchens under Queen Victoria when he was a teenager, was told by older staff that the Queen ate her breakfast boiled egg from a gold egg-cup with a gold spoon, attended by two Indian servants resplendent in gold and scarlet; the rest of the family began with eggs, followed by bacon, grilled fish, cutlets, chops or steak, and finished with roast woodcock, snipe or chicken.

Royalty were at least useful employers of the labour force; their establishments required thousands of workers, often moving across country buying up all the produce as they went. A royal household was in effect like a great army and the royal progress was often dreaded, for the country behind them was left bare and desolate. The Duc de Saint Simon describes in his memoirs the military camp at Compiègne of Louis XIV, designed to 'astonish Europe'. Indeed, it still astonishes us, the ingenuity and the wealth expended, the intricate arrangements to have supplies of food sent from all over Europe, even the water which was brought from the Seine. Inescapably, one comes to the conclusion that food is used by the rich in a different way: the more you squander, the greater you are.

Monarchs on the whole tend to be intemperate creatures. Throughout history the rich and the powerful fell ill and died from diseases associated with overeating, while the poor died from overwork and malnutrition. Gluttony is described here as the 'coarsest bolter of bacon' by Launcelot Sturgeon. The avid gorging of Trimalchio – thought to be a portrait of Nero – is not unlike that of the Emperor's short-lived successor, Vitellius, who banqueted four times a day. Only a slightly more moderate form of gluttony is depicted by Zola at his Parisian dinner where they are all 'stuffed to suffocation'. What those diners and others could not eat was collected from the Paris hotels and restaurants and put on display, garnished for resale, in the market at Les Halles. It is an astonishing picture, going against all modern notions of hygiene and food safety, yet poverty compels the hungry to appease their stomachs with whatever is at hand. Such revelations give an insight into the diet of the poor and how they survive on the edge of disease.

What of the cooks themselves? Do not even bother to interview the cook who believes in 'plain cooking', was the advice given by Ruth Lowinsky – 'They boil everything and serve it with a garnish of water'. And though the 'Chef-trained' send up 'marvellous looking mousses', it is 'only by their position in the menu and the fact that they taste vaguely of sugar or salt that you know whether they be made of lobsters or of strawberries'.

Some cooks were competent but unnerving, such as the Mrs Jelinik described by Harold Acton, who endured her 'distinctly sinister' hors-d'oeuvre, the 'unsettling' soups and vegetables 'calculated to give you a vague feeling of impending doom' before the celestial Chong Sung arrived in his life. Incompetents might be fired, but for every cook who was dismissed there were probably an equal number who left of their own accord. The president of Trinity College told Richardson Wright in the 1940s that he was well past fourteen before he realized that 'high-dudgeon wasn't a high-wheeled vehicle in which cooks departed'.

It is interesting to see how often the art of preparing food is measured by the simplest dish – salad and how to dress it. We include, naturally, Sydney Smith's famous verse on the art of dressing a salad, in a letter written to his friend Lady Holland. Such skill was certainly lacking earlier: in 1614 Castelvetro commented that the English put so much vinegar into the salad bowl it was enough for a footbath. Nor would we much care, I suspect, for Hannah Glasse's advice on how to grow a salad in the space of two hours, from mustard seeds placed between two layers of fresh horse dung.

It is surprising to see how much bad food was acceptable, so long as it conformed to the conventions of the time. Bad food required more planning and preparation, often simply to mask its identity. One can imagine how insipid the mock cutlets at Buckingham Palace must have been. One also wonders at the nature of some of the dishes, what, for example, is Filet de Sole Mountbatten served at the Wedding Breakfast of our present monarch? Such a dish never surfaced afterwards at Wheelers or elsewhere.

Entertaining almost always involves pretension. Madame de La Tour du Pin had to be in full dress wearing jewels for dinner at three o'clock in Montpellier in the 1780s. In 1798 Elisabeth Vigée-Le Brun relates with a touch of schadenfreude the bad luck of one of her sitters, the Duchess de Mazarin, who 'could do absolutely nothing, not even throw a party without it being ruined by some catastrophe'. The most famous was a disastrous live-bird pie at a supper party for sixty.

But there are more modest modes of entertaining. Pliny remonstrated with a guest who did not appear by detailing what he missed: 'One lettuce each, three snails, two eggs, barley-cake and wine with honey chilled with snow'. His contemporary Martial took the cynical view that a man 'your dinner has made your friend' loves 'mullet, boar and oysters', not his host.

Food carries with it a whole armoury of social expectations. There was nothing intrinsically wrong with the navettes Jeannette Ferrary made for M. F. K. Fisher when she was asked to 'Bring Something Silly'; the fact that they didn't have the desired effect was not even her fault. Mrs Fisher herself was not enchanted with a blue violet salad after she had read George Ellwanger's purple prose describing it – the salad she was eventually served wasn't bad, it just wasn't *right*. Indeed, food does not necessarily have to be actually bad to be disappointing; and skill, or lack of it, does not always matter. The soufflé that doesn't

rise or the listing cake are not inedible and, given the right circumstances, even enjoyable.

Extravagant praise frequently precedes a gastronomic disappointment. Long before she tasted one, Betty Macdonald heard geoduck
spoken about in Seattle with 'the mystic reverence usually associated
with an eclipse of the sun or the aurora borealis'. They were, she
discovered, 'tougher than tyre casing and tasted exactly like clams'.

Goethe and Norman Douglas both experienced disappointments in
Southern Italy. Goethe found the raw thistles everyone else was
consuming with relish 'tasteless', and Norman Douglas fulminates
against the 'diabolical preparation known as *zuppa di pesce*'. But
Goethe is constantly impressed throughout Italy by the hospitality – as
when, for example, he was given accommodation by a family of
macaroni makers in a village where there was no inn.

To the stranger there can be no aspect of food more seductive than
the generosity with which it is given. In the beginning, as James Laver
wrote, 'hospitality to strangers was a great advance in civilisation,
when it began to be thought desirable not to kill any foreigner at sight'.
Food offered to travellers is all the more touching when it comes from
people who have very little. George Borrow was moved to tears in a
humble cottage in Wales, having 'never experienced so much genuine
hospitality'. Gerald of Wales wrote about the hospitality and eating
habits of the Welsh as well as the converse, 'their greediness and the
demands they make'. Even during periods of war and rationing there
can be generosity and the warmth of friendship: Ambrose Heath tells
in his broadcast of groups of people eating a jolly communal meal in
the same street where bombs had fallen.

Survival in times of hardship, privation and war can become a
driving force, a kind of iron will centred on the gut. This is seen most
intensely in the portrait of young Jim in J. G. Ballard's *Empire of the
Sun*. During the seige of Paris in 1870 Goncourt to his astonishment
sees his local butcher's shop hung with carcases from the Paris zoo.
Alexandre Dumas is appalled at what the Russian soldier has to
survive on: sodden black bread and cabbage soup. Froissart notes that
when the Scots invaded England in 1327 they won their campaign
because of swiftness and surprise – their secret being the frugality of
the food they carried with them.

War for civilians meant rationing. Books were published during the
Second World War that told civilians how to plan meals with meagre
amounts and very few ingredients. The Vicomte de Mauduit wrote one
on 'Nature's Larder' that included a recipe for squirrel-tail soup.

Theodora Fitzgibbon later recalled that 'it is difficult to realize now that we were always hungry. There simply wasn't enough to eat.' She made pâtés out of horse liver and jellied their tongues, but when they were eaten never confessed their source. In the first years of the war, the onion completely vanished and 'the taste of this humble vegetable so long taken for granted, seemed suddenly the peak of gastronomic pleasure'.

The urge for survival clashed with traditional instincts, and it was the latter which triumphed over new foods, whether whale or other sea creatures. A powerful embedded instinct told the British people that they were being conned, as the years of rationing continued and allowances shrank, and they finally rebelled over snoek. The snoek saga is told by Susan Cooper, who quotes one woman as saying, 'the name frightened me'. It is questionable in any case whether anyone who had read Melville's vivid and moving account of the killing of the whale in *Moby Dick* would want to eat whale meat.

From earliest times humankind was aware that in the food which represented their survival was a cruel paradox. It is a theme which Mary Douglas explores, that what is life-giving entails an act of slaughter, and the paradox has always exercised the minds of philosophers. The ideal state described in Plato's *Republic* is a vegetarian one, for slaughter of animals leads inevitably, according to Socrates, to war among people. Three hundred years later Plutarch wrote a long and passionate essay against the eating of flesh. And how old is the practice of inflicting cruelty on animals immediately prior to slaughtering to improve flavour and tenderness? Certainly it was common when Plutarch wrote his essay, around AD 90, and it still continues today, as in the preparation of rats in Canton. The more we are divorced from the sights and sounds of the slaughterhouse, the more easy it is to forget that meat was until very recently living flesh, as Jane Legge explains in her poem. Perhaps the most terrifying reading in this book are the recent accounts by Andrew Tyler of workers in a slaughterhouse. His writing is all the more powerful and moving for it being so sober, detailed and direct.

The last chapter, 'The Wilder Shores of Gastronomy', ranges from the enjoyment of turtle to the taste of man himself. It deals with one tribe's taboos and another's favourites – always what is revolting to some may be the height of deliciousness to others. Because Arnold Bennett quailed before terrapin he shocked his Philadelphian hosts, revealing to them 'that he was no gentleman'. Turtle was popular in early America, as it was in Bristol, according to Sydney Smith, who noted 'everybody's stomach is full of green fat'. Turtle, in fact, remained a highly fashionable dish, the soup always appearing in the banquets up to the 1930s. Rattlesnakes, alligator and bear meat were all eaten with gusto in Florida, the flavour of the last being like 'choicest prime beef with an added rich gaminess'. A curiously named creature called Baby Fish in Northern China turned out to be a kind of salamander: when the cook stirred the water in the vat, the creature with small handlike paws tried to climb out, crying like a baby.

Paul Levy refuses to believe that live monkey brains are eaten, but in a spirit of enquiry he tucks into a stew of dogs, while noting that a Hong Kong gastronome would prepare a whole dog using various parts of the carcass, including the penis and testicles, in four distinctly different ways. Horse and insects are enjoyed by some; there are recipes for earthworm broth and roasted palmworms; and menus are proposed that include wasp grubs and curried cockchafers. Possibly the most fascinating meal was the one eaten by William B. Seabrook, who decided, after discussing the question with a priest, a professor of philosophy and a doctor, that it would be of interest to learn why cannibals eat human flesh. His stay with the Guéré and what he experienced is told in some detail, disabusing the reader about some of the myths attending the taste, aroma and texture of human flesh. Seabrook includes recipes for cooking the carcase and tells how the cooked meat was garnished.

Perhaps the deepest, most lasting pleasure we derive from food is the one most difficult to pin down. It is perhaps best seen and caught in imagining two people glowingly in love, dining in some perfect setting where the ambiance is enhanced by soft music, the flickering light of candles, the aromas of fruits, herbs and flowers on the evening air; where the meal is subtly seasoned, the textures creamy, the wines velvety, the foods perhaps spiced with sage and cinnamon, the salad leaves glistening with walnut oil. Eating is sexual – and there is a good biological reason why it stimulates us. We have nerve endings, called Krause's end bulbs, shaped like closed tulips in our lips and in the penis and clitoris. Upon this subject, people urged us to include the food scene in Fielding's *Tom Jones*, but they were, of course, thinking of the film, in which Albert Finney and Joyce Redman eat a meal while devouring each other with their eyes.

Inevitably, there have been omissions. We tried to avoid the over-anthologized, so you will find no Charles Lamb on roast pig, no Christmas goose or Sam Weller's oysters from Dickens. Neither is there any Samuel Pepys or John Evelyn, as both are so frequently quoted; nor another anthologists' favourite, Parson Woodforde. We must confess to finding this country parson a huge bore, for though he painstakingly lists the foods contained in each meal he rarely has anything interesting to say about them. There is no James Boswell, Isaac Walton or Sir Walter Scott, simply because they seem too familiar; and for the same reason we avoided pieces by Lewis Carroll, Mark Twain and Ogden Nash. We also omitted plays, mainly because written dialogue takes up space.

Yet you will find some familiar pieces within these pages. From Petronius to Melville, from Martial to E. M. Forster, a few favourites begged to be included. This anthology attempts to straddle the divide between a recipe of Apicius and the wit of Noël Coward, between Gerald of Wales and Nancy Mitford, between Plato's stricture that cooking is nothing but a form of flattery and three men in a boat taking hours to peel some potatoes. At times the path of the anthologist seemed to be an endless one, for once we had thrown the net wide, refusing to be limited by either literature or gastronomy, the possibilities were well nigh infinite.

Childhood

❦

Hunger

After the success of her novel Good Behaviour *in 1981 Molly Keane
was asked to write* Nursery Cooking *at the height of the cookery
book boom. She remarked with delight and some astonishment
during a television interview that she had been paid a larger
advance for it than for any of her novels. In the introduction she
recalls both the good and bad food of her childhood, and her
family's stern attitude towards greed, which she happily discarded.*

I was born in 1904, and by 1908 I had accepted the fact that nursery
food was so disgusting that greed, even hunger, must be allayed
elsewhere.

In my childhood there was little or no communication between the
nurseries, at the top of the house, and the kitchen, three flights of stairs
beneath in the basement. Nanny and Mrs Finn, the cook, had no liking
for each other. Nanny, considering herself socially superior, would
send Mrs Finn acid messages via the nursery maid (with meagre effect)
on the quality or quantity of the food that travelled up on black tin
trays wreathed with roses for nursery breakfast, dinner and tea.
Today, given there was a nanny, and a cook, Nanny would have
enough sense to crawl to the cook – but not at that date . . .

Food in the dining-room was better, but not a great deal so, than
food in the nursery. I think Mrs Finn gave of her best only at dinner-
time. Rabbit came to the dining-room in a proper pie. In the nursery it
was a black-veined leg, sitting humped in a thin cornflour sauce; for
the dining-room its bones were removed and it was layered with bacon
and hard-boiled egg, onions, parsley and bayleaf. Roast chicken was
always first favourite, perhaps because of the tiny sausage and curl of

I

bacon that went with the helping. As to puddings, stewed apple and junket were far too much of an everyday occurrence, but Mrs Finn had a genius for glorifying summer fruits. A syrup was made – only squashed berries supplying its liquid – and in this syrup whole raspberries, red currants and black currants were simmered for the shortest possible time, then cooled and eaten with toasted cake and cream. To think of it revives the exuberant strength of a child's sense of taste, a sense as irrecoverable as the mythical length of those summer days.

We ate under the watchful eyes of the sad gardening aunt, sitting with her and our governess at one end of the long table while my father and mother, at a holy distance from us, ate and talked undisturbed at the other. Aunt Marjorie was always alert for greed in the young: a vice that was a depravity to be commented on and corrected whenever evident. She herself ate her soufflé in as abstracted a manner as though receiving Holy Communion, more careful than dainty. For years I had a sensation of shame as well as guilt about second helpings; a deep-rooted sense that the enjoyment of food was unattractive, something to conceal. This corresponds with another axiom of my later youth: 'An eager girl [greed again] never gets her man'. In my time I have proved the falsity of both.

Nursery Cooking, 1985

Sweet Corn

GARRISON KEILLOR 1941–

Sweet corn – or corn on the cob in North America – eaten within minutes of being picked is regarded by many as the quintessential American delicacy. Maize was discovered in the New World and nowhere else is it so keenly appreciated.

Sweet corn was our family's weakness. We were prepared to resist atheistic Communism, immoral Hollywood, hard liquor, gambling and dancing, smoking, fornication, but if Satan had come around with sweet corn, we at least would have listened to what he had to sell. We might not have bought it but we would've had him in and given him a cup of coffee. It was not amazing to learn in eighth-grade science that corn is sexual, each plant containing both genders, male tassel and female flower, propagating in our garden after dark. Sweet corn was so delicious, what could have produced it except sex? Sunday after church, when the pot roast was done and the potatoes were boiled and mashed and a pot of water was boiling – only then would Dad run out with a bushel basket and pick thirty ears of corn. We shucked it clean in five seconds per ear and popped it in the pot for a few minutes. A quick prayer, a little butter and salt, and that is as good as it gets. People have searched the world over for something better and didn't find it because it's not there. There's nothing better, not even sex. People have wanted sex to be as good as sweet corn and have worked hard to improve it, and afterwards they lay together in the dark, and said, 'Det var dejligt.' ('That was so wonderful.') 'Ja, det var.' 'Men det var ikke saa godt som frisk mais.' ('But it wasn't as good as fresh sweet corn.') 'Ney.'

Leaving Home, 1987, from the foreword to the 1988 edition

Lawnwood Crammer

HAROLD ACTON 1904–

Harold Acton recalls the food at his crammer in 1917.

During this phase of the war one could not expect good food, but the food at Lawnwood was so unpalatable that I smuggled as much of it as possible into my handkerchief and threw it down the lavatory later. Goaded by repulsion for the hairy brawn and knobbly porridge, my sleight of hand became so dexterous that I whisked whole platefuls into my pocket without being detected. The blotched oily margarine that accompanied our meals flavoured my entire stay at this institution, where faded photographs of Greek sculpture on the walls filled me with a prejudice against Greek art which it took me years to shake off.

Memoirs of an Aesthete, 1948

Baked Potatoes
ANNE TYLER 1941–

For supper they had Rose's pot roast, a salad with Macon's dressing, and baked potatoes. Baked potatoes had always been their favorite food. They had learned to fix them as children, and even after they were big enough to cook a balanced meal they used to exist solely on baked potatoes whenever Alicia left them to their own devices. There was something about the smell of a roasting Idaho that was so cozy, and also, well, *conservative*, was the way Macon put it to himself. He thought back on years and years of winter evenings: the kitchen windows black outside, the corners furry with gathering darkness, the four of them seated at the chipped enamel table meticulously filling scooped-out potato skins with butter. You let the butter melt in the skins while you mashed and seasoned the floury insides; the skins were saved till last. It was almost a ritual. He recalled that once, during one of their mother's longer absences, her friend Eliza had served them what she called potato boats – restuffed, not a bit like the genuine article. The children, with pinched, fastidious expressions, had emptied the stuffing and proceeded as usual with the skins, pretending to overlook her mistake. The skins should be crisp. They should not be salted. The pepper should be freshly ground. Paprika was acceptable, but only if it was American. Hungarian paprika had too distinctive a taste. Personally, Macon could do without paprika altogether.

The Accidental Tourist, 1985

'Gentleman's Relish'
NANCY MITFORD 1904–73

'Now, Linda darling,' said Aunt Sadie, 'if Fanny has finished her tea why don't you show her your toad?'

'He's upstairs asleep,' said Linda. But she stopped crying.

'Have some nice hot toast, then?'

'Can I have Gentleman's Relish on it?' she said, quick to make capital out of Aunt Sadie's mood, for Gentleman's Relish was kept strictly for Uncle Matthew, and supposed not to be good for children.

4

The others made a great show of exchanging significant looks. These were intercepted, as they were meant to be, by Linda, who gave a tremendous bellowing boo-hoo and rushed upstairs.

The Pursuit of Love, 1945

Harold's 95 Theses
GARRISON KEILLOR 1941–

1. You have fed me wretched food, vegetables boiled to extinction, fistfuls of white sugar, slabs of fat, mucousy casseroles made with globs of cream of mushroom, until it's amazing my heart still beats. Food was not fuel but ballast; we ate and then we sank like rocks. Every Sunday, everyone got stoned on dinner except the women who cooked it and thereby lost their appetites – the rest of us did our duty and ate ourselves into a gaseous stupor and sat around in a trance and mumbled like a bunch of beefheads.
2. Every Advent, we entered the purgatory of *lutefisk*, a repulsive gelatinous fishlike dish that tasted of soap and gave off an odor that would gag a goat. We did this in honor of Norwegian ancestors, much as if the survivors of a famine might celebrate their deliverance by feasting on elm bark. I always felt the cold creeps as Advent approached, knowing that this dread delicacy would be put before me and I'd be told, 'Just have a little.' Eating 'a little' was, like vomiting 'a little,' as bad as 'a lot.'

Lake Wobegon Days, 1985

Christmas at Cliveden
JOYCE GRENFELL 1910–79

We came down and sat at the children's table near the fire, where Uncle Waldorf chose to join us. He poured out our milk and sliced the wholesome loaf and plain cake baked for us to eat. At the grown-up table, where Aunt Nancy presided, there were delectable little scones in a lidded silver dish, kept hot over a spirit lamp. There was also a special, almost black, rich fruit-cake topped with marzipan, chocolate

5

éclairs and very short crisp shortbreads, all made in the still-room by two full-time cake-and-pastry-cooks. Sometimes we were allowed special treats from the grown-ups' table, but Aunt Nancy kept an eye on the goodies, and we were strictly rationed.

After tea Aunt Nancy went to her present-room, a small dark panelled study next to her boudoir used for storage. No child was allowed to go there, paticularly at Christmas-time, but, once when I was about sixteen and was sent in there to fetch something for her, I saw it was like a little shop. Piles of sweaters of all colours and sizes, men's, boys', women's and girls'; silk stockings, silk scarves, chiffon squares and boxes of linen handkerchiefs, from the Irish Linen Stores, initialled for everyone in the party. There were evening bags, men's ties, golf-balls in boxes, little packs of tees, diaries, toys, games, books and candy. *Lots* of candy. There was never a more generous present-giver than Aunt Nancy, but she was always careful about her candy store; most of it came from American friends, and she didn't let it out of her keeping except in very occasional bestowals of a caramel here and a sour-ball there. She also had a great many boxes of chewing-gum and was never without a supply in her pocket.

In Pleasant Places, 1979

The Flavor of Jackson
EUDORA WELTY 1909–

As a child I heard it said that two well-traveled bachelors of the town, Mr. Erskine Helm and Mr. Charles Pierce, who lived on Amite Street, had 'brought mayonnaise to Jackson.' Well they might have, though not in the literal way I pictured the event. Mayonnaise had a *mystique*. Little girls were initiated into it by being allowed to stand at the kitchen table and help make it, for making mayonnaise takes three hands. While the main two hands keep up the uninterrupted beat in the bowl, the smaller hand is allowed to slowly add the olive oil, drop-by-counted-drop. The solemn fact was that sometimes mayonnaise didn't make. Only the sudden dash of the red pepper onto the brimming, smooth-as-cream bowlful told you it was finished and a triumph.

For sure, you couldn't *buy* mayonnaise, and if you could, you wouldn't. For the generation bringing my generation up, everything made in the kitchen started from scratch, too. There was a barrel of flour standing in the kitchen! Perhaps a sugar barrel too. The household may have provided (ours did) its own good butter (which implies a churn and, of course, a cow) and its own eggs, and most likely it grew its own tomatoes, beans, strawberries, even asparagus. Why, your mother called up the butcher, talked to him, asked what was especially nice today, and let him send it. There was communication with butchers. And my father sometimes *saw* them, for he'd stop by on his way from the office and come bringing home by hand the little squared-off, roofed-over white-cardboard bucket with the wire handles, fragrant and leaking a little – and produced oysters for supper, just ladled out of the oyster barrel that the butcher got in from New Orleans.

And they grated from whole nutmegs, they ground coffee from the beans, went to work on whole coconuts with the hatchet. Some people knew how to inveigle for the real vanilla bean. (Vanilla must have had a central importance in those days – think of all the cakes. Wasn't there a local lady who made her living, and her entertainment, just selling vanilla extract over the telephone?)

Our mothers were sans mixes, sans foil, sans freezer, sans blender, sans monosodium glutamate, but their ingredients were as fresh as the day; and they knew how to make bread.

Jackson believed in and knew how to achieve the home flavor. And if ever there were a solid symbol of that spirit, one that radiates its pride and joy, it is the hand-cranked ice cream freezer. I see it established in a shady spot on a back porch, in the stage of having been turned till it won't go around another time; its cylinder is full of its frozen custard that's bright with peaches, or figs, or strawberries, its dasher lifted out and the plug in tight, the whole packed with ice and salt and covered with a sack to wait for dinner – and right now, who bids to lick the dasher?

The Jackson Cookbook, 1971

Feeding Children

GERMAINE GREER 1939–

Dr Germaine Greer gave the second annual Badoit lecture to the
Guild of Food Writers in London. Dr Greer, whose first book The
Female Eunuch *is one of the seminal texts of the feminist*
movement, is an accomplished cook.

Now let's think about the meal table. It is an altar. Thirty inches off the
ground, i.e., over the head of the average toddler. An altar consecrated
to the abilities of the bread winner, who presides over it, traditionally
like Melchizedech. This altar must be covered with a clean cloth and
with a conglomeration of unnecessary articles. Eating is thus rendered
awesome, and it goes on being awesome for every foray up the ladder
of consumption, exposing us to new hazards and new humiliations.
The terror of the fondue, eating asparagus, extracting snails from
shells, what to do with bones, what to do with something that is
making you gag, and worst of all the selection of the right instrument.
Decent eating is carried out sitting up at the table. Chairs do not
particularly aid the digestive process, either when food is being
ingested or the debris is being excreted, but they are considered part of
the proper decorum of eating and excreting. Chairs are a particular
problem for children, who can barely climb onto them and barely keep
from slipping off them, while the edge of the table beetles over them
and they are in constant danger of putting too much pressure on the
rim of the plate and ending up with the whole lot on their faces. I
would venture to say that every child alive in England has had an
accident involving the edge of a table and some have even died as a
result. Every family either carries on the nonsense of getting children to
sit up, keep elbows off the table or allowing them to get down when
they're finished or else let the children hell around the table at risk to
themselves and everybody else. Eating is dangerous, and children learn
this fact very early.

By far the worst aspect of weaning in my view is coming to terms
with cold steel. For some reason, the rich world, in this imagining itself
civilised insists on presenting its food to itself on the end of metal
implements, of which as many as twenty may be used by the eater in
the course of a meal. This is curious, in view of the fact that human

beings have at the end of each arm an extremely versatile, prehensile instrument which is capable of doing all the actions involved in preparation and feeding. These things are easily cleaned, even if one is not prepared to do as they do in some parts of India, put the whole thing in your mouth and suck it clean. We are only allowed to use fingers at the table for very specific foods, for the rest we must adopt what I call the surgical approach, dissecting and partitioning the food with sterile instruments.

'Sex and Food', *Badoit Lecture*, 1989 (unpublished)

Nanny on France
NANCY MITFORD 1904–73

So Park society was not what it had been. There was no wide range of choice, as in the past, and the few nannies who were left clung together, a sad little bunch, like the survivors in an autumnal poultry yard, most of whose fellows had already gone to the pot. Nanny had few friends among them and pronounced them to be, on the whole, a very inferior type of person. But at Bunbury she had congenial gossips, the old housekeeper, the groom's wife, Mrs. Atkin the butler's wife, and Mrs. Black, to whom she was able to boast and brag about her year in France until they stretched their eyes. Anybody who knew how terribly she had complained during the whole of her sojourn there, or who could have heard her comments to Nanny Dexter on every aspect of French civilization, would have been amazed by the attitude she now assumed over the clanking cups of tea with her cronies.

'Say what you choose, France is a wonderful country – oh it is wonderful. Take the shops, dear, they groan with food, just like pre-war. I only wish you could see the meat, great carcasses for anybody to buy – the offal brimming over on to the pavement – animals like elephants. They could have suet everyday if they knew how to make a nice suet pudding. But there is one drawback, nobody there can cook. They've got all the materials in the world but they cannot serve up a decent meal – funny, isn't it? It's the one thing I'm glad to be back for, you never saw such unsuitable food for a child – well I ended with a spirit lamp in the nursery, cooking for ourselves.'

The Blessing, 1951

J is for Juvenile Dining

M. F. K. FISHER 1908–92

M. F. K. Fisher was the undisputed doyenne of American cookery writers. W. H. Auden called her 'as talented a writer as she is a cook. Indeed, I do not know of anyone in the United States today who writes better prose . . . The Art of Eating is a book which I think Colette would have loved and wished she had written.'

My child likes a kind of pattern to her meals: I put raisins in rows, instead of willy-nilly, on a slice of buttered toast, or rounds of banana in an X or an A over the top of her applesauce – A is for Anne, and X is, but naturally, for X-citing! Now and then, pure gastronomical fillip, there is a faint dash of cinnamon, a touch of nutmeg.

In five years she has been sick only once, in the good old English sense of the word, and that was psychosomatic rather than digestive, when a brush fire threatened us.

She seems to have a constant and lively speculation about taste and a truly 'curious nose', which reassures me when I remember her first instinctive shudder, and which keeps me watching, trying, testing, and always using my wits to avoid havoc. I want her to have a keen palate, inquisitive but never tyrannical. I want her to be able to eat at least one taste of anything in the world, from Beluga caviar to porcupine grilled with locusts, with social impunity and a modicum of inquisitive gusto.

An Alphabet for Gourmets, 1949

Bread-and-Butter before Cake

MOLLY KEANE 1904–

I feel strongly that, to be acceptable, children's food should be varied, even a little startling, and pretty enough to please the eye. I am all for the flower in the fish's mouth and the daisy in the salad. On the practical side, a croûton is a perfect exchange for a crisp, besides which, it is an addition to popularize any vegetable soup.

I have always been against the 'the-bread-and-butter-before-cake' line of thought since, in my long-and-long-ago, an enlightened hostess excited a solemn children's tea-party to ecstasy by the magical words, 'Now! Let's start with the strawberries and cream', I have felt sure that change is good for man and beast – and children too.

In contrast to that blessed hostess, there stays in my mind another children's party when Nanny stood behind my chair denying me all the pleasures of the table, and proclaiming to the hostess nanny, who was proffering sponge cake: 'Thank-you, Nanny, no. We have our acid tum. We stick to bread and butter. Eat up, dear.' The shame of it is with me still. So are the sideways glances of nice, healthy children stuffing down sardine sandwiches and chocolate biscuits.

Nursery Cooking, 1985

Family Life
JONATHAN RABAN 1942–

If I have a single image of family life, it is of a meal table. There is a high chair in the picture, dirty bibs, spilt apple puree, food chaotically laid out in saucepans, a squeal, a smack, my father's suffering brow creased with migraine, my mother's harassed face ('Oh, *Blow!*'), and the line 'William's made a smell' spoken by my younger brother through his adenoids. And over all this, the ancestors glower from their frames and the crested silver mocks from the tabletop. It isn't just the noise, the mess, the intrusive intimacies; it is that hopeless collision between the idea of Family as expounded by my father and the facts of family as we lived them out. We had ideas that were far beyond our means.

'Living on Capital', New Review, 1977

Don't Be Dainty
DIANA COOPER 1892–1986

And so back to dinner at one o'clock. I was the baby and in consequence Nanny's special charge and favourite. As I sat perched high in my baby's chair, strapped in with a tray for my food that, attached to the chair, came whirling over my head and imprisoned me safely, Nanny would feed me bread and milk, teach me to use my right hand, give me a crust to suck and later a chicken drumstick to gnaw – a bone I see to this day as the symbol of the soul. On my feeder in red cross-stich was written 'Don't be dainty' and I wasn't, but poor Letty, like so many children, while not dainty, could not swallow her food. Round and round it went in her mouth, colder and more congealed grew the mutton-fat, further away receded the promising pudding, and very often I saw her unfinished plate put cold into the cupboard for tea.

The Rainbow Comes and Goes, 1958

Jam
CLAUDIA RODEN 1936–

Jams remind me vividly of my childhood, of visiting relatives, of sitting on low sofas surrounded with bright silk cushions, of being enveloped by perfumes, faint and delicate or rich and overpowering.

My father's sisters, whom we visited regularly, were always fragrant with their favourite home-made soaps perfumed with violets, rose water, orange blossom and jasmine. Their homes were intoxicating with the frankincense which they used in every room – *bakhoor el barr*, benzoin or aloes-wood – with musk and ambergris, and the jasmin, orange blossom and rose petals which were left soaking in water in little china or crystal bowls.

Candied orange peel, quince paste, coconut, fig, date, rose, tangerine and strawberry jams would be brought in as soon as we arrived, together with pyramids of little pastries, and accompanied by the tinkling of tiny silver spoons, trembling on their stands like drops on a chandelier. Delicately engraved and inlaid silver trays carried small crystal or silver bowls filled with the shiny jams: orange, brilliantly white, mauve, rich brown, deep rose or sienna red. They were arranged around the spoon stand, next to which was placed a glass of water, ornate with white or gold arabesques.

The trays were brought round to each of us in turn as the coffee was served, for us to savour a spoonful of each jam, or more of our favourite one, with one of the little spoons, which was then dropped discreetly into the glass of water.

At our beautiful Aunt Régine's we would be served the best date jam in existence, our favourite rose jam was made by our gentle Aunt Rahèle, and Camille made an inimitable *wishna*. *Harosset* and coconut jam were traditionally made for our Passover celebrations by my mother. We ate them all the more rapturously because they appeared so rarely.

A Book of Middle Eastern Food, 1968

Breakfast

FLANNERY O'CONNOR 1925–64

Sheppard sat on a stool at the bar that divided the kitchen in half, eating his cereal out of the individual pasteboard box it came in. He ate mechanically, his eyes on the child, who was wandering from cabinet to cabinet in the panelled kitchen, collecting the ingredients for his breakfast. He was a stocky blond boy of ten. Sheppard kept his intense blue eyes fixed on him. The boy's future was written in his face. He would be a banker. No, worse. He would operate a small loan company. All he wanted for the child was that he be good and unselfish and neither seemed likely. Sheppard was a young man whose hair was already white. It stood up like a narrow brush halo over his pink sensitive face.

The boy approached the bar with the jar of peanut butter under his arm, a plate with a quarter of a small chocolate cake on it in one hand and the ketchup bottle in the other. He did not appear to notice his father. He climbed up on the stool and began to spread peanut butter on the cake. He had very large round ears that leaned away from his head and seemed to pull his eyes slightly too far apart. His shirt was green but so faded that the cowboy charging across the front of it was only a shadow.

'Norton,' Sheppard said, 'I saw Rufus Johnson yesterday. Do you know what he was doing?'

The child looked at him with a kind of half attention, his eyes forward but not yet engaged. They were a paler blue than his father's as if they might have faded like the shirt; one of them listed, almost imperceptibly, towards the outer rim.

'He was in an alley,' Sheppard said, 'and he had his hand in a garbage can. He was trying to get something to eat out of it.' He paused to let this soak in. 'He was hungry,' he finished, and tried to pierce the child's conscience with his gaze.

The boy picked up the piece of chocolate cake and began to gnaw it from one corner.

'Norton,' Sheppard said, 'do you have any idea what it means to share?'

A flicker of attention. 'Some of it's yours,' Norton said.

'Some of it's *his*,' Sheppard said heavily. It was hopeless. Almost any fault would have been preferable to selfishness – a violent temper, even a tendency to lie.

The child turned the bottle of ketchup upside-down and began thumping ketchup on to the cake.

Sheppard's look of pain increased. 'You are ten and Rufus Johnson is fourteen,' he said. 'Yet I'm sure your shirts would fit Rufus.' Rufus Johnson was a boy he had been trying to help at the reformatory for the past year. He had been released two months ago. 'When he was in the reformatory, he looked pretty good, but when I saw him yesterday, he was skin and bones. He hasn't been eating cake with peanut butter. on it for breakfast.'

The child paused. 'It's stale,' he said. 'That's why I have to put stuff on it.'

Everything That Rises Must Converge, 1965

Diet for Children
RUTH LOWINSKY d. 1958

Hippocrates, the doctor from Cos who was a contemporary of Socrates, wrote, 'With regard to food and drink, it is better to take something slightly less suitable but pleasing than something more suitable but less pleasing.'

When we were children it was considered good for our souls as well as our bodies to be continually fed on any food we disliked. Lucky children of the present day are benefiting by a reversal of this theory. Doctors have discovered that only what you eat with relish nourishes you, so the children's tastes are given due consideration, and variety in diet is thought essential.

The result is that the child of to-day is not greedy, rarely over-eats, and generally prefers savouries to sweets. If a child has a passion for sugar or sweet things, it is often because he needs them. Children love prettily served food. Milk puddings need not be sent up every day to be eaten before something more appetising. Most people owe their hatred of tapioca, known in everybody's nursery as 'frogs' eggs' or 'fishes' eyes,' to their childhood. If accompanied by grated chocolate, or coloured pink, or sprinkled with hundreds and thousands, any milk pudding will meet with success. Never heap up the plate of a child who does not seem hungry. If the first helping be small enough he will ask for more. Supper does not exist for the modern child, whose last meal is tea. He seems able to digest pastry and sugary cakes in large quantities without ill effects, and ices, if they follow a meal.

A NURSERY MENU

VEAL CAKES

VEGETABLES OR SALAD

*

CREAMED RICE

OR

VEGETABLE FRITTERS

Lovely Food, 1931

Brain Food

MADHUR JAFFREY 1933–

The beginning of summer inevitably meant the coming of examination time, a period that fell, inexorably, during late April and early May. This is when hot *loo* winds blow with the ferocity of furnaces gone wild, picking up sand from the deserts of Central India and scattering it over North Indian cities. We would sit up late, learning about Moghul architecture or Tudor intransigence (we studied as much British history as Indian history), our fevered, overworked brains sustained by watermelon from across the river, orange-fleshed, sweet-sweet *Dassheri* mangoes that an aunt parcelled to us from Lucknow, and *kakris*, pencil-thin – and just as long – skinless, seedless cucumbers that were hawked in the bazaar as '*Laila ki ungliyan, Majnu ki pasliyan*', 'The fingers of Juliet, the ribs of Romeo!'

Early in the morning, before we left to take our exams, my mother would appear with a plate of *badaam-ki-golis*, small almond balls made by soaking the nuts overnight, grinding them with sugar and cardamom and finally covering them with real silver tissue, *varak*. My mother firmly believed that almonds were brain food and that any child sent off to write two examination papers for six hours unfortified with almond balls was surely suffering from the severest form of neglect.

A Taste of India, 1985

Learning to Cook
BETTY MACDONALD 1908–58

When the enormously popular book The Egg and I *was made into a film, Claudette Colbert played the author. Her stories about her neighbours inspired the series of 'Ma and Pa Kettle' films of the 1950s*

While he and Cleve were practising archery, Mary and I were learning to cook. Mother supervised this herself as she was a marvellous cook and Gammy was the world's worst. Mother taught us to put a pinch of clove and lots of onion in with a pot roast; to make French dressing with olive oil and to rub the bowl with garlic; to make mayonnaise and Thousand Island dressing; to cook a sliver of onion with string beans; never to mash potatoes until just before serving; to measure the ingredients for coffee; and always to scald out the teapot.

Gammy taught us that when you bake a cake you put in anything you can lay your hands on. A little onion, several old jars of jam, left over batter-cake dough, the rest of the syrup in the jug, a few grapes, cherries, raisins, plums or dates, and always to use drippings instead of butter or shortening. Her cakes were simply dreadful – heavy and tan and full of seeds and pips. She made a great show of having her feelings hurt if we didn't eat these cakes but I really think she only offered them to us as a sort of character test because, if we were strong and refused, she's throw them out to the dogs or chickens without a qualm.

Gammy said she did not believe in waste and she nearly drove our maids crazy by filling up the ice-box with little dishes containing one pea, three string beans, a quarter of a teaspoonful of jam or a slightly used slice of lemon. If Mother finally demanded a clean-up and began jerking dishes out of the refrigerator and throwing stuff away, Gammy would become very huffy and go out and get a twenty-five pound sack of flour and hand it to Mother, saying, 'Go on, throw this away too. Waste seems to be the order of the day.' Gammy made great big terrible cookies too. Into these she put the same ingredients she put in the cakes but added much more flour. These cookies were big and round and about half an inch thick. They stuck to the roof of the mouth and had no taste. What to do with them became quite a problem when we finally settled down and weren't moving around any more. They were stacking up alarmingly in the kitchen and lying around the back porch untouched when the Warrens moved across the street from us. The Warrens had a beautiful colonial house and two cars, but their children – there were four of them, two boys and two girls – ate dog biscuits. Why, I don't know, but they did. Mrs. Warren kept a one-hundred pound sack on the back porch and the little Warrens filled their pockets after school and nibbled at them while playing Kick the Can. We tried some once, and they weren't much of a shock after Gammy's cakes but we didn't care for the rather bitter tang they had – it was no doubt the dried blood and bone. One day the Warren children stopped at our house before going home for their dog biscuits and Gammy happened to be baking cookies (she happened to be baking cookies about six days a week – she said that they were cheap and filling and would save on the grocery bill) and she forced us all to take some. The Warrens liked them. We were amazed and took a few tentative bites ourselves to see if these cookies might be different. But they weren't. They were the same big, stuffy, tasteless things they had always been, but I guess compared to dog biscuit they were delicious because the Warrens begged for more and the suckers got them. All they could eat and all we couldn't eat. From that day on they ate all Gammy's output and we didn't have to flinch as we watched her pour the rest of the French dressing and a jar of 'working' plums into her cookie dough.

The Egg and I, 1947

Pig

NANCY MITFORD 1904–73

My mother, whose views on health were rudimentary, who had never heard of hygiene and did not really believe in illness, had one medical superstition which nothing could shake. Pig, she thought, was unclean and, like the Jews and the Arabs, we were strictly forbidden to eat it. The perfect health of Arabs is a very current English belief. How many times have I been told not to expose myself to the sun because they wear blankets in heatwaves! (Most of those I see are noticeable for their poor physique, but let that pass.) Of course, we don't go so far as to copy their ablutions; true cleanliness is considered rather immoral by my compatriots, who lie for hours in hot baths, but are maddened at the sight of a bidet.

The ruling that deprived us children of pig also forbade horse and oysters; that was not a real hardship, because no other member of the family ate horse, and oysters are seldom seen in the Cotswolds. But pig! Whiffs of fried bacon from my father's breakfast and the sight of him tucking into sausage rolls or sausage mash, cold gammon and cranberry sauce, pork chops with apple sauce, pigs' thinkers and trotters and Bath chaps were daily tortures; the occasional sucking-pig which crackled into the dining-room hardly bears contemplating, even now. Our craving for the stuff amounted to an obsession. Others have told how my young sisters were to be seen concealing sausages up their knickers and running off to eat them in some secluded spot; the first letter my brother Tom wrote from his private school simply stated 'We have sossages every day.' Blor must have thought this 'no pig' rule eccentric, if not rather mad; she never commented on it and always upheld it, except on one occasion. She and convalescent Debo were sent to a seaside hotel for a breezy fortnight. Ordering luncheon on the first day Debo said to the waiter, in what she thought was a grown-up voice: 'I'll have a very little bit of ham.' Then she looked at Blor to see what the reaction would be. Blor gave her a disapproving sniff, but she only said: 'Well, it must be a very, very little bit of ham.'

'Blor', The Water Beetle, 1962

Merry Supper Parties
ELISABETH VIGÉE-LE BRUN 1755–1842

Finally, although barely out of childhood, I can perfectly remember the merry supper parties my father used to hold. I was made to leave the table before dessert, but the sound of laughter and the strains of an occasional song would float up to my room. If the truth be told I never really understood the words to these songs, but this did little to lessen my enjoyment of those delicious holidays.

Having made my first communion at the age of eleven, I left the convent for good. Davesne the oil painter invited me to his studio so that I might learn to make up a palette; his wife came to fetch me and when I saw how poor they were I was struck with pity. One day I wished to remain longer to finish a painting and they invited me to join them for dinner. The 'dinner' consisted of some soup together with a few baked apples. I am sure that the only decent meal they ever had was at my father's supper table and that this alone kept them alive.

Memoirs, TRANS. Siân Evans, 1989

Louis XV at La Muette in 1719
DUC DE SAINT-SIMON 1675–1755

La Muette was a small hunting lodge situated out in the country at Passy. Louis was nine when the Regent lent it to him as a royal Wendy house.

The Duc d'Orléans paid the king a charming compliment, well-suited to his years, by proposing that he should use La Muette for his amusements, and go out there and have collations. The king was enchanted. He thought he was really having something of his own; and he took delight in going there and eating bread and milk and fruit and vegetables, and amusing himself with all that diverts a boy of his age.

Memoirs of the Duc de Saint-Simon, TRANS. Katherine Wormeley, 1899

Porridge with Salt – No Sugar
GWEN RAVERAT 1885–1957

Surely our feeding was unnecessarily austere? We had porridge for breakfast, with salt, not sugar; and milk to drink. Porridge always reminds me of having breakfast alone with my father, when I was so small that I put the porridge into the spoon with my fingers, while he told me stories in French. My mother came down later, perhaps with the sensible idea of avoiding me and the porridge and the French. There was toast and butter, but I never had anything stronger for breakfast, till I tasted bacon for the first time in my life when I went to stay with Frances, at the age of nearly ten.

It is true that twice a week we had, at the end of breakfast, one piece of toast, spread with a thin layer of that dangerous luxury, Jam. But, of course, not butter, too. Butter and Jam on the same bit of bread would have been an unheard-of indulgence – a disgraceful orgy. The queer thing is that we none of us like it to this very day. But these two glamorous Jam-days have permanently coloured my conception of Sundays and Wednesdays, which are both lovely dark-red days. Though Wednesday, being also Drawing Class Day, is much the redder of the two. Sunday's delicious jam colour has been considerably paled down by Church.

Just occasionally our father used to give us, as a breakfast treat, a taste of special food, called by us *Speissums*; but, schismatically, by our cousins: *Purr Meat*. There was a continual controversy over the correct name. Fortnum and Mason called it *Hung Beef*. Some of it was freshly grated every morning into a fluffy pile on a plate; and you put a bit of toast, butter side down, on it, and some of it stuck on. It was delicious. But that was later on, when the decay of morals had set in. Margaret got it when she was quite young. I didn't.

There was only bread-and-butter and milk for tea, as Jam might have weakened our moral fibre; and sponge-cakes when visitors came. One of my major crimes was a propensity for nibbling the edges off the sponge-cakes before the visitors arrived. Our cousins did not consider that our tea-parties were very good; they were rather sorry for us. We were generally given one piece of Maple Sugar after tea; my mother imported it from the States. It was delicious but not nearly enough; and we might not ever buy sweets, which were considered very unwholesome; except, oddly enough, butterscotch out of the penny-in-the-slot machines at the railway stations. There was a blessed theory that the slot machines were pure, that the Railways guaranteed their Virtue. But we did not travel often, so I was obliged to steal sugar whenever I could. Certainly I was greedy, but one really had to do the best one could for oneself, in those days, when sugar was thought to be unwholesome; and fruit, though a pleasant treat, rather dangerous.

As we grew older, our moral fibre was weakened by having either Jam or very heavy dough-cake for tea. But not both; never both. However, this relaxation was the beginning of the end; under our continual pressure the food laws wore thinner and thinner, till by the time they got down to Billy – who is nine years younger than I am – there were no regulations left at all, and he could eat whatever was going for breakfast and tea, just like the grown-ups themselves. And I cannot see that his character is any the worse for it; in fact, he is probably less greedy that I am. Ah, innocent child, he little knew how much he owed to my self-sacrificing campaign for liberty, equality and fraternity over the victuals.

Period Piece, 1954

Supper

JON 1906–84 AND RUMER GODDEN 1907–

One by one we were summoned to our bath, supper and bed. The bath water arrived in kerosene tins and always smelled a little of smoke. When we were in our dressing-gowns, cotton crepe kimonas from Japan printed with mimosa and cherry blossom, and our hair had been brushed with one hundred strokes, Abdul would serve our suppers in the nursery-half of the dining-room, a supper of soup, or potatoes and gravy, or egg with bread and butter or – a dish often given to children in India – a stew of chicken and rice called pish-pash. To eat alone in the big dining-room was always solitary, sometimes a little frightening, and we hurried back to the populated nursery where Hannah was folding clothes, perhaps talking with the mata rani in hushed tones because the little ones were asleep, but when teeth had been brushed, the last excuse to stay was gone and we would go up the stairs, slippers flip-flapping, books under our arms.

Two under the Indian Sun, 1966

Green Stew

ALICE THOMAS ELLIS 1932–

After lunch Rose tidied the kitchen completely, and began to prepare the twins' supper. She had made a pink blancmange, of which anachronistic confection the twins were very fond. It was shaped like a cowering rabbit and quivered oleaginously on a green wedgwood plate. She had put fresh raspberries in little glass bowls decorated with damask rose petals, and washed nasturtium leaves and wild sorrel to put in their salad. Now she began to make their stew. She cut a long slice from a shoulder of lamb and chopped it into neat little squares. These she put to brown in some green gold olive oil in a heavy pan. She quartered three green tomatoes and sliced three courgettes, and chopped up a bunch of green spring onions, adding a clove of garlic for its stomachic properties and its efficacy against evil. These she added to the oil and meat in the pan, together with a chopped green pepper. She stirred it once and put on the lid. Later she would drop in ten tiny new potatoes. Five each. Lastly she took some spinach leaves and a handful of watercress and minced them up finely, saving all the juice. At the last minute she would add this, and the whole thing would turn a marvellous faery green. With it she would serve bright buttered carrots. Sometimes she made them an episcopally gorgeous beetroot stew with rosy cubes of chicken and green peas, but green stew was their favourite.

The Sin Eater, 1977

The Child as Epicure

G. B. STERN 1890–1973

My favourite food, as a child, was cheese, and cheese had to be stolen; for authority did not think that large wedges of gorgonzola were good for delicate, highly-strung little Gladys. I would rob the sideboard, whenever I had a chance, of a hunk about the size of my fist, and carrying it away to the nursery or a quiet part of the garden, nibble it in solitude, and think beautiful thoughts of fairies and ladybirds and how nice it was to be good. I stole lumps of sugar, too, from the dining-room sideboard, but more casually, in the spirit of 'I might as well, as I'm passing!' and absently I used to snatch muscat grapes from the Salviati glass fruit-dishes, and could never understand why authority should object to my methods, or, indeed, how they ever found out. I realize now that it did not improve the appearance of that cool, golden-green bunch to have seven or eight beheaded stems, and carelessly beheaded at that. Question: 'Do you still like muscat grapes?' Answer: 'Yes, I do' . . .

The Epicure's Companion, ED. Edward and Lorna Bunyard, 1937

Simple Pleasures

❦

Medlars
EDWARD BUNYARD 1872–1939

Medlars require reverential consideration, after Mr. Saintsbury's declaration that they are the ideal fruit to join with wine. Each of us has some blind spots in our make-up, and it may be that a liking for Dickens and Medlars are in some strange way connected, as these are the only two things in which I cannot follow the author of the *Cellar Book* with reverence and gratitude.

The Anatomy of Dessert, 1933

Honey and Mushrooms
KATHERINE MANSFIELD 1888–1923

Katherine Mansfield suffered her first lung haemorrhage in 1918 and spent the remaining years of her life in Switzerland and France. In February 1921 she wrote to a friend in London, 'I shall never live in England again. I recognise England's admirable qualities, but we simply don't get on. We have nothing to say to each other; we are always meeting as strangers.' Her husband John Middleton Murry had given up his job editing The Athenaeum *to join her, and in June they rented the Chalet des Sapins. At the beginning of this letter to one of her oldest friends she wrote of her 'high fever, deadly sickness and weakness . . . How I do abominate any kind of illness! Oh God, what it is to live in such a body! Well, it doesn't bear thinking about . . .'*

TO DOROTHY BRETT

Chalet des Sapins, Montana-sur-Sierre [29 August 1921]
They have just taken the new honey from the hives. I wish I could send
you a jar. All the summer is shut up in a little pot. But summer is on the
wane – the wane. Now Murry brings back autumn crocuses and his
handkerchief is full of mushrooms. I love the satiny colour of
mushrooms, & their *smell* & the soft stalk. The autumn crocuses push
above short, mossy grass. Big red pears – monsters jostle in Ernestine's
apron. Yes, ça commence, ma chere [it begins, my dear]. And I feel as I
always do that autumn is loveliest of all. There is such a sharpness with
the sweetness – there is the sound of cold water running fast in the
stream in the forest. Murry says the squirrels are tamer already. But
Heavens Brett – Life is so marvellous, it is so rich – such a store of
marvels that one cant say which one prefers.

Selected Letters, 1988

Medlars

GIACOMO CASTELVETRO 1546–1616

Medlars are gathered at the end rather than the beginning of autumn.
They ripen, as the proverb says, with a little time and a little straw.
Medlars are quite well known in England, and well liked for their
pleasant flavour. They are eaten raw after meals, with or without
sugar.

Children are particularly fond of medlars because of their association with the feast of St Martin [the night of 10 November], which
we call the *Ventura*. I must explain what this is all about. Just as the
rulers of Italy in olden times established public amusements to keep the
populace docile and entertained, our heads of households set aside
certain days of innocent games and pastimes for their children, one of
these being the *Ventura*. This is the night when the new wines are
tasted and the order in which the wines should be drunk is established,
and no one would tempt providence by broaching them before this
ceremony. Hence the somewhat trite local saying:

A San Martino,
oqni mosto è buon vino.
On St Martin's night we think
any must is good to drink.

And so, when this special evening arrives, the father of the family
settles himself by the fire and has a basket brought to him. In it he puts
as many pairs of medlars as there are people under his roof, and one
extra for the poor. Then he covers the basket with a cloth so that he
can hide three small coins in three of the fruit, gives the basket a good
shake, and announces: 'Let it be known to one and all that I have put
three coins inside these fruit – a *denaio*, a two-*denaio* piece and a
soldo. Whoever finds the smallest of them shall win one *scudo*, the
next size up wins one half of one, and the largest he keeps and gets a
third of a *scudo* as well.'

Then he calls his youngest child to him and says: 'Put your hand into
the basket and take out two medlars for the poor and put them on the
table', making sure the child does not peep to see if they have any
money in them. This continues until the child has distributed all the
medlars, except the last two, which it keeps for itself. Then everyone
looks inside their fruit, and if there is any money in the ones for the
poor, it will be given to the first beggar who knocks on the door the
next morning. Then follows a big celebration, tinged for some with
sadness at not winning the *Ventura*, and with noisy merriment for
others. I well remember the indescribable joy I once felt on finding the
money in a fruit.

When this cheerful commotion has died down, the medlars are eaten
and the wines sampled. There are so many wines to taste, that even
though everyone takes only a sip, some of the party have been known
to go up to bed somewhat merrier than usual, much to the delight of
the rest of the family.

The Fruit, Herbs and Vegetables of Italy, TRANS. Gillian Riley, 1989

Homely Meats

DAVIES OF HEREFORD

THE AUTHOR LOVING THESE HOMELY MEATS SPECIALLY, VIZ.:
CREAM, PANCAKES, BUTTERED PIPPIN-PIES (LAUGH, GOOD
PEOPLE) AND TOBACCO; WRIT TO THAT WORTHY AND
VIRTUOUS GENTLEWOMAN, WHOM HE CALLETH MISTRESS, AS
FOLLOWETH

If there were, oh! an Hellespont of cream
Between us, milk-white mistress, I would swim
To you, to show to both my love's extreme,
Leander-like – yea! dive from brim to brim.
But met I with a buttered pippin-pie
Floating upon 't, that would I make my boat
To waft me to you without jeopardy,
Though sea-sick I might be while it did float.
Yet if a storm should rise, by night or day,
Of sugar-snows and hail of caraways,
Then, if I found a pancake in my way,
It like a plank should bring me to your kays;
    Which having found, if they tobacco kept,
    The smoke should dry me well before I slept.

The Scourge of Folly, 1610

Mangosteen in Malucca

WILLIAM HICKEY 1749–1830

We accordingly came to an anchor and immediately went on shore to a neat, pretty-looking town, in which we fixed our abode at a tavern close to the sea, the room in which we sat commanding a view of the roads and shipping. Captain Elphinstone joined our party, who, being a most gentlemanlike and pleasing man, proved a great acquisition. We likewise had his first officer, Mr. Parsloe, with us, a coxcomb of the superlative degree, who afforded us considerable entertainment from an extraordinary propensity to the marvellous, or, in plain terms, lying. Our table fare was very tolerable, the fish and poultry excellent, but marred from their cooking, everything swimming in oil; the fruits delicious, one especially so, the mangosteen, which I thought the most exquisite I ever tasted anywhere. The flavour, although sweet and rich, is extremely delicate, and any quantity of it might be eaten without risk of injuring the health. Captain Elphinstone was at them morning, noon, and night, the whole time lamenting he had so short a period to enjoy them, for it is impossible to keep them long; even on shore they spoil in twenty-four hours after being gathered.

Memoirs, ED. Peter Quennell, 1960

Mangosteen from Fauchon
JANE GRIGSON 1928–90

I went into Fauchon's in the Place Madeleine in Paris one day via the fruit department. I always go in by that door because the moment you push it open paradise wafts towards you. No need for blue sea, palm trees, since the exquisite blend of guava and passion-fruit smells, pineapple, oranges, mango, cantaloup and charentais melons, figs, apples and perfect pears with tiny wood strawberries, provide an incomparable sweetness of distant places. The next move is to check on all the trays and punnets to see if there is anything I've never encountered before. There always is. On one visit it was a heap of purple-brown fruit, rounder than apples, but about the same size. They might have been carved from some dark unknown wood, each one finished with a top ruff of firm, rounded petal shapes. They had no scent at all. They played no part in the wafts of scent around them. I took advice – 'Mangoustans, Madame!' – and bought three for the family supper.

Away from the splendours of Fauchon, they looked drab. Sniffs all round. I said firmly, 'They are the most delicious fruit in the world!' The family thought I had been robbed.

With a sharp knife I cut into the firm shape, which was not as hard as it looked, and moved it round until a cap came off with those winged petal shapes. Inside was a jewel of plump, white, sectioned translucency, set in a case of glorious pink. As we admired it, the pink faded into a deeper deader tone, and I lifted out the small sections.

THE FABER BOOK OF FOOD

Even thousands of miles from Malaysia, they tasted fragrant, unlike anything else, except that the flesh had the consistency of lychees.

The most delicious fruit in the world? Yes, perhaps, in Malaysia – at any rate, off the tree, or from a market-seller's plaited tray in Thailand. To someone living in the British Isles I would judge the most delicious fruit would be a yellow raspberry direct from the cane on a warm day, or a William pear at the exact moment of perfection. But most of us have as much chance of these two experiences, or perhaps less chance, as of going one day to south-east Asia and eating a mangosteen in its perfection.

Exotic Fruits & Vegetables, 1986

Apple Butter
J. HECTOR ST JOHN CRÈVECOEUR 1735–1813

We often make apple-butter, and this is in the winter a most excellent food, particularly where there are many children. For that purpose, the best, the richest of our apples are peeled and boiled; a considerable quantity of sweet cider is mixed with it; and the whole is greatly reduced by evaporation. A due proportion of quinces and orange peels is added. This is afterwards preserved in earthern jars, and in our long winters is a very great delicacy and highly esteemed by some people. It saves sugar and answers in the hands of an economical wife more purposes than I can well describe. Thus our industry has taught us to convert what Nature has given us into such food as is fit for people in our station. Many farmers make excellent cherry and currant wines, but many families object to them on account of the enormous quantity of sugar they require. In some parts of this country, they begin to distil peaches and cider, from which two species of brandy are extracted, fiery and rough at first, but with age very pleasant. The former is the common drink of the people in the southern provinces.

Letters from an American Farmer and Sketches of Eighteenth-Century America, 1963

Nectarine

CHARLOTTE DU CANN 1956–

I am quite grown up at fifteen, and have taken to ordering nectarines in the fruit order book.

Who taught me to eat the nectarine?

My grandfather with his eyes like sparrowhawks and his nineteenth-century suits. We had started a correspondence.

Previously he had enjoyed a correspondence with Bernard Shaw. In tiny crabbed handwriting he advised me to burn my cello and to be instead like Arnold Bennett who wrote two thousand words before breakfast, he sent me articles about snuff-boxes and postcards of Florentine painting and quotations from Shakepeare, especially 'to thine own self be true'; he told me that on no account was I to become a librarian as advised by the school's careers officer: 'I have been in the London Library today and had a good look at the girls there and they *all* have dirty fingernails. Next time you are in London I suggest we meet and I will tell you how to be a journalist. School can only teach you how to read books but journalism will teach you how to read people.'

And so the next holidays, in the Easter holidays, we sat in Fortnum's in the greeneygilt Fountain Room and ate sandwiches with cress inside and drank China tea. He showed me his diamond watches and gave me one of his beloved coins, one that celebrated the marriage of the doomed Queen Charlotte. My grandfather had a lock of Thomas Hardy's hair and a quill pen belonging to Dickens. His father had been a travelling lecturer in the occult in the West Country, his mother had died of consumption in the workhouse and been buried in a pauper's grave. He refused to talk about them, as my parents did about him. To me he appeared like an appendix to the Novel.

After tea, that first tea, he took me to the fruit department and bought me a nectarine (later we tasted guavas, a passion fruit, pomegranates, mango, kiwi fruit, lychees . . . long, long before these were fashionable).

'Have a nectarine when possible,' said my grandfather, who was also a member of the Fruiterers Association. 'It is a finer fruit than the peach and has no unpleasant furry skin.'

The assistant put one into a paper bag.

'Well, go on, taste it,' said my grandfather loudly in the middle of Piccadilly. 'Tell me what you think.'

'In the street?' I asked. Eating in the street was one of the grave sins, as bad as not writing thank you letters or cheating in exams.

I looked into his fierce sparrowhawk eyes and decided to disobey my upbringing. I took the nectarine and bit slowly into the sweet slippery juicy goldeny-pink flesh, there in the grey street. The juice ran down my chin.

'Well?' he said.

'It's decadent,' I replied.

'Yes, yes,' said my grandfather, 'but I prefer the muscat grape.'

I remain loyal to the nectarine, perhaps more than to my upbringing. Each year, as the summer creeps into the city waving his dusty hat, I seek out a barrow selling fruit in the street. And I buy, not a kilo, not several, not even two, but one ripe nectarine. And I take it out of its paper prison and, standing quite still with my eyes closed, I eat the glorious fruit while the traffic roars away.

Offal and the New Brutalism, 1985

Lemons

J. W. GOETHE 1749–1832

December 13 [1786] [Rome]

Here you do not notice the winter. The only snow you can see is on the mountains far away to the north. The lemon trees are planted along the garden walls. By and by they will be covered with rush mats, but the orange trees are left in the open. Hundreds and hundreds of the loveliest fruits hang on these trees. They are never trimmed or planted in a bucket as in our country, but stand free and easy in the earth, in a row with their brothers. You can imagine nothing jollier than the sight of such a tree. For a few pennies you can eat as many oranges as you like. They taste very good now, but in March they will taste even better.

April [1788] [Rome]

In our garden, an old secular priest looked after a number of lemon trees of medium height, planted in ornamented terracotta vases. In summer these enjoyed the fresh air but in winter they were kept in a greenhouse. When the lemons were ripe, they were picked with care, wrapped singly in soft paper, packed and sent off. They were particularly choice specimens and much in demand on the market.

Such an orangery was regarded by middle-class families as a capital investment which would pay a certain interest every year.

Italian Journey 1786–88, TRANS. W. H. Auden
and Elizabeth Mayer, 1962

Strawberries

EMILE ZOLA 1840–1902

Leaning over the balustrade, she was gazing at the grounds below her. They consisted of seven or eight acres of land, enclosed within a wall. Then the sight of the kitchen garden seized her attention. She darted back into the house and pushed past the maid on the stairs, stammering:

'It's full of cabbages! . . . You've never seen such big cabbages! . . . And lettuces, and sorrel, and onions, and everything! Come quick!'

The rain was falling more heavily now. She opened her white silk parasol, and ran down the garden walks.

'Madame will catch cold!' shouted Zoé, who had stayed safely under the glass porch over the steps.

But Madame wanted to see, and at each new discovery there was an exclamation.

'Zoé, there's spinach! Do come and see. . . . Oh! Artichokes! They *are* funny. So artichokes have flowers, do they? . . . Now, what can that be? I've never seen that before. . . . Do come, Zoé, perhaps you know.'

The maid did not budge. Madame must be raving mad. For now the rain was coming down in torrents, and the little white silk parasol was already completely black; it didn't shelter Madame either, and her skirts were wringing wet. Not that that seemed to bother her. In the pouring rain she toured the kitchen garden and the orchard, stopping in front of every tree, and bending over every bed of vegetables. Then she ran and looked down the well, lifted up a frame to see what was underneath it, and became engrossed in the contemplation of a huge pumpkin. She felt an urge to go along every path in the garden, and to take immediate possession of all the things she had dreamt of in the old days, when she had been a poor working-girl in Paris. The rain was getting heavier, but she did not feel it, her only complaint being that the daylight was fading. She could not see clearly any longer, and had to touch things with her fingers to find out what they were. All of a sudden, in the twilight, she made out a bed of strawberries, and all the longings of her childhood burst forth.

'Strawberries! Strawberries! There are some here: I can feel them! . . . A plate, Zoé. Come and pick strawberries.'

And Nana squatted in the mud, dropping her parasol and exposing herself to the full force of the downpour. Her hands dripping with water, she began picking strawberries among the leaves.

Nana, TRANS. George Holden, 1972

Country Dance
EDITH SITWELL 1887–1964

One of the poems from Façade *which was set to music by Sir William Walton and first performed at her brother's house in Carlyle Square, Chelsea in the winter of 1922. When Dame Edith recorded* Façade *with Peter Pears and the English Opera Group Ensemble the sleeve notes quoted her on the first public performance, 'which took place at the Aeolian Hall on June 12, 1923, caused alarm and raised an uproar among such custodians of the purity of our language, such upholders of tradition in Aesthetics, as writers of Revue, firemen on duty in the hall, and passing postmen, who, on being lassoed and consulted by journalists, expressed the opinion that we were mad. And that in no uncertain terms.'*

That hobnailed goblin, the bob-tailed Hob,
Said, 'It is time I began to rob.'
For strawberries bob, hob-nob with the pearls
Of cream (like the curls of the dairy girls),
And flushed with the heat and fruitish-ripe
Are the gowns of the maids who dance to the pipe.
Chase a maid?
She's afraid!
'Go gather a bob-cherry kiss from a tree,
But don't, I prithee, come bothering me!'
She said –

As she fled.
The snouted satyrs drink clouted cream
'Neath the chestnut-trees as thick as a dream;
So I went,
And I leant,
Where none but the doltish coltish wind
Nuzzled my hand for what it could find.
As it neighed,
I said,
'Don't touch me, sir, don't touch me, I say!
You'll tumble my strawberries into the hay.'
Those snow-mounds of silver that bee, the spring,
Has sucked his sweetness from, I will bring
With fair-haired plants and with apples chill
For the great god Pan's high altar . . . I'll spill
Not one!
So, in fun,
We rolled on the grass and began to run
Chasing that gaudy satyr the Sun;
Over the haycocks, away we ran
Crying, 'Here be berries as sunburnt as Pan!'
But Silenus
Has seen us . . .
He runs like the rough satyr Sun.

Come away!

Façade, 1922

Okra

MARJORIE KINNAN RAWLINGS 1896–1953

Okra is a Cinderella among vegetables. It lives a lowly life, stewed stickily with tomatoes, or lost of identity in a Creole gumbo. I do not know whether the magic wand with which I wave it into something finer than mere edibility is original, but I know no other cook who serves it as I do. To bring it to its glamorous fulfillment, only the very small tender young pods must be used. These are left with the stem end uncut and are cooked exactly seven minutes in rapidly boiling salted water. I serve them arranged like the spokes of a wheel on individual small plates, with individual bowls of Hollandaise sauce set in the center. The okra is lifted by the stem end as one lifts unhulled strawberries, dipped in the Hollandaise and eaten much more daintily than is possible with asparagus. The flavor is unique.

Cross Creek, 1942

Melon

EDWARD BUNYARD 1872–1939

Of all the ideals which our poor humanity cherishes, the concept of the ideal Melon stands alone, for we know in our inmost souls that it will never be realised. With a peach or an apple full satisfaction is often attained, but in our search for perfection the Melon eludes us again and again!

There is but little doubt that a dark chapter in melonic history lies concealed in the mists of antiquity. I suspect a family scandal, a *tertium quid*, and, if I may so far offend the delicacy of my readers, I would hint that a vegetable marrow played the dastard part. From that day the Melon has never quite recovered its self-respect, and we ourselves are uncertain whether to treat it as a fruit or a vegetable. Those of the Marrovian school take it with pepper, and their opponents – sugar.

The Anatomy of Dessert, 1933

Ode to the Tomato

PABLO NERUDA 1904–73

The street
drowns in tomatoes:
noon,
summer,
light
breaks
in two
tomato

halves,
and the streets
run
with juice.
In December
the tomato
cuts loose,
invades
kitchens,
takes over lunches,
settles
at rest
on sideboards,
with the glasses,
butter dishes,
blue salt-cellars.
It has
its own radiance,
a goodly majesty.
Too bad we must
assassinate:
a knife
plunges
into its living pulp,
red
viscera,
a fresh,
deep,
inexhaustible
sun
floods the salads
of Chile,
beds cheerfully
with the blonde onion,
and to celebrate
oil
the filial essence
of the olive tree
lets itself fall
over its gaping hemispheres,
the pimento

adds
its fragrance,
salt its magnetism –
we have the day's
wedding:
parsley
flaunts
its little flags,
potatoes
thump to a boil,
the roasts
beat
down the door
with their aromas:
it's time!
let's go!
and upon
the table,
belted by summer,
tomatoes,
stars of the earth,
stars multiplied
and fertile
show off
their convolutions,
canals
and plenitudes
and the abundance
boneless,
without husk,
or scale or thorn,
grant us
the festival
of ardent colour
and all-embracing freshness.

Selected Poems, 1970, TRANS. Nathaniel Tarn

H is for Happy

M. F. K. FISHER 1908–92

When I was a child my Aunt Gwen (who was not an aunt at all but a large-boned and enormous-hearted woman who, thank God, lived next door to us) used to walk my little sister Anne and me up into the hills at sundown. She insisted on pockets. We had to have at least two apiece when we were with her. In one of them, on these twilight promenades, would be some cookies. In the other, oh, deep sensuous delight! would be a fried egg sandwich!

Nobody but Aunt Gwen ever made fried egg sandwiches for us. Grandmother was carefully protected from the fact that we had ever even heard of them, and as for Mother, preoccupied with a second set of children, she shuddered at the thought of such grease-bound proteins with a thoroughness which should have made us chary but instead succeeded only in satisfying our human need for secrets.

The three of us, Aunt Gwen weighing a good four times what Anne and I did put together, would sneak out of the family ken whenever we could, into the blue-ing air, our pockets sagging and our spirits spiraling in a kind of intoxication of freedom, breathlessness, fatigue, and delicious anticipation. We would climb high above other mortals, onto a far rock or a fallen eucalyptus tree, and sit there, sometimes close as burrs and sometimes apart, singing straight through *Pinafore* and the Episcopal Hymn Book (Aunt Gwen was British and everything from contralto to basso profundo in the Whittier church choir), and biting voluptuously into our tough, soggy, indigestible and luscious suppers. We flourished on them, both physically and in our tenacious spirits.

An Alphabet for Gourmets, 1949

Nourish Me on an Egg
STEVIE SMITH 1902–71

Nourish me on an egg, Nanny,
And ply with bottled stout,
And I'll grow to be a man
Before the secret's out.

Nourish me on an egg, Nanny,
With bottled stout to drink,
And I'll grow to be a man
Before you can think.

Nourish me on an egg, Nanny,
Don't wring your hands and weep,
Bring me a glass of stout
And close my eyes in sleep.

Collected Poems, 1975

Welsh Mutton
GEORGE BORROW 1803–81

For dinner we had salmon and leg of mutton; the salmon from the Dee, the leg from the neighbouring Berwyn. The salmon was good enough, but I had eaten better; and here it will not be amiss to say, that the best salmon in the world is caught in the Suir, a river that flows past the beautiful town of Clonmel in Ireland. As for the leg of mutton it was truly wonderful; nothing so good had I ever tasted in the shape of a leg of mutton. The leg of mutton of Wales beats the leg of mutton of any other country, and I had never tasted a Welsh leg of mutton before. Certainly I shall never forget that first Welsh leg of mutton which I tasted, rich but delicate, replete with juices derived from the aromatic herbs of the noble Berwyn, cooked to a turn, and weighing just four pounds.

'O its savoury smell was great,
Such as well might tempt, I trow,
One that's dead to lift his brow.'

Let any one who wishes to eat leg of mutton in perfection go to Wales, but mind you to eat leg of mutton only. Welsh leg of mutton is superlative; but with the exception of the leg, the mutton of Wales is decidedly inferior to that of many other parts of Britain.

Wild Wales, 1854

The Dairy
ANDRÉ GIDE 1869–1951

The third door is the door of the dairy.

Peace; silence; endless dripping of the wicker trays where the cheeses are set to shrink; curds, heaped and pressed in metal moulds; on hot July days, the smell of curdled milk seemed cooler and sicklier – no, not sickly, but so mildly sour, so washed out, that it could only be smelt at the very back of one's nose, where it was already more a taste than a smell.

Churn, scoured to the utmost cleanliness. Little pats of butter lying on cabbage leaves. Red-handed dairy-maid. Windows, always kept open, but stretched with wire gauze to keep out cats and flies.

The pans are ranged in rows, full of milk which gradually turns yellow until all the cream has risen. The cream rises to the surface slowly; it puffs and wrinkles and separates from the whey. When the whey has lost all its richness, it is time to skim. . . . (But Nathaniel, I can't enter into all this. I have a friend who goes in for farming and who nevertheless can talk about it marvellously; he explains the use of everything and tells me that even the butter-milk is not wasted.) (In Normandy, they give it to the pigs, but it appears there is better to be done with it than that.) . . .

The fourth door opens into the cowhouse.

It is intolerably warm, but the cows smell sweet. Ah! if only I could go back to the time when the farmer's children who smelt so pleasantly of sweat used to scamper about with us in and out of the cows' legs; we searched for eggs in the corners of the hay-racks; we watched the cows for hours on end; we watched the dung fall and squelch on the ground;

we had bets, as to which would let drop first, and one day I fled terrified, because I thought one of them was suddenly going to give birth to a calf.

Fruits of the Earth, TRANS. Dorothy Bussy, 1952

Sicily

J. W. GOETHE 1749–1832

April 13 [1787] [Sicily]
So far I have said nothing about the food – an important subject, after all. The vegetables are delicious, especially the lettuce, which is very tender and tastes like milk; one can understand why the Ancients called it *lactuca*. The oil and wine are also good, but would be even better if prepared with greater care. The fish – excellent and of a most delicate flavour. We have always had good beef, too, though most people here do not recommend it.

Italian Journey 1786–88, TRANS. W. H. Auden
and Elizabeth Mayer, 1962

Apples

EDWARD BUNYARD 1872–1939

No fruit is more to our English taste than the Apple. Let the Frenchman have his Pear, the Italian his Fig, the Jamaican may retain his farinaceous Banana, and the Malay his Durian, but for us the Apple.

In a careful pomological study of my fellow-men I have met but one who really disliked apples, but as he was a Scotsman born in Bavaria, educated in England, domiciled in Italy, he is quite obviously ruled out.

What fruit can compare with the Apple for its extended season, lasting from August to June, keeping alive for us in winter, in its sun-stained flush and rustic russet, the memory of golden autumnal days?

Through all the seven ages of man it finds a welcome, and we now learn that not only does it keep the doctor from our doors but ourselves from the dentists.

Is there any other edible which is at once an insurance, a pleasure, and an economy?

The Anatomy of Dessert, 1933

Manners and Apples
RICHARDSON WRIGHT 1887–1961

Manners and Apples. To sink one's teeth in the crisp living tissue of an apple fresh picked from the tree (better dentifrice by far than powder or wash), to let the juice trickle down the throat and then to toss the core as far as you can throw it into the farther reaches of the orchard – ah, that's one of the best of the countryman's Autumnal delights. The polite eating of an apple with knife and fork at table brings no such satisfaction. To be enjoyed thoroughly, an apple must be eaten lustily and without manners.

And what sweet music are their names – Northern Spy, Red McIntosh, Alexander, Rhode Island Greening, Baldwin, Cortland, Wolf River, Winter Banana, Roxbury Russets, Delicious, Jonathan.

A confirmed apple-eater will develop as much of a 'nose' for their fragrance as a wine drinker for his Ports and Burgundies and Clarets. Each kind has its own aroma, and just as the wine drinker sniffs of his glass first, before a drop passes his lips, so does the epicure sniff at the skin before he plunges his teeth into it.

The Bed-Book of Eating and Drinking, 1943

Pomegranates
ANDRÉ GIDE 1869–1951

Nathaniel, what of pomegranates?
They were sold for a few pence in that Eastern market
Where they had been tumbled on to reed trays.
Some had rolled away into the dust
And naked children picked them up.

43

Their juice is tart like unripe raspberries.
Their flowers look made of wax;
They are coloured like the fruit.

Guarded treasure, honeycomb partitions,
Richness of flavour,
Pentagonal architecture.
The rind splits; the seeds fall –
Crimson seeds in azure bowls,
Or drops of gold in dishes of enamelled bronze.

Fruits of the Earth, TRANS. Dorothy Bussy, 1952

Custard Apple
D. H. LAWRENCE 1885–1930

Richard bought himself a big, knobbly, green, soft-crusted apple, at a Chinese shop, and a pretty mother-of-pearl spoon to eat it with. The queer Chinese, with their gabbling-gobbling way of speaking – were they parasites too? A strange, strange world. He took himself off to the gardens to eat his custard apple – a pudding inside a knobbly green skin – and to relax into the magic ease of the afternoon. The warm sun, the big, blue harbour with its hidden bays, the palm-trees, the ferry steamers sliding flatly, the perky birds, the inevitable shabby-looking, loafing sort of men strolling across the green slopes, past the red poinsettia bush, under the big flame-tree, under the blue, blue sky – Australian Sydney, with a magic like sleep, like sweet, soft sleep – a vast, endless, sun-hot, afternoon sleep with the world a mirage. He could taste it all in the soft, sweet, creamy custard apple. A wonderful sweet place to drift in. But surely a place that will some day wake terribly from this sleep.

Yet why should it? Why should it not drift marvellously for ever, with its sun and its marsupials?

Kangaroo, 1923

Asparagus
E. S. DALLAS 1828–79

The greatest defect of the English arrangement of dinner is that almost always vegetables are of no account save as adjuncts. It is not understood, except in the dinners of the poor, that a vegetable may make an excellent dish to be eaten by itself alone. To this rule, however, there are two exceptions made – in favour of artichokes and asparagus. It is a question whether this exception is due to a pure admiration of the vegetable, or to the circumstance that, having to be eaten with the fingers, it is necessary to put down either knife or fork in order to seize the vegetable. The probability is, that if the Creator had thought fit, in His wisdom, to endow the Englishman with three or four hands, he would never be seen eating the artichoke or the asparagus alone, but always in conjunction with some other food.

Kettner's Book of the Table, 1877

Asparagus
CONSTANCE SPRY 1886–1960

I suppose it will be considered *lèse-majesté* to say that English garden asparagus is the best in the world, the most delicately flavoured and the sweetest. Already I think I hear ghostly voices calling 'Argenteuil, Argenteuil,' and a vision springs up of a stately waiter in an expensive restaurant bearing a dish of gigantic stems of pale out-of-season asparagus to his most rich and valued clients. I am not going to say that I wouldn't like to eat it too, because I would eat asparagus whenever I had an opportunity, but it is a moment when I feel sorry for people who have to feed chiefly at hotels and who do not have a vegetable garden of their own, for the difference between the taste of these two kinds of the same vegetable is great. They are indeed poles apart. Early forced bunches of large stems are expensive and succulent, but lack the delicious flavour of the fresh green stems from the garden asparagus bed. Freshness with asparagus is a *sine qua non*; even this delicate

45

vegetable can acquire an unpleasant flavour if it has been kept too long at the vegetable shop.

The Constance Spry Cookery Book, 1956

Asparagus
JANE GRIGSON 1928–90

I have this image of early summer, May and June. We walk home slowly up the village street, which runs across the cliff at a kindly slope. The midday angelus rings from the church tower above us. Children stream out of school, and flow politely past our slower feet into open cottage doors. The air pulses with the warm smell of lilac, but as we pass each door, the lilac dominance is subdued by heady wafts of asparagus cooking.

This is not Utopia. It's a poorish village, less than 300 miles south of London.* The inhabitants have the sense to grow asparagus, that's all. If they haven't a garden patch across the river, they can buy it at 35p the lb. bunch in the village shop. No aristocratic aura. Not even a whiff of bourgeois privilege, just a universal smell of asparagus.

Good Things, 1971

Raw Artichokes
J. W. GOETHE 1749–1832

April 26 [1787] [Sicily]
Our *vetturino* eats raw artichokes and kohlrabi with the greatest gusto; it must be said, though, that they are much tenderer and more succulent here than they are in our climate. The same is true of other vegetables. When one passes through the fields, the peasants let one eat, for example, as many young broad beans as one likes, pods and all.

Italian Journey 1786–88, TRANS. W. H. Auden
and Elizabeth Mayer, 1962

* Trôo, Loire et Cher.

Artichoke

E. S. DALLAS 1828–79

Artichoke – It is good for a man to eat thistles, and to remember that he is an ass. But an artichoke is the best of thistles, and the man who enjoys it has the satisfaction of feeling that he is an ass of taste. There are several elaborate ways of dressing the artichoke – the Barigoule way and the Lyonnese way, for example, which have little to recommend them but their elaboration. Each is a mountain of labour for a mouse of result. The result is not bad; but it is always melancholy to see waste – and in art especially the pleasure of it is destroyed when we are made conscious of effort. The Barigoule and Lyonnese receipts are frantic attempts to paint the lily and to perfume the violet. When a great cook brings the whole battery of his kitchen to bear upon a simple artichoke bottom, one is reminded of Victor Hugo's comparison: 'It is as if the Deity were to bombard a lettuce with a thunderbolt.' Depend upon it that the simplest way of dressing the artichoke is the best. Trim it, boil it in salt and water, and let it be eaten with oil and vinegar, with English sauce or with Holland sauce. There is a special receipt for these sauces when served with vegetables. Some French cooks, before sending the artichoke to table, are careful to remove the choke, or as they call it, the hay. For this purpose the artichoke must either be allowed to cool, or must be dipped in cold water, and heated again after the removal of the hay – which might too vividly remind us how much we are asses. That hay in the artichoke certainly raises a delicate question, and it must be left to the good feeling of cooks whether they will or will not send it up to table.

Kettner's Book of the Table, 1877

Rice

ERICA JONG 1942–

The rice is pregnant.
It swells past its old transparency.
Hard, translucent worlds inside the grains
open like fans. It is raining rice!

The peasants stand under oiled
rice paper umbrellas cheering.

Someone is scattering rice from the sky!
Chopper blades mash the clouds.
The sky browns like cheese soufflé.
Rice grains puff & pop open.

'What have we done to deserve this?'
the peasants cry. Even the babies
are cheering. Cheers slide from their lips
like spittle. Old men kick their clogs
into the air & run in the rice paddies
barefoot. This is a monsoon! A wedding!

Each grain has a tiny invisible parachute.
Each grain is a rain drop.

'They have sent us rice!' the mothers scream,
opening their throats to the smoke . . .

Fruits and Vegetables, 1971

An Elizabethan Grace before Meat

ANON

'For bread and salt, for grapes and malt,
For flesh and fish, and euery dish:
Mutton and beefe, of all meates cheefe:
For cow-heels, chitterlings, tripes and sowse,
And other meate thats in the house:
For backs, for brests, for legges, for loines,
For pies with raisons, and with proines:
For fritters, pancakes, and for freyes,
For venison pasties, and minc't pies:
Sheephead and garlick, brawne and mustard.
Wafers, spic'd cakes, tart and custard,
For capons, rabets, pigges and geese,
For apples, carawaies and cheese:

For all these and many moe
Benedicamus Domino.'
Two Fifteenth Century Cookery Books, ED. Thomas Austin, 1888

Any Part of Piggy
NOËL COWARD 1899–1973

Any part of piggy
Is quite all right with me
Ham from Westphalia, ham from Parma
Ham as lean as the Dalai Lama
Ham from Virginia, ham from York,
Trotters, sausages, hot roast pork.
Crackling crisp for my teeth to grind on
Bacon with or without the rind on
Though humanitarian
I'm not a vegetarian.
I'm neither crank nor prude nor prig
And though it may sound infra dig
Any part of darling pig
Is perfectly fine with me.

Not Yet the Dodo, 1967

Truffles
GIACOMO CASTELVETRO 1546–1616

In the year of our Lord 1572 I found myself in Germany, studying the
somewhat cumbersome language of that noble nation. I was living in
the village of Rotteln in Baden Baden, about three miles outside the
beautiful city of Basle, which was so full of students from Italy, France
and Spain that I had been unable to find lodgings there.

One day I was invited to dine with the lord of that village and the
surrounding countryside. The company consisted of a group of
gentlemen, one of whom, a charming young baron, had just returned
from a visit to Italy. When he heard where I was from, he said, 'Can

49

you tell me, my friend, since you are Italian, why it is that the noblemen of the most civilized nation in the world perambulate their estates in the company of pigs?'

I assumed that he must have seen someone out hunting truffles, in the way I have just described, and could not help laughing at his bewilderment. He took this in bad part, as if I had been calling him a liar or making fun of him. 'Well,' he said crossly, 'is it true, or isn't it?' So to placate him I quickly replied, 'You are absolutely right, you may well have seen quite a few of these gentlemen walking along behind a pig, tied to one of its back legs with a piece of string. But you must also have noticed that the gentleman was followed by a peasant with a spade or shovel over his shoulder.' 'Well, yes, that's true,' he said, 'but there they all were, out walking with pigs.'

'What you saw,' I went on, 'was not an Italian nobleman leading his pig to pasture, but a gentleman following his pig on a treasure hunt. And great fun it is, too. The pig has a keen sense of smell, without which it would never be able to find the treasure, which is hidden deep in the ground under the snow. If you had waited long enough you would have seen the animal rootling in the ground with its snout, and the gentleman pulling the pig back, while the peasant dug away with his spade.'

The young nobleman replied, 'Now that I understand what was going on, I am no longer scandalized by such behaviour, and am very much obliged to you. But I still cannot imagine what on earth it was that they could have been searching for. If you do not mind, I should be vastly obliged to you for an explanation.'

'Well,' I replied, 'the treasure is not a lump of earth, as some people think, but a sort of mushroom that grows in the ground and never shows above it, called *tartufo*.'

When he heard its name, so like the German *der Teufel* (which means 'devil'), he said, 'Good heavens, how can you bear to eat that sort of monster!' At which I could not prevent myself from laughing out loud, and said, 'I wish to God we had some of these little devils here today, for I am sure that you and all the present company would enjoy them enormously.'

'Well, I must confess,' he said, 'I can well believe that, for I remember how I used to refuse to eat frogs and snails, when I was in your country. I thought they were quite repellent, and now I enjoy them so much I eat them the way other people do chickens or partridges.'

The Fruit, Herbs and Vegetables of Italy, TRANS. Gillian Riley, 1989

Cornish Cream
SACHEVERELL SITWELL 1897–1988

Many children have been tasting Devonshire cream for the first time in their lives. And they have been luckier still if it was scalded cream from Cornwall. For that is even better. This, and grouse from Scotland, are our two epicurean advantages over the French. Cornish cream has a furry, brown crust to it. I was taken to see an old gentleman of eighty who had eaten it all his life, four times a day, and he seemed none the worse. Eaten with ginger cake and black-currant jam it is an epicurean feast.

Truffle Hunt, 1953

Simple Pleasures
KATHERINE MANSFIELD 1888–1923

TO VERA BEAUCHAMP

[4 Fitzherbert Terrace] In the Smoking Room
June 19th [1908]

Digression no 2 – I had to leave this letter – go into the kitchen & cut myself an entire round of bread & bloater paste – tin loaf – because the body refuses to consider itself dined on one piece of flounder & an orange – I didn't know that Life held anything so ineffably delicious as this bread – was für Warheit [that's the truth!] Simple pleasures are the refuge of the complex, nicht?

Selected Letters, 1988

Cheese
EDWARD BUNYARD 1872–1939

Cheese is milk that has grown up. Every one feels a tinge of revulsion when strong, bearded men are caught in the act of milk drinking; we feel that this food, ordained for the mouths of babes and sucklings, is not for them.

But with cheese it is otherwise; it is pre-eminently the food of man – the older it grows the more manly it becomes, and in the last stages of senility it almost requires a room to itself, like the jokes consecrated to the smoking-room.

Cheese is one of the best indications of national character. In England, you will note, most cheeses are Cyclopean in size, not for a day but for a long time; no kickshaw cheeses for the countrymen of Fielding and Thackeray, and if it is a good cheese why try another? How different in France, where variety and adventure in taste is welcomed for its own sake! There you can run your course from the La Fontaine-like simplicity of Petit Suisse to the tingling Rabelaisian pungency of Roquefort; the Hugo-like romanticism of Pont-l'Évêque, and finally plunge into the abyss of decadence with Livarot, the very Verlaine of all cheeses. We may, indeed, divide cheeses into two groups, the romantic and the classic. They are easily distinguished. The romantics are apt to run over and become a little offensive when over-ripe. Classic cheeses do not; age may set them a little more firmly, but they never give way to it. Pungency and sting they may and do have, but all within the limits of decency. To the epics of Cheshire or Stilton, a Camembert stands as a sonnet thrown off in a moment of emotion, having perhaps all the poetic qualities save nobility.

The Epicure's Companion, ED. Edward and Lorna Bunyard, 1937

Black Pudding
JOHN FULLER 1937–

Butter a hot pan and therein slice,
Thumb-thick, a whole black quoit
Of black pudding. Add half a dozen lean

52

Rashers, cut to the size of the side
Of a box of matches; two large Bramleys
In chunks; and stir. The pudding's purple,
Flecked with white, blackens as you turn it
Until it shines with fat, a winning set
Of draughts. The bacon shrinks and crisps.
Before the apple does much more than soften
Add a whole tin of anchovies, each cut
In three. Stir once again, and serve.
Afterwards you may walk the block,
Or collect your daughter from judo, noticing
In the jut of lip and foot in the jostling
For a fall, an equal determination.
Then coffee, and music. And perhaps a cigar.

The Beautiful Inventions, 1983

Sorrel

JOHN FULLER 1937–

Apologies to the snail
For gathering his dinner
    And perhaps tomorrow's,
With whom I have no quarrel
As fingers search for sorrel.

The leaves are stacked against
The thumb, ready to spring
    Apart again
As from the packed plastic
They dump their green elastic

And stir upon the table,
A dark dealt freshness,
    In gathered mounds
Of vegetable life
That moisten to the knife.

With butter in a pan
They fall to a khaki slime
    As sharp as a lemon.

53

Outside, it continues to rain
And the snails walk again.

The Beautiful Inventions, 1983

Pork-pie
REBECCA WEST 1892–1983

'And if there's those who don't know what a pork-pie hat is, there's lots more that don't know what a pork-pie is. It's a very rare thing, let me tell you, a good pork-pie, and I can say so, for I'm one of the few people who can make one, though I say it myself.'

Richard stood up, advanced on her crying, 'A magic?'

'Well, cooking is,' she answered.

'Make me a magic pork-pie, make me a magic pork-pie with spell and onions,' he bade her, laughing.

'Well, I will, but there's a whole lot of things you have to get in,' she warned him; 'there's conger eel, for one thing.'

'Conger eel,' exclaimed Mamma, coming out of her musical remoteness, as she was willing to do if just cause were shown.

'Conger eel, conger eel, conger eel,' cried Richard Quin, in triplicate.

'Yes, indeed, conger eel,' said Aunt Lily, gravely, as if she did not want us to make a joke of something serious, 'veal and ham pie you can have without conger eel, that's quite natural, but you can't have a real pork-pie without a nice bit of conger eel in it.'

Richard Quin clasped her knees and laid his head in her lap, chuckling, 'This is lovely like the *Arabian Nights*,' while Mamma, gazing into the upper air at vast interlacing forms, like supple drainpipes, murmured, 'Conger eels, conger eels,' and the name, by reiteration, became something else, even more extraordinary.

'You are a funny crowd,' said Aunt Lily, delighted at the sensation she was creating, 'everybody who can make a good pork-pie knows that, though as I say there's few enough of us who can. I never would have learned the trick, if it hadn't been that old Uncle Joe Salter who did the cold table for the Admiral Benbow down at the Old Harbour took a fancy to me and showed me.'

Richard Quin seized on this superb supply of raw material for nonsense. 'Admiral Benbow, he had a cold table, a very – cold – table – a table dripping with stalactites,' he chanted in ecstasy, shuddering

and turning up an imaginary coat collar, 'down by the harbour, the
very old harbour the one they don't use any more, it's far too old and
far too deep, and there's the thing with two heads that eats the
anchors, so nobody goes there now except Uncle Joe Salter, and Uncle
Joe Salt, and Uncle Joe Saltest – Aunt Lily, Aunt Lily, do, do go on.'

'Hark at the child,' said Aunt Lily, 'goodness, I do wish old Uncle
Joe Salter was alive to hear that, Uncle Joe Salt and Uncle Joe Saltest,
he'd have died of laughing. But now, since you're all so interested in
pork-pies, I wonder if I could make one tonight. Do you know if the
girl's got a good stock-pot going?'

Kate had indeed. And Mamma did what was almost unthinkable,
she gave us permission to go out after dark, and presently Richard
Quin and I were scurrying through the night beside Aunt Lily, who
walked with excessive speed and frequently burst into excessive
laughter, and threaded her way through alleys we had never noticed
before, into little black shops where Aunt Lily demanded the ingredients necessary to a real pork-pie with an air of adept cunning and
troglodytish shop-keepers sold them to her with an equally zestful air
of complicity. She paused to tell us that whereas there were a great
many good butchers, ordinary butchers, a good *pork* butcher was as
rare as an archbishop. After that she shot with an air of having dodged
a barrier into an establishment where she found some good lean fillets
of pork and some lard, which, we gathered from her unctuous
explanation, was white as the new snow because it came from the farm
belonging to the father-in-law of the plump gentleman in a blue overall
behind the marble counter. This increased Richard Quin's sense of the
magic inherent in a pork-pie, and thereafter a pork-butcher wizard
and his father-in-law, a djinn who lived in a haystack and wore a
smock, constantly appeared in our games and stories. In a shop crusted
like a bottle of port an old grocer with whitening eyes sold us what
Aunt Lily certified as by far the best black pepper-corns to be bought in
the whole of London. There was a conspiracy of silence over the
impossibility of obtaining conger eel. We pretended we had done all in
order. Then we came back into the commonplace high street and
hurried contemptuously by the people who were going to buy the
usual things in the shops everyone knew about, and got back to the
kitchen just about the right time to take off the bones that had been
simmering on the range for gravy since morning.

At length Aunt Lily came to, as it were, her cadenza. She had to build
the pastry she had made with the lard into a tower; we called the others
down to look, and Kate stood behind us, her hands on her hips,

nodding in professional sympathy. It was really very clever, because not only did Aunt Lily have to build the pastry into a tower, she had to fill it with pieces of meat and hard-boiled egg, and pour in some gravy, and put on a pastry hat just to fit, and as you have to make that sort of pastry by boiling the lard with some water and mixing it into the flour it was quite warm and soft, so that the whole thing might have fallen down if she had not been quick and careful. There was an easy way of making it by moulding the pastry on a jar, but Aunt Lily said that that was a mug's game, and one had one's pride; and she smiled proudly as she watched her hands perform the remembered trick. 'Nancy never saw me do this,' she sighed. 'Queenie would never let the children eat anything vulgar. Harry liked it, when he went out in his boat, but I could never get into the kitchen, with those blessed maids always hanging about.' She gave Kate a quick smile. 'Not like you.'

'I know what you mean,' said Kate. 'That's why I am a general. I know what girls are like when there's more than one kept.'

They nodded in understanding. We all felt safe in the warm cave of our kitchen.

'Haven't any reason, now I come to think of it, to think Clara isn't a good woman,' meditated Aunt Lily, her fingers still busy. 'She's from the North. They say North Country people are very homely.'

So we got through that sad evening; and we ate the pork-pie the following day at luncheon and we thought it wonderful, though Aunt Lily suffered over it as artists do when they have to make compromises for the sake of their friends, for Kate had reminded her that, like most children at that time, we were allowed no condiments, and she had been obliged to leave out the unique peppercorns. But she owned it was as good as could be expected, considering that omission.

The Fountain Overflows, 1957

The Oddest of Dinners

EMILE ZOLA 1840–1902

'I say, aren't you going to have anything to eat this evening? *I'm* dying of hunger. I haven't had any dinner.'

Nana was cross with him. The great booby, to sneak out of his mama's house on an empty stomach, just to go and fall in a waterhole? But she was as hungry as a hunter too. Of course they must eat! Only they would have to make do with what they could get. And they set to work to improvise the oddest of dinners on a small table they rolled up in front of the fire. Zoé ran down to the gardener's, who had cooked a cabbage soup in case Madame didn't dine at Orléans before she arrived, because Madame had forgotten to tell him in her letter what he was to get ready. Fortunately the cellar was well furnished. So they had cabbage soup, with a piece of bacon. Then, rummaging in a bag, Nana found a whole heap of provisions which she had taken the precaution of stuffing into it: a *pâté de foie gras*, a bag of sweetmeats and some oranges. The two of them ate like wolves, with the healthy appetite of twenty-year-olds, not standing on ceremony with each other. Nana kept calling Georges 'my sweet', a form of address which struck her both as affectionate and familiar. At dessert, so as not to disturb Zoé, they used the same spoon in turn to empty a pot of jam they found at the top of a cupboard.

'My sweet,' said Nana, pushing back the table. 'I haven't had such a good dinner these past ten years!'

Nana, TRANS. George Holden, 1972

Supper with Mole

KENNETH GRAHAME 1859–1932

'Rat,' he moaned, 'how about your supper, you poor, cold, hungry, weary animal? I've nothing to give you – nothing – not a crumb!'

'What a fellow you are for giving in!' said the Rat reproachfully. 'Why, only just now I saw a sardine-opener on the kitchen dresser, quite distinctly; and everybody knows that means there are sardines about somewhere in the neighbourhood. Rouse yourself! pull yourself together, and come with me and forage.'

They went and foraged accordingly, hunting through every cupboard and turning out every drawer. The result was not so very depressing after all, though of course it might have been better; a tin of sardines – a box of captain's biscuits, nearly full – and a German sausage encased in silver paper.

'There's a banquet for you!' observed the Rat, as he arranged the table. 'I know some animals who would give their ears to be sitting down to supper with us to-night!'

'No bread!' groaned the Mole dolorously; 'no butter, no –'

'No *pâté de foie gras*, no champagne!' continued the Rat, grinning, 'And that reminds me – what's that little door at the end of the passage? Your cellar, of course! Every luxury in this house! Just you wait a minute.'

He made for the cellar door, and presently reappeared, somewhat dusty, with a bottle of beer in each paw and another under each arm. 'Self-indulgent beggar you seem to be, Mole,' he observed. 'Deny yourself nothing. This is really the jolliest little place I ever was in.'

The Wind in the Willows, 1908

Ma Kettle's Cinnamon Rolls
BETTY MACDONALD 1908–58

I turned into a driveway that led along the side of the house but there arose such a terrific barking and snarling and yapping from a pack of mongrels by the back porch, that I was about to leap over the fence into the orchard when the back door flew open and someone yelled to the dogs to 'stop that god-damn noise!' Mrs. Kettle, a mountainously fat woman in a very dirty housedress, waddled to the corner of the porch and called cordially, 'Come in, come in, glad to see you!' but as I drew timidly abreast of the porch my nostrils were dealt such a stinging blow by the outhouse lurking doorless and unlovely directly across from it that I almost staggered. Apparently used to the outhouse, Mrs. Kettle kicked me a little path through the dog bones and chicken manure on the back porch and said, 'We was wonderin' how long afore you'd git lonesome and come down to see us,' then ushered me into the kitchen, which was enormous, cluttered and smelled deliciously of fresh bread and hot coffee. 'I'll have a pan of rolls baked by the time the coffee's poured, so set down and make yourself comfortable.' She indicated a large black leather rocker by the stove and so I sat down gratefully and immediately a long thin cat leaped into my lap, settled himself carefully and began purring like a buzz saw. As he purred I stroked him until I noticed a dark knot of fleas between his eyes from which single fleas were disentangling themselves and crawling down on to his nose and into the corners of his eyes and then unhurriedly going back into the knot again. I gently lifted him off my lap and put him down by the stove but he jumped back again and I pushed him off and he jumped back and so finally I gave up and let him stay but stopped stroking him and tried to keep track of the fleas to be sure they went back after each sortie.

The Kettles' kitchen was easily forty feet long and thirty feet wide. Along one wall were a sink and drain-boards, drawers and cupboards. Along another wall was a giant range and a huge woodbox. Back of the range and woodbox were pegs to hang wet coats to dry but from which hung parts of harness, sweaters, tools, parts of cars, a freshly painted fender, hats, a hot-water bottle and some dirty rags. On the floor behind the stove were shoes, boots, more car parts, tools, dogs, bicycles and a stack of newspapers. In the centre of the kitchen was a table about nine feet square, covered with a blue and white oilcloth tablecloth, a Rochester lamp, a basket of sewing, the Sears, Roebuck and Montgomery Ward catalogues, a large, thick white sugar bowl and cream pitcher, a butter dish with a cover on it, a jam dish with a cover on it, a spoon-holder, a fruit jar filled with pencil stubs, an ink bottle and a dip pen. Spaced along other walls were bureaus, bookcases, kitchen queen, work tables and a black leather sofa. Opening from the kitchen were doors to a hall, the parlour, the pantry (an enormous room lined with shelves) and the back porch. The floor was fir and evidently freshly scrubbed, which seemed the height of useless endeavour to me in view of the chicken manure and refuse on the back porch and the muddy door yard.

While I was getting my bearings and keeping track of the fleas, Mrs. Kettle waddled between the pantry and the table setting out thick white cups and saucers and plates. Mrs. Kettle had pretty light brown hair, only faintly streaked with grey and skinned back into a tight knot, clear blue eyes, a creamy skin which flushed exquisitely with the heat, a straight delicate nose, fine even white teeth, and a small rounded chin. From this dainty pretty head cascaded a series of busts and stomachs which made her look like a cookie jar shaped like a woman. Her whole front was dirty and spotted and she wiped her hands continually on one or the other of her stomachs. She had also a disconcerting habit of reaching up under her dress and adjusting something in the vicinity of her navel and of reaching down the front of her dress and adjusting her large breasts. These adjustments were not, I learned later, confined to either the privacy of the house or a female gathering – they were made anywhere – any time. 'I itch – so I scratch – so what!' was Mrs. Kettle's motto.

But never in my life have I tasted anything to compare with the cinnamon rolls which she took out of the oven and served freshly frosted with powdered sugar. They were so tender and delicate I had to bring myself up with a jerk to keep from eating a dozen. The coffee was so strong it snarled as it lurched out of the pot and I girded up my loins for the first swallow and was amazed to find that when mixed with plenty of thick cream it was palatable. True it bore only the faintest resemblance to coffee as I made it but still it had a flavour that was good when I got my throat muscles loosened up again.

The Egg and I, 1947

Oysters

ELEANOR CLARK 1913–

The human race is said to be growing taller, but its stomach is evidently shrinking. In the past, where oysters were eaten at all, a plate of six or a dozen would have been considered ridiculous. Another important fact of mollusc-lore is that although oysters have had certain ups and downs in popularity as food in some parts of the world, in general man seems to have been eating them, if not gorging on them, from the minute he appeared. Or since he was kicked out of the garden, since Adam is pictured as a vegetarian before that, and there is no mention of any seacoast nearby. Anyhow, if you could bring together the shells of all the oysters consumed by humans since we have been around they would probably stack up to something like the Himalayas and then some, and this has mostly not been a matter of word getting around from one area to another. Oyster-eating was world-wide long before the Phoenicians and the Vikings. Apparently people took to it independently, while still in the grunting stage, on all the temperate-zone coasts of the world where the oyster of any sort was available.

The Oysters of Locmariaquer, 1965

Love and Oysters
CHARLES DICKENS 1812–70

Mr. John Dounce was returning one night from the Sir Somebody's Head, to his residence in Cursitor Street – not tipsy, but rather excited, for it was Mr. Jennings's birthday, and they had had a brace of partridges for supper, and a brace of extra glasses afterwards, and Jones had been more than ordinarily amusing – when his eyes rested on a newly-opened oyster shop, on a magnificent scale, with natives laid, one deep, in circular marble basins in the windows, together with little round barrels of oysters directed to Lords and Baronets, and Colonels and Captains, in every party of the habitable globe.

Behind the natives were the barrels, and behind the barrels was a young lady of about five-and-twenty, all in blue, and all alone – splendid creature, charming face, and lovely figure! It is difficult to say whether Mr. John Dounce's red countenance, illuminated as it was by the flickering gas-light in the window before which he paused, excited the lady's risibility, or whether a natural exuberance of animal spirits proved too much for that staidness of demeanour which the forms of society rather dictatorially prescribe. But certain it is that the lady smiled: then put her finger upon her lip, with a striking recollection of what was due to herself; and finally retired, in oyster-like bashfulness, to the very back of the counter. The sad-dog sort of feeling came strongly upon John Dounce; he lingered – the lady in blue made no sign. He coughed – still she came not. He entered the shop.

'Can you open me an oyster, my dear?' said Mr. John Dounce.

'Dare say I can, sir,' replied the lady in blue with playfulness. And Mr. John Dounce ate one oyster, and then looked at the young lady; and then ate another, and then squeezed the young lady's hand as she was opening the third, and so forth, until he had devoured a dozen of those at eightpence in less than no time.

'Can you open me half a dozen more, my dear?' inquired Mr. John Dounce.

'I'll see what I can do for you, sir,' replied the young lady in blue, even more bewitchingly than before; and Mr. John Dounce ate half a dozen more of those at eightpence.

Sketches by 'Boz', 1836–7

Oyster Soup
LADY HARRIET ST CLAIR d. 1867

*In the preface Lady Harriet wrote that a relation of hers expressed
the opinion that, 'Original English, or what is called plain cooking,
is the worst, and the most ignorant, and the most extravagant, in
the known world!' The author herself agreed with the French chef
Louis Eustache Ude who had written on the subject of the English
sauce a few decades earlier. 'What can be more unpalatable than the
horrible attempts at entrées, dignified with some high-sounding
French name, made by the general run of English cooks? The
sodden pieces of meat, soaking in a mess of flour and butter,
commonly called roux, which, with the addition of a little melted
glaze, forms the English cook's universal idea of a sauce, and which
they liberally and indiscriminately bestow on fish, flesh and
fowl . . .' she wrote. She obviously did not regard a lavish use of
oysters extravagant in the days when they were cheap and plentiful.*

Take eighty oysters and their liquor; place them in a pan with salt,
cayenne pepper, and a teaspoonful of chopped chervil; when boiling
add three yolks of eggs beat up in half a pint of cream, and serve. This
is enough for five persons. If the oysters have not sufficient liquor, a
little water and salt may be added, and parsley may be used if
preferred, instead of chervil.

Dainty Dishes, 1866

Poem in Praise of Fish
SYDNEY SMITH 1771–1845

Much do I love, at civic treat,
The monsters of the deep to eat;
To see the rosy salmon lying,
By smelts encircled, born for frying;
And from the china boat to pour,
On flaky cod, the flavour'd shower.

Thee, above all, I much regard,
Flatter than Longman's flattest bard,
Much honour'd turbot! – sore I grieve
Thee and thy dainty friends to leave.

Receipt to Roast Mutton

SYDNEY SMITH 1771–1845

Gently stir and blow the fire,
Lay the mutton down to roast,
  Dress it quickly, I desire;
In the dripping put a toast,
  That I hunger may remove; –
  Mutton is the meat I love.

  On the dresser see it lie;
Oh! the charming white and red!
  Finer meat ne'er met the eye,
On the sweetest grass it fed;
  Let the jack go swiftly round,
  Let me have it nicely brown'd.

  On the table spread the cloth,
Let the knives be sharp and clean,
  Pickles get and salad both,
Let them each be fresh and green.
  With small beer, good ale, and wine,
  O ye gods! How shall I dine!

Fish Feast

THOMAS LOVE PEACOCK 1785–1866

All day we sat, until the sun went down –
'Twas summer, and the Dog-star scorched the town –
At fam'd Blackwall, O Thames! upon thy shore,
Where Lovegrove's tables groan beneath their store;

We feasted full on every famous dish
Dress'd many ways, of sea and river fish –
Perch, mullet, eels, and salmon, all were there,
And whitebait, daintiest of our fishy fare;
Then meat of many kinds, and venison last,
Quails, fruits, and ices, crowned the rich repast.
Thy fields, Champagne, supplied us with our wine,
Madeira's Island, and the rocks of Rhine.
The sun was set, and twilight veiled the land:
Then all stood up, – all who had strength to stand,
And pouring down, of Maraschino, fit
Libations to the gods of wine and wit,
In steam-wing'd chariots, and on iron roads,
Sought the great city, and our own abodes.

The Greying of John Major

CAL McCRYSTAL

Mr Major has only one proven personal weakness: food. At the Treasury he often would be seen sitting on his own consuming hamburgers in a nearby greasy-spoon establishment. While at the DHSS, he feasted on baked beans and sausages. On his way to this year's Young Conservative conference in Scarborough, he refreshed himself at a roadside Happy Eater.

The Independent on Sunday, 21 April 1991

National Styles

❦

The Germans
TACITUS 55–120 AD

As soon as they wake, which is often well after sunrise, they wash, generally with warm water – as one might expect in a country where winter lasts so long. After washing they eat a meal, each man having a separate seat and table. Then they go out to attend to any business they have in hand, or, as often as not, to partake in a feast – always with their weapons about them. Drinking-bouts lasting all day and all night are not considered in any way disgraceful. The quarrels that inevitably arise over the cups are seldom settled merely by hard words, but more often by killing and wounding. Nevertheless, they often make a feast an occasion for discussing such affairs as the ending of feuds, the arrangement of marriage alliances, the adoption of chiefs, and even questions of peace or war. At no other time, they think, is the heart so open to sincere feelings or so quick to warm to noble sentiments. The Germans are not cunning or sophisticated enough to refrain from blurting out their inmost thoughts in the freedom of festive surroundings, so that every man's soul is laid completely bare. On the following day the subject is reconsidered, and thus due account is taken of both occasions. They debate when they are incapable of pretence but reserve their decision for a time when they cannot well make a mistake.

Their drink is a liquor made from barley or other grain, which is fermented to produce a certain resemblance to wine. Those who dwell nearest the Rhine or the Danube also buy wine. Their food is plain – wild fruit, fresh game, and curdled milk. They satisfy their hunger without any elaborate cuisine or appetizers. But they do not show the same self-control in slaking their thirst. If you indulge their intemperence by plying them with as much drink as they desire, they will be as easily conquered by this besetting weakness as by force of arms.

The Agricola: The Germania, TRANS. H. Mattingly
and S. A. Handford, 1970

Demoralizing the Britons
TACITUS 55–118 AD

The following winter was spent on schemes of social betterment. Agricola had to deal with people living in isolation and ignorance, and therefore prone to fight; and his object was to accustom them to a life of peace and quiet by the provision of amenities. He therefore gave private encouragement and official assistance to the building of temples, public squares, and good houses. He praised the energetic and scolded the slack; and competition for honour proved as effective as compulsion. Furthermore, he educated the sons of the chiefs in the liberal arts, and expressed a preference for British ability as compared with the trained skills of the Gauls. The result was that instead of loathing the Latin language they became eager to speak it effectively. In the same way, our national dress came into favour and the toga was everywhere to be seen. And so the population was gradually led into the demoralizing temptations of arcades, baths, and sumptuous banquets. The unsuspecting Britons spoke of such novelties as 'civilization', when in fact they were only a feature of their enslavement.

The Agricola: The Germania, TRANS. H. Mattingly
and S. A. Handford, 1970

Expensive v Cheap
THEODORE ZELDIN 1933–

Once upon a time, the Swiss produced the best watches, the Germans made the best cameras and every rich man aspired to have a French cook. For most of this century, the most expensive hotels all over the world have felt obliged to offer French food, or a parody of it, and at least a menu in French. But the supremacy of French cooking is threatened. The mistake the French made was to export expensive food, that is, for a minority. The Chinese have countered by appealing to the hungry student. Since every nation has a fundamental hostility to foreign food, the Chinese were able to overcome resistance by giving the masses a good reason for accepting their food: they made it cheap. The result is that today in Britain there are eight times as many Chinese restaurants as there are French ones[1] and in the United States the Chinese also lead the field (in equality with the Italians). Simple French peasant food has not entered the homes of the masses: Heinz Baked Beans has been preferred to Cassoulet Toulousain and the Americans have mastered the fast food business. The refrain in every French discussion of their attitudes to foreigners is their inability to tolerate foreign cooking. Food isolates the French almost as much as their language. That would not be serious if France were at least certain of remaining a refuge for good food. But that is in doubt.

The French, 1983

Clinging to the Old
CLAUDIA RODEN 1936–

The changes that occur to regional foods when they travel and become ethnic foods in other lands do not depend solely on their gastronomic value nor on the produce available in the new territory. Many other factors are involved: economic, social and ideological, and not least the need to cling to an old identity or the wish to discard it. For cooking is the part of culture which remains closest to people and matters most; more than music and painting and clothing, more than language and sometimes even more than religion. For some generations of some peoples it may be all that is left, long after everything else has been lost; for it is that which makes people happy and comfortable.

'*Cooking in Israel: A Changing Mosaic*',
Oxford Food Symposium, 1981

---

[1] 4000 Chinese restaurants, 2000 Indian and Pakistani, 1500 Italian, 1200 Greek and Turkish and 500 French.

Meat

NANCY MITFORD 1904–73

Meat: People here have been very much upset by an account in the newspapers of the horrible, long, waterless journey undergone by the poor horses sent from the British Isles to be killed and eaten here. The French think it not only cruel but also extremely odd that a country so short of meat that whales and reindeer are sold in the butchers' shops should export perfectly good *biftek de cheval* to this land of plenty.

'Paris Column', *Sunday Times*, 17 August 1952

American Cooking

FRANCES TROLLOPE 1780–1863

In relating all I know of America, I surely must not omit so important a feature as the cooking. There are sundry anomalies in the mode of serving even a first-rate table; but as these are altogether matters of custom, they by no means indicate either indifference or neglect in this important business; and whether castors are placed on the table or on the side-board; whether soup, fish, patties, and salad be eaten in orthodox order or not, signifies but little. I am hardly capable, I fear, of giving a very erudite critique on the subject; general observations therefore must suffice. The ordinary mode of living is abundant, but not delicate. They consume an extraordinary quantity of bacon. Ham and beef-steaks appear morning, noon, and night. In eating, they mix things together with the strangest incongruity imaginable. I have seen eggs and oysters eaten together; the sempiternal ham with apple-sauce; beef-steak with stewed peaches; and salt fish with onions. The bread is everywhere excellent, but they rarely enjoy it themselves, as they insist upon eating horrible half-baked hot rolls both morning and evening. The butter is tolerable; but they have seldom such cream as every little dairy produces in England; in fact, the cows are very roughly kept, compared with our's. Common vegetables are abundant and very fine. I never saw sea-cale, or cauliflowers, and either from the want of summer rain, or the want of care, the harvest of green vegetables is much sooner over than with us. They eat the Indian corn in a great variety of forms; sometimes it is dressed green, and eaten like peas; sometimes it is broken to pieces when dry, boiled plain, and brought to table like rice; this dish is called hominy. The flour of it is made into at least a dozen different sorts of cakes; but in my opinion all bad. This flour, mixed in the proportion of one-third, with fine wheat, makes by far the best bread I ever tasted.

I never saw turbot, salmon, or fresh cod; but the rock and shad are excellent. There is a great want of skill in the composition of sauces; not only with fish, but with every thing. They use very few made dishes, and I never saw any that would be approved by our savants. They have an excellent wild duck, called the Canvass Back, which, if delicately served, would surpass the black cock; but the game is very inferior to our's; they have no hares, and I never saw a pheasant. They seldom indulge in second courses, with all their ingenious temptations to the eating a second dinner; but almost every table has its dessert, (invariably pronounced desart) which is placed on the table before the cloth is removed, and consists of pastry, preserved fruits, and creams. They are 'extravagantly fond', to use their own phrase, of puddings, pies, and all kinds of 'sweets', particularly the ladies; but are by no means such connoisseurs in soups and ragoûts as the gastronomes of Europe. Almost every one drinks water at table, and by a strange contradiction, in the country where hard drinking is more prevalent than in any other, there is less wine taken at dinner; ladies rarely exceed one glass, and the great majority of females never take any. In fact, the hard drinking, so universally acknowledged, does not take place at jovial dinners, but, to speak plain English, in solitary dram-drinking. Coffee is not served immediately after dinner, but makes part of the serious matter of tea-drinking, which comes some hours later. Mixed dinner parties of ladies and gentlemen are very rare, and unless several foreigners are present, but little conversation passes at table. It certainly does not, in my opinion, add to the well ordering a dinner table, to set the gentlemen at one end of it, and the ladies at the other; but it is very rarely that you find it otherwise.

Domestic Manners of the Americans, 1832

Aboriginal Life
MICHAEL SYMONS 1945–

The British government exploded a handful of nuclear bombs at Maralinga and Woomera in South Australia between 1953 and 1957 and fired various missiles into the 1960s. The British chose central Australia because they considered it was so arid that few pastoral stations, let alone towns, blocked their path. Nevertheless, they had to despatch patrols to round up remnants of the 10,000 or more Aborigines who once roamed the Western desert. Deposited in the care of mission stations and government settlements and no longer permitted to wander the distances necessary to find food and water, the refugees soon picked the nearby desert clean. Dependent on White rations, they began to lose the complicated skills and culture which had sustained them perhaps 40,000 years in apparently inhospitable conditions. And so, Australia's last completely self-sufficient hunter-gatherers were brought into the fringe of industrial society.

Studying the last of the tribes in 1966–67, anthropologist Dr Richard Gould gave a glimpse of how food was consumed in Australia before the arrival of the Europeans. He found that these Aborigines covered the greatest distance of any nomads – walks of 400 and 550 km were not unusual, particularly in times of drought. Groups shifted camp as many as nine times in three months, foraging over roughly 2,500 square km. he said. Moving typically in groups of 10 to 30, they came together in groups of 100 or more when food was plentiful.

The monotonous Western desert of long, low sandhills and gravel knolls lacked real seasons, making food unpredictable. Yet with 38 edible plants and 47 varieties of meats available to them, the Aborigines considered food less a problem than the terrifying lack of water. The rains averaged about 250 mm annually, but that figure is misleading since many years came with scarcely a drop. There were no freshwater lakes, flowing rivers or permanent springs in the desert, and the Warburton-Musgrave and Rawlinson-Petermann ranges were landmarks without streams. Instead, the Aborigines relied on occasional shaded pools in rocky areas or sub-surface water tables, the so-called 'native wells', where they dug. Dr Gould, who happened to visit in the last months of a record drought, summed this habitat up as the world's 'most unreliable and impoverished'. Yet these Australians lived a healthy, contented and fulfilled life. They survived not so much through great physical endurance as through knowledge – their 'cognitive map' of where to find food and, especially, water.

The women sought the berries, seeds, leaves, bulbs, roots and fruits which made up the bulk of the primarily vegetarian diet. The main daily staple was about 1.5 kg each of desert tomatoes. Good rain would bring wild figs. Drought meant relying more on dried fruit, like quandong desiccated on the tree. Some dried fruit was preserved in balls. The women and children also caught small game, such as goannas, mice, birds, grubs and, more recently, rabbits and cats. Yet the food quest did not require more than four or five hours of work for each woman daily, and generally less. Even in drought, two or three hours' collecting could be sufficient. The women's work, in a sense, freed the men for their longer hours of more chancy hunting. As with the women, they collected small game but also hoped for a feast like a kangaroo or emu. It still left plenty of time for people to rest, gossip and make tools and artworks. Their adaptation was an 'impressive human achievement,' Dr Gould concluded. Ironically, the tough environment protected the desert nomads nearly two centuries longer than their amply-provided coastal counterparts, as European invasion reduced an estimated 314,500 Aboriginal population to one-fifth by the 1930s.

One Continuous Picnic, 1982

Shopping in Australia
D. H. LAWRENCE 1885–1930

She still had in her mind's eye an Australia with beautiful manorial farm-houses and dainty, perfect villages. She never acquiesced in the *uncreatedness* of the new country, the rawness, the slovenliness. It seemed to her comical, for instance, that no women in Australia would carry a basket. Harriet went shopping as usual with her pretty straw basket in the village. But she felt that the women remarked on it. Only then did she notice that everybody carried a suit-case in this discreet country. The fat old woman who came to the door with a suit-case must, she thought, be a visitor coming to the wrong house. But no. 'Did you want a cabbage?' In the suitcase two cabbages and half a pumpkin. A little girl goes to the dairy for six eggs and half a pound of butter with a small, elegant suit-case. Nay, a child of three toddled with a little six-inch suit-case, containing, as Harriet had occasion to see, two buns, because the suit-case flew open and the two buns rolled out. Australian suit-cases were always flying open, and discharging groceries or a skinned rabbit or three bottles of beer. One had the impression that everybody was perpetually going away for the week-end: with a suit-case. Not so at all. Just a new-country bit of convention.

Ah, a new country! The cabbage, for example, cost tenpence in the normal course of things, and a cauliflower a shilling. And the tradesmen's carts flew round in the wilderness, delivering goods. There isn't much newness in *man*, whatever the country.

Kangaroo, 1923

London Supper – Restaurant
EVELYN WAUGH 1902–66

On the night of my return I dined in London. After dinner we were in some doubt where to go. The names I suggested had long ceased to be popular. Eventually we decided, and drove to a recently opened supper-restaurant which, they said, was rather amusing at the moment.

It was underground. We stepped down into the blare of noise as into a hot swimming-pool, and immersed ourselves; the atmosphere caught our breath like the emanation in a brewery over the tanks where fermentation begins. Cigarette-smoke stung the eyes.

A waiter beckoned us to a small table, tight-packed among other tables, so that our chairs rubbed backs with their neighbours. Waiters elbowed their way in and out, muttering abuse in each others' ears. Some familiar faces leered through the haze: familiar voices shrilled above the din.

We chose some wine.

'You'll have to take something to eat with it.'

We ordered seven-and-sixpenny sandwiches.

Nothing came.

A Negro in fine evening-clothes was at the piano, singing. Afterwards, when he went away, people fluttered their hands at him and tried to catch his eye. He bestowed a few patronizing nods. Someone yelled, 'He's losing his figure.'

A waiter came and said, 'Any more orders for drinks before closing time?' We said we had had nothing yet. He made a face and pinched another waiter viciously in the arm, pointing at our table and whispering in Italian. That waiter pinched another. Eventually the last-pinched waiter brought a bottle and slopped out some wine into glasses. It frothed up and spilt on the tablecloth. We looked at the label and found that it was not the wine we had ordered.

Someone shrilled in my ear: 'Why, Evelyn, where *have* you been? I haven't seen you about anywhere for days.'

My friends talked about the rupture of an engagement which I did not know was contracted.

The wine tasted like salt and soda water. Mercifully a waiter whisked it away before we had time to drink it. 'Time, if you please.'

I was back in the centre of the Empire, and in the spot where, at the moment, 'everyone' was going. Next day the gossip-writers would chronicle the young M.P.s, peers, and financial magnates who were assembled in that rowdy cellar, hotter than Zanzibar, noisier than the market at Harar, more reckless of the decencies of hospitality than the taverns of Kabalo or Tabora. And a month later the wives of English officials would read about it, and stare out across the bush or jungle or desert or forest or golf links, and envy their sisters at home, and wish they had the money to marry rich men.

Why go abroad?

See England first.

Just watch London knock spots off the Dark Continent.

I paid the bill in yellow African gold. It seemed just tribute from the weaker races to their mentors.

Remote People, 1931

The Pavlova

MICHAEL SYMONS 1945–

Not surprisingly, the great promoters of daintiness, which turned mere 'feeding' into 'dining', were the modern food companies. They could not make much sales progress with the rough tastes of workmen. However, they could coax housewives to adopt profitable frills. They could persuade shoppers to ask for highly-advertised embellishments like chocolate, desiccated coconut, custard powder and jelly. They could convince women to accept a new role as consumers. Daintiness – which embodied 'feminine' qualities like lightness, prettiness and gentility – was part of a long campaign to pervert the traditional caring concerns of women into petty materialist preoccupations . . .

In 1934, Mrs Elizabeth Paxton succeeded her husband as licensee of the Esplanade and under her invigorated guidance the afternoon teas became very desirable occasions for the wives of Perth's fortune-makers. One day she called in her manager, Harry Nairn, and they approached their chef to devise something special. Tall, upright and what his second wife described as 'a very ordinary chef', Bert Sachse experimented for a month. 'I had always regretted that the meringue cake was invariably too hard and crusty, so I set out to create something that could have a crunchy top and would cut like marsh-mallow,' he recalled for a reporter. He lit on the secret of adding cornflour and vinegar to the whipped egg whites. These were his ingredients, slightly more complicated than usual: six egg whites, six ounces of sugar, ounce of cornflour, just under a dessertspoon of vinegar, few drops of vanilla essence, good pinch of cream of tartar, one-third pint of cream, three or four passionfruit.

According to Paxton family tradition, the pavlova was named at a meeting at which Sachse presented the now familiar cake. The family say that either the licencee, Elizabeth, or the manager, Harry Nairn (as Sachse also said), remarked, 'It is as light as Pavlova'.

One Continuous Picnic, 1982

The Other Island
NANCY MITFORD 1904–73

There is still a feudal flavour about [Irish] domestic life, for servants abound, and delightful they are. The kitchen teems with scullions and the servants' hall nourishes many more people than actually work in the house. The atmosphere below stairs is jolly; quarrels are rare. Food is of paramount importance and the houses vie with each other to delight the guests. It is rather too rich for me, based on cream. A typical Irish dinner would be: cream flavoured with lobster, cream with bits of veal in it, green peas and cream, cream cheese, cream flavoured with strawberries. I crave skim milk from an English coalmine, but then I have not been on the river all day to sharpen my appetite. Sometimes we lunch, on cold cream, in the fishing-hut.

The Water Beetle, 1962

No. 8

F. T. CHENG 1884–1970

The late Mr Ernest Bevin, former British Foreign Secretary, dined several times at the Chinese Embassy and, every time, was given, partly, Chinese food. One evening he was asked whether he had ever had Chinese food before, and he answered 'yes', adding that he often went to Chinese restaurants before he took office. Hearing this I naturally asked him what dish he liked best and his answer was, 'No. 8.' This sounded like a conundrum. Therefore I followed up my question with a series of queries like 'Animal? Mineral? Vegetable?' In other words, I asked him whether it was meat, poultry, or sea food, and his replies were a successive 'No.' Then I said, 'I know it now!' He dined at the Embassy a few weeks later and 'No. 8' prominently figured in the menu. After he had tasted it, I asked him whether it was right, and his answer was 'Quite right, but you have improved it!' This was, in fact, 'Chop Suey'. As 'No. 8' became so well known afterwards as a gastronomic choice of the Foreign Secretary, it always formed an item of the menu in subsequent 'diplomatic' dinners during my term of office, even on the occasion when their Royal Highnesses, Princess Elizabeth (now Her Majesty the Queen) and the Duke of Edinburgh, honoured us with their presence at an informal dinner in April 1949.

To conclude, it may be observed that culture has nothing to do with motor, radiator, refrigerator, elevator, or waste, but something to do with eating, drinking, cooking, living and taste.

Musings of a Chinese Gourmet, 1954

Scottish Tea

REBECCA WEST 1892–1983

Then Constance called us because it was teatime. It was good that she was Scottish, it meant that she gave us a good tea. Our family was still shocked by the nullity of Lovegrove bakeries compared to what we had become accustomed to in Edinburgh. Constance gave us hot oatmeal scones, which we spread with butter and golden syrup, and she had some home-made Scotch bun, the rich cake in a pastry case which is known as 'black death.'

The Fountain Overflows, 1957

White Bacon

MARJORIE KINNAN RAWLINGS 1896–1953

When you say 'meat' in the north, you mean beef or lamb or something of the sort. 'Meat' in Florida is one thing – white bacon. We call it white bacon to distinguish it from breakfast bacon, or side meat, and it is, simply, salt pork, or, to the army, sow belly. If it is under-rated in the north and by the military, it is perhaps over-rated in Florida, for it is the staple meat. Affluent rural families serve it three times a day, no matter what other meats may be on the table, poor families have it as often as they can afford it, and town families of rural antecedents serve it when the nostalgic hunger becomes too great. The other evening I found my colored maid Idella laughing to herself in the kitchen. I inquired the source of her mirth.

'Guess what I had for my supper,' she said.

I could not guess.

'Well, I had cornpone and white bacon. When we were growing up and there were so many of us in the family, all we had most of the time was cornpone and white bacon, and we had to eat it or go hungry. I thought I'd just like to see how it tasted when I didn't have to eat it.'

It tasted very good indeed, she reported.

White bacon is cooked everywhere in about the same fashion. It is usually soaked a little while in warm water or in milk, squeezed dry, dipped in flour and fried to a crisp golden brown. The large amount of grease that fries from it is poured into a bowl and this to the backwoodsman is 'gravy.' It is solid grease, and it is poured over grits, over sweet potatoes, over cornbread or soda biscuits, and how country stomachs survive ten hundred and ninety-five servings of this a year is a mystery past my solving.

Cross Creek, 1942

A French Recipe and English Waste
VIRGINIA WOOLF 1882–1941

'It is a triumph,' said Mr Bankes, laying his knife down for a moment. He had eaten attentively. It was rich; it was tender. It was perfectly cooked. How did she manage these things in the depths of the country? he asked her. She was a wonderful woman. All his love, all his reverence had returned; and she knew it.

'It is a French recipe of my grandmother's,' said Mrs Ramsay, speaking with a ring of great pleasure in her voice. Of course it was French. What passes for cookery in England is an abomination (they agreed). It is putting cabbages in water. It is roasting meat till it is like leather. It is cutting off the delicious skins of vegetables. 'In which,' said Mr Bankes, 'all the virtue of the vegetable is contained.' And the waste, said Mrs Ramsay. A whole French family could live on what an English cook throws away.

To the Lighthouse, 1927

The Inn at Terracina
WASHINGTON IRVING 1783–1859

The supper, as it was termed by the Italian, or dinner, as the Englishman called it, was now served. Heaven and earth, and the waters under the earth, had been moved to furnish it, for there were birds of the air and beasts of the earth and fish of the sea. The Englishman's servant, too, had turned the kitchen topsy-turvy in his zeal to cook his master a beefsteak; and made his appearance loaded with ketchup, and soy, and Cayenne pepper, and Harvey sauce, and a bottle of port wine, from that warehouse, the carriage, in which his master seemed desirous of carrying England about the world with him. Every thing, however, according to the Englishman, was execrable. The tureen of soup was a black sea, with livers and limbs and fragments of all kinds of birds and beasts, floating like wrecks about it. A meagre winged animal, which my host called a delicate chicken, was too delicate for his stomach, for it had evidently died of a consumption. The macaroni was smoked. The beefsteak was tough buffalo's flesh, and the countenance of mine host confirmed the assertion. Nothing seemed to hit his palate but a dish of stewed eels, of which he ate with great relish, but had nearly refunded them when told that they were vipers, caught among the rocks of Terracina, and esteemed a great delicacy.

In short, the Englishman ate and growled, and ate and growled, like a cat eating in company, pronouncing himself poisoned by every dish, yet eating on in defiance of death and the doctor. The Venetian lady, not accustomed to English travellers, almost repented having persuaded him to the meal; for though very gracious to her, he was so crusty to all the world beside, that she stood in awe of him. There is nothing, however, that conquers John Bull's crustiness sooner than eating, whatever may be the cookery; and nothing brings him into good humor with his company sooner than eating together; the Englishman, therefore, had not half finished his repast and his bottle, before he began to think the Venetian a very tolerable fellow for a foreigner, and his wife almost handsome enough to be an Englishwoman.

Tales of a Traveller, 1824

Italian Attitudes

ELIZABETH ROMER

All Italians are very conscious of food, almost, one might say, obsessed with the table and the quality of cooking, and the subject of food is never very far from the lips of men or women. I once overheard a conversation in an Italian train between two businessmen who were strangers to each other. For the entire two-hour journey they discussed with passion their particular way of making *Spaghetti alla Carbonara* and other pasta sauces, behaviour which would appear distinctly odd in an English railway carriage but is very normal in Italy. So, Silvana in this remote valley is daily preparing food for critics and what is more for critics who, although bucolic, know what they are talking about.

The Tuscan Year, 1984

Vegetables

CLAUDIA RODEN 1936–

Vegetables in the Middle East do not play second fiddle as do the 'two veg' to meat in England. They hold a dignified, sometimes splendid position in the hierarchy of food. They are, in turn, *mezze*, pickles and salads. They can be stuffed and ranked as a main dish, an adornment to meat in a stew, or deep-fried, sautéed or steamed. In cooking, their nature is taken into account, and their flavour, texture and colour are treated with respect. They are expected to give of their best.

They do not come in polythene bags or packed tight in little boxes, synthetically remote from their buyers. They are hunted, eyed covetously, handled and smelt, chosen and bargained for, and at last brought home in triumph.

Early in the morning, people leave their houses to do their shopping at the market stalls spilling over with vegetables and fruits fresh from the villages. Men often do this pleasant task before going to work or on the way home.

To look for aubergines for one's *Imam Bayildi* or for courgettes for one's *kousa bi gebna* is a pleasure. Will the courgettes be good for stuffing? Or will they be too small? Will the aubergines be round today, or thin and long? Which stall will have the best tomatoes, and at what price? It is a challenge and a triumph to find a truly good, unblemished vegetable at a good price.

There is also the pleasure of bargaining, an ancient ritual. How dull it would be to have fixed prices and not to indulge in this game which daily sharpens the wits and brings shopping to a personal, human level!

A Book of Middle Eastern Food, 1968

Russian Dinner

MARQUIS DE CUSTINE 1790–1857

It is the custom of the north to precede the principal repast by a smaller refection, which is served in the saloon, a quarter of an hour before entering the dining-room. The preliminary, which is destined to sharpen the appetite, is called in Russian, if my ear has not deceived me, zacuska. The servants bring upon trays small plates filled with fresh caviare, such as is only eaten in this country, dried fish, cheese, salt meats, sea biscuits, and pastry; with these, bitter liqueurs, French brandy, London porter, Hungarian wine, &c., are also brought in; and these things are eaten and drunk standing. A stranger, ignorant of the usages of the country, or an appetite easily satisfied, might very soon here make a meal, and remain afterwards a spectator only of the real dinner. The Russians eat plentifully, and keep a liberal table; but they are too fond of hashes, stuffing, little balls of mince-meat, and fish in pâtés.

One of the most delicate fishes in the world is caught in the Volga, where it abounds. It is called the sterled, and unites the flavour of the sea and fresh water fishes, without, however, resembling any that I have eaten elsewhere. This fish is large, its flesh light and fine; its head, pointed and full of cartilages, is considered delicate; the monster is seasoned very skilfully, but without many spices: the sauce that is served with it unites the flavour of wine, strong meat broth, and lemon-juice. I prefer this national dish to all the other ragoûts of the land, and especially to the cold and sour soup, that species of fish-broth, iced, that forms the detestable treat of the Russians. They also make soups of sugared vinegar, of which I have tasted enough to prevent my ever asking for any more.

The governor's dinner was good and well served, without super-fluity, and without useless *recherche*. The abundance and excellent quality of the watermelons astonishes me: it is said that they come from the environs of Moscow, but I should rather imagine they send to the Crimea for them. It is the custom in this country to place the dessert upon the table at the commencement of the dinner, and to serve it plate by plate. This method has its advantages and its inconveniences: it seems to me only perfectly proper at great dinners.

The Empire of the Czar, 1843

English Cookery
ISABELLE VISCHER d. 1963

I have constantly tried to explain and demonstrate to my friends across the Channel the beauty and delights of good English cookery. They have always been surprised, often interested, sometimes dazzled. In France, where feminine characteristics are prevalent, cooking perfects itself through elaboration; in England, more exclusively masculine, through simplification. Surely, both these approaches are wise and both show deep discernment in matters concerning good food. If the French school of cookery goes in for subtle researches and learned combinations, in England the main object seems to be what is after all one of the most, if not *the* most, important gastronomic principle: always bring out and keep the individual flavour. 'The greatest achievement in cookery,' a connoisseur said to me once (and he was a Continental), 'the greatest achievement is when each viand or cooked food retains its own *fumet*.' The French word *fumet* for flavour is, I think, much more expressive. But when a French recipe happens to be apparently plain and simple, it is then that one may be sure that it is elusive, imponderable and difficult to follow successfully. And of such, before any other, is the omelette. That is why, I imagine, every cook has a different way of making it, and why most writers and experts – especially the most famous – devote a special and long chapter to it. If each one gives a different method, they all agree on one point: that it is a bit of a conjuring trick.

Now to the Banquet, 1953

Porridge or Prunes, Sir?
E. M. FORSTER 1879–1970

These are grim words, and they fell grimly on my ear that bleak October morning. I was returning to England, my country, by one of her boat trains. We had landed at Tilbury at an unearthly hour, and the pale ferrety-faced Customs Officials had given us their usual welcome home. To their attentions succeeded the inattentiveness of the Restaurant Car. We sat in a vacuum waiting, waiting for breakfast.

The carriage was stuffy, yet cold, the table cloths drooped as if they too had lain awake half the night, and now and then a passenger fidgeted, but in vain. Breakfast could not be served until the train started. More passengers, more porters, more luggage with chalk scriggles on it loomed in the murk outside, faint variants in the eternal monotone. I opened my book and tried to read – it was a novel by François Mauriac; the Customs Officer had not liked the look of it at all. But I could not attend to the exquisite prose; the fever, the loveliness, the tenderness in hatred, the light and the scents of the south, would none of them come through. Breakfast, oh for breakfast! Mauriac cannot stay an empty stomach. At last the engine gave a jerk, the knives and forks slid sideways and sang against one another sadly, the cups said 'cheap, cheap' to the saucers, as well they might, the door swung open and the attendants came in crying 'Porridge or Prunes, sir? Porridge or Prunes?' Breakfast had begun.

That cry still rings in my memory. It is an epitome – not, indeed, of English food, but of the forces which drag it into the dirt. It voices the true spirit of gastronomic joylessness. Porridge fills the Englishman up, prunes clear him out, so their functions are opposed. But their spirit is the same: they eschew pleasure and consider delicacy immoral. That morning they looked as like one another as they could. Everything was grey. The porridge was in pallid grey lumps, the prunes swam in grey juice like the wrinkled skulls of old men, grey mist pressed against the grey windows. 'Tea or coffee, sir?' rang out next, and then I had a haddock. It was covered with a sort of hard yellow oilskin, as if it had been out in a lifeboat, and its inside gushed salt water when pricked. Sausages and bacon followed this disgusting fish. They, too, had been up all night. Toast like steel, marmalade a scented jelly. And the bill, which I paid dumbly, wondering again why such things have to be.

They have to be because this is England, and we are English. We often eat well in our homes or in clubs or in small restaurants which have not yet been spoiled, but we do not demand good food in public, and when we eat upon an object that moves, such as a train or a boat, we expect, and generally get, absolute muck. Some people go in for complaining, cursing the waiters, calling for the manager, writing to the head office and so on, but complaints seem to me the wrong end of the stick. It is no use scorning a system which can't understand how you feel. One of my friends, who does complain, was travelling recently upon a patriotic and pretentious liner. He laid about him at meals until one of his fellow passengers said acidly: 'You seem somewhat hard to please.' He replied: 'I am not hard to please. I am merely trying to find some dish which a working-class boy would not throw in his mother's face.' This made all concerned sit up, but the menus continued as before. If you do not need prunes there is porridge; if you cannot manage the bottled coffee there is the stewy tea.

Well, I drink to the cuisine of my country in the glass of warm beer which was recently served me in a smart railway buffet at Birmingham. On that occasion I did complain. The barmaid turned pert and said: 'Something warm ought to be just right for this cold day.' Then she softened and said, yes, other customers had complained, too, but the only place she was given to keep the beer was over the hot water pipes. I drink in the beer which had to be kept over the hot water. I drink in the soup which stood in the draught. May they mingle with the porridge and the prunes, and bring oblivion!

We Shall Eat And Drink Again, ed. Louis Golding
and André L. Simon, 1944

Food as a System of Communication

MARY DOUGLAS 1921–

The combination of the food system as it has developed autonomously and the economic factors explains the extraordinary phenomenon of the British cheap biscuit. Here is an example of a national preference, the kind of taste-formation which the economists are only too glad to leave aside as not susceptible of economic analysis. The British like to have cheap biscuits and they do not mind whether they all taste much the same so long as they are varied in their shapes and sizes, colours and geometrical decoration. The same designs of biscuits are found in other European nations but they are generally expensive and of good quality materials, with considerable difference between one biscuit and another as to its taste. The explanation that is offered here of the British demand for cheap biscuits is that the biscuit is a condensed symbol of all the food events and the social events of a day and a week and a lifetime. It has to be cheap because it has to be used so often to make the regular summation of the symbolic system which in the case of the food patterning that we have described occurs very frequently. It has to be cheap because it is an integral part of the working-class food system. From the perspective of this system the wedding cake can be

83

presented plausibly as the most formal pile of biscuits offered in the course of a lifetime. As the ordinary biscuit sums up the daily and the weekly food system, so does the wedding cake sum up the high moment in the life-cycle. It is a sweet cereal confection on which a white liquid dressing has been poured, but the dressing has set into the hardest, shiniest and most improbably patterned crust. The icing of the wedding cake is able to express what it does because it is the pinnacle of a very rigorously formalized set of rules which segregate liquid from solid with complete consistency right through all the constituent food occasions.

In the Active Voice, 1982

Russian Profusion
ROBERT BYRON 1905–41

Judged by Russian standards, which differ from ours, the food was not really profuse; indeed how could it be? though they had bought, at considerable expense we discovered afterwards, the last sardines in the town. But it had that *air* of profusion which Russians always create about them, and as new guests kept wandering in, and new tables were brought, and new chairs, and the children hopped up on people's laps, the dishes kept pace and were still as full as ever of the sardines from India, paprika from Russia, fresh meat with onion salad, and bread. A decanter of yellow vodka, in which fruit was swimming, was endlessly replenished. The Russians, who gulped it off in cups, complained furiously of our slow sipping. But that was only at first.

The Road to Oxiana, 1937

Why Italians Eat More Fruit and Vegetables
GIACOMO CASTELVETRO 1546–1616

When you consider the reasons, it is hardly surprising that we Italians eat such a profusion of fruit and vegetables, some of them quite unknown and unappreciated elsewhere. Firstly, Italy, though beautiful, is not as plentifully endowed as France or this fertile island with meat, so we make it our business to devise other ways of feeding our excessive population.

The other equally powerful reason is that the heat, which persists for almost nine months of the year, has the effect of making meat seem quite repellent, especially beef, which in such a temperature one can hardly bear to look at, let alone eat. Even mutton is not eaten much, for we keep the animals closed in stalls at night, not in the fields as you do, and this gives the meat a somewhat unpleasant taste.

This is why we prefer our fruit and vegetables, for they are refreshing, they do not thicken the blood and above all they revive the flagging appetite.

The Fruit, Herbs and Vegetables of Italy, TRANS. Gillian Riley, 1989

English Salad
EDWARD BUNYARD 1872–1939

In most of the comings and goings of life one feels quietly proud to be an Englishman. But at table there is one awful moment of doubt – when the English salad appears. Will it be, as it all too often is, like Niobe, all tears? Or will it be really dry and crisp, prepared for its final benediction of vinegar and oil.

At the worst, will it have been 'made' an hour beforehand, 'to save time'? How well we know those limp and soddened leaves, devoid of crispness, resembling a copy of *The Times* which has floated down from Hammersmith to Deptford. The English salad! True emblem of lost hope, drenching skies, and 'approaching depressions.'

Come, come, we really must pull ourselves together. Look in the garden, where there are admirable lettuce, taut and strict in the strength of their youth. Crisp as hoar-frost and brittle as glass, why should they fail so lamentably in their last hour?

The Epicure's Companion, ED. Edward and Lorna Bunyard, 1937

The Greediness of the Welsh

GERALD OF WALES 1147–1223

*Gerald of Wales was half Norman and half Welsh. He was one of
the most dynamic and colourful churchmen of the 12th century,
determined to become Bishop of St David's, and be consecrated
without having to acknowledge the supremacy of Canterbury. He
knew almost everyone worth knowing, kings, popes, Welsh princes
and prelates. He wrote seventeen books and planned a number of
others, all in Latin. His* Journey through Wales *and* The Description
of Wales *are invaluable source books for the history of the period.
He died in obscurity, his dream unfulfilled.*

If they come to a house where there is any sign of affluence and they are
in a position to take what they want, there is no limit to their demands.
They lose all control of themselves, and insist on being served with vast
quantities of food and more especially intoxicating drink. With the
Apostle they say: 'I know both how . . . to abound and to suffer
need,'[1] but they do not add with him that they are 'made all things to
all men' so that they 'might by all means save some'[2] for God. In times
of scarcity their abstinence and frugality are most remarkable, but,
when they have gone without food for a long time, their appetite
becomes enormous, especially when they are sitting at someone else's
table. In this they resemble wolves and eagles, which live by plunder
and are rarely satisfied. In difficult times they have to fast, but in times
of plenty they glut themselves. All the same, no one in Wales
mortgages his property to satisfy his greed and gluttony, as I have seen
the English do.

They want everyone else to share their bad habits and then provide
the wherewithal to pay for them,

> For crime makes us equal, corrupting us all.[3]

The Description of Wales, TRANS. Lewis Thorpe, 1978

[1] Philippians, 4.12.
[2] I Corinthians, 9.20–22.
[3] Lucan, *Pharsalia,* V.290.

English Butchers
MADAME DE LA TOUR DU PIN 1770–1853

England, a country, where there are immense fortunes and people who live in sumptuous elegance, is also the country where the poor can live most comfortably. For instance, there is no need to go to market. The butcher never forgets to call regularly at the same hour every day, coming to the door and shouting 'Butcher' to announce his presence. You open and tell him what you want. A leg of lamb, perhaps? He will bring it to you all prepared and ready to be put on the spit. Cutlets? They are laid neatly on a little wooden tray, which he collects the following day. A small wooden skewer fastens a paper to the meat showing the weight and price of whatever you have bought. There are no useless pieces or so-called 'make-weights'. The same system is followed by all the other tradesmen. There are no arguments or complications.

Memoirs, ED. TRANS. Felice Harcourt, 1969

Brolairs?
NANCY MITFORD 1904–73

Meanwhile Mrs H, who came from England an hour ago, is recounting her news, all bad. 'My doctor I was so fond of has gone into broilers.' *'Brolairs? Qu'est ce que c'est que ça?'* 'A kind of chicken you keep in the dark and feed with injections. He says they can't ring him up in the night – oh, it is too hard.'

'But these broilairs must be very nasty?' They are more concerned with the sufferings of the consumer than those of the hen.

'Oh, very. But nobody cares. Veal in England now tastes of blotting-paper – why? Because the calves live in Turkish baths,' she adds, conjuring up a picture of Hammams all over England's green and pleasant land.

'Portrait of a French Country House', The Water Beetle, 1962

One English Sauce

LOUIS EUSTACHE UDE

It is very remarkable, that in France, where there is but one religion, the sauces are infinitely varied, whilst in England, where the different sects are innumerable, there is, we may say, but one single sauce. Melted butter, in English cookery, plays nearly the same part as the Lord Mayor's coach at civic ceremonies, calomel in modern medicine, or silver forks in the fashionable novels. Melted butter and anchovies, melted butter and capers, melted butter and parsley, melted butter and eggs, and melted butter for ever: this is a sample of the national cookery of this country.

The French Cook, 1813

Butter

DR JOHN DORAN 1807–78

The illustrious Ude, or some one constituting him the authority for the nonce, has sneered at the English as being a nation having twenty religions, and only one sauce, – melted butter. A French commentator had added, that we have nothing polished about us but our steel, and that our only ripe fruit is baked apples. Guy Pantin traces the alleged dislike of the French of his day for the English, to the circumstances that the latter poured melted butter over their roast veal. The French execration is amusingly said to have been further directed against us, on account of the declared barbarism of eating oyster-sauce with rump-steak, and 'poultice,' as they cruelly characterize 'bread sauce,' with pheasant. But, to return to butter: – the spilling of it has more than once been elucidative of character. When, in the days of the old *régime*, an English servant accidentally let a drop or two of melted butter fall upon the silken suit of a French *petit-maître*, the latter indignantly declared that 'blood and butter were an Englishman's food.' The conclusion was illogical, but the arguer was excited. Lord John Townshend manifested better temper and wit, when a similar accident befell him, as he was dining at a friend's table, where the coachman was the only servant in waiting. 'John,' said my Lord, 'you should never grease anything but your coach-wheels.'

It was an old popular error that a pound of butter might consist of any number of ounces. It is an equally popular error, that a breakfast cannot be, unless bread and butter be of it. Marcus Antoninus breakfasted on dry biscuits; and many a person of less rank, and higher worth, is equally incapable of digesting any thing stronger. Solid breakfasts are only fit for those who have much solid exercise to take after it; otherwise heartburn may be looked for. Avoid new bread and spongy rolls; look on muffins and crumpets as inventions of men of worse than sanguinary principles, and hot buttered toast as of equally wicked origin. Dry toast is the safest morning food, perhaps, for persons of indifferent powers of digestion; or they may substitute for it the imperial fashion set by Marcus Antoninus.

Table Traits, 1854

Sunday Lunch

PENELOPE LIVELY 1933–

There is roast chicken for Sunday lunch, bread sauce, bacon rolls, all the trimmings . . . Mother has done everything herself, valiantly, with little self-deprecating comments. She has taught herself to cook, brave Mother, since the defection of the last of the village helps. Claudia gave her Elizabeth David's *French Country Cooking* for Christmas which was received politely but without enthusiasm; no *coq au vin* or *quiche lorraine* has appeared on the table at Sturminster Newton.

Moon Tiger, 1987

Decent English Waste
KATHERINE MANSFIELD 1888–1923

TO FREDERICK GOODYEAR

Villa Pauline, Bandol (Var) Sunday.
[4 March 1916]
In fact, now I come to ponder on your last letter I don't believe you want to write to me at all and Im hanged if Ill shoot arrows in the air. But perhaps that is temper on my part; it is certainly pure stomach. Im so hungry, simply empty, and seeing in my minds eye just now a surloin of beef, well browned with plenty of gravy *and* horseradish sauce and baked potatoes I nearly sobbed. There's nothing here to eat except omelettes and oranges and onions. Its a cold, sunny windy day – the kind of day when you want a tremendous feed for lunch & an armchair in front of the fire to boaconstrict in afterwards. I feel sentimental about England now – English food, *decent* English *waste!* How much better than these thrifty French whose flower gardens are nothing but potential salad bowls. There's not a leaf in France that you cant 'faire une infusion avec [make tea with]', not a blade that isn't bon pour la cuisine [good for cooking]. By God, Id like to buy a pound of the best butter, put it on the window sill and watch it melt to spite em.

Selected Letters, 1988

French Food
ALICE B. TOKLAS 1878–1967

The French approach to food is characteristic; they bring to their consideration of the table the same appreciation, respect, intelligence and lively interest that they have for the other arts, for painting, for literature and for the theatre. By French I mean French men as well as French women, for the men in France play a very active part in everything that pertains to the kitchen. I have heard working men in Paris discuss the way their wives prepare a beef stew as it is cooked in Burgundy or the way a cabbage is cooked with salt pork and browned in the oven. A woman in the country can be known for kilometres about for the manner in which she prepares those sublimated dumplings known as *Quenelles*, and a very complicated dish they are. Conversation even in a literary or political *salon* can turn to the subject of menus, food or wine.

The French like to say that their food stems from their culture and that it has developed over the centuries. It has its universal reputation for these reasons and on account of the mild climate and fertile soil.

We foreigners living in France respect and appreciate this point of view but deplore their too strict observance of a tradition which will not admit the slightest deviation in a seasoning or the suppression of a single ingredient. For example, a dish as simple as a potato salad must be served surrounded by chicory. To serve it with any other green is inconceivable. Still, this strict conservative attitude over the years has resulted in a number of essential principles that have made the renown of the French kitchen.

The Alice B. Toklas Cook Book, 1954

Travelling in France
EDMOND 1822–96 AND JULES 1830–70
GONCOURT

Travelling in France, it is a misfortune to be a Frenchman. The wing of the chicken at a *table d'hôte* always goes to the Englishman. He is the only person the waiter serves. Why is this? Because the Englishman does not look upon the waiter as a man, and any servant who feels that he is being regarded as a human being despises the person considering him in that light.

Pages from the Goncourt Journals, ED., TRANS. Robert Baldick, 1962

Romany Dinner

RUPERT CROFT-COOKE 1903–79 AND NOËL BARBER 1909–88

It was in Liverpool, also, that there was given probably the only public dinner of gypsy food. It was to celebrate the Jubilee of the Gypsy Lore Society, a circle of erudite enthusiasts dedicated to the study of the Dark Race, of which Augustus John is the President. The late Lady Eleanor Smith and Professor Walter Starkie were among the guests, but there were also gypsies from Wales and the North Country. The menu will seem a strange document to non-gypsies, for it was printed in Romanes, the gypsy language, and would make a unique item in one of those collections which most of us spend our lives in meaning to make, and somehow never starting, a collection of unusual menus. This one was headed *Hobbensko Lil*, which might be literally translated as Food Paper. First was *Zumin* (soup), of which the two varieties were called simply *Goshti* (thick) and *Korodi* (clear). Then *Macho* (fish) was something familiar to all Northern and Welsh gypsies, salmon, called the *Baro-Macho* or big fish. The menu specified that it would be *Kerado – kek chordino*, which means boiled, not poached, a harmless play on words, since *chordino*, let us own, means stolen. The *Mas*, or meat, took the form of *Romani Xeliax*, or gypsy stew, with *Neve Phuvengre* (new potatoes) and *Chimerimen Puruma* (braised onions). The *Gudlibena* (sweet) was one which any gypsy might have made over his fire, *Durilengi Goi tha Smentena*, bilberry pudding and cream, and there was *Kial* (cheese) and *Chinkudi* (coffee).

Cities, 1946

Swamp Guinea's $4.50 All You Can Eat

WILLIAM LEAST HEAT MOON 1921–

The road through the orange earth of north Georgia passed an old, three-story house with a thin black child hanging out of every window like an illustration for 'The Old Woman Who Lived in a Shoe'; on into hills and finally to Swamp Guinea's, a conglomerate of plywood and two-by-fours laid over with the smell of damp pine woods.

Inside, wherever an oddity or natural phenomenon could hang, one hung: stuffed rump of a deer, snowshoe, flintlock, hornet's nest. The place looked as if a Boy Scout troop had decorated it. Thirty or so people, black and white, sat around tables almost foundering under piled platters of food. I took a seat by the reproduction of a seventeenth-century woodcut depicting some Rabelaisian banquet at the groaning board.

The diners were mostly Oglethorpe County red-dirt farmers. In Georgia tones they talked about their husbandry in terms of rain and nitrogen and hope. An immense woman with a glossy picture of a hooked bass leaping the front of her shirt said, 'I'm gonna be sick from how much I've ate.'

I was watching everyone else and didn't see the waitress standing quietly by. Her voice was deep and soft like water moving in a cavern. I ordered the $4.50 special. In a few minutes she wheeled up a cart and began off loading dinner: ham and eggs, fried catfish, fried perch fingerlings, fried shrimp, chunks of barbecued beef, fried chicken, French fries, hush puppies, a broad bowl of cole slaw, another of lemon, a quart of ice tea, a quart of ice, and an entire loaf of factory-wrapped white bread. The table was covered.

'Call me if y'all want any more.' She wasn't joking. I quenched the thirst and then – slowly – went to the eating. I had to stand to reach plates across the table, but I intended to do the supper in. It was all Southern fried and good, except the Southern-style sweetened ice tea; still I took care of a quart of it. As I ate, making up for meals lost, the Old-Woman-in-the-Shoe house flashed before me, lightning in darkness. I had no moral right to eat so much. But I did. Headline: STOMACH PUMP FAILS TO REVIVE TRAVELER.

The loaf of bread lay unopened when I finally abandoned the meal. At the register, I paid a man who looked as if he'd been chipped out of Georgia chert. The Swamp Guinea. I asked about the name. He spoke of himself in the third person like the Wizard of Oz. 'The Swamp Guinea only tells regulars.'

'I'd be one, Mr. Guinea, if I didn't live in Missouri.'

'Y'all from the North? Here, I got somethin' for you.' He went to the office and returned with a 45 rpm record. 'It's my daughter singin'. A little promotion we did. Take it along.' Later, I heard a husky north Georgia voice let go a down-home lyric rendering of Swamp Guinea's menu:

That's all you can eat
For a dollar fifty,
Hey! The barbecue's nifty!

And so on through the fried chicken and potatoes.

As I left the Swamp Guinea, a former antique dealer whose name was Rudell Burroughs, said, 'The nickname don't mean anything. Just made it up. Tried to figure a good one so we can franchise someday.'

Blue Highways, 1983

Pilau

MARJORIE KINNAN RAWLINGS 1896–1953

The pilau is almost a sacred Florida dish, and for making a small amount of meat feed a large number, it has no equal. A Florida church supper is unheard of without it. Bartram found the dish here those many years ago, and called it 'pillo,' and once, 'pilloe.' We pronounce the word purr-loo. Almost any meat, but preferably chicken or fresh pork, is cut in pieces and simmered in a generous amount of water until tender. When it falls from the bones, as much rice is added as is needed for the number to be fed, and cooked to a moist flakiness. The flavor of meat and gravy permeates the last grain of rice. Fred Tompkins once cooked a coot liver and gizzard pilau at the Creek. It was very good, and the only time I have been able to down coot in any form. The rest of the Creek considers coots almost as edible as ducks. I have followed Martha's directions faithfully, soaking the coots overnight in vinegar-water and parboiling with soda before roasting, but they still taste rankly of the marsh mud on which they have fed.

We are all in complete agreement on squirrel meat. Fried, smother-fried with a rich gravy, or made into a pilau, we esteem it highly. There are, however, strong differences of opinion on the edibility of the head. I saw his disagreement flare up violently at the doings at Anthony.

Word came that Fatty Blake, a snuff and tobacco salesman, and Anthony's richest citizen – wealth at Anthony, as elsewhere, is relative – was having a big doings on a certain Thursday night. The world was invited. Fatty himself stopped at the village store to verify the invitation. He was inviting two counties to his doings, and all was free. There would be squirrel pilau and Brunswick stew. Fatty couldn't likker folks, as he would like to do, but if you brought your own 'shine and were quiet about it, why, he'd meet you at the gate for a drink, and God bless you.

'I got boys in the woods from can't-see to can't-see,' he said, 'getting me squirrels for that pilau. I got a nigger coming to stir that pot of rice all day long. And my wife, God bless her, is walking the county, getting what she needs for Brunswick stew, the kind her mammy made ahead of her in Brunswick, Georgia.'

Cars and wagons and lone horses and mules began coming in to Anthony long before dark. They brought women in homemade silks and in ginghams, men in mail-order store clothes with stiff collars and men in the blue pin-checks of the day's work. Children screamed and played all over the swept sand about Fatty's two-story house. The wives of Anthony bustled up and down a forty-foot pine-board table. Each had brought her contribution, of potato salad made by stirring cut onion and hard-boiled eggs into cold mashed potatoes, of soda biscuits and pepper relish, of pound cake and blueberry pie. Back of the house a Negro stirred rice in a forty-gallon iron kettle with a paddle as big as an oar. It grew dark and the crowd was hungry. . . .

At seven-thirty the Methodist preacher rose to his feet beside the organ. He lauded Fatty Blake as a Christian citizen. He prayed. Here and there a devout old woman cried 'Amen!' And then the parson asked that any one so minded contribute his mite to help Brother Blake defray the expense of his great free feast.

'Will Brother Buxton pass the hat?' . . .

The crowd packed tight around the table, weaving and milling. The pilau and stew were passed around in paper dishes. The passing hat reached a lean, venerable farmer just as he had completed a tour of exploration through his pilau.

'No!' he shrilled, with the lustiness of an old man with a grievance.

'No, I ain't goin' to give him nothin'! This here was advertised as a free meal and 'tain't nothin' but a dogged Georgia prayer-meetin'. Get a man here on promises and then go to pickin' his pocket. This food ain't fitten to eat, dogged Georgia rations, Brunswick stew and all. And he's done cooked the squirrel heads in the pilau, and that suits a damned Georgia Cracker but it don't suit me.

'I was born and raised in Floridy, and I'm pertickler. I don't want no squirrel eyes lookin' at me out o' my rations!'

Cross Creek, 1942

95

Aunt Doe Rae's Packaged-up World

ERNEST MATTHEW MICKLER

Aunt Doe Rae was working her mind awful hard, trying to write up an announcement of this year's homecoming-and-dinner-on-the-ground for the New Mt. Nebo Creek Baptist Church. She, especially, was trying to find the language strong enough to put a stop to the onslaught of all the cardboard cartons and Styrofoam platters of food that could be bought at any corner convenient store. She was in tears thinking about last year's dinner and how it seems that almost everyone lost the feeling and the spirit of the dinner on the ground. She knew it would take some powerful words, but at this point she was willing to say anything she could to get this occasion back on the ground. She wrote and scratched for days until she had come up with what she considered some of the dos and don'ts for a homecoming dinner. It was mostly don'ts. When she had finished, she stood up at her kitchen table and began to read it out loud, as if the entire Mt. Nebo congregation was listening.

'Do any of you, or can any of you, remember when Nuvell was just Raenelle's twin-sister, plain ol, and not some skimpy kinda French cookin. I mean, last year at our dinner, I saw a three bean salad that consisted of egxactly that! Three beans, and a sprig of somethin that looked everbit like dogfennel to me. They a-fiddlin with our fat. That's what they doin. Now, I ain't advocatin un-healthy food but what can you say against Miss Lyddie's fried pork chops, she et 'em for 96 years. And she ain't never robbed, raped er murdered nobody. She did die, but it weren't her pork chops. She simply wore out. However, take the other fence, these young folks that's been a eatin all this messa enbombed cardboard since they was knee high, they are up to their eye-teeth in dope, akahal, an devilmint. I'll tell ya, it's got to be this fast, superized eatin, cause it ain't, no matter what they say, the coloreds, the communists, nor the poor ol kudzu vine. And cholesterol was nothing compared to the repercussion of this soulless eatin.

'Anyways, it was a shameful sight last year, at our homecomin dinner. They was cartons and boxes on every tablecloth from all the fast food stores in the country. An not a one, an I mean, not a one had the decency to even cover 'em up with a nice piece of tinfoil er something. But ebem that wouldn'ta helped the taste none. Just, for instance, you take Viney's ol Chocolate Sheath Cake, she bakes it year after year after year, and then slips it down in a nest of foil on the bottom of any cutoff box. It ain't much. But, looks to high heaven. An'll melt in yo mouth, too. So you see, it . . . don't . . . TAKE . . . much. I ain't askin for the sky. I'm just layin out the law this year. Not a one can bring a thing that they ain't cooked er made with their own two hands. Except for Miss Lucy, of course, she ain't got but one hand. It's got to come from your kitchen or you cain't bring it to the dinner. I don't care how many boxes and cans you use to make it, just so it come off your stove.

'Now, I'm aware that the Devil'll be workin overtime tryin to fool me, but I'll catch you, cause the Man Upstairs is gone be workin on my side. An you ladies out there, that works hard in your kitchens, I know I can depend on you to help me spot all that store-bought stuff and we'll throw it straight to the dawgs, where it belongs. Can you imagine seein Mrs. Bridie duMac's delicious Shoesoles and Grits sittin right nex ta a slice of some nasty frozen Pizza. Is that what we want our dinner affair to turn out to. No, it ain't!! An I'm puttin my foot right here to stop it. Now!! (She puts her foot out as if to trip somebody.) I know we ain't got no reason to go and get uppity about our food, cause we eat some pretty low . . . down . . . stuff ourselves. We not only eat the egg but there is them that eats 'the where it come from'. So, I know, we ain't fancy and we don't have all kinds a stuff that others has, but we'll take anything, and I do mean anything, an turn it till it hollers. An there is one thing you can always, just about, count on. FRESH . . . right off the stove, fresh. Everything from scratch, well, at least as much as you can get by with in this packaged-up world. You ain't got to mummafy food, if it's fresh made. Maybe, one warm-up, and then out it goes to the hawgs. So y'all, hear . . . me . . . good. It's them poisons in all the fast eatin that's caused this lack of pride, idle-handedness, and general no-count. It ain't the Fat. An, if I'm standin here as Aunt Doe Rae Dollar, I betcha ninety percent of them rapers, robbers and killers is skinny, skinny. An it ain't two of 'em that has ever said the blessin an eat on the ground.'

Sinkin Spells, Hot Flushes, Fits and Cravings, 1988

An Ode to English Food

GEORGE MACBETH 1932–92

O English Food! How I adore looking forward to you, Scotch trifle at the North British Hotel, Princes Street, Edinburgh. Yes, it is good, very good, the best in Scotland.

Once I ate a large helping at your sister establishment, the Carlton Hotel on Waverley Bridge overlooking the cemetery on Carlton Hill. It was rich, very rich and pleasant. O, duck, though,

roast, succulent duck of the Barque and Bite, served with orange sauce, mouth-meltingly delicious! You I salute. Fresh, tender and unbelievable English duck. Such

luscious morsels of you! Heap high the groaning platter with pink fillets, sucking pig and thick gammon, celestial chef. Be generous with the crackling. Let your hand slip with the gravy trough, dispensing plenty. Yes, gravy, I give you your due, too. O savoury and delight-some gravy, toothsome over

the white soft backs of my English potatoes, fragrant with steam. Brave King Edwards, rough-backed in your dry scrubbed excellence, or with butter, salty. Sweet

potatoes! Dear new knobbly ones, beside the oiled sides of meaty carrots. Yes, carrots. Even you, dumplings,

with indigestible honey, treacle-streaky things. You tongue-burners. You stodgy darlings. Tumbled out of the Marks and Spencer's tin or Mr Kipling silver paper wrapper, warm and ready except in summer. Cold strawberry sauce, cream and raspberries. O sour gooseberry pie, dissemble nothing, squeezed essence

of good juice. Joy in lieu of jelly at children's parties, cow-heel that gives the horn a man seeing my twelve-year-old buttocks oiled in hospital by a nurse assured me, dirty

old bugger. I eat my six chosen slices of bread, well buttered, remembering you and your successor the tramp who stole a book for me. Cracked

coffee cup of the lucky day, betokening mother-love, nostalgic.

Fill with Nescafé and milk for me. It is all great, sick-making allure of old food, sentiment of the belly. I fill with aniseed's

parboiled scagliola, porphyry of the balls. With, O with, licorice, thin straws of it in sherbert, sucked up, nose-bursting explosives of white powders! Yes,

montage of pre-European Turkish delights obtained under the counter in wartime, or during periods of crisis, and

O the English sickness of it. Food, I adore you. Pink-faced and randy! Come to me, mutton chops. Whiskers of raw chicken-bones, wishes

and plastic cups. Unpourable Tizer. Take me before I salivate. I require your exotic fineness, taste

of the English people, sweep me off my feet into whiteness, a new experience. With beer. And with blue twists of salt in the chip packets. Grease of newspaper. Vinegar of the winter nights holding hands in lanes after *The Way to the Stars*. It

is all there. Such past and reticence! O such untranslatable grief and growing pains of the delicate halibut. The heavy cod, solid as gumboots. And the wet haddock, North Sea lumber of a long Tuesday's lunch. Fish and sauce. Nibbles and nutshells. Gulps of draught ale, Guinness or cider made with steaks. English food, you are all we have. Long may you reign!

Collected Poems, 1989

Roast Beef Dinner in Iraq

H. V. MORTON 1892–1979

The distance between Damascus and Baghdad is five hundred and twenty-seven miles, and the Nairn coaches accomplish the journey in twenty-four hours, with only two official stops: one, at Rutba Fort, half-way, and the other at Ramadi, the Iraq passport station. Before cars crossed the desert, the journey was possible only by camel caravan, and these sometimes took two months. I do not know whether the two New Zealanders who have originated this extraordinary adventure in transport will make a fortune, but no one can deny that they have made history.

NOTICE

Passengers are warned when leaving the fort always to keep the fort in sight. Cases have occurred of passengers becoming lost (through losing their bearings) when out for a stroll, owing to darkness falling suddenly and the fort not being in sight. The result of this causes danger to the passengers and trouble to the police.

By Order.
Administrative Commandant.

My eye lingered lovingly over 'when out for a stroll,' which brought memories of Eastbourne into Mesopotamia. No-one but an Englishman could have talked about having 'a stroll' at Rutba.

While I was wondering from whom all these blessings flowed, my curiosity was answered by the appearance of a short, stout man in a grey flannel suit, who passed rapidly through the dining-room, talking like a machine-gun in sudden rapping bursts of fluent Arabic. Every waiter addressed by him seemed to have been given an electric shock. Some fled into the kitchen, some attempted to hide, and several stumbled over chairs and upset the salt in a passion of obedience. He smoked a cigarette all the time, rapping out his orders between puffs of smoke and with a glance of pale blue eyes which had the fixed expression of expecting the worst; a look which men acquire from long contact with foreign troops. I put him down as an old soldier, and from the quick way he moved and the way he held himself, as a boxer or an athlete. And in none of these things was I far wide of the mark.

He was George Bryant, commandant of the rest-house. As I sat down to dinner, we attempted to talk, but this was difficult because he was interrupted every two seconds by one of his waiters. He would spring lightly to his feet and disappear with a terrifying gleam of frosty blue eyes, to return a minute later with the air of having quelled a rebellion. During his first absence I gazed incredulously at the card which was propped against the cruet.

DINNER
Tomato Soup
Fried Fish.
Tartar Sauce.
Roast Beef.

Horse-Radish Sauce.
Roast Potatoes.
Cauliflower.
Yorkshire Pudding.
Raisin Pudding, Lemon Syrup.
Fruit. Coffee.

I invite you to look at the map which is at the beginning of this book, and, having found Rutba, to believe that this very night a meal of such superb Englishness is probably being eaten in that hut behind the fortress wall. In an age of half-belief, it is inspiring to meet that mood of stern faith which will recognise in no part of the earth a place that cannot be made a little like home; that must, in fact, be made like home before it can be called good. And although we may laugh at people who go about the world taking England wherever they may be, what finer thing is there to take about the world? For one brief hour, as we sat at the parting of the ways in this desert, some of us to travel towards the Mediterranean, others towards the Indian Ocean, we sat in peace, sharing the solid comfort of a tradition built up in generations of English families.

When George Bryant returned, I looked at him with renewed interest. No; he had no woman to help him. He had trained the cooks and the waiters himself. Where did he come from? Born at Bath, played rugger for Bristol, entered the Palestine police force, stationed at Nazareth, left the force, and had been in the desert ever since. So much I got out of him in a quick-fire way between his jumpings-up and his sittings-down.

'Enjoy your dinner? Not too bad, is it?' And a frosty smile came into his eyes for a second. 'Difficult? It's not too easy. You've got to keep them up to the scratch. That's the secret. You can't let one detail escape you.'

Through Lands of the Bible, 1938

Szechuanese Cuisine
PETER GOULLART d. 1978

I always felt hungry because the food at the farm was almost uneatable. The Szechuanese only had two meals during the day. One was at about ten o'clock in the morning and another roughly at about five in the afternoon. During breakfast, which was also called lunch, we had butter tea and *momos* with some salted turnips or cabbage and a little kanbar. *Momos* were lozenge-shaped baps made of roughly milled Indian corn. They were baked right in the stove before the yak-dung fire and were always mixed with ashes by the time they were ready. If they had been fully baked, they were as hard as bricks; if they were underdone, they were unpleasantly soggy inside. During the afternoon meal we had the same kind of *momos* and a soup which was brought in a small wooden tub. It was usually made of dried peas or chick-peas and, infrequently, of turnips, rutabagas or potatoes, the only vegetables that could grow at this altitude, with an addition of sliced pig intestines or a piece of old salted pork. Although the Tibetan women started cooking this evening meal soon after breakfast, nothing was properly boiled or stewed when dinner time came. Of course, it was not their fault; at this altitude the water appeared to boil quickly, but it was not really very hot and a hand could be put into it without being scalded. It took many hours to boil anything and even eggs required something like ten minutes to get them soft-boiled. Thus we sat down to a meal of these sodden *momos*, and soup in which the peas, still as hard as stones, lay on the bottom of the bowl. The intestines, only half-washed and improperly cleaned, were loathsome in the extreme. Remembering what the pigs ate, I could not control a feeling of nausea when such food was served. The soup with other ingredients was no better, the potatoes, turnips or rutabagas being half-raw floating together in a greasy, murky liquid with unsavoury pieces of salt pork which was unpalatable and stringy. However, I had to eat at least something to keep myself alive. But this diet effectively ruined my stomach and left its mark on my digestion for many years. I believe I would have died if it had not been for a bowl of rich yak milk which I wangled as my daily due from the unrelenting farm manager, who was clearly enjoying my discomfiture. I always suspected that he and his assistant had their own stores and ate much better on the sly.

Princes of the Black Bone, 1959

The English Pastry-cook
FANNY TROLLOPE 1780–1863

We have been on a regular shopping tour this morning; which was finished by our going into an English pastry-cook's to eat buns. While thus engaged, we amused ourselves by watching the proceedings of a French party who entered also for the purpose of making a morning goûter upon cakes.

They had all of them more or less the air of having fallen upon a terra incognita, showing many indications of surprise at sight of the ultramarine compositions which appeared before them – but there was a young man of the party who, it was evident, had made up his mind to quiz without measure all the foreign dainties that the shop afforded, evidently considering their introduction as a very unjustifiable interference with the native manufacture.

'Est-il possible!' said he, with an air of grave and almost indignant astonishment, as he watched a lady of his party preparing to eat an English bun, – 'Est-il possible that you can prefer these strange-looking comestibles à la pâtisserie française?'

'Mais goûtez-en,' said the lady, presenting a specimen of the same kind as that she was herself eating: 'ils sont excellens.'

'No, no! it is enough to look at them!' said her cavalier, almost shuddering. 'There is no lightness, no elegance, no grace in any single gâteau here.'

'Mais goûtez quelque chose,' reiterated the lady.

'Vous le voulez absolument!' exclaimed the young man; 'quelle tyrannie! . . . and what a proof of obedience I am about to give you! . . . Voyons donc!' he continued, approaching a plate on which were piled some truly English muffins – which, as you know, are of a somewhat mysterious manufacture, and about as palatable if eaten untoasted as a slice from a leathern glove. To this *gâteau*, as he supposed it to be, the unfortunate connoisseur in pâtisserie approached, exclaiming with rather a theatrical air, 'Voilà donc ce que je vais faire pour vos beaux yeux!'

As he spoke, he took up one of the pale, tough things, and, to our extreme amusement, attempted to eat it. Any one might be excused for making a few grimaces on such an occasion – and a Frenchman's privilege in this line is well known: but this hardy experimentalist outdid this privilege; – he was in a perfect agony, and his spittings and reproachings were so vehement, that friends, strangers, boutiquier, and all, even down to a little befloured urchin who entered at the moment with a tray of patties, burst into uncontrollable laughter, which the unfortunate, to do him justice, bore with extreme good humour, only making his fair countrywoman promise that she would never insist upon his eating English confectionary again.

Paris and the Parisians, 1835

Lent in the Castiles 1722
DUC DE SAINT-SIMON 1675–1755

Lent put an end to what *fêtes* there were; and their Catholic Majesties left the palace and went to that of the Buen-Retiro. Lent is very grievous in the Castiles. Inertness and distance from the sea result in a fish-market being unknown. The largest rivers have scarcely any fish; the small ones still less, because they are torrents. There are few or no vegetables, except garlic, onions, cardoons, and a few herbs; neither milk nor butter. They have salt-fish, which might be good if the oil were sweet; but it is usually so rancid that the stench infects the streets of Madrid through Lent, which is kept by every one, young and old, men, women, seigneurs, bourgeois, and populace. One is therefore reduced to eggs cooked in every possible way, and chocolate, which is their great resource. But I tasted some buffalo milk at Aranjuez, which is most excellent, and by far the best of any. It is smooth, sweet, but not insipid; thicker than the best cream, without any taste of the animal, or of cheese or butter. I am surprised that they make no use in Madrid of such a delicious milk product. Spaniards, though always very moderate, eat as much as we do, with taste, selection, and pleasure; but as for drink they are very abstemious.

Memoirs of the Duc de Saint-Simon, TRANS.
Katharine Wormeley, 1899

Picnics

❦

Vatel's Suicide
MME DE SÉVIGNÉ 1626–96

TO MADAME DE GRIGNAN

[Paris, Sunday 26 April 1671]

The King arrived on Thursday evening. Hunting, lanterns, moonlight, a gentle walk, supper served in a spot carpeted with daffodils – everything was perfect. They had supper. There was no roast at one or two tables because of several unexpected guests. That upset Vatel, and he said more than once, 'I am dishonoured; this is a humiliation I will not bear.' He said to Gourville, 'I don't know where I am, I haven't slept for twelve nights. Help me give orders.' Gourville comforted him as far as he could, but this roast missing, not from the King's table but from the twenty-fifth down, constantly came back to his mind. Gourville told all this to Monsieur le Prince. Monsieur le Prince went to Vatel's room and said to him, 'Vatel, everything is all right, nothing was so perfect as the King's supper.' But he answered, 'Monseigneur, your kindness is overwhelming, but I know that there was no roast at two tables.' 'Not at all,' said Monsieur le Prince, 'don't upset yourself, everything is going splendidly.' Night falls. The fireworks are a failure owing to fog, and they cost 16,000 francs. By four in the morning Vatel was rushing round everywhere and finding everything wrapped in slumber. He found a small supplier who only had two loads of fish. 'Is that all?' he asked. 'Yes, Sir.' He did not know that Vatel had sent round to all the seaports. Vatel waited a short time, the other suppliers did not turn up, he lost his head and thought there would be no more fish. He went and found Gourville and said, 'Sir, I shall never survive this disgrace, my honour and my reputation are at stake.' Gourville laughed at him. Vatel went to his room, put his sword up against the door and ran it through his heart. But that was only at the third attempt, for the first two were not mortal. Then he fell dead. Meanwhile the fish was coming in from all quarters. They looked for Vatel to allocate it, went to his room, broke in the door and found him lying in his own blood. They rushed to Monsieur le Prince, who was terribly upset. Monsieur le Duc wept, for the whole of his trip to Burgundy depended on Vatel. Monsieur le Prince told the King very sadly, explaining that it was a matter of honour as he saw it; he was greatly praised. His courage was both praised and blamed. The King said that he had been putting off his visit to Chantilly for five years because he realized what an extreme embarrassment it would be. He told Monsieur le Prince that he ought to have two tables and not undertake all the rest. He swore that he would not allow Monsieur le Prince to take all this trouble, but it was too late for poor Vatel. However, Gourville tried to make up for the loss of Vatel. He did so, and there was a very good dinner, light refreshments later, and then supper, a walk, cards, hunting, everything scented with daffodils, everything magical. Yesterday, Saturday, the same thing and in the evening the King went on to Liancourt, where he had commanded a *medianoche*; he is to stay there today.

Selected Letters, TRANS. Leonard Tancock, 1982

Compiègne
DUC DE SAINT-SIMON 1675–1755

In his memoirs for 1698 Saint-Simon described the military camp at Compiègne, designed by Louis XIV to 'astonish Europe by a show of his power'. On Thursday, August 28 the Court departed for Compiègne where the King invited the King of England, James II, who was in exile, to dine with the Maréchal. 'The singularity of entertaining two kings together was great', he wrote.

The colonels, and many of the simple captains, kept abundant and delicate tables; six lieutenant-generals, and fourteen brigadier-generals distinguished themselves by vast display; but Maréchal de Boufflers astonished all by his lavishness, and by the surprising order of his profusion, with its choiceness, its magnificence, and its courtesy, throughout the whole period of the camp and at all hours of the day and night, teaching even the king himself what it was to give a really superb and magnificent fête, and M. Le Prince, whose art and taste were thought to surpass those of everybody else, what elegance, novelty, and exquisite choiceness really were. Never was there a spectacle so brilliant, so dazzling, and it must be said, so alarming, while, at the same time nothing was more composed than the maréchal and his surroundings amid this universal hospitality, nothing more silent than all the preparations, more easy than this prodigious splendour, nothing so simple, modest, and free of all care as the great general who had ordered all and was ordering it unceasingly, although he seemed to be occupied only by the duty of commanding the army. Tables without number, freshly replenished and served at all moments as officers, courtiers, or spectators, even the most unknown idlers, came to them; all were received, invited, and as if captured by the attention, civility, and promptitude of the multitude of officials. All sorts of hot and cold liquors were also served, everything, in short, that could be most splendidly included in that class of refreshment; French wines, foreign wines, the choicest liqueurs were lavished in profusion; and measures were so carefully taken that an abundance of game and venison arrived from all directions; and the seas of Normandy, Holland, England, Brittany, and even the Mediterranean furnished whatever they had that was rarest and most costly day after day at the right moment, with inimitable order, and by means of couriers and small post-chaises. Even the water, which it was feared might be exhausted or made turbid by so many mouths, was brought from Sainte-Reine, from the Seine, and other esteemed sources. It is not possible to imagine anything of any kind that was not there to hand, and for the poorest comer as for the most important and well attended guest. Wooden houses furnished like the most superb Parisian houses, all being new and made expressly for the purpose with taste and charming gallantry; immense and magnificent tents, the number of which alone formed a camp in themselves; kitchens, offices, and the innumerable officials required for this uninterrupted service of the tables, the butlers, the cellars – all these things formed a spectacle the order, silence, punctuality, rapidity, and perfect cleanliness of which filled every one with surprise and admiration.

Memoirs of the Duc de Saint-Simon, TRANS. Katharine Wormeley,

1899

Tinned Supper
C. S. FORESTER 1899–1966

'We'll have a good supper tonight,' said Rose, jumping up. 'No, don't you move, dear. You just sit still and smoke your old cigarette.'

They had their good supper, all of the special delicacies which the Belgian manager of the mine received in his fortnightly consignment – tinned tomato soup, and tinned lobster and a tin of asparagus, and a tin of apricots with condensed milk, and a tin of biscuits. They experimented with a tin of *pâté de foie gras*, but they neither of them liked it, and by mutual consent they put it over-side half finished. And, swilling tea afterwards, they were both of them firmly convinced that they had dined well. They were of the generation and class which had been educated to think that all good food came out of tins, and their years in Africa had not undeceived them.

The African Queen, 1935

Sheep-shearer's Dinner
GEORGE EWART EVANS 1909–88

Village life in Suffolk, at Blaxall.

When the company was working at a farm in, or not very far from the village their families would go out to them to have their main meal of the day – usually after the work had been completed. The wives and children carried out the food in big baskets covered with cloths. The sheep-shearing platform would then be cleared and covered with white table-cloths. The food was then placed all together on the improvised table and shared in common by all the clippers and their families. The fare eaten at these open-air dinners was traditionally pork, dumplings, spring cabbage and new potatoes, followed by suet pudding. The meat and the vegetables would be boiled in the same pot. The dumplings were called *fillers*, as the father would have most of the meat while the rest of the family filled up with the dumplings and the gravy; but the children often called them *swimmers* as they always floated on top of the pot of meat and vegetables. The men had home-brewed beer to drink, the children *small* or very weak beer. As at harvest-time this was kept in large earthenware bottles and was served in horn-beakers, one of which each man would carry in his bag with his shears and whetstones. As it was horn it was less likely to be broken. Often the farmer would supply drink – beer or cider – for the shearers. It was brought to them in a large earthenware jug called a *gotch*: on one farm in this village the beer was brought into the fields in a copper jug called a *ranter*.

Ask the Fellows who Cut the Hay, 1956

Haymaker's Dinner
L. N. TOLSTOY 1828–1910

As they were walking back over the cut grass, the old man drew Levin's attention to the little girls and boys approaching from different sides, along the road and through the long grass – hardly visible above it – carrying the haymakers pitchers of rye-beer stoppered with rags, and bundles of bread which dragged their little arms down.

'Look'ee, little lady-birds crawling along!' he said, pointing to them and glancing at the sun from under his hand.

They completed two more rows; the old man stopped.

'Come, master, dinner-time!' he said briskly. And on reaching the stream the mowers moved off across the cut grass towards their pile of coats, where the children who had brought their dinners sat waiting for them. The men who had driven from a distance gathered in the shadow of their carts; those who lived nearer went under a willow bush, over which they threw grass.

Levin sat down beside them; he did not want to go away.

All constraint in the presence of the master had disappeared long ago. The peasants began preparing for dinner. Some had a wash, the young lads bathed in the stream, others arranged places for their after-dinner rest, untied their bundles of bread and unstoppered their pitchers of rye-beer.

The old man crumbled up some bread in a cup, pounded it with the handle of a spoon, poured water on it from the dipper, broke up some more bread and, having sprinkled it with salt, turned to the east to say his prayer.

'Come, master, have some of my dinner,' he said, squatting on his knees in front of the cup.

The bread and water was so delicious that Levin changed his mind about going home. He shared the old man's meal and chatted to him about his family affairs, taking the keenest interest in them, and told him about his own affairs and all the circumstances that could be of interest to the old peasant.

Anna Karenin, TRANS. Rosemary Edmonds, 1954

Cossack Bread

ALEXANDRE DUMAS 1802–70

So while four of our Cossacks unloaded our tent from the *telega* and erected it on the far side of the road, beside a dried-up well, my friends and I went forward to join the main group of Tatars by the ruined wall. They were sitting round their fire on sacks of flour that they were taking from Baku to army headquarters for the troops fighting in the Caucasus, and were busy making bread for their evening meal. It was a simple operation. From a large lump of fresh dough they cut a piece about the size of a man's fist, placed it on a kind of iron drum over a charcoal fire and rolled it out with a wooden stick. When one side was cooked they turned it over to cook the other, then passed it round and ate it hot. It looked and tasted very much like the crusty girdle-cakes sold in France at village fairs.

As we approached, a man who seemed to be the chief of this little group came forward to greet us and presented each of us with some of this bread and a crystal or two of rock-salt – symbols of hospitality. We seated ourselves by the fire on sacks of flour, while another man rose and cut a thick slice from a large lump of meat hanging on the wall (I think it was the forequarter of a horse), divided it into cubes and tossed them on to the iron drum where the bread had just been cooked. Soon they began to smoke and splutter and curl up. In five minutes they were ready and our host indicated with a gesture that they were for us. We speared the succulent morsels with the little knives that are kept in the sheaths of *kinjals* for this purpose, and ate them with our bread and salt. I have often eaten a worse meal at tables far more elegantly served.

There was something particularly romantic about eating supper with the descendants of Gengis-Khan and Tamerlane on the steppes beside the Caspian Sea, in the shadow of a ruined *caravanserie* built by Shah Abbas! In the distance lay the mountains of Daghestan, whence at any moment a troop of brigands might sweep down upon us and force us to fight for our very lives. All around us we could hear the bells of fifty camels as they cropped the shrivelled grass, or see them lying with their necks stretched out on the sand. The sight of our little tent, with the French tricolour fluttering above it in this vast empty space where in all probability our flag had never flown before, moved me so profoundly that, even now, I only have to close my eyes to see it all again!

We shook hands with our hosts as we left them for the night, and were offered more bread and salt for our morning meal. But at daybreak, when we awoke and looked around, we were quite alone. The Tatars, their camels and their bags of flour had all vanished in the night and the steppes were as empty as the sea.

Adventures in the Caucasus, TRANS. A. E. Murch 1962

Bull-fight Breakfast
MME CALDERÓN DE LA BARCA 1804–82

The lively letter and journals written by the bride of the first Spanish envoy to Mexico found an appreciative audience when they were published in 1843. Don Angel Calderón de la Barca married Frances Erskine Inglis in 1838, the year he took up his Mexican post. She was already widely travelled: Fanny's family had moved from Scotland to Normandy when her father lost his fortune. After his death Fanny, her mother and her married sister went to America where they set up a school, first in Boston, then in Staten Island and Baltimore.

After an enormous number of bulls had been caught and *labelled*, we went to breakfast. We found a tent prepared for us, formed of bows of trees intertwined with garlands of white moss, like that which covers the cypresses of Chapultepec, and beautifully oramented with red blossoms and scarlet berries. We sat down upon heaps of white moss, softer than any cushion. The Indians had cooked meat under the stones for us, which I found horrible, smelling and tasting of smoke. But we had also boiled fowls, and quantities of burning chile, hot tortillas, atole, or *atolli*, as the Indians call it, a species of cakes made of very fine maize and water, and sweetened with sugar or honey; *embarrado*, a favourite composition of meat and chile, very like *mud*, as the name imports, which I have not yet made up my mind to endure; quantities of fresh tunas, granaditas, bananas, aguacates, and other fruits, besides pulque, *á discrétion*.

The other people were assembled in circles under the trees, cooking fowls and boiling eggs in a gipsy fashion, in caldrons, at little fires made with dry branches; and the band, in its intervals of tortilla and pulque, favoured us with occasional airs. After breakfast, we walked out amongst the Indians, who had formed a sort of temporary market, and were selling pulque, chia, roasted chestnuts, yards of baked meat, and every kind of fruit. We then returned to see a great bull-fight, which was followed by more *herraderos* – in short, spent the whole day amongst the *toros*, and returned to dinner at six o'clock, some in coaches, some on horseback.

. . .The animal, when dead, was given as a present to the *torcadores*; and this bull, cut in pieces, they bury with his skin on, in a hole in the ground previously prepared with fire in it, which is then covered over with earth and branches. During a certain time, it remains baking in this natural oven, and the common people consider it a great delicacy, (in which I differ from them).

Life in Mexico, 1843

The Feast of St Soulas

LAWRENCE DURRELL 1912—91

We bowl over the crown of the last hillock and there before us lies the site of the shrine; the ground slopes away on all sides in a series of thinly-forested hillocks, leaving a level space of perhaps four acres. Here the villages of Soroni have performed their usual task in digging a dozen large pits which will be filled with glowing charcoal and over which sheep and oxen will be roasted. At strategic points, too, huge bundles of dry brushwood lie piled, waiting for the night. Lofty pine-trees give a good deal of shade, and here out-door cafés have sprung up all round the shrine, which looks something like a small provincial bus-station. Paul jockeys us out of the line of lorries and we bump across the dusty soil toward the cover of the trees where he draws up with a triumphant smile. Everybody piles out of the bus into the sunny afternoon light, eager to see what is going on.

The sky above the eastern hollows is suffused with clouds of pinkish dust kicked up by the heels of mules; apparently some of the races have already started, as one can discern the gesticulating figures who ride them, with coloured scarves tied round their heads. The course itself has been squared out neatly with tent-pegs, and in one corner, on a wooden dais, sit the Brigadier and senior members of his staff, half choked with dust, and busily trying to memorise speeches in demotic which they will have to deliver at the prizegiving. To the westward, under the pines, stand groups of black-coated figures – each looking for all the world like a spiny black hedgehog in the shadow; this must be a cluster from various parts of the island. The low grumble of their chanting can be dimly heard above the prodigious hubbub of the crowd which fills the middle distance. They too have a dais from which prizes will be distributed, gaily decked with Greek and English flags stencilled all over it in waterpaint. Overhead is a roof of plaited palm-leaves which contributes a faintly central-African flavour to the scene.

Around the shrine itself (which resembles an ant-hill) streets have begun to improvise themselves as if a boom-town were suddenly growing up under one's very eyes. Yet the streets are lined, not with houses, but with stalls packed to the sky with sweetmeats, lemonade, almonds, cheese. There is hardly an unfamiliar face here, for every itinerant pedlar of Rhodes has made the pilgrimage on foot. Here for example is the old one-armed man who trundles a barrow about the town, loaded with chestnuts which he roasts on a brazier; I have often watched the skill with which he fills the little paper bags, shouting all the time in a deep croaky voice, 'Chestnuts . . . Chestnuts.' Next to him stand several of the itinerant fresh-water sellers, each with his little white municipal cart shaded by a cluster of green. Next again come the sweet-meat sellers, shouting as if their hearts were broken 'Sweeeeets . . . Sweeeeets.' There is chocolate, nougat, almond paste, marzipan, pistachio nougat as well as those heavier confections like *galactobour-iko* and *baklava*, which Gideon claims are made from waste blotting paper and honey. At intervals too stand the *loukumades* experts, their long spoons at the ready to seize the roasted doughnut when it is fried brown and crisp, and then to duck it in honeyed sauce. Small children stand round these stalls breathing in the flowery scent of the ovens with appreciation, each holding a slip of paper on his small brown palm, waiting for the hot sweetmeat to be plumped into it. Here too pine-nuts are being roasted, and there spools of mastic (the Aegean chewing-gum) are being wound out and pressed into shapes, or being merely loaded into spoons and dropped into glasses of water.

At one end of this gallery of smells and sound is a section inhabited by a number of ferociously unshaven gentlemen, each stripped to the buff and liberally coated with soot. They dwell in an absolute forest of entrails out of which they stick their heads from time to time in order to utter a shriek before they return to their work at the spits; all round them on biscuit tins loaded with fine charcoal roast the entrails of Gideon's luckless sheep and lambs. Every sort of offal is here accorded expert treatment; tripe is wound round and round a giant spit, plugged with clove, nutmeg and garlic, and is roasted slowly; sheep's entrails receive horizontal roasting, being basted quickly with fat and lemon juice as they turn. Testicles, hearts and livers are all given an exacting professional attention and distinctive treatment on spits of various kinds. The cooks themselves carry long knives between their lips which gives them a terrifying look, and they dart from side to side of their stalls, now shaving off a tiny piece of beef to see if it tastes right, now banging a whole cluster of kebab off a spit on to a tin plate. They seem never to stop shouting for a moment, even when their knives are between their teeth. The attitudes they strike are magnificent, gladiatorial. Pools of hot dripping fall in the deep dust beneath the stalls, and here whole colonies of cats and dogs lounge, waiting for tit-bits. The pandemonium which reigns the whole length of this street is indescribable; but set back twenty yards on either side of it, the cafés are less noisy. Chairs and tables have sprung up like mushrooms everywhere, and here the peasant families have seated themselves in bright semicircles to drink and eat. Here and there, too, small bevies of musicians are tuning up their accordions, guitars and violins, standing back to back to play a few stray phrases from time to time. Somewhere a big drum is banging, slow and paunch-like, which suggests that already a dance has begun, but I cannot see where; meanwhile the upper air is hoarse with the sickening braying of asses and the fever-shrill bleating of sacrificial lambs.

On the high ground where the green grass is thickest and where the line of myrtle and arbutus begins, lorries are slowly straying, like lost camels, looking for good camping-sites. Here whole families have unpacked their belongings, spread coloured rugs and pillows, and have settled down with no intention of moving before tomorrow. Stately peasant matrons are unpacking their squamous litters of small children, and their saddle bags full of bottles and cans and immense loaves of home-made bread. I wander in this forest of human beings with the loving detachment of a child in a familiar countryside, drinking it all in – even the savour of the harsh reddish dust which coats the air and dries the throat: all the weird mixture of smells which together compose the anthology of a Greek holiday under the pines – petrol, garlic, wine and goat.

Reflections on a Marine Venus, 1953

Thirty People in Two Cars

MADHUR JAFFREY 1933–

Preparations for the picnic would begin in the wee hours of the morning. All the short ladies of the house – and they were all short – would begin scurrying around in the kitchen. One would be stirring potatoes in a gingery tomato sauce; another, sitting on a low stool, would be rolling out *pooris* (small, puffed breads) by the dozen; yet another would be forming meatballs with wetted palms. Pickles had to be removed from pickling jars, fruit packed in baskets, and disposable terracotta *mutkainas* – our tea cups – given a thorough rinse. Two cars, the gleaming Plymouth and the well-worn Ford, would stand at the ready in the brick driveway.

The art of getting thirty people into two cars had long been mastered. The first layer consisted of alternating teenagers and short ladies, with the teenagers sitting perched on the edge of the seat. On their laps went the second layer of slim ten to twelve year olds. The third layer, sitting on the laps of the second layer, consisted of those under ten. The tall men and servants sat in the front seat. On *their* laps sat the fat ten to twelve year olds holding all the baskets and pots that could not be stuffed into the trunk.

A Taste of India, 1985

Outdoor Lunch
L. N. TOLSTOY 1828–1910

When he and Kitty returned from the springs, the prince, who had invited the colonel and Maria Yevgenyevna and Varenka all to come and have coffee with them, had a table and chairs brought into the garden under the chestnut tree and lunch laid there. The landlord and the servants grew brisker under the influence of his cheerfulness. They knew his open-handedness; and half an hour later the invalid doctor from Hamburg, who lived on the top floor, was looking enviously out of the window at the jolly party of healthy Russians gathered under the chestnut tree. Beneath the trembling circles of shadow from the leaves, at one end of a table covered with a white cloth and set with coffee-pot, bread-and-butter, cheese, and cold game, sat the princess in a high cap with lilac ribbons, handing out cups of coffee and sandwiches. At the other end sat the prince, eating heartily, and talking loudly and merrily. The prince had spread out in front of him his purchases: carved boxes, little ornaments, paper-knives of all kinds, of which he had bought a heap at every watering-place, and was giving them away to everybody, including Lieschen, the servant-girl, and the landlord, with whom he jested in his comically bad German, assuring him that it was not the waters that had cured Kitty but his splendid cooking, especially his prune soup.

Anna Karenin, TRANS. Rosemary Edmonds, 1954

English Picnics
LESLEY BLANCH 1907–

I was brought up to believe no meal could be eaten indoors if it was possible to be eaten outside, in the garden, on a balcony or wherever the sky was all around. I remember raw, winter days of watery sunshine when my mother, a fragile woman, wrapped in rugs and wearing woolly gloves, presided over rapidly congealing luncheons on our terrace overlooking the Thames. While this might have conditioned me to loathe al fresco eating, it did not, and I still feel stifled indoor, or in those restaurants which deny daylight, with table lamps and heavy curtains . . .

The wildest, most improbable things, eaten out of doors, preferably in some remote setting, seem absolutely right and put to shame the uninspiring cold chicken and thermos flasks which nestle so smugly in the well-equipped picnic-baskets of convention.

Picnics have always been part of the English scene. Ginger biscuits and a thermos of sloshy tea with Nanny, on some bracing beach. The midnight dormitory feasts of school-days, cocoa, sardines and sausages. Romantic picnics in punts, at Henley Regatta; elaborate hampers at Glyndbourne; tea-urns at Lords. Etonian excesses on the fourth of June. Hampers full of sustenance for those banging away in the butts on 'the glorious twelfth' (though some of us find the adjective inappropriate when applied to that organised slaughter which goes by the name of sport). And finally there is our present-day adaptation of the picnic, now domesticated, or brought indoors in terms of the TV dinner-snack, a tray full of mysterious cartons and fast foods, or unwisely ambitious versions of Irish stew or trifle, to accompany those singular versions of life to which the Box has accustomed the British, as well as the American public.

From Wilder Shores, 1989

Let's Have Lunch in the Garden
ALICE THOMAS ELLIS 1932–

'Let's have lunch in the garden, a picnic.' She slid her sunglasses back down from her hairline to her nose and her sandals back on to her feet.

Rose made no objection. Henry hated eating out of doors, and so, she was sure, did the others. 'You are kind,' she said, as though Angela had offered to do it by herself. 'You'll find the fish in the scullery and a nice sharp knife hanging on the wall.'

Angela played this one well. 'Oh,' she cried. 'I hate cutting things' heads off. You must help me, Edward.'

'Angela's giving us a picnic,' explained Rose to the others as they gathered to look hopefully in the dining-room. They dragged the garden table out of the out-house where it was kept and carried it, cursing, to the terrace, where they had to pull it around a good deal until it ceased staggering. Michael and Henry sat down exhausted.

'Open a bottle,' said Henry. 'I hope it's well chilled.'

Edward and Angela came trotting merrily out, like runners in a relay race, with plates of fried fish. Angela had taken trouble to make it look nice, garnishing it with radishes cut to look like flowers and slices of lemon with castellated edges. It was very reminiscent of hotel food, from the thinly sliced brown bread and butter to the selection of small cheeses which Angela had gathered from the refrigerator. The plaice had the limp and glistening aspect usual to English cookery; and the midday sun, just turning its attention to the luncheon table, did not enhance its appearance.

'I can't eat this,' said Henry after a while. 'It's too hot.'

'Then I'll have it,' said Edward, scooping half-eaten fish and skin on to his plate.

'Sensible,' said Angela. 'It's wicked to waste good food.'

The Sin Eater, 1977

Picnic Food
RUTH LOWINSKY d. 1958

Picnics are not as popular to-day as they were in the time of Watteau and Queen Victoria. Now it nearly always rains and at least two of the guests hate picnics, and say so, but refuse to be left behind. The food must be good enough to put everyone in an amiable frame of mind. This is not as difficult as it sounds, as most of the party do not expect anything more enticing than ham sandwiches. Ask everyone before the start what they would like to drink, and on no account forget a Thermos flask of hot black coffee, or more important still, the salt. For a picnic you must have drinking cups, plates and dishes of papier-mâché. This means that there is very little of the disgusting business of packing up dirty crockery. Afterwards, a bonfire preserves the good looks of the countryside as papier-mâché burns easily. Everything should be neatly done up in grease-proof paper, and placed in separate boxes or in papier-mâché dishes, otherwise, when the basket is unpacked, the food is already squashed and unappetising.

Lovely Food, 1931

Ratty's Luncheon Basket

KENNETH GRAHAME 1859–1932

'Look here! If you've really nothing else on hand this morning, supposing we drop down the river together, and have a long day of it?'

The Mole waggled his toes from sheer happiness, spread his chest with a sigh of full contentment, and leaned back blissfully into the soft cushions. '*What* a day I'm having!' he said. 'Let us start at once!'

'Hold hard a minute, then!' said the Rat. He looped the painter through a ring in his landing-stage, climbed up into his hole above, and after a short interval reappeared staggering under a fat, wicker luncheon-basket.

'Shove that under your feet,' he observed to the Mole, as he passed it down into the boat. Then he untied the painter and took the sculls again.

'What's inside it?' asked the Mole, wriggling with curiosity.

'There's cold chicken inside it,' replied the Rat briefly; 'coldtongue-coldhamcoldbeefpickledgherkinssaladfrenchrollscresssandwidges-pottedmeatgingerbeerlemonadesodawater –'

'O stop, stop,' cried the Mole in ecstasies: 'This is too much!'

'Do you really think so?' inquired the Rat seriously. 'It's only what I always take on these little excursions; and the other animals are always telling me that I'm a mean beast and cut it *very* fine!'

The Wind in the Willows, 1908

Tea

C. S. FORESTER 1899–1966

'Now I can think about supper,' he said. 'What about a cup o' tea, miss?'

Tea! Heat and thirst and fatigue and excitement had done their worst for Rose. She was limp and weary and her throat ached. The imminent prospects of a cup of tea roused her to trembling excitement. Twelve cups of tea each Samuel and she had drunk daily for years. Today she had had none – she had eaten no food either, but at the moment that meant nothing to her. Tea! A cup of tea! Two cups of tea!

Half a dozen great mugs of tea, strong, delicious, revivifying! Her mind was suffused with rosy pictures of an evening's tea drinking, a debauch compared with which the spring sowing festivities at the village by the mission station were only a pale shade.

'I'd like a cup of tea,' she said.

'Water's still boiling in the engine,' said Allnutt, heaving himself to his feet. 'Won't take a minute.'

The tinned meat that they ate was, as a result of the heat, reduced to a greasy semi-liquid mass. The native bread was dark and unpalatable. But the tea was marvellous. Rose was forced to use sweetened condensed milk in it, which she hated – at the mission they had cows until von Hanneken commandeered them – but not even that spoilt her enjoyment of the tea. She drank it strong, mug after mug of it, as she had promised herself, with never a thought of what it was doing inside her to the lining of her stomach; probably it was making as pretty a picture of that as ever she had seen at a Band of Hope lantern lecture where they exhibited enlarged photographs of a drunkard's liver. She gulped down mug after mug. For a moment her body temperature shot up to fever heat, but presently there came a blissful perspiration – not the sticky, prickly sweat in which she moved all day long, but a beneficent and cooling fluid, bringing with it a feeling of ease and well-being.

'Those Belgians up at the mine wouldn't never drink tea,' said Allnutt, tilting the condensed milk tin over his mug of black liquid. 'They didn't know what was good.'

'Yes,' said Rose. She felt positive friendship for Allnutt welling up within her. She slapped at the mosquitoes without irritation.

The African Queen, 1935

August Bank Holiday

DYLAN THOMAS 1914–1953

August Bank Holiday – a tune on an ice-cream cornet. A slap of sea and a tickle of sand. A fanfare of sunshades opening. A wince and whinny of bathers dancing into deceptive water. A tuck of dresses. A rolling of trousers. A compromise of paddlers. A sunburn of girls and a lark of boys. A silent hullabaloo of balloons.

I remember the sea telling lies in a shell held to my ear for a whole harmonious, hollow minute by a small, wet girl in an enormous bathing suit marked Corporation Property.

I remember sharing the last of my moist buns with a boy and a lion. Tawny and savage, with cruel nails and capacious mouth, the little boy tore and devoured. Wild as seedcake, ferocious as a hearthrug, the depressed and verminous lion nibbled like a mouse at his half a bun and hiccupped in the sad dusk of his cage.

I remember a man like an alderman or a bailiff, bowlered and collarless, with a bag of monkeynuts in his hand, crying 'Ride 'em, cowboy!' time and again as he whirled in his chairaplane giddily above the upturned laughing faces of the town girls bold as brass and the boys with padded shoulders and shoes sharp as knives; and the monkeynuts flew through the air like salty hail.

Children all day capered or squealed by the glazed or bashing sea, and the steam-organ wheezed its waltzes in the threadbare playground and the waste lot, where the dodgems dodged, behind the pickle factory.

And mothers loudly warned their proud pink daughters or sons to put that jellyfish down; and fathers spread newspapers over their faces; and sandfleas hopped on the picnic lettuce; and someone had forgotten the salt.

In those always radiant, rainless, lazily rowdy and sky-blue summers departed, I remember August Monday from the rising of the sun over the stained and royal town to the husky hushing of the roundabout music and the dowsing of the naphtha jets in the seaside fair: from bubble-and-squeak to the last of the sandy sandwiches.

There was no need, that holiday morning, for the sluggardly boys to be shouted down to breakfast; out of their jumbled beds they tumbled, and scrambled into rumpled clothes; quickly at the bathroom basin they catlicked their hands and faces, but never forgot to run the water loud and long as though they washed like colliers; in front of the cracked looking-glass, bordered with cigarette cards, in their treasure-trove bedrooms, they whisked a gap-tooth comb through their surly hair; and with shining cheeks and noses and tidemarked necks, they took the stairs three at a time.

But for all their scramble and scamper, clamour on the landing, catlick and toothbrush flick, hair-whisk and stair-jump, their sisters were always there before them. Up with the lady lark, they had prinked and frizzed and hot-ironed; and smug in their blossoming dresses, ribboned for the sun, in gymshoes white as the blanco'd show, neat and silly with doilies and tomatoes they helped in the higgledy kitchen. They were calm; they were virtuous; they had washed their necks; they did not romp, or fidget; and only the smallest sister put out her tongue at the noisy boys.

And the woman who lived next door came into the kitchen and said that her mother, an ancient uncertain body who wore a hat with cherries, was having one of her days and had insisted, that very holiday morning, in carrying, all the way to the tram-shop, a photograph album and the cutglass fruit bowl from the front room.

This was the morning when father, mending one hole in the thermos-flask, made three; when the sun declared war on the butter, and the butter ran; when dogs, with all the sweet-binned backyards to wag and sniff and bicker in, chased their tails in the jostling kitchen, worried sandshoes, snapped at flies, writhed between legs, scratched among towels, sat smiling on hampers.

And if you could have listened at some of the open doors of some of the houses in the street you might have heard:

'Uncle Owen says he can't find the bottle-opener –'
    'Has he looked under the hallstand?'
'Willy's cut his finger –'
    'Got your spade?'
'If somebody doesn't kill that dog –'
'Uncle Owen says why should the bottle-opener be under the hall-stand?'
    'Never again, never again –'
'I know I put the pepper somewhere –'
    'Willy's bleeding –'
'Look, there's a bootlace in my bucket –'
    'Oh come *on*, come *on* –'
'Let's have a look at the bootlace in your bucket –'
    'If I lay my hands on that dog –'
'Uncle Owen's found the bottle-opener –'
    'Willy's bleeding over the cheese –'

And the trams that hissed like ganders took us all to the beautiful beach.

'Holiday Memory', Collected Stories, 1980

Shooting Lunch

RUTH LOWINSKY

Shooting lunches sent miles out on the hill, carried by a pony or heavily laden ghillie, are best packed separately for each person, with his name written on the outside. A small aluminium box, preferably jointed at sides, back and lid, is lined with grease-proof paper. Then half a grouse is put in, some thinly cut bread and butter, a couple of savoury sandwiches, a jam puff, cheese, biscuits, and an apple, salt and pepper, each item being wrapped separately in grease-proof paper.

Here are a few more suggestions for those who are not so conservative as to demand the same lunch every day.

SAUSAGES   MUTTON PIES   VENISON

*

CUTLETS   TOMATOES

*

PICKLES AND GHERKINS

*

BAKED POTATOES   SMALL TARTS

*

COLD PLUM PUDDING   FRUIT CAKES

Lovely Food, 1931

Shooting Party, Balmoral, 1906

GABRIEL TSCHUMI

Quite a lot of these visitors at shooting-parties brought their own dogs with them, and we fed them and the gun-dogs on scraps of meat from the kitchens. But the German Kaiser, for some reason, did not trust the food the ordinary royal gun-dogs received from the cooks and insisted that an equerry should feed his favourite dog with scraps from his own plate.

A picnic lunch at a shooting-party might sound a fairly impromptu affair, but often we provided a full hot meal for the King and his guests during a break in the shooting. At Balmoral in October 1906 the lunch provided for the stag-shooting party led by King Edward consisted of Scotch broth and Mulligatawny soup, hashed venison, stewed mutton, game pies, Irish stew, and ended with plum pudding and apple fard. For some reason plum pudding was always popular at shooting-parties, particularly with the King.

Royal Chef, 1954

King Ludwig II – 17 October
LESLEY BLANCH 1907–

In the pine-dark forests of Bavaria, the mad King Ludwig II knew all about the pleasures of picnicking, and contrived the *ne plus ultra* in picnic menus, or so he saw them, when he took to dashing about his kingdom by night – one-night stands generally – the destination being decided on the spur of the moment. This capricious monarch would usually only eat one meal, or sleep one night, in any of his numerous palaces, hunting-lodges or grandiose architectural fantasies, before dashing on again.

But the whole thing was a cheat, picnic-wise, for a retinue of cooks, scullions, pages and grooms had to precede his torch-lit sleigh with its plumed white horses caracoling across the snow. The minions were compelled to go at an even more furious pace, in order to arrive well before the king, to set up every imaginable luxury, gold plate, crystal, china, portable ovens and lavish ingredients for spectacular spreads. Here is a typical royal menu, as cited in a curious book I possess, written by one of the royal scullions.

MENU

17 October

SWEETBREAD SOUP
GOOSELIVER ON TOAST

FRIED CARP WITH PARMESAN SAUCE

ROAST VEAL STUFFED WITH KIDNEY, ANCHOVY AND SOUR CREAM
ROEBUCK STEWED IN CIDER
SEMOLINA DUMPLINGS

NUT CAKE WITH RUM AND CHOCOLATE SAUCE
TROUBLED THOUGHTS* (A SUGAR-ICED BISCUIT)

BEER AND CHAMPAGNE

From Wilder Shores, 1989

Picnic Addicts

ELIZABETH DAVID 1913–92

Picnic addicts seem to be roughly divided between those who frankly make elaborate preparations and leave nothing to chance, and those others whose organization is no less complicated but who are more deceitful and pretend that everything will be obtained on the spot and cooked over a woodcutter's fire, conveniently to hand; there are even those, according to Richard Jefferies, who wisely take the precaution of visiting the site of their intended picnic some days beforehand and there burying the champagne.

Not long before the war I was staying with friends in Marseille. One Saturday night a picnic was arranged for the next day with some American acquaintances; it was agreed that the two parties should proceed in their own cars to a little bay outside Marseille, and that we should each bring our own provisions. On Sunday morning I and my friends indulged in a delicious hour of shopping in the wonderful market of the rue de Rome, buying olives, anchovies, salame sausages, pâtés, yards of bread, smoked fish, fruit and cheese. With a provision of cheap red wine we bundled the food into the car and set off, stopping now and again for a drink; so that we arrived at our rendezvous well disposed to appreciate the sun, the sea and the scent of wild herbs and Mediterranean pines. Presently our friends drove up and started to unload their car. One of the first things to come out was a hatchet, with which they efficiently proceeded to chop down olive branches, and in no time at all there was a blazing fire. Out of their baskets came cutlets, potatoes, bacon, skewers, frying pans, jars of ice, butter, tablecloths, all the trappings of a minor barbecue. Our reactions as we watched these proceedings were those of astonishment, admiration, and finally, a realization of the inadequacy of our

---

* which might well follow such a menu.

own catering dawned, dismay. How wilted they seemed, those little packets wrapped up in rather oily paper; the olives which had glowed with colour in the market stalls of the rue de Rome looked shabby now; the salame seemed dried up and the anchovies a squalid mess. Miserably, like poor relations, we sat with our shameful bundles spread out on the grass and politely offered them to our friends. They were kind, but obviously preferred their own grilled cutlets and fried potatoes, and we were too embarrassed to accept their proffered hospitality. Presently they produced ice cream out of a thermos, but by now we were past caring, and finally it was their turn for surprise when they found we hadn't even provided ourselves with the means of making a cup of coffee.

Then there was the hospitable family I remember in my childhood; they owned a beautiful house and an elegant garden and were much given to out-of-door entertainments, pageants and picnics. On picnic days a large party of children and grown-ups would be assembled in the hall. Led by our host and hostess we proceeded through the exquisite formal Dutch garden, across the lane and over a fence into a coppice. Close on our heels followed the butler, the chauffeur and the footman, bearing fine china plates, the silver and tablecloths, and a number of vast dishes containing cold chickens, jellies and trifles. Arrived at the end of our journey, five minutes from the house, our host set about making a fire, with sticks which I suspect had been strategically placed by the gardener, over which we grilled quantities of sausages and bacon, which were devoured amidst the customary jokes and hilarity. The picnickers' honour thus satisfied, we took our places for an orderly meal, handed round by the footman, and in composition resembling that of an Edwardian wedding breakfast.

Since those days I have had a good many opportunities of evolving a picnic technique on the lines laid down by Henry James, 'not so good as to fail of an amusing disorder, nor yet so bad as to defeat the proper function of repasts'.

Summer Cooking, 1955

Irish Stew

JEROME K. JEROME 1859–1927

We roamed about sweet Sonning for an hour or so, and then, it being too late to push on past Reading, we decided to go back to one of the Shiplake islands, and put up there for the night. It was still early when we got settled, and George said that, as we had plenty of time, it would be a splendid opportunity to try a good, slap-up supper. He said he would show us what could be done up the river in the way of cooking, and suggested that, with the vegetables and the remains of the cold beef and general odds and ends, we should make an Irish stew.

It seemed a fascinating idea. George gathered wood and made a fire, and Harris and I started to peel the potatoes. I should never have thought that peeling potatoes was such an undertaking. The job turned out to be the biggest thing of its kind that I had ever been in. We began cheerfully, one might almost say skittishly, but our lightheartedness was gone by the time the first potato was finished. The more we peeled, the more peel there seemed to be left on; by the time we had got all the peel off and all the eyes out, there was no potato left – at least none worth speaking of. George came and had a look at it – it was about the size of a pea-nut. He said:

'Oh, that won't do! You're wasting them. You must scrape them.'

So we scraped them, and that was harder work than peeling. They are such an extraordinary shape, potatoes – all bumps and warts and hollows. We worked steadily for five-and-twenty minutes, and did four potatoes. Then we struck. We said we should require the rest of the evening for scraping ourselves.

I never saw such a thing as potato-scraping for making a fellow in a mess. It seemed difficult to believe that the potato-scrapings in which Harris and I stood, half-smothered, could have come off four potatoes. It shows you what can be done with economy and care.

George said it was absurd to have only four potatoes in an Irish stew, so we washed half-a-dozen or so more, and put them in without peeling. We also put in a cabbage and about half a peck of peas. George stirred it all up, and then he said that there seemed to be a lot of room to spare, so we overhauled both the hampers, and picked out all the odds and ends and the remnants, and added them to the stew. There were half a pork pie and a bit of cold boiled bacon left, and we put them in. Then George found half a tin of potted salmon, and he emptied that into the pot.

He said that was the advantage of Irish stew: you got rid of such a lot of things. I fished out a couple of eggs that had got cracked, and we put those in. George said they would thicken the gravy.

I forget the other ingredients, but I know nothing was wasted; and I remember that, towards the end, Montmorency, who had evinced great interest in the proceedings throughout, strolled away with an earnest and thoughtful air, reappearing, a few minutes afterwards, with a dead water-rat in his mouth, which he evidently wished to present as his contribution to the dinner; whether in a sarcastic spirit, or with a general desire to assist, I cannot say.

We had a discussion as to whether the rat should go in or not. Harris said that he thought it would be all right, mixed up with the other things, and that every little helped; but George stood up for precedent. He said he had never heard of water-rats in Irish stew, and he would rather be on the safe side, and not try experiments.

Harris said:

'If you never try a new thing, how can you tell what it's like? It's men such as you that hamper the world's progress. Think of the man who first tried German sausage!'

It was a great success, that Irish stew. I don't think I ever enjoyed a meal more. There was something so fresh and piquant about it. One's palate gets so tired of the old hackneyed things: here was a dish with a new flavour, with a taste like nothing else on earth.

And it was nourishing, too. As George said, there was good stuff in it. The peas and potatoes might have been a bit softer, but we all had good teeth, so that did not matter much: and as for the gravy, it was a poem – a little too rich, perhaps, for a weak stomach, but nutritious.

Three Men in a Boat, 1917

The Englishman's Grand Gesture
GEORGINA BATTISCOMBE 1905–

A picnic is the Englishman's grand gesture, his final defiance flung in the face of fate. No climate in the world is less propitious to picnics than the climate of England, yet with a recklessness which is almost sublime the English rush out of doors to eat a meal on every possible and impossible occasion. The more prudent continental, whose climate is nevertheless so much more dependable than ours, has wisely developed the café habit; he indeed eats and drinks out of doors, but with the protection of an awning overhead and the safe retreat of a restaurant at his back. In spite of many attempts on the part of progressive *restaurateurs* the Englishman refuses to frequent an outdoor café of any sort, obstinately clinging to his picnic-basket in a wet and wasp-haunted field.

Whatever may have been its origin, today the picnic is a predominately British institution. Maybe the lamentably low standard of English cooking has something to do with the matter. Abroad the traveller may be sure of good food and good drink in the smallest village inn, but in England he may well prefer to pack a picnic meal and eat in the open air, regardless of the weather, rather than face the gastronomic rigours of the British hotel. It is significant that the greatest vogue of the picnic occurred during the middle of the nineteenth century, thus coinciding with the decline of the English inn due to the development of the railways. Today the wayside inn is showing signs of recovery and perhaps the time will come when its food and its fireside will be so inviting that picnics will fall out of fashion. But, fashionable or unfashionable, when spring comes round again the young will always go picnicking and the old remember the picnic pleasures of their youth.

English Picnics, 1951

Rules for Al Fresco Eating
RICHARDSON WRIGHT 1887–1961

Rules for Al Fresco Eating. While eating unexpectedly in various rooms of a house will add zest to any meal, best of all it is to eat in unexpected parts of a garden. This habit of dining al fresco is one to which Americans have still to become accustomed. Somehow, we have not shaken ourselves free from the orthodox Victorian notion that any meal not served in a dining room is a picnic – the sort of thing you do once in a great while to please the children. Picnics at best are messy affairs. Any meal at which one eats off one's knees, juggling a mélange of plates and cups and consuming prodigious quantities of greasy food prepared by men who have never recovered from having been Boy Scouts – a little of that sort of dining goes a long way.

The barbecue is a different matter and, now that it has been accepted through most of the country, picnics face a steep decline in popularity. However, the barbecue is only an outdoor kitchen and dining-room combined; it is not mobile; you go to the same spot to eat. Unless it can be moved about, it has the same disadvantage as the static dining-room indoors.

The first rule for dining in a garden is to be comfortable. One's feet should be under some sort of table. This table should be so placed that no one is exposed to the pitiless glare and heat of the Summer sun or the penetrating chill of winds or the curious gaze of strangers.

The second rule for al fresco dining is that it should never have the slightest air of haste or responsibility. Any meal which is eaten hastily and under pressure, whether in town or country, is merely a matter of temporary stimulation.

The third rule is that is should be colorful and informal – colorful in the fitments of the table and informal in both the foods and the clothes one wears. A rural meal served in a garden or on a terrace should be composed mainly of such ingredients as the local countryside affords. It should be eaten in loose and comfortable clothes that in no wise are reminiscent of formal dining in town. To dine between the grass and the infinite stars in dinner gowns and dinner jackets is a silly affectation, a sure sign that one fears the country lest he or she 'go native' under its intimate contact.

The Bed-Book of Eating and Drinking, 1943

Whelks with Vinegar and Pepper
JEREMY ROUND 1957–89

I am not a fan of eating outside at the best of times; unless on chairs at a table on the terrace of some restaurant with a view of the Alps and an adjustable sun-shade, it flies in the face of evolution. Certainly, the romanticised English plan – pootling off to a flowery meadow by a clear, lazily flowing stream backed by an inviting wood, with a couple of dressed crabs, a pot of home-made garlic mayonnaise, a mixed salad and a bottle of something fizzy chucked into the insulated cool-box in the boot of the car – is rarely matched by the reality. Nobody washed out the cool-box since that avocado mousse spilt all over the bottom last year, the meadow is full of vast yellow slugs, the stream foams with effluent, the ants and wasps eat more than you do and the wood is surrounded by impassable barbed wire.

The only acceptable British circumstance for a picnic, as far as I'm concerned, is whelks with vinegar and pepper in the car parked on the seafront somewhere, with headscarves on and the windows rolled down.

The Independent Cook, 1988

Custom and Style

❦

Englishmen Loveth Sweet Meats
ANTHONY MUNDAY 1553–1633

*The English College in Rome was where English Catholics hatched
plots against the Protestant state. Munday on his return to England
became a government agent, identifying and assisting in the arrest
of Jesuits who came to England.*

The English College, is a house both large and fair, standing in the way
to the Pope's Palace, not far from the Castle Sante Angello . . . As for
their fare, trust me it is very fine and delicate, for every man hath his
own trencher, his manchet, knife, spoon and fork laid by it, and then a
fair white napkin covering it, with his glass and pot of wine set by him.
And the first mess, or 'antepast' (as they call it) that is brought to the
table, is some fine meat to urge them have an appetite, as sometimes
the Spanish anchovies, and sometimes stewed prunes and raisins of the
sun together, having such fine tart syrup made to them, as I promise
you a weak stomach would very well digest them. The second, is a
certain mess of pottage of that country manner, no meat sod in them,
but are made of divers things, whose proper names I do not remember,
but me thought they were both good and wholesome. The third, is
boiled meat, as kid, mutton, chicken, and such like; every man a pretty
modicum of each thing. The fourth is roasted meat of the daintiest
provision, that they can get, and sometimes stewed and baked meat,
according as pleaseth master cook to order it. The fifth and last is
sometime cheese, some time preserved conceits, sometime figs,
almonds and raisins, a lemon and sugar, a pomegranate, or some such
sweet gear; for they know that Englishmen loveth sweet meats.

The English Romayne Lyfe, 1582

133

Before the Revolution – Trifling Observations
LOUIS-SÉBASTIEN MERCIER 1740–1814

Mercier was one of the first French dramatists to present bourgeois life on the stage. He wrote more than sixty plays, two of them considered so radically anti-clerical and anti-royal that they were not performed until after the Revolution. However, he was one of the members of the revolutionary Convention opposed to passing the death sentence on Louis XVI. He was imprisoned during the Terror and only released after Robespierre went to the scaffold in 1794.

The manners of the period have immensely shortened ceremonies, and it is now very provincial to stand on ceremony. Of all ancient and trivial customs that of saying 'God bless you' when you sneeze is the only one that still exists. One almost dare boast of having a good stomach, which one would not have dared to do twenty years ago.

Lackeys do not leave the room with the dessert, they remain till the end of the repast. Meals are no longer drawn out, they are shorter, and it is impossible any longer to talk freely or to tell amusing stories.

I do not advise the good man who has no valet of his own to go and dine in a big house. For you drink only at the servant's discretion. At your modest orders they twirl on their heels, rush to the sideboard to fetch a drink for someone else. Soon the dryness of your throat will prevent you from raising your voice; and your suppliant looks will be no better interpreted than your request. You feel your palate on fire and you can no longer taste any of the viands on the table. You must wait till the end of dinner to moisten your throat with a glass of water. This has become a method of exclusion for people who have no servants. Thus do the rich preserve their tables from too great an influx of guests.

The majority of women only begin their dinner with the sweets.

The Picture of Paris, TRANS. Wilfred and Emilie Jackson, 1929

Five Hours at Table

LAUNCELOT STURGEON

'Launcelot Sturgeon, Esq. Fellow of the Beef-Steak Club, and an Honorary Member of several Foreign Pic Nics, &c, &c, &c.' is how the author of Essays, Moral, Philosophical, and Stomachical, of the Important Science of Good-Living, *is described on the title page of this amusing little volume. The name is a pseudonym, but it is not known for whom.*

As eating is the main object of life, so, dining being the most important action of the day, it is impossible to pay too great attention to every thing which has any affinity to it.

It is convenient to dine late; because, the more trivial concerns of the morning being by that time despatched, all our thoughts may then be concentrated upon our plate, and our undivided attention may be bestowed on what we are eating.

A true epicure would as soon fast as be obliged to hurry over a good dinner.

Five hours are a reasonable time to remain at table, when the dinner is tolerable: but, as a well-bred man never looks at his watch in company, so, no man of sense ever regulates the period of his sitting by aught but the quality of the entertainment; and time is never so well employed as in doing justice to good-fare.

Punctuality is, in no transaction of life, of such importance as in cookery: three turns too many may spoil a haunch: the *critical minute* is less difficult to be hit in the boudoir than in the kitchen; and every thing may be put into a *stew* – except the cook.

The Importance of Good Living, 1822

Hot for Sunday, Cold for Monday
FORD MADOX FORD 1873–1939

In those days people seem to have been extraordinarily slow. It was not only that they dined at seven and went about in four-wheelers; it was not only that they still asked each other to take pot luck (I am just informed that no really modern young person any longer understands what this phrase means). It is not only that nowadays if we chance to have to remain in town in August we do not any longer pull down the front blinds, live in our kitchen, and acquire by hook or by crook a visitor's guide to Homburg, with which we could delude our friends and acquaintances on their return from Brighton into the idea that in the German spa we had rubbed shoulders with the great and noble. It is not only that our menus now soar beyond the lofty ideal of hot roast beef for Sunday, cold for Monday, hash for Tuesday, leg of mutton for Wednesday, cold on Thursday, and so on; it is that we seem altogether to have changed. It is true that we have not grown up, but we are different animals. If we should open a file of the *Times* for 1875 and find that the leader writer agreed with some of our sentiments today, we should be as much astonished as we are when we find on Egyptian monuments that the lady who set snares for the virtue of Joseph was dissatisfied with the state of her linen when it came home from the wash.

Ancient Lights, 1911

Tea-Time
CONSTANCE SPRY 1886–1960

The very word tea-time has a nostalgic ring for those of us who remember the past with delight. In those days the disposition of a woman's time made tea-time possible, and the taste for, shall I say, the cosier figure gave no cause for apprehension. I have to admit that tea-time beyond the stimulant of the tea itself is not really necessary when other meals are adequate, but the hour, the association, and the food proper to it are all pleasant. So when, for example, on highland holidays tea-time falls naturally into place, it can be delightful. There is

an argument concerning the serving of the tea itself that might be aired
here. China tea offered plain or with thin slices of lemon is pleasant to
many of us, and the connoisseur will not accept it in any other way,
considering the addition of milk to so delicately flavoured a beverage
as barbaric; even those who like to take it with milk insist that this
shall be put in last. This brings us to the real argument. Leaving China
tea out of the question, should tea be served with the milk poured in
first or last? Those in favour of milk being put into the cup first will
maintain, and rightly, I think, that the resulting cup of tea has a more
blended taste. This is natural enough, because in pouring on to a small
quantity of milk a larger quantity of scalding tea the milk becomes ever
so slightly cooked. The difference in the taste of tea poured out in this
way is less obvious in subsequent cups. Now those on the other side of
the argument will say that in polite circles tea is poured first into the
cups, and then they will add in good old-fashioned parlance 'and
cream and sugar handed separately'; and it is when they use the word
cream that they undermine their own argument. If you are serving tea
with cream, then the cream should not be put first into the cup because
the scalding of it spoils its flavour. In old-fashioned tea parties cream
was *de rigueur* with tea and should certainly have been put in last, but
a little ordinary milk, or milk, shall we say, on the thin side, poured
into a full cup of tea does not really appeal to a discerning taste. In the
old days, when it was correct to hand the cream after the tea had been
poured out, there was another custom. The hostess would rinse out the
tea-cups with boiling water from her silver kettle before pouring in the
tea. This was not with the sole object of warming the cups, but also to
prevent her delicate china from becoming cracked by the sudden
impact of hot tea. Now we are no longer all of us so meticulous in the
matter of pouring out, the putting in of the milk first will have the same
advantageous effect.

As real tea-time belongs to conventional days, it is perhaps not out
of place to discuss it in conventional fashion and to lay stress on the
finer points of what was then considered *de rigueur*.

It was not then considered good taste to have too many small things
– one good plum cake, one light cake, perhaps of the sponge or
sponge-sandwich variety, or an orange cake, iced, might appear, and a
hot dish of crumpets or buttered toast, anchovy toast or hot tea-cakes,
and, in particular, that admirable hot cake described as Irish Sally
Lunn. Even on the most elegant of tea tables it was then, and is now,
permissible to leave jam in its pot set on a plate unless you possessed a
nice, plain glass jam pot. It was the fancy dish that was inelegant. Then

I hear the shadow of one old lady saying to me 'and never biscuits out of a tin, my dear!' although the same old lady would allow that for the country tea you might have a loaf of home-made bread, a pat of butter, watercress, radishes, and, if you were hungry from exercise, a boiled egg. If what I have just said sounds ridiculous and snobbish to you, and meaningless into the bargain, I will excuse myself by saying that as tea-time was in its glory in the old, conventional days, it is forgivable to report what was then *de rigueur*. This expression, which applies to far fewer things to-day than it did long ago, may be boring, as conventions can be. But when too many conventions disappear a certain grace goes with them.

The Constance Spry Cookery Book, 1956

Favourable for Love
JANE AUSTEN 1775–1817

Letter from Jane Austen to her sister Cassandra, dated Chawton, Sunday Evening, Jany 24 (1813).

I could see nothing very promising between Mr. P. and Miss P. T. She placed herself on one side of him at first, but Miss Benn obliged her to move up higher; and she had an empty plate and even asked him to give her some mutton without being attended to for some time. There might be design in this . . . on his side; he might think an empty stomach the most favourable for love . . .

Venerous Roots
WILLIAM HARRISON 1534–93

Eroticism was certainly a sub-text of 'banquetting stuffe' as so many of the ingredients were thought to be aphrodisiacs. Anything rare and expensive was regarded as stimulating, and this included sugar and spices. All roots, particularly eringo or sea holly roots,

candied and flavoured with orange or rose flower waters or musk
were particularly effective. Even parsnips and carrots were said to
provoke Venus and the sweet potato, being the newest and strangest
root, was credited with powerful restorative properties.

In number of dishes and change of meat, the nobility of England
(whose cooks are for the most part musical-headed Frenchmen and
strangers) do most exceed, since there is no day in manner that passeth
over their heads, wherein they have not only beef, mutton, veal, lamb,
kid, pork, cony, capon, pig, or so many of these as the season yieldeth,
but also some portion of the red or fallow deer, beside great variety of
fish and wild fowl . . . jellies of all colors, mixed with a variety of the
representation of sundry flowers, herbs, trees, forms of beasts, fish,
fowls, and fruits, and thereunto marchpane wrought with no small
curiosity, tarts of divers hues, and sundry denominations, conserved of
old fruits, foreign and homebred, suckets, codinacs, marmelades,
marchpane, sugar-bread, gingerbread, florentines, wild fowls, venison
of all sorts, and sundry outlandish [foreign] confections, altogether
seasoned with sugar (which Pliny calleth *mel ex arundinibus*, a device
not common nor greatly used in old time at the table, but only in
medicine, although it grew in Arabia, India and Sicily) . . . Of the
potato, and such venerous roots as are brought out of Spain,
Portingale and the Indies to furnish up our banquets, I speak not . . .
But among all these, the kind of meat which is obtained with most
difficulty and cost, is commonly taken for the most delicate, and
thereupon each guest will soonest desire to feed.'

A Description of England, 1577

Decorating the Table
ELSIE DE WOLFE 1856–1950

Just a few words to add as to the decoration of your table.

Never have high flower vases, or other things that obstruct the view
of the beautiful woman across the table, or prevent the witticism of the
clever man, who is your opposite, reaching you, unless by dodging to
one side or the other.

A very successful decoration I have used in Paris is a table cloth of silver (lamé) with a lovely crystal ship, having all its glass sails and its pennants set and flying, mirrored in a sheet of glass which forms the centre. Added to this, according to the size of the table, are two rock-crystal birds and four rock-crystal candlesticks.

In the year 1929, I used two rock-crystal vases in which were branches of white orchids, but those days are gone, I fear, forever, and a few white carnations have to suffice now. *Enfin*, perhaps the orchids will bloom again.

Recipes for Successful Dining, 1934

Elsie de Wolfe

CECIL BEATON 1904–80

Elsie de Wolfe passed through a number of fashion periods, yet each phase found her picking the creative vibrations of esoteric people and exploiting them commercially with great flair. This may seem strange, since she was such a very individual personality in her own life and way of living, to which she brought the ruthlessness of a company director, even planning her entertainments with an inspired perfectionism. Her businesslike attention to life's minutiae created an entirely new standard of technique, and she was seldom without a suave, efficient secretary at her side, taking down notes of any detail, however small, that could be filed for later reference. It was inscribed that Her Ladyship would not allow gladioli to be used in a vase of mixed flowers, just as three, not four, cigarettes were allotted to each place at table. She invented a cross-filing system by which she could check on the specific number of times a guest had been entertained, with full descriptions of the menu, the company invited, and the table decorations. Thus Lady Mendl could vary the pleasures of her guests on each occasion. If a hot cheese biscuit was served with the wrong dish or a cocktail was insufficiently shaken, there would more than likely be a court-martial. When a new sandwich proved to be successful, she would dictate a memorandum that it must be photographed for *Vogue*. This fetishistic concern for trivialities was to inspire the Duchess of Windsor to organize her entertainments for café society with an equal unction and determination.

The way that Elsie de Wolfe's own houses were run, lit, heated, scented, the manner in which the food was presented, were all the result of a genius for taking infinite pains. Nothing was left to chance. Only when the scene was set, the perfumes burnt in the censers, and the last candle lit was the element of spontaneity encouraged.

The Glass of Fashion, 1954

Elsie de Wolfe
COLETTE 1873–1954

TO MARGUERITE MORENO

Paris, February 1947

Trying to escape the heat, we went on to Versailles, where we dined with Lady Mendl. She is ninety-one, with the thinness of a schoolgirl, and no longer lives on anything but alcohol. Dressed in white muslin, with a choker of sapphires and a silk scarf knotted into a turban to hide the absence of a wig.

All but weightless and tottering about her grounds, which are flowerless and entirely green, with hedges clipped in the British manner, in fantastic animal shapes. An evening for you, for us.

Letters from Colette, TRANS. Robert Phelps, 1982

One of Those Fellows Who Call Twice for Soup
LAUNCELOT STURGEON

To commence with your entrance into the drawing room – don't stand bowing at the door, as if you had a petition to present; but stride confidently up to the lady of the house, and so close before you make your obeisance, that you nearly thrust your head into her face.

When dinner is announced – if you should follow a lady to the dining room, don't tread upon her train, nor step back, to avoid it, upon the toes of her behind you; and if it should be your lot to hand one to her seat – endeavour to avoid tumbling over the chairs in your hurry to place her.

When seated – don't stare up at the lamps, as if you were an oilman calculating their contents; but look inquisitively round the table, and if you have got an eye glass – which, by the bye, is a great help to gentility – apply it steadily to the object that is nearest to you: those at a distance require no such help.

Whatever may be your inclination, cautiously abstain from being helped a second time from the same dish: a man's character has been damned in society in consequence of being stigmatized as 'one of those fellows who call twice for soup!'

The Importance of Good Living, 1822

White Peacocks
DIANA COOPER 1892–1986

A memory of California, 1927, while touring with The Miracle.

One dinner I remember at Burlingame, where a clubroom had been converted by two old ladies (whose profession it was) into a fairy orchard in Persia at dawn. The walls, seemingly of transparent ice flushed pink, held silver espalier trees bearing golden apples. On the table for 120 guests were tall staves on which white peacocks perched, with garlands of flowers linking them. At the corners were white china elephants as big as genuine newborns, with white peacock-tails spreading in pride from their howdahs.

The Light of Common Day, 1959

A Castle for Queen Isabella
JEAN DE FROISSART 1337?–1410?

Froissart describes the state banquet held after Queen Isabella's ceremonial entry into Paris in 1389, four years after she was married to King Charles VI.

On the next day, which was Monday, the King gave a dinner at the Palace for the ladies, of whom there were a great number. But first the

Queen was escorted by the four dukes already named to high mass in the Sainte-Chapelle of the Palace. During mass she was consecrated and anointed, as a Queen of France should be. The Archbishop of Rouen, who at that date was Guillaume de Vienne, officiated.

After mass had been solemnly sung, the King and Queen went back to their rooms in the Palace, and all the ladies retired to theirs. Soon afterwards, the King and Queen entered the banqueting-hall, followed by the ladies.

I should say that the great marble table which is always in the Palace and is never moved had been covered with an oak top four inches thick, on which the dinner was laid. Behind this great table, against one of the pillars, was the King's sideboard, large, handsome and well arranged, covered with gold and silver plate. Many an eye looked covetously at it on that day. In front of the King's table was a stout wooden barrier with three openings guarded by serjeants-at-arms, royal ushers and mace-bearers, whose duty it was to see that none came through except the serving-men. For you must know that the crowd in the hall was so dense that it was very difficult to move. There were numbers of entertainers, each showing their skill in their different arts. The King, the prelates and the ladies washed their hands. They took their places at table, in this order: at the King's high table, the Bishop of Noyon was at one end, then the Bishop of Langres, then, next to the King, the Archbishop of Rouen. The King wore an open surcoat of crimson velvet lined with ermine and had a very rich gold crown on his head. Next to the King, at a slight distance, sat the Queen, also wearing a rich gold crown. Next to her sat the King of Armenia, then the Duchess of Berry, then the Duchess of Burgundy, then the Duchess of Touraine, then Madame de Nevers, then Madame de Bar, then the Lady de Coucy, then Mademoiselle Marie d'Harcourt. There were no others at the King's high table, except, right at the lower end, the Lady de Sully, wife of Sir Guy de La Trémoille.

At two other tables, running right round the sides of the hall, sat over five hundred other ladies, but the crowd round the tables was so great that they could only be served with the greatest difficulty. Of the courses, which were abundant and excellently prepared, I need not speak. But I will say something of the interludes which were performed. They could not have been better planned, and they would have provided a delightful entertainment for the King and the ladies if those who had undertaken to perform had been able to do so.

In the middle of the great hall a castle had been set up, twenty feet square and forty feet high. It had a tower at each of the four corners and a much higher one in the middle. The castle represented the city of Troy, and the middle tower the citadel of Ilium. On it were pennons bearing the arms of the Trojans, such as King Priam, the knightly Hector his son and his other children, as well as the kings and princes who were besieged in Troy with them. This castle moved on wheels which turned very ingeniously inside it. Other men came to attack the castle in an assault-tower which was also mounted on ingeniously hidden wheels, with none of the mechanism showing. On this were the arms of the kings of Greece and other countries who once laid siege to Troy. There was also, moving in support of them, a beautifully made model ship, on which there must have been a hundred men-at-arms. The three things, castle, assault-tower and ship, moved about thanks to the skilful mechanism of the wheels. The men on the tower and the ship made a fierce attack on one side of the castle, and the men in the castle defended it stoutly. But the entertainment could not last long because of the great crush of people round it. Some were made ill by the heat, or fainted in the crowd. A table near the door of the parliament chamber was overturned by force. The ladies who were sitting at it had to get up hurriedly, without ceremony. The great heat and the stink of the crowd almost caused the Queen to faint, and a window which was behind her had to be broken to let in the air. The Lady de Coucy was also seriously affected. The King saw what was happening and ordered the performance to stop. This was done and the tables were quickly cleared and taken down, to give the ladies more room. The wine and spices were served hurriedly and, as soon as the King and Queen had gone to their apartments, everyone else left also.

Froissart Chronicles, TRANS. Geoffrey Brereton, 1968

A Pyramid of Twenty Dishes
MME DE SÉVIGNÉ 1626–96

Wednesday 5 August, 1671, to Mme de Grignan:
I must tell you a bit of news about our States as your penalty for being Breton. M. de Chaulnes arrived on Sunday evening to the sound of all the din that Vitré can muster. On Monday morning he wrote me a letter and sent it by one of his gentlemen. I answered by going to dine with him. Food was served at two tables in the same room, which made a pretty good feed with fourteen covers at each table. Monsieur

presided at one, Madame at the other. There was far too much to eat, roasts were taken back again as though untouched. For the pyramids of fruit the doorways had to be raised. Our forefathers never foresaw mechanics like these, since they didn't imagine a door had to be higher than themselves. A pyramid wants to come in (one of those pyramids that means you are obliged to write notes from one side of the table to the other, not that there is anything upsetting about that, on the contrary it is very pleasant not to see what they conceal). This pyramid, with twenty dishes, was so satisfactorily knocked down at the door that the din drowned the violins, oboes and trumpets.

Selected Letters, TRANS. Leonard Tancock, 1982

Clock-work Table – Bath

FANNY BURNEY 1752–1840

June, 1780
Mr. Ferry is a Bath alderman; his house and garden exhibit the house and garden of Mr. Tattersall, enlarged. Just the same taste prevails, the same paltry ornaments, the same crowd of buildings, the same unmeaning decorations, and the same unsuccessful attempts at making something of nothing.

They kept us half an hour in the garden, while they were preparing for our reception in the house, where after parading through four or five little vulgarly showy closets, not rooms, we were conducted into a very gaudy little apartment, where the master of the house sat reclining on his arm, as if in contemplation, though everything conspired to show that the house and its inhabitants were carefully arranged for our reception. The Bishop had sent in his name by way of gaining admission.

The Bishop, with a gravity of demeanour difficult to himself to sustain, apologised for our intrusion, and returned thanks for seeing the house and garden. Mr. Ferry started from his pensive attitude, and begged us to be seated, and then a curtain was drawn, and we perceived through a glass a perspective view of ships, boats, and water! This raree-show over, the maid who officiated as show-woman had a hint given her, and presently a trap-door opened, and up jumped a covered table, ornamented with various devices. When we had expressed our delight at this long enough to satisfy Mr. Ferry, another hint was given, and presently down dropped an eagle from the ceiling, whose talons were put into a certain hook at the top of the covering of the table, and when the admiration at this was over, up again flew the eagle, conveying in his talons the cover, and leaving under it a repast of cakes, sweetmeats, oranges, and jellies.

Diary and Letters, 1842–6

Salad with His Fingers
EDMOND 1822–96 AND JULES 1830–70
GONCOURT

14 November [1867]
This evening Sainte-Beuve gave a dinner for the Princess. His little cook, Marie, showed us into the dining-room, where the table was laid as if for a banquet arranged by a parish priest entertaining his bishop, and then into a ground-floor drawing-room, all bare and white and gold, with brand-new daffodil-yellow furniture looking like a suite chosen by an upholsterer for a tart.

The guests arrived: the Princess, Nieuwerkerke, Mme Espinasse, Dr. Philips, and old Giraud of the Institut. The Princess looked gay and in high spirits: she was looking forward to the evening as if it were a bachelor party. At dinner she insisted upon serving everything and carving everything. Her father, she said, always carved. He had very pretty hands. He used to eat salad with his fingers, and when he was told that it was an unclean habit, he answered: 'In my day, if we had eaten it in any other way, we should have been scolded and told that our hands were dirty.'

Pages from the Goncourt Journals, ED., TRANS. Robert Baldick, 1962

Coronation Balls, 1911
DIANA COOPER 1892–1986

But the summer brought a Coronation and a London at its most brilliant. Not that the balls were half as elaborate as today's. Derby, Lansdowne, Londonderry, Bridgewater and Stafford Houses were all magnificent, gilded and marbled, and not to be tampered with. There was no imaginative bedizening, no floodlit trees, temples or ruins, no flowery merry-go-rounds and swing-boats or statues made of moss erected for a night. Marquees there were – uncompromising red-and-white-striped tents and discreet fairy lamps twinkling red, white and blue along the grimy garden paths. It didn't look in the least like fairyland, though we always said it did. Florists were ordered to bring suitable begonias and smilax to edge the stairs and sprawl over dinner and supper tables. A crude blaze of electric-light bulbs from chandeliers and sconces did nothing for the beauties and robbed the fabulous crowns and jewels of their smoulder and sparkle. I remember no candles except on dinner-tables. At supper there were quails, too fat to need stuffing, and *chaud-froids* with truffle designs on them, hot and cold soup, lobsters and strawberries, ices and hothouse peaches. It never varied.

The Rainbow Comes and Goes, 1958

Cambridge Dinner Parties in the 1880s
GWEN RAVERAT 1885–1957

The regular round of formal dinner-parties was very important in Cambridge. In our house the parties were generally of twelve or fourteen people, and everybody of dinner-party status was invited strictly in turn. The guests were seated according to the Protocol, the Heads of Houses ranking by the dates of the foundations of their colleges, except that the Vice-Chancellor would come first of all. After the Masters came the Regius Professors in the order of their subjects, Divinity first; and then the other Professors according to the dates of the foundations of their chairs, and so on down all the steps of the hierarchy. It was better not to invite too many important people at the same time, or the complications became insoluble to hosts of only ordinary culture. How could they tell if Hebrew or Greek took precedence, of two professorships founded in the same year? And some of the grandees were very touchy about their rights, and their wives were even more easily offended.

The latest bride had to wear her wedding-dress, and was taken in by the host. It was terrifying for her, poor young thing, to walk out before all those hawk-eyed matrons; and to remember to be ready for the hostess to 'catch her eye' at the end of dinner. This was the signal for the ladies to gather up their belongings and to sweep demurely out of the room, leaving the gentlemen to their wine. And it was worst of all for her in the drawingroom, where the ladies all fell into intimate, low-voiced conversations about their illnesses, their children and their servants, for she had as yet no illnesses, nor children, and knew very little about servants. At the end – about 10.15 – no one could leave until the bride rose; and cases have been known of the bride being so petrified by fear that, after a long wait, the kindest of the elder ladies had to rise and propel her into doing her duty.

We children used to huddle on the stairs in our nightgowns to watch the formal procession going from the drawing-room to the dining-room, led by my father with the principal lady on his arm, while my mother brought up the rear, on the arm of the most important gentleman. After they had all swept grandly by, we could dash down and warm ourselves by the drawingroom fire, before taking up our stations by the serving-hatch to help finish up the good things as they came out. The strident roar of conversation pointed by the clatter of knives and forks came through the hatch in bursts, cut off suddenly when it was closed.

Dinner was at 7.45, and there were eight, nine, or even ten courses: I have some of the menus. Such dinners needed good organization, especially as they were all prepared and served by our own ordinary three servants, with very little extra help, beyond a waitress. Some people had special dishes sent in from the college kitchens, but my mother considered that extravagant. Here is a dinner given by my parents on 31st October 1885, when Sir William and Lady Thomson (the Kelvins) came to stay. This is clearly rather a grand dinner.

> Clear Soup
> Brill and Lobster Sauce
> Chicken Cutlets and Rice Balls
> Oyster Patties
> Mutton, Potatoes, Artichokes, Beets
> Partridges and Salad
> Caramel Pudding ⎫
> Pears and Whipped Cream ⎬
> Cheese and Ramequins ⎫
> Cheese Straws ⎬
> Ice
> Grapes, Walnuts, Chocolates and Pears

But on 1st April 1885, there were only four people at dinner: my mother, my father, Edmund Gosse and Dew Smith, and yet they had:

Tomato Soup
Fried Smelts and Drawn Butter Sauce
Mushrooms on Toast
Roast Beef, Cauliflower and Potatoes
Apple Charlotte
Toasted Cheese
Dessert: Candied Peel, Oranges, Peanuts,
Raisins and Ginger

I know this because after dinner my mother left the three men alone and came into the drawing-room and wrote it all down in a letter to her sister. This was five months before I was born; she was twenty-three, and she clearly felt very grand and grown-up, with three servants of her own.

Period Piece: A Cambridge Childhood, 1952

Good Taste in Food
ELSIE DE WOLFE 1856–1950

Since food, like fashion, changes with the times, the standard of food in our day is very different from the pre-War standard of 'lavish hospitality.' To-day, good taste in food is just the reverse of lavish and is stamped with the same restraint and elimination as the dress worn at dinner in 1934, compared to the dress worn at dinner in 1900.

It is for this reason that my book includes a section devoted to menus as well as to recipes. These menus are intended to be a guide for the modern repast, as I see it, and an inspiration to the hostess who can no longer think of what to order. She, I hope, will find consolation, as I often have when at my wit's end, by referring to these menus, chosen from among my own files of reference on the subject, covering many years.

In my philosophy of food, the perfect meal is the short meal. Naturally, one presupposes in a short meal that the few dishes served will be perfection and served generously. I always have a réchaud (dish-warmer) on the side-table on which dishes are kept hot under covers so that they are properly presented a second time. The short meal must have a perfectly balanced menu. There should be one simple dish and one richer one. With a careful choice of dishes in this short, well-balanced meal, there is no need for the prolongation of the time spent at table which, in these days of Spartan eating, is the greatest trial to at least fifty per cent of the people who have learned how to eat wisely and well.

Furthermore, I think that at every meal there should be what I call a 'surprise' – a dish that, if possible, is a new dish presented in a new manner. So it has been my object in presenting this collection of recipes to give you as many such dishes as possible, in order that there may be a note of surprise in the short menu, to take the place of an extra and unnecessary dish, too often resorted to when imagination fails.

Recipes for Successful Dining, 1934

Luncheon

LADY LLANOVER 1802–96

I lately maintained a fierce argument with the Hermit on the word 'Luncheon,' which I said was often called 'Lunch.' The Hermit insisted upon it that no educated person in refined society could possibly talk of 'Lunch,' or 'Lunching,' but that they must always say 'Luncheon.' I assured him that I had heard persons who, for their birth and rank in life, might be supposed to belong to refined society, speak of '*Lunch*' instead of '*Luncheon*,' and of '*Lunching*' instead of '*eating Luncheon*,' and who said, '*I never Lunch*,' instead of '*I never eat Luncheon*.' My good host, however, maintained that the origin of the word was from 'clutch' or 'clunch,' the meaning of which was a *handful*, in contra-distinction to a *full meal* – a small quantity – to appease hunger when there was no time to sit down to the table; and whether he is right or wrong, I do not pronounce, but it was impossible to help laughing when he said, 'How would it be possible for a refined gentleman when he means to imply that he has eaten a small quantity of food in the *forenoon*, to exclaim, "*I clutched*," which,' (added he,) 'he might just as well say as "*I lunched*." Johnson himself quoted Gay as authority for the word "*Luncheon*."'

'I sliced the *luncheon* from the barley loaf;
With crumbled bread I thicken'd well the mess.'
The First Principles of Good Cookery, 1867

Classic Cuisine

HSIANG JU LIN AND TSUIFENG LIN

The tone set by the hors d'oeuvre should be developed in the rest of the menu. What belongs to classic cuisine? A certain number of tastes and textures. Understand that it is a gathering together of the best ideas, hence a creation of the mind. It therefore contains a preponderance of those total creations of texture and flavour. It consists of the sophistications of the cuisine, but is not necessarily the best of the cuisine. To it belong all the plays on texture. The mild, mellow, bland, rich and convoluted flavours are emphasized to the exclusion of the very salty, sour and hot. Red peppers are not allowed. Coarseness is excluded; minces and pastes, tender, suave substances that glide down the throat, have a central place. It is the ultimate in gastronomy, as far removed from savage cooking as can be imagined. That is why this creation of the mind is considered in gastronomy as the highest order of cooking.

No item in classic cooking is brought in casually. Each one is the result of perhaps an exorbitant amount of thought and labour. Considering all these things, why is it that many feasts are so unsatisfying? It is because they lack style, because the host has little taste. Taking the most expensive things and putting them together on a menu is foolish. We encounter it so often that we call it 'the usual'. It consists of the fins, the nest, the duck, the squab, *ad nauseam*. It is possible to stay well within the boundaries of classic cuisine and escape common vulgarity. The art of making up menus, like the art of dress, is not what you put on, but how everything is put together.

OPULENT

(suitable for visiting dignitaries, merchant princes and rich relatives)
Shark's Fins with Crab Sauce
Happy Family
Stuffed Duck

Whole Chicken Stuffed with Bird's Nest
Pastry Peaches

PSEUDO-RUSTIC
(suitable for artists, gourmets, noted authors)
Black Hen Soup, with Black Mushrooms
Tungpo Pork, with pinwheels
Soochow Cabbage Stew
Duck Steamed in Wine
Sweet Bird's Nest

RECHERCHÉ
(for entertaining good cooks and distinguished company)
Bêche-de-mer Gourmet
Crisp Spiced Duck, with Buns
Bird's Nest with Bean Sprouts
Carp in Lamb Broth
Silver Fungus with Candy Sugar Syrup

THE BEST
(neither too showy nor mock simple, it is excellent for all occasions)
Velvet, Chicken I
Prawn (Shrimp) Balls
Peking Duck
Minute Beef
Steamed Fish
Peking Dust*

Chinese Gastronomy, 1969

Ortolans and Wheatears
SACHEVERELL SITWELL 1897–1988

In Royal Chef, Gabriel Tschumi writes that King Edward VII 'enjoyed Ortolans sautés in brandy, a favourite Edwardian dish made from a small Egyptian bird with a piquant flavour which was always cooked in brandy'; and that the last time he prepared Zéphire d'Ortolans à la Sueullus was at King George V's coronation banquet, 'the last really magnificent one held at Buckingham Palace'.

* A mound of chestnut purée covered with whipped cream.

I have just been told of a retired Italian waiter who finds cèpes in the woods near Dorking and supplies them, regularly, to a grocer in Soho. Are not these mushrooms supposed to grow in cellars in Bordeaux?

At one time ortolans were sold in large numbers in the London market. I have been shown a telegram from Oscar Wilde, who was recovering from 'flu, announcing that he was 'to be allowed ortolans, to the sound of flutes, at eight o'clock'. They are never sold in London now. These delicious birds come from the Landes, south of Bordeaux, and are served up in little paper cases.

Wheatears used to be snared in great numbers in Kent and Sussex and were a famed delicacy at Tunbridge Wells, but I have never tasted one. I believe their Latin name is *Saxicola ænanthe*.

Truffle Hunt, 1953

Tea and Muffins
FORD MADOX FORD 1873–1939

The writer has very strongly the vision of Mr Wilde, who was a common object of the countryside, who sat in a high-backed chair, consuming tea and muffins with the luxury of a great Persian cat coiled up before the fire. And wasn't that in all probability the real Wilde? The man who sighed with relief to find himself in the one house in London where he did not have to stand on his head?

Memories of Oscar Wilde, 1939

How to Get On in Society
JOHN BETJEMAN 1906–84

Originally set as a competition in 'Time and Tide'

Phone for the fish-knives, Norman
As Cook is a little unnerved;
You kiddies have crumpled the serviettes
And I must have things daintily served.

Are the requisites all in the toilet?
　　The frills round the cutlets can wait
Till the girl has replenished the cruets
　　And switched on the logs in the grate.

It's ever so close in the lounge dear,
　　But the vestibule's comfy for tea
And Howard is out riding on horseback
　　So do come and take some with me.

Now here is a fork for your pastries
　　And do use the couch for your feet;
I know that I wanted to ask you –
　　Is trifle sufficient for sweet?

Milk and then just as it comes dear?
　　I'm afraid the preserve's full of stones;
Beg pardon, I'm soiling the doileys
　　With afternoon tea-cakes and scones.

Collected Poems, 1958

Sauce Robert

GEORGE AUGUSTUS SALA 1828–96

Diana Cooper, youngest child of the 8th Duke of Rutland, wrote in her memoirs that her mother regarded a 'great many things' as 'common', even 'tomatoes and lemon as flavouring', dyed fur and holding hands.

This is one of the most ancient sauces, and also one of the most appetising, only you must clear your head of the nonsensical notion that a cuisine into which onions enter must be of necessity a vulgar one. Indeed, the whole Temple of Cookery, as far as flavouring is concerned, may be said to rest on four pillars – the onion and its congeners, the lemon, the anchovy, and the faggot of sweet herbs. The dome of the edifice is the spice-box, and it is flanked on each side by smaller cupolas, the salt-box and the pepper-box.

The Thorough Good Cook, 1895

Pastel Shades

PATRICK WHITE 1912–90

Mrs Jolley was a lady, as she never tired of pointing out. She would repeat the articles of her faith for anybody her instinct caught doubting. She would not touch an onion, she insisted; not for love. But was partial to a fluffy sponge, or butter sandwich, with non-parelles. A lady could never go wrong with pastel shades.

Riders in the Chariot, 1961

Garlic and a Lady

FORD MADOX FORD 1873–1939

In our experience eating prodigious quantities of garlic does not adequately 'school the organs to assimilate' and thereby eliminate the lingering smell. After consuming three heads of garlic at lunch one day while travelling to Brittany, we were firmly disabused of this theory by the travelling companion who shared a cabin on the ferry.

I came yesterday, also in Fitzroy Street, at a party, upon a young Lady who was the type of young lady I did not think one ever could meet. She was one of those ravishing and, like the syrens of the Mediterranean and Ulysses, fabulous beings who display new creations to the sound of harps, shawms and tea-cups. What made it all the more astounding was that she was introduced to me as being one of the best cooks in London – a real *cordon bleu*, and then some. She was, as you might expect, divinely tall and appeared to appear through such mists as surrounded Venus saving a warrior. But I found that she really could talk, if awfully, and at last she told me something that I did not know – about garlic. . . .

As do – as *must* – all good cooks, she used quantities of that bulb. It occurred to me at once that this was London and her work was social. Garlic is all very well on the bridge between Beaucaire and Tarascon or in the arena at Nîmes amongst sixteen thousand civilized beings . . .

But in an *atelier de couture* in the neighbourhood of Hanover Square!
. . . The lady answered mysteriously; No: there is no objection if only
you take enough and train your organs to the assimilation. The
perfume of *allium officinale* attends only on those timorous creatures
who have not the courage as it were to wallow in that vegetable. I used
to know a London literary lady who had that amount of civilization so
that when she ate abroad she carried with her, in a hermetically sealed
silver container, a single clove of the principal ingredient of *aioli*. With
this she would rub her plate, her knife, her fork and the bread beside
her place at the table. This, she claimed, satisfied her yearnings. But it
did not enchant her friends or her neighbours at table.

My instructress said that that served her right. She herself, at the
outset of her professional career, had had the cowardice to adopt
exactly that stratagem that, amongst those in London who have seen
the light, is not uncommon. But, when she went to her studio the
outcry amongst her comrades, attendants, employers, clients and the
very conductor of the bus that took her to Oxford Circus, had been
something dreadful to hear. Not St Plothinus nor any martyrs of Lyons
had been so miscalled by those vulgarians.

So she had determined to resign her post and had gone home and
cooked for herself a *poulet Béarnais*, the main garniture of which is a
kilo – two lbs – of garlic per chicken, you eating the stewed cloves as if
they were *haricots blancs*. It had been a Friday before a Bank holiday
so that the mannequins at that fashionable place would not be
required for a whole week.

Gloomily, but with what rapture internally, she had for that space of
time lived on hardly anything else but the usually eschewed bulb. Then
she set out gloomily towards the place that she so beautified but that
she must leave for ever. Whilst she had been buttoning her gloves she
had kissed an old aunt whose protests had usually been as clamant as
those of her studio-mates. The old lady had merely complimented her
on her looks. At the studio there had been no outcry and there too she
had been congratulated on the improvement, if possible, of her skin,
her hair, her carriage. . . .

She had solved the great problem; she had schooled her organs to
assimilate, not to protest against, the sacred herb. . . .

Provence, 1935

A Pink Pudding for a Marquis
LADY JEKYLL 1861–1937

*Lady Jekyll's Kitchen Essays first appeared in The Times in 1921–
1922. Agnes Jekyll and her husband Sir Herbert lived at Munstead
House in Surrey, next door to Sir Herbert's sister Gertrude, the
celebrated garden designer. Gertrude Jekyll and the architect Sir
Edwin Lutyens were frequent collaborators and the families were
close. His daughter Mary remembered the soothing atmosphere of
Munstead House: 'the apogee of opulent comfort and order without
grandeur, smelling of pot-pourri, furniture polish and wood smoke.
As well as the perfect food there were always the latest books laid
out on a long stool in front of the fireplace.'*

The dishes which will befit a king's banquet or a Lord Mayor's feast
look strange and out of place in modest surroundings. Turtle soup,
plum-pudding, and champagne for an August Sunday luncheon in a
seaside villa would be, to say the least, incongruous, but have been
experienced.

A blue-blooded and conservative marquis may be forgiven his
temporary loss of self-control when the newly-engaged cook sent on
its gay career round a decorous dinner-party of county neighbours a
transparent and highly decorated pink ice pudding concealing within
inmost recesses a fairy light and a musical box playing the 'Battle of
Prague.' Words were spoken, and, like the chord of self in Locksley
Hall, this over-elaborated creation 'passed in music out of sight.'

Matters of taste must be felt, not dogmatized about. A large crayfish or lobster rearing itself menacingly on its tail seems quite at home
on the sideboard of a Brighton hotel-de-luxe, but will intimidate a shy
guest at a small dinner party.

Kitchen Essays, 1922

The Dinner Gong
ARNOLD PALMER 1886–1973

Among the innumerable domestic casualties of recent years an unnoticed stillness in the air, a modest gap in the hall, commemorate negatively the once vibrant gong. It used to summon us to meals, mysterious affairs prepared out of sight by unseen hands and popping up deliciously, in a setting of snow and silver, every four hours. It even bade us, in the more splendid mansions and hotels, prepare ourselves for the supreme evening rite. Beneath the master touch of one of those butlers whose glance, like Medusa's, one never dreamed of meeting, it could murmur, hum, and finally mount to a reverberating crescendo that made ears sing, temples throb, that drowned speech and thought and almost consciousness itself. It was the Victorians' monitory *apéritif*, the Edwardian version of the cocktail – and how, at its accents, those gastric juices flowed! Now that meals, like women, have lost their mystery, it is superfluous, it has gone. As father finishes laying the table, mother enters with the tureen, followed by the children with soup plates and toastrack. Everybody knows that dinner is ready, knows it only too well and is already half-sick of the knowledge. As for evening clothes, they would only stress the fact that father has become a waiter and that mother has failed to become a cook. Who, then, wants a gong? Nobody. A generation has arisen which believes, rightly, that gongs have only one purpose – to usher in the films of J. Arthur Rank.

Movable Feasts, 1952

Changes
CONSTANCE SPRY 1886–1960

Wars and rationing have brought about many changes in the culinary world, none greater, perhaps, than in the food which we may now serve with propriety for a luncheon party, or indeed for everyday family fare. It is amusing to look through old-fashioned books and study the menus; one is beset by a constant wonder as to how they did it.

But I do not need to go to books to recall a luncheon menu of considerable proportions. When I was about the age of some of our Winkfield students, that is to say had put up my hair and was therefore 'out,' I was invited to a family luncheon before a concert at the Albert Hall. Borne in the arms of a stiffly capped maid came first of all an enormous tureen of rich oyster cream soup, very full of oysters. This rich soup was followed by roast turkey with all the trimmings, including a separate dish of chestnuts – and it was not Christmas, mind you. Then there was apple pie or treacle pudding, cheese, celery, and dessert. Of the concert afterwards I remember nothing, but after all these years I recall the food and think of it when I pass the great block of flats which has replaced the imposing Victorian house near the concert hall.

If such a menu were considered necessary for a luncheon party to-day we should think twice before asking our friends, and I find it fortunate that simplicity is in fashion. Friendliness and easy hospitality are more important than grandeur.

The Constance Spry Cookery Book, 1956

Embarrassing Moments
SACHEVERELL SITWELL 1897–1988

SALAD DAYS

To the Englishman abroad there is no experience more embarrassing than that dread moment in a restaurant when a violinist comes up and plays something immediately underneath his chin. I have often wondered why a resident Tzigane was not attached to those country house courses where students are given tests in psychology. Probably it is only because of the difficulty of providing suitably glamorous female companions.

LE MOT JUSTE

Another awkward moment is when the *maître d'hôtel* approaches, carrying a silver dish, and lifts off the cover. What are you to say or do? Jean Cocteau solved this problem. They brought him a chicken on a silver dish. He inspected it, and told the waiter: 'Merci, c'est bien ressemblant!'

Truffle Hunt, 1953

The Rise to Power of the Avocado Pear
CHARLOTTE DU CANN 1956–

I was sitting opposite a film writer one day in this studio off Ladbroke Grove. We were eating pasta and everyone had this good Chianti glow inside and suddenly I heard him say:

'I just *had* to get out of LA. I FELT I WAS TURNING INTO AN AVOCADO!'

(The Avocado, native of America, drops in the height of the season onto the sidewalks of Los Angeles where it lies rotting.)

It was weird because the rest of us, the English ones, felt shocked. The Avocado was a golden fruit. To compare it to a mushy state of despair was like saying someone was as dull as champagne.

The Avocado Pear made its first brief appearance on the English table three centuries ago but did not start its illustrious career until the 1960s, when it was imported from its adopted country, Israel, and began to sit on supermarket shelves with all the smug assurance of the Cheshire Cat.

London then was Boom Town. Suddenly there was more money to spend on life's little luxuries and more chance to get where you wanted to be. Up there with the rest. And the Avocado knew all this. O so well. The people had begun to travel, broadening their photograph albums and their palates. The people had begun to eat out in restaurants. They liked the sound of the pear. Eating the pear meant one was civilized, metropolitan, ate in restaurants frequently, knew the form. Knew what hors d'oeuvres *were* for a start. It became the most upwardly mobile foodstuff around.

The Avocado was:
Round like a pear (but it wasn't a fruit).
Savoury like spinach (but it wasn't a vegetable).
Rich like cream (but it wasn't from a cow).
Perfectly contained like an egg (but needing no cooking).

Everyone could eat the pear (except macrobiotics but did they count?). Vegetarians could eat it, those with no teeth, models ('I know it's got LOTS of calories but it has practically every mineral in the book. And so good for my hair'), hassled mothers with children (it was convenient and nutritious without the stigma of, say, fishfingers) and of course babies. There was even a book for babies who might grimace at the greeny pulp, John Burningham's *The Avocado Baby*, a modern tale of a baby who became superstrong and righted all wrong after he had eaten up his nice magic golden pear. Just like Popeye and the tinned spinach.

Except the Avocado was never *that* cheap. It wasn't for poor or lazy people. It kept its chic as a reward. Just so. Its divine goldenness never tarnished.

Soon you could find the pear in every supermarket and grocer's shop. It had Terrific Shelf Life. Bought rock hard you could keep it until the next week, bought soft you could have it for lunch. You bought it anyway. Which could not be said of the other vegetables.

You could order it in every restaurant. English, French, Italian, Indian, you name it places. Up and down the land the pear appeared as if from nowhere, lashed with bite-your-tongue-off vinaigrette and prawn cocktails.

And when it was felt that the Golden Fruit was just too relatively available in the uneven 'eighties when difference was IN, the pear took other forms. Fussy restaurants, for example, cooked it (the taste was always 'surprising'), the wine bars tossed it with bacon and lettuce (*so* New York) or mashed it into guacamole (*so* West Coast), the Nouvelle Restaurant made it into sorbet or sliced it prettily in a shallow pool of fruit coulis. It remained throughout these strange transformations golden still. The Avocado was always a media star, being naturally photogenic. It looked so confident, so aesthetically pleasing in the advertisements and colour pages. And unlike its cheesy counterpart, the Brie, which at the same time was undergoing trial by garlic, pepper, herbs and deep frying with gooseberries, the Avocado never looked stupid, never lost its cool. It stayed put.

Why did we love it so? Good Lord it wasn't even English! We loved it because it was reliable. It never went out of season. And unlike the Golden Delicious, it wasn't French. It had kept cleverly out of the Common Market rumpus. The pear was a real survivor.

It appeared in fact to have no nationality at all and therefore no cultural misunderstandings. Above all it had no history. Until the Avocado arrived smart food in restaurants or on dinner tables of the rich had comprised oysters, smoked salmon, game, lobster, suckling pig and a pâté made from the liver of a fatted goose. Dishes for gentlemen who had land to catch and breed them and servants to cook them.

The Avocado could be eaten by anyone, anywhere, anytime. So long as the person could pay the price. It needed no inherited trick or ritual and carried no squire-in-the-big-house, let-them-eat-cake associations. No one felt embarrassed, awkward or guilty when they ate the Golden Fruit.

The Avocado was and is a triumph of the New Guard, a bourgeois without gentility who has fought off the aristocratic sniggerings about doilies and the Mitfordian slips of the past.

If a classless society arrives, it will not be the one imagined by the romantic left, a proletariat of honest folk eating kippers and brown bread and drinking English beer. Nor will it be the vision of poets, a nobility of souls who will dine like kings upon roasted peacock and wine. No, the classless society will be brought about by a populist conservatism for which freedom means consumer choice, the inability to tell between margarine and butter. A society bound by materialism and no art, convenience and no season, convention and no tradition.

It will be a society in which we can be free to eat avocados without fear.

O Brave New World that bears such fruit!

Offal and the New Brutalism, 1985

The Best

FRANCINE DU PLESSIX GRAY

'What's the best tonight?' Barbara Walters asked a few weeks later at the nine-fifteen sitting of Nicolas's restaurant.

'I'd say the shad roe with rhubarb and leeks, and to start with, you might consider the lobster steamed in tea and cinnamon, Malaysian style. As a special tonight we also have calves' liver marinated in Maine cider . . .'

It was an evening off from my Hamlet. I was sitting at a corner table alone to see how Nicolas was getting on, pretending I was one of the food editors who were flocking to The Best to do their reviews. He seemed very pleased as he glanced about the room, waiting for the Walters party to put in their orders. In the past few weeks Lauren

Bacall, Walter Cronkite, Calvin Klein had already made an appearance. Barbra Streisand and John Irving had reserved tables for the weekend.

'Your veal is angelic!' a client called out as Nicolas passed one of the tables. 'We love the chiaroscuro of the brains in fennel sauce!'

'I tried to make it epigrammatic,' Nicolas said modestly. 'It's a complication that works.'

At another table a man and a woman were arguing about the state of gastronomy while waiting for two late guests.

'Nouvelle is one of the genuine trends of the future, it's to cuisine what Saint-Laurent is to couture . . .'

'Well I miss the Nantuas, the brioche doughs, the sustenance of the ancienne style,' the dissenter said. He had a large, florid face and was sipping his second Bellini. 'At least Hollins has the vision to include cassoulet and pot roast in his menu. Out with the itsy-bitsy vegetable abortions, they aren't going to sell through another season.'

'You're missing the whole mystique: in for keeps, health!' The woman's black hair was cut into short zigzags and she kept a notebook by her plate.

'I'm all for freshness,' the dissenter persisted, as they began to sample one of Nicolas's soups, 'but the trout over there looks as if it had passed out right on the plate. And that grilled Long Island goat cheese smells like melted crayon.'

'Your parsley soup transcends itself!' he called out to Nicolas. 'Truly verdant! What aura!'

'Edible jade!' his colleague agreed. 'Adele!' she exclaimed as one missing member of the party appeared at the door. 'Where have you been for the last hour?'

'I am . . . just back . . . from L.A.!' the late guest announced slowly. She was a plump blond with a pale masklike face who had swept a fold of her black shawl dramatically over her shoulder, like a toreador. 'Do you realize what happened yesterday in L.A.?'

'Calm down and order a drink,' the ancienne fan grumbled.

'But you don't understand what happened!' the blond continued, still standing by the table. 'Wolfgang Puck . . . has saved us! Our dear Los Angeles is saved!'

'Make yourself clear, Adele.'

'Wolfgang Puck! The chef of our generation!' The traveler raised her arm in an oracular gesture. 'Puck opened a new restaurant on Wilshire Boulevard last night . . . it is . . . sheer genius! The flair! The surprises!'

'How does he pull it off?'

'Is it the sauces?'

'Sauces!' the blond laughed derisively. 'Out, out months ago! It's all in the grilling! Puck's variety of perfumed woods – grapevine, mesquite, peach! Pigeon breast and figs on a grill of apricot wood . . . pure charisma!'

'Served with what?' one of her friends inquired, scribbling.

'Guess! What would you do with chestnuts?'

'Stone Puck with them,' the man grumbled.

'Chestnut gnocchi!' the blond exclaimed. 'Wolfgang Puck! A boy of twenty-six . . . The irony, the suspense he creates, the intermezzos of aquavit sherbet! What theater!'

October Blood, 1986

New Cooking

JEREMY ROUND 1957–89

I am not hungry tonight
For *délice de volaille farci à la banane.*
I have eaten already. Elsewhere.

I do not care how long
It took to sieve prawns or *monté jus-de-viande.*
I snatched a roll at King's Cross. With Maureen.

I am no longer excited by the
Stiffness of your meringues, soft bite of your asparagus spears.
And haven't been really. For months.

I am not hungry tonight;
Nothing here wets my tongue; from now on for a while
I just want hamburgers. Standing up.

Other Poetry 15, ED. Anne Stevenson

Hunger and Death
NOËL COWARD 1899–1973

Sunday 19 November 1961 [Jamaica]
Cole and I had a long and cosy talk about death the other evening, sitting up here watching the dark come and waiting for the fireflies to appear. He is so sensible. We discussed what would happen if I died and what would happen if he died, and came to the sensible conclusion that there was nothing to be done. We should have to get on with life until our turn came. I said, 'After all, the day had to go on and breakfast had to be eaten', and he replied that if I died he might find it a little difficult to eat breakfast but would probably be peckish by lunch-time.

The Noël Coward Diaries, ED. Graham Payn and
Sheridan Morley, 1982

Dogmas and Doctrines

❦

A Babylonian Toothache Remedy, 3000 BC
ANON.

The Babylonians believed that the various diseases to which they were subject were due to the attacks of evil spirits, or to the malice of wizards or witches. Hence while such remedies as were known were used in the treatment of bodily ailments, the treatment was always accompanied by the recitation of one or more incantations. The colophon at the end of this incantation says that it should be repeated three times over the sufferer after the prescribed treatment has been applied.

After Anu had created heaven,
Heaven had created the earth,
The earth had created the rivers,
The rivers had created the canals,
The canals had created the marsh,
And the marsh had created the worm,
The worm went weeping before Shamash,
His tears flowing before Ea:
'What wilt thou give me for my food?
What wilt thou give me for my sucking?'
'I shall give thee the ripe fig.
And the apricot.'
'Of what use are they to me, the ripe fig
And the apricot?
Lift me up and among the teeth
And the gums cause me to dwell!
The blood of the tooth will I suck,

And of the gum I will gnaw
Its roots!'
    Fix the pin and seize its foot.*
'Because thou has said this, O worm!
May Ea smite thee with the might
Of his hand!'

Middle Eastern Mythology, 1963

Calvary Was An Abattoir

JONATHAN MEADES 1947–

Jesus Christ is the food that is most often represented in western art. Calling Him the Lamb doesn't make the eucharist any the less cannibalistic. It's a *man's* body and blood that Christians eat. This elemental meat is shown us at many stages of its development: The first is when it's a babe, when it is indeed lamb, or veal or sucking pig. There follow childhood, miracles, feasts, trials, calumnies; betrayals. The greatest image though is when it's dead, when it's a casualty that has died for our plates, when it's a bull that has undergone the physical change that makes it beef, when it's a pig that has undergone the change that makes it pork. Calvary was an abattoir. The last stage is when it is bread and wine – or, in the case of the artotyrites, bread and cheese – when, anyway, it is no longer recognizable as the creature save by faith in transsubstantiation.

Now, with other meats, more literal meats, the central and most potent image in that progress is missing. Painting that shows the killing of animals for human consumption is not a genre – there is not a word for it: slaughterscape, still death, conversion piece . . . None of these is currency. And hunting scenes are not primarily concerned with the death of the prey, let alone with its evisceration and preparation for the market. Of course there are films like Georges Franju's *La Sang Des Bêtes* which show the horror of abattoirs, but their concern and effect is to hit the senses rather than to preach. They are not works of vegan propaganda. Jesus's death is crucial to the Christian mystery, to its morbidity and pathos. It must not be forgotten. The death of calves

---

* This is the instruction given to the dentist.

168

and of pigs shrieking as they try to keep their foothold is simply not part of the tradition of alimentary art.

'Meat on Canvas', Peter Knows What Dick Likes, 1989

Nothing Is Repeated
EDMOND 1822–96 AND JULES 1830–70
GONCOURT

15 April [1867]
Everything is unique, nothing happens more than once in a lifetime. The physical pleasure which a certain woman gave you at a certain moment, the exquisite dish which you ate on a certain day – you will never meet either again. Nothing is repeated, and everything is unparalleled.

Pages from the Goncourt Journals, ED., TRANS. Robert Baldick, 1962

An Anthropologist from Mars
MARY DOUGLAS 1921–

Imagine a competent young anthropologist arriving on this planet from Mars and setting out to study the culture of the English natives. He would try to attend all their ceremonies. Sooner or later he would start being invited to weddings and there he would be perhaps baffled to make up his mind whether the central focus of the ceremony was the marriage or the cake. He would of course have read about Kava ceremonial in Tonga and tea ceremonial in Japan. Their complexity of ritual would pale into insignificance compared with the ceremonial surrounding the cutting and distribution of the wedding cake. At military weddings he would see the bride try to cut the cake with a sword, unable to succeed without the help of her spouse. He would see in photographs the bride standing near the cake about to cut it. He would observe the bride's mother in tears, the cake being parcelled into minute portions to be distributed around the room; a large section of the cake being distributed even more elaborately in small postal packets to be eaten by absent friends. Asking about the mythology of the cake, he would hear that those young maidens who receive a portion should sleep with it under their pillow and dream of their future husband, and also that the top portion of this towering three-tier confection should be put aside and kept for the christening ceremony of the first child, etc., etc. Taking an old-fashioned diffusionist approach, he could trace this cake through the history and geography of weddings in Europe. He would conclude that he had seen the apotheosis of the cake form, something as worthy of study as the American Indians' sun dance. He would have no difficulty in getting pictorial records of the cake for he would find that no bakery that produces wedding cakes is without its album of photographs of famous cakes that it has made. If he had Marxist leanings he might be worried to see the extraordinary uniformity of the wedding cake formula across the class structure. Although there will be many discernible differences in quality and price between one cake and another, for any guest standing at the other end of the room it is hard to see the difference; the wedding cake seems to be relatively classless – perhaps a symptom of the embourgeoisement of the European workers or perhaps the reverse process. When he had completed filling in the diffusionist and sociological background of the cake ceremony, the researcher would embark upon the structural analysis which I shall not describe in detail. Essentially this technique of study would require him never to consider the cake as a genre, still less the wedding cake alone apart from the food system in which it appears. The food system would be seen as a series of events using a defined medium combined according to clearly understood rules. He would have to set all the cake forms that he could record into the context of all other food forms habitually used by the people under study.

In the Active Voice, 1982

French Spending

THEODORE ZELDIN 1933–

In 1960 the French spent 42% of their household budgets on food, but at the last census (1975) they were down to 24%. This is slightly more than one would expect, compared to other prospering nations who always spend less on food as they get richer, but there is undoubtedly a new tendency for the French to shift more of their spending from food to housing, following the American pattern. The sociologist Pierre Bourdieu has claimed that there is now a tension between two different attitudes to food. The old working-class and lower-middle-class attitude, he says, is that eating and drinking copiously is part of the art of the good life: when they have guests, they like above all to offer them plentiful helpings; they esteem above all the kind of cooking their mothers produced; they have little taste for experiment, inventiveness or exotic dishes; it is important to them that the meal should be eaten in a relaxed and friendly, jovial atmosphere, because eating is a feast. By contrast, the educated classes are cultivating a taste for light food, delicately and artistically prepared with 'amusing' or 'interesting' dishes; their concern is not to fill their guests up, but to ensure they are not bored. The workers' priorities are seen in the budgets of those of them who become foremen: these spend as much money on food as managers, devoting a far larger proportion of their budget to pleasures of the table.

The French, 1983

On Cookery

PLATO 427–347 BC

Gorgias is a professor of oratory, and though the dialogue opens with a discussion between him and Socrates on the nature of art, it soon concerns itself wholly with ethics. It is clear that Plato did not rate the art of cooking very highly at all; it is to him a form of flattery that merely tries to gratify and give pleasure, without investigating the nature of pleasure and giving a rational account of itself.

SOCRATES: You set a high value on giving gratification; will you gratify me in a small matter?
POLUS: By all means.
SOCRATES: Just ask me, will you, what sort of art I take cookery to be.
POLUS: Very well; what sort of art is cookery?
SOCRATES: It isn't an art at all, Polus.
POLUS: What is it then? Explain.

SOCRATES: A kind of knack gained by experience, I should say.
POLUS: A knack of doing what, pray?
SOCRATES: Producing gratification and pleasure, Polus.

Cookery puts on the mask of medicine and pretends to know what
foods are best for the body; and, if an audience of children or of men
with no more sense than children had to decide whether a confectioner
or a doctor is the better judge of wholesome and unwholesome
foodstuffs, the doctor would unquestionably die of hunger. Now I call
this sort of thing pandering and I declare that it is dishonourable – I'm
speaking to you now, Polus – because it makes pleasure its aim instead
of good, and I maintain that it is merely a knack and not an art because
it has no rational account to give of the nature of the various things
which it offers. I refuse to give the title of art to anything irrational,
and if you want to raise an objection on this point I am ready to justify
my position.

Cookery then, as I say, is the form of pandering which corresponds
to medicine, and in the same way physical training has its counterfeit
in beauty-culture, a mischievous, swindling, base, servile trade, which
creates an illusion by the use of artificial adjuncts and make-up and
depilatories and costume, and makes people assume a borrowed
beauty to the neglect of the true beauty which is the product of
training. In short, I will put the matter in the form of a geometrical
proportion – perhaps now you will be able to follow me – and say that
cookery is to medicine as beauty-culture is to physical training, or
rather that popular lecturing is to legislation as beauty-culture to
training, and oratory to justice as cookery to medicine.

Gorgias, TRANS. Walter Hamilton, 1960

Three Hours Per Day
MARVIN HARRIS 1927–

The notion that palaeolithic populations worked round the clock in
order to feed themselves now also appears ludicrous. As collectors of
food plants they were certainly no less effective than chimpanzees.
Field studies have shown that in their natural habitat the great apes
spend as much time grooming, playing, and napping as they do
foraging and eating. And as hunters our upper palaeolithic ancestors

must have been at least as proficient as lions – animals which alternate bursts of intense activity with long periods of rest and relaxation. Studies of how present-day hunters and collectors allocate their time have shed more light on this issue. Richard Lee of the University of Toronto kept a record of how much time the modern Bushman hunter-collectors spend in the quest for food. Despite their habitat – the edge of the Kalahari, a desert region whose lushness is hardly comparable to that of France during the upper palaeolithic period – less than three hours per day per adult is all that is needed for the Bushmen to obtain a diet rich in proteins and other essential nutrients.

The Machiguenga, simple horticulturalists of the Peruvian Amazon studied by Allen and Orna Johnson, spend a little more than three hours per day per adult in food production and get less animal protein for this effort than do the Bushmen. In the rice-growing regions of eastern Java, modern peasants have been found to spend about forty-fours per week in productive farm work – something no self-respecting Bushman would ever dream of doing – and Javanese peasants seldom eat animal proteins. American farmers, for whom fifty-and-sixty-hour work weeks are commonplace, eat well by Bushman standards but certainly cannot be said to have as much leisure.

Cannibals and Kings, 1977

Silent Cuisine

JEAN-FRANÇOIS REVEL 1924–

Masking error or banality is fortunately not the only function of gastronomical literature. But the difficulty when one explores the past (and even the present) lies in appreciating the difference between silent cuisine and cuisine that talks too much, between the cuisine that exists on the plate and the one that exists only in gastronomical chronicles. Or else, to state the matter in a different way, the difficulty lies in discovering, behind the verbal façade of fancy cuisines, the popular, anonymous, peasant or 'bourgeois' cuisine, made up of tricks and little secrets that only evolve very slowly, in silence, and that no individual in particular has invented. It is above all this latter cuisine, the average cuisine, the gastronomical art of the 'depths,' that is responsible for there being countries where one 'eats well' and others where one 'eats badly.' But by itself, cuisine that is merely practical, traditional family cooking does not suffice either. If it is not stimulated by the inno-vation, the reflection, and indeed the extravagance of a handful of artists, popular cuisine itself becomes atrophied, dull and uninterest-ing. The gastronomical serial written by the centuries has as its 'plot' the constant battle between the good amateur cook and the thinking chef, a lover's quarrel that, as in all good adventure novels, ends, after many a stormy scene, with a marriage.

Culture and Cuisine, TRANS. Helen R. Lane and C. Doubleday, 1982

I Don't Care What I Eat
NORMAN DOUGLAS 1868–1952

The railway station at Rome has put on a new face. Blown to the winds is that old dignity and sense of leisure. Bustle everywhere; soldiers in line, officers strutting about; feverish scurrying for tickets. A young baggage employé, who allowed me to effect a change of raiment in the inner recesses of his department, alone seemed to keep up the traditions of former days. He was unruffled and polite; he told me, incidentally, that he came from –. That was odd, I said; I had often met persons born at –, and never yet encountered one who was not civil beyond the common measure. His native place must be worthy of a visit.

'It is,' he replied. 'There are also certain fountains . . . .'

That restaurant, for example – one of those few for which a man in olden days of peace would desert his own tavern in the town – how changed! The fare has deteriorated beyond recognition. Where are those succulent joints and ragoûts, the aromatic wine, the snow-white macaroni, the café-au-lait with genuine butter and genuine honey?

War-time!

Conversed awhile with an Englishman at my side, who was gleefully devouring lumps of a particular something which I would not have liked to touch with tongs.

'I don't care what I eat,' he remarked.

So it seemed.

I don't care what I eat: what a confession to make! Is it not the same as saying, I don't care whether I am dirty or clean? When others tell me this, I regard it as a pose, or a poor joke. This person was manifestly sincere in his profession of faith. He did not care what he ate. He looked it. Were I afflicted with this peculiar ailment, this attenuated form of *coprophagia*, I should try to keep the hideous secret to myself. It is nothing to boast of. A man owes something to those traditions of our race which has helped to raise us above the level of the brute. Good tastes in viands has been painfully acquired; it is a sacred trust. Beware of gross feeders. They are a menace to their fellow-creatures. Will they not act, on occasion, even as they feed? Assuredly they will. Everybody acts as he feeds.

Alone, 1921

Essay on Flesh Eating
PLUTARCH 40–120 AD

1. Can you really ask what reason Pythagoras had for abstaining from flesh? For my part I rather wonder both by what accident and in what state of soul or mind the first man who did so, touched his mouth to gore and brought his lips to the flesh of a dead creature, he who set forth tables of dead, stale bodies and ventured to call food and nourishment the parts that had a little before bellowed and cried, moved and lived. How could his eyes endure the slaughter when throats were slit and hides flayed and limbs torn from limb? How could his nose endure the stench? . . .

But you who live now, what madness, what frenzy drives you to the pollution of shedding blood, you who have such a superfluity of necessities? Why slander the earth by implying that she cannot support you? Why impiously offend law-giving Demeter and bring shame upon Dionysus, lord of the cultivated vine, the gracious one, as if you did not receive enough from their hands? Are you not ashamed to mingle domestic crops with blood and gore? You call serpents and panthers and lions savage, but you yourselves, by your own foul slaughters, leave them no room to outdo you in cruelty; for their slaughter is their living, yours is a mere appetizer.

3. It is certainly not lions and wolves that we eat out of self-defence; on the contrary, we ignore these and slaughter harmless, tame creatures without stings or teeth to harm us, creatures that, I swear, Nature appears to have produced for the sake of their beauty and grace. . . .

What a terrible thing it is to look on when the tables of the rich are spread, men who employ cooks and spicers to groom the dead! And it is even more terrible to look on when they are taken away, for more is left than has been eaten. So the beasts died for nothing! There are others who refuse when the dishes are already set before them and will not have them cut into or sliced. Though they bid spare the dead, they did not spare the living.

5. We declare, then, that it is absurd for them to say that the practice of flesh-eating is based on Nature. For that man is not naturally carnivorous is, in the first place, obvious from the structure of his body. A man's frame is in no way similar to those creatures who were made for flesh-eating: he has no hooked beak or sharp nails or jagged teeth, no strong stomach or warmth of vital fluids able to digest and assimilate a heavy diet of flesh. It is from this very fact, the evenness of our teeth, the smallness of our mouths, the softness of our tongues, our possession of vital fluids too inert to digest meat that Nature disavows our eating of flesh. If you declare that you are naturally designed for such a diet, then first kill for yourself what you want to eat. Do it, however, only through your own resources . . .

For what sort of dinner is not costly for which a living creature loses its life? Do we hold a life cheap? I do not yet go so far as to say that it may well be the life of your mother or father or some friend or child, as Empedocles declared. Yet it does, at least, possess some perception, hearing, seeing, imagination, intelligence, which last every creature receives from Nature to enable it to acquire what is proper for it and to evade what is not. Do but consider which are the philosophers who serve the better to humanize us: those who bid us eat our children and friends and fathers and wives after their death, or Pythagoras and Empedocles who try to accustom us to act justly toward other creatures also? You ridicule a man who abstains from eating mutton. But are we, they will say, to refrain from laughter when we see you slicing off portions from a dead father or mother and sending them to absent friends and inviting those who are at hand, heaping their plates with flesh.

Moralia, TRANS. Harold Chermiss and William Helmbold, 1978

Simple Cooking

MARY DOUGLAS 1921–

Sometimes at home, hoping to simplify the cooking, I ask, 'Would you like to have just soup for supper tonight? I mean a good thick soup – instead of supper. It's late and you must be hungry. It won't take a minute to serve.' Then an argument starts: 'Let's have soup now, and supper when you are ready.' 'No, no, to serve two meals would be more work. But if you like, why not start with the soup and fill up with pudding?' 'Good heavens! What sort of a meal is that? A beginning and an end and no middle.' 'Oh, all right then, have the soup as it's there, and I'll do a Welsh rarebit as well.' When they have eaten soup, Welsh rarebit, pudding, and cheese: 'What a lot of plates. Why do you make such elaborate suppers?' They proceed to argue that by taking thought I could satisfy the full requirements of a meal with a single, copious dish. Several rounds of this conversation have given me a practical interest in the categories and meaning of food. I needed to know what defines the category of a meal in our home.

Implicit Meanings, 1975

Men Are Like Plants

J. HECTOR ST JOHN DE CRÈVECOEUR
1735–1813

Men are like plants; the goodness and flavour of the fruit proceeds from the peculiar soil and exposition in which they grow. We are nothing but what we derive from the air we breathe, the climate we inhabit, the government we obey, the system of religion we profess, and the nature of our employment. Here you will find but few crimes; these have acquired as yet no root among us. I wish I were able to trace all my ideas; if your ignorance prevents me from describing them properly, I hope I shall be able to delineate a few of the outlines, which is all I propose.

Those who live near the sea feed more on fish than on flesh and often encounter that boisterous element. This renders them more bold and enterprising; this leads them to neglect the confined occupations of the land. They see and converse with a variety of people; their intercourse with mankind becomes extensive. The sea inspires them with a love of traffic, a desire of transporting produce from one place to another, and leads them to a variety of resources which supply the place of labour. Those who inhabit the middle settlements, by far the most numerous, must be very different; the simple cultivation of the earth purifies them, but the indulgences of the government, the soft remonstrances of religion, the rank of independent freeholders, must necessarily inspire them with sentiments, very little known in Europe among a people of the same class. What do I say? Europe had no such class of men; the early knowledge they acquire, the early bargains they make, give them a great degree of sagacity. As freemen, they will be litigious; pride and obstinacy are often the cause of lawsuits; the nature of our laws and governments may be another. As citizens, it is easy to imagine that they will carefully read the newspapers, enter into every political disquisition, freely blame or censure governors and others. As farmers, they will be careful and anxious to get as much as they can, because what they get is their own.

Letters from an American Farmer and Sketches of Eighteenth-Century
America, 1963

I Eat Everything Except Corpses
LADY JEKYLL 1861–1937

One guest scored off a solicitous hostess who, when accepting a proffered visit for luncheon, asked for some guidance as to the then preferred diet – was it vegetarian or uncooked fruit, were vitamines and proteids desired or taboo? The reply came short and incisive: 'Thank you, I eat everything except *corpses*,' thereby making a lamb cutlet or the wing of a boiled chicken seem positively tigerish. Some people let their moderation be known to all men, never, according to their own account, partaking of anything grosser than twelve almonds and six raisins in the twenty-four hours. Others boast of a cup of milk with two slices of brown bread and a lettuce. Do not fear overmuch to put such resolution to the test. They have been known often to enjoy copious and diversified meals – only their doing so must never be noticed.

Kitchen Essays, 1922

Emptiness
SHEILA MACLEOD 1939–

Most people know when they are hungry and will eat, more or less, accordingly. Bruch contrasts this fortunate majority with both the anorexic and the obese person, neither of whom knows how to gauge the state of her own stomach or assess what is a reasonable requirement of food for her own bodily needs. The obese person cannot recognise that her stomach is full, nor the anorexic that hers is empty. It is easy enough to see how someone, especially someone who has suffered a childhood of poverty, can be led to a fear of emptiness, of not getting enough to eat, of starvation itself, and so in later life to stave off or compensate for such a fear. And indeed obesity is a disease of the poor rather than the rich. It is perhaps less easy to see how someone from a privileged background can be led to seek emptiness as a physical state, when it is obviously such an unpleasant, even painful, one. Repletion is probably a more pleasurable state for most people than is emptiness, and its metaphorical implications are now widely understood: to be well-fed is to feel safe from poverty and death; it is to engage in an enjoyable activity; and it is to feel loved, if only by oneself. But the metaphorical implications of emptiness are less clear. Because it is both difficult and painful to maintain one's stomach in a state of emptiness, we cannot doubt that there are powerful psychic motivations for sustaining such an activity, which is not only abnormal, but directly contrary to both physiological and social pressures.

The Art of Starvation, 1981

Hebraic Laws
JEAN SOLER

How can we explain the dietary prohibitions of the Hebrews? To this day these rules – with variations, but always guided by the Mosaic laws – are followed by many orthodox Jews. Once a number of false leads, such as the explanation that they were hygienic measures, have been dismissed, the structural approach appears to be enlightening.

Lévi-Strauss has shown the importance of cooking, which is

peculiar to man in the same manner as language. Better yet, cooking is a language through which a society expresses itself. For man knows that the food he ingests in order to live will become assimilated into his being, will become himself. There must be, therefore, a relationship between the idea he has formed of specific items of food and the image he has of himself and his place in the universe. There is a link between a people's dietary habits and its perception of the world.

Moreover, language and dietary habits also show an analogy of form. For just as the phonetic system of a language retains only a few of the sounds a human being is capable of producing, so a community adopts a dietary regime by making a choice among all the possible foods. By no means does any given individual eat everything; the mere fact that a thing is edible does not mean that it will be eaten. By bringing to light the logic that informs these choices and the inter-relation among its constituent parts – in this case the various foods – we can outline the specific characteristics of a society, just as we can define those of a language.

Food and Drink in History, Vol. 5, ED. R. Forster and O. Ranum,

TRANS. E. Forster and P. M. Ranum, 1979

The Stomach

JEROME K. JEROME 1859–1927

It is very strange, this domination of our intellect by our digestive organs. We cannot work, we cannot think, unless our stomach wills so. It dictates to us our emotions, our passions. After eggs and bacon, it says, 'Work!' After beefsteak and porter, it says, 'Sleep!' After a cup of tea (two spoonsful for each cup, and don't let it stand more than three minutes), it says to the brain, 'Now, rise, and show your strength. Be eloquent, and deep, and tender; see, with a clear eye, into Nature and into life; spread your white wings of quivering thought, and soar, a god-like spirit, over the whirling world beneath you, up through long lanes of flaming stars to the gates of eternity!'

After hot muffins, it says, 'Be dull and soulless, like a beast of the field – a brainless animal, with listless eye, unlit by any ray of fancy, or of hope, or fear, or love, or life.' And after brandy, taken in sufficient quantity, it says, 'Now, come, fool, grin and tumble, that your fellow-men may laugh – drivel in folly, and splutter in senseless sounds, and show what a helpless ninny is poor man whose wit and will are drowned, like kittens, side by side, in half an inch of alcohol.'

We are but the veriest, sorriest slaves of our stomach. Reach not after morality and righteousness, my friends; watch vigilantly your stomach, and diet it with care and judgment. Then virtue and contentment will come and reign within your heart, unsought by any effort of your own; and you will be a good citizen, a loving husband, and a tender father – a noble, pious man.

Before our supper, Harris and George and I were quarrelsome and snappy and ill-tempered; after our supper, we sat and beamed on one another, and we beamed upon the dog, too. We loved each other, we loved everybody. Harris, in moving about, trod on George's corn. Had this happened before supper, George would have expressed wishes and desires concerning Harris's fate in this world and the next that would have made a thoughtful man shudder.

As it was, he said, 'Steady, old man; 'ware wheat.'

And Harris, instead of merely observing, in his most unpleasant tones, that a fellow could hardly help treading on some bit of George's foot, if he had to move about at all within ten yards of where George was sitting, suggesting that George never ought to come into an ordinary sized boat with feet that length, and advising him to hang them over the side, as he would have done before supper, now said: 'Oh, I'm so sorry, old chap; I hope I haven't hurt you.'

And George said: 'Not at all;' that it was his fault; and Harris said no, it was his.

It was quite pretty to hear them.

Three Men in a Boat, 1917

Chinese Criteria of Excellence

HSIANG JU LIN AND TSUIFENG LIN

Chinese cuisine is known to some only by its curiosities, but it actually differs from Western cuisine in a number of fundamental aspects. Its peculiar character comes from the realization that cooking is a form of artifice. This attitude accounts for its triumphs, its faults and its sophistications. Because of the trickery involved, the psychology of eating is different. The criteria of excellence in cuisine are somewhat different and are discussed as a lesson in Chinese. The pursuit of flavour has resulted more often in the blending of flavours, sometimes successful, often mismatched. Chinese cuisine is uniquely distinguished by textural variation, which has also led to the use of parts. And it is one of the few cuisines in which some kinds of fat are treated as delicacies.

Cooking is a form of artifice, because the taste of food is both good and bad. Good taste cannot be achieved unless one knows precisely what is bad about each ingredient, and proceeds to correct it. The curious, omnivorous cook knows that the taste of raw fruit is quite delicious and cannot be improved upon. Raw fish is insipid, raw chicken metallic, raw beef is palatable, but for the rank flavour of blood. It is pointless to talk about the natural taste of these things, as many people like to do. We take it to mean the characteristic flavour of each thing, which is mainly in the fat and in the juices. This is brought out by artifice and appreciated as the *hsien* and *hsiang*, the flavour and aroma. They are to food what soul is to man. Cooking is essentially the capturing of these qualities, gastronomy the appreciation of them. *Hsien* and *hsiang* are not associated with any form of cooking. Here is the pivotal point where Chinese cuisine swings away from the others and takes off on its own. Note that Western pastry-making is a departure from the natural form and perhaps the 'natural taste' of food. The *pâtissier* works only with butter, eggs, flour and sugar. But because he does not feel compelled to preserve the natural form, and present the flavour of each ingredient individually, he is often able to evolve something better. The palate can then perceive the taste of the ingredients interlocked in his inventions. The Chinese cook has done the same for food in general. (But Chinese sweet pastry is deplorably heavy and monotonous, often made up of glutinous rice, fat pork and sweet bean paste.) One discerns the *hsien* and *hsiang* of each ingredient in dishes of novel texture and appearance, these qualities having been brought out by artifice.

Criteria of Excellence
The unique qualities of the cuisine are contained in some almost untranslatable words. The words *hsien*, *hsiang*, *nung* and *yu-er-pu-ni* are the criteria of excellence in flavour. 'Flavours must be rich and robust, never oily, or they must be delicate and fresh without being too thin. A flavour which is *nung* means that the essences are concentrated and the scum has been removed. Those who like greasy food might just as well dine on lard. When some dish is *hsien*, its true flavour is

present. Not the least particle of error can be tolerated or you will have missed the mark.' (Yuan Mei)

Chinese Gastronomy, 1969

Bacon
WILLIAM COBBETT 1763–1835

A couple of flitches of bacon are worth fifty thousand Methodist sermons and religious tracts. They are great softeners of temper and promoters of domestic harmony.

Cottage Economy, 1821

Hamlet the Bull
JONATHAN MEADES 1947–

Take a bull. Call him Hamlet, not after the Dane from the problem family, but after his dad who was Dublin District Milk Board's most prolific sire, an Aberdeen Angus with 75,000 offspring. That Hamlet died in 1977 and was made into dog meat. Our Hamlet is destined for human consumption, not for bovine generation and canine delight. His nativity will not be recorded – we don't want to be reminded of the vulnerability and cuteness of future meat. And no one will snap the moment when he is about to be led into a windowless building and he glances a pair of eyes through the slats of a cattle truck and recognizes them as those of his father who was forced to give him life so he'd have an early death. No, not that sort of stuff. No, what suits next is the triumphal pastoral. This is where Hamlet, full grown and in the flush of early manhood – which is the only manhood he'll get – is found in a field with a famous chef. The weather is great. There are lots of variables: the landscape may be fell or fen; there can be trees – anything but species like the stone pine or the cypress which are suggestive of parched rather than of lush ground; houses are OK so long as they're yeoman vernacular or grand, and farm buildings have got to be old ones – no metal sheds no matter how gleamy they may be, no silage towers. Cars are Range Rover, not greedy farmer Volvos and

183

Mercs parked in front of rancho bungalows. There can be a farmer provided he's got outdoorsy clothes. The chef is got up for the country too, and of course what he's doing is inspecting his raw materials on the hoof the way an agent of murder meets his victim before he puts out a contract. He's claiming Hamlet's life with a gingerly made pat to the flank. The next time we see Hamlet he has shrunk, he has changed shape and colour, he has stopped being a quadruped. The chef has put on new clothes, white for absolution – but anyway, it wasn't him, *he* didn't give Hamlet the old volt jolt, did he? The sun's gone in too. These suns you see were brought along and lugged in by the photographer's assistant. No landscape – everything's tempered metal now, blades and flame. Chef is making his first incision, he's a surgeon and an artist. And we only know that these lumps of amputee used to fit together to make Hamlet because we are told so.

Often we won't see Hamlet in the field; often the story begins posthumously, with no reference to the life save in terms of the sort of pasture where it was led, maybe. And absolutely no reference to the death. Often Hamlet, who of course won't have a name – you don't give names to dark red cushions with wax spilled on them – often he'll be in a state of very quick metamorphosis, bumping through a serial Hell of mallets and blades and drownings.

'Meat on Canvas', *Peter Knows What Dick Likes*, 1989

No Cheaper Form of Bread
DODIE SMITH 1896–1990

Goodness, Topaz is actually putting on eggs to boil! No one told me the hens had yielded to prayer. Oh, excellent hens! I was only expecting bread and margarine for tea, and I don't get as used to margarine as I could wish. I thank heaven there is no cheaper form of bread than bread.

How odd it is to remember that 'tea' once meant afternoon tea to us – little cakes and thin bread-and-butter in the drawing-room. Now it is as solid a meal as we can scrape together, as it has to last us until breakfast. We have it after Thomas gets back from school.

I Capture the Castle, 1949

What is Raw?
CLAUDE LÉVI-STRAUSS 1908–

What each society understands by 'raw', 'cooked' and 'rotten' can only be determined through ethnographical observation, and there is no reason why they should all be in agreement about the definitions. The recent increase in the number of Italian restaurants in France has given French people a taste for raw food in a much 'rawer' state than was traditional with us: the vegetables are simply washed and cut up, without being prepared with an oil and vinegar dressing, according to the usual French custom – except for radishes, which, however, are significantly felt to require a generous accompaniment of butter and salt. Through Italian influence we have, then, extended our category of the raw. Certain incidents which occurred after the Allied landings in 1944 show that American soldiers had a broader conception of the category of the rotten than the French; under the impression that the Normandy cheese dairies stank of corpses, they sometimes destroyed the buildings.

The Origin of Table Manners, TRANS. John and
Doreen Weightman, 1968

Potential Disaster
MIREILLE JOHNSTON

Potentially every meal is a disaster, ready to fail because of boredom, tensions, rivalries, long nurtured grudges. But because of this incredible operation where we give the best of ourselves, planning, selecting, preparing, even improvising a last-minute extra treat, because of the excitement and the delight in sharing delicious things, everyone forgets differences and old feuds.

'Educating a Palate', *The Journal of Gastronomy*, Vol. 1, 1985

The Ideal Vegetarian State
PLATO 428–347 BC

*One of the world's best-kept secrets is that Plato's vision of the
ideal state was vegetarian.*

'But let us consider the matter and not draw back. And first, let us
consider what will be the manner of life of men so equipped. Will they
not spend their time in the production of corn and wine and clothing
and shoes? And they will build themselves houses; in summer they will
generally work without their coats and shoes, but in winter they will
be well clothed and shod. For food they will make meal from their
barley and flour from their wheat, and kneading and baking them they
will heap their noble scones and loaves on reeds or fresh leaves, and
lying on couches of bryony and myrtle boughs will feast with their
children, drink wine after their repast, crown their heads with
garlands, and sing hymns to the gods. So they will live with one
another in happiness, not begetting children above their means, and
guarding against the danger of poverty or war.'

Here Glaucon interrupted and said: 'Apparently you give your men
dry bread to feast on.'

'You are right,' I said; 'I forgot that they would have a relish with it.
They will have salt and olives and cheese, and they will have boiled
dishes with onions and such vegetables as one gets in the country. And
I expect we must allow them a dessert of figs, and peas and beans, and
they will roast myrtle berries and acorns at the fire, and drink their
wine in moderation. Leading so peaceful and healthy a life they will
naturally attain to a good old age, and at death leave their children to
live as they have done.'

'Why,' said Glaucon, 'if you had been founding a city of pigs,
Socrates, this is just how you would have fattened them.'

'Well, Glaucon, how must they live?'

'In an ordinary decent manner,' he said. 'If they are not to be
miserable, I think they must have couches to lie on and tables to eat
from, and the ordinary dishes and dessert of modern life.'

'Very well,' I said, 'I understand. We are considering, apparently,
the making not of a city merely, but of a luxurious city. And perhaps
there is no harm in doing so. From that kind, too, we shall soon learn,

if we examine it, how justice and injustice arise in cities. I, for my part, think that the city I have described is the true one, what we may call the city of health. But if you wish, let us also inspect a city which is suffering from inflammation. There is no reason why we should not. Well, then, for some people the arrangements we have made will not be enough. The mode of living will not satisfy them. They shall have couches and tables and other furniture; rich dishes too, and fragrant oils and perfumes, and courtesans and sweetmeats, and many varieties of each. Then again we must make more than a bare provision for those necessities we mentioned at the first, houses and clothes and shoes. We must start painting and embroidery, and collect gold and ivory, and so on, must we not?'

'Yes,' he said.

'Then we must make our city larger. For the healthy city will not now suffice. We need one swollen in size, and full of a multitude of things which necessity would not introduce into cities. There will be all kinds of hunters and there will be the imitators; one crowd of imitators in figure and colour, and another of imitators of music; poets and their servants, rhapsodists, actors, dancers and theatrical agents; the makers of all kinds of articles, of those used for women's adornment, for example. Then, too, we shall need more servants; or do you think we can do without footmen, wet-nurses, dry-nurses, lady's maids, barbers, and cooks and confectioners, besides? Then we shall want swineherds too; we had none in our former city – there was no need – but we shall need them along with all the others for this city. And we shall need great quantities of all kinds of cattle if people are to eat them. Shall we not?'

'Surely.'

'Then if we lead this kind of life we shall require doctors far more often than we should have done in the first city?'

'Certainly.'

'Then I dare say even the land which was sufficient to support the first population will be now insufficient and too small?'

'Yes,' he said.

'Then if we are to have enough for pasture and ploughland, we must take a slice from our neighbours' territory. And they will want to do the same to ours, if they also overpass the bounds of necessity and plunge into reckless pursuit of wealth?'

'Yes, that must happen, Socrates,' he said.

'Then shall we go to war at that point, Glaucon, or what will happen?'

'We shall go to war,' he said.

The Republic, TRANS. A. P. Lindsay, 1935

Mayonnaise Proves the Existence of God

ALICE THOMAS ELLIS 1932–

Aunt Irene really inclined to that simplest of all views: the one expressed so cogently in the book of Genesis, which explained everything with appealing clarity. This was the only view that explained, for instance, mayonnaise. It was patently absurd to suppose that mayonnaise had come about through random chance, that anyone could ever have been silly or brilliant enough to predict what would happen if he slowly trickled oil on to egg yolks and then gone ahead and tried it. An angel must have divulged that recipe and then explained what to do with the left-over whites. Meringues – there was another instance of the exercise of superhuman intelligence. To Aunt Irene the Ten Commandments seemed almost insignificant compared with the astonishing miracle of what you could do with an egg. As the angel had left in his fiery chariot he must have added, 'And don't forget omelettes, and cake and custard and soufflés and poaching and frying and boiling and baking. Oh, and they're frightfully good with anchovies. And you can use the shells to clarify soup – and don't forget to dig them in round the roots of your roses', the angelic tones fading into the ethereal distance.

The 27th Kingdom, 1982

A Rolex Oyster That You Swallow

JONATHAN MEADES 1947–

Loss of meaning is manifest in the death of ritual – no one says grace any more. Ritual is not a cosmetic. It is a means of transportation to sublimity and awe. Without it the multiplicity of responses to food vanishes. Food is reduced to fuel. I believe the current preoccupation with effortfully gimmicky photographs of food is an attempt to regain some sort of meaning, to invest food with a new set of non-nutritional properties. The properties I'm talking about are banally temporal ones – they're concerned with status, social placement and so on. Food has become chic, it's an OK subject. The food photography in the glossy magazines and the colour supplements and the specialist magazines is ineffably vulgar and manages to disassociate posh eating from the notions of glut and excess: it invariably shows food that is cooked to be photographed. The tyranny of the visual over the gustatory suits the English very well: the English suffer, as we all know, a collectively defective palate and a sense of embarrassment about eating well. If food can be made to look so nice, why, then it can be counted a decorative art, and to taste it must be a quasi-aesthetic experience, quite as intellectually demanding and emotionally trying as an interior by John Fowler or a design by Cecil Beaton.

As a result of the efforts of the food photographers who see themselves as the heirs to Arcimboldo and Miro and god knows which minor Nip print makers chefs have submitted to the dictates of art direction. They make food which is to be looked at. It is *not* sustaining. They talk about presentation, *all the time*, believe me, they do. High cooking is not something you eat and are thankful for, it is not celebratory of nature's fecundity. It is like a disposable and expensive accoutrement, a prop to what we must call a lifestyle. A Rolex Oyster that you swallow.

'Meat on Canvas', *Peter Knows What Dick Likes*, 1989

Cookery Books
JOSEPH CONRAD 1857–1924

Of all the books produced since the most remote ages by human talents and industry those only that treat of cooking are, from a moral point of view, above suspicion. The intention of every other piece of prose may be discussed and even mistrusted; but the purpose of a cookery book is one and unmistakable. Its object can conceivably be no other than to increase the happiness of mankind . . . Conscientious cooking is an enemy to gluttony. The trained delicacy of the palate like a cultivated delicacy of sentiment stands in the way of unseemly excesses. The decency of our life is for a great part a matter of good taste, of the correct appreciation of what is fine in simplicity. The intimate influence of conscientious cooking by rendering easy the processes of digestion promotes the serenity of mind, the graciousness of thought, and that indulgent view of our neighbours' failings which is the only genuine form of optimism. Those are its titles to our reverence.

Preface to A Handbook of Cookery for a Small House, 1923

Olive Oil
EDWARD BUNYARD 1872–1939

This, one of the greatest blessings that the generous Mediterranean has bestowed upon mankind, is, unfortunately, only too easily adulterated, and a cheap oil is likely to be a bad one. The only remedy for this is to obtain supplies from a house of integrity. Olive oil is the very soul of a salad, and far beyond this, for it is one of the finest natural foods and medicines ever bestowed upon man. Let us away with salines and the depressing salts and substitute olive oil, which not only lubricates, but feeds the nerves, stimulates a proper functioning of the liver, upon which the happiness of man depends, and benevolently protects the mucous membranes from the noxious effects of biting acids. True wisdom would cause dictators to administer olive, rather than castor, oil. And there is no need to cause the repulsion of a heavy dosage. A teaspoonful a day, taken with vegetables in the course of the daily meals, will calm the troubles of many a storm-tossed digestion, and make the world a better place for the brief dwelling of man.

The Epicure's Companion, ED. Edward and Lorna Bunyard, 1937

Salt
MARGARET VISSER 1940–

The first of the salt men on record was found in 1573. He was bearded and fully clothed in a woollen jacket and trousers, leather shoes, and a conical cap. His flesh was yellow and hard as a rock, but perfectly preserved because he was buried in salt. After the people of the village had had a good look at him, spread out in church 'like a salted codfish,' he was given a Christian burial in the mountain, 'to get him out of men's thoughts.' At least three other bodies in a similar state have been found in the shafts of salt-mines in the same region near Salzburg (Salt Town), Austria. They were all victims of mine accidents between two and three thousand years ago.

In 1836 a cemetery dating back to the age of the Salt Men was found in the vicinity of the nearby village of Hallstatt (which also means Salt Town). So far, well over two thousand graves have been excavated at this site, many of them royal burials equipped with gold jewellery, chariots, iron weapons, and joints of salt beef for the journey to the other world. Tiny Hallstatt has given its name to a whole civilization whose confines stretched from Spain to Yugoslavia during the First Millennium BC. These were the early Celts, who made the transition from the Bronze to the Iron Age in Europe. Hallstatt princes could import the finest art works from ancient Greece. They traded with the Etruscans, the Egyptians, and the Romans, and their merchant subjects continually travelled back and forth for distances as great as that between southern France and Cornwall.

Neither the riches nor the travel would have been possible without these people's knowledge of salt deposits, salt mining, and the properties of salt. Hallstatt miners knew exactly how and at what angle best to sink a shaft through surface layers of soil to the richest salt seams in the mountains. As they walked down into the tunnel they had made, they would grip their 'lamps' in their teeth: long pine sticks soaked in resin and lighted at the end. Down below, roped bunches of burning pine lit the work-face. Remains of these torches have been found, together with many miners' tools, the goatskin sacks they strapped to their backs for hauling back precious lumps of salt, wooden buckets, water bags – even a Wagnerian-looking musical instrument made of horn, used, perhaps, to signal a miner's where-abouts in case of mishap.

These Iron-Age men used old-fashioned bronze in the mines, for they had found out that bronze resists salt corrosion better than iron does. They were prepared to live and work high in the cold and dangerous mountains in order to get salt, even though contemporary settlements are almost invariably to be found in sheltered valleys. The miners knew how and where to find salt, and this gave the Hallstatt Celts an endlessly useful headstart in trading relations with other people less fortunate, less energetic, or less informed than themselves.

Like corn, salt has received the full blast of modern man's scientific attention, but until recently salt has been available only in relatively tiny amounts: its historic importance has been a direct function of its rarity. Salt has never been thought of as motherly or bountiful like maize. On the contrary, its mythical character is habitually dry and sterile. Salt is clever and sly and hard to get; a little of it goes a very long way. It is a thing of fate and malediction, both necessary and absolutely irreplaceable.

'God has distributed His benefits in such a manner that there is no area on the earth so rich that it does not lack all sorts of goods,' wrote the French political theorist Jean Bodin in 1568. 'It appears that God did this in order to induce all the subjects of His Republic to entertain friendly relations with one another.' For many thousands of years human beings have longed for salt. Until one hundred years ago, salt was to be had only from great distances; at the cost of long, skilled, and watchful labour; or with the aid of enormous courage and technological expertise. Salt has forced man to explore, to think, to work, to travel. To obtain salt he has erected whole political and economic systems; he has fought, built, destroyed, extorted, and haggled.

Much Depends on Dinner, 1986

Diet and Digestion

·⧉·

The Diet of Pythagoras
PORPHYRY 253–306 AD

*Only a fragment of this work has survived, in which Porphyry gives
these details of the diet of Pythagoras. It was written some 800
years after the philosopher and mathematician died, so it is
impossible to say how reliable it is. Schools of Pythagoreanism
flourished throughout the ancient world, and most of them followed
a vegan diet, but this was not publicised, as such ideas were often
frowned upon by the authorities. In 600 BC the sacrifice of live
animals on the altar of the gods was commonplace: Pythagoras was
the first to eschew it. He believed in the theory of metempsychosis,
the transmigration of souls, which was his reason for not killing
animals, though here we see he ate some dairy products.*

Of his diet, the breakfast was honeycomb or honey, the dinner bread
of millet or barley and vegetables, whether boiled or raw. He would
eat only rarely of the flesh of sacrificial victims, and this not from every
part of the body. Generally, when he was about to descend into adyta
(shrines) of the gods and remain there for some time, he used foods
that would keep away hunger and thirst. That which would keep away
hunger he composed of poppy seed and sesame and the skin of a squill
(a herb) washed carefully until cleansed of the juice around it, and
flower stalks of asphodel, and leaves of mallow and barley groats and
barley corns and chick peas, all of which he chopped up in equal
quantities and soaked the choppings with honey from Hymettus. That
which would keep away thirst he made of cucumber seeds and juicy
raisins, from which he took out the seeds, and coriander flowers and
seed of mallow and purslane and cheese gratings and the finest wheat

meal and cream, all of which he mixed with honey from the islands. He said Hercules had learned these recipes from Demeter when he was sent into waterless Libya. . . . In sacrificing to the gods he practiced simplicity, propitiating them with barley groats and a cake and frankincense and myrtle, and occasionally with cocks and with the tenderest of pigs. He once sacrificed an ox, however (but according to the more accurate authorities, it was an ox made of dough), when he found the square of the hypotenuse of a right triangle equal to the sum of squares of the other sides.

Life of Pythagoras, quoted in *The Philosophy of Vegetarianism*,

D. A. Dombrowski, 1984

Plain Food

CLEMENT OF ALEXANDRIA 150–215 AD

One of the most important early Christian Fathers, a missionary theologian, apologist and polemicist, his surviving works are a trilogy: Protreptikos (Exhortation), Paedagogus *(The Instructor), Stromatos (Miscellanies). In the middle work he deals with diet, and was one of the first Christian writers to link gluttony with sin.*

'Some men live that they may eat, as the irrational beings "whose life is their belly and nothing else." But the Instructor enjoins us to eat that we may live. For neither is food our business, nor is pleasure our aim. Therefore discrimination is to be used in reference to food: it must be plain, truly simple, suiting precisely simple and artless children – as ministering to life not to luxury. And the life to which it conduces consists of two things, health and strength; to which plainness of fare is most suitable, being conducive both to digestion and lightness of body, from which come growth, and health, and right strength: not strength that is violent or dangerous, and wretched, as is that of the *athletes* which is produced by artificial feeding.

Paedagogus, TRANS. Rev. William Wilson, 1867

No Butcher's Meat

ADAM SMITH 1723–90

*The Scottish moral philosopher and political economist made
several shrewd comments on food.*

It may, indeed, be doubted whether butchers' meat is *anywhere* a
necessary of life. Grain and other vegetables, with the help of milk,
cheese, and butter, or oil (where butter is not to be had), it is known
from experience, can, *without any butchers' meat, afford the most
plentiful, the most wholesome, the most nourishing, and the most
invigorating diet.*

The Wealth of Nations, 1776

Regular, Constipated and Lax

JEAN-ANTHELME BRILLAT-SAVARIN 1755–1826

INFLUENCE OF DIGESTION

Of all corporeal operations, digestion is the one which has the most
powerful influence on the mental state of the individual.

Nobody should be surprised by this assertion, for it could not
possibly be otherwise.

The most elementary rules of psychology teach us that the mind can
only be impressed by means of its subject organs, which keep it in
touch with external things; whence it follows that, when those organs
are in poor condition, weak or inflamed, the deterioration inevitably
influences the sensations, which are the intermediary and occasional
means of intellectual activity.

Thus our accustomed manner of digesting, and particularly the
latter part of the process, makes us habitually sad or gay, silent or
talkative, morose or melancholy, without our being aware of it, and
above all without our being able to avoid it.

In this respect it would be possible to separate the civilized portion of mankind into three great divisions, namely, the regular, the constipated, and the lax.

The Philosopher in the Kitchen, TRANS. Anne Drayton, 1970

Diet and Digestion
DR JOHN DORAN 1807–78

'No digest of law's like the law of digestion.' – Moore

Our good neighbours the French, or rather, the philosophers among them, have asserted that the perfecting of man and his species depends upon attention to diet and digestion; and, in a material point of view, they are not far wrong; and, indeed, in a non-material point of view, it may be said that the spirit, without judgment, is very likely to be exposed to indigestion; and perhaps ignorance complete is to be preferred to an ill-digested erudition. With diet and patience, Walpole thought all the diseases of man might be easily cured. Montesquieu, on the other hand, held that health purchased by rigorously watching over diet, was but a tedious disease. But Walpole was nearly correct, while Montesquieu was not very distant from the truth. Dieting, like other things, must be undertaken on common-sense principles; for, though there be multitudes of mad people in the world, society generally is not to be put upon the *régime* of 'Bedlam.'

We live, not by what we eat, but by what we digest; and what one man may digest, another would die of attempting. Rules on this subject are almost useless. Each man may soon learn the powers of his stomach, in health or disease, in this respect; and this ascertained, he has no more business to bring on indigestion than he has to get intoxicated or fall into debt. He who offends on these three points, deserves to forfeit stomach, head, and his electoral franchise!

Generally speaking, fat and spices resist the digestive power; and too much nutritious food is the next evil to too little. Good cookery, by developing flavour, increases the nutritiousness of food, which bad cookery would perhaps render indigestible. Hence a good cook rises to the dignity of 'artist.' He may rank with the chemists, if not with the physicians.

Table Traits, 1854

Cakes are Unwholesome
THOMAS TRYON 1634–1703

Thomas Tryon wrote many books in his lifetime on diet and health. He influenced the playwright, Aphra Behn, and a work of his induced Benjamin Franklin to become vegetarian in his youth, though the phase only lasted some seven years. Tryon was first put to work by his father at the age of ten, spinning and carding, but he longed to be a shepherd and so tended a flock of sheep from the ages of eleven to eighteen, by which time he had taught himself to read and write. He then read the works of the German philosopher Behem and was persuaded to become a 'Pythagorean'. His books all preach the healthy life on a diet of grains, vegetables and fruits. Much of what he says strikes a highly contemporary note, as in this passage about sugary cakes.

'Observe the composition of cakes, which are frequently oaten and given especially to children as food; in them there are commonly flour, butter, eggs, milk, fruit, spice, sugar, salt, rosewater and sweetmeats as citron or the like; now here are ten ingredients which are of so many several natures and operations, but being intermixt all in one mass, the simple and natural virtues of all and each of them are destroyed and changed into another nature, so that the predominant quality of each of them suffers violence and loseth its natural power.'

The Way to Health and Love, Life and Happiness, 1683

Feed or Starve into Virtue
SYDNEY SMITH 1771–1845

TO ARTHUR KINGLAKE

Combe Florey, Sept. 30th, 1837

Dear Sir,
I am much obliged by the present of your brother's book. I am convinced digestion is the great secret of life; and that character,

talents, virtues, and qualities are powerfully affected by beef, mutton, pie-crust, and rich soups. I have often thought I could feed or starve men into many virtues and vices, and affect them more powerfully with my instruments of cookery than Timotheus could do formerly with his lyre. Ever yours, very truly,

SYDNEY SMITH

Selected Letters, ED. Nowell C. Smith, 1956

The Un-Fussy Diet of Dr Bigg
NOËL COWARD 1899–1973

Friday 15 July [1955]   Wisconsin
Yesterday was fairly restful except for the hydraulic drills which happily stopped at 4.30 p.m., having been going since 7.30 a.m. At about five o'clock I had a long talk to Dr Bigg. He lectured me firmly about my future health with emphasis on my 'nervous' stomach. He said nothing organic was wrong with me, except a slight curving of the spine which can be remedied or at least prevented from curving more by watching my posture and walking and sitting with more care, but that I must remember that I am fifty-five and not twenty-five, and live sensibly and moderately and *not* give myself so much to other people and their problems. He also said that I should create more and perform less and, for the rest of my life, drink as little alcohol as socially possible. He also told me not to be fussy about my diet, but to eat little and well. He specified that roughage was bad for my colon, which apparently is over-sensitive, like so many of my friends. He said that all the old wives' tales about cooked green vegetables being good for me was nonsense and that meat and fish, eggs, potatoes, bread and sugar were much better! He advised the latter in moderation on account of my figure. In fact he advised moderation in everything. We then got into a long discussion of morals and sex taboos and homosexuality, which convinced me that he is one of the wisest and most thoroughly sensible men I have ever met. I shall go to him once a year.

The Noël Coward Diaries, ED. Graham Payn and Sheridan Morley,

1982

How to Sit Out Every Man at the Table
WILLIAM HICKEY 1749–C.1830

The life of a rake, described with lively relish in William Hickey's memoirs, was expensive. He stole and squandered a small fortune from his long-suffering father who eventually packed him off to join the East India Company when he was nineteen, to remove him from temptations such as these. It was not a success.

The fact is, I always was ambitious of sitting out every man at the table where I presided; which by a little management I generally accomplished, eating sparingly of some one plain dish, avoiding malt liquor, and desiring the servants to take away my glass after a hob-nob the moment I put it down, by which means I was better enabled to do the duty of president when the cloth was removed; from which moment I never flinched, and contrived to send my guests away quite happy and contented. When, as was sometimes the case, I felt the wine disposed to revolt, chewing two or three French olives without swallowing the pulp would relieve and enable me to get down half a dozen more glasses. By these little fair manoeuvres I established the character of being a capital host.

Memoirs, ED. Peter Quennell, 1960

Gruel, Vermicelli and Sago
SYDNEY SMITH 1771–1845

TO LADY CARLISLE

56, Green-street, Oct. 1844

My dear Lady Carlisle,

From your ancient goodness to me, I am sure you will be glad to receive a bulletin from myself, informing you that I am making a good progress; in fact, I am in a regular train of promotion: from gruel, vermicelli, and sago, I was promoted to panada, from thence to minced meat, and (such is the effect of good conduct) I was elevated to a mutton-chop. My breathlessness and giddiness are gone – chased away by the gout. If you hear of sixteen or eighteen pounds of human flesh, they belong to me. I look as if a curate had been taken out of me. I am delighted to hear such improved accounts of my fellow-sufferer at Castle Howard. Lady Holland is severe in her medical questions; but I detail the most horrible symptoms, at which she takes flight.

Accept, my dear Lady Carlisle, my best wishes for Lord Carlisle and all the family –

SYDNEY SMITH
Selected Letters, ED. Nowell C. Smith, 1956

Uncle Davey's Red and White Meals
NANCY MITFORD 1904–73

'You shouldn't,' said Davey, 'read in trains, ever. It's madly wearing to the optic nerve centres, it imposes a most fearful strain. May I see the menu, please? I must explain that I'm on a new diet, one meal white, one meal red. It's doing me so much good. Oh, dear, what a pity. Sadie – oh, she's not listening – Logan, could I ask for an egg, very lightly boiled, you know. This is my white meal, and we are having saddle of mutton, I see.'

'Well, Davey, have your red meal now and your white meal for breakfast,' said Uncle Matthew. 'I've opened some Mouton Rothschild, and I know how much you like that – I opened it specially for you.'

'Oh, it is too bad,' said Davey, 'because I happen to know that there are kippers for breakfast, and I do so love them. What a ghastly decision. No! it must be an egg now, with a little hock. I could never forgo the kippers, so delicious, so digestible, but, above all, so full of proteins.'

'Kippers,' said Bob, 'are brown.'

'Brown counts as red. Surely you can see that.'

But when a chocolate cream, in generous supply, but never quite enough when the boys were at home, came round, it was seen to count as white. The Radletts often had cause to observe that you could never entirely rely upon Davey to refuse food, however unwholesome, if it was really delicious.

The Pursuit of Love, 1945

Food Fads

RICHARDSON WRIGHT 1887–1961

Horace Fletcher, the American inventor of Fletcherism, was said to have taught the world to chew via his book The A–B–Z of Our Own Nutrition, *published in 1903. He was an advocate of an almost meatless diet and prolonged mastication. He lived in a palazzo on the Grand Canal in Venice and celebrated his fiftieth birthday by making a 190-mile trip on his bicycle.*

Anyone who has lived to respectable middle age and has enjoyed his meals along the way, experimenting withal, cannot have escaped being exposed to food fads. There was the Nut Period and the Dried Fruit Era, and both of these we managed to survive by not indulging in them. But one of the darkest chapters in my boyhood opened when our father read about Fletcherizing. There we sat, two parents and their seven offspring ranging from five to nineteen, solemnly munching away and rebelling at every munch. Conversation, of course, was impossible till we finally swallowed what we had chewed forty times. Such aching jaws we had and such solemn-faced brats we must have been! Eventually Father grew tired of his newfound fad and the family table became normal again.

The Bed-Book of Eating and Drinking, 1943

Vegetarian Diet

GEORGE BERNARD SHAW 1856–1950

Mr Shaw's correspondents are reminded that current vegetarianism does not mean living wholly on vegetables. Vegetarians eat cheese, butter, honey, eggs, and, on occasion, cod liver oil.

On this diet, without tasting fish, flesh, or fowl, Mr Shaw has reached the age of 92 (1948) in as good condition as his meat eating contemporaries. It is beyond question that persons who have never from their birth been fed otherwise than as vegetarians are at no disadvantage, mentally, physically, nor in duration of life, with their carnivorous fellow-citizens.

Nevertheless Mr Shaw is of opinion that his diet included an excess of protein. Until he was seventy he accumulated some poison that exploded every month or six weeks in a headache that blew it off and left him quite well after disabling him for a day. He tried every available treatment to get rid of the headaches: all quite unsuccessful. He now makes uncooked vegetables, chopped or grated, and their juices, with fruit, the staple of his diet, and finds it markedly better than the old high protein diet of beans, lentils and macaroni.

His objection to carnivorous diet is partly aesthetic, partly hygienic, mainly as involving an unnecessary waste of the labor of masses of mankind in the nurture and slaughter of cattle, poultry, and fish for human food.

He has no objection to the slaughter of animals as such. He knows that if we do not kill animals they will kill us. Squirrels, foxes, rabbits, tigers, cobras, locusts, white ants, rats, mosquitoes, fleas, and deer must be continually slain even to extermination by vegetarians as ruthlessly as by meat eaters. But he urges humane killing and does not enjoy it as a sport.

Ayot Saint Lawrence,
Welwyn, Herts.

One of George Bernard Shaw's postcards (undated)

Black Honey Cure
ROBERT BYRON 1905–41

Ak Bulagh (c. 5500 ft), 20 October. Christopher was ill when he woke up, from the fleas. Seeing this, the steward brought him a cone of black honey and said that if he ate this for four days, at the same time abstaining from curds and rogand, the rancid butter in which everything is cooked, the fleas would avoid him as they do me. While we breakfasted by the fire off milk and eggs, a boy of some fourteen years old walked in attended by an old man and a train of servants. This, it appeared, was the squire, to whom we owed so much good food and attention, and the old man was his uncle. His name is

Mohammad Ali Khan, and our host of tonight describes him as 'the lord of all the villages'.

The Road to Oxiana, 1937

A Vindication of Natural Diet
PERCY BYSSHE SHELLEY 1792–1822

It is only by softening and disguising dead flesh by culinary preparation that it is rendered susceptible of mastication or digestion, and that the sight of its bloody juices and raw horror does not excite intolerable loathing and disgust. Let the advocate of animal food force himself to a decisive experiment on its fitness, and, as Plutarch recommends, tear a living lamb with his teeth, and, plunging his head into its vitals, slake his thirst with the steaming blood; when fresh from the deed of horror let him revert to the irresistible instincts of nature that would rise in judgment against it, and say, Nature formed me for such work as this. Then, and then only, would he be consistent . . .

Surely the bile-suffused cheek of Buonaparte, his wrinkled brow and yellow eye, the ceaseless inquietude of his nervous system, speak no less plainly the character of his unresting ambition than his murders and victories. It is impossible that had Buonaparte descended from a race of vegetable feeders that he could have had either the inclination or the power to ascend the throne of the Bourbons . . .

Seventeen persons of all ages (the families of Dr Lambe and Mr Newton) have lived for seven years on this diet [vegetables and pure water], without a death and almost without the slightest illness. Surely, when we consider that some of these were infants, and one a martyr to asthma now nearly subdued, we may challenge any seventeen persons taken at random in this city to exhibit a parallel case . . .

The quantity of nutritious vegetable matter consumed in fattening the carcase of an ox would afford ten times the sustenance, undepraving indeed, and incapable of generating disease, if gathered immediately from the bosom of the earth. The most fertile districts of the habitable globe are now actually cultivated by men for animals, at a delay and waste of aliment absolutely incapable of calculation. It is only the wealthy that can, to any great degree, even now, indulge the unnatural craving for dead flesh, and they pay for the greater licence of the privilege by subjection of supernumerary diseases . . .

The advantage of a reform in diet is obviously greater than that of any other. It strikes at the root of the evil . . .

The pleasures of taste to be derived from a dinner of potatoes, beans, peas, turnips, lettuce, with a dessert of apples, gooseberries, strawberries, currants, raspberries, and in winter, oranges, apples, and pears, is far greater than is supposed. Those who wait until they can eat this plain fare, with the sauce of appetite, will scarcely join with the hypocritical sensualist at a lord mayor's feast, who declaims against the pleasures of the table. Solomon kept a thousand concubines and owned in despair that all was vanity.

A Vindication of Natural Diet, 1813

Half of What You Could Eat and Drink
SYDNEY SMITH 1771–1845

TO J. A. MURRAY

Combe Florey, Sept. 29th 1843
You are, I hear, attending more to diet than heretofore. If you wish for anything like happiness in the fifth act of life, eat and drink about one-half what you *could* eat and drink. Did I ever tell you my calculation about eating and drinking? Having ascertained the weight of what I could live upon, so as to preserve health and strength, and what I did live upon, I found that, between ten and seventy years of age, I had eaten and drunk forty four-horse waggon-loads of meat and drink more than would have preserved me in life and health! The value of this mass of nourishment I considered to be worth seven thousands pounds sterling. It occurred to me that I must, by my voracity, have starved to death fully a hundred persons. This is a frightful calculation, but irresistably true; and I think, dear Murray, your waggons would require an additional horse each!

Selected Letters, ED. Nowell C. Smith, 1956

Scurvy
WILLIAM HICKEY 1749–1830

Smith (the surgeon) was grievously distressed at seeing the ravages made by the cruel distemper without having it in his power to prevent or alleviate the misfortune, though he made various experiments for that purpose. Wine, sugar, spruce, and every other anti-scorbutic procurable were abundantly supplied without material benefit . . .

The 1st February 1780, we struck soundings upon the Bank off Cape Lagullas, early the next morning saw the land; and, as it was then blowing very strong onshore, the two commanders determined to make for False Bay instead of rounding the Cape, as the most likely way to avoid any French cruisers. We accordingly (certainly at considerable risk) went close in under the land, running alongshore until four in the afternoon of the 2nd, at which hour we opened False Bay, stood directly in, and at six both ships came to an anchor. Our invalid, Smith [a midshipman], after we made the land, enquired every quarter of an hour with extreme earnestness when we should get in. About noon of the 2nd, he gave up all hopes, lay in the most melancholy state, uttering nothing but, 'Oh, fruit, fruit, or I die.' Soon after we anchored, a boat from the shore brought off a variety of fruits, vegetables, and refreshments. Everybody ran with the utmost anxiety to Smith's cot with fruit of all sorts. The doctor held a bunch of grapes to him, which the poor fellow (then speechless and entirely exhausted) by an effort raised to his lips, and with a deep groan expired. His death was sincerely lamented by all on board.

Memoirs, ED. Peter Quennell, 1960

The Mouth
DIANE ACKERMAN 1948–

We normally chew about a hundred times a minute. But, if we let something linger in our mouth, feel its texture, smell its bouquet, roll it around on the tongue, then chew it slowly so that we can hear its echoes, what we're really doing is savoring it, using several senses in a gustatory free-for-all. A food's flavor includes its texture, smell, temperature, color, and painfulness (as in spices), among many other features. Creatures of sound, we like some foods to titillate our hearing more than others. There's a gratifying crunch to a fresh carrot stick, a seductive sizzle to a broiling steak, a rumbling frenzy to soup coming to a boil, an arousing bunching and snapping to a bowl of breakfast cereal. 'Food engineers,' wizards of subtle persuasion, create products to assault as many of our senses as possible. Committees put a lot of thought into the design of fast foods.

Companies design potato chips to be too large to fit into the mouth, because in order to hear the high-frequency crackling you need to keep your mouth open. Chips are 80 percent air, and each time we bite one we break open the air-packed cells of the chip, making that noise we call 'crispy'. These are high-tech potato chips, of course. The original potato chip was invented in 1853 by George Crum, a chef at Moon Lake Lodge in Saratoga Springs, New York, who became so angry when a guest demanded thinner and thinner French fries that he sliced them laughably thin (he thought) and fried them until they were varnish-brown. The guest loved them, envious fellow guests requested them, word spread, and ultimately Crum started up his own restaurant, which specialized in potato chips.

The mouth is what keeps the prison of our bodies sealed up tight. Nothing enters for help or harm without passing through the mouth, which is why it was such an early development in evolution. Every slug, insect, and higher animal has a mouth. Even one-celled animals like paramecia have mouths, and the mouth appears immediately in human embryos. The mouth is more than just the beginning of the long pipeline to the anus: It's the door to the body, the place where we greet the world, the parlor of great risk. We use our mouths for other things – language, if we're human; drilling tree bark if we're a woodpecker; sucking blood if we're a mosquito – but the mouth mainly holds the tongue, a thick mucous slab of muscle, wearing minute cleats as if it were an athlete.

A Natural History of the Senses, 1990

Cooks and Cooking

◈

A Chef in Classical Greece
ATHENAEUS C. 200 AD

The great value of Athenaeus is that he has preserved many fragments of lost works. This monologue by a chef, Athenaeus tells us, is from a comedy by Sotades called Locked-up Women, *written around 350 BC.*

CHEF: First I took the shrimps: I fried them all in a skillet. A great dogfish has been given to me. I roasted the middle slices and boiled the inferior parts after making a mulberry sauce. I fetch two very big head sections of greyfish in a large casserole, lightly adding herbs, cummin, salt, water, and a little oil. After this I bought a really fine sea-bass which will be boiled in an oil and brine pickle with herbs, once I have served the meats roasted on spits. I purchased some fine red mullet and some fine wrasse: these I tossed on the charcoal without more ado, and to an oil and brine pickle I add origano. To these I added cuttle-fish and squid. Elegant is boiled squid stuffed with chopped meat and so are the tentacles gently roasted. To these I added a fresh sauce of many herbs. Afterwards came some boiled dishes with a sauce of vinegar and oil. On top of this I bought a really fat conger-eel which I smothered in a really nice fresh pickle. Some gobies and some rock-fish next: I nipped off their heads and smeared them with batter . . . by such a method I send them on the same journey as the shrimps. A widowed bonito, a really fine beast, I passed through just enough oil and then swaddled it in fig leaves, sprinkled it with origano and hid it like a firebrand in a heap of hot ashes. To go with it I got some Phalerum small fry. A gill of water poured over this is ample. I then cut up plenty of fine herbs, and even if the jug holds a quart, I empty it all. What remains? Nothing more. This is my art, and it doesn't come from books or notes.

Connoisseurs in Dining, TRANS. C. B. Gulick, 1987

Aunt Chloe

HARRIET BEECHER STOWE 1811–96

A cook she certainly was, in the very bone and centre of her soul. Not a chicken or turkey or duck in the barn-yard but looked grave when they saw her approaching, and seemed evidently to be reflecting on their latter end; and certain it was that she was always meditating on trussing, stuffing and roasting, to a degree that was calculated to inspire terror in any reflecting fowl living. Her corn-cake, in all its varieties of hoe-cake, dodgers, muffins, and other species too numerous to mention, was a sublime mystery to all less practised compounders; and she would shake her fat sides with honest pride and merriment, as she would narrate the fruitless efforts that one and another of her compeers had made to attain to her elevation.

The arrival of company at the house, the arrangement of dinners and suppers 'in style,' awoke all the energies of her soul; and no sight was more welcome to her than a pile of travelling trunks launched on the verandah, for then she foresaw fresh efforts and fresh triumphs . . .

'Yes,' said George, 'I says to him, "Tom, you ought to see some of Aunt Chloe's pies, they're the right sort," says I.'

'Pity, now, Tom couldn't,' said Aunt Chloe, on whose benevolent heart the idea of Tom's benighted condition seemed to make a strong impression. 'Ye oughter jest ask him here to dinner, some o'these times, Mas'r George,' she added; 'it would look quite pretty of ye. Ye know, Mas'r George, ye oughtenter feel 'bove nobody, on 'count yer privileges, 'cause all our privileges is gi'n to us, we ought al'ays to 'member that,' said Aunt Chloe, looking quite serious.

'Well, I mean to ask Tom here, some day next week,' said George; 'and you do your prettiest, Aunt Chloe, and we'll make him stare. Won't we make him eat so he won't get over it for a fortnight?'

'Yes, yes, – sartin,' said Aunt Chloe, delighted; 'you'll see. Lor! to think of some of our dinners! Yer mind dat ar great chicken-pie I made when we guv de dinner to General Knox? I and missis, we come pretty near quarrelling about dat ar crust. What does get into ladies sometimes, I don't know; but, sometimes, when a body had de heaviest kind o' 'sponsibility on 'em, as ye may say, and is all kinder "*seris*" and taken up, dey takes dat ar time to be hangin' round and kinder interferin'! Now, missis, she wanted me to do dis way, and she wanted me to do dat way; and, finally, I got kinder sarcy, and says I, "Now, missis, do jist look at dem beautiful white hands o'yourn, with long fingers, and all sparkling with rings, like my white lilies when de dew's on 'em; and look at my great black stumpin' hands. Now don't ye think that de Lord must have meant *me* to make de pie-crust, and you to stay in de parlour?" Dar! I was jist so sarcy, Mas'r George.'

'And what did mother say?' said George.

'Say? why, she kinder larfed in her eyes – dem great handsome eyes o'hern; and says she, "Well, Aunt Cloe, I think you are about in the right on 't," says she; and she went off in de parlour. She oughter cracked me over de head for bein' so sarcy; but dar's whar't is, I can't do nothin' with ladies in de kitchen!'

'Well, you made out well with that dinner; I remember everybody said so,' said George.

'Didn't I? And wan't I behind de dinin'-room door dat bery day? and didn't I see de Gineral pass his plate three times for some more dat bery pir? – and says he, "You must have an uncommon cook, Mrs. Shelby." Lor! I was fit to split myself.

'And de Gineral, he knows what cookin' is,' said Aunt Chloe, drawing herself up with an air. 'Bery nice man, de Gineral! He comes of one of de bery *fustest* familes in Old Virginny! He knows what's what, now, as well as I do – de Gineral. Ye see, there's *pints* in all pies, Mas'r George; but tan't everybody knows what they is, or orter be. But the Gineral, he knows; I knew by his 'marks he made. Yes, he knows what de pints is!'

Uncle Tom's Cabin, 1848

High Dudgeon
RICHARDSON WRIGHT 1887–1961

Rev. Remsen B. Ogilby, president of Trinity College, assures me that he was one of the charter members of the Cook-of-the-Month Club, and that not until he was well past fourteen did he know that 'high dudgeon' wasn't a high-wheeled vehicle in which cooks departed.

The Bed-Book of Eating and Drinking, 1943

·Mrs Jelinek

HAROLD ACTON 1904–

Since there was little choice we had to take what cooks were available. A drunken Irishwoman was the most capable of them. I had heard that before employing a cook in England one should ask her if she drank: if she denied it she would not be worth considering, for alcohol is wont to supply the defects of imagination and technique. But this Irishwoman overdid it from the start. I forgot to ask her if she had been a friend of James Joyce, but I think she must have been: much of her talk was recognizable in his *Anna Livia Plurabelle* – the flowing of the Liffey with a potent current of poteen as a chaser. She poured increasing doses of sherry into the soup: every dish was alcoholized by progressive degrees. Brandy cherries and pineapples with kirsch are delectable variations, but she drowned every other sweet in brandy or kirsch: sometimes she mixed them and would add a dash of whisky or maraschino. In the meantime her Irish keening would reach the dining-room, a never-ending wail: it was a sound that might have soothed the ears of Yeats but that filled mine with dull dismay and terrified Pasqualino, as it was usually followed by breakages and knife-throwings. When we were about to complain of her caprices, she would disarm us with a gift of beautiful roses. But there was little peace in the house while she remained. We resolved to rid ourselves of her, after submitting to Banshee howlings which culminated in an attack of delirium tremens. Often did I lament Chong Sung, for his ancient civilization had evolved a sublime gastrology which can satisfy the appetite and appeal to the intellect as well. He was happily free, moreover, from any neurosis.

After our Irishwoman, the *proxime accessit* was Mrs. Jelinek, a Czech. Her cooking was rich in literary associations, reminding me forcibly of Apollinaire's Doctor Merrytart. One could never guess what culinary tragedies or comedies were in store for one, and approached each meal with a certain trepidation. Her hors-d'oeuvre had a distinctly sinister aspect and her soups could be most unsettling.

Her vegetables were calculated to give you a vague feeling of impending doom: lurid egg-plant, depressing parsnips or lugubrious potato salad besprinkled with bleeding red cabbage, just like Doctor Merrytart's dinners. But her jocular moods were equally droll. Her version of *minestrone* was a parody of the original: an altogether foreign conception of Italy, derived from opera as played by organ-grinders, had entered into it. The basis was vermicelli of inordinate length, and curious trailing weeds and frivolous parsley were added with floating particles of scrambled egg. Her savouries were obviously designed to give one the giggles: I remember certain cheese tartlets and arrangements of mushrooms and curly bacon which one simply had to laugh at: their appearance, smell and texture were excruciatingly funny if one really examined them.

Sometimes we were without a cook for days together, when my brother and Pasqualino would concoct appetizing Italian dishes, especially *tortini* of onions and artichokes. Often the temptation to dine out was overwhelming, and once one acquires that habit it is like a drug. Eventually my existence, apart from the Last Medici, was almost a procession of dinners, at which I became a spectator of other people's ambitions, intrigues and animosities.

Memoirs of an Aesthete, 1948

How to Interview a Cook
RUTH LOWINSKY d. 1958

A most difficult task is to find just the cook one is looking for. Most of us have some drawback from the cook's point of view, such as too large or too small a kitchen – either is an unsuperable difficulty – or too large a nursery. How often have I been told 'Well, madam, if you had *one* little boy, I might have tried your place.' I have always pointed out that, had the cook and I met each other earlier, something might have been done, but, with four already in the nursery . . .

It never pays even to interview the 'good plains,' and very seldom the chef-trained or 'equal to chef.' The first think that, as they call themselves plain cooks, they are entitled to boil everything and to serve it with a garnish of water. Any sweet above a trifle – there is nothing below – has no place in their repertoire.

On the other hand, the chef-trained cook is quite unable either to roast or to grill meat, though she can send up the most marvellous looking mousses. It is only by their position on the menu and the fact that they taste vaguely of sugar or salt that you know whether they be made of lobsters or of strawberries. Remember that food is not a 'still life,' but made to be eaten. Never correspond with a cook – see her, and then ask for her idea of a good menu for a dinner party. If she suggests as an inspiration that it should start with grapefruit, then goes on to consommé à la royal, a nice sole, and a bird, you can stop her before she proceeds to the inevitable meringues and sardines on toast. Give her up as hopeless and renew your quest.

Two very good test questions are: 'What ices do you know?' and 'Can you make a vol-au-vent?' You will be surprised to find how these two simple questions reduce the number of possible cooks.

Beware the cook who calls any chicken which is neither roasted nor boiled 'done up'! . . .

As a final word of advice, do not be surprised if, when you have praised a certain dish, your cook suggests it for every meal for the next fortnight. Go on praising her – but remember that food must above all things be varied, surprising and original.

Lovely Food, 1931

Françoise
MARCEL PROUST 1871–1922

But – and this more than ever from the day on which fine weather definitely set in at Combray – the proud hour of noon, descending from the steeple of Saint-Hilaire which it blazoned for a moment with the twelve points of its sonorous crown, would long have echoed about our table, beside the 'holy bread', which too had come in, after church, in its familiar way; and we would still be found seated in front of our Arabian Night plates, weighed down by the heat of the day, and even more by our heavy meal. For upon the permanent foundation of eggs, cutlets, potatoes, preserves, and biscuits, whose appearance on the table she no longer announced to us, Françoise would add – as the labour of fields and orchards, the harvest of the tides, the luck of the markets, the kindness of neighbours, and her own genius might provide; and so effectively that our bill of fare, like the quatrefoils that were carved on the porches of cathedrals in the thirteenth century, reflected to some extent the march of the seasons and the incidents of human life – a brill, because the fish-woman had guaranteed its freshness; a turkey, because she had seen a beauty in the market at Roussainville-le-Pin; cardoons with marrow, because she had never done them for us in that way before; a roast leg of mutton, because the fresh air made one hungry and there would be plenty of time for it to 'settle down' in the seven hours before dinner; spinach, by way of a change; apricots, because they were still hard to get; gooseberries, because in another fortnight there would be none left; raspberries, which Mr Swann had bought specially, cherries, the first to come from the cherry-tree, which had yielded none for the last two years; a cream cheese of which in those days I was extremely fond; an almond cake, because she had ordered one the evening before; a fancy loaf, because it was our turn to 'offer' the holy bread. And when all these had been eaten, a work composed expressly for ourselves, but dedicated more particularly to my father, who had a fondness for such things, a cream of chocolate, inspired in the mind, created by the hand of Françoise would be laid before us, light and fleeting as an 'occasional piece' of music, into which she had poured the whole of her talent. Anyone who refused to partake of it, saying: 'No, thank you, I have finished; I am not hungry,' would at once have been lowered to the level of the Philistines who, when an artist makes them a present of one of his works, examine its weight and material, whereas what is of value is the creator's intention and his signature. To have left even the tiniest morsel in the dish would have shown as much discourtesy as to rise and leave a concert hall while the 'piece' was still being played, and under the composer's very eyes.

Swann's Way, TRANS. C. K. Scott-Moncrieff, 1928

Ratatouille

DOUGLAS DUNN 1942–

I

Consider, please, this dish of ratatouille.
Neither will it invade Afghanistan
Or boycott the Olympic Games in a huff.
It likes the paintings of Raoul Dufy.

213

It feeds the playboy and the working-man.
Of wine and sun it cannot get enough.
It has no enemies, no, not even
Salade niçoise or phoney recipes,
Not Leonid Brezhnev, no, not Ronald Reagan.
It is the fruits of earth, this ratatouille,
And it has many friends, including me.
Come, lovers of ratatouille, and unite!

II

It is a sort of dream, which coincides
With the pacific relaxations called
Preferred Reality. Men who forget
Lovingly chopped-up cloves of *ail*, who scorn
The job of slicing two good peppers thinly,
Then two large onions and six aubergines –
Those long, impassioned and imperial purples –
Which, with six courgettes, you sift with salt
And cover with a plate for one round hour;
Or men who do not care to know about
The eight ripe *pommes d'amour* their wives have need of,
Preparing ratatouille, who give no thought to
The cup of olive oil that's heated in
Their heaviest pan, or onions, fried with garlic
For five observant minutes, before they add
Aubergines, courgettes, peppers, tomatoes;
Or men who give no thought to what their wives
Are thinking as they stand beside their stoves
When seasoning is sprinkled on, before
A *bouquet garni* is dropped in – these men
Invade Afghanistan, boycott the Games,
Call off their fixtures and prepare for war.

III

Cook for one hour, and then serve hot or cold.
Eat it, for preference, under the sun,
But, if you are Northern, you may eat
Your ratatouille imagining Provence.
Believe me, it goes well with everything,
As love does, as peace does, as summers do

Or any other season, as a lifetime does.
Acquire, then, for yourselves, ingredients;
Prepare this stew of love, and ask for more.
Quick, before it is too late. *Bon appétit*!

Saint Kilda's Parliament, 1981

Cooks in Mexico
MME CALDERÓN DE LA BARCA 1804–82

As for taking a woman-cook in Mexico, one must have strong nerves
and a good appetite to eat what she dresses, however palatable, after
having seen her. One look at her flowing locks, one glance at her
reboso, *et c'est fini*. And yet the Mexican servants have their good
qualities, and are a thousand times preferable to the foreign servants
one finds in Mexico; especially the French. Bringing them with you is a
dangerous experiment. In ten days they begin to fancy themselves
ladies and gentlemen – the men have *Don* tacked to their name; and
they either marry and set up shops, or become unbearably insolent. A
tolerable French cook may occasionally be had, but you must pay his
services their weight in gold, and wink at his extortions and robberies.
There are one or two French *restaurants*, who will send you in a very
good dinner at an extravagant price: and it is common in foreign
houses, especially amongst the English, to adopt this plan whenever
they give a large entertainment . . .

I have lately been engaged in search of a *cook*, with as much
pertinacity as Japhet in search of his father, and with as little success as
he had in his preliminary inquiries. One, a Frenchman, I found out had
been tried for murder – another was said to be deranged – a third, who
announced himself as the greatest *artiste* who had yet condescended to
visit Mexico, demanded a salary which he considered suitable to his
abilities. I tried a female Mexican, in spite of her flowing hair. She
seemed a decent woman and tolerable cook; and, although our French
housekeeper and prime minister had deserted us at our utmost need,
we ventured to leave the house, and to spend the day at Tacubaya. On
our return, found the whole establishment unable to stand! Cook tipsy
– soldiers ditto – galopine slightly intoxicated – in short, the house
taking care of itself – no *standing force* but the coachman and
footman, who have been with us some time, and appear to be excellent

servants. I am, however, promised a good Mexican housekeeper, and trust that some order will be established under her government; also, a Chinese cook, with a *celestial* character . . .

Life in Mexico, 1843

Social Position
JEAN-PAUL ARON 1925–88

Social position. Since their very existence was born out of the fall of the aristocracy, restaurant cooks – and, by analogy, those in bourgeois households – enjoy an unrivalled prestige. They play an outstanding role in Parisian mythology. They preside over social life, love affairs, business; their elegant settings lend wings to the imagination. The memory of the pioneers hovers over the dinner tables throughout the entire century. If they had failed in their task in 1815, what would have become of France, for was not Alexandre I won over by Carême? At Carême's death, men clamour to pay their respects. Talleyrand writes: 'It will take a hundred years to find another Carême.' Mlle Carême receives three hundred letters of condolence. Magny and Brébant speak to Sainte-Beuve, the Goncourts, Flaubert, Zola and Renan as to equals. One scarcely dares approach Dugléré. Bignon treats notables in cavalier fashion, Catcomb shows them the door at the slightest sign of trouble. However, about 1890–1900, this esteem begins to wane. Democracy, new techniques, gas, electricity, the overpopulation of Paris, the multiplicity and the general levelling-down of restaurants brings in its train a deconsecration of the highest. The masters are still respected but the cook is no longer shielded by his legend: 'We have come to be regarded as labourers, who are sent for when needed and dismissed with thanks when the whim has passed.' And so, at the height of the egalitarian Republic, one sees the true artists, whom the merchants of the nineteenth century had treated as distinguished men, begin the surreptitious slide into domesticity.

The Art of Eating in France, TRANS. Nina Rootes, 1975

Elsie and the Piece of Steak

ARNOLD BENNETT 1867–1931

When she reached her kitchen with the remains of tea, the steak was to her a sacrosanct object. Even the fragment of it was a sacrosanct object; she put the fragment with her fingers on the same plate as the steak, and then she licked her fingers – not a very wise action – and proceeded to wash up. She was still full of remorse for the theft – yes it was a theft! – of the egg. That incident was to be a lesson to her; it was to teach her the lamentable weakness of her character. Never again would she fall into sin. Absurd to fancy that she did not have enough to eat at Riceyman Steps, and that she was continually hungry! She had more to eat, and more regularly, than many persons in her experience. Appetite was a sign of good health, and she ought to be thankful for good health; good health was a blessing. She ought not to be greedy, and above all she ought not to seek to excuse her greed by false excuses about appetite and lack of food. She continued calmly with her washing up.

The steak, during its cooking, had caused her a lot of inconvenience; the smell of it had awakened desires which she had had difficulty in withstanding; it had made her mouth water abundantly; and she had been very thankful to get the steak safely into the dining-room without any accident happening to it. But now the steak did not challenge her weakness. Resolution had triumphed over the steak. Her too active and ingenious mind became, however, entangled in the conception of the tiny fragment lying by the steak itself. She examined the fragment. A mouthful; no more! In the morning it would be dried up and shrunk to nothing. It would be wasted. She picked up the fragment out of curiosity, just to see exactly what it was like, and in an instant the fragment had vanished. The fragment did not seem to go into her stomach; it subdivided itself into a thousand parts, which ran through all her veins like fire, more potent than brandy, more dreadfully inspiring than champagne.

From this moment the steak was turned into a basilisk, with a devilish, sinister fascination for her. She ceased to wash up. She was saddened by the domestic infelicity of her employer; she was cast down and needed a tonic. She felt that without some pick-me-up she could not bear the vast grief of the world. She went through the agonies of the resisting drunkard dragged by ruthless craving nearer and nearer to the edge of the fatal precipice. Would her employers themselves eat the steak on the morrow? Very probably not. Very probably Mrs Earlforward on the morrow would authorize her, Elsie, to eat the steak. If she might eat it to-morrow she might eat it tonight. What difference to her employers whether she ate it to-morrow or to-night? Moreover, if Mrs Earlforward had not been upset she would quite possibly have given Elsie express permission to eat the steak. Elsie began to feel her self-respect slipping away, her honour slipping away, all rightmindedness slipping away, under the basilisk's stare of the steak. A few minutes later she knocked at the bedroom door, and, receiving no answer, went in. The room was dark, but she could distinguish the form of Mrs Earlforward in the bed.

'What is it? What is it?' demanded a weak, querulous mournful voice.

Mrs Earlforward vaguely extended her hand, and it touched something which for several seconds she could not identify. It touched Elsie's cap. Elsie had sunk to her knees by the bedside. She burst into weeping.

'Oh, 'm!' sobbed Elsie. 'Oh, 'm! I've gone and eaten the steak. I don't know what made me do it, 'm, but I've eaten the steak and I run straight in to tell you, 'm.'

Riceyman Steps, 1923

French Chefs

THEODORE ZELDIN 1933–

The cuisine of France has been created not just by cooks, but by gastronomes who have produced a whole literature out of their discussion of their meals; they have often been professional men, bankers, lawyers, doctors, priests, for whom eating has been their main hobby; the most dedicated have been bachelors who know no other love. Puritanism and modesty are incompatible with whole-hearted gastronomy, which is unashamedly dedicated to the enjoyment of sensuality, to the subtle analysis of man's appetites and to delight in their satisfaction. The restaurant has played an essential part in the creation of French cooking, because it has stimulated it by constant public discussion and competition. The great chefs are, therefore, 'inspired' not only by the food they find in the market, but also by their relations with their clientele; they come into the dining room after the meal to see the results. Charles Barrier, the three-star chef of Tours, says, 'When I cook, I imagine the pleasure I am going to give to someone – seeking pleasure for oneself is just masturbation.' Alain Chapel insists that he needs a response from his customer; he likes to meet every guest as they arrive so that each dish is perfect for each individual who eats it; cooking for him is 'an act of love'; since monotony is the great threat, he gets most pleasure from cooking dishes that are specially requested. His conclusion is that of an artist: 'What matters is that I should evolve and search for my truth.' He condemns all attempts to turn cooking into snobbery; he refuses to offer 'elaborate food'. The simplicity of the artist, however, is inevitably revealed as elaborate when it is analysed; and it is seldom capable of being imitated. That is why one is so often disappointed in restaurants. Genius cannot be consistent, and routine is its great enemy.

The French, 1983

Chong Sung

HAROLD ACTON 1904–

My quick-lunch lounge meals were squalid after the cooking of the Quai Bourbon, but Robert's company helped me to forget what I was eating. When I found a flat at number five, John Street, Adelphi, I also decided to find a Chinese cook. After various inquiries I went to the Chinese Labour Club in Goodge Street, a basement which must have been unique in that quarter, seething with activity in a placid minor key. I blinked, fascinated by the restful choreographic arrangement of the scene before me, the groups of polished ivory faces in the crepuscular light. One party of Chinese sailors were playing chess, some were dandling benevolent babies on their laps, others were smoking long pipes intent on the latest newspapers from home, and a cheerful tune was wafted from a two-stringed fiddle above the sing-song talk. Graceful cups were replenished with green tea. Hardly anyone could speak English, but I managed to make myself intelligible, and a little man in a Homburg hat too big for him poured me a cup of tea and suggested coming to cook for me there and then. He had a smooth serious face, bristly black hair and a pleasing expression of intelligence. Apart from the hat crushed over his ears he was neatly dressed, in blue serge with two fountain pens displayed in his breast pocket. He had a mere handful of English, which he had picked up in the Chinese restaurant at Wembley; he was a Cantonese by birth and his name was Chong Sung. The question of his wages settled, he accompanied me to my flat and drew up a list of necessities which he set off at once to procure.

Father Christmas could not have surprised me more than Chong Sung on his return. He was loaded with packages which he proceeded to unravel one by one, a handsome teapot in a silk-padded container of woven bamboo, innumerable bowls, cups, saucers, porcelain spoons of charming design, a lacquered canister of tea, cumquats, a pot of ginger, and myriads of smaller parcels of rice, vermicelli, ly-chees, mushrooms and other dainties like precious herbal and geological specimens. To my untutored eye the bill appeared an elegant sample of calligraphy, brushed on an oblong sheet of rice-paper. While I was lost in contemplation of this array, Chong Sung reappeared from the kitchen with fresh-made tea, pale green. How wise I had been, how wise! I thought to myself. But had I been a serious novelist I would have engaged the Cockney slut who had 'done' for my predecessor, to study her character and note her tricks of speech. Bit by bit I would have inveigled her into intimate confessions, and having steeped myself in the Goncourts, I would have compiled another *Esther Waters*. But I was not a serious novelist, I was a poet. And Chong Sung was a perfect minister to my Muse.

Each meal excelled the last in delicate flavours. I banished European impediments and ate with chopsticks. Besides cooking and catering for me, Chong Sung was my valet. In his quiet way he wished to educate me. He was anxious for me to understand his country and since he could not converse with so restricted a vocabulary, he brought me papers and pamphlets that had been issued in English for propaganda by the Kuomintang party. For the first time I read about Dr. Sun Yat-sen and his programme of national reconstruction.

Except *Humdrum* my worries dwindled. I was seldom tempted to dine out. On the other hand I could tempt few friends to dinner. They associated Chinese food with snakes and scorpions, and more than one kind lady was concerned about my health. But I grew plumper. The green tea I drank at all hours cleared my brain and induced a greater serenity. I was half in China, and as time went on I wished to be wholly in China. For if one Chinese could render existence so agreeable, what couldn't some four hundred millions do?

Memoirs of an Aesthete, 1948

Tests for Cooks
RICHARDSON WRIGHT 1887–1961

Tests for Cooks. Each housewife has her own test for a new cook – she must make impeccable mayonnaise or feather-light pastry or never suffer a soufflé to fall. For my own taste I would try her on beefsteak and kidney pie. In fact, I would make her jump all the meat hurdles – a steak properly broiled, lamb roasted to the exact pinkness, beef neither raw nor incinerated. To me the one unforgivable sin against the gods of good eating is to spoil meat. Mayonnaise is a necessity, slim and flaky pastry I enjoy and praise to the skies, the soufflé may fall because guests are laggard in their eating. These are trifles, but a spoiled roast throws me into a towering temper.

The Bed-Book of Eating and Drinking, 1943

Invitations to Dinner
WILLIAM KITCHINER 1775?–1827

It is a common fault with *Cooks who are anxious about Time, to overdress every thing* – the Guests had better wait than the Dinner – a little delay will improve Appetite; but if the Dinner waits for the Guests, it will be deteriorated every minute: – The Host who wishes to entertain his friends with food perfectly well dressed, while he most earnestly endeavours to impress on their minds the importance of being punctual to the appointed hour, – will still allow his Cook a quarter of an hour's grace.

The Cook's Oracle, 1831

Keep to Your Own Rooms
ANON

When you dine out, if you have the opportunity of speaking to the cook and if she deserves it, compliment her on her cooking. She will be grateful and it is only right to think of the person who has prepared your meal.

When you are at home, unless you have a good excuse, unless you propose to help, never enter the kitchen.

The cook is in her own domain there. You will look as if you were spying on her, or, still worse, meddling in what only concerns her. She does not allow herself to sit down in a chair in the drawing-room or to come to your study. Keep to your own rooms, each of you.

Never invite anybody by chance, or bring home a friend you meet in the street.

You may, on that particular day, put your servant in a most awkward position. Or, if you allow yourself to do such things, always bring with you a *pâté* and some dessert.

You cannot battle against a cook; the victory would be hers from the start.

Clarisse or The Old Cook, 1926

Pastry-cooks and Cookshops
LOUIS-SÉBASTIEN MERCIER 1740–1814

Pastry-cooks, pork-butchers and cookshops catch the eye on all sides. Their sign-board is the thing itself. You see rolled tongues, hams encircled with bay leaves, plump chickens, rosy pâtés, and sugar-covered cakes all lying before you: you have but to put out your hand and take them; even if you have no appetite you may well do so, if, as according to Boërhaave, the food you prefer has an influence on the juices of the stomach. If at seventeen one prefers the pretty young women in the milliners' shops, at the age of eight or ten one's eyes are fixed on the pastry-cook's.

When Saint Louis regulated the Statutes of pastry-cooks in the month of May, A.D., 1270, he confirmed the old custom then prevalent of working on all holidays without any distinction, for feasts and junketings usually take place on Sundays and Saints' days, and from time immemorial Saint Martin's Eve, Twelfth Night, and many other Patron Saints' days have been celebrated by different banquets.

That is the case now; pastry-cooks are far busier on Sundays and holidays than at any other times. On these days the oven is alight from morning to evening, and the scullions are far more exhausted when they go to bed than on any other night in the week.

The cookshops are sold out and there is not a chicken left.

Modest households who have only one fireplace send their meat to be cooked in the pastry-cook's oven. Fifty suppers cook in the one oven. The cook with his larding pin extracts the gravy from the leg or shoulder of mutton, or from a sirloin; but it is not wasted, he sells it back to you again in small pasties which taste all the better for it. You pay two *sous* for the cooking of these dishes; the modest householder thus saves ten *sous* in wood and his roast is dry, blackened, and nearly always burnt.

Round about nine o'clock in the evening, you may see, or rather smell, the roast meats being carried forth in their covered dishes. Dirty scullions leave the platters at the street corners, spill the sauce, and the piping hot dish reaches you all cold.

It is always agreeable to have a good chicken or capon at hand, which only awaits your signal to be placed on the spit and thence on your table. By this method the friend who comes to call on you is never in the way. You welcome him without embarrassment. There are wretched countries where even by paying in gold you get neither fowl nor succulent pastry, but in Paris 1200 cooks are always at your disposal; you are served in the wink of an eye, nothing could be more convenient nor more fitting to strengthen the fond ties of friendship, for no sooner is the tablecloth laid than the dishes are spread, and appetite smiles on friendship.

The Picture of Paris, TRANS. Wilfred and Emilie Jackson, 1929

A Knowledge of Housemaids
LADY CLODAGH ANSON 1879–1957

When we were older and did the housekeeping he used to break our
hearts sometimes by looking down the menu at dinner and then saying
to the butler in a resigned voice, 'Order two poached eggs for me,
please,' which we looked on as a frightful slam on our choice of foods.
One night the housekeeper came rushing into his sitting-room to say
that one of the housemaids had got hysterics and was lying on her back
unconscious. He went down to the servants' quarters with the butler
carrying his chair, as he could not walk more than a short way at a
time; when he got to the housemaid's room he suggested that the
housekeeper should put a mustard plaster over the invalid's heart,
which drastic remedy brought her to with a shriek. Granny Beaufort,
who was staying with us at Curraghmore at the time, was very
shocked about it. She said that he ought not to have known that there
were such things as housemaids! – which seemed rather an old-
fashioned idea to us.

Another Book, 1937

Carême Dinner
LADY MORGAN 1776?–1859

*Lady Morgan, born Sydney Owenson in Dublin, was a novelist as
well as a travel writer. O'Donnel, published in 1814, was admired
by Maria Edgeworth, Mary Russell Mitford and Sir Walter Scott.
She wrote two books on life in France in 1817 and 1829, and
published another on Italy in 1821.*

We happened to have with us two noted Amphitryons, (English and
French,) when a dinner invitation from Monsieur et Madame de
Rothschild was brought in by the servant. '*Quel bonheur*,' exclaimed
my French friend, as I read aloud. 'You are going to dine at the first
table in France; – in Europe. You are going to judge, from your own
personal experience, of the genius of Carême.'

'In England,' said my British Apicius, 'I remember immense prices being given for his second-hand *pâtés*, after they had made their appearance at the Regent's table.'

Anecdotes beyond number were then given of the pomps and vanities of the life of Carême; the number of the aids attached to his staff; his box at the opera, and other proofs of sumptuosity and taste, which, whether true or false, were very amusing; and increased my desire to make the acquaintance, through his 'œuvres complettes,' of a man who was at the head of his class . . .

To do justice to the science and research of a dinner so served, would require a knowledge of the art equal to that which produced it. Its character, however, was, that it was in season, that it was up to its time, that it was in the spirit of the age, that there was no *perruque* in its composition, no trace of the wisdom of our ancestors in a single dish; no high-spiced sauces, no dark-brown gravies, no flavour of cayenne and allspice, no tincture of catsup and walnut pickle, no visible agency of those vulgar elements of cooking, of the good old times, fire and water. Distillations of the most delicate viands, extracted in 'silver dews,' with chemical precision,

'On tepid clouds of rising steam,'

formed the *fond* of all. Every meat presented its own natural aroma; every vegetable its own shade of verdure. The *mayonese* was fried in ice, (like Ninon's description of Sévigné's heart,) and the tempered chill of the *plombière* (which held the place of the eternal *fondu* and *soufflets* of our English tables) anticipated the stronger shock, and broke it, of the exquisite *avalanche*, which, with the hue and odour of fresh gathered nectarines, satisfied every sense, and dissipated every coarser flavour.

With less genius than went to the composition of this dinner, men have written epic poems; and if crowns were distributed to cooks, as to actors, the wreath of Pasta or Sontag, (divine as *they* are,) were never more fairly won than the laurel which should have graced the brow of Carême, for this specimen of the intellectual perfection of an art, the standard and gauge of modern civilization! On good cookery, depends good health; on good health, depends the permanence of a good organization; and on these, the whole excellence in the structure of human society. Cruelty, violence, and barbarism, were the characteristics of the men who fed upon the tough fibres of half-dressed oxen. Humanity, knowledge, and refinement belong to the living generation, whose tastes and temperance are regulated by the science of such philosophers as Carême, and such amphitryons as his employers.

As I was seated next to Monsieur Rothschild, I took occasion to insinuate, after the soup, (for who would utter a word before?) that I was not wholly unworthy of a place at a table served by Carême; that I was already acquainted with the merits of the man who had first declared against '*la cuisine epicée et aromatisée;*' and that though I had been accused of a tendency towards the *bonnet rouge*, my true vocation was the *bonnet blanc*. I had, I said, long *gouté les ouvrages de Monsieur Carême* theoretically; and that now a practical acquaintance with them, filled me with a still higher admiration for his unrivalled talents.

'*Eh! bien,*' said Monsieur Rothschild, laughing, 'he, on his side, has also relished your works; and here is a proof of it.'

I really blush, like Sterne's accusing spirit, as I give in the fact: but he pointed to a column of the most ingenious confectionary architecture, on which my name was inscribed in spun sugar. *My* name written in sugar! Ye Quarterlies and Blackwoods, and *tu Brute*, false and faithless Westminster! – ye who have never traced my proscribed name but in gall, – think of 'Lady Morgan' in sugar; and that, too, at a table surrounded by some of the great supporters of the holy alliance! – *je n'en revenais pas!*

All I could do, under my triumphant emotion, I did. I begged to be introduced to the celebrated and flattering artist, and promised, should I ever again trouble the public with my idleness, to devote a tributary page to his genius, and to my sense of his merits, literary and culinary. Carême was sent for after coffee, and was presented to me, in the vestibule of the chateau, by his master. He was a well-bred gentlemen, perfectly free from pedantry, and, when we had mutually complimented each other on our respective works, he bowed himself out, and got into his carriage, which was waiting to take him to Paris.

Lady Morgan in France, ED. Elizabeth Sudderby
and P. J. Yarrow, 1971

Mrs Powell

OSBERT SITWELL 1892–1969

In the morning, she would go out, for she liked to do her own shopping. Just as, herself an artist in her own profession, she had, as I have said, esthetic feelings, so that in later years she was the only person who warned me not to sell a magnificent picture by Modigliani which hung in my London house, and she could understand also the full scope of the masterpiece Arthur Waley had created in his great translation of Lady Murasaki's novel, *The Tale of Genji*, so, too, she found a pleasure, comparable to the gratification that can be provided by pictures or books, in the material of food, and when she came in would greet one with such words as, 'I saw the loveliest piece of turbot in the King's Road: a really *lovely* thing' or 'They've a *beautiful* saddle of lamb at Bowen's, sir, I wish you'd go and see it'. And the phrases she used, after this style, were perfectly sincere, the meaning to be accepted literally. She loved her art and was expert at it. In illustration of this, it is no less indicative of Mrs. Powell's nature than of Mrs. Greville's special understanding of character, that towards the end of Mrs. Powell's life, when she had made a transient recovery from a severe illness and operation, and when Mrs. Greville wished, because of what my housekeeper had been through, to show her kindness of a sort that would really appeal to her, suddenly the inspiration came: would Mrs. Powell, she asked, care to spend the evening of the following day in the kitchen at 16 Charles Street, watching the celebrated French chef who was in charge there cook and dish up for a dinner party of some forty people? Mrs. Powell accepted the invitation with rapture, and it was my opinion that the employment she derived from, and interest she took in, all she saw on that occasion benefited her health more than would have a whole month spent by the seaside. She returned at about midnight, in an entranced condition at the splendour of the batteries, the china, the service: though she told me, with the confidence that a perfect knowledge of her own great gifts inspired, that she knew she could have turned out a finer, better dinner herself, had she possessed a kitchen equally well equipped, and similar aids and accessories.

It is a singular instance of poetic injustice that the only direct mention of a dinner cooked by her, in the journal of a well-known writer, records a curious culinary solecism, which I remember, and of which it was always impossible to find any explanation. This entry occurs in Arnold Bennett's Journal for 15th June 1919,[1] and I reproduce it here, since it a little gives the impression of life at Swan Walk at that time.

> Dined at Osbert Sitwell's. Good dinner. Fish before soup. Present W. H. Davies, Lytton Strachey, Woolf, Nichols, S. Sassoon, Aldous Huxley, Atkin (a very young caricaturist), W. J. Turner and Herbert Read (a very young poet). The faces of Woolf, Atkin and Read were particularly charming in their ingenuousness. Davies, I liked. He had walked all the way from Tottenham Court Road to Swan Walk. A house with much better pictures and bric-à-brac than furniture.[2] In fact there was scarcely any what I call furniture. But lots of very modern pictures of which I liked a number. Bright walls and bright cloths and, bright glass everywhere. A fine Rowlandson drawing. Osbert is young. He is already a very good host. I enjoyed this evening. . . .

Though fish before soup was an unique aberration, sometimes Mrs. Powell's enthusiasm, no less than the inherent profusion so evident in all she did or said, carried with it consequences equally unusual, and always to herself unexpected. Thus when, for example, she purchased cranberries, in order to make a sauce to accompany a turkey, there might arrive – admittedly because calculation was not her strongest point, but also, no doubt, because this lavishness fitted in with her entire temperament – a whole scarlet mountain of these bitter berries. After the fashion of goats on the hills we would be obliged to feed on them for weeks on end, and even then many would ultimately have to be given away. But her esthetic perception seldom led her astray, she never bought any food that was not perfect in its own fashion, nor did she ever purchase an ugly object for use in the house. Once, however, it is true, I returned from abroad to find that in my absence she had made for me a cushion of black satin, and had embroidered upon it an ice-cream-pink rose, with a few leaves of an arsenical green, and had placed it in the drawing-room: but she quickly saw her mistake, and before I had been home two days, and though I had thanked her most

---

[1] *The Journals of Arnold Bennett, 1911–21.* Edited by Newman Flower. (Cassell, 1932.)

[2] This is quite true, but may I modestly point out that the pictures and bric-à-brac were things I had bought? The furniture belonged to the owner of the house.

gratefully for her present, and I believe had shown no signs of my real feelings, it was withdrawn. It just disappeared, and was never seen or mentioned again. But to pictures she brought an eye unafraid, observant, receptive, and unaffected by the current trends of respectability and condemnation. Almost the only time I saw traces of her having been annoyed was when a contemporary chat-spinner had contributed the following item to an evening journal: 'The Sitwell brothers have achieved the impossible, and persuaded their cook to work in a kitchen hung with pictures of the modern school.' I came in late the night that this had appeared, and found on the table a piece of paper addressed to myself. On it, scrawled in Mrs. Powell's straggling hand, was written:

SIR,
　　Please tell the young gentleman who wrote about the kitchen that servants are individuals like other people, and not a separate race. I happen to like modern pictures. – Your obedient servant,

E. POWELL.

Laughter in the Next Room, 1949

Frederick

LADY CLODAGH ANSON 1879–1957

When my father and mother went out to Egypt for the winter in 1891, we were at Badminton with Granny and Grandpa Beaufort till after Christmas, and then went to Curraghmore picnicking in a corner of the house, being waited on by the odd boy, a quaint creature called Frederick who did the strangest things. He had a habit of carrying wineglasses between his fingers, so when someone slammed a door behind him, he jumped and clenched his fist, thereby breaking off all the stems of the glasses and cutting himself severely; but instead of getting someone to bind up his wounds he put his hand into a pudding basin and wound the bandages round the basin and all. We met him and his basin in the passage, and our governess gave him a long lecture on his foolish way of carrying glasses, to which he listened patiently for a long time until he could bear it no longer, when he said meekly,

'Yes, miss. I'm sure all you say is quite right, but meanwhile I'm losing a deal of blood,' and promptly fainted away.

Another Book, 1937

Dark Meat

GWEN RAVERAT 1885–1957

It is quite likely that the dark chicken meat never went beyond the green baize door.

I have defined Ladies as people who did not do things themselves. Aunt Etty was most emphatically such a person. She told me, when she was eighty-six, that she had never made a pot of tea in her life; and that she had never in all her days been out in the dark alone, not even in a cab; and I don't believe she had ever travelled by train without a maid. She certainly always took her maid with her when she went in a fly to the dentist's. She asked me once to give her a bit of the dark meat of a chicken, because she had never tasted anything but the breast.

Period Piece, 1954

Dormice

APICIUS FIRST CENTURY AD

TETRAPUS. IX GLIRES

Glires: isicio porcino, item pulpis ex omni membro glirium, trito cum pipere, nucleis, lasere, liquamine farcies glires, et sutos in tegula positos mittes in furnum aut farsos in clibano coques.

THE QUADRUPED. IX DORMICE

Stuff the dormice with minced pork, the minced meat of whole dormice, pounded with pepper, pine-kernels, asafoetida, and *liquamen*. Sew up, place on a tile, put in the oven, or cook, stuffed, in a small oven (*clibanus*).

The Roman Cookery Book, TRANS. Barbara Flower
and Elisabeth Rosenbaum, 1958

Cooking Ought Not to Take Too Much of One's Time
JESSIE CONRAD 1873–1936

Cooking ought not to take too much of one's time. One hour and a half to two hours for lunch, and two and a half for dinner is sufficient, providing that the servant knows how to make up the fire in order to get the stove ready for use. Most girls will quickly learn to do that and how to put a joint properly in the oven. For my part I never went into the kitchen before half-past eleven for a half-past one lunch of three dishes. But once the cooking is begun one must give all one's attention and care to it. No dish, however simple, will cook itself. You must not leave the kitchen while the cooking is going on – unless of necessity and only for a very few minutes at a time.

A Handbook of Cookery for a Small House, 1923

Cookery Cannot Be Done Like Pharmacy
LOUIS EUSTACHE UDE

Louis Eustache Ude states on the title page of The French Cook *that it is 'a system of fashionable and economic cookery adapted to the use of English families'. He describes himself as 'ci-devant cook to Louis XVI, and the Earl of Sefton; late steward to the United Service Club; to his Late Royal Highness the Duke of York; and now Maître d'Hotel at Crockford's Club, St. James's Street'.*

Cookery cannot be done like pharmacy: the Pharmacist is obliged to weigh every ingredient that he employs, as he does not like to taste it;

the Cook, on the contrary, must taste often, as the reduction increases the flavour. It would be blind work, indeed, without tasting: the very best soups or entrées, in which you have omitted to put salt, are entirely without flavour; seasoning is in Cookery what chords are in music; the best instrument, in the hand of the best professor, without its being in tune, is insipid.

The French Cook, 1813

Whale Steak Must Be Tough
HERMAN MELVILLE 1819–1891

About midnight that steak was cut and cooked; and lighted by two lanterns of sperm oil, Stubb stoutly stood up to his spermaceti supper at the capstan-board, as if that capstan-head were a side-board. Nor was Stubb the only banqueter on whale's flesh that night. Mingling their mumblings with his own mastications, thousands on thousands of sharks, swarming round the dead leviathan, smackingly feasted on its fatness. The few sleepers below in their bunks were often startled by the sharp slapping of their tails against the hull, within a few inches of the sleepers' hearts. Peering over the side you could just see them (as before you heard them) wallowing in the sullen, black waters, and turning over on their backs as they scooped out huge globular pieces of the whale of the bigness of a human head. This particular feat of the shark seems all but miraculous. How, at such an apparently unassailable surface, they contrive to gouge out such symmetrical mouthfuls, remains a part of the universal problem of all things. The mark they thus leave on the whale, may best be likened to the hollow made by a carpenter in counter-sinking for a screw.

But, as yet, Stubb heeded not the mumblings of the banquet that was going on so nigh him, no more than the sharks heeded the smacking of his own epicurean lips.

'Cook, cook! – where's that old Fleece?' he cried at length, widening his legs still further, as if to form a more secure base for his supper; and the same time darting his fork into the dish, as if stabbing with his lance; 'cook, you cook! – sail this way, cook!'

The old black, not in any very high glee at having been previously roused from his warm hammock at a most unseasonable hour, came shambling along from his galley, for, like many old blacks, there was something the matter with his knee-pans, which he did not keep well scoured like his other pans; this old Fleece, as they called him, came shuffling and limping along, assisting his step with his tongs, which, after a clumsy fashion, were made of straightened iron hoops; this old Ebony floundered along, and in obedience to the word of command, came to a dead stop on the opposite side of Stubb's sideboard; when, with both hands folded before him, and resting on his two-legged cane, he bowed his arched back still further over, at the same time sideways inclining his head, so as to bring his best ear into play.

'Cook,' said Stubb, rapidly lifting a rather reddish morsel to his mouth, 'don't you think this steak is rather overdone? You've been beating this steak too much, cook; it's too tender. Don't I always say that to be good, a whale-steak must be tough? There are those sharks now over the side, don't you see they prefer it tough and rare? What a shindy they are kicking up! Cook, go and talk to 'em; tell 'em they are welcome to help themselves civilly, and in moderation, but they must keep quiet. Blast me, if I can hear my own voice.'

Moby Dick, 1851

Civilization in Peaches
JANE GRIGSON 1928–90

When one thinks of the civilization implied in the development of peaches from the wild fruit, or of apricots, grapes, pears, plums, when one thinks of those millions of gardeners from ancient China right across Asia and the Middle East to Rome, then across the Alps north to France, Holland and England of the eighteenth and nineteenth centuries, how can we so crassly, so brutishly, reduce the exquisite results of their labour to cans full of syrup and cardboard-wrapped blocks of ice? These gardeners were concerned to grow better-tasting fruit or vegetable, a larger and more beautiful one too, but mainly a better-tasting one. Would they believe us if we told them that now tomatoes are produced to regular size and regular shape, that only two or three kinds of potato are regularly on sale, that peas taste like mealy bullets? It's odd that we should have clung on to traditions that hardly matter – beefeaters, Swiss guards, monarchies, the paraphernalia of the past – and forgotten the true worth of the past, the long labouring struggle to learn to survive as well and as gracefully as possible.

Cooking something delicious is really much more satisfactory than painting pictures or throwing pots. At least for most of us. Food has the tact to disappear, leaving room and opportunity for masterpieces to come. The mistakes don't hang on the walls or stand on the shelves to reproach you for ever. It follows from this that kitchens should be thought of as the centre of the house. They need above all space for talking, playing, bringing up children, sewing, having a meal, reading, sitting and thinking. One may have to walk about a bit, but where's the harm in that? Everything will not be ship-shape, galley-fashion, but it's in this kind of place that good food has flourished. It's from this secret retreat that the exploration of man's curious and close relationship with food, beyond the point of nourishment can start.

Good Things, 1971

Cooking is an Art
CONSTANCE SPRY 1886–1960

The fact is that cooking is a combination of science, art, invention, and a few other things; it calls for individual taste and latitude in adjustment of the formulae. There is another word to be underlined – taste – taste of course in both its meanings, of discrimination of quality and perception of flavour, but primarily here the latter. If you won't taste as you work you will never be a first-class cook; what other possible guide have you to rely on for nicety of seasoning and flavouring and all the subtleties of a dish – even of what you may be pleased to call good, plain food? There can be a smug sound about these words as sometimes uttered, especially when they are used to cover the bad cooking that produces overcooked meat, gluey gravy, waterlogged vegetables, and heavy puddings. Good plain food can be the best, the apotheosis of good fare; it can be very expensive and still plain. Good cooking owes a great deal to attention to detail, whatever the exponents of a more slapdash method may aver.

Cooking is an art; it demands hard and sometimes distasteful work, but on the whole it is the creative side that prevails. The kitchen should be raised to the status of a studio, as indeed it is in some homes where the mistress of the house is a cook. If it should ever become universally so regarded, then to earn a living in a domestic kitchen would become a more attractive calling to young, educated, qualified cooks, who at present are more attracted to posts in commercial and institutional kitchens. This is a pity, for it is in the private kitchen that opportunity presents itself for experiment and invention. As it is, the contemporary cook-hostess has the best of it, for she sees her efforts appreciated and hears the dishes discussed, which is a pleasant innovation, for talk about food used to be taboo.

Something else is new too: the immensely better and fairer distribution of food among all grades of society. This is due to a variety of causes, not the least of which was the rationing system at which we grumbled so incessantly and to which we so thankfully said good-bye. Remembering as I do the days of immensely long, boring, wasteful dinners, remembering too the starvation which was all too often at our very doors, I cannot forbear to remind you how much respect ought to be paid to food, how carefully it should be treated, how shameful waste is. Forgive me for this, but you see it is fortunately unlikely that your hearts will be wrung or your consciences nudged by the sight of starving people.

The Constance Spry Cookery Book, 1956

Menus for Holiday Feasts and Banquets
ANON

A NEW YEAR'S MENU
Menu Pour Le Jour De l'An.

BREAKFAST

Oranges.
Oatmeal, Cream.
Radishes. Cress. Olives.
Broiled Trout, Sauce à la Tartare.
Potatoes à la Duchesse.
Creamed Chicken. Omelette aux Confitures.
Salade à la Créole.
Batter Cakes. Louisiana Syrup. Fresh Butter.
Café au Lait.

DINNER

Oysters on Half Shell.
Spanish Olives. Celery. Pickles.
Salted Almonds.
Green Turtle Soup, Croûtons.
Broiled Spanish Mackerel,
Sauce à la Maître d'Hôtel.
Julienne Potatoes.
Lamb Cutlets Breaded, Sauce Soubise.
Green Peas.
Sweetbreads à la Créole.
Ponche à la Romaine.
Roast Turkey, Cranberry Sauce.
Baked Yams.   Cauliflower au Gratin.
Asparagus à la Maître d'Hôtel.
Lettuce, Salad Dressing.
Broiled Snipe on Toast.
Pouding à la Reine, Wine Sauce. Mince Pie.
Cocoanut Custard Pie.
Biscuit Glacé. Petits Fours. Fruits. Nuts.
Raisins.
Cheese. Toasted Crackers.
Café Noir.

SUPPER

Cold Turkey, Currant Jelly.
Celery Salad.
French Rolls. Butter. Assorted Cakes.
Fruit. Nuts.
Tea.

A MORE ECONOMICAL NEW YEAR'S MENU

BREAKFAST

Sliced Oranges.
Oatmeal and Cream.
Broiled Spring Chicken. Julienne Potatoes.
Radishes. Celery.

Egg Muffins. Fresh Butter. Louisiana Syrup.
Café au Lait.

DINNER

Consommé.
Radishes. Celery. Olives. Pickles.
Boiled Sheepshead. Cream Sauce.
Mashed Potatoes.
Vol-au-Vent of Chicken.
Salami of Wild Duck. Green Peas.
Banana Fritters.
Roast Turkey. Cranberry Sauce.
Baked Yams, Sliced and Buttered.
Green Pepper and Tomato Salad, French Dressing.
Pointes d'Asperges au Beurre.
Mince Pie. Roquefort.
Vanilla Ice Cream. Sponge Cake.
Assorted Fruits. Nuts. Raisins.
Café Noir.

SUPPER

Cold Turkey, Cranberry Sauce.
Tomato Salad.
Cake. Fruit. Tea.

A NEW YEAR'S DECORATION

On New Year's Day, no matter how humble her circumstances, the Creole housewife will have freshly blooming roses on her table. In our delightful climate, where flowers bloom the year round, and where, in winter especially, roses are in their zenith of glory, there are few homes, indeed, in which a patch of ground is not set aside for the cultivation of flowers; while in the lovely open gardens in the "Garden District of New Orleans" roses in exquisite bloom overrun the trellises and arbors and smile upon you from the fancifully laid-out garden beds. It is wonderful how a bit of green, with a few roses nestling between, will brighten up the homeliest table. With the linen spotless, the crystal shining, a few loose clusters of rose-buds, typical of the budding year, blooming on the mantels and in low, glass bowls in the center, a charm is imparted to the feast, the graceful idea of beginning anew suggested, and a lingering fragrance thrown over memory's page that will remain as an incentive to nobler effort for many a day.

The Picayune's Creole Cook Book, 1901

Two Recipes

HANNAH GLASSE 1708–70

TO RAISE A SALLAT IN TWO HOURS AT THE FIRE

Take fresh Horse-Dung hot, and lay it in a Tub near the Fire, then sprinkle some Mustard-seeds thick on it, and lay a thin Lay of Horse-Dung over it, cover it close and keep it by the Fire, and it will rise high enough to cut in two Hours.

TO MAKE AN EGG AS BIG AS TWENTY

Part the Yolks from the Whites, strain them both separate through a Sieve, tye the Yolks up in a Bladder, in the Form of a Ball; boil them hard, then put this Ball into another Blader, and the Whites round it; tie it up oval Fashion, and boil it. These are used for grand Sallads. This is very pretty for a Ragoo, boil five or six Yolks together, and lay in the Middle of the Ragoo of Eggs; and so you may make them of any Size you please.

The Art of Cookery Made Plain and Easy, 1747

Haschich Fudge

BRIAN GYSEN

(which anyone could whip up on a rainy day)
This is the food of Paradise – of Baudelaire's Artificial Paradises: it might provide an entertaining refreshment for a Ladies' Bridge Club or a chapter meeting of the DAR. In Morocco it is thought to be good for warding off the common cold in damp winter weather and is, indeed, more effective if taken with large quantities of hot mint tea. Euphoria

and brilliant storms of laughter; ecstatic reveries and extensions of one's personality on several simultaneous planes are to be complacently expected. Almost anything Saint Theresa did, you can do better if you can bear to be ravished by '*un évanouissement reveillé*.'

Take 1 teaspoon black peppercorns, 1 whole nutmeg, 4 average sticks of cinnamon, 1 teaspoon coriander. These should all be pulverised in a mortar. About a handful each of stoned dates, dried figs, shelled almonds and peanuts: chop these and mix them together. A bunch of *canibus sativa* can be pulverised. This along with the spices should be dusted over the mixed fruit and nuts, kneaded together. About a cup of sugar dissolved in a big pat of butter. Rolled into a cake and cut into pieces or made into balls about the size of a walnut, it should be eaten with care. Two pieces are quite sufficient.

Obtaining the *canibus* may present certain difficulties, but the variety known as *canibus sativa* grows as a common weed, often unrecognised, everywhere in Europe, Asia and parts of Africa; besides being cultivated as a crop for the manufacture of rope. In the Americas, while often discouraged, its cousin called *canibus indica*, has been observed even in city window boxes. It should be picked and dried as soon as it has gone to seed and while the plant is still green.

'*Recipes from Friends*', *The Alice B. Toklas Cook Book*, 1954

Ginger
BRUCE COST 1945−

Ginger spiced up the language as well as the cuisine when it invaded England probably via the Romans, according to Elizabeth David. The use of the seasoning was so pervasive in the Middle Ages that the word ginger became synonymous with spice in certain contexts. It even had a canister of its own at the table, a concept that startles those of us who thought salt and pepper were a mandate from when human beings first sat down to eat. Besides adding flavor to food, ginger's ability to warm people and stimulate their circulation was common knowledge. 'It heateth in the third degree', according to Elizabethan herbalist John Gerard. Ginger, in other words, meant zing in food, life and conversation.

Today the noun ginger means pep or liveliness to the British, and there are vestiges of this usage in New England. The verb form, which means 'to pep up', or 'give life to', is also bandied about. Applying the name Ginger to redheaded females because of their supposedly hot temperaments is as standard as using Red for males. In fact, red hair today is sometimes described as gingerous. The adjective gingery, when used to describe one's complexion, means ruddy brown; a gingery morning is invigorating. The adverb gingerly meaning cautious seems contradictory; yet as an old modifier applied to dance it meant lively but graceful.

Gerard also wrote that ginger 'provoketh Venerie'; so eventually, to 'ginger it up' or 'add spice to your life' meant stimulating more than your palate. Most don't know that ginger gave us 'racy' as in 'racily clad'. The English called knobs of ginger 'races', from the Portuguese-Spanish *raices*, meaning root. Thus food laced with ginger came to be called racy as well as spicy, both suggestive of all ginger's qualities. In the United States, the predominant connotation of racy is 'suggestive', while in Britain it can as easily mean lively, strong-flavored or piquant – another word that may have broadened its meaning due to its link with ginger. I should also mention the word 'sauce', from which we get saucy, sauciness, sass and sassy. Sauce originally meant just the spices added to give it life and came from the French sallere (to salt). A seventeenth century recipe might instruct, "Add no sauce but salt", meaning leave out the ginger for once.

The Journal of Gastronomy, Vol. 1, 1984

Crab Newburg

MARJORIE KINNAN RAWLINGS 1896–1953

We boil the crabs immediately, twenty minutes in salted water. We like best to eat them just so, with homemade mayonnaise and Cuban bread and cold bitter ale. The meat comes from the shells in enormous flakes, snow-white and incredibly sweet and flavorsome. There are two schools of crab-eaters. Some like to eat as fast as they pick. I find this an infuriating process, for one works for an hour or more, getting a small mouthful at a time, and is never satisfied. I take the long view and patiently pick out the meat from my share of the crabs until I have built up a fine mound to be eaten in luxury. There is considerable risk in this procedure, for the still famished piecemeal pickers eye my luscious pile greedily and have been known to saunter past my place at table and one by one snatch a forkful from my plate in selfish jealousy, all because of their own improvidence.

When we have crab meat to spare, I make a crab Newburg so superlative that I myself taste it in wonder, thinking, 'Can it be I who has brought this noble thing into the world?'

It is impossible to give proportions, for I never twice have the same amount of crab meat to work with, and here indeed I have no mother, but only instinct, to guide me. In an iron skillet over a low fire I place a certain amount of Dora's butter. As it melts, I stir in the flaked crab meat, lightly, tenderly. The flakes must not become disintegrated; they must not brown. I add lemon juice, possibly a tablespoonful for each cup of crab meat. I add salt and pepper frugally, paprika more generously, and a dash of powdered clove so temporal that the flavor in the finished Newburg is only as though the mixture had been whisked through a spice grove. I add Dora's golden cream. I do not know the exact quantity. It must be generous, but the delicate crab meat must never become deluged with any other element. The mixture bubbles for a few moments. I stir in dry sherry, the quantity again unestimable. Something must be left to genius. I stir in well beaten eggs, perhaps an egg, perhaps two, for every cup of flakes. The mixture must now no more than be turned over on itself and removed in a great sweep from the fire. I stir in a tablespoonful, or two, of the finest brandy, and turn the Newburg into a piping hot covered serving dish. I serve it on toast points and garnish superfluously with parsley, and a Chablis or white Rhine wine is recommended as an accompaniment. Angels sing softly in the distance.

We do not desecrate the dish by serving any other, neither salad nor dessert. We just eat crab Newburg. My friends rise from the table, wring my hand with deep feeling, and slip quietly and reverently away. I sit alone and weep for the misery of a world that does not have blue crabs and a Jersey cow.

Cross Creek, 1942

French Cooks and French Tricks

HANNAH GLASSE 1708–70

If I have not wrote in the high, polite Stile, I hope I shall be forgiven; for my Intention is to instruct the lower Sort, and therefore must treat them in their own Way. For Example; when I bid them lard a Fowl, if I should bid them lard with large Lardoons, they would not know what I meant: But when I say they must lard with little Pieces of Bacon, they know what I mean. So in many other Things in Cookery, the great Cooks have such a high Way of expressing themselves that the poor Girls are at a Loss to know what they mean: And in all Receipt Books yet printed there are such an odd Jumble of Things as would quite spoil a good Dish; and indeed some Things so extravagant, that it would be almost a Shame to make Use of them, when a Dish can be made full as good, or better without them. For Example; when you entertain ten or twelve People you shall use for a Cullis a Leg of Veal and a Ham; which with the other Ingredients, makes it very expensive, and all this only to mix with other Sauce. And again, the Essence of a Ham for Sauce to one Dish; when I will prove it for about three Shillings I will make as rich and high a Sauce as all that will be, when done . . . So that really one might have a genteel Entertainment for the Price the Sauce of one Dish comes to. But if Gentlemen will have *French* Cooks, they must pay for *French* tricks. A *Frenchman*, in his own Country, would dress a fine Dinner of twenty Dishes, and all genteel and pretty, for the Expence he will put an *English* Lord to for dressing one Dish. But then there is the little petty Profit. I have heard of a Cook that used six Pounds of Butter to fry twelve Eggs; when every Body knows, that understands Cooking, that Half a Pound is full enough, or more than need be used: But then it would not be *French*. So much is the blind Folly of this Age, that they would rather be impos'd on by a *French* Booby, than give Encouragement to a good *English* Cook!

The Art of Cookery Made Plain and Easy, 1747

Advice to Cooks

LOUIS EUSTACHE UDE

Cookery is an art which requires much time, intelligence, and activity, to be acquired in its perfection. Every man is not born with the qualifications necessary to constitute a good Cook. The difficulty of attaining to perfection in the art will be best demonstrated by offering a few observations on some others. Music, dancing, fencing, painting, and mechanics in general, possess professors under twenty years of age; whereas, in the first line of cooking, pre-eminence never occurs under thirty. We see daily at Concerts, and Academies, young men and women who display the greatest abilities; but in our line, nothing *but the most consummate* experience can elevate a man to the rank of Chief Professor. It must be admitted, that there are few good Cooks, though there are many who advance themselves as such. This disproportion of talent among them is the cause of the little respect in which they are held; if they were *all* provided with the necessary qualities, they would certainly be considered as artists.

What science demands more study than Cookery? You have not only, as in other arts, to satisfy the general eye, but also the individual taste of the persons who employ you; you have to attend to economy, which every one demands; to suit the taste of different persons at the same table; to surmount the difficulty of procuring things which are necessary to your work; to undergo the want of unanimity among the servants of the house; and the mortification of seeing unlimited confidence sometimes reposed in persons who are unqualified to give orders in the kitchen, without assuming a consequence, and giving themselves airs which are almost out of reason, and which frequently discourage the Cook.

The French Cook, 1813

Recipes for Jellies

THE GOODMAN OF PARIS C.1392

*The Goodman of Paris was at least sixty when he wrote a
household manual for his bride of fifteen. Evidently, life was not
too short in the fourteenth century to gild a jelly.*

Item, on a fish day, jelly is made as above of luce, tench, bream, eels
and crayfish and of pike. And when the fish is cooked, you set it to dry
on a fair white cloth, and skin it and clean it very well, and throw away
the skins and the broth.

Item TO MAKE BLUE JELLY, take of the aforesaid broth, be it of flesh
or fish, and set it in a fair pan and boil it again on the fire, and get from
the spicer two ounces of tournsole and set it to boil therewith until it be
of a good colour, then take it off; and then take a pint of loach and
cook it somewhere else, and spread the loach on your dishes and let the
broth run onto it as above and then leave it to cool. *Item*, thus is made
a blue jelly. And if you would make armorial bearings on the jelly, take
gold or silver, whichsoever pleaseth you best, and trace [your design]
with the white of an egg on a feather, and put the gold thereon with a
brush.

The Goodman of Paris, TRANS. Eileen Power, 1928

Dinner Menus

RUTH LOWINSKY D. 1958

*The amusing menus and the clever situations Ruth Lowinsky
invented to introduce them in* Lovely Food, *one of the three cookery
books she wrote in the 1930s, are almost more interesting now than
her recipes. The delightful little book is illustrated with witty line
drawings by her husband Thomas Lowinsky, the painter she met
when they were both students at the Slade. As Arabella Boxer noted
in her book on English food, Mrs Lowinsky, who inherited her
father's gold and diamond fortune, didn't actually learn to cook
until after the war. She was a friend of Constance Spry, and one of*

the many much-admired hostesses of her day who wrote about the
food their fortunate guests might encounter when invited to dine.

A slightly more pompous dinner for about ten people, none of whom
have met before, and who are neither young nor amusing. They think
they know all about food, but actually know only what they like.
Therefore the cocktails and the wine, champagne if possible, are
chosen for their mellowing effect. It is as well to start with a cold hors
d'œuvre, as several of these guests may be late.

HORS D'OEUVRES À LA SUÉDOISE
CONSOMMÉ À L'ASPERGE
SOLE GRAND SUCCÈS
POULET SPATCHCOCK SAUCE VERTE
ORLÉANS SALAD
MARRONS GLACÉS ICE

*

Most of us have had to take a party to a Charity Dance. The following
dinner may start the evening well. Remember that the tickets – £2.2.0
each or 18 guineas for 10 – a doubtful economy – include a large
supper. So dinner can be quite short, just something to fill in the time,
and give the young men a chance of making up their minds which girls
to avoid.

MOCK TURTLE SOUP
SOLE ORLOFF
BOILED CHICKEN
FRUIT
COFFEE

—

MOCK TURTLE SOUP
Remove brains from calf's head. Bring to boil and then place under
cold water tap and thoroughly wash. Put in clean stewpan and cover
with stock. Add vegetable stock. Next day remove fat, clarify, add one
turtle tablet and some turtle soup tablets. When clear, strain through
thick cloth, add sherry, salt and pepper to taste. Just before serving put
in glutinous squares from calf's head – two for each person. Enough
for eight people.

*

Chosen to create a favourable impression on a father-in-law, who comes prepared to judge you as either the laziest housekeeper in Europe, or the most extravagant, or even a subtle combination of the two. On no account burst into caviare or pâté de foie gras to do him honour, but be very careful to bring in the fact that the sweets come from Fortnum & Mason, the fruit, chosen by yourself, from Jessie Smith, and the coffee from Lyles, and he cannot, at any rate, accuse you of being lazy.

CLEAR MUSHROOM CONSOMMÉ
SMELTS À LA TARTARE
ROMANY CHICKEN
MERINGUES À LA SUISSE
—

CLEAR MUSHROOM CONSOMMÉ

Make a good consommé. Chop some mushrooms, fry them in a little butter, add the mushrooms to the consommé, and add a little hock to taste.

Lovely Food, 1931

Red-currant Fool

E. F. BENSON 1867–1940

By this time Isabel Poppit had advanced as far as the fish shop three doors below the turning down which Mrs Plaistow had vanished. Her prancing progress paused there for a moment, and she waited with one knee highly elevated, like a statue of a curveting horse, before she finally decided to pass on. But she passed no farther than the fruit shop next door, and took the three steps that elevated it from the street in a single prance, with her Roman nose high in the air. Presently she emerged, but with no obvious rotundity like that of a melon projecting from her basket, so that Miss Mapp could see exactly what she had purchased, and went back to the fish shop again. Surely she would not put fish on the top of fruit, and even as Miss Mapp's lucid intelligence rejected this supposition, the true solution struck her. 'Ice', she said to herself, and, sure enough, projecting from the top of Miss Poppit's basket when she came out was an angular peak, wrapped up in paper already wet.

Miss Poppit came up the street and Miss Mapp put up her illustrated paper again with the revolting picture of the Brighton sea-nymphs turned towards the window. Peeping out behind it, she observed that Miss Poppit's basket was apparently oozing with bright venous blood, and felt certain that she had bought red currants. That, coupled with the ice, made conjecture complete. She had bought red currants slightly damaged (or they would not have oozed so speedily), in order to make that iced red-currant fool of which she had so freely partaken at Miss Mapp's last bridge party. That was a very scurvy trick, for iced red-currant fool was an invention of Miss Mapp's, who, when it was praised, said that she inherited the recipe from her grandmother. But Miss Poppit had evidently entered the lists against Grandmother Mapp, and she had as evidently guessed that quite inferior fruit – fruit that was distinctly 'off' – was undetectable when severely iced. Miss Mapp could only hope that the fruit in the basket now bobbing past her window so much 'off' that it had begun to ferment. Fermented red-currant fool was nasty to the taste, and, if persevered in, disastrous in its effects. General unpopularity might be needed to teach Miss Poppit not to trespass on Grandmamma Mapp's preserves.

Miss Mapp, 1922

Rossini

CHARLES NEILSON GATTEY 1921–

More cordon-bleu recipes have been named after Rossini than any other composer – the most prized of all honours for a gourmet such as he was. He once wrote: 'The stomach is the conductor who rules the grand orchestra of our passions. An empty stomach is to me like a bassoon which growls with discontent or a piccolo flute which expresses its desire in shrill tones. A full stomach, on the other hand, is the triangle of pleasure, or the drum of joy. To eat, to love, to sing, to digest – these are, in truth, the four acts of the comic opera we call life. Who ever let it pass without having enjoyed them is a consummate ass.'

When the owner of Rossini's favourite provisions store asked him for an autographed photograph, the composer gave him one signed: '*To my stomach's best friend.*' He would astonish people by maintaining that he had taken up the wrong profession and that his artistry in dressing a salad pleased him more than all his successes in music. He once wrote to a friend: 'What is going to interest you much more than my opera is the discovery I have just made of a new salad [dressing] for which I hasten to send you the recipe. Take Provence oil, French vinegar, a little lemon juice, pepper and salt. Whisk and mix all together. Then throw in a few truffles, which you have taken care to cut into tiny pieces. The truffles give to this seasoning a kind of nimbus to plunge the gourmet into an ecstasy.'

At home, Rossini enjoyed himself most when he was cooking in the kitchen. He was extremely fond of pasta and in particular of *cappelletti in brodo*, which was full of cheese, buttermilk curd, egg, nutmeg, cloves and grated bread cooked in meat broth. He would gulp it all down at a tremendous rate, as if he feared someone might steal it from him. As a result of the ill-effects on his health of such gorging he was continually resorting to cures of various kinds.

When asked why he had not become a chef, Rossini replied, 'Because my education as a boy was so bad.' The aroma of his favourite foods helped him to compose. The day before his opera, *Tancredi*, had its première in Venice, Mme Malanotte who was to play the title role found fault with her first aria. Rossini went home wondering what he could compose in its stead to please her. He told his servant to fry some rice and as he supervised its cooking he had an inspiration and noted down the beautiful melody, 'Di tanti palpiti', afterwards known as the *aria di rizzi* – the rice aria.

Foie Gras and Trumpets, 1984

The Woman Who Loved to Cook
ERICA JONG 1942–

Looking for love, she read cookbooks,
She read recipes for *tartlettes*,
terrines de boeuf, timbales,
& Ratatouille.
She read cheese fondue
& Croque Monsieur,
& Hash High Brownies
& Lo Mein.

If no man appeared who would love her
(her face moist with cooking,
her breasts full of apple juice
or wine),
she would whip one up:
of gingerbread,
with baking powder
to make him rise.

Even her poems
were recipes.
'Hunger,' she would write, 'hunger.'
The magic word to make it go away.
But nothing filled her up
or stopped that thump.
Her stomach thought it was a heart.

Then one day she met a man,
his cheeks brown as gingerbread,
his tongue a slashed pink ham
upon a platter.
She wanted to eat him whole
& save his eyes.
Her friends predicted he'd eat her.

How does the story end?
You know it well.

She's getting fatter
& she drinks too much.

Her shrink has read her book
& heard her tale.

'Oral,' he says,
& coughs
& puffs his pipe.

'Oral,'
he says,
& now
'time's up.'

Half-Lives, 1973

Broth

LOUIS EUSTACHE UDE

Broth is the foundation of Cookery.

Any trimmings of meat will serve to make the first broth, provided the scum and fat be carefully removed – the broth will otherwise be too highly coloured to mix with the sauce. If the broth be properly prepared it will serve to moisten all the sauces.

When there is a good kitchen, broth should be always in the larder; as the stock-pot must be settled according to the dinner intended to be given. For a small dinner with four entrées (or dishes of the first course), twenty pounds of beef would be required to be used for broth only, independent of the roast; for it should be observed, that any joint roasted in the kitchen is entirely wasted for cooking.

The French Cook, 1813

Western-style Butter

PETER GOULLART D. 1978

Peter Goullart was born in Russia at the beginning of the century but brought up in the Orient. He came from a long line of merchants who travelled through Mongolia, Turkistan and Tibet, dealing in cattle, herbs, musk and saffron. In 1939 he became the representative of the Chinese Industrial Co-operatives and travelled from Shanghai to the ancient Chinese kingdom of Nakhi in Yunnan, by the Tibetan border.

In accordance with my instructions, I went into the problems of making Western-style butter on the farm. There were several hundred yaks, and many cows gave good milk. The yak milk was very rich and sweet, almost like pure cream and its fat content was very high. Of course, it was still winter and the yield was small, but, anyway, there was enough milk for demonstration purposes. However, the enormity of my task became apparent all at once. The first process, the milking, as it was done on the farm and, for that reason, all over Tibet, appalled me. A dirty copper pail, merely rinsed in the ice-cold muddy water of the brook, was thrust by a Tibetan man or woman under the filthy, woolly fur of the yak, hanging almost to the ground, and the milk was led from its udder to a piece of rough yak-wool mat spread over the pail, serving as a strainer. By the time the product has been delivered to the farm, it was already cold. The only cream separator, although they were inordinately proud of it, was a mere toy capable of producing, perhaps, one pound of butter an hour. They had never operated it before and I found it all rusty and dirty and almost beyond hope of repair. Of course, it could not operate with cold milk. So the milk was warmed in the kitchen over a yak-dung fire and, naturally, by the time it had been heated, it smelled, like other cooked food, of the dung. Then there was no proper churn except the long, barrel-like churns used in making Tibetan-style butter. They were too big for the amount of cream obtained by hours of separation through the small machine; they were also too filthy and begrimed by months of use. The Tibetans made their yak butter in their own way. They simply collected the newly produced milk, without straining it once more, and poured it into these big churns. Then several persons, men and women, took their turn in churning, moving the handle up and down all day long until a large lump of butter had been produced; the lump was fished out, pressed into convenient cakes of about two catties each and wrapped in birch bark. It had a cheesy flavour and contained plenty of yak hair among other impurities; in warm weather it became quickly rancid. Rancidness was considered rather desirable by the Tibetans as they liked their butter with a kick just as many people prefer Gorgonzola cheese to milder varieties.

Princes of the Black Bone, 1959

The Epistle

SIR HUGH PLAT 1552–1608

Of sweetes the sweetest I will now commend,
To sweetest creatures that the earth doth beare:
These are the Saints to whome I sacrifice
Preserues and conserues both of plum and peare.
Empaling now adieu: tush, marchpane wals,
Are strong enough and best befits our age:

Let pearcing bullets turne to sugar bals,
The Spanish feare is husht and all their rage.
Of marmelade and paste of Genua,
Of musked sugar I intend to wright,
Of Leach, of Sucket, and Quidinea,
Affording to each Ladie, her delight.
I teach both fruites and flowers to preserue,
And candie them, so Nutmegs, Cloues, and Mace;
To make both marchpane paste, and sugred plate,
And cast the same in formes of sweetest grace,
Each bird and foule, so moulded from the life,
And after cast in sweet compounds of Arte,
As if the flesh and forme which Nature gaue,
Did still remaine in euery lim and part.
When crystall frost hath nipt the tender grape,
And cleane consum'd the fruits of euerie vine,
Yet heere behold the clusters fresh and faire,
Fed from the branch, or hanging on the line,
The Wallnut, small nut, and the chesnut sweet,
Whose sugred kernels lose their pleasing taste,
Are heere from yeere to yeere preserued meet,
And made by arte with strongest fruits to last:
Th' artichoke, and th' Apple of such strength,
The Quince, Pomgranate, with the Barberie,
No sugar vs'd, yet colour, taste and smell,
Are heere maintain'd and kept most naturally.
For Ladies closets and their stillatories,
Both waters, ointments and sweet smelling bals,
In easie tearmes without affected speech,
I heere present most ready at their cals.
And least with carelesse pen I should omit
The wrongs that Nature on their persons wrought
Or parching sun with his hot firie rayes,
For these likewise relieuing meanes I sought.
No idle thoughts, nor vaine surmised skils.
By fancie framde within a theorique braine,
My Muse presents vnto your sacred eares:
To win your fauours falsly I disdaine.
From painefull practise, from experience,
I sound, though costly mysteries deriue:
With firie flames in scorching *Vulcans* forge.

To teach and fine each secret I doe striue.
Accept them well, and let my wearied Muse
Repose her selfe in Ladies laps awhile.
So when she wakes, she happely may record,
Her sweetest dreames in some more pleasing stile.

Delightes for Ladies, 1602

Pojarky de Volaille

GABRIEL TSCHUMI

Few people realised how easy it was for an elaborate dish like *Pojarky de volaille*, the chicken dish from the menu of October 9, 1900, to be spoilt by any delay in serving. When cuisine classique was taken for granted no one realised, either, the amount of preparation that might go into one dish, such as pheasant consommé garnished with force-meat.

It took three days to prepare. On the first day the pheasant meat and bones were boiled for about five hours in huge stewpans to obtain the full richness of flavour, and on the second the meat was passed through a machine, returned to the consommé with vegetables, clarified, and strained through a very fine soup cloth. The third day was spent making the forcemeat garnishing or quenelles, which Queen Victoria liked. They consisted of breast of chicken mixed with a thick white sauce and cream and passed through a sieve, shaped into small ovals and cooked in boiling water.

Forcemeat was used a good deal for garnishing clear soup, and at banquets might be served in three colours: red, white and green. I have seen cooks spend hours making these quenelles, using tomato purée to colour them red, and spinach purée to colour them green. The secret of good quenelles was in the blending of the chicken with the white sauce and cream. Each small piece had to retain the flavour of chicken but melt in the mouth.

Royal Chef, 1954

Far Too Much Flavouring
NOËL COWARD 1899–1973

Sunday 26 February 1956

Cole and I have cooked dinner every night this week. I am inclined to put in far too much flavouring, as in painting I put in far too much colour, but I am learning restraint. I am also learning to be fearless with eggs and undismayed by deep fat and flour and breadcrumbs. It all comes under the heading of living dangerously and maybe the day will come when I can cook a joint, stuff a chicken's arse with butter, and make pastry so light that it flies away at a touch. My solo triumphs to date have been a chocolate mousse (plus cinnamon, Nescafé and Crème de Cacao), some rather curiously shaped croquettes, Kitchener eggs, sensational salad dressing with bacon rinds, various experimental soups originating from tins but rising to ambrosial heights after my pudgy fingers have been busy with herbs and garlic, and last but by no means least a *coquille* of shrimps and smoked oysters.

The Noël Coward Diaries, ED. Graham Payn
and Sheridan Morley, 1982

High Church Ham
SYDNEY SMITH 1771–1845

TO LADY HOLLAND

January 10th, 1809

My dear Lady Holland,

Many thanks for two fine Gallicia hams; but as for boiling them in wine, I am not as yet high enough in the Church for that; so they must do the best they can in water.

Selected Letters, ED. Nowell C. Smith, 1956

Art and Drama in the Kitchen
LORNA BUNYARD

Both art and drama dwelt in the kitchen in the days when the jack and shining meat-screen ruled the roast. Many a sexagenarian can recall his own absorbed interest when the cook, suitably serious, and not lightly to be questioned, fixed the meat to the jack. The real artist used yarn or worsted, that the meat might not be pierced. The plain workman pushed in a hook. Then the works were wound up, and there began that regular clack, syncopated by the broken dropping of fat, which induced the true theatre spirit, where the onlooker watches the play unroll before him, in the tranced interest of a being from another world. What drama in the sudden blaze of heat when the screen door was opened, the long spoon unhooked, and sizzling dripping basted the twisting joint with careful skill! What a thrill when a cinder jumped from the bars, with a burst of flame and sudden explosion of fat from the pan! How deep the sympathy for cook as she lamented: 'Oh, my poor hearth!' Art shone in the basting, and art, too, in the tending of the fire. There was a judicious measure of fresh coal at the back, a careful arrangement of the glowing cinders, and the final top-dressing of slack, which kept up a steady glow. What a clutch caught the throat at the expression on the lolling head of a dead cockerel! How the childish heart was torn, to no diminution of subsequent appetite, by the puzzled, wrinkled snout, sad tail, and little pink bottom of the sucking-pig. No more can the budding epicure take his stool and, sitting under the kitchen table, revel in each detail of the initiation. The twentieth-century cook sets a dial, shuts a door, and sits down to a study of the stars. Roasting is no more! 'On prend son bien où l'on s'y trouve.' Baking takes the place of roasting, and every one must try out the method and adjust it to his pleasure. An oven large enough for a pan which holds a generous measure of fat is a prime concern. There are ovens where the joint can hang, and at least pretend that it is roasting. But cooks do not look with favour on the subsequent cleaning of the oven, which must be done if the house is not to reek of burnt fat.

The Epicure's Companion, ED. Edward and Lorna Bunyard, 1937

Our Simple Cookery

J. HECTOR ST. JOHN DE CRÈVECOEUR 1735–1813

It is in the art of our simple cookery that our wives all aim at distinguishing themselves. This wife is famous for one thing, that for the other. She who has not fresh comb-honey, some sweetmeats of her own composing, and smoked beef at tea would be looked upon as very inexpert indeed. Thus these light repasts become on every account the most expensive of any; and as we dine early and work until tea-time, they often are very serious meals at which abundance of biscuits and shortcakes are always eaten. Some people would think it a disgrace to have bread brought on these round tables. Our beef by smoking becomes so compact that we commonly shave it with a plane. The thin, transparent peelings, when curled up on a dish, look not only neat and elegant but very tempting. Thus going to drink tea with each other implies several very agreeable ideas: that of riding sometimes five or six miles; that of chatting much and hearing the news of the county; and that of eating heartily. Considering that our women are never idle but have something to do from one year's end to another, where is the husband that would refuse his wife the pleasure of treating her friends as she has been treated herself?

Letters from an American Farmer and Sketches of Eighteenth-Century
America, 1963

Mustard

LAUNCELOT STURGEON

In the first place – never entrust the composition of your mustard to any hand but your own, unless you should be fortunate enough to possess a maître d'hotel, or a butler, in whom you can place the most implicit confidence: next, let the powder be invariably mixed with champagne in lieu of water; then, add a small quantity of essence of anchovy, and one drop – light as the morning dew upon a rose-bud – of assafœtida. And here we may remark, that whenever the aid of garlick is required, assafœtida will equally answer the purpose of adding a high flavor, while it is more easily incorporated with other ingredients. As to the root itself, when used in a small quantity its odour is scarcely perceptible; but were it 'rank as the dull weed that grows on Lethe's banks,' it is more fragrant than any flower that blows, and he is but a mere pretender to the name of epicure who does not prefer its savoury pungency to the mawkish effluvia of attar of roses. It is this that was, in days of yore, the incense of the gods: when the heroes of Homer – who, by the bye, were every man of them cooks – broiled their offerings of beef-steaks for the deities, this was the seasoning they used to render them acceptable; and the steam that was snuffed with such ineffable delight upon Olympus, was always strongly impregnated with garlick. Its perfume raises the spirits, and awakens the appetite by its association in idea with a good dinner; it braces the nerves, and overpowers all unpleasant scents more effectually than any of the essences in use; and the most agreeable effects would be perceptible in our drawing rooms, if, instead of the lavender, musk, and bergamot, which we are forced to inhale in them, ladies would but consent to sprinkle their handkerchiefs with assafœtida.

The Importance of Good Living, 1822

Truffles

ANON

Do not make a fetish of truffles as the bourgeois do. Truffles are excellent, but they are not sublime.

I do not deny that they add a pleasant flavour to a chicken or to scrambled eggs, but people who speak of them solemnly with pursed-up lips are not sincere.

Their aroma is dry and coarse and my master never ate them except as the ebony heart in the centre of *foie gras*. I blame them for not being really worthy either of their high price, or of their legendary reputation. They date too much and have become bad company.

The stout little guardian who, in the reign of the worthy Louis Philippe, would arrive from the provinces and surprise his nephew, with his feet on the mantelpiece, and Amanda beside him in undress, would carry them off to the Palais-Royal to eat something stuffed with truffles.

Truffles have come to suggest private rooms in restaurants and secret dissipations. They are brilliant, but not serious. All the same, you can use them to flavour a chicken at the end of the month that follows November. Christmas gives them absolution.

Clarisse or The Old Cook, 1926

Sauces

CHARLES LAMB 1775–1834

It is a desideratum in works that treat *de re culinariâ*, that we have no *rationale* of sauces, or theory of mixed flavours: as to show why cabbage is reprehensible with roast beef, laudable with bacon; why the haunch of mutton seeks the alliance of currant jelly, the shoulder civilly declineth it; why loin of veal (a pretty problem), being itself unctuous, seeketh the adventitious lubricity of melted butter, – and why the same part in pork, not more oleaginous, abhorreth from it; why the French bean sympathises with the flesh of deer; why salt fish points to parsnip, brawn makes a dead-set at mustard; why cats prefer valerian to heart's-ease, old ladies *vice versa*, – though this is rather travelling out of the road of the dietetics, and may be thought a question more curious than relevant; why salmon (a strong sapor *per se*) fortifieth its condition with the mighty lobster sauce, whose embraces are fatal to the delicater relish of the turbot; why oysters in death rise up against the contamination of brown sugar, while they are posthumously amorous of vinegar; why the sour mango and the sweet jam by turns court and are accepted by the compliable mutton hash, – she not yet decidedly declaring for either. We are as yet but in the empirical stage of cookery. We feed ignorantly, and want to be able to give a reason of the relish that is in us; so that, if Nature should furnish us with a new meat, or be prodigally pleased to restore the phœnix, upon a *given* flavour, we might be able to pronounce instantly, on philosophical principles, what the sauce to it should be, – what the curious adjuncts.

Essays and Sketches, 1834

Fundamental Flavourings
DOROTHY HARTLEY 1893–1985

It was considered very important to flavour the joint of meat *with the flavour of the food the animal ate*. Thus, for mutton from sheep bred on the mountains, the flavouring was the wild thyme whose small purple flowers made the mutton itself so spicy.

The marsh mutton (our equivalent of the pres salé of Paris) had a distinct iodine tang, from the seaweed and salt grasses of the estuary.

Therefore the laver weed, that grows there, made the hot laver sauce, a delicacy still sold at Bath spa and in Bideford and other places down west.

Fat Midland mutton from the orchards had fruit sauces, such as redcurrant jelly. This very old sauce is also used for game. Actually the rowan jelly is better for moorland mutton or venison.

Most sheep had their lambs down in the warm valley grazing lands where the streams ran, and mint grew in abundance. Hence mint sauce with lamb. Beef quite naturally has the milk and corn adjuncts from meadow and dairy – Yorkshire puddings, milky horse radish and corn bake.

Food in England, 1954

The Right Way to Make a Good Salad
GIACOMO CASTELVETRO 1546–1616

Giacomo Castelvetro, a Protestant, was saved from the Inquisition in Venice in 1611 by the British ambassador, Sir Dudley Carleton. He lived the rest of his life in exile in England, where he was horrified at the vast quantities of meat and sugar consumed. He dreamed of teaching the English how to make a perfect salad, and his book was an attempt to describe the gastronomic delights of his beloved Italy so as to convince his hosts of the benefits of fresh fruit and vegetables.

It takes more than good herbs to make a good salad, for success depends on how they are prepared. So, before going any further, I think I should explain exactly how to do this.

It is important to know how to wash your herbs, and then how to season them. Too many housewives and foreign cooks get their greenstuff all ready to wash and put it in a bucket of water, or some other pot, and slosh it about a little, and then, instead of taking it out with their hands, as they ought to do, they tip the leaves and water out together, so that all the sand and grit is poured out with them. Distinctly unpleasant to chew on . . .

So, you must first wash your hands, then put the leaves in a bowl of water, and sir them round and round, then lift them out carefully. Do this at least three or four times, until you can see that all the sand and rubbish has fallen to the bottom of the pot.

Next, you must dry the salad properly and season it correctly. Some cooks put their badly washed, barely shaken salad into a dish, with the leaves still so drenched with water that they will not take the oil, which they should to taste right. So I insist that first you must shake your salad really well and then dry it thoroughly with a clean linen cloth so that the oil will adhere properly. Then put it into a bowl in which you have previously put some salt and stir them together, and then add the oil with a generous hand, and stir the salad again with clean fingers or a knife and fork, which is more seemly, so that each leaf is properly coated with oil.

Never do as the Germans and other uncouth nations do – pile the badly washed leaves, neither shaken nor dried, up in a mound like a pyramid, then throw on a little salt, not much oil and far too much vinegar, without even stirring. And all this done to produce a decorative effect, where we Italians would much rather feast the palate than the eye.

You English are even worse; after washing the salad heaven knows how, you put the vinegar in the dish first, and enough of that for a footbath for Morgante, and serve it up, unstirred, with neither oil nor salt, which you are supposed to add at table. By this time some of the leaves are so saturated with vinegar that they cannot take the oil, while the rest are quite naked and fit only for chicken food.

So, to make a good salad the proper way, you should put the oil in first of all, stir it into the salad, then add the vinegar and stir again. And if you do not enjoy this, complain to me.

The secret of a good salad is plenty of salt, generous oil and little vinegar, hence the text of the Sacred Law of Salads:

Insalata ben salata,
poco aceto e ben oliata.

Salt the salad quite a lot,
then generous oil put in the pot,
and vinegar, but just a jot.

And whosoever transgresses this benign commandment is condemned
never to enjoy a decent salad in their life, a fate which I fear lies in store
for most of the inhabitants of this kingdom.

OLLA PODRIDA

In Italy we make another salad with the outlandish name of *olla
podrida* because as well as the profusion of salad ingredients I have
just described, we go on to add white endive, blanched chicory shoots,
the cooked roots of these two vegetables, raisins, angelica, stoned
olives, salted capers soaked in tepid water, some little Genoese capers,
thin slices of salted ox tongue, small pieces of candied citron and
lemon peel, spring onions if they are in season, radishes, horseradish,
and the white shoots of alexanders.

The Fruit, Herbs and Vegetables of Italy, TRANS. Gillian Riley, 1989

Salad
SYDNEY SMITH 1771–1845

Oil 4 Tables
Vinegar 2
Salt 3 Tea Spoons
Essence of Anchovy 1
Mustard 1
the Yellow of two Eggs boild hard
2 or 3 potatoes boild and straind through a Sieve
½ a Tea Spoon of onion chopped very fine
Mix the Salad thoroughly just before it is used.
                                        Turn over
too cold for Mrs. Sydney – many thanks.

This is the 'very *excellent* receipt for a salad' which Lady
Holland, writing to Henry on 3 March 1840, says S. 'has put into
verse' . . . It is natural to suppose that the rhymed version had
not been long in circulation, though as early as 1823 S. had
boasted to Lady Holland of his skill in dressing salads. . . . As
this celebrated *Recipe for a Salad* has been generally printed with
a bad mistake, 'brown' for 'crown' in l. 11, I take this opportunity of reprinting it with the correction.

RECIPE FOR A SALAD

To make this condiment your poet begs
The pounded yellow of two hard-boil'd eggs;
Two boiled potatoes, passed through kitchen sieve,
Smoothness and softness to the salad give.
Let onion atoms lurk within the bowl,
And, half-suspected, animate the whole.
Of mordant mustard add a single spoon,
Distrust the condiment that bites so soon;
But deem it not, thou man of herbs, a fault
To add a double quantity of salt;
Four times the spoon with oil of Lucca crown,
And twice with vinegar procur'd from town;
And lastly o'er the flavour'd compound toss
A magic soupçon of anchovy sauce.
Oh, green and glorious! Oh, herbaceous treat!
Twould tempt the dying anchorite to eat;
Back to the world he'd turn his fleeting soul,
And plunge his fingers in the salad-bowl!
Serenely full, the epicure would say,
'Fate cannot harm me, I have dined today.'

Selected Letters, ED. Nowell C. Smith, 1956

Salad

GEORGE H. ELLWANGER 1848–1906

To remember a successful salad is generally to remember a successful dinner; at all events, the perfect dinner necessarily includes the perfect salad. The mere process of salad-making is among the most simple of all those that appertain to the table: a little oil, a little vinegar, of salt and pepper each a little, the onion and the mixing, with such other herbs and condiments as the artist may elect. And yet an unexceptionable salad is as rare in the average household as a piece of old Gubbio, or a fine old Ghiordes prayer-rug. Seldom, indeed, is this refreshing dish met with as one usually finds it in France – crisp, tender, and appetising, with none of its ingredients perceptibly dominant in the *liaison* which, first pleasingly addressing the taste, is afterwards destined to soothe and tranquillise digestion. The reason is not difficult to analyse; the happy touch which is necessary in salads and sauces being largely a matter of individual address and a growth of advanced gastronomy. For in the preparing of salads no formula that is absolute may be given, success depending upon practice, a correct taste, and minute attention to detail. Here, as in everything else that is faultless, care and experience are factors requisite to attainment.

The Pleasures of the Table, 1902

Tracking the Gazpacho

ALICE B. TOKLAS 1878–1967

From murder to detection is not far. And here is a note on tracking a soup to its source. It was as a result of eating *gazpacho* in Spain lately that I came to the conclusion that recipes through conquests and occupations have travelled far. After the first ineffable *gazpacho* was served to us in Malaga and an entirely different but equally exquisite one was presented in Seville the recipes for them had unquestionably become of greater importance than Grecos and Zurbarans, than cathedrals and museums. Surely the calle de las Sierpes, the liveliest, most seductive of streets, would produce the cook-book that would answer the burning consuming question of how to prepare a *gaz-*

pacho. Down the narrow Sierpes where only pedestrians are permitted to pass, with its de luxe shops of fans, boots and gloves, toys and sweets, its smart men's clubs on either side whose members sit three tables deep sipping iced drinks and evaluating the young ladies who pass, at the end of the street was the large book shop remembered from a previous visit forty years before. Cook-books without number, exactly eleven, were offered for inspection but not a *gazpacho* in any index. Oh, said the clerk, *gazpachos* are only eaten in Spain by peasants and Americans. Choosing the book that seemed to have the fewest French recipes, I hurried back to Zurbaran and Greco, to museums and cathedrals.

At Cordoba there was another and suaver *gazpacho*, at Segovia one with a more vulgar appeal, outrageously coarse. There was nothing to do but to resign oneself to an experimental laboratory effort as soon as a kitchen was available. Upon the return from Spain my host at Cannes, a distinguished Polish-American composer, a fine *gourmet* and experienced cook, listened to the story of the futile chase for *gazpacho* recipes, for their possible ingredients. Ah, said he, but you are describing a *chlodnik*, the Polish iced soup. Before he had had time to prepare it for us a Turkish guest arrived and he hearing about the *gazpachos* and the *chlodnik* said, You are describing a Turkish *cacik*. Perhaps, said I. It was confusing. He said he would prepare a *cacik* for us. It was to be sure an iced soup, but the Turk had not the temperament of a great cook, he should not have accepted olive oil as a substitute for the blander oil of Sesame. Then we had the *chlodnik*, a really great dish worthy of its Spanish cousins. But that was not the end. There was the Greek *tarata*. Yes indeed, it was confusing, until one morning it occurred to me that it was evident each one of these frozen soups was not a separate creation. Had the Poles passed the recipe to their enemy the Turks at the siege of Vienna or had it been brought back to Poland much earlier than that from Turkey or Greece? Or had it been brought back by a crusader from Turkey? Had it gone to Sicily from Greece and then to Spain? It is a subject to be pursued.

The Alice B. Toklas Cook Book, 1954

Mock Cutlets

GABRIEL TSCHUMI

When at last there were Courts held again at Buckingham Palace we threw ourselves into preparing food for them with enthusiasm.

Of course, the lamb cutlets the size of a saucer and the enormous servings of chicken of Edwardian Courts were a thing of the past, but we found ways of keeping up the standard of royal food. A good chef can do a great deal by illusion, and a lot of guests were astonished at the amount of meat and chicken available at these courts.

What they were eating really were cutlets and pieces of chicken which might not have contained enough meat to cover a half-crown. The same thing, I am sorry to say, has to be done by chefs at Buckingham Palace today owing to scarcity of materials. It is amazing how good these mock cutlets and mock chicken slices can look if they are well prepared.

To make the meat cutlets served at the Courts of 1918 we prepared a purée of leg of mutton which had been minced up small, mixed this with a very strong brown sauce, and with a cutter shaped each piece to look like a cutlet, serving it with brown chaudfroid sauce. The chicken consisted of nothing more or less than old ends of poultry made into forcemeat, cooked in cutlet moulds and chaudfroided with white chicken sauce. It was a great deal of work, but we did our best to make these mock dishes look effective. Sometimes the chicken was served with a salad consisting of rice, diced pimentos, tomatoes and mayonnaise to give it a green-and-red colour scheme. We got a black-and-white effect from slices of truffles and the chopped-up whites of poached eggs.

Royal Chef, 1954

Entertaining and Hospitality

❧❧❧

Three Dinners

PLINY THE YOUNGER 61?–113 AD

TO CATILIUS SEVERUS

I will come to dinner, but only on condition that it is simple and informal, rich only in Socratic conversation, though this too must be kept within bounds; for there will be early-morning callers to think of. Cato himself could not escape reproach on meeting them, though Caesar's adverse comment is tinged with admiration. The passers-by whom Cato met when drunk, blushed when they discovered who it was, and (says Caesar) 'You would have thought they had been found out by Cato, not Cato by them'. What better tribute to Cato's prestige than to show him still awe-inspiring when drunk! But our dinner must have a limit, in time as well as in preparations and expense; for we are not the sort of people whom even our enemies cannot blame without a word of praise.

TO SEPTICIUS CLARUS

Who are you, to accept my invitation to dinner and never come? I have a good case and you shall pay my costs in full, no small sum either. It was all laid out, one lettuce each, three snails, two eggs, barley-cake, and wine with honey chilled with snow (you will reckon this too please, and as an expensive item, seeing that it disappears in the dish), besides olives, beetroots, gherkins, onions, and any number of similar delicacies. You would have heard a comic play, a reader or singer, or all three if I felt generous. Instead you chose to go where you could have oysters, sow's innards, sea-urchins, and Spanish dancing-girls. You will suffer for this – I won't say how. It was a cruel trick done to spite one of us – yourself or most likely me, and possibly both of us, if you think what a feast of fun, laughter and learning we were going to have. You can eat richer food at many houses, but nowhere with such free and easy enjoyment. All I can say is, try me; and then, if you don't prefer to decline invitations elsewhere, you can always make excuses to me.

TO JULIUS GENITOR

Thank you for your letter. You complain about a dinner party, a grand affair which filled you with disgust at the mimes and clowns and the male 'dancers' going the round of the tables. Please don't be for ever frowning – I have nothing of that kind in my own house, but I can put up with those who do. The reason why I don't have them is that I find nothing novel or amusing to attract me in that sort of 'dancer's' charms, in a mime's impudence, or a clown's folly. But you see I am not pleading my principles but my personal taste; and think how many people there are who dislike the entertainments which we find fascinating, and think them either pointless or boring. How many take their leave at the entry of a reader, a musician, or an actor, or else lie back in disgust, as you did when you had to endure those monstrosities as you call them! Let us then be tolerant of other people's pleasures so as to win indulgence for our own.

Letters, TRANS. Betty Radice, 1969

Two Epigrams
MARTIAL 42?–102 AD

Book IX, XIV. This man, whom your table, whom your dinner has made your friend – think you his heart one of loyal friendship? 'Tis boar he loves, and mullet, and sow's paps, and oysters, not you. Were I to dine so well, he will be my friend.

Book X, XLVIII. My crescent couch takes seven . . . my bailiff's wife has brought me mallows that will unburden the stomach, and the various wealth the garden bears; amongst which is squat lettuce and clipped leek, and flatulent mint is not wanting nor the salacious herb; sliced eggs shall garnish lizard-fish served with rue, and there shall be a paunch dripping from the tunny's brine. Herein is your whet: the modest dinner shall be served in a single course – a kid rescued from the jaws of a savage and meat-balls to require no carver's knife, and beans, the food of artisans, and tender young sprouts; to these a chicken, and a ham that has already survived three dinners, shall be added. When you have had your fill I will give you ripe apples, wine without lees from a Nomenton flagon . . .

(salacious herb: rocket)

Martial, TRANS. W. C. A. Ker

Montpellier in the Early 1780s

MME DE LA TOUR DU PIN 1770–1853

Henriette-Lucy Dillon was born in Paris in 1770. Her father Arthur Dillon was the second son of Henry, 11th Viscount Dillon. He commanded the Dillon regiment serving France until the Revolution – he was executed in 1794. Her mother Lucie de Rothe was lady-in-waiting to Queen Marie Antoinette – she died in 1782. Nineteen when the Revolution began, the intrepid Lucy used her considerable wit to elude the Terror – the thrilling story of the family's escape to America is described in her memoirs.

We had to be in full dress, even wearing jewels, by three o'clock exactly, ready for dinner. We would go up to the drawing-room where, except on Fridays, we always found about fifty guests. On Saturdays, my uncle dined out, either with the Bishop, or with some other important member of the States. My grandmother and I were always the only ladies present and the most important of the guests would be placed between us. When there were foreigners, especially Englishmen, they were put beside me. It was training for me in the art of conversation and behaviour, in learning to decide which subjects would most interest my neighbour, often a person of importance and sometimes of learning, too.

In those days, everyone with a decently dressed servant was waited on by him at table. No decanters or wine glasses were put on the table. At big dinners, there were silver buckets on a sideboard to hold the wine for the various courses. There was also a stand of a dozen glasses and anyone wishing for a glass of one of the wines sent his servant to fetch it. This servant always stood behind his master's chair.

I had a servant of my own who also dressed my hair. He wore my livery which, since our braidings exactly resembled those of the Bourbons, had to be in red. The dark blue used by my family in England would have made our livery resemble that of the King, which was not allowed.

After dinner, which did not last more than an hour, we went to the drawing-room where there would be a gathering of members of the States come to drink coffee with us. We all remained standing, and after half an hour, my grandmother and I would go downstairs to our own apartments. Afterwards, we often went visiting, carried in sedan chairs, which were the only possible means of transportation in the streets of Montpellier. The fine new parts of the city did not exist then. The Place Peyrou was still outside the town and the great ditches which surrounded the city were laid out in gardens, well sheltered from the cold.

Memoirs, ED., TRANS., Felice Harcourt, 1969

Greek Supper 1788
ELISABETH VIGÉE-LE BRUN 1755–1842

Siân Evans, who translated the memoirs, writes that Jean-Jacques Barthelmy published Voyage de Jeune Anacharsis en Grèce *in 1788. (Anacharsis was a 'legendary' Scythian sage mentioned by Herodotus.) She quotes a footnote from the* Voyage: *'the black brew of the Spartans is believed to have been made with pork fat, salt and vinegar. Such was the reputation of this sauce that Denis, tyrant of Sparta, wished to see it served at his table. The sauce was brought, the king tasted it and pushed it away indignantly. 'But my lord,' said the cook from Laconia, 'you have forgotten the essential seasoning.' 'And pray what is that?' asked the tyrant. 'Hearty exercise before the meal,' replied the slave.*

My dear, I will now give you, dear friend, an exact account of the most lavish supper I ever held in the days when people talked continually about my extravagance and high living.

One evening I invited between twelve and fifteen people to come and hear a poetry recital by the poet Le Brun. My brother had come earlier to read a few pages of the *Voyages d'Anacharsis* to me whilst I was resting. When he came to the passage describing a Greek dinner with its recipes for various sauces, he suggested that we try some of the recipes that very evening. Straightaway I asked my cook to come up and we enlisted her support. We agreed that she would make a certain sauce for the poultry and another for the eels; as my guests included some very pretty women I thought it would be a good idea if we all dressed in Greek costume in order to surprise M. de Vaudreuil and M. Boutin for I knew they would not arrive until ten o'clock. My studio was full of pieces of fabric that I used to drape about my models and I thought this would be perfect for the costumes; what is more, the Comte de Parois, who lodged in the same house, owned a very fine collection of Etruscan vases. As chance would have it, he came to see me that very day around four o'clock and soon he too was involved in our plan. Later the Count returned with a quantity of bowls and vases and choosing several from among them I cleaned them and placed them on a bare mahogany table. Having done this, I placed a huge screen behind the chairs and took care to disguise it by draping some more materials across it, securing it at intervals as in the paintings of Poussin. A hanging lamp was fixed above the table throwing its powerful beams upon it and finally everything was ready, except for the costumes. The daughter of Joseph Vernet, the charming Mme Chalgrin, was the first to arrive. I set about styling her hair and dressing her. Then came Mme de Bonneuil, renowned for her beauty and soon after Mme Vigée, my sister-in-law, who, although not exactly pretty, had the most beautiful eyes in the world; so there they were, transformed, the three of them, into veritable Athenian ladies. As soon as Le Brun-Pindare came in, off came his powder; we ruffled the curls on either side of his face and placed a laurel leaf upon his head. I had just used the wreath whilst painting the young prince, Henry Lubomirski, in *The Love of Glory*; I had depicted him kneeling before a laurel bush weaving a crown from its leaves. The picture remained in his family and the King of Poland once told me that he wanted it but the prince would not sell it at any price. The Comte de Parois had, so it happened, a huge purple cloak which I used to drape about my poet and in the blink of an eye Pindare became Anacréon. The Marquis de Cubières was next to arrive and I dressed him whilst someone else went to fetch his guitar which he had transformed into a golden lyre. I also dressed M. de Rivière (my sister-in-law's brother), Guinguené and Chaudet, the famous sculptor.

Time crept on; but I had a little left to prepare myself. However since I always wore white tunic style dresses, nowadays known as smocks, it seemed sufficient to don a veil and place a garland of flowers upon my head. I took particular care with my daughter, a charming little girl by now, and with Mlle de Bonneuil, now Mme Regnault d'Angély, who was as pretty as an angel. Both were delightful to behold as they prepared to serve us wine from one of the fragile antique vases.

By half past nine the preparations were complete, and as soon as we had sat down the effect was so original and so picturesque that each of us rose in turn to view who remained seated.

At ten o'clock we heard the coach of the Comte de Vaudreuil and de Boutin draw up outside; I had opened both doors to the dining room and when those two gentlemen reached the doorway, they found us singing Gluck's chorus, *Le dieu de Paphos et de Gnide*, with M. de Cubières accompanying us on his lyre.

In all my life I never saw two more surprised or astonished faces as those of M. de Vaudreuil and his companion. They were so stunned, so charmed, that they stood for ages before deciding to take the seats we had kept for them.

As well as those mentioned earlier we also had two vegetable dishes and a cake made with honey and Corinthian raisins. Truth be told, our only extravagance that evening was a bottle of old Cyprus wine, given to me as a present. Nevertheless we stayed hours at the table and Le Brun recited several odes from Anacréon which he himself had translated; indeed I can scarcely remember a more enjoyable evening.

M. Boutin and M. Vaudreuil were so taken with the whole evening that they talked about it the next day to all their friends. A few ladies from the Court asked me to perform the joke for a second time. I refused for various reasons and I believe several were offended by my refusal. Soon the word spread about society that my little dinner party had cost twenty thousands francs. The King, aggrieved by these reports, spoke to the Marquis de Cubières, who as luck would have it had been one of our guests; he managed to persuade His Majesty that the rumour was a gross exaggeration.

However, the stories which spoke of a modest twenty thousand francs in Versailles had grown to forty thousand by the time they reached Rome. In Vienna, the Baronne Stroganoff informed me, to my great surprise, that I had spent sixty thousand francs on my Greek supper. As you know, the sum finally settled upon in St. Petersburg was eighty thousands francs; in fact the real cost of the meal was nearer fifteen francs!

Memoirs, TRANS. Siân Evans, 1989

Curious Fire-works
and a Sumptuous Banquet for Her Majesty
JOHN LYLY 1554?–1606

John Lyly was a playwright whose rambling prose romances were written in such an affected, high-flown style that his character Euphues has given us the term euphuism.

By 1530 the banquet had become a separate meal served after dinner, which on this occasion ended before 3 o'clock, and after supper. It was the sweet course which we would now call dessert, and was taken in banqueting houses, rooms or out of doors and for grand parties entertainment was usual.

The Honourable Entertainment given to the Queen's Majesty in Progress, at Elvetham in Hampshire, by the Right Honourable the Earl of Hertford, 1591 . . . after supper there were two delights presented unto her Majesty; curious fire-works and a sumptuous banquet: the first from the three islands in the pond, the second in a low gallery in Her Majesty's privy garden . . . during the time of these fire-works in the water, there was a banquet served all in glass and silver into the low gallery in the garden, from a hill-side fourteen score off, by two hundred of my Lord of Hertford's gentlemen, every one carrying so many dishes that the whole number amounted to a thousand, and there were to light them in their way a hundred torch-bearers. To satisfy the curious I will here set down some particulars in the banquet: Her Majesty's Arms in sugar-work. The Several Arms of all our nobility in sugar-work. Many men and women in sugar-work, and some enforced by hand. Castles, forts, ordnance, drummers, trumpeters, and soldiers of all sorts, in sugar-work. Lions, unicorns, bears, horses, camels, bulls, rams, dogs, tigers, elephants, antelopes, dromedaries, apes, and all other beasts. Eagles, falcons, cranes, bustards, heronshawkes, bitterns, phesants, partridge, quails, larks, sparrows, pigeons, cocks, owls and all that fly in sugar-work. Snakes, adders, vipers, frogs, toads and all kind of worms in sugar-work. Mermaids, whales, dolphins, congers, sturgeons, pikes, carps, brawms, and all sorts of fishes in sugar-work. The self same devices were also there in flat-work. Moreover these particulars following and many such like, were in flat sugar-work and cinnamon, marchpanes, grapes, oysters, mussels, cockles, periwinkles, crabs, lobsters. Apples, pears and plums of all sorts. Preserves, suckets, jellies, leaches, marmalades, pastes, comfits, of all sorts.

Euphues, 1632

Wedding Feast
MME DE SÉVIGNÉ 1626–96

To Mme de Grignan, Les-Rochers,
Wednesday 15 July 1671
Mlle du Plessis often honours us with her presence. She was saying yesterday that in Lower Brittany the food is admirable, and that at the wedding of her sister-in-law they ate twelve hundred chickens in one day. At this exaggeration we were all turned to stone. I plucked up my courage and said, 'Mademoiselle, think a moment, don't you mean twelve? Everyone makes mistakes sometimes.' 'No, Madame, it was twelve hundred, or eleven hundred. I won't swear to you whether it was eleven or twelve, for fear of telling a lie, but I am sure it was one or the other.' And she repeated that a score of times, and wouldn't knock off a single chicken. We felt that there must have been at least three hundred dressers to prepare the birds with larding fat, and that the scene must have been a big field in which marquees had been set up, and that if they had numbered only fifty they would have had to start a month in advance. This table-talk was good and you would have enjoyed it. Have you got some exaggerating female like that?

Selected Letters, TRANS. Leonard Tancock, 1982

Let Me Make Lunch
FAY WELDON 1931–

The children were hungry so Martha opened them a can of beans and sausages and heated that up. ('Martha, do they have to eat that crap? Can't they wait?': Martin)

Katie was hungry: she said so, to keep the children in face. She was lovely with children – most children. She did not particularly like Colin and Janet's children. She said so, and he accepted it. He only saw them once a month now, not once a week.

'Let me make lunch,' Kate said to Martha. 'You do so much, poor thing!'

And she pulled out of the fridge all the things Martha had put away for the next day's picnic lunch party – Camembert cheese and salad and salami and made a wonderful tomato salad in two minutes and opened the white wine – 'not very cold, darling. Shouldn't it be chilling?' – and had it all on the table in five amazing competent minutes. 'That's all we need, darling,' said Martin. 'You are funny with your fish-and-chip Saturdays! What could be nicer than this? Or simpler?'

Nothing, except there was Sunday's buffet lunch for nine gone, in place of Saturday's fish for six, and would the fish stretch? No.

'Weekend', *Cosmopolitan*, 1978

What Would You Like For Breakfast?
JULIAN STREET 1879–1947

If a guest but realized it, he would save his hostess minutes of patient inquiry if, when asked what he likes to eat for breakfast, he would cast shyness away and speak up. We set down a typical dialogue overheard in our household on one occasion, after the first question had been asked:

'Oh, anything – anything at all. Toast and coffee'd be fine.'

'No fruit?'

'Well yes, of course, if you have fruit . . . Yes, I'd like fruit, thanks.'

'Any particular choice? There's grapefruit, and I think prunes and orange juice.'

'Oh, orange juice – yes, thanks very much.'

'Nothing else? How about cereal, or bacon and eggs?'

'Oh, that would put you to a lot of trouble. I *would* like bacon and eggs, but –'

He wanted a big breakfast all along, but was too diffident to say so. It would have been simpler for everyone concerned if he had.

Table Topics, 1959

Country Weddings
LADY JEKYLL 1861–1937

Country weddings must often take place early in the day, and so necessitate a more substantial sitting-down meal for everybody, small tables supplementing the large ceremonial one where are gathered the guests of honour. There the complicated foods we are so erroneously supposed to like, and so seldom do, are offered in bewildering variety; and mayonnaises, mousses, aspics, succeeded by elaborate creams, jellies, pastries, and ornamental cakes, appear in profusion, whilst confidential butlers pour champagne encouragingly into frugal glasses as the anxious moment for speeches draws near. Might it not be better to concentrate effort and expenditure on two or three really first-rate dishes of universal acceptance? Silvery salmon or sea trout, lobsters fresh from their rocky homes, peach-fed hams, abundant chickens hot, young, and undisguised, crisp lettuces, and perfect potatoes; compotes of fruit with generous bowls of whipped cream, cakes of the best, but not masquerading as flowers or towering into castellated buildings, all these would be welcome!

In both types of wedding breakfasts there is a tendency towards the conventional, the stereotyped, unworthy of this greatest day in life.

Kitchen Essays, 1922

Three Dinners

L. N. TOLSTOY 1828–1910

Oblonsky liked a good dinner, but what he liked better still was a dinner-party at his own house: not a big affair, but very choice, both as regards the food and drink, and the guests. He was well satisfied with the programme for that day's dinner: there would be perch (brought alive to the kitchen), asparagus, and *la pièce de résistance* – a superb but quite plain joint of roast-beef, and the appropriate wines: so much for the food and drink.

The efforts of Agatha Mihalovna and the cook to prepare a specially good dinner only ended in the two hungry friends sitting down to the preliminary course and filling themselves up with bread and butter, smoked goose, and pickled mushrooms, and in Levin's ordering the soup to be served without waiting for the little pies with which the cook had particularly meant to impress their visitor. But Oblonsky, though he was accustomed to very different dinners, found everything delicious: the herb brandy, the bread and the butter, and, above all, the smoked goose and the mushrooms, the nettle soup and the chicken in white sauce, the Crimean white wine – everything was superb and marvellous.

The dinner was as choice as the dinner-service, and Oblonsky was a connoisseur of china. The soup *Marie-Louise* had succeeded to perfection, the tiny patties melted in the mouth and were flawless. Matvey and two footmen in white ties manipulated the dishes and wines unobtrusively, noiselessly, and skilfully. On the material side the dinner was a success; it was no less so on the non-material side. The conversation, sometimes general and sometimes tête-à-tête, never flagged, and towards the end became so animated that the men got up from the table still talking, and even Karenin was completely thawed.

Anna Karenin, TRANS. Rosemary Edmonds, 1954

Fig-pecker
ALEXIS SOYER 1809–58

Alexis Soyer was perhaps the most famous of Victorian chefs. He left Paris in 1830 because of the July revolution and served in the kitchens of the Duke of Cambridge in London. In 1837 he was appointed chef at the Reform Club. He patented various cooking devices and wrote many best-selling cookery books. He also reorganized the victualling of the army hospitals at Scutari and Constantinople during the Crimean War.

The Pantropheon, sub-titled The History of Food and its Preparation in Ancient Times, *is quite unlike any other book written by Soyer. There is now grave doubt that he wrote it at all, and how it came to be published under Soyer's name is still a mystery.*

The Duke of C**** had received from nature one of those culinary organizations which the vulgar assimilate with gluttony, and the man of arts calls genius. Greece would have raised statues to him; the Roman emperor Vitellius would have shared the Empire with him. In France he gained the esteem of all parties by inviting them to sumptuous banquets.

This rich patrician brought up with tender care a young *chef de cuisine*, whom his *major-domo* had bequeathed to him on his death-bed, as Mazarin did Colbert to Louis XIV. The disciple profited by the learned lessons of the Duke; already the young *chef*'s head, eye, and hand possessed that promptitude and certainty whose union is so rarely combined: there remained for him only the instruction of experience.

One day, in the month of September, some guests of the highest class, all professed judges in the order of epicureans, met together at the residence of the noble Amphitryon, who often claimed the authority of their enlightened judgment. The learned Areopagitæ had to pronounce on certain new dishes: it was necessary, by dint of seduction, to captivate the favour and patronage of these judges by disarming their severity.

Everything was served to the greatest nicety, everything was deemed exquisite, and they only awaited the dessert – that little course which causes the emotion of the great culinary drama to be forgotten – when the young *chef* appeared, and placed in the centre of the table a silver dish, containing twelve eggs. 'Eggs!' exclaimed the Duke. The astonished guests looked at each other in silence. The cook took one of the eggs, placed it in a little china boat, slightly broke the shell, and begged his master to taste the contents. The latter continued to remove the white envelope, and at length discovered a savoury and perfumed ball of fat. It was a fig-pecker of a golden colour – fat, delicate, exquisite – surrounded by a wonderful seasoning.

The good old man cast on his pupil a look full of tenderness and pride; and, holding out his hand to him: 'You are inspired by Petronius,' said he; 'to imitate in such a manner is to create. Courage! I am much pleased with you.'

This classic dish – a revival from the feasts of Trimalcio – enjoyed only an ephemeral glory. Europe was on fire; a warlike fever raged everywhere; and Paris soon forgot the eggs of Petronius.

The fig-pecker merits the attention of the most serious gastronomists. The ancients reckoned it among the most refined of dishes. The Greeks made delicate pies of this bird, which exhaled an odour so tempting, that criticism was disarmed beforehand.

The Romans gave it their entire esteem, and prepared it with truffles and mushrooms. Among them, men who knew what good cheer means, thought there was nothing worth eating in birds but the leg and lower part of the body. Fig-peckers were the only exception to this rule: they were served and eaten entire.

The Pantropheon, 1853

How to Ensure a Hearty Welcome
WILLIAM KITCHINER 1775?–1827

The Guest who wishes to ensure a hearty welcome, and frequent invitation to the board of hospitality, may calculate that the 'easier he is pleased, the oftener he will be invited.' Instead of unblushingly demanding of the fair Hostess that the prime '*tit-bit*' of every dish be put on your plate – receive (if not with pleasure – or even content) with the liveliest expressions of thankfulness, whatever is presented to you – and forget not to praise the Cook, and the same shall be reckoned unto you even as the praise of the Mistress.

I once heard a gentle hint on this subject, given to a *Blue-Mould Fancier*, who by looking too long at a Stilton cheese, was at last completely overcome, by his Eye exciting his Appetité, till it became quite ungovernable; and unconscious of every thing but the *mity* object of his contemplation, he began to pick out in no small portions, the primest parts his eye could select from the centre of the Cheese.

The good-natured founder of the Feast, highly amused at the Ecstasies each morsel created in its passage over the palate of the enraptured *Gourmand*, thus encouraged the perseverance of his Guest – 'Cut away my dear sir, cut away, use no Ceremony, I pray: – I hope you will pick out all the best of my Cheese – *don't you think that* THE RIND *and the* ROTTEN *will do very well for my Wife and Family?*' There is another set of terribly *Free and Easy* folks, who are 'fond of taking possession of the Throne of Domestic Comfort,' – and then, with all the impudence imaginable, simper out to the ousted Master of the Family – 'Dear me, I am afraid I have taken your place!'

The Cook's Oracle, 1831

The Dinner Was Indescribably Grand

DORA CARRINGTON 1893–1932

TO LYTTON STRACHEY

Saturday [September 26th, 1925]   Ham Spray House, Hungerford
Darling Lytton, Your letter has just come. I wrote you a long letter on Thursday, and Friday, but didn't post it. So now I will write it all over again. All Wednesday was very hot, and exquisite, I spent the entire morning gossiping to Helen and inventing a dinner for our party. We drove to Hungerford before lunch; otherwise the entire day seemed to be spent in meandering conversations. The Japp world arrived at half past seven. The dinner was indescribably grand. Epoch making; grapefruit, then a chicken covered with fennel and tomato sauce, a risotto with almonds, onions, and pimentos, followed by sack cream, supported by Café Royal red wine, *perfectly* warmed. (The cradle took Mrs Japp's breath away.) I shall repeat this grand dinner for our next weekend. We all became very boozed. You would hardly have recognized old Japp. He became so flirtatious and talkative. Helen was a great support and was very polite to the Japps. We tippled sherry

over the fire till after 11 o'ck. The next morning I manoeuvred and got Dorelia to promise to come down, on her way to Alderney. She arrived at half past six. Henry came over. We again had a *superb* dinner ending with crême brulé and two bottles of champagne and more sherry afterwards! Dorelia became completely boozed and very gay. Even Henry was less gloomy and rather amusing. We played Haydn, made endless jokes and talked without stopping. Somehow I thought it was the most lovely evening I'd ever spent. I wished you could have been with us . . . Helen and I go to Japps tonight to a return dinner. Apparently Mrs Japp is renowned for exquisite cuisine and was very agitated by our gorgeous display. So this is a rival supper party.

Letters, 1979

First Class Chinese Banquet
LADY MACARTNEY 1877–1949

Catherine Borland was another Scottish-born diplomatic bride who, like Fanny Calderón de la Barca, wrote about her life in an exotic foreign land a very long way from home. Catherine began her book: 'Long years ago, one Saturday morning in early autumn, I, a girl of twenty-one, was busy in the kitchen making cakes. I had been engaged to be married for the past two years, and my fiancé as I supposed, was away at his post in Kashgar. As my future was to be spent in the wilds of Central Asia, I was doing my best to learn things that would be useful to me in such a remote place.' They were married the following Saturday. It was 1898 and Catherine was to spend the next seventeen years in China where the Macartneys maintained a hospitable household in the British residence in Chini Bagh – the Chinese Garden.

One day invitations arrived for us from the Ti-tai and his wife to a Chinese dinner in the New City.

It was to be a first class banquet, that is to say, one that included both swallow's-nest soup and sucking-pig. The invitations were in the form of a long strip of red paper, about two feet long and six inches wide, folded backwards, and forwards, and placed in a red envelope. Some tiny characters were written on the invitation that in English would read something like this: 'Respectfully, with goblet in hand, I await the light of your countenance on the sixth day of the first moon at midday.' As we accepted we kept the documents to show that we did so.

If it had been a dinner of the second class we were invited to, that is, one at which sucking-pig would be served, but not swallow's nest, the invitations would have been written on a small red card, with a list of the guests on it. Each one invited would have written beside his name something in very flowery language to the effect that he accepted or refused, and have returned the card to the messenger who brought it.

But we were to be honoured with the very best of entertainments, and I was quite excited at the prospect.

Everyone was very friendly and crowded round me, the newcomer, to see how I was dressed. They opened my fur coat to see what I wore beneath it, stroked the feather in my hat, and seemed highly amused at my serviceable winter clothing. My black shoes and stockings caused quite an excitement, and I am afraid were not admired. The little ladies put out their tiny embroidered satin shoes to compare with them, and went into peals of laughter at mine, till I tucked them away under me, hoping they would forget all about the ugly black things. I began to feel so embarrassed, and was much relieved when dinner was announced.

Our hostess led me to my place on her left hand, and taking a tiny wine cup from a servant, raised it to her forehead before placing it on the table before my chair. Then she went through the same ceremony with a pair of chopsticks; she shook my chair to make certain that it would bear me, and passed her sleeve over the seat to brush away the dust. This performance had to be gone through for each guest before we could sit down.

We sat round a big square table on which were a number of small bowls containing sauces and condiments; then the serving began. We started with ancient eggs that had been buried in lime for a very long time; they were not as bad as I expected they would be, and when one tried to imagine that they were what they very much resembled, gorgonzola cheese, and not bad eggs, they were quite possible to eat. Then followed about forty courses – meat, vegetables, poultry, dried fish of many kinds, sea slugs, ducks, shark's fins, seaweed, lotus seeds, and roots, fungi of various sorts, sweet dishes, and the very special delicacies, sucking-pig, which seemed to be simply the crackling served sweet, and swallow's nest soup. Everything was cut into small pieces, for convenience of eating with chopsticks, I suppose.

I was very curious to see, and try, the swallow's-nest soup I had heard so much about, but I was quite disappointed in it. It tasted just as though it had been made with vermicelli, highly flavoured with onion and garlic, and I could not find anything very delicious about it whatever. It is made from the gelatinous lining of the nest of a special breed of swallow that lives in the south of China and builds in most inaccessible places on the cliffs. The nest lining is about the size of half a tablespoon; one side, where it has been stuck against the cliff, being cut off just like a spoon cut in half. It is very beautifully made, and looks like fine vermicelli woven into a tiny basket. The idea is not a very nice one, I know, but it seems that the birds themselves make this gelatinous stuff with their saliva to line their little nests.

At a dinner of men, this great dish must be honoured by being eaten with hats on; and before it is put on the table, the servant of each guest brings his master's hat to him. As we were all wearing our hats, no difference was made; and perhaps mere womenfolk are not expected to observe all these niceties of etiquette.

All through the long meal a servant kept coming round with a kettle of boiling spirit to replenish the wine cups, and I am afraid we rather gave offence by not drinking it.

Another servant wandered about with a very greasy-looking wet cloth, ready to wipe anyone's hands and face who needed the attention. Needless to say I did not make use of him!

It is as well that the table had an upstanding edge all round, for most of the dishes were served in soup or gravy, which slopped over the bowls and dripped off the dainty morsels as they were being conveyed about by the chopsticks.

We found on the table in our places, besides the chopsticks, knives, forks and spoons. When I took up mine, to my surprise, I found they were my own and wondered how they had got there. Afterwards I learned that the Ti-tai had most thoughtfully sent a servant to suggest to Jafar Ali that he should bring a supply with him, and Jafar Ali had sensibly brought a cruet too. I tried valiantly to use the chopsticks and provided much amusement for the company; nothing got as far as my mouth, for if I managed to pick up a bit of something from the bowl after long, patient efforts, I promptly dropped it on the table.

To the Chinese guests the dinner was most recherché. Many of the things had come from China and were very costly. But I found it difficult to swallow some of them, in spite of the mustard and salt Jafar Ali had provided. Any very dainty titbit my hostess insisted on my eating, conveying the choicest bits from the bowl with her own chopsticks to my mouth. I managed pretty well till the sea slugs came along: if they had been minced or disguised in some way, they might not have been so bad, but they were served boiled whole, and when I saw these huge black slugs, covered with lumps, wobbling about in front of me, I wondered how I should live through the ordeal of swallowing one. But there was no getting out of it and I was faced with the choice of eating it or giving offence. So I covered one well with mustard, shut my eyes, and swallowed it whole. The ladies were so pleased with me that they insisted on me eating another; and three or four times I had to go through the awful ordeal. It was many days before I forgot those sea slugs, for eating the tough, gelatinous things whole like that made me horribly ill afterwards.

One little lady, seeing us apparently enjoying mustard, insisted on trying it; we warned her to be careful, but she took a spoonful and put it in her mouth; then there was a scene better imagined than described!

But, oh! I did get tired, and how I longed for the cup of tea to appear which would be the signal for us to go; we sat there from twelve till past five, and my head ached violently.

The Ti-tai and his wife escorted us again to the gate and we took an elaborate farewell. Again the nerve-wracking salute was fired, and again I bumped along in that awful cart, reaching home a complete wreck for the time being.

The polite thing to say to the host who has entertained you when you see him after a week or so is: 'The taste of your dinner is still in my mouth.' I could have said that with great feeling and perfect truth!

An English Lady in Chinese Turkestan, 1931

Fancy-Dress-Frenzy, 1931
DIANA COOPER 1892–1986

Palazzo Mocenigo [Venice]   *6 September [1931]*
I missed writing yesterday because I was in my typical fancy-dress-frenzy from dawn to eve. I was also turned out of Byron's bedroom and put in the dining-room, to allow eighty people to dine in it – two tables of forty, everyone in white, a Cartier-bag prize for the best lady and links for the lucky man. I went as the Ghost of Byron's dream of the Levant, and was admired by artists (Lifar, Oliver Messel and Madame Sert). The party had no *entrain* and there are a lot of

complaints on the beach this morning. The funniest is one going round
the bars where the hang-overers are having hairs of dogs. Their
headaches are attributed to too many tuberoses.

The Light of Common Day, 1959

Entertaining Pons

HONORÉ DE BALZAC 1799–1850

At the moment when Pons was mechanically making his way into the
house, Madame Cibot was putting the last touches to Schmucke's
dinner. This dinner consisted of a kind of stew whose aroma
permeated the entire courtyard: the remains of a joint of boiled beef
bought from a cookshop whose owner did some trade in left-overs,
hashed up in butter with thin slices of onion until the meat and onions
soaked up the butter, so that this concierge's fare looked quite like a
freshly fried dish. La Cibot had lovingly concocted it for sharing
between her husband and Schmucke, and it went in company with a
bottle of beer and a morsel of cheese: it answered the needs of the old
German music-master. And you may take it that Solomon in all his
glory dined no better than Schmucke. Sometimes it would be this same
dish of boiled beef with onions *en fricassée*, sometimes remnants of
poulet sauté, sometimes a cold beef salad with parsley, or fish served
up with a sauce of La Cibot's own invention – a mother could
unsuspectingly have eaten her own child with this – and sometimes
venison, all depending on the quality and quantity of food sold off by
the boulevard restaurants to the man who ran the cookshop in the rue
Boucherat. Such was Schmucke's ordinary fare, and he was content to
eat, without comment, anything set before him by the 'goot Matame
Cipot'. And, as time went on, the good Madame Cibot had reduced
this menu until it cost her no more than a franc to produce.

Cousin Pons, TRANS. H. J. Hunt, 1968

Life at Nohant with Mme Sand

EDMOND 1822–96 AND JULES 1830–70
GONCOURT

14 September [1863]

Dinner at Magny's. Afterwards, Sainte-Beuve left us drinking the mixture of rum and curaçao he always prepares for us at dessert.

'By the way, Gautier, you are just back from Madame Sand's at Nohant, aren't you? Is it amusing?'

'As amusing as a Moravian monastery! I arrived in the evening. It's a long way from the station. They left my box in a bush. I reached the house by way of the farm, with the most frightening dogs following me. They gave me dinner. The food's good, but there's too much game and chicken, and that doesn't suit me. There was Marchal, the painter, there and Alexandre Dumas *fils* and Madame Calamatta.'

'And how's Dumas *fils*? Still ill?'

'Oh, terribly unhappy. You know what he does these days? He sits down in front of a sheet of paper and stays there for four hours. He writes three lines. He goes off to have a cold bath or do some exercises, because he's full of ideas on hygiene. Then he comes back and decides that his three lines are damn stupid.'

'Well, that shows some sense!' said somebody.

'And he crosses out everything except three words. Every now and then his father arrives from Naples and says: 'Get me a cutlet and I'll finish your play for you', writes the scenario, brings in a whore, borrows some money and goes off again. Dumas *fils* reads the scenario, likes it, goes and has a bath, reads the scenario again, decides that it's stupid, and spends a year revising it. And when his father comes back, he finds the same three words from the same three lines as the year before!'

'And what sort of life do they lead at Nohant?'

'You breakfast at ten. On the last stroke, when the hand is exactly at ten o'clock, everybody sits down without waiting for Mme Sand, who arrives looking like a sleepwalker and stays asleep throughout the meal. After breakfast, you go into the garden and play bowls; that wakes her up. She sits down and begins to talk. The conversation at that hour of the day is usually about pronunciation, for instance how to pronounce *ailleurs* and *meilleur*. But the chief conversational pleasure in that company is the scatological joke.'

'Get along with you!'

'Yes, all their fun comes from farting. Marchal was wildly popular with his wind. But never a word about relations between the sexes. I do believe they would throw you out of the house if you made the slightest allusion to the subject. . . . At three o'clock Madame Sand goes back upstairs to churn out copy till six. Then you have dinner, but in rather a hurry, to give Marie Caillot time to eat. She's the housemaid, a *petite Fadette* Madame Sand found near Nohant to play in her private theatre, and who comes to the sitting-room in the evening after her meal. After dinner Madame Sand plays patience until midnight without uttering a single word.'

Pages from the Goncourt Journals, ED., TRANS. Robert Baldick, 1962

College Dinner
EDNA O'BRIEN 1932–

Dinner was in one of the most esteemed of the colleges and they foregathered in a small overheated sitting-room, that was full of furniture and pieces of china. Her host, a professor, had invited a young professor and two freshmen. They sat and awkwardly sorted each other out, the young men laughing lightly at everything and constantly interjecting their remarks with bits of French as they bantered with each other about their sleeping habits and their taste for sherry or classical music. It was stiff. Her son should have had a different introduction, something much less formal, a bit of gaiety. The conversation centred for a long time on a professor who had the nickname of a woman and who received students in his long johns and thought nothing of it. Incongruously he was described as a hermit even though he seemed to be receiving students most mornings in his cluttered room. It was stifling hot. To calm herself, Lena thought of the beautiful mist like fine gauze sparkling on the courtyard outside, and above it a sky perfectly pictorial with its new moon and its thrilling stars.

They went down a short flight of stairs and then climbed some other steps to their early dinner. The host had done everything to make it perfect – smoked salmon, grouse, chantilly, different wines for each course and all this printed alongside each person's nameplace. The old servant was so nervous that he trembled as he stood over her and kept debating with his long hands whether to proffer the entrée dish or the gravy jug. It was touch and go. His master told him for God's sake to put the jug down. A movement that caused his neck to tremble like that of a half-dead cockerel's. Yes, 'It was so' that students were sent down but they had to be awfully bad or else awfully unlucky and of course it was an awfully amusing thing. 'I am in a modern English play,' she thought, the kind of play that portrayed an intelligent man or woman going to seed and making stoical jokes about it. Academic life was not for her. She would rather be a barbarian. She sucked on the word as if it were sherbet. Barbarian.

The grouse was impossible to tackle. Everyone talked too much and tried too eagerly and this all-round determination to be considerate caused them instead to be distracted and noisy. Little bright jets of blood shot up as knives vainly attacked the game. To conceal his embarrassment the young professor said it was too delicious. The host said it was uneatable and if young Freddie's was delicious to give it to Lena since hers was like a brick. She demurred, said it was lovely, while at the same time resolved that she would eat the sprouts and would drink goblets of wine. A toast was raised to her son and he went scarlet as he heard himself being praised. Looking downwards she saw that the various plates contained a heap of little bones, decked with bits of torn pink flesh, and true to her domestic instinct she said they would make good broth, those leavings. A most tactless slip. Everyone raved over the nice raspberry chantilly and enormous portions of it were lolloped on the young men's dessert plates.

'In the Hours of Darkness', Mrs Reinhardt and Other Stories, 1978

I Am Now Dining with a Maiden Aunt
SYDNEY SMITH 1771–1845

TO LADY HOLLAND

[Probably March–April 1810]

Dear Lady Holland,

It is barely possible I may come to your recollection before you set down to dinner: and therefore I write to account for my absence. You invited me to dine with you on this day a week past, and in consequence I have refused to dine with the Marquis of Stafford, and again with Lord Crewe; but as you said nothing to me about it this morning, and said I should see you at the Opera, I presumed you had forgotten it and did not come for fear of another *surprise*. The consequence of your forgetfulness of me has been that I am now dining with a *Maiden Aunt*, and that dinner will be over before you have read this. When the happiness of your fellow creatures is at stake you should really be more careful.

Yrs &c.
SYDNEY SMITH
Selected Letters, ED. Nowell C. Smith, 1956

Luncheon

PATRICK WHITE 1912–90

There were the luncheons, and the dinners, but preferably the luncheons, for there the wives were without their husbands, and their minds could move more nimbly divested of the weight: wives who had stupid husbands were in a position to be as clever as they wished, whereas stupid wives might now put their stupidity to its fullest, its most profitable use.

It was the period when hostesses were discovering *cuisine*, and introducing to their tables *vol-au-vent*, *sole Véronique*, *beignets au fromage* and *tournedos Lulu Wattier*, forcing their husbands into clubs, hotels, even railway stations, in their longing for the stench of corned beef. Mrs Chalmers-Robinson in particular, was famous for her amusing luncheons, at which she would receive the wives of graziers – so safe – barristers, solicitors, bankers, doctors, the Navy – but never the Army – and with discretion, the wives of storekeepers, some of whom, by that time, had become rich, useful, and therefore, tolerable. Many of the ladies she entertained, the hostess hardly knew, and these she liked best of all . . .

But before a luncheon, Mrs Chalmers-Robinson would invariably dazzle. She would come into the dining-room, to move the cutlery about on the table, and add two or three little Murano bowls filled with different brands of cigarettes.

Even if she felt like frowning, she would not let herself. She might say:

'How I wish I could sit down on my own to a nice, quiet grill, with you to wait on me, and tell me something interesting. But I must congratulate you, Ruth. You have everything looking perfect.' . . .

Before one lunch, which Ruth Joyner had cause to remember, a lady told the company of some acquaintance common to them all who was dying of cancer. It seemed ill-timed. Several of the ladies withdrew inside their sad fur, others began knotting the fringes. One spilled her brandy cruster, and at least her immediate neighbours were able to assist in the mopping. Until the conversation could resume its trajectory of smoke, violet-scented, where for a moment there had been the stench of sick, drooping monkeys.

Everyone felt far better in the dining-room, where Ruth and an elderly woman called May, who came in when help was needed, were soon moving in their creaking white behind the chairs of monkey-ladies.

Mrs Chalmers-Robinson kept her eye on everyone, while giving the impression she was eating. She could knit any sort of party together. She heard everything, and rumbles too.

She whispered:

'Another of the little soles, Ruth, for Mrs du Plessy. Ah, yes, Marion, they are too innocent to refuse!'

Or, very, very soft:

'Surely you have not forgotten, May, which is the left side?'

But the wine had contented everyone. And already, again, there was a smoke, blurry and blue, of released violets, it could have been.

At the end, when a big swan in spun sugar was fetched in, the ladies clapped their rings together. It was so successful.

Ruth herself was delighted with the cook's triumphant swan. She could not resist remarking to a lady as she passed behind:

'It was the devil to make, you know. And has got a bomb inside of it.'

Which the visitor considered inexperienced, though comical.

Riders in the Chariot, 1961

Genuine Hospitality

GEORGE BORROW 1803–81

I entered the house, and the kitchen, parlour, or whatever it was, a nice little room with a slate floor. They made me sit down at a table by the window, which was already laid for a meal. There was a clean cloth upon it, a teapot, cups and saucers, a large plate of bread-and-butter, and a plate, on which were a few very thin slices of brown, watery cheese.

My good friends took their seats, the wife poured out tea for the stranger and her husband, helped us both to bread-and-butter, and the watery cheese, then took care of herself. Before, however, I could taste the tea, the wife, seeming to recollect herself, started up, and hurrying to a cupboard, produced a basin full of snow-white lump sugar, and taking the spoon out of my hand, placed two of the largest lumps in my cup, though she helped neither her husband nor herself; the sugar-basin being probably only kept for grand occasions.

My eyes filled with tears; for in the whole course of my life I had never experienced so much genuine hospitality. Honour to the miller of Mona and his wife; and honour to the kind hospitable Celts in general! How different is the reception of this despised race of the wandering stranger from that of –. However, I am a Saxon myself, and the Saxons have no doubt their virtues; a pity that they should be all uncouth and ungracious ones!

Wild Wales, 1854

Arab Hospitality

A. W. KINGLAKE 1809–91

You who are going into their country have a direct personal interest in knowing something about 'Arab hospitality'; but the deuce of it is, that the poor fellows with whom I have happened to pitch my tent were scarcely ever in a condition to exercise that magnanimous virtue with much *éclat*; indeed Mysseri's canteen generously enabled me to outdo my hosts in the matter of entertainment. They were always courteous, however, and were never backward in offering me the *youart*, a kind of whey, which is the principal delicacy to be found amongst the wandering tribes.

Eothen, 1844

Haute Cuisine
GIUSEPPE DI LAMPEDUSA 1896–1957

The Prince was too experienced to offer Sicilian guests, in a town of the interior, a dinner beginning with soup, and he infringed the rules of *haute cuisine* all the more readily as he disliked it himself. But rumours of the barbaric foreign usage of serving an insipid liquid as first course had reached the citizens of Donnafugata too insistently for them not to quiver with a slight residue of alarm at the start of a solemn dinner like this. So when three lackeys in green, gold and powder entered, each holding a great silver dish containing a towering macaroni pie, only four of the twenty at table avoided showing pleased surprise; the Prince and Princess from fore-knowledge, Angelica from affectation and Concetta from lack of appetite. All the others (including Trancredi, I regret to say), showed their relief in varying ways, from the fluty and ecstatic grunts of the notary to the sharp squeak of Francesco Paolo. But a threatening circular stare from the host soon stifled these improper demonstrations.

Good manners apart, though, the aspect of those monumental dishes of macaroni was worthy of the quivers of admiration they evoked. The burnished gold of the crusts, the fragrance of sugar and cinnamon they exuded, were but preludes to the delights released from the interior when the knife broke the crust; first came a smoke laden with aromas, then chicken livers, hard boiled eggs, sliced ham, chicken and truffles in masses of piping hot, glistening macaroni, to which the meat juice gave an exquisite hue of suède.

The beginning of the meal, as happens in the provinces, was quiet. The arch-priest made the sign of the Cross and plunged in head first without a word. The organist absorbed the succulent dish with closed eyes; he was grateful to the Creator that his ability to shoot hare and woodcock could bring him ecstatic pleasures like this, and the thought came to him that he and Teresina could exist for a month on the cost of one of these dishes; Angelica, the lovely Angelica, forgot her Tuscan affectations and part of her good manners and devoured her food with the appetite of her seventeen years and the vigour given by grasping her fork half-way up the handle. Tancredi, in an attempt to link gallantry with greed, tried to imagine himself tasting, in the aromatic forkfuls, the kisses of his neighbour Angelica, but he realised at once that the experiment was disgusting and suspended it, with a mental reserve about reviving this fantasy with the pudding; the Prince, although rapt in the contemplation of Angelica sitting opposite him, was the only one at table able to notice that the *demi-glace* was overfilled, and made a mental note to tell the cook so next day; the others ate without thinking of anything, and without realising that the food seemed so delicious because sensuality was circulating in the house.

The Leopard, TRANS. Archibald Colquhoun, 1960

Paris Dinners
EDMOND 1822–96 AND JULES 1830–70
GONCOURT

November [1852]
We are supping out a great deal this year: mad suppers where they serve mulled wine made from Léoville and peaches *à la Condé* costing 72 francs the dish, in the company of trollops picked up at Mabille and shopsoiled sluts who nibble at these feasts with a bit of the sausage they had for dinner stuck in their teeth. One of them once exclaimed naively: 'Why, it's four o'clock . . . Ma's just peeling her carrots.'

Wednesday, 3 April [1878]
House-warming dinner at Zola's.

A study in which the young master works on a massive Portuguese throne in Brazilian rosewood, a bedroom with a carved four-poster bed and twelfth-century stained-glass in the window, tapestries showing greenish saints on the walls and ceilings, altar frontals over the doors, a whole houseful of ecclesiastical bric-à-brac: all this makes a somewhat eccentric setting for the author of *L'Assommoir*.

He gave us a very choice, very tasty dinner, a real gourmet's dinner, including some grouse whose scented flesh Daudet compared to an old courtesan's flesh marinaded in a bidet.

10 April [1886]

At seven o'clock we met again, the Zolas and I, at Daudet's, where there was a big dinner. Right at the beginning, with regard to the delicate pastel drawing of his daughter which Raffaelli has put on show and which I praised, Zola declared that Raffaelli had a laborious talent and lacked 'sincerity'. . . . We sat down at table. Daudet called out to me: 'Goncourt, I've been to Joret's to get some morels for you.' At this Mme Zola's shrill voice could be heard saying: 'Oh, morels are quite common now; they only cost three francs. . . .' And she went on making amiable remarks of that kind all the way through dinner. Poor Mme Charpentier, who did her best to calm her down and who, in connexion with a bouillabaisse which the Daudets had had sent from Marseilles, spoke to her of her skill at cooking that particular dish, was rewarded with the sharp retort: 'Really, Madame, you are going to make people think that I spend the whole of my life in the kitchen!'

Pages from the Goncourt Journals, ED., TRANS. Robert Baldick, 1962

Every Mark of Refinement

ROSAMOND LEHMANN 1901–90

Dinner was over, they were back in the drawing-room. Half an hour to be got through before one could hope to hear Walker's taxi come chugging up the drive, and gracefully rise to assume one's cloak.

Dinner had gone off with every mark of refinement. There had been candles on the table under hand-painted floral shades, chocolates in little silver dishes; the best dinner service, *croûtons* in the creaming potato soup, roast pheasant, a trifle liberally strewn with cherries, angelica and whipped cream, and definitely tasting of sherry. Mrs. Curtis was stately in black velvet with transparent black chiffon sleeves, her diamond necklace and several rings in old-fashioned settings. And though Mr. Curtis had unfortunately not thought fit to change out of his dark grey tweed suit, he had behaved quite impressively, offering white wine or whisky and soda, circulating the port. He had said nothing queer at all, scarcely mentioning Simpkin, confining himself chiefly to questions about Oxford, addressing their guest as Kershaw. Only, as the meal wore on, he seemed a little out of spirits: that was all.

And though completely silent, Uncle Oswald had, after two glasses of wine and two of port, begun to smile a good deal in a pleasant way, and when Mrs. Curtis rose after coffee, had hastened forward to open the door for her. And though he had tripped over the rug, his old-world courtesy, his deep bow as they passed out, had been almost as much a pleasure as a surprise.

Invitation to the Waltz, 1932

Kate Pulls It Off

CYRA MCFADDEN 1937–

At two in the morning, when the Wilsons, the Gallaghers and the Steins finally finished off the last of the Courvoisier and left, each of them assuring her that dinner had been 'fabulous,' Kate surveyed the rubble in her tract house kitchen in a happy glow of accomplishment. All that work had paid off; she was back in the mainstream again, her credentials as a Marin hostess reestablished.

And she'd pulled off her party without Harvey, who's always driven her up the wall, on similar occasions in the past, worrying about whether she hadn't served the Gallaghers *ris de veau* the last time they were there, whether or not Petrini's pâté was overexposed as an hors d'oeuvre, and whether the people she'd invited would really relate to each other or have to fake it.

One of Harvey's uptight ideas, for instance, was that you never invited a doctor and a lawyer to the same party because they'd spend the evening hassling each other about the malpractice insurance crisis. Scratch *that* little bit of folk wisdom. Frank Gallagher was a surgeon, Tony Wilson an attorney; and not only had they never even *mentioned* malpractice insurance tonight, they'd scarcely even made eye contact.

As for Petrini's pâté, Angela Stein had greeted its entrance, over the perfect Manhattans, with glad little cries. She said she loved Petrini's pâté and *nobody* ever served it anymore.

Of course there *were* minor hassles over the evening. A dinner party wasn't a well-oiled machine or something. It was sort of more like a compost heap, where you just put everything in and turned the hose on it and hoped it would turn into mulch. But you couldn't expect pyracantha trimmings and potato peels to break down into organic matter at exactly the same rate, and sometimes you got a lot of fruit flies . . .

Scraping congealed Bordelaise off her Heath ware plates, Kate abandoned the comparison. Her party hadn't *decomposed*, though she had been kind of freaked out when it developed that Marsha Wilson had become a lacto-vegetarian since Kate had last seen her. Marsha had accordingly preempted the entire wilted-spinach salad. And Kate thought it insensitive of Ginger Gallagher to hold forth, over the beef Wellington, about *Diet for a Small Planet* and how selfish it was for middle-class WASPs to eat meat instead of soybeans and screw up the entire protein chain.

Ginger's remark burned Kate especially since she hadn't been invited to dinner parties herself lately, because friends apparently felt she needed space, and she'd had some heavy anxieties about the menu anyway. She wasn't sure what was really *au courant* right now, and the Marin dinner-party number went through like *cycles*.

Ten years ago, when she and Harvey had first moved to Mill Valley and started making the scene, it was easy; if you had people to dinner, you just cooked yourself blind. Kate and all her women friends competed with each other to serve the first really authentic couscous or the first Mongolian hotpot, complete with those little mesh dippers from Cost Plus you passed around so each guest could fish out his own individual bits of bok choy.

At that point in time, food was *big*, because everybody else, too, had just discovered it, after migrating to the Bay Area from Indiana or some godforsaken place, and gourmet tripping was the name of the game. You could just wipe everybody *out* by stuffing your own grape leaves, making your own phyllo dough or pickling your own pickled squid.

Then came phase two, when everybody got tired of pickled squid and stuffed grape leaves and decided food was *fuel* and that placing all that emphasis on it was 'decadent.' During phase two, Kate planted her Mongolian hot-pot with Swedish ivy. She no longer cooked three-day Julia Child spectaculars but instead called people at five o'clock, just off the wall, to ask them to drop around and take pot luck with 'the family' if they didn't have anything else going. She promised not to fuss and said she'd 'just dump another quart of water into the lentil soup.'

For the last three weeks she'd worried about whether phase two was still in effect or not. Had 'getting back to the basics' also become decadent, while she was still too hung up in her own scene with Harvey to pick up on it? She seemed to remember her ex-friend Martha recently describing some real losers as 'the kind of people who still serve California wines.'

Kate started the first load of Heath ware in the Kitchenaid, started hand-washing her tulip glasses, and consigned the last of the beef Wellington to the Afghan (nothing was worse than puff paste on the second day). There wasn't much left, so she must have been doing something right, and certainly the high-energy rap they'd had over the evening reinforced her sense of really having made it dinner-partywise.

The Serial, 1976

Form in Tilling
E. F. BENSON 1867–1940

Tea, followed by a bridge-party, was, in summer, the chief manifestation of the spirit of hospitality in Tilling. Mrs Poppit, it is true, had attempted to do something in the way of dinner-parties, but though she was at liberty to give as many dinner-parties as she pleased, nobody else had followed her ostentatious example. Dinner-parties entailed a higher scale of living; Miss Mapp, for one, had accurately counted the cost of having three hungry people to dinner, and found that one such dinner-party was not nearly compensated for, in the way of expense, by being invited to three subsequent dinner-parties by your guests. Voluptuous teas were the rule, after which you really wanted no more than little bits of things, a cup of soup, a slice of cold tart, or a dished-up piece of fish and some toasted cheese. Then, after the excitement of bridge (and bridge was very exciting in Tilling) a jig-saw puzzle or Patience cooled your brain and composed your nerves. In winter, however, with its scarcity of daylight, Tilling commonly gave evening bridge-parties, and asked the requisite number of friends to drop in after dinner, though everybody knew that everybody else had only partaken of bits of things. Probably the ruinous price of coal had something to do with these evening bridge-parties, for the fire that warmed your room when you were alone would warm all your guests as well, and then, when your hospitality was returned, you could let your sitting-room fire go out.

Miss Mapp, 1922

Fork-Supper in the Villa Diodati, 1938
DIANA COOPER 1892–1986

TO DUFF COOPER

11 September
I half-think of giving a fork-supper in Byron's house, the Villa Diodati, above the Eaux Vives. Carl showed it me. I could have the lovely *salle* lit with candles and get a local restaurant to provide food. It's a scheme that needs courage. What do you think? I must repay.

13 September
On Friday I am throwing my Byronic fête in the empty Villa. The room was decorated by Jean Jaquet in *boiserie* and busts. The chairs are covered with chintz that Byron himself chose. John Julius and I have collected sixty candelabra from various *antiquaires*. I've ordered the collation – *consommé chaud, langoustes, pâté de canard de Périgord, entremets, friandises et fruits.*

14 September
A lovely sight-seeing evening last night with Carl in first twilight, then lunatic moonlight, then total darkness, ending up at Lausanne and all that you like in bar and restaurant – an exquisite *truite flambée* for Madame, a *châteaubriand saignant pour Monsieur.* Hanging over this fantastic evening were the spectre words *état de siège* and 'ultimatum.' We heard them over the strains of 'The Lambeth Walk.' My Byron festa tomorrow threatens to be another Brussels Ball.

16 September
My party is tonight. I quail. I spent the day transporting candelabra from Town up to Villa and winding rose-wreaths for the busts. Maurice is to supply Montrachet, red Burgundy, Château Yquem, Champagne and Cognac. It's to be a surprise. No one knows but Carl, who is ordered to produce six Swiss Venuses for the delegates' delectation. I remembered suddenly and sadly the need of women. I'll write results tomorrow.

17 September
It was glorious! We even illuminated the big chandelier with redundant candles. Four tables, two waiters, a chef in cap, a barman and a radio for the dance (this last a near-impossibility because of no electricity). The six *indigènes* were breath-taking – Elisabeth

Burckhardt in a red Watteau coat – all *hochgeboren* and dressed in Paris with flowers in their hair and a tiger lily round one of their wrists. We were thirty-two strong and I'm sorry to say that forty-two bottles of wine were drunk, excluding the cocktails and *apéritifs* and thirty Armagnacs. It cost a fortune and was worth it. They danced until about 1 (it began at 7.30) and then they moved on to somebody's ball, which is all rather blurry. 'I can't remember how I went to bed.' I can't really. I was deposited relatively intact by a favourite at 2. a.m. Enclosed are two Collinses. Rab's is very winning:

> I write to thank you very much for a delightful party. I thought it was going to be the Eve of Waterloo, only the other way round, and now it's over I'm sure it will be a prelude to preserving *'notre civilisation,'* as the Radio and M. Bonnet say.
>
> In one of my most exalted moments I asked an apocryphal figure in white, *la femme du Vice-Consul*, to come with me onto the *balcon* to see the view. I started a verse of Lamartine's '*Le Lac*' but when I looked round, the *balcon* was bare and my partner had ratted. So I went round the garden and down the avenue alone, and thought of the history of the house and wondered where Claire Clairmont's slipper was found, and thought how nice it would be to live there with no Committees of the Assembly.
>
> > *Yours gratefully,*
> > R. A. BUTLER
> > *The Light of Common Day,* 1959

Pound Party

MARJORIE KINNAN RAWLINGS 1896–1953

'I'm Ella May, and Mama says we're having a pound party tomorrow evening and she'd be proud did you come.'

It came to me that this was the first neighborly gesture I had encountered at the Creek. I was touched.

I said, 'I'd be glad to. But what is a pound party?'

'Everybody brings a pound of something. Sugar, or butter, or candy, or a cake. A cake's fine. Such as that.'

The evening of the party was clear as glass and I walked the half-mile to Cow Hammock. Remembering the swarm of little Townsends, and adding a houseful of guests in my mind's eye, I had doubled my largest cake recipe and baked it in a roasting pan. I thought I must be early, for there was no one in the shabby house but the Townsends. The children were watching and at sight of me scattered within.

I heard a sibilant, 'Here she comes.'

The suspicion had not yet touched me not only that they knew I should be the sole arrival, but that the party had been built around the probability of my innocent acceptance. The Townsends were in their Sunday best, fresh-scrubbed and uncomfortable. The girls were starched, the boys in stiff clean blue overalls and shirts. I was given a seat on a bench along a wall. Behind me a ragged screen over the open window let in a steady stream of mosquitoes, attracted by the oil lamp on the table. Ella May was assigned with a newspaper to sit beside me and fan my legs to keep them from biting me. When Ella May lagged, Beatrice took up the paper. Their work was enthusiastic but inadequate to the ingenuity of mosquitoes. I slapped furtively. My cake had the place of honor on the bare deal table in the center of the room. A Townsend layer cake dripping sticky icing was pushed modestly to one side. The rest of the refreshments provided by the hostess consisted of a bucket of water, a ten-cent jar of peanut butter and a nickel box of soda crackers.

She said easily, 'We'll wait a while to eat, just in case.'

I made conversation as best I could. We talked of the heavy crop of blackberries, of the Hamon sow that could not be kept up, no matter how one tried, of the summer rains and of the fishing. Mr. Townsend spoke up brightly when we reached the fishing. Fishing was not only the family livelihood but its delight. The Townsends would have sat all day with poles if they had been millionaires.

'I'll bring you a mess of bream one day,' he said.

The talk ebbed. The mosquitoes buzzed and the Townsends slapped automatically. The lamp flickered in a gust of wind.

Mrs. Townsend said, 'Be nice, did you blow some, Floyd.'

Mr. Townsend echoed, 'Blow some, Floyd.'

Floyd, the oldest, long, thin and pale, brought out a mouth organ from his pocket and drew up a straight wooden chair. He began to pat his foot before he started his tune. Into the patting came suddenly the whine of the mouth organ. The tune, formless, unrecognizable, was mournful. One sad phrase repeated itself over and over. Other Townsends took up the patting and the rickety floor shook to the thumping. Floyd stopped abruptly.

Mrs. Townsend said to the air, 'Be nice, did Preston dance.'

Preston was five, the youngest weaned Townsend. The older children seized him and dragged him from the doorway. He hung his head but made no resistance. They seemed to prop him up, then retreated and left him standing alone. Floyd took up his tune. Preston stood staring vacantly. The tune and the party seemed no concern of his. As though one note had set off a mechanical spring, he began to shuffle his feet. His body was still. His arms jerked a little, like a broken jack-in-the-box. His feet shuffled back and forth without rhythm. He might have been trying to keep his footing on a slippery treadmill. This was the dance. I expected him to stop in a moment but he kept it up. The tune, the dance, were endless.

Mrs. Townsend said complacently, 'Preston holds out good, don't he?'

The compliment seemed a signal, for he stopped as suddenly as he had begun.

Mrs. Townsend said, 'We just as good to eat.'

She passed the crackers in one hand and the tiny jar of peanut butter, with a spoon in it, in the other. Eyes followed her hungrily. I refused, to the relief of the eyes. I had a dipper of water and as small a piece of cake as I dared take and yet be courteous. The two cakes disappeared as though a thunder-shower had melted them. The party was obviously over. Mrs. Townsend accompanied me outside the house and to the head of the path. She looked up into a cloudless and star-lit sky.

'I reckon the threat of bad weather kept the others away,' she said placidly.

I inquired about pound parties at the Creek, and my gullibility was verified. Yet the occasion had been truly a party, and the Townsends had done their best to make it festive. I decided that I should go any time I was invited, and should see to it that a larger jar of peanut butter was provided. After the party, the Townsend children and I were great friends. Ella May and Beatrice came almost every day to visit me. Dorsey and Floyd and Glenwood came to do odd chores. They were thin, grave boys and very capable. They moved slowly, like old men, and had the look of age that hunger puts on children. The boys were the right size to climb into the pecan trees and shake down and gather the nuts. The crop was heavy that year, and the filled sacks and baskets amounted to many hundred pounds.

The boys were asked, 'What would you do if you had a dollar for every one of those pecans?'

There was silence while the thought of wealth was contemplated.

Dorsey said slowly, 'First off, I'd get me a whole plug of Brown Mule tobaccy, all for myself.'

Floyd said, 'I'd have all I want of rich folks' rations – light bread and jelly.'

The questioner went on, 'What, no cornbread?'

Glenwood said quickly, 'Oh yes. We know you got to have cornbread to grow on.'

Cross Creek, 1942

Lemon Jellies and Punches Afterwards!!!

DORA CARRINGTON 1893–1932

TO LYTTON STRACHEY

Sunday [February 4th, 1917]   *Asheham House, Rodmell, Sussex*
We had a party on Friday evening, Vanessa, Duncan and Bunny, and the beautiful Maynard – Bull-boy. Such a dinner. Soups, Beef sausages and Leeks, Plum Pudding, Lemon Jellies, and Punches afterwards!!! – The conversation was instructive, and serious.

Letters, 1979

Two Fêtes in Canton, 1769

WILLIAM HICKEY 1749–1830

After spending three very merry days at Whampoa, we returned to Canton, where Maclintock gave me a card of invitation to two different entertainments on following days, at the country house of one of the Hong merchants named Pankeequa. These fêtes were given on 1st and 2nd October, the first of them being a dinner, dressed and served *à la mode Anglaise*, the Chinamen on that occasion using, and awkwardly enough, knives and forks, and in every respect conforming to the European fashion. The best wines of all sorts were amply supplied. In the evening a play was performed, the subject warlike, where most capital fighting was exhibited, with better dancing and music than I could have expected. In one of the scenes an English naval officer, in full uniform and fierce cocked hat, was introduced, who strutted across the stage, saying 'Maskee can do! God damn!' whereupon a loud and universal laugh ensued, the Chinese, quite in an ecstasy, crying out 'Truly have muchee like Englishman.'

The second day, on the contrary, everything was Chinese, all the European guests eating, or endeavouring to eat, with chopsticks, no knives or forks being at table. The entertainment was splendid, the victuals superiorly good, the Chinese loving high dishes and keeping the best of cooks. At night brilliant fireworks (in which they also excel) were let off in a garden magnificently lighted by coloured lamps, which we viewed from a temporary building erected for the occasion and wherein there was exhibited sleight-of-hand tricks, tight- and slack-rope dancing, followed by one of the cleverest pantomimes I ever saw. This continued until a late hour, when we returned in company with several of the supercargoes to our factory, much gratified with the liberality and taste displayed by our Chinese host.

Memoirs, ED. Peter Quennell, 1960

Land of Plenty

ROBERT BYRON 1905–1941

The Governor of Maimena was away at Andkhoi, but his deputy, after refreshing us with tea, Russian sweets, pistachios and almonds, led us to a caravanserai off the main bazaar, a Tuscan-looking old place surrounded by wooden arches, where we have a room each, as many carpets as we want, copper basins to wash in, and a bearded factotum in high-heeled top-boots who has laid down his rifle to help with the cooking.

It will be a special dinner. A sense of well-being has come over us in this land of plenty. Basins of milk, pilau with raisins, skewered kabob well salted and peppered, plum jam, and new bread have already arrived from the bazaar; to which we have added some treats of our own, patent soup, tomato ketchup, prunes in gin, chocolate, and ovaltine.

The Road to Oxiana, 1937

Chickens with Wilfred Thesiger
ERIC NEWBY 1939–

We crossed the river by a bridge, went up through the village of Shāhnaiz and downhill towards the Lower Panjshir.

'Look,' said Hugh, 'it must be Thesiger.'

Coming towards us out of the great gorge where the river thundered was a small caravan like our own. He named an English explorer, a remarkable throwback to the Victorian era, a fluent speaker of Arabic, a very brave man, who has twice crossed the Empty Quarter and, apart from a few weeks every year, has passed his entire life among primitive peoples.

We had been on the march for a month. We were all rather jaded; the horses were galled because the drivers were careless of them, and their ribs stood out because they had been in places only fit for mules and forded innumerable torrents filled with slippery rocks as big as footballs; the drivers had run out of tobacco and were pining for their wives; there was no more sugar to put in the tea, no more jam, no more cigarettes and I was reading *The Hound of the Baskervilles* for the third time; all of us suffered from a persistent dysentery. The ecstatic sensations we had experienced at a higher altitude were beginning to wear off. It was not a particularly gay party.

Thesiger's caravan was abreast of us now, his horses lurching to a standstill on the execrable track. They were deep-loaded with great wooden presses, marked 'British Museum', and black tin trunks (like the ones my solicitors have, marked 'Not Russel-Jones' or 'All Bishop of Chichester').

The party consisted of two villainous-looking tribesmen dressed like royal mourners in long overcoats reaching to the ankles; a shivering Tajik cook, to whom some strange mutation had given bright red hair, unsuitably dressed for Central Asia in crippling pointed brown shoes and natty socks supported by suspenders, but no trousers; the interpreter, a gloomy-looking middle-class Afghan in a coma of fatigue, wearing dark glasses, a double-breasted lounge suit and an American hat with stitching all over it; and Thesiger himself, a great, long-striding crag of a man, with an outcrop for a nose and bushy eyebrows, forty-five years old and as hard as nails, in an old tweed jacket of the sort worn by Eton boys, a pair of thin grey cotton trousers, rope-soled Persian slippers and a woollen cap comforter.

'Turn round,' he said, 'you'll stay the night with us. We're going to kill some chickens.'

We tried to explain that we had to get to Kabul, that we wanted our mail, but our men, who professed to understand no English but were reluctant to pass through the gorges at night, had already turned the horses and were making for the collection of miserable hovels that was the nearest village.

Soon we were sitting on a carpet under some mulberry trees, surrounded by the entire population, with all Thesiger's belongings piled up behind us.

'Can't speak a word of the language,' he said cheerfully. 'Know a lot of the Koran by heart but not a word of Persian. Still, it's not really necessary. Here, you,' he shouted at the cook, who had only entered his service the day before and had never seen another Englishman. 'Make some green tea and a lot of chicken and rice – three chickens.'

'No good bothering the interpreter,' he went on, 'the poor fellow's got a sty, that's why we only did seventeen miles today. It's no good doing too much at first, especially as he's not feeling well.'

The chickens were produced. They were very old; in the half-light they looked like pterodactyls.

'Are they expensive?'

'The Power of Britain never grows less,' said the headman, lying superbly.

'That means they are very expensive,' said the interpreter, rousing himself.

Soon the cook was back, semaphoring desperately.

'Speak up, can't understand a thing. You want sugar? Why don't you say so?' He produced a large bunch of keys, like a housekeeper in some stately home. All that evening he was opening and shutting boxes so that I had tantalizing glimpses of the contents of an explorer's luggage – a telescope, a string vest, the *Charterhouse of Parma*, *Du Côté de Chez Swann*, some fish-hooks and the 1/1000000 map of Afghanistan – not like mine, a sodden pulp, but neatly dissected, mounted between marbled boards.

'That cook's going to die,' said Thesiger; 'hasn't got a coat and look at his feet. We're nine thousand feet if we're an inch here. How high's the Chamar Pass?' We told him 16,000 feet. 'Get yourself a coat and boots, do you hear?' he shouted in the direction of the camp fire.

After two hours the chickens arrived; they were like elastic, only the rice and gravy were delicious. Famished, we wrestled with the bones in the darkness.

'England's going to pot,' said Thesiger, as Hugh and I lay smoking the interpreter's King Size cigarettes, the first for a fortnight. 'Look at this shirt, I've only had it three years, now it's splitting. Same with tailors; Gull and Croke made me a pair of whipcord trousers to go to the Atlas Mountains. Sixteen guineas – wore a hole in them in a fortnight. Bought half a dozen shotguns to give to my headmen, well-known make, twenty guineas apiece, absolute rubbish.'

He began to tell me about his Arabs.

'I give them powders for worms and that sort of thing.' I asked him about surgery. 'I take off fingers and there's a lot of surgery to be done; they're frightened of their own doctors because they're not clean.'

'Do you do it? Cutting off fingers?'

'Hundreds of them,' he said dreamily, for it was very late. 'Lord, yes. Why, the other day I took out an eye. I enjoyed that.

'Let's turn in,' he said.

The ground was like iron with sharp rocks sticking up out of it. We started to blow up our air-beds. 'God, you must be a couple of pansies,' said Thesiger.

A Short Walk in the Hindu Kush, 1958

Inviting a Friend to Supper

BEN JONSON 1572–1637

To night, grave sir, both my poore house, and I
Doe equally desire your companie:
Not that we thinke us worthy such a ghest,
But that your worth will dignifie our feast,
With those that come; whose grace may make that seeme
Something, which, else, could hope for no esteeme.
It is the faire acceptance, Sir, creates
The entertaynment perfect: not the cates.
Yet shall you have, to rectifie your palate,
An olive, capers, or some better sallade
Ushring the mutton; with a short-leg'd hen,
If we can get her, full of eggs, and then,
Limons, and wine for sauce: to these, a coney
Is not to be despair'd of, for our money;
And, though fowle, now, be scarce, yet there are clarkes,

The skie not falling, thinke we may have larkes.
He tell you more, and lye, so you will come:
Of partrich, pheasant, wood-cock, of which some
May yet be there; and godwit, if we can:
Knat, raile, and ruffe too. How so ere, my man
Shall reade a piece of Virgil, Tacitus,
Livie, or of some better booke to us,
Of which wee'll speake our minds, amidst our meate;
And Ile professe no verses to repeate:
To this, if ought appeare, which I not know of,
That will the pastrie, not my paper, show of.
Digestive cheese, and fruit there sure will bee;
But that, which most doth take my Muse, and mee,
Is a pure cup of rich Canary-wine,
Which is the Mermaids, now, but shall be mine:
Of which had Horace, or Anacreon tasted,
Their lives, as doe their lines, till now had lasted.
Tabacco, Nectar, or the Thespian spring,
Are all but Luthers beere, to this I sing.
Of this we will sup free, but moderately,
And we will have no Pooly, or Parrot by;
Nor shall our cups make any guiltie men:
But, at our parting, we will be, as when
We innocently met. No simple word,
That shall be utter'd at our mirthfull boord,
Shall make us sad next morning: or affright
The libertie, that wee'll enjoy to night.

Milk! from Where?

LUCIE DUFF-GORDON 1821–69

TO SIR ALEXANDER DUFF-GORDON

Cairo, 14 November, 1863
We saw the spectacle of devastation – whole villages gone, submerged
and melted, mud to mud, and the people with their animals encamped
on spits of sand or on the dykes in long rows of ragged makeshift tents,
while we sailed over where they had lived. Cotton rotting in all

directions and the dry tops crackling under the bows of the boat. When we stopped to buy milk, the poor woman exclaimed: 'Milk! from where? Do you want it out of my breasts?' However, she took our saucepan and went to get some from another family. No one refuses it if they have a drop left, for they all believe the murrain to be a punishment for churlishness to strangers – by whom committed no one can say. Nor would they fix a price, or take more than the old rate. But here everything has doubled in price.

Letters from Egypt, 1869

Kyrenia

LAWRENCE DURRELL 1912–91

While I was finding my bearings and conducting an initial exploration I lodged with my friend Panos, a schoolmaster, in two small clean rooms overlooking the harbour of Kyrenia, the only port in Cyprus which – diminutive, cleanly coloured, beautiful – has some of the true Cycladean *allure*. It is on the seaward side of the Kyrenia hills opposite the shaggy Turkish coastline whose mountains sink and rise out of the sea, dissolve and reappear with the transparent promise of a desert mirage.

Panos lived with his wife and two small sons in a house which must once have been part of the Church of Saint Michael the Archangel – up forty whitewashed steps, brilliant with sunshine, into a stone court-yard: the obvious site of the ancient acropolis of the town. The belfry of the church towered over us, its bell banging aggressively for every service, the lazy blue-and-white ensign of Greece softly treading the wind above the blue harbour.

The schoolmaster himself was very typical of Greek Cyprus – a round curly head, stocky body, with strong arms and legs; sleepy good-natured eyes. Through him I made my first acquaintance with the island temperament which is very different from the prevailing extrovert disposition of the metropolitan Greek. The styles of polite-ness were more formalized, I noticed, even between Cypriots. Forms of address were somewhat old-fashioned and lacking in spontaneity; there was a certain thoughtful reserve in conversation, a sense of measure. Hospitality was unobtrusive and shyly offered – as if the donor feared rebuff. Voices were lower and laughter set in a lower key.

But the Greek Panos spoke was true Greek, with here and there an unfamiliar word from the *patois* of the island.

Every evening we took a glass of sweet, heavy Commanderia on his little terrace, before walking down the tiny winding lanes to the harbour in order to watch the sunset melt. Here by the lapping water I was formally and civilly introduced to his friends, the harbourmaster, the bookseller, the grocer, who sat by the lapping water sipping *ouzo* and watching the light gradually fade over the stubby bastions of Kyrenia Castle, and the slender points of the Mosque. Within a week I had a dozen firm friends in the little town and began to understand the true meaning of Cypriot hospitality which is wrapped up in a single word – '*Kopiaste*' which roughly speaking means 'Sit down with us and share.' Impossible to pass a café, to exchange a greeting with anyone eating or drinking without having the word fired at one as if from the mouth of a gun. It became dangerous even to shout 'Good appetite', as one does in Greece, to a group of labourers working on the roads when one passed them at their lunch-hour seated under an olive-tree. At once a dozen voices would reply and a dozen hands would wave loaves or cans of wine . . . After ten days of this I began to feel like a Strasbourg goose.

Bitter Lemons, 1957

Talleyrand's Turkish Luncheon, 1797
MME DE LA TOUR DU PIN 1770–1853

A Turkish embassy arrived in Paris and M. de Talleyrand gave a magnificent luncheon in honour of the Ambassador and his suite. Instead of having the luncheon at a table, a buffet was arranged along one side of a large salon. It rose in tiers half way up the windows and was laden with exquisite dishes of every kind and decorated with vases of the rarest flowers. Around the other three sides of the room were sofas for the guests, and small tables, already laid, were carried in and set before them. M. de Talleyrand led the Ambassador to a divan, seated himself in Eastern fashion and invited his guest, through an interpreter, to choose the lady whose company he would like at luncheon. The Ambassador did not hesitate and indicated me. I did not feel unduly flattered, for of all the ladies present, none could stand the

brilliant light of a mid-August noon, whereas my own complexion and
fair hair had nothing to fear from it.

Memoirs, ED., TRANS., Felice Harcourt, 1969

Persian Kittens

LESLEY BLANCH 1907–

Seventeenth-century travellers and diplomats who succeeded in reaching the glittering Safavid court of Shah Abbas at Isfahan were dumb-
founded, for after many wearisome months struggling across the
barren wastes of Central Asia they were confronted by unparalleled
splendours. Their memoirs also recorded a curious custom designed to
refresh revellers at the Shah's table. Between the courses, by way of
diversion, a basket of kittens (Persian of course) were often circulated,
the guests fondling the little creatures ecstatically. Cats were ever the
Persians' especial delight, and at the banquets they provided a kind of
furry variation to the customary undulating houris or their rivals, the
painted dancing boys. All of them were seen as a *détente* between the
sumptuous sequence of gold, jewel-studded dishes the Shah, 'Allah's
Shadow on Earth', offered the assemblage crouched before him on
silken rugs beside pearl-tasselled bolsters.

From Wilder Shores, 1989

The Convent of Encarnacion

MME CALDERÓN DE LA BARCA 1804–82

Having visited the whole building, and admired one virgin's blue satin
and pearls, and another's black velvet and diamonds, sleeping holy
infants, saints, paintings, shrines, and confessionals, – having even
climbed up the Azotea, which commands a magnificent view, we came
at length to a large hall, decorated with paintings and furnished with
antique high-backed arm-chairs, where a very elegant supper, lighted
up and ornamented, greeted our astonished eyes; cakes, chocolate,
ices, creams, custards, tarts, jellies, blancmangers, orange and lemonade, and other profane dainties, ornamented with gilt paper cut into

little flags, etc. I was placed in a chair that might have served for a pope under a holy family; the Señora – and the Señorita – on either side. The elder nuns in stately array, occupied the other arm-chairs, and looked like statues carved in stone. A young girl, a sort of *pensionnaire*, brought in a little harp without pedals, and while we discussed cakes and ices, sung different ballads with a good deal of taste. The elder nuns helped us to everything, but tasted nothing themselves. The younger nuns and the novices were grouped upon a mat *à la Turque*, and a more picturesque scene altogether one could scarcely see.

Life in Mexico, 1843

Spanish Habits
MME CALDERÓN DE LA BARCA 1804–82

Many of the elements of Spanish-style hospitality which impressed and amused Mme Calderón de la Barca in Mexico exist today in Spanish-speaking countries. Nuns in many convents still make a dazzling array of sweets, and an invitation to dine in a private home, unless the occasion is very formal, automatically extends to whoever happens to be in your party. Arriving late with a handful of uninvited guests is not considered a breach of etiquette.

On Sunday we had a number of people to dinner, by chance, it being Spanish fashion to dine at a friend's house without invitation. . . .

Some Mexican visits appear to me to surpass in duration all that one can imagine of a visit, rarely lasting less than one hour, and sometimes extending over a greater part of the day. And gentlemen, at least, arrive at no particular time. If you are going to breakfast, they go also – if to dinner, the same – if you are asleep, they wait till you awaken – if out, they call again. An indifferent sort of man, whose name I did not even hear, arrived yesterday, a little after breakfast, sat still, and walked in to a late dinner with us! These should not be called visits, but visitations, – though I trust they do not often occur to that extent. An open house and an open table for your friends, which includes every passing acquaintance; these are merely Spanish habits of hospitality transplanted.

Life in Mexico, 1843

How Are We to Give Him a Dinner?
FANNY BURNEY (MME D'ARBLAY) 1752–1840

TO HER SISTER, CHARLOTTE

November, 1797
[Charlotte has proposed to bring Mr. Broome, who is to be her second husband, to spend a day with the d'Arblays.]

I need not say how I shall rejoice to see you again, nor how charmed we shall both be to make a nearer acquaintance with Mr. Broome but, for Heaven's sake, my dear girl, how are we to give him a dinner? – unless he will bring with him his poultry, for ours are not yet arrived from Bookham; and his fish, for ours are still at the bottom of some pond we know not where; and his spit, for our jack is yet without one; and his kitchen grate, for ours waits for Count Rumford's next pamphlet; not to mention his table-linen; and not to speak of his knives and forks, some ten of our poor original twelve having been massacred in M. d'Arblay's first essays in the art of carpentering; – and to say nothing of his large spoons, the silver of our plated ones having feloniously made off under cover of the whitening-brush; – and not to talk of his cook, ours being not yet hired; – and not to start the subject of wine, ours, by some odd accident, still remaining at the wine-merchant's!

With all these impediments, however, to convivial hilarity, if he will eat a quarter of a joint of meat (his share, I mean), tied up by a packthread, and roasted by a log of wood on the bricks, – and declare no potatoes so good as those dug by M. d'Arblay out of our garden – and protest our small beer gives the spirits of champagne – and make no inquiries where we have deposited the hops he will conclude we have emptied out of our tablecloth – and pronounce that bare walls are superior to tapestry – and promise us the first sight of his epistle upon visiting a new-built cottage – we shall be sincerely happy to receive him in our Hermitage; where I hope to learn, for my dearest

Charlotte's sake, to love him as much as, for his own, I have very long admired him.

Manage all this, my dear girl, but let us know the day, as we have resumed our Norbury Park excursions, where we were yesterday. God bless you, my love, and grant that your happiness may meet my wishes!

Diary and Letters, 1842–6

Native Californians

GENERAL JOHN BIDWELL 1819–1900

The kindness and hospitality of the native Californians have not been overstated. Up to the time the Mexican régime ceased in California they had a custom of never charging for anything; that is to say, for entertainment, food, use of horses, etc. You were supposed, even if invited to visit a friend, to bring your blankets with you, and one would be very thoughtless if he traveled and did not take a knife along with which to cut his meat. When you had eaten, the invariable custom was to rise, deliver to the woman or hostess the plate on which you had eaten the meat and beans – for that was about all they had – and say, *Muchas gracias, Senora* ('Many thanks, Madam'); and the hostess as invariably replied, *Buen provecho* ('May it do you much good'). The missions in California invariably had gardens with grapes, olives, figs, pomegranates, pears, and apples, but the ranches scarcely ever had any fruit, with the exception of the tuna or prickly pear. These were the only cultivated fruits I can call to mind in California, except oranges, lemons, and limes in a few places.

Echoes of the Past, 1842

Contrast of Customs

GIACOMO CASTELVETRO 1546–1616

When we come to making wine, which all our townsfolk do, and the grapes are brought in from the estates, we keep back large amounts of the must from the pressing. We boil this with flour until all the water has evaporated, to make *sugolo*. As the wagons of grapes come into town, all the artisans with no plot of land of their own come running up with pots and jars to beg for some of the must, which it would be shameful to refuse them. I can remember one gentleman who parted with over half his load in this way.

How very different from France and Germany, where the people very rarely let you eat any of the grapes, and as soon as they start to ripen post public watchmen to guard them day and night and punish anyone who so much as dares to pick one in passing. This could never happen in my country and, if it did, the amount of money saved would be totally insignificant. As it is, we not only let people help themselves to what they want, but any traveller has the right to eat grapes growing on the public highway, and take as much as he wants away with him as well, without the owner daring to complain. This I think must be derived from the Laws of Moses, which command that the farmer should leave every seventh sheaf of corn for the poor.

If growers in my region did not send barges piled high with their surplus wine to Venice, they would find themselves with more on their hands than they knew what to do with. In fact they often produce more wine than barrels to put it in, and sometimes end up giving it away in exchange for the empty barrel.

This reminds me of when I was a lad in Germany, where there was a rather delightful custom for marriageable young women to invite the neighbouring young men to help them with the grape harvest. I was in Basle at the time, among those invited by a charming young lady to gather her grapes. When she saw me eating some of them, she exclaimed in a peevish voice: 'Hey! Those are for making wine with, not for eating!'

The contrast with our own custom made me laugh. In Italy, if a stranger or peasant passes by without asking for some grapes, the harvesters take offence and shower them with abuse. They will give them away gladly, and thank you for taking them. And if a traveller in the intense heat asks these peasants for a drink of water, they reply: 'The water's rotting away in the ditch, friend, we couldn't give you that, but if you'd like some wine, you'd be very welcome.' If he were alive today, my Lord Sir John North, father of the present baron, would recall how we were surprised and pleased when this happened to us in Brescia in 1575, when I was his tutor on a tour of the beauties of Italy.

The Fruit, Herbs and Vegetables of Italy, TRANS. Gillian Riley, 1989

Voluntary Catering
JAMES LAVER 1899–1975

Voluntary catering, which is simply hospitality to strangers, is a long and honourable story in itself. It was already a great advance in civilization when it began to be thought desirable not to kill any foreigner at sight, but to provide him with what he needed and send him on his way in peace. The rules which gradually grew up about this practice seem to the commercial modern mind almost extravagant in their highmindedness. In some remote communities it was thought necessary to offer the stranger not only a bed for the night but a wife – the wife of the host. Arab legend is full of stories of heroic generosity even to enemies once they had 'eaten salt', and among the Japanese we hear of a host destroying the ancestral dwarf trees in order to provide fuel for his guest.

Eating Out: An Historical Dissertation, 1947

The Duchesse de Mazarin's Bird-Pie Disaster
ELISABETH VIGÉE-LE BRUN 1755–1842

During my pregnancy I had painted the Duchesse de Mazarin, who though no longer young, was still very beautiful. I thought my daughter's eyes remarkably like those of the Duchess. They used to say of this lady that she had been blessed by three fairies at her birth: the fairies of wealth, beauty and bad luck. It is true indeed that the poor woman could do absolutely nothing, not even throw a party, without it being ruined by some catastrophe. There were a number of well known stories concerning her various misfortunes; here is one of the lesser known incidents. One evening she held a supper party for sixty people and had the idea of placing an enormous pie in the middle of the table, inside of which there were a hundred small live birds. At a sign from the Duchess the pie was broken open and a mad flurry of wild birds flew into the faces of the guests, burying themselves in the ladies' carefully coiffed hair. You can imagine the screams, the frayed tempers! It was almost impossible to get rid of the infernal creatures.

Finally, everyone rose from the table, swearing and cursing the stupidity of the idea.

Memoirs, TRANS. Siân Evans, 1989

Sicily

J. W. GOETHE 1749–1832

Since there are no inns in Girgenti, a family kindly made room for us in their own house and gave us a raised alcove in a large chamber. A green curtain separated us and our baggage from the members of the household, who were manufacturing macaroni of the finest, whitest and smallest kind, which fetches the highest price. The dough is first moulded into the shape of a pencil as long as a finger; the girls then twist this once with their finger tips into a spiral shape like a snail's. We sat down beside the pretty children and got them to explain the whole process to us. The flour is made from the best and hardest wheat, known as *grano forte*. The work calls for much greater manual dexterity than macaroni made by machinery or in forms. The macaroni they served us was excellent, but they apologized for it, saying that there was a much superior kind, but they hadn't enough in the house for even a single dish. This kind, they told us, was only made in Girgenti and, what is more, only by their family. No other macaroni, in their opinion, can compare with it in whiteness and softness.

In the evening, our guide again managed to appease our impatient longing to walk down the hill by leading us to other points on the heights from which, as we gazed at the noble view, he gave us a general survey of the position of all the remarkable things we were to see on the morrow.

Italian Journey 1786–88, TRANS. W. H. Auden
and Elizabeth Mayer, 1962

Dinner in Mexico

MME CALDERÓN DE LA BARCA 1804–82

I have now formed acquaintance with many Mexican dishes; *molé* (meat stewed in red chile), boiled nopal, fried bananas, green chile, etc. Then we invariably have *frijoles* (brown beans stewed), hot tortillas – and this being in the country, pulque is the universal beverage. In Mexico, tortillas and pulque are considered unfashionable, though both are to be met with occasionally, in some of the best old houses. They have here a most delicious species of cream cheese made by the Indians, and ate with virgin honey. I believe there is an intermixture of goats' milk in it; but the Indian families who make it, and who have been offered large sums for the receipt, find it more profitable to keep their secret.

Every dinner has *puchero* immediately following the soup; consisting of boiled mutton, beef, bacon, fowls, garbanzos (a white bean), small gourds, potatoes, boiled pears, greens, and any other vegetables; a piece of each put on your plate at the same time, and accompanied by a sauce of herbs or tomatoes.

As for fruits, we have mameys, chirimoyas, granaditas, white and black zapotes; the black, sweet, with a green skin and black pulp, and with black stones in it; the white resembling it in outward appearance and form, but with a white pulp, and the kernel, which is said to be poisonous, is very large, round, and white. It belongs to a larger and more leafy tree than the black zapote, and grows in cold or temperate climates; whereas the other is a native of *tierra caliente*. Then there is the chicozapote, of the same family, with a whitish skin, and a white or rose-tinged pulp; this also belongs to the warm regions. The capulin, or Mexican cherry; the mango, of which the best come from Orizaba and Cordova; the cayote, etc. Of these I prefer the chirimoya, zapote blanco, granadita, and mango; but this is a matter of taste.

Life in Mexico, 1843

Between Ourselves

ELSIE DE WOLFE d. 1950

Do you have a menu in which there is one simple dish for those who diet, and one rich dish for those who do not?

Do you have menus on the table so that your guests may choose the dish they prefer, if they do not eat all and everything? How often has one heard a guest say: 'Oh, dear, if I'd known *this* was coming, I wouldn't have taken *that*.'

Are your plates hot, Hot, HOT? Do you feel them yourself when they are placed before you at the table?

Are your dishes in the short meal presented the second time as hot as when first served?

Do you serve coffee at the table at the psychological moment when your guests are relaxed and happy, and when good conversation flows? Do not interrupt it by taking them into the drawing-room where the thread of what might have been interesting is broken. (This is not a rule.)

Recipes for Successful Dining, 1934

Lord Mayor's Banquet c. 1781

WILLIAM HICKEY 1749–1830

The 9th being the Lord Mayor's day, I arrayed myself in my full suit of velvet. Alderman Woolridge called at my father's and conveyed me in his chariot to Guildhall at half-past four o'clock; about half an hour after which the procession arrived from Westminster. At six, we sat down to a profusion of turtle and venison, followed by all the etceteras of French cookery, with splendid dessert of pines, grapes, and other fruits. I was seated between Mrs. Healy, sister to Wilkes, and Lord Lewisham, eldest son of the Earl of Dartmouth. Mrs. Healy almost enveloped me in her immense hoop, but was vastly attentive to me, whom she perceived to be a stranger, ordering one of her servants to wait upon me, and naming to me the different persons who sat at the same table, amongst whom were most of the great officers of state, the Lord Chancellor, judges, and Master of the Rolls. The heat from the crowd assembled and immense number of lights was disagreeable to all, to many quite oppressive and distressing.

The Lord Mayor's table, at which I was, and nearly opposite his Lordship, was less so than other parts of the hall, from being considerably elevated above the rest. The wines were excellent, and the dinner the same, served, too, with as much regularity and decorum as if we had been in a private house; but far different was the scene in the body of the hall, where, in five minutes after the guests took their stations at the tables, the dishes were entirely cleared of their contents, twenty hands seizing the same joint or bird, and literally tearing it to pieces. A more determined scramble could not be; the roaring and noise was deafening and hideous, which increased as the liquor operated, bottles and glasses flying across from side to side without intermission. Such a bear garden altogether I never beheld, except my first visit to Wetherby's, which it brought very forcibly to my recollection.

This abominable and disgusting scene continued till near ten o'clock, when the Lord Mayor, Sheriffs, the nobility, etc., adjourned to the ball and card rooms, and the dancing commenced. Here the heat was no way inferior to that of the hall, and the crowd so great there was scarce a possibility of moving. Rejoiced, therefore, was I upon Alderman Woolridge's saying he would take me home whenever I wished it; I eagerly answered, 'This moment, if you please.' He thereupon took me through some private apartments and down a flight of stairs to a door opening into a back lane where his carriage was ready, into which we stepped without the smallest difficulty or impediment, and were driven home. Completely exhausted, I retired to bed, perfectly satisfied with having once partaken of a Lord Mayor of London's feast.

Memoirs, ED. Peter Quennell, 1960

French Society
ELISABETH VIGÉE-LE BRUN 1755–1842

It is impossible to understand what was meant by 'French Society' if one has not experienced the time when twelve or fifteen charming people would gather together to end their day in the house of some grand lady. The relaxed and easy good humour which presided over these light evening meals gave them a charm no formal dinner could ever hope to attain. An air of shared confidence and intimacy prevailed among the happy guests and since well bred people rarely suffer from awkwardness, these suppers made Parisian high society superior to any other in Europe.

At my house, for example, we met around nine. We never talked of politics, but we did discuss literature and recount the anecdote of the day. Sometimes we even amused ourselves playing charades and on other occasions the Abbé Delille or Le Brun-Pindare read us some of their verse. We usually sat down to eat at ten. My suppers were the simplest imaginable; they always included some fowl, fish, a vegetable dish and a salad; so little in fact that if I forgot myself and invited too many people to supper there would not be enough food to go around. It mattered little however, we were happy and content; the hours passed like minutes and people would not start to drift home until midnight.

Memoirs, TRANS. Siân Evans, 1989

Uncle Goes A-Hunting
JULIAN STREET 1879–1947

A story that has amused us since we were a child was told at his own expense by an uncle of ours who graduated from West Point in time to join the old Indian-fighting army of the 1870's.

When he was a young lieutenant at Fort Assiniboine, Montana, word came one day that a general, on a tour of inspection, would arrive at the post that evening. A dinner party was planned, and our uncle borrowed his colonel's hunting-dogs and went out with an orderly to get wild ducks.

It was the time of year when ducks were usually plentiful, and he was a good shot, but on this day he failed to get a single bird. He gave his orderly some money and told him to ride to the nearest town, buy game birds at the market, and deliver them to the colonel's wife.

But the orderly could find no game in the town. He felt that he must get something else and hit upon canned oysters. These he delivered to the colonel's lady with a card on which our uncle had written: 'I shot these for your dinner.'

Table Topics, 1959

Burra Sahibs' Party in Calcutta c. 1778
WILLIAM HICKEY 1749–1830

A succession of large and formal dinners followed Mr. Francis's, beginning with the Governor-General, Mr. Wheler, General Stibbert, Mr. Barwell, and in fact all the *Burra Sahibs* (great men) of Calcutta. The first really pleasant party I was at, after my illness, was given by Daniel Barwell, who, as I have before observed, kept house with Pott and others. The most highly dressed and splendid hookah was prepared for me. I tried, but did not like it, which being perceived by my friend Robert, he laughed at me, recommending me to funk away and I should accomplish the matter without choking myself. As, after several trials, I still found it disagreeable, I with much gravity requested to know whether it was indispensably necessary that I should become a smoker, which was answered with equal gravity, 'Undoubtedly it is, for you might as well be out of the world as out of the fashion. Here everybody uses a hookah, and it is impossible to get on without.' Mr. Gosling, less volatile and flighty than the rest of the party, immediately said, 'Don't mind these rattling young men, Mr. Hickey, there is no sort of occasion for your doing what is unpleasant; and, although hookahs are in pretty general use, there are several gentlemen that never smoke them.' I directly dismissed the hookah, never after tasting one. Often since have I rejoiced that I did not happen to like it, as I have seen the want of it, from servants misunderstanding where they were ordered to attend their masters, or some other accident, a source of absolute misery, and have frequently heard men declare they would much rather be deprived of their dinner than their hookah.

In this party I first saw the barbarous custom of pelleting each other with little balls of bread, made like pills, across the table, which was even practised by the fair sex. Some people could discharge them with such force as to cause considerable pain when struck in the face. Mr. Daniel Barwell was such a proficient that he could, at the distance of three or four yards, snuff a candle, and that several times successively. This strange trick, fitter for savages than polished society, produced many quarrels, and at last entirely ceased from the following occurrence. A Captain Morrison had repeatedly expressed his abhorrence of pelleting, and that, if any person struck him with one, he should consider it intended as an insult and resent it accordingly. In a few minutes after he had so said, he received a smart blow in the face from one, which, although discharged from a hand below the table, he saw by the motion of the arm from whence it came, and that the pelleter was a very recent acquaintance. He therefore without the least hesitation took up a dish that stood before him and contained a leg of mutton, which he discharged with all his strength at the offender, and with such well-directed aim that it took place upon the head, knocking him off his chair and giving a severe cut upon the temple. This produced a duel in which the unfortunate pelleter was shot through the body, lay upon his bed many months, and never perfectly recovered. This put a complete stop to the absurd practice.

Memoirs, ED. Peter Quennell, 1960

Gebbur in Ethiopia
EVELYN WAUGH 1903–66

There was a cheerful, friendly tea-party that afternoon at the American Legation and a ball and firework display at the Italian, but the party which excited the keenest interest was the *gebbur* given by the emperor to his tribesmen. These banquets are a regular feature of Ethiopian life, constituting, in fact, a vital bond between the people and their over-lords, whose prestige in time of peace varied directly with their frequency and abundance. Until a few years ago attendance at a *gebbur* was part of the entertainment offered to every visitor in Abyssinia. Copious first-hand accounts can be found in almost every book about the country, describing the packed, squatting ranks of the diners; the slaves carrying the warm quarters of newly slaughtered, uncooked beef; the dispatch with which each guest carves for himself; the upward slice of his dagger with which he severs each mouthful from the dripping lump; the flat, damp platters of local bread; the great draughts of *tedj* and *talla* from the horn drinking-pots; the butchers outside felling and dividing the oxen; the emperor and notables at the high table, exchanging highly seasoned morsels of more elaborate fare. These are the traditional features of the *gebbur* and, no doubt, of this occasion also. It was thus that the journalists described their impressions in glowing paraphrases of Rhey and Kingsford. When the time came, however, we found that particular precautions had been taken to exclude all Europeans from the spectacle. Perhaps it was felt that the feast might give a false impression of the civilizing pretensions of the Government. Mr Hall loyally undertook to exercise his influence for each of us personally, but in the end no one gained admission except two resolute ladies and, by what was felt to be a very base exploitation of racial advantage, the coloured correspondent of a syndicate of Negro newspapers.

Remote People, 1931

A Literary Dinner
WASHINGTON IRVING 1783–1859

A few days after this conversation with Mr. Buckthorne, he called upon me, and took me with him to a regular literary dinner. It was given by a great bookseller, or rather a company of booksellers, whose firm surpassed in length even that of Shadrach, Meschach, and Abednego.

I was surprised to find between twenty and thirty guests assembled, most of whom I had never seen before. Buckthorne explained this to me by informing me that this was a 'business dinner,' or kind of field day, which the house gave about twice a year to its authors. It is true, they did occasionally give snug dinners to three or four literary men at a time, but then these were generally select authors; favorites of the public; such as had arrived at their sixth and seventh editions. 'There are,' said he, 'certain geographical boundaries in the land of literature, and you may judge tolerably well of an author's popularity, by the wine his bookseller gives him. An author crosses the port line about the third edition and gets into claret, but when he has reached the sixth and seventh, he may revel in champagne and burgundy.'

'And pray,' said I, 'how far may these gentlemen have reached that I see around me; are any of these claret drinkers?'

'Not exactly, not exactly. You find at these great dinners the common steady run of authors, one, two, edition men; or if any others are invited they are aware that it is a kind of republican meeting. – You understand me – a meeting of the republic of letters, and that they must expect nothing but plain substantial fare.'

These hints enabled me to comprehend more fully the arrangement of the table. The two ends were occupied by two partners of the house. And the host seemed to have adopted Addison's ideas as to the literary precedence of this guests. A popular poet had the post of honor, opposite to whom was a hot-pressed traveller in quarto, with plates. A grave-looking antiquarian, who had produced several solid works, which were much quoted and little read, was treated with great respect, and seated next to a neat, dressy gentlemen in black, who had written a thin, genteel, hot-pressed octavo on political economy that was getting into fashion. Several three-volume duodecimo men of fair currency were placed about the centre of the table; while the lower end was taken up with small poets, translators, and authors, who had not as yet risen into much notice.

Tales of a Traveller, 1824

Life at Woburn c. 1935
DIANA COOPER 1892–1986

The head of Conrad's house was the Duke of Bedford, grandfather of the present Duke. His wife, 'the Flying Duchess,' often 'flipping about the Gold Coast in her Puss Moth,' one day did not return, and the old Duke, then lonely, began to invite very occasionally members of his family to Woburn Abbey in Bedfordshire. When Conrad received his summons I made him promise to leave no detail unnoted. The following description of the Duke's paramount rule compares strangely with today's mobocracy:

Dinner was a choice of fish and a whole partridge each. No drink except inferior claret and not much of it. Nothing else. The second that I had swallowed my peach Herbrand [the Duke] sprang up and we all trooped out. He read the *Evening Standard* for 1½ hours. Miss Green (companion librarian) had been reading the Flying Duchess's account of coming to my farm in her diary. She had liked it more than any she had ever seen. 'She was envious of having a house like that.' Odd! it's an ordinary sort of very small house and suits me all right. When we arrived Herbrand was wearing a white silk tie, tweed coat, dark waistcoat, gabardine trousers (much stained and frayed around the bottoms) and very thick black buttoned boots. For dinner he wore a long-tailed coat, black tie, black waistcoat. I've got a lovely bedroom, all rosebud curtains and rosebud chintz. It's the room that Papa always had at Christmas. The bathroom is huge and stinks fearfully on account of rubber flooring. Herbrand said: 'I've put you on the first floor so that you can see the birds and squirrels better.' As it's dark I can see neither.

This is how the day passed. At 9 minutes to 9 we are all assembled in the Canaletto room. At 9 the butler knocks loudly at the door, comes in and bawls: 'Breakfast on the table, Your Grace.' Herbrand says: 'Well, shall we go to breakfast?' We all file in then. There are five men to wait on us, one for each. Everyone has their own tea or coffee pot. You help yourself to eggs and bacon. The butler takes your plate from you and carries it to your place. You walk behind him. It makes a little procession. As soon as the last person is helped he leaves the room. Herbrand eats a prodigious number of spring onions.

Glasses of milk, apples and biscuits at 11.30 to keep one going until lunch, which is at 2. Later a comic-opera Rolls dating to 1913 picked us up. Man on box as well as driver, and the back wheels fitted with chains as if for snowy weather. Miss Green held a small butler's tray on her lap and on the tray stood a Pekinese the size of a basset hound. The tray was supported by a single leg and hitched to the front of the car by green baize straps. By this means the dog's behind is brought to within a half-inch of one's nose. There's no escape.

We called on Constance and Romola, Lord Ampthill's daughters. They were sitting indoors in immense beefeater hats and thick cloth coats with brown braid. We all talked and screamed and said the same thing over and over again for forty minutes. Lunch at the Abbey, and afterwards Herbrand offered to send me to Whipsnade: 'There's nothing to do here, you know.' I refused and walked to the Chinese Dairy alone.

Dinner a repetition of last night. Rough claret, and Herbrand puts a lot of ice in his. Miss Green's stinking dog sits on a tray on a high chair next to me. On the table is a wooden bowl hollowed out to hold a glass bowl full of ice. The dog licks the ice from time to time during dinner. Clear soup, choice of two fish, grouse, ice, peaches. A.1.

I enclose a card stolen from my bedroom: 'You are particularly requested to refrain from giving a gratuity to any servant.'

It's been an experience coming here. Poor Herbrand! What an extraordinary business it is, and how odd that the world should contain places like Woburn and people like Herbrand. It sometimes strikes me as quite unnatural. My family is a zoo, only instead of lions and bears in the cages there are unicorns, chimaeras, cockatrices and hippogriffs.

The Light of Common Day, 1959

Tea in Maryland
FRANCES TROLLOPE 1780–1863

Frances Trollope was the mother of Anthony, the novelist. She was a novelist too, and published many novels, as well as producing books on her travels to America, Belgium, Paris and Vienna. Her stay in America was not a success: her descriptions incensed American society, while her husband was ruined by a scheme for selling fancy goods in Cincinnati.

When in Maryland, I went into the houses of several of these small proprietors, and remained long enough, and looked and listened sufficiently, to obtain a tolerably correct idea of their manner of living.

One of these families consisted of a young man, his wife, two children, a female slave, and two young lads, slaves also. The farm belonged to the wife, and, I was told, consisted of about three hundred acres of indifferent land, but all cleared. The house was built of wood, and looked as if the three slaves might have overturned it, had they pushed hard against the gable end. It contained one room, of about twelve feet square, and another adjoining it, hardly larger than a closet; this second chamber was the lodging-room of the white part of the family. Above these rooms was a loft, without windows, where I was told the 'staying company' who visited them, were lodged. Near this mansion was a 'shanty', a black hole, without any window, which served as kitchen and all other offices, and also as the lodging of the blacks.

We were invited to take tea with this family, and readily consented to do so. The furniture of the room was one heavy huge table, and about six wooden chairs. When we arrived the lady was in rather a dusky dishabille, but she vehemently urged us to be seated, and then retired into the closet-chamber above mentioned, whence she continued to address to us from behind the door, all kinds of 'genteel country visiting talk', and at length emerged upon us in a smart new dress.

Her female slave set out the great table, and placed upon it cups of the very coarsest blue ware, a little brown sugar in one, and a tiny drop of milk in another, no butter, though the lady assured us she had a '*deary*' and two cows. Instead of butter, she 'hoped we would fix a little relish with our crackers', in ancient English, eat salt meat and dry biscuits. Such was the fare, and for guests that certainly were intended to be honoured. I could not help recalling the delicious repasts which I remembered to have enjoyed at little dairy farms in England, not *possessed*, but rented, and at high rents too; where the clean, fresh-coloured, bustling mistress herself skimmed the delicious cream, herself spread the yellow butter on the delightful brown loaf, and placed her curds, and her junket, and all the delicate treasures of her dairy before us, and then, with hospitable pride, placed herself at her board, and added the more delicate 'relish' of good tea and a good cream. I remembered all this, and did not think the difference atoned for, by the dignity of having my cup handed to me by a slave.

Domestic Manners of the Americans, 1832

High Tea

D. H. LAWRENCE 1885–1930

They put down the Trewhellas at their house in North Sydney, and went on to Murdoch Road over the ferry. Jack had still to take the car down to the garage in town. Victoria said she would prepare the high tea which takes the place of dinner and supper in Australia, against his return. So Harriet boldly invited them to this high tea – a real substantial meal – in her own house. Victoria was to help her prepare it, and Jack was to come straight back to Torestin. Victoria was as pleased as a lamb with two tails over this arrangement, and went in to change her dress.

Somers knew why Harriet had launched this invitation. It was because she had had a wonderfully successful cooking morning. Like plenty of other women Harriet had learned to cook during war-time, and now she loved it, once in a while. This had been one of the whiles. Somers had stoked the excellent little stove, and peeled the apples and potatoes and onions and pumpkin, and looked after the meat and the sauces, while Harriet had lashed out in pies and tarts and little cakes and baked custard. She now surveyed her prize Beeton shelf with love, and began to whisk up a mayonnaise for potato salad.

Victoria appeared in a pale gauze dress of pale pink with little dabs of gold – a sort of tea-party dress – and with her brown hair loosely knotted behind, and with innocent sophistication pulled a bit untidy over her womanly forehead, she looked winsome. Her colour was very warm, and she was gawkily excited. Harriet put on an old yellow silk frock, and Somers changed into a dark suit. For tea there was cold roast pork with first-class brown crackling on it, and potato salad, beetroot, and lettuce, and apple chutney; then a dressed lobster – or crayfish, very good, pink and white; and then apple pie and custard-tarts and cakes and a dish of apples and passion fruits and oranges, a pineapple and some bananas: and of course big cups of tea, breakfast-cups.

Victoria and Harriet were delighted, Somers juggled with colour-schemes on the table, the one central room in the bungalow was brilliantly lighted, and the kettle sang on the hearth. After months of India, with all the Indian decorum and two silent menservants waiting at table: and after the old-fashioned gentility of the P. and O. steamer, Somers and Harriet felt this show rather a come-down maybe, but still good fun. Victoria felt it was almost 'society'. They waited for Jack.

Jack arrived bending forward rather in the doorway, a watchful look on his pale, clean-shaven face, and that atmosphere of silence about him which is characteristic of many Australians.

'Kept you waiting?' he asked.

'We were just ready for you,' said Harriet.

Jack had to carve the meat, because Somers was so bad at it and didn't like doing it. Harriet poured the great cups of tea. Callcott looked with a quick eye round the table to see exactly what he wanted to eat, and Victoria peeped through her lashes to see exactly how Harriet behaved. As Harriet always behaved in the vaguest manner possible, and ate her sweets with her fish-fork and her soup with her pudding spoon, a study of her table manners was not particularly profitable.

To Somers it was like being back twenty-five years, back in an English farm-house in the Midlands, at Sunday tea. He had gone a long way from the English Midlands, and got out of the way of them. Only to find them here again, with hardly a change. To Harriet it was all novel and fun. But Richard Lovat felt vaguely depressed.

Kangaroo, 1923

Gluttony

❦

Trimalchio's Feast
PETRONIUS d. 66 AD

'Then an extremely grand first course was served, as all the company was now seated except Trimalchio, for whom the first place at table was still reserved according to a new fashion. For the hors d'oeuvre there was a large dish with the figure of an ass on it, in Corinthian bronze, and loaded with panniers containing olives, pale on one side and black on the other. The ass was sheltered by two flat plates engraved round the rims with Trimalchio's name and their weight as silver. Then little bridges, soldered together, held dormice conserved in honey and sprinkled with poppy-seed. There were piping-hot sausages over a silver grid, with damsons and the seeds of pomegranates below.' . . .

'Yes,' said Trimalchio, 'but what did you have to eat?'

'I'll tell you if I can,' replied the other, 'but my memory is so good I often forget my own name. Well, first of all we had a pig crowned with a cup, and round it sausages and liver very well done, some beetroot of course, wholemeal bread baked at home, which I prefer to white, because it builds you up, and it makes me do my duty without tears. Then came a dish of cold tart and vintage Spanish wine poured over warm honey. I didn't touch a bit of tart, but I gorged myself on the honey. Chick-peas and lupins came round, nuts to choice and an apple apiece. I lifted two of them myself, and here they are wrapped in my napkin. There would be trouble if I didn't bring my little slave a present. Ah! My wife has just reminded me – we had a portion of bear on display. Scintilla was rash enough to try some, and she nearly brought her inside up. Yet I guzzled over a pound of it myself, for it smacked of real wild boar. What I say is, when the bear devours puny man, how much more ought our puny man to eat up the bear? To round off we had cream cheese and boiled wine, every man his snail, bits of tripe, livers on tiny plates, capped eggs, turnips, mustard, a plate of muck – whoa, Palamedes! They brought round a bowl of cummin in vinegar, and some were perverse enough to take three handfuls, for we had waved the ham aside.'

Satyricon, TRANS. Paul Dinnage, 1953

Vitellius

SUETONIUS 69?–140? AD

Vitellius's ruling vices were extravagance and cruelty. He banqueted three and often four times a day, namely morning, noon, afternoon, and evening – the last meal being mainly a drinking bout – and survived the ordeal well enough by taking frequent emetics. What made things worse was that he used to invite himself out to such meals at the houses of a number of different people on one and the same day; and these never cost his various hosts less than 4,000 gold pieces each. The most notorious feast of the series was given him by his brother on his entry into Rome; 2,000 magnificent fish and 7,000 game birds are said to have been served. Yet even this hardly compares in luxuriousness with a single tremendously large dish which Vitellius dedicated to the Goddess Minerva and named 'Shield of Minerva the Protectress of the City'. The recipe called for pike-livers, pheasant brains, peacock-brains, flamingo-tongues, and lamprey-milt; and all these ingredients, collected in every corner of the Empire from the Parthian frontier to the Spanish Strait, were brought to Rome by naval captains and triremes. Vitellius paid no attention to time or decency in satisfying his remarkable appetite. While a sacrifice was in progress, he thought nothing of snatching lumps of meat or cake off the altar, almost out of the sacred fire, and bolting them down; and on his travels would devour cuts of meat fetched smoking hot from wayside cookshops, and even yesterday's half-eaten scraps.

The Twelve Caesars, TRANS. Robert Graves, 1957

Greediness

LOUIS-SÉBASTIEN MERCIER 1740–1814

I know a man who maintains that the pleasures of the table are the greatest of pleasures. Mankind, says he, begins by feeding at the breast, and never loses his appetite till he dies. The pleasure is renewed two or three times a day, and if it is not a pleasure for every man it is because only one man in fifty thousand has a first-class cook. This man is the slave of his belly which is already very big. He exults over a succulent dish. He maintains that there is all the difference in the world between feeding and eating – he *eats*. When his cook is ill he hastens to the best doctor in town and begs him to spare no art or pains to restore health to one whom he regards as a second self, and the joy of his life.

He makes the finest distinctions in viands, even as a trained ear catches the semitones in music. He glories in his greed, and pities, not the hungry, but the eater of bad dinners.

It is not his appetite that governs him, but an artificial hunger he has created for himself; which goes to prove what habit can form, and how astonishing are the latent powers of the stomach, since it leads us from victory to victory until that day comes when the battle is lost and indigestion kills him.

The Picture of Paris, TRANS. Wilfred and Emilie Jackson, 1929

Gluttony

THE GOODMAN OF PARIS C. 1392

This sin of gluttony, which, as I have said, is divided into two parts, has five branches. The first branch is when a person eateth before he ought, to wit too early in the morning, or before saying hours and going to church and hearing the word of God and His commandments; for every creature ought to have the good sense and discretion not to eat before the hour of tierce, save by reason of illness, or weakness or some constraining thereto.

The second branch of gluttony is when a person eats more often than behoveth and without need. For, as the Scripture saith: once upon the day to eat and drink it is angelic, and to eat twice a day is human, and thrice or four times or more often is the life of a beast and not of a human being.

The third branch of gluttony is when a person eats and drinks so much in a day that ill befalls him, and he is drunk and sick and must take to his bed, and is sore burdened thereby.

The fourth branch of gluttony is when a person eats so greedily of a dish that he doth not chew it and swallows it whole and before he ought, as the Scripture telleth of Esau, that was the firstborn of all his brothers, and made such haste to eat that he was nigh choked.

The fifth branch of gluttony is when a person seeks out delicious viands, howsoever costly they be, and can do good to fewer others and cannot withhold himself so that he may help a poor man, or two, or more. And it is this sin concerning which we read in the Gospels of the wicked rich man, that was clad in purple, and each day ate so plenteously of meat and would do no kindness to the poor lazar, and concerning him, we read that he was damned, for that he lived too delicately and gave not for God's sake as behoved him.

Afterwards cometh the sin of lechery, which is born of gluttony, for when the wicked man has well drunken and eaten more than he ought, then is he moved and warmed to this sin and then come disordered thoughts and evil meditations and from the thought he goeth to the deed.

The Goodman of Paris, TRANS. Eileen Power, 1928

Gluttony Murders
LUIGI CORNARO 1465–1566

Luigi Cornaro was born into one of the leading families of Venice and led a life of great indulgence until his mid-thirties, when his health broke down. He then changed his diet to an austere regime of vegetables and water, supplemented occasionally with the yolk of an egg and dry bread. He was eighty-two when he began to write books exhorting all who value their health to follow his example.

O wretched and unhappy Italy! can you not see that gluttony murders every year more of your inhabitants than you could lose by the most cruel plague or by fire and sword in many battles! Those truly shameful feasts (*i tuoi veramente disonesti banchetti*), now so much in fashion and so intolerably profuse that no tables are large enough to hold the infinite number of the dishes – those feasts, I say, are so many battles. And how is it possible to *live* amongst such a multitude of jarring foods and disorders? Put an end to this abuse, in heaven's name, for there is not – I am certain of it – a vice more abominable than this in the eyes of the divine Majesty. Drive away this plague, the worst you were ever afflicted with – this new kind of death – as you have banished that disease which, though it formerly used to make such havoc, now does little or no mischief, owing to the laudable practice of attending more to the goodness of the provisions brought to our markets. Consider that there are means still left to banish intemperance, and such means, too, that every man may have recourse to them without any external assistance.

quoted in *The Ethics of Diet*, 1883

Challenge
JEAN-PAUL ARON 1925–88

Challenge. This is the gentlest form of aggression and presents a fascinating spectacle: a solitary eater working his way through a lunatic feast, impassive under the gaze of his table-companions, his petrified neighbours. During the July Monarchy, the Vicomte de Viel-Castel wagered that he would despatch a dinner costing 500 francs (the annual income of an average worker) in one hundred and twenty minutes. At seven o'clock precisely, at the *Café de Paris*, the meal began. First, twelve dozen Ostend oysters, which he swallowed so quickly that, perfectly at his ease, he asked for the same again, and washed them down with a bottle of Johannisberg. The oysters do not count, since dinner proper begins with the soup: in this case, swallows' nest. Getting into his stride, the Vicomte ordered an extra dish: stew with potatoes, which he rapidly devoured. From this point on, the menu unfolded in its usual sequence: a splendid *féra* – a breed of salmon from Lake Geneva – which he ate right down to the bones; an enormous pheasant crammed with truffles; a salmis of ten ortolans which he polished off in as many mouthfuls; asparagus, petits pois. The desserts were simple: a pineapple and some strawberries. With the remove and the entreé, Viel-Castel drank two bottles of Bordeaux;

another of the same with the roast, and a bottle of sherry with the desserts. Naturally, there were liqueurs with the coffee. He paid 518 francs 50, slightly more than the specified cost, and at nine o'clock he left the table, as fresh as a rose.

The Art of Eating in France, TRANS. Nina Rootes, 1975

Balzac

GILES MACDONOGH 1955–

Balzac himself, despite a genuine admiration for Grimod de La Reynière, was more of a glutton than a Lucullus. His own one recorded visit to Véry is a record of a truly gargantuan appetite. In theory Balzac had offered to take his publisher Werdet out to lunch. The latter, fearing perhaps that his writer was unwise to choose such an expensive restaurant, ordered a bowl of soup, and a chicken wing. Balzac for his part had no such false modesty and swallowed a hundred Ostend oysters, twelve Pré-Salé mutton cutlets, a duckling with turnips, a brace of roast partridges, a sole Normande, without counting hors d'oeuvres, entremets, fruits, etc., including a dozen pears. All of this was washed down with the most famous wines, liqueurs and coffee; all disappeared without so much as the writer pausing to catch his breath. Having finished this prodigious feat of gluttony, Balzac confessed to having no money on him; 'By the way my dear fellow, you wouldn't have any cash on you would you?'

Werdet was stunned; he had been invited out to lunch and yet Balzac had not a sou to pay the bill.

'I must have some forty francs on me,' he replied.

'That's not enough, give me five francs.' Taking the money, Balzac called for the bill with an imperious tone. 'This,' he said to the waiter, giving him the coin, 'is for you.' Then, writing a few words on the bottom of the bill, he said, 'This is for the lady at the counter, tell her it is from Honoré de Balzac.'

The next day an outraged Werdet received a bill for sixty-two francs fifty. He deducted it from the author's account, not forgetting the five francs for the tip.

A Palate in Revolution, 1987

A Dominican at Breakfast, 1770
W. A. MOZART 1756–91

To His Mother and Sister

Bologna, 21 August 1770
I too am still alive and, what is more, as merry as can be. I had a great
desire today to ride on a donkey, for it is the custom in Italy, and so I
thought that I too should try it. We have the honour to go about with a
certain Dominican, who is regarded as a holy man. For my part I do
not believe it, for at breakfast he often takes a cup of chocolate and
immediately afterwards a good glass of strong Spanish wine; and I
myself have had the honour of lunching with this saint who at table
drank a whole decanter and finished up with a full glass of strong wine,
two large slices of melon, some peaches, pears, five cups of coffee, a
whole plate of cloves, and two full saucers of milk and lemon. He may,
of course, be following some sort of diet, but I do not think so, for it
would be too much; moreover he takes several little snacks during the
afternoon. *Addio.* Farewell. Kiss Mamma's hands for me. My greet-
ings to all who know me.

WOLFGANG MOZART
Mozart's Letters, TRANS. Emily Anderson, 1938

Zola's Only Vice, 1875
EDMOND 1822–96 AND JULES 1830–70
GONCOURT

Monday 25 January
The Flaubert dinners are unlucky. Coming away from the first, I
caught pneumonia. Today, Flaubert himself was missing: he is
confined to bed. So there were only four of us: Turgenev, Zola,
Daudet, and myself . . .
   Zola was tucking into the good food, and when I asked him whether
by any chance he was a glutton, he replied: 'Yes, it's my only vice; and
at home, when there isn't anything good for dinner, I'm miserable,

utterly miserable. That's the only thing that matters; nothing else really exists for me.'

Pages from the Goncourt Journals, ED., TRANS. Robert Baldick, 1962

Triumphs of Gluttony

GIUSEPPE DI LAMPEDUSA 1896–1957

Beneath the candelabra, beneath the five-tiers bearing towards the distant ceiling pyramids of home-made cakes that were never touched, spread the monotonous opulence of buffets at big balls: coraline lobsters boiled alive, waxy *chaud-froids* of veal, steely-tinted fish immersed in sauce, turkeys gilded by the ovens' heat, rosy *foie-gras* under gelatine armour, boned woodcocks reclining on amber toast decorated with their own chopped guts, and a dozen other cruel, coloured delights. At the end of the table two monumental silver tureens held limpid soup, the colour of burnt amber. To prepare this supper the cooks must have sweated away in the vast kitchens from the night before.

'Dear me, what an amount! Donna Margherita knows how to do things well. But it's not for me!'

Scorning the table of drinks, glittering with crystal and silver on the right, he moved left towards that of the sweetmeats. Huge blond *babas, Mont Blancs* snowy with whipped cream, cakes speckled with white almonds and green pistachio nuts, hillocks of chocolate-covered pastry, brown and rich as the top soil of the Catanian plain from which, in fact, through many a twist and turn they had come, pink ices, champagne ices, coffee ices, all *parfaits* and falling apart with a squelch at a knife cleft, a melody in major of crystallised cherries, acid notes of yellow pineapple, and those cakes called 'Triumphs of Gluttony,' filled with green pistachio paste, and shameless 'Virgin's cakes' shaped like breasts. Don Fabrizio asked for some of these, and as he held them on his plate looked like a profane caricature of Saint Agatha. 'Why ever didn't the Holy Office forbid these puddings when it had the chance? Saint Agatha's sliced-off breasts sold by convents, devoured at dances! Well! Well!'

Round the room smelling of vanilla, wine, *chypre*, wandered Don Fabrizio looking for a place. Tancredi saw him from his table and clapped a hand on a chair to show there was room there; next to him was Angelica, peering at the back of a silver dish to see if her hair was in place. Don Fabrizio shook his head in smiling refusal. He went on looking; from a table he heard the satisfied voice of Pallavicino, 'The most moving moment of my life . . .' By him was an empty place. What a bore the man was! Wouldn't it better, after all, to listen to Angelica's refreshing if forced cordiality, to Tancredi's dry wit? No: better bore oneself than bore others.

With a word of apology he sat down next to the Colonel, who got up as he arrived – a small sop to Salina pride. As he savoured the subtle mixture of blancmange, pistachio and cinnamon in the puddings he had chosen, Don Fabrizio began conversing with Pallavicino and realised that, beyond those sugary phrases meant perhaps only for ladies, the man was anything but a fool.

The Leopard, TRANS. Archibald Colquhoun, 1960

Triumph of Gluttony

MARY TAYLOR SIMETI 1941–

Prince Fabrizio really wasn't at all hungry, or he would have succumbed to the 'triumph of gluttony.' This is another of the great convent specialties, but each order of nuns seems to have had its own idea of Waterloo, for the number and content of the different layers changes from place to place. One recipe I have seen called for a bottom layer of *pan di Spagna* soaked with rum, on which were spread pistachio preserves, followed by a layer of *pasta frolla*, then a layer of egg-custard cream covered with more *pasta frolla* and still more custard, each layer slightly smaller than the one below. Once this basic cone was formed, its entire surface was spread with apricot jelly, covered with a thin sheet of *pasta reale*, and decorated with candied fruit and chopped pistachios.

The only triumph of gluttony that I have actually tasted, one made by a convent in Palermo, was quite different but equally irresistible. There were five layers of *pan di Spagna*, each less than $\frac{1}{2}$ inch thick, which alternated with deep layers of what seemed to be just enough of a rather liquid *biancomangiare* to hold together coarsely chopped pistachios and candied *zuccata*. The cone-shaped cake was covered with preserves – possibly pistachio – with a patterned decoration of candied fruit and frills and curlicues fashioned of *pasta reale*. A large green almond of marzipan was balanced on the top of the cone.

If its outward appearance was touchingly naïve, within the golden stripes of *pan di Spagna* framed bright green chips of pistachio and greeny-gold cubes of glistening *zuccata*, which floated in the pale *biancomangiare* like so many tesserae from the mosaic wall of an Arab-Norman chapel. This harmony of color was echoed by equal sophistication in the balance of the flavors: the *zuccata* was a miracle of delicacy; the pistachio was present yet not obtrusive; the faint suggestion of jasmine gave context to an affirmation of stick cinnamon, crushed in a mortar and sprinkled over every layer.

Even if I were fortunate enough to have it, a recipe for this triumph of gluttony would be useless without the secret of the sisters' *zuccata*. The best I can offer is a recipe for pistachio preserves, which are very simple to make. If you were to use them in a *zuppa imprescia* that was sprinkled with abundant crushed stick cinnamon, you would be brought close enough to a triumph of gluttony to feel that you were succumbing in style.

Sicilian Food, 1989

Thank Goodness I Am Greedy
BERNARD DARWIN 1876–1961

'I am not hungry,' says a gentleman enshrined in one of the dear old bound volumes of Mr. Punch, 'but thank goodness I am greedy.' It is a very proper subject for thanksgiving. There can breathe nobody with soul so dead that he has not said to himself, on the eve of a visit, rubbing his hands in expectant ecstasy, that here he will meet with potted shrimps of a quality to make a man wink, or there a treacle tart come from beyond the skies. Whether this paradise be a private house or a club or an inn, there dwells in it the tradition, founded on the recipe of some long forgotten artist, of a dish of peculiar and superlative excellence belonging to nowhere else in the world. Extend this principle and we connect some of these particular delights with whole regions.

Receipts and Relishes, 1950

On the *Stella*

EVELYN WAUGH 1903–66

The dining-room had the advantage over many ships that it could seat all the passengers at once, so that meals did not have to be arranged in two services. These, allowing for the limitations of cold storage, were admirable, and almost continuous in succession. It seems to be of the tenets of catering on board ship that passengers need nutrition every two and a half hours. On shore the average civilized man, I suppose, confines himself to two or at the most three meals a day. On the *Stella* everybody seemed to eat all the time. They had barely finished breakfast – which included on its menu, besides all the dishes usually associated with that meal, such solid fare as goulash and steak and onions – before tureens of clear soup appeared. Luncheon was at one o'clock and was chiefly remarkable for the cold buffet which was laden with every kind of Scandinavian delicatessen, smoked salmon, smoked eels, venison, liver pies, cold game and meat and fish, sausage, various sorts of salad, eggs in sauces, cold asparagus, in almost disconcerting profusion. At four there was tea, at seven a long dinner, and at ten dishes of sandwiches, not of the English railway-station kind, but little rounds of bread covered with caviare and *foie gras* with eggs and anchovies. Drinks and tobacco were sold, of course, duty free, and were correspondingly cheap. There were some interesting Scandinavian spirits, drunk as apéritifs, which made me feel rather sick.

Labels, 1930

Killing for the Kitchen

❦

Essay on Flesh Eating
PLUTARCH 40–120 AD

'In slaughtering swine, for example, they thrust red-hot irons into their living bodies, so that, by sucking up or diffusing the blood, they may render the flesh soft and tender. Some butchers jump upon or kick the udders of pregnant sows, that by mingling the blood and milk and matter of the *embryos* that have been murdered together in the very pangs of parturition, they may enjoy the pleasures of feeding upon unnaturally and highly inflamed flesh! Again, it is a common practice to stitch up the eyes of cranes and swans, and shut them up in dark places to fatten. In this and other similar ways are manufactured their dainty dishes, with all the varieties of sauces and spices [καρυκείαις – Lydian sauces, composed of blood and spices] – from all which it is sufficiently evident that men have indulged their lawless appetites in the pleasures of luxury, not for necessary food, and from no necessity, but only out of the merest wantonness, and gluttony, and display . . .'

Moralia, TRANS. Harold Chermiss and William Helmbold, 1978

Rats in Canton
ANDREW HIGGINS

The idea that if you inflict cruelty on the living animal immediately before slaughter the result will be greater flavour and tenderness in the carcass still exists today.

A restaurant devoted exclusively to exploring the culinary potential of rat, though, is a first, even in Canton, where most animals end up in the

343

cooking-pot. Mr Zhang, 31, says the idea came to him in a flash one night early last year. He was walking home when a rat scampered across his path: a restaurant – and the beginnings of a small fortune – was born. He now serves up around 30 rats a day and takes deliveries of fresh, live rats every second day.

The key to preparing good rat, he says, is in the killing: 'Put the rat in hot water. The temperature must be just right, about 65 degrees. Wait until it stops squirming, fish it out before it dies and pluck its hair, cut open its belly and chop off its tail and head.' The finished product is stored in a freezer.

The Independent on Sunday, 25 August 1991

Can Civil and Human Eyes Yet Abide the Slaughter

DR. W. MOFFET 1553–1604

'Nay, tell me, can civil and human eyes yet abide the slaughter of an innocent "beast," the cutting of his throat, the smashing him on the head, the flaying of his skin, the quartering and dismembering of his limbs, the sprinkling of his blood, the ripping up of his veins, the enduring of ill-savours, the heaving of heavy sighs, sobs, and groans, the passionate struggling and panting for life, which only hard-hearted butchers can endure to see?

'Is not the earth sufficient to give us meat, but that we must also rend up the bowels of "beasts," birds, and fishes? Yes, truly, there is enough in the earth to give us meat; yea, verily, and choice of meats, needing either none or no great preparation, which we may take without fear, and cut down without trembling which, also, we may mingle a hundred ways to delight our taste, and feed on safely to fill our bellies.'

Health's Improvement, 1655

Arguments in Favour of a Vegetable Diet
ANON 1801

From the texture of the human heart arises a strong argument in behalf of persecuted animals. Mercy is an amiable quality, admired by those who do not practice it. There exists within us a rooted repugnance to the spilling of blood; a repugnance which yields only to custom, and which even the most inveterate custom can never entirely overcome. Hence the horrid task of shedding the tide of life, for the gluttony of the table, has, in every country, been committed to the lowest class of men; and their profession is almost every where an object of abhorrence. On the carcase we feed, without remorse, because the dying struggles of the butchered creature are secluded from our sight; because his cries pierce not our ear; because his agonizing shrieks sink not into our souls; but were we forced with our own hands to assassinate the animals we readily devour, there are some amongst us that would throw down, with detestation the knife; and rather than embrue his hands in the murder of the lamb, consent, for ever, to forego the favourite repast? How is it possible, possessing in our breasts an abhorrence of cruelty, and sympathy for misery, that we can act so barbarously. Certainly the feelings of the heart point more unerringly than the dogmas and subtilties of men who sacrifice to custom the dearest sentiments of humanity. Had nature intended man an animal of prey, would she have implanted in his breast a principle so adverse to her purpose? Could she mean the human race should eat their food with compunction and regret; that every morsel should be purchased with a pang, and every meal of man be impoisoned with remorse? Can nature have imparted the milk of kindness in the same bosom which should be filled with unfeeling ferocity? Would she not rather have wrapped his heart in ruthless ribs of brass; and, have armed him, with iron entrails, to grind, without remorse, the palpitating limbs of agonizing life? Has nature winged with fleetness the feet of man to overtake the flying prey, or given him fangs to tear assunder the creatures destined for his food? Glares in his eyeballs the lust of carnage? Does he scent from afar the footsteps of his victim? Does his soul pant for the feast of blood? Is the bosom of man the rugged abode of bloody thoughts; and from that sink of depravity and horror, does the sight of other animals excite his rapacious desires to slay, to mangle, to devour?

On the Primeval Diet of Man, 1801

Whale

HERMAN MELVILLE 1819–91

'Haul in – haul in!' cried Stubb to the bowsman! and, facing round towards the whale, all hands began pulling the boat up to him, while yet the boat was being towed on. Soon ranging up by his flank, Stubb, firmly planting his knee in the clumsy cleat, darted dart after dart into the flying fish; at the word of command, the boat alternately sterning out of the way of whale's horrible wallow, and then ranging up for another fling.

The red tide now poured from all sides of the monster like brooks down a hill. His tormented body rolled not in brine but in blood, which bubbled and seethed for furlongs behind in their wake. The slanting sun playing upon this crimson pond in the sea, sent back its reflection into every face, so that they all glowed to each other like red men. And all the while, jet after jet of white smoke was agonizingly shot from the spiracle of the whale, and vehement puff after puff from the mouth of the excited headsman; as at every dart, hauling in upon his crooked lance (by the line attached to it), Stubb straightened it again and again, by a few rapid blows against the gunwale, then again and again sent it into the whale.

'Pull up – pull up!' he now cried to the bowsman, as the waning whale relaxed in his wrath. 'Pull up! – close to!' and the boat ranged along the fish's flank. When reaching far over the bow, Stubb slowly churned his long sharp lance into the fish, and kept it there, carefully churning and churning, as if cautiously seeking to feel after some gold watch that the whale might have swallowed, and which he was fearful of breaking ere he could hook it out. But that gold watch he sought was the innermost life of the fish. And now it is struck; for, starting from his trance into that unspeakable thing called his 'flurry,' the monster horribly wallowed in his blood, overwrapped himself in impenetrable, mad, boiling spray, so that the imperilled craft, instantly dropping astern, had much ado blindly to struggle out from that phrensied twilight into the clear air of the day.

And now abating in his flurry, the whale once more rolled out into view; surging from side to side; spasmodically dilating and contracting his spout-hole, with sharp, cracking, agonized respirations. At last, gush after gush of clotted red gore, as if it had been the purple lees of red wine, shot into the frighted air; and falling back again, ran

dripping down his motionless flanks into the sea. His heart had burst!
'He's dead, Mr. Stubb,' said Daggoo.

Moby Dick, 1851

Murder by Smothering
ALICE B. TOKLAS 1878–1967

It was in the market of Palma de Mallorca that our French cook tried
to teach me to murder by smothering. There is no reason why this
crime should have been committed publicly or that I should have been
expected to participate. Jeanne was just showing off. When the crowd
of market women who had gathered about her began screaming and
gesticulating, I retreated. When we met later to drive back in the carry-
all filled with our marketing to Terreno where we had a villa I refused
to sympathise with Jeanne. She said the Mallorcans were bloodthirsty,
didn't they go to bullfights and pay an advanced price for the meat of
the beasts they had seen killed in the ring, didn't they prefer to chop off
the heads of innocent pigeons instead of humanely smothering them
which was the way to prevent all fowl from bleeding to death and so
make them fuller and tastier. Had she not tried to explain this to them,
to teach them, to show them how an intelligent humane person went
about killing pigeons, but no they didn't want to learn, they preferred
their own brutal ways. At lunch when she served the pigeons Jeanne
discreetly said nothing. Discussing food which she enjoyed above
everything had been discouraged at table. But her fine black eyes were
eloquent. If the small-sized pigeons the island produced had not
achieved jumbo size, squabs they unquestionably were, and larger and
more succulent squabs that those we had eaten at the excellent
restaurant at Palma.

Later we went back to Paris and then there was war and after a
lifetime there was peace. One day passing the *concierge's loge* he called
me and said he had something someone had left for us. He said he
would bring it to me, which he did and which I wished he hadn't when
I saw what it was, a crate of six white pigeons and a note from a friend
saying she had nothing better to offer us from her home in the country,
ending with But as Alice is clever she will make something delicious of
them. It is certainly a mistake to allow a reputation for cleverness to be
born and spread by loving friends. It is so cheaply acquired and so

dearly paid for. Six white pigeons to be smothered, to be plucked, to be cleaned and all this to be accomplished before Gertrude Stein returned for she didn't like to see work being done. If only I had the courage the two hours before her return would easily suffice. A large cup of strong black coffee would help. This was before a lovely Brazilian told me that in her country a large cup of black coffee was always served before going to bed to ensure a good night's rest. Not yet having acquired this knowledge the black coffee made me lively and courageous. I carefully found the spot on poor innocent Dove's throat where I was to press and pressed. The realization had never come to me before that one saw with one's fingertips as well as one's eyes. It was a most unpleasant experience, though as I laid out one by one the sweet young corpses there was no denying one could become accustomed to murdering. So I plucked the pigeons, emptied them and was ready to cook.

The Alice B. Toklas Cook Book, 1954

Killing A Pig

ETHELIND FEARON

Jonathan has been killing a pig. It sounds simple enough, and was a regular occurrence several times during the winter.

You popped a net over your pig, carted him comfortably to the brew-house, knocked him behind the ear just once with the traditional 'blunt instrument', in this case a slab of oak, and while he was senseless cut his throat. And no one, least of all the pig, was a button the worse.

As he lay supine upon his bier, as dignified as any marble crusader upon a tombstone, one knelt before him with a basin full of oatmeal to catch his bright life-blood and produce black-puddings. He was singed, scalded, disembowelled and otherwise tidied up, and every conceivable portion of him, from trotters to ears, was utilised in some way.

Most Happy Husbandman, 1946

Prosciutto

ELIZABETH ROMER

In years gone by the slaughtering of the pigs was a messy noisy business. Silvana remembers when she and her sister were girls and used to feed the pigs on their little farm high in the mountains. When the day for slaughtering came her sister would rise early and run far up into the woods so that she would not hear the pigs screaming and there in the shelter of the trees she would cry her heart out. Silvana, being made of sterner material, would often assist in the killing and hold the bowl for the blood. Orlando is also soft hearted and insists that a humane killer be used to prevent the creature suffering; a small pistol fires a retractable bolt into the pig's brain and death is instantaneous. Then the heart is pierced to let the blood flow. Silvana stresses that the animal must be properly bled or the *prosciutto* will not cure properly. She also observes that the only animal whose death the old Tuscan people really mourned was the ox, the beautiful white beast that drew the plough; they were mourned almost as if they were human because they too need nine months in the womb before they are ready to be born.

The Tuscan Year, 1984

Ritual Significance

PATIENCE GRAY

In Apollona one felt that the eating of meat still had its ritual significance, that invisible thighbones were being offered to the gods. Zeus still held sway on that high peak that dominates the solid wall of mountains on the eastern side of Naxos. Meat only figured on feast days. Butchery, as we understand it, did not exist.

The signal for the feast was usually a small boy running past our dwelling on the lip of the bay, pursuing a horned goat. The carcase, freshly killed and skinned, was suspended by its Achilles tendon from a tamarisk on the village quay, and its owner hacked off portions with a blunt instrument which were then weighed on an old iron balance and rapidly seized by the contestants who stood around screaming their preferences.

There was no interval between the animal's death and its conversion into rough joints of meat, one reason why the meat was tough. The goat's meat was boiled with sage, thyme, slices of lemon, onions, carrots, celery, and was served in the invariably liquid sauce with boiled spaghetti.

The lamb was better, but at first sight the carcase was a shock. A skeleton, one realised why, seeing the flocks trotting at speed among the mountain boulders with the shepherd Apostólyi leaping after them as they nibbled the few live shoots of herbs, amongst the scrub, which had survived the sun's withering glance.

It was therefore no surprise to us when the two old peasants from up the mountain, who had rented us our lofty muleshed on the condition, inexorable, that they spend 20 days with us in July, while the old man took his annual sand-bath on the little beach, despatched a kid on a Saint's day, which they cooked and consumed in a short time between them on the seashore.

This operation bore all the aspects of a domestic crime. The guilt one feels is an old legacy from which we are saved by slaughterhouse and butcher, and which was once expunged by sacrifice. So the goat is boiled, and the kid and lamb are grilled in sections on a driftwood fire. I am speaking of what happens in Apollona. All that was left of this particular kid I found with horror and surprise next morning in the communal black pot – the unskinned head and the little furry paws.

Perhaps I should add that in the port of Naxos which had suffered the beneficial effects of four centuries of Venetian occupation, there were butcher's shops – red caverns hung with carcases and solid three-legged chopping blocks painted the colour of blood. There too, the pig entire was skilfully roasted on a charcoal spit with fragrant herbs. In the eating-houses one could eat goat which had been braised.

In Apollona we were living among the vestiges of neolithic and bronze age life: the wild almond, wild fig, wild olive and the vine which all came, if sporadically, into cultivation seven or eight thousand years ago, these staples along with wheat, rye and barley were staples still, as were the original sources of sweetness, honey, the carouba tree, wild pears, grapes, mulberry, figs. It was not hard to imagine that the same nimble flocks of long-tailed sheep and little black goats had been treading the mountain for many thousands of years, or that the acorns of ilex and dwarf kermes oaks had always been munched by little grey-skinned pigs.

Honey from a Weed, 1986

Our Bullock

AMANDA GOODFELLOW

Few of us like to face up to the realities of what is involved in the preparation of the meat we eat. We did, and I must say it was a sobering experience which nearly put us off eating meat altogether, and has certainly reduced my enthusiasm for shop bought meat. For several years we bought in bullocks, one or two at a time, to help our little flock of Jacob sheep keep down the summer grass in the large meadow behind our house. They were friendly, handsome animals, full of character, and we grew fond of them. They were happier in pairs, but when single made friends with the ram. The two of them, Charlie the ram and the solitary bullock, could be seen on summer evenings, standing under the trees at the top of the meadow, scratching each others backs with their horns.

By the time November came, bringing with it the cold weather, and our itinerant butcher, it seemed a crime to deprive our bullock of the life he so evidently enjoyed. The deed was quickly done, the great beast stunned and destroyed with a bolt through the head, while contentedly munching an apple. Then began the gory process of skinning and gutting the carcase. A metal bar was inserted through the hind locks of the animal and a block and tackle attached to the stout branch of a neighbouring oak, some way above the ground. By means of the tackle hooked to the metal bar, the bullock was hauled up to swing free of the ground. With belly split from top to bottom, his guts were spilled into the waiting buckets, then the skin, head and hooves were removed. Finally the carcase was sawn into four manageable pieces, which we hung in a neighbouring shed for three weeks to mature. A pall of gloom enveloped the household that day.

Three weeks later, the butcher returned to cut up the quarters into joints for the freezer, working on the kitchen table. It took him most of two days, despite our help in packing and labelling. There is an awful lot of meat on one bullock. Our beasts were killed when not much over a year old. Commercially raised animals are slaughtered at between eighteen months and two years, when they have put on considerably more weight. Nevertheless the carcase weight of our bullock was around 400 lb and it provided joints of meat totalling over 300 lb in weight, together with bags full of bones for soup and abundant suet for Christmas puddings and mince pies. This amount of meat was more than enough to supply the needs of our household of six, with intermittent guests, for a year, together with five or six lambs. When we had a second bullock, we sold the meat to friends, which just about covered our outlay. And it was delicious meat too, the best I have ever tasted, certainly outclassing ordinary butchers' meat. Of course the animals had eaten nothing but our untreated grass for eight months, and before that had been raised naturally by a smallholder. By the time we came to eat them, guilt and regret at having deprived these charming creatures of their lives had diminished. At least they had spent their days contentedly and been spared the horrors of a slaughterhouse, we reassured ourselves. We felt grateful to them for having provided us with such excellent food, and remembered them, as we chewed, with affection – Smokey, John Paul, Patch and Billy. Such is the curious relationship between farmers and their animal 'victims'. They love them in life, as much as they take pride in them in death. So it was with the butcher too. He had great understanding of animals, especially his first love, pigs. But he also enjoyed cutting them up, which he did with great skill, and appraising the quality of their dead flesh.

The slaughtering and dismembering of the sheep were less traumatic experiences – partly because they were much smaller animals, and partly because they had lost the delightful, individual characters they had as lambs, and had become dull, undistinguished members of the flock. They took much less time to 'process'. Their meat too was excellent – fairly small, very lean joints. The quality, I should say, was not so much above that of the first class English lamb from our local butcher, whereas our beef was decidedly superior.

A Household Legacy, 1989

Learning to be a Dutiful Carnivore

JANE LEGGE

Dogs and cats and goats and cows,
Ducks and chickens, sheep and sows
Woven into tales for tots,
Pictured on their walls and pots.
Time for dinner! Come and eat
All your lovely juicy meat.

One day ham from Percy Porker
(In the comics he's a corker),
Then the breast from Mrs Cluck
Or the wing from Donald Duck.
Liver next from Clara Cow
(No, it doesn't hurt her now).
Yes, that leg's from Peter Rabbit
Chew it well; make that a habit.
Eat the creatures killed for sale,
But never pull the pussy's tail.
Eat the flesh from 'filthy hogs'
But never be unkind to dogs.
Grow up into double-think –
Kiss the hamster; skin the mink.
Never think of slaughter, dear,
That's why animals are here.
They only come on earth to die,
So eat your meat, and don't ask why.

Eating Meat and Eating People, 1978

Turtle

ANDRÉ LAUNAY 1930–

In England, traditionally, *turtle soup* is the aristocratic soup which is held in the highest esteem, served at great ceremonial banquets, diplomatic dinners and sometimes on Royal occasions. It is considered to combine the two essential qualities for a good soup – delicate taste and valuable nourishment. If, however, in previous chapters the reader has found that foreigners are apt to put their stomachs before the animal's feelings, it might be well to dwell a little on this all-English recipe.

How many, who dip their silver spoons into the clear, hot, sticky, sherry-tanged liquid, have asked themselves how a turtle is killed? The problem, on the face of it, seems to be the same as the lobster's, except that a rather larger saucepan might be needed to boil a turtle.

Turtles measure anything up to four feet in length and three feet in width, and the truth of the matter is that turtles are hanged.

They arrive alive in this country from South America, Africa, the

West Indies and Australia, and are taken to the kitchens where the soup is to be made. They are put down in a corner somewhere and watched over by an apprentice chef, whose sole job it is to call out 'action stations' the moment he sees one of the turtles move. The sport is to wait till the turtle pokes its head out from beneath its shell and either lasso it or hook it by the chin.

If this is achieved successfully the turtle is hanged from a suitable scaffold, not to kill it, but to get the beast to expose enough neck so that its throat can be cut. It sounds barbarous, but in the end it's kindness itself.

The turtle, having been told by friends what may happen to it, does not help in any way and, being unbelievably strong and stubborn, can stay hanging for three or four days before its sheer weight exhausts it and obliges it to give up the struggle. When at last it exposes its leathery neck, an experienced slaughterer quickly flicks a razor-sharp knife in the right direction, after which everyone relaxes and thinks of soup.

Once the animal is dead no time is lost. Experts, equipped with hammers, chisels, saws and pliers get down to dismantling the beast, for getting the meat from the turtle is similar to decarbonising an engine. A heave here, a pull there, the top comes off, then the bottom, then the flippers, and so on.

The top and bottom shells are cut, or sawn, into easily-managed pieces, and, with the flippers, boiled till the meat can be easily removed. The meat is then blanched for a few minutes, put in a stew pan with a specially-prepared richly-flavoured consommé, vegetables and herbs, and cooked for about seven hours.

Caviare and After, 1964

Tenderizing
ANDREW JOHNSON

Methods of 'tenderizing' continue today, though EC proposals may ban this process. We are told that injections of papain in cattle are common in the USA, where the population has a large percentage of elderly people who wear dentures, and who like their steak to be the consistency of pâté.

Chemical methods are also used to 'improve' the quality of beef carcasses. More than 10 per cent of cattle slaughtered in Britain in 1989 received an injection of papain, a protein-digesting enzyme derived from the pawpaw, about half an hour before they were killed. This has a remarkable effect on the resulting meat: it can make 'the toughest old cow as tender as the most expensive rump steak'. In fact, the tenderizing effect is so dramatic that the liver and kidneys of treated cattle cannot be sold for normal use, because they disintegrate on cooking. The process was developed by Swifts of Chicago, a major meat wholesaler, who market the resulting meat under the label Pro Ten beef. At first the practice was restricted to elderly dairy cows, but it has increasingly been used to obtain more roast-quality cuts from prime beef cattle. The process was criticized by the Farm Animal Welfare Council, as the injection of 100 ml of enzyme into the jugular vein sometimes causes the cow to collapse with shock, or even drop dead. The uncooked meat contains about 4 parts per million of papain, which is activated and largely broken down during cooking. As far as health hazards from meat treated in this way are concerned, there is no reliable evidence, but in November 1989 David Maclean, Britain's Minister for Food Safety, announced that the practice was to be banned in compliance with draft European proposals forbidding the marketing of enzyme-treated meat after 1992.

Factory Farming, 1991

Slaughterhouse Tales

ANDREW TYLER 1946–

Andrew Tyler is a vegan campaigning journalist who works to expose the following conditions.

I had spent the morning at a south of England abattoir watching truckloads of pigs being briskly slaughtered and was returning home when the bus was halted by a funeral procession. Looking down from the top deck, I could see the hearse with its polished coffin and gleaming brass rails, the half-dozen other hired limousines and, beyond them, a string of family saloons.

I'd seen 300 pigs go down that morning, creatures known in vivisection circles as 'horizontal man' because of the way the arrangement of their internal organs exactly matches our own; heart for heart, liver for liver, and because of that same warm, soft slappy feeling to their bellies. I looked down at the creeping ceremonial marking the passing of one human and reflected on the neurotic haste with which the pigs had been killed: two and a half hours on the journey, then 15 minutes per animal, as it was electrocuted, stabbed, degutted and dispatched to the chillers. Speed forced by a piece-rates system, was the essence and many a rule on welfare and hygiene was trampled on the way. Where the animals would not cooperate in their own slaughter – and even when they did – they were punched, kicked and cursed the way women are cursed: 'Come on, you dozy bitch. . . you stupid cunt!'

What do you make of pigs? I had asked slaughterman Barry Frame, some weeks earlier.

'Absolutely bloody stupid.'

Why is that?

'They've got a mind of their own. If they make up their mind they don't want to go where you want them to go, they won't.'

Our truck driver was a mild-tempered man named Steve Fallow who works for his father's haulage firm. We met at 6 a.m. for the first of half a dozen calls that fetched up some 125 animals.

The picture drawn by pigmen is of a cussed creature that refuses to abbreviate the passage from its mother's teat to the breakfast plate. But even the many farmers I've visited, who in the main kept their animals in a deep crust of unattended excreta, confining the breeding females to crates and stalls for the greater part of their lives that allowed scarcely the room to sink to the ground, subjecting them to a constant cycle of pregnancies; even they will admit that the pig, if permitted, is a clean animal that will strain to deposit its waste well away from its living area; also a good mother with a talent for nest building; resourceful, physically powerful, unusually sensitive and, yes, with an appetite, sharpened by the tedium of lifelong confinement, as voracious as our own.

The first thing that probably strikes the pigs on arrival is the noise, in some locations like a roaring mechanical tide, elsewhere the explosive sound of metallic slamming and clanking, chains and hooks coupling and uncoupling, the hiss of power hoses, the bang of the 'captive bolt' as it penetrates the skulls of cattle, and, mingling throughout, the shrieks of terror from doomed beasts.

Then they would notice how the air is heavy with a demonic mist, a mixture of blood and foul water. It splashes and froths up from the bleeding troughs where animals are hung by a back leg after their throat is cut. And it washes, in great black waves, from the scalding tank as each newly slaughtered pig is dumped in.

Our truckload of pigs is ready for opening. As the first dozen are driven into the stunning pen, one urinates on the trot and makes a screeching noise I hadn't heard before. Blood and mucus flies from its snout. The eyes close, the front legs stiffen and when Hammond opens the tongs, it falls, like a log, on its side. It lies there, back legs kicking, as Hammond turns to the next candidate. Most huddle against the entrance with their rumps towards him, heads passively bowed, snout to snout. They wait quietly until Hammond clamps another and then a couple break from the huddle and sniff a fallen comrade.

He tells me that the tongs should be held on for a minimum of seven seconds to ensure a proper stun before the throat is cut. But, urged on by his mates further along the slaughterline, he is giving them $1\frac{1}{2}$ or less. ('If you were from the ministry, I'd do it longer.')

When he has stunned three or four, he shackles each of them with a chain around a back leg. They are then mechanically lifted and carried to an adjoining stone room where his colleague, Dave, cuts deep into the neck and the still pumping heart gushes out blood. Hammon is supposed to stun and shackle one animal at a time since the delay involved in doing them in groups means they could go wide awake to the knife. The animals are probably conscious anyway, given the stunning time he allows them. But the pair were to depart further still from the rule book.

Suddenly an electrocuted animal slips its shackle en route to the 'sticking room', drops five feet to the stone floor and crash lands on its head. Hammond continues jolting more creatures while its back legs paddle furiously. Without re-stunning it, he hooks it up again and sends it through to the knife.

This crash-landing routine is to be repeated several more times in the next few minutes – caused by a combination of haste and incompetence, particularly on the part of Dave, who takes over the shackling after a third man replaces him on the knife.

One animal slams down twice. Dave curses it as it lies paddling, blood seeping from anus and mouth. Hammond, meanwhile, is ear-wrestling a would-be escapee that is leaping at a small opening in the metal gate. 'You can have it another fucking way then you idiot,' Dave cries, as he helps slap the animal down.

There is just one more waiting for the tongs, a small quiet creature which, from its position near the gate, looks me directly in the eye, breaking my heart. Hammond chases it a few steps. The tongs firstly ineptly clasp its neck; the eyes close in a strange blissful agony. The tongs are adjusted, and like a rock it falls.

It is interesting what still reaches a slaughterman's calloused heart – calloused, that is, by the job of work he is commissioned to do by the consumer. For one ex-slaughterman I spoke to, it was young goats: 'They cry just like babies.' For a veteran blood-and-guts disposal man at this plant, it is carrying three-day-old calves to the shooting box and destroying them with a captive bolt.

As abattoirs go, this was not a rogue outfit but regarded as top notch, practising 'humane slaughter' and supplying both supermarket chains and corner butcher shops. And Hammond is not an outrageous example but a typical and experienced practitioner. If he seems from this account to be monstrous, then he was contracted to his monstrous work by the rest of us, who then avert our eyes and hold our nostrils.

The Independent, 30 March 1989

Spiritual Chickens
STEPHEN DOBYNS 1941–

A man eats a chicken every day for lunch,
and each day the ghost of another chicken
joins the crowd in the dining room. If he could
only see them! Hundreds and hundreds of spiritual
chickens, sitting on chairs, tables, covering
the floor, jammed shoulder to shoulder. At last
there is no more space and one of the chickens
is popped back across the spiritual plain to the earthly.
The man is in the process of picking his teeth.
Suddenly there's a chicken at the end of the table,
strutting back and forth, not looking at the man
but knowing he is there, as is the way with chickens.
The man makes a grab for the chicken but his hand
passes right through her. He tries to hit the chicken
with a chair and the chair passes through her.
He calls in his wife but she can see nothing.
This is his own private chicken, even if he
fails to recognize her. How is he to know
this is a chicken he ate seven years ago
on a hot and steamy Wednesday in July,

with a little tarragon, a little sour cream?
The man grows afraid. He runs out of his house
flapping his arms and making peculiar hops
until the authorities take him away for a cure.
Faced with the choice between something odd
in the world or something broken in his head,
he opts for the broken head. Certainly,
this is safer than putting his opinions
in jeopardy. Much better to think he had
imagined it, that he had made it happen.
Meanwhile, the chicken struts back and forth
at the end of the table. Here she was, jammed in
with the ghosts of six thousand dead hens, when
suddenly she has the whole place to herself.
Even the nervous man has disappeared. If she
had a brain, she would think she had caused it.
She would grow vain, egotistical, she would
look for someone to fight, but being a chicken
she can just enjoy it and make little squawks,
silent to all except the man who ate her,
who is far off banging his head against a wall
like someone trying to repair a leaky vessel,
making certain that nothing unpleasant gets in
or nothing of value falls out. How happy
he would have been to be born a chicken,
to be of good use to his fellow creatures
and rich in companionship after death.
As he is he is constantly being squeezed
between the world and his idea of the world.
Better to have a broken head – why surrender
his corner on truth? – better just to go crazy.

Cemetery Nights, 1991

Dirty Business
ANDREW TYLER 1946–

The swill boiling unit was in the centre of the farm overlooking the
main driveway. It comprised three adjoining stone rooms. Room one
contained an old black boiler that looked like the thing Bogart kicked

and stoked in *The African Queen*: with taps, stud rivets, glass portals, gauges and a rusty chimney pipe that rose through a gash in the metal roof. It was powered, if that's the word, by coal dust that Berry got cheap from local yards. The steam it produced was carried by pipe through to room two where it was injected into three adjoining cooking troughs. Raw swill was kept in dustbins in the third room.

The stench up close was mesmerising and it seemed incredible that his pigs could be fed such a suppurating mess, thick with its head of fungus and still littered with chunks of crockery and the odd spoon or knife. We get used to the idea of pig equalling foulness and stench. But a pig, if given the chance, is a clean animal who'll endeavour to muck well away from its eating and bedding areas. Nor is it disposed to eat the kind of mixture Berry feeds it, or, for that matter, the powdery compound feeds that is its typical diet on non-swill farms. Its preference is for roots, fruits, herbs and buds, tree shoots, mushrooms and larvae . . .

The circuit takes some three hours and embraces two hospitals, a number of hotels and a couple of holiday camps. At the latter, several residents ostentatiously held their noses and gagged as we walked past. They were telling us that we reeked. 'And they feed that to the pigs!' one commented loudly. And yes, I marvelled, and you probably eat the end result, which is the swill pig, either as sausages or pies, or, more commonly these days, because swillmen sell their pigs wherever they can, in the form of everyday pork and bacon. Round and round it went. Here was discarded bacon in the bins, which was fed to the pigs, who were converted into bacon, a proportion of which wound up back in the bins.

It was as we called at a hospital that the full circular irony hit home. The image that arrested me was of an old man in bed, tubercular maybe, chewing on his hospital gruel. He spits out a mouthful, pushes the plate aside, whereupon his bronchial scraps end up in the pigs. Via the slaughterhouse, they then enter the high street customer.

The Independent, 1990

Disappointments and Dangers

✥

Napalm Sauce

MARTIN AMIS 1949–

'I'll be right over,' Keith had said. He now doubleparked outside the Indian Mutiny on Cathcart Road. Seated at his usual table, Keith ate poppadams and bombay duck while the staff fondly prepared his mutton vindaloo. 'The napalm sauce, sir?' asked Rashid. Keith was resolved, in this as in all things. 'Yeah. The napalm sauce.' In the kitchen they were busy responding to Keith's imperial challenge: to make a curry so hot that he couldn't eat it. The meal arrived. Lively but silent faces stared through the serving-hatch. The first spoonful swiped a mustache of sweat on to Keith's upper lip, and drew excited murmurs from the kitchen. 'Bit mild,' said Keith when he could talk again. That day, the Indian Mutiny had no other customers. Keith chewed steadily. His lion's hair looked silver in the shadows. Tears inched their way over his dry cheeks. 'Bland, Rashid,' said Keith, later, as he paid and undertipped. 'What you looking at? It's five per cent. Bland. Dead bland.'

London Fields, 1989

Fugu

KAZUO ISHIGURO 1954–

Fugu is a fish caught off the Pacific shores of Japan. The fish has held special significance for me ever since my mother died through eating one. The poison resides in the sexual glands of the fish, inside two fragile bags. When preparing the fish, these bags must be removed with caution, for any clumsiness will result in the poison leaking into the veins. Regrettably, it is not easy to tell whether or not this operation has been carried out successfully. The proof is, as it were, in the eating.

Fugu poisoning is hideously painful and almost always fatal. If the fish has been eaten during the evening, the victim is usually overtaken by pain during his sleep. He rolls about in agony for a few hours and is dead by morning. The fish became extremely popular in Japan after the war. Until stricter regulations were imposed, it was all the rage to perform the hazardous gutting operation in one's own kitchen, then to invite neighbours and friends round for the feast.

At the time of my mother's death, I was living in California. My relationship with my parents had become somewhat strained around that period, and consequently I did not learn of the circumstances surrounding her death until I returned to Tokyo two years later. Apparently, my mother had always refused to eat fugu, but on this particular occasion she had made an exception, having been invited by an old schoolfriend whom she was anxious not to offend. It was my father who supplied me with the details as we drove from the airport to his house in the Kamakura district. When we finally arrived, it was nearing the end of a sunny autumn day.

'Did you eat on the plane?' my father asked. We were sitting on the tatami floor of his tea-room.

'They gave me a light snack.'

'You must be hungry. We'll eat as soon as Kikuko arrives.'

A Family Supper, 1982

Melon

EDWARD BUNYARD 1872–1939

The Melon, perhaps more than any other fruit, requires to be taken in moderation. History has been turned in its course, and dynasties hurled from their destinies, by the fatal effects of immoderate indulgence in this fruit.

Few of us could emulate Claudius Albinus with his ration of ten per diem, or even that moderate Maréchal of Belle-Isle who contented himself with three. Who can forget the sad fate of Pope Paul II., who, in 1471, died from a surfeit of melons; or that of Frederick of Germany, named the 'Peaceful', whose immoderate taste for this fruit led him to an untimely tomb in 1493; and, horror upon horror's head, the terrible fact that his son, Maximilian I., impelled by the relentless laws of heredity, followed him in 1519 to the same place and for the same reason? Thus do we see how hardly may a man learn from experience other than his own.

The Anatomy of Dessert, 1933

Rabbit Mousse

MOLLY KEANE 1905–

'I wonder are you wise, Miss Aroon, to give her the rabbit?'

'And why not?' I can use the tone of voice which keeps people in their places and usually silences any interference from Rose. Not this time.

'Rabbit sickens her. Even Master Hubert's first with his first gun. She couldn't get it down.'

'That's a very long time ago. And I've often known her to enjoy rabbit since then.'

'She never liked rabbit.'

'Especially when she thought it was chicken.'

'You couldn't deceive her, Miss Aroon.' She picked up the tray. I snatched it back. I knew precisely what she would say when she put it down on Mummie's bed. I had set the tray myself. I don't trust Rose. I don't trust anybody. Because I like things to be right. The tray did look charming: bright, with a crisp clean cloth and a shine on everything. I lifted the silver lid off the hot plate to smell those quenelles in a cream sauce. There was just a hint of bay leaf and black pepper, not a breath of the rabbit foundation. Anyhow, what could be more delicious and delicate than a baby rabbit? Especially after it has been forced through a fine sieve and whizzed for ten minutes in a Moulinex blender . . .

'Luncheon,' I said cheerfully, the tray I carried making a lively rattle. 'Shall I sit you up a bit?' She was lying down among her pillows as if she were sinking through the bed. She never makes an effort for herself. That comes of having me.

'I don't feel very hungry,' she said. A silly remark. I know she always pretends she can't eat and when I go out makes Rose do her fried eggs and buttered toast and all the things the doctor says she mustn't touch.

'Smell that,' I said, and lifted the cover off my perfect quenelles.

'I wonder if you'd pull down the blind –' not a word about the quenelles – 'the sun's rather in my eyes.'

'You really want the blind down?'

She nodded.

'All the way?'

'Please.'

I went across then and settled her for her tray, pulling her up and putting a pillow in the exact spot behind her back, and another tiny one behind her head. She simply refused to look as if she felt comfortable. I'm used to that. I arranged the basket tray (straight from Harrods) across her, and put her luncheon tray on it.

'Now then,' I said – one must be firm – 'a delicious chicken mousse.'

'Rabbit, I bet,' she said.

I was still patient: 'Just try a forkful.'

'Myxomatosis,' she said. 'Remember that? – I can't.'

I held on to my patience. 'It was far too young to have myxomatosis. Come on now, Mummie –' I tried to keep the firm note out of my voice – 'just one.'

She lifted the small silver fork (our crest, a fox rampant, almost handled and washed away by use) as though she were heaving up a load of stinking fish: 'The smell – I'm –' She gave a trembling, tearing cry, vomited dreadfully, and fell back into the nest of pretty pillows.

I felt more than annoyed for a moment. Then I looked at her and I was frightened. I leaned across the bed and rang her bell. Then I shouted and called down to Rose in the kitchen. She came up fast, although her feet and her shoes never seem to work together now; even then I noticed it. But of course I notice everything.

'She was sick,' I said.

'She couldn't take the rabbit?'

Rabbit again. 'It was a mousse,' I screamed at the old fool, 'a cream mousse. It was perfect. I made it so I ought to know. It was RIGHT. She was enjoying it.'

Rose was stooping over Mummie. 'Miss Aroon, she's gone.' . . .

'I'll telephone to the doctor and ask him to let Nurse know. Just take that tray down and keep the mousse hot for my luncheon.'

Rose lunged towards me, over the bed, across Mummie's still feet. I think if she could have caught me in both her hands she would have done so.

'Your lunch,' she said. 'You can eat your bloody lunch and she lying there stiffening every minute. Rabbit – rabbit chokes her, rabbit sickens her, and rabbit killed her – call it rabbit if you like. Rabbit's a harmless word for it – if it was a smothering you couldn't have done it better.'

Good Behaviour, 1981

Salt 1717
DUC DE SAINT-SIMON 1675–1755

The Maréchal de Montrevel, whose name will not be found in history, the pet of silly women, of fashion and the gay world, of the Maréchal de Villeroy, and almost of the late king, from whom he had drawn more than a hundred thousands francs a year in benefits which he still received, a man noted for nothing but that in which he had the smallest part, namely, a face which made him all his life the idol of women, a great birth, and brilliant valour, died about this time, cheating his creditors by leaving nothing but three thousand louis, and much plate and porcelain, and fearing nothing so much as an overturned salt-cellar. He was just preparing to go to Alsace. Dining with Biron (afterwards duke, peer, and marshal of France), a salt-cellar was overturned and the salt scattered over him. He turned pale, felt ill, and said he was a dead man; they were obliged to leave the table and take him home. There was no restoring the small amount of brains he had. Fever seized him that night and he died four days later, leaving no regrets but those of his creditors.

Memoirs of the Duc de Saint-Simon, TRANS. Katherine Wormeley, 1899

Ship's Biscuit
WILLIAM HICKEY 1749–1830

There was nothing I felt the want of so much as bread; for in those days it was not customary to make that article on board East Indiamen, and it unluckily happened that the biscuit was uncommonly bad and flinty, so that it was with difficulty I could penetrate it with my teeth. This being the subject of conversation one day at table, a question arose as to the time in which a person might eat one of these biscuits, which ended in a wager of five guineas between Rider and

Grant, the former laying the latter that he did not get rid of one by his teeth in four minutes. He was to have no liquid to aid him. A bag of biscuits being brought to table, the doctor by mutual consent put his hand in and brought out one, which was to be that of trial. Chance here operated against Grant, for it proved an uncommonly hard one, and he had difficult in breaking it in two. A watch being laid upon the table, at it he went with a set of remarkably strong teeth; but, strong as they were, we all thought he must lose his bet, and he was twice in extreme danger of choking, by which he lost several seconds. Notwithstanding this, however, he, to our great surprise, accomplished his object, and won the wager, being six seconds within the given time.

Memoirs, ED. Peter Quennell, 1960

Insulting the Cook

ALICE THOMAS ELLIS 1932–

The other most important thing to remember in life was the total inadvisability of insulting the cook. What could be more misguided and reckless? When you thought of the power wielded by the cook, it was tantamount to taunting the driver on a hairpin bend. Even for cooks without access to datura or chopped-up panthers' whiskers there were umpteen varieties of dubious fungi – to some of which there was absolutely no antidote. Once eaten, that was it. You were sick on the first day, better on the second and dead on the third. The horror. What an ass you would feel on that second day, knowing you were doomed to death by something masquerading as a mushroom and had a mere twenty-four hours to order your effects. Then there were foxgloves and the autumn crocus, not to mention the teaspoonful of putrefied catfood lurking in the fragrant depths of the curry. There were wringing out the floor-cloth into the soup and spitting in the hollandaise. There was the slow but sure method known as English cookery, which meant white flour, white sugar, too much animal fat, too much salt, murdered vegetables, bicarbonate of soda, puddings and puddings and puddings, and salad once a year as a treat for Sunday tea – lettuce, tomato, cucumber and hard-boiled egg all layered together. And tinned fruit-salad. No wonder they were such a pasty lot. And so self-righteous about it, with their boundless contempt for garlic and messed-up foreign food with sauces. An exasperating people. Aunt Irene always maintained that she would eat boiled bloodhound and cassava root if they were properly cooked. The war had done a great deal to improve the health of the British – except, of course, for those who'd been killed or maimed, and Major Mason – since they'd been forced to eat less meat and sugar and more vegetables and the dark National Loaf, which was a splendid foodstuff with all the nutrients left in. Everyone had hated it.

The 27th Kingdom, 1982

Navettes for Mrs Fisher

JEANNETTE FERRARY

'Bring something silly,' she suggested. 'Or bring dessert.'

That seemed easy enough. She would take care of the lunch and the wine. Maybe she would even warm up a handful of almonds, the way she sometimes did, and then bundle them in the folds of some sort of French tea towel set in an olivewood bowl. Something silly: it was one of those suggestions that couldn't have been more informal, or more intimidating.

If only she weren't such a fine cook herself, someone who cared as much about what you put in your mouth as whom you were with at the time and whether it was raining. Silly: but not like jellybeans or glazed donuts. Silly, not ridiculous.

Making cookies seemed light-hearted enough to qualify. But which of the world's millions of recipes was the right one to make for her? I knew, of course, that she had spent a good part of her life in the south of France, in Aix-en-Provence, in Marseille. Maybe some French cookie would be nice, but not one of those dressy ones that look like pearl-studded brooches or the latches of satin evening bags. They weren't her style: she'd say they were too beautiful to eat, and then she would tell about other things she had known that were too beautiful to eat, and then she wouldn't eat them. Whatever I chose, it had to be absolutely correct: intellectually, culturally, personally. I was seeking a cookie with so many levels of meaning that she would know at a glance the great measure of thought behind it. I wanted to please her, not with my baking abilities, which were less than honed, but with my informed appreciation. I was looking for the recipe that would show her my sensitivity to her life, my gratitude for what she had so generously shared of it in her writings. And I wanted it to taste good, or I'd never hear the end of it.

I began by reading up on the subject, raiding the cookie jargon of shapes and baking sheets, the national origins of doughs and batters and exotic mixtures. Many of these cookies seemed nice enough, but none was truly relevant. The only one even remotely apropos bore the unfortunate name Gallic Goodies. I knew she was not the Gallic Goodies type. Just as the whole matter was becoming altogether too important, I turned to Richard Olney's *Simple French Food* in the hope that I could find an alternative to the endless Drops, Crescents and Twists. I expected to discover nothing so meaningful as an entire section of his book devoted to the little Christmas cakes of Provence.

Even more timely, these Provencal cookies didn't stop at Christmas. They didn't even end with the Epiphany. According to Olney, the non-stop confections continued to commemorate miracles and other events right on through to Candlemas Day, the second of February. On that day, a simple buttery cookie called Navettes de la Chandeleur was baked all over Marseille: A most considerable cookie, I thought to myself, knowing better than to say it aloud, then or ever. Surely she would know of these Navettes. She had travelled so often to Marseille, and food was always so central to her special perspective on the life of everything. Whatever Candlemas Day was, it was just about that time of year now. And whether or not anybody in Marseille was still making Navettes for the occasion, I was certainly going to do so in California.

For a while I tried to figure out if Navettes, which appeared to be a form of the word Navet, or turnip, were actually supposed to be shaped like turnips. Perhaps they symbolized the Winter harvest, a belated homage to root vegetables. The word Chandeleur was equally intriguing. Ah, Marseille and its mysteries, I thought, where the rough coexists with the regal, the turnip with the chandelier. Most import-ant, I knew I was doing the right thing. This was no mere batch of cookies: this was transcendence, palpable communication between me and the past, her past. I couldn't wait for her to open the tin into which I had carefully packed my Navettes, or 'our' Navettes as I began thinking of them, allowing myself a bit of nostalgia by proxy. The recipe made twelve, I made twenty-four. The next day when I packed the little tin next to me for the long drive north to Sonoma, it still felt warm.

The woman who was leaving as I pulled in the driveway had no doubt just delivered a batch of her very own home-grown-onion compote. She had that kind of smile on her face. People were forever dropping off things like red pepper marmalades or a day's gathering of fleshy, brash chanterelles. The kitchen drainboard, the heavy refectory table, even the couch, were always laden with harvests of things that had probably just been dropped off unexpectedly, since they seldom got incorporated into that day's lunch. A quick glance proved that today was no exception, though a lot of something was going into the oven as I walked in.

She didn't hear me. I tried to cough in a non-startling way, but she was taking something off the top of the stove. It looked like a wrought iron tree with holes in the branches, each of which held a blue-white egg. As she set it down on top of a pile of mail, I decided it was time for a big cough.

'Is that you, dear?' she said, turning around. 'I thought it was Charlie shuffling around over there. He's always packing himself into some cozy corner, purring and fussing.'

Her cheeks were the color that is meant when anyone speaks of healthy pink cheeks. She looked happy to see me.

'I'm so happy to see you, you funny one. It's been too long again.'

We had our wine and, from the wood-burning stove, the delicious warm fire that was, on this rain chilling Tuesday noon, the only thing better than almonds. It was one of those days so nasty that everyone unites against it. No one holds out and tries to make a case for how refreshing it is to have a day like this once in a while. With the weather as our scapegoat, a mood of agreeability set in and we soon found ourselves assenting about matters which, on a nicer day, would surely have started some good arguments. It was into this atmosphere of universal acceptance that I introduced my turnips.

'When you were in Marseille around this time of year,' so coyly I began, 'did you ever hear of a local confection called Navettes de la Chandeleur?'

'Navettes!' she announced back at me, before I'd really finished mispronouncing the last syllable. I could almost hear her mind loading up the appropriate reel of Navette-entangled memories. Her blue eyes sparkled, sharpening the focus, getting the details as clear and current as the present moment. She was a veritable genius at this sort of recall. 'Navettes! Oh, yes! They were awful!'

Awful?

'They were little cookies. They were made only in two places in Marseille and at one time I lived directly above one of them.'

Awful?

369

'They were hard as bricks. Inedible really. People would buy them every year for Candlemas Day and the next year they would still have them from the year before. They were so hard and dry, they kept all year. The Candlemas ceremony itself was quite lovely, though, flickering with white and green candles. That Provence green, you only see it there.'

'Well, what about the turnips? Why were the cookies named after turnips?'

'Turnips?' she echoed, her brow, even her voice, furrowed. The cat that never left the room ran out into the rain.

'I thought perhaps that the word Navettes was a variation of Navets. I mean, maybe the shape or something. Olney doesn't elaborate,' I added weakly. Blame it on him.

'Navettes refer to the little boat that Mary Magdalene was supposed to have come in. That's why the cookies are shaped that way. Like little canoes with hooks on either end. The slit down the center is the inside of the boat.'

My mind chased away images of the bifurcated turnips awaiting in the tin. I think it was the way I said 'Oh' that made her ask.

'Why all this curiosity about Navettes anyway?'

'Oh, well, it was just that I came across this recipe and I thought maybe since it was about that time of the year and Marseille and everything. And since you did mention about bringing something silly . . .' Silly, I remembered: not preposterous.

'You mean you made Navettes? You actually made them? I can't imagine anyone making those bone dry, impenetrable stones. I suppose they could be made edible, though it wouldn't be consistent with the way they actually were.'

I had never thought of food that way before. That there are some things which are by nature or tradition not terribly delicious. That it is not our place, we who are interested in food, to 'improve' them, to alter the attributes which give them their own special faults. I knew there was nothing wrong with the cookies in the tin; that was the problem. When she found out that they were in fact delicious, she would have to be disappointed. She would realize that the recipe had been bastardized, that it had sacrificed truth for taste. The idea is not to make something taste good if it doesn't, but rather to make something else altogether. That's the trouble with cookbooks and photographs and art in general: despite all the best intentions, the artist gets in the way.

I felt better after the split-second philosophizing. I was an innocent bystander after all. I could dump it all on Olney for caring more about pleasure than history. Anyway, I could see by her pursed lips that she was planning to enter into this Navettes reverie, no matter how unfaithful this particular reproduction. She was squinting meaningfully into the box.

'Navettes,' she savored. 'All over Marseille, on the days around Candlemas, you could smell them cooking. It was the orange peel, the bitter Seville orange peel they folded into the dough. That was the characteristic thing about Navettes.'

Damn Olney. I proceeded cautiously.

'What if,' I ventured, 'There were no orange peel in the recipe. What would you say of that?'

'No orange peel?' She was bewildered.

'I mean, wouldn't you say that was silly?'

'No,' she said. 'Not necessarily.'

The Journal of Gastronomy, Vol. 1, 1984

E is for Exquisite
M. F. K. FISHER 1908–92

I remember deciding once, long ago and I believe after reading Ellwanger's Pleasures of the Table for the first time, that the most exquisite dish I had ever heard of was a salad of satiny white endive with large heavily scented Parma violets scattered through it. It meant everything subtle and intense and aesthetically significant in my private gastronomy, just as, a few years earlier, a brown-skinned lover with a turquoise set in one ear lobe epitomized my adolescent dream of passion. It is a misfortune perhaps that not many months ago the salad was set before me in a bowl.

That it was not very good was relatively unimportant: the dressing was light to the point of being innocuous, and it was unable to stand up under the perfumed assault of the blossoms. What disappointed me, finally and forever, was that it was served neither exquisitely, nor by an exquisite, nor with an exquisite disregard of the vulgar.

Instead it was concocted and presented with both affectation and awkwardness and was at best an attempt at that insidious decadence which is a prerequisite of my definition. It suddenly became ridiculous.

I blushed for my long dream of it and felt a hollowness, for where again will I know so certainly that such and such a dish is it? What will it be? Expense is not enough, for sure, and no intricate silverware, no ritual of serving and compounding, can guarantee the magic. There must, for me at least, be a faint nebular madness, dignified no matter how deliberate, to a dinner that is exquisite.

An Alphabet for Gourmets, 1949

Blue Violet Salad

GEORGE H. ELLWANGER 1848–1906

'There was a great bunch of double violets on the table, the lovely dark variety (*Viola odoratissima flore pleno*) with their short stems, freshly plucked from the garden, and the room was scented by their delicious breath.

'A bowl of broad-leaved Batavian endive, blanched to a nicety and alluring as a siren's smile, was placed upon the table. I almost fancied it was smiling at the violets. A blue-violet salad, by all means! there are violets and to spare.

'On a separate dish there was a little minced celery, parsley, and chives. Four heaped salad-spoonfuls of olive-oil were poured upon the herbs, with a dessert-spoonful of white wine vinegar, the necessary salt and white pepper, and a tablespoonful of Bordeaux. The petals of two dozen violets were detached from their stems and two thirds of them were incorporated with the dressing. The dressing being thoroughly mixed with the endive, the remaining flower petals were sprinkled over the salad and a half-dozen whole violets placed in the centre.

'The lovely blue sapphires glowed upon the white bosom of the endive.

'A white-labelled bottle, capsuled Yquem, and the cork branded "Lur Saluces," was served with the salad. You note the subtle aroma of pineapple and fragrance of flower ottos with the detonation of the cork – the grand vintages of Yquem have a pronounced *Ananassa* flavour and bouquet that steeps the palate with its richness and scents the surrounding atmosphere.

'Now try your blue-violet salad.

'Is it fragrant? is it cool? is it delicious? is it divine?'

The Pleasure of the Table, 1902

Geoduck
BETTY MACDONALD 1908–58

Sharkey gave me my first geoduck. I had been hearing about geoducks ever since first coming to Seattle. People spoke of them with the mystic reverence usually associated with an eclipse of the sun or the aurora borealis. I had heard that geoducks are giant clams and, like dinosaurs, now extinct. I had heard that geoducks have to be dug by flashlight at night. I had heard that they moved like greased lightning, opening and closing their great shells like a clam-shell dredge and getting down to the bowels of the earth in a matter of seconds. I had heard that geoducks have to be dug by a crew of strong men all armed with shovels and all working like demons. I had heard that the only way to catch a geoduck was to take a hatpin and pinion his neck and then excavate under him. I had heard that geoducks were worth driving hundreds of miles and digging all night to get, for they were the most subtly flavoured, most succulent of all sea food.

Geoduck, by the way, is pronounced by the Indians gooey-duck.

I had heard all of this about geoducks but like most of the people living in the Pacific North-west I had not taken the trouble to find out about geoducks for myself, and was therefore shivery with anticipation when Sharkey told me that he had one for me over at his shack, and went over to fetch it. He came back presently and handed me the largest clam I had ever seen. The shell was oblong, about eight inches long and five or six inches wide, squarish and covered with yellowish skin. The siphon, or what we commonly call the neck, was about two inches in diameter, seven or eight inches long and covered with a heavy, wrinkled yellowish skin. The whole thing, including the shell, must have weighed five or six pounds and was definitely unlovely. Sharkey told me to peel the neck and to grind it up for chowder. He said to clean the body part of the stomach and things, cut it into steaks and fry them in butter.

I did as he told me and found that geoduck had been vastly overrated. It was tougher than tyre casing and tasted exactly like clams.

The Egg And I, 1947

Plum Pudding
LADY MACARTNEY 1877–1949

The first big plum pudding I made for our Chinese entertainment at the
New Year came to a sad end. I left the puddings I had made boiling
until evening in Isa's charge, telling him to take them out of the pots
and hang them by their strings on nails to drain, when he had finished
his work in the kitchen. As we were settling down to a cosy evening
after dinner, Isa came in, looking very scared and said: 'I don't think
the big pudding is quite well, will the Memsahib come and see?' I
rushed out to the kitchen, and there was my beautiful pudding a
shapeless mass on the floor. Isa had never thought to see that the knot
of the string was firm before hanging it up, and so the poor pudding
looked very unwell indeed. I will not enlarge on my feelings, but it was
a very real tragedy to me when I knew I could not easily replace the
ingredients it had been made of. At that time I had not got enough
words to say much, and poor Isa was nearly as upset as I was at the
accident. One does not mind these things so much when one can send
to a shop and get just what one wants, but it is rather heartbreaking to
see stores wasted that one will have to wait months to replace.

An English Lady in Chinese Turkestan, 1931

Dining with Mrs Cozens
NANCY MITFORD 1904–73

The food at dinner, served by the slut in a gaunt dining-room, was so
terrible that I felt deeply sorry for Mrs. Cozens, thinking that
something must have gone wrong. I have had so many such meals since
then that I do not remember exactly what it was; I guess, however, that
it began with tinned soup and ended with dry sardines on dry toast,
and that we drank a few drops of white wine. I do remember that the
conversation was far from brilliant, a fact which, at the time, I
attributed to the horrible stuff we were trying to swallow, but which I
now know was more likely to have been due to the presence of
females; dons are quite used to bad food but become paralysed in
mixed company. As soon as the last sardine tail had been got down,

Mrs. Cozens rose to her feet, and we went into the drawing-room, leaving the men to enjoy the one good item of the whole menu, excellent vintage port. They only reappeared just before it was time to go home.

Love in a Cold Climate, 1949

Perhaps the Signore Would Prefer a Hen?
NORMAN DOUGLAS 1868–1952

No, thank you. I know those hens and how they are caught. This is the manner of it. The careful housewife singles out the scraggiest of her fowls, which forthwith stops eating and watches her steadily with one eye, doubtless aware of her intentions. The preliminary coaxing being of no avail (it is merely done for form's sake), five small boys are despatched in pursuit with sticks and stones. They begin by liking the job, for their prey, sure of victory, marches straight in front of them without deigning to look round, an easy mark for projectiles. One stone grazing its tail, it takes flight and settles in the vineyards on the hill-side, amid howls of execration from the boys. Other pursuers are roused and join in the chase; a cloud of missiles envelopes the bird as it gallops and flutters over stones and up trees, into gullies and thickets; the rabble vanishes from sight – you can hear them shouting a mile off.

An hour or so having elapsed, the hen is seen, a speck on the horizon, flying down from the mountains in a straight line, pressed hard by an undaunted knot of pursuers. *Sant' Antonio!* It is going into the water like last year! And, sure enough, it slides into the waves about three hundred yards from the shore and begins to preen its remaining feathers. May its mother be barren! May its children die unblest! The boat – the boat! It is launched, and at the very moment when the oar is about to descend with a crash upon the muscular frame of the victim, it rises like a lark and perches upon the roof of the church. *A chi t'è morto!* Out with the ladder! All work ceases in the village, the school is closed for the day; the priest and the tobacconist, mortal enemies, are observed to exchange a few breathless words. Bedridden hags crawl into the piazza and ask whether there is an earthquake. No, the hen! The church! The signore! The foreign signore wants the hen – the hen on the church! Just as the nimble *figlio di Luisella* has placed his foot upon that last rung of the ladder – *Ah,*

Santo Dio! It has flown away, away into the brushwood, where none but the swiftest and surest-footed can hope to follow.

Towards Ave Maria it is carried in, vanquished. The conqueror, streaming with perspiration and attended by the entire populace, proudly holds it up for your inspection by one leg – the other is missing. A small boy, reluctantly, produces it from his pocket.

Is this a hen?

There is not a vestige of feathers on its body; the head, too, seems to have come off in the heat of the fray. The conqueror tells you that he could have shot it, but was afraid of spoiling its plumage. The careful housewife asks whether you will have it boiled or *al cacciatore?*

What is left of the bird looks as if it were already half cooked . . .

Siren Land, 1911

Welsh Rarebit

ERIC NEWBY 1919–

'I'll cook,' I said, feeling heroic. Each night, unless we were eating Irish stew, we took it in turn to prepare some primitive delicacy. It was really Hugh's night. This evening I chose Welsh rarebit.

Fascinated by this dish that was outside their experience, the drivers gathered round me whilst I assembled the ingredients, opened the tins of cheese and started the primus. Soon, just as the mixture was turning from liquid to the required consistency, the stove went out. It had been snuffing out all the time in the wind but this time it went out for good because it had run out of fuel. Abdul Ghiyas rushed off and returned with a can of what I soon found, when he started to pour it into the stove, to be water, and Badar Khan, on this the only recorded time during the entire journey that he ever did anything that was not in his contract, produced another containing methylated spirits that would have blown us all to glory. Faced with the failure of the Welsh rarebit and the rapidly cooling stove I got up to find the paraffin can myself, caught the trousers of my windproof suit in the handle of the frying-pan and shot the whole lot over the rocks.

At this moment, looking sleek and clean, Hugh returned from the stream where he had combed his hair and put on a clean shirt and thick sweater.

'Ready?' he asked pleasantly.

'It – well isn't.'

'Taking a long time.'

Was it possible that he couldn't see us all trying to scrape it off the rocks?

'You'll have to wait a long time for this one. I should go to bed.'

A Short Walk in the Hindu Kush, 1958

Thistles

J. W. GOETHE 1749–1832

As we were solemnly making strategic plans for our war on the thistles, we were put to shame by the discovery that they were not quite as useless as we thought. At a lonely inn where we had halted to fodder our mules, two Sicilian noblemen had just arrived. They were on their way across country to Palermo to settle a lawsuit. To our amazement, we saw these two dignified gentlemen standing in front of a clump of thistles and cutting off the tops with their sharp pocket knives. Carefully holding their prickly acquisitions by the finger tips, they pared the stalk and consumed the inner portion with great gusto, an operation which took them some time. Meanwhile we refreshed ourselves with some wine, undiluted for once, and some good bread. Our *vetturino* prepared some of this thistle pith for us, insisting that it was both healthy and refreshing, but to us it seemed as tasteless as the raw kohlrabi of Segesta.

Italian Journey 1786–88, TRANS. W. H. Auden
and Elizabeth Mayer, 1962

Bunni

H. V. MORTON 1892–1979

On the way back to the Ziggurat I fell in with a group of people, several men, three or four women, and some children, all modern Iraqis. The leader of the party introduced himself as the post-master of Ur, and told me that he was entertaining some friends, railway officials, their wives and families. They were going to have a picnic in the ruins and would I care to join them? I replied I would gladly do so, and we mounted a sand-hill near the temple of the Moon Goddess and sat on the ground.

It was going to be a feast of *bunni*. I did not know what *bunni* was, but asked no questions, knowing that the *bunni* would soon reveal itself. Two young Arabs came up the hill carrying a wooden box in which lay six monstrous fish, very thick in the body and covered with large iridescent scales the size of a finger nail. They had come out of the Euphrates, from a village called Nasariya, about ten miles away. Any one of these fish would have been a meal for us, but all six were split open with a knife and prepared for cooking.

While this was going on the Arabs lit a fire and added to it pieces of hard, dark wood which they had brought with them, for in this treeless country no wood can ever be picked up. I asked what kind of wood this was, and they told me that it came from India, and was part of an old railway sleeper.

The split *bunni* was pegged upright in a circle on the sand with their scales away from the flames, and allowed to grill. Now and then a *bunni* fell into the ashes, to be swiftly rescued by a lean, dark hand. Soon the first fish was ready. The post-master produced a lemon, a bag of curry powder, a packet of salt, and a bottle of Lea and Perrins Sauce. These were dashed with rough artistry on the *bunni*, which was then placed on the ground in the centre of the circle, and we were soon detaching portions of it with our fingers.

If you can imagine an oily cod-fish tasting of smoke and wood ashes, you have a rough idea of roast *bunni*. It is white, flaky, and extremely rich. The greediest cat on earth would slink away defeated from a fraction of a full grown *bunni*. But at our feast *bunni* succeeded *bunni* with oriental lavishness. Into some we just dipped our fingers as if in a finger bowl and let the Arab lads take it away to devour over the embers.

When I made a remark about the size of the fish, my friends smiled and said that another fish found in the Euphrates, called a *bizz*, was often seven feet long and weighed as much as a hundred pounds.

Through Lands of the Bible, 1938

Nuts

EDWARD BUNYARD 1872–1939

The fresh Brazil, which Nature has decreed shall not be ready for the English Christmas, is a good nut and worthy of a limited attention. When, however, it has been kept for a year or so it takes an oily nature which only the most active of livers can painlessly discuss. At this stage it should be lighted with a match to amuse the children, and its yellow flame has brought many an uncle a deserved popularity.

And of the other nuts what can be said? Coco Nuts, good food for tomtits, and to enliven the Nonconformist bun.

I am informed that Monkey, Ground, or Pea Nuts are eaten in America, and certainly Film villains seem to have contracted the habit. Well-groomed heroes, I gather, abstain; and who shall grudge them their reward?

The Anatomy of Dessert, 1933

Chester Cheese

GEORGE BORROW 1803–81

On arriving at Chester, at which place we intended to spend two or three days, we put up at an old-fashioned inn in Northgate Street, to which we had been recommended; my wife and daughter ordered tea and its accompaniments, and I ordered ale, and that which always should accompany it, cheese. 'The ale I shall find bad,' said I; Chester ale had a villainous character in the time of old Sion Tudor, who made a first-rate englyn upon it, and it has scarcely improved since; 'but I shall have a treat in the cheese, Cheshire cheese has always been reckoned excellent, and now that I am in the capital of the cheese country, of course I shall have some of the very prime.' Well, the tea, loaf and butter made their appearance, and with them my cheese and ale. To my horror the cheese had much the appearance of soap of the commonest kind, which indeed I found it much resembled in taste, on putting a small portion into my mouth. 'Ah,' said I, after I had opened the window and ejected the half-masticated morsel into the street, 'those who wish to regale on good Cheshire cheese must not come to

379

Chester, no more than those who wish to drink first-rate coffee must go to Mocha. I'll now see whether the ale is drinkable;' so I took a little of the ale into my mouth, and instantly going to the window, spirted it out after the cheese. 'Of a surety,' said I 'Chester ale must be of much the same quality as it was in the time of Sion Tudor, who spoke of it to the following effect:

> Chester ale, Chester ale! I could ne'er get it down,
>   'Tis made of ground-ivy, of dirt, and of bran.
> 'Tis as thick as a river below a huge town!
> 'Tis not lap for a dog, far less drink for a man.

Well! if I have been deceived in the cheese, I have at any rate not been deceived in the ale, which I expected to find execrable. Patience! I shall not fall into a passion, more especially as there are things I can fall back upon. Wife! I will trouble you for a cup of tea. Henrietta! have the kindness to cut me a slice of bread and butter.'

Wild Wales, 1884

Hors d'oeuvres
SAKI (HECTOR HUGH MUNRO) 1870–1916

'Hors d'œuvres have always a pathetic interest for me,' said Reginald: 'they remind me of one's childhood that one goes through, wondering what the next course is going to be like – and during the rest of the menu one wishes one had eaten more of the hors d'œuvres'.

'Reginald at the Carlton', Penguin Complete Saki, 1976

On Board the *Messenger*
CHARLES DICKENS 1812–70

We are to be on board the *Messenger* three days: arriving at Cincinnati (barring accidents) on Monday morning. There are three meals a day. Breakfast at seven, dinner at half-past twelve, supper about six. At each there are a great many small dishes and plates upon the table, with very little in them; so that, although there is every appearance of a mighty 'spread,' there is seldom really more than a joint: except for those who fancy slices of beet-root, shreds of dried beef, complicated entanglements of yellow pickle, maize, Indian corn, apple sauce, and pumpkin.

Some people fancy all these little dainties together (and sweet preserves besides), by way of relish to their roast pig. They are generally those dyspeptic ladies and gentlemen who eat unheard-of quantities of hot corn bread (almost as good for the digestion as a kneaded pin-cushion) for breakfast and for supper. Those who do not observe this custom, and who help themselves several times instead, usually suck their knives and forks meditatively until they have decided what to take next; then pull them out of their mouths; put them in the dish; help themselves; and fall to work again. At dinner there is nothing to drink upon the table but great jugs full of cold water. Nobody says anything, at any meal, to anybody. All the passengers are very dismal, and seem to have tremendous secrets weighing on their minds. There is no conversation, no laughter, no cheerfulness, no sociality, except in spitting; and that is done in silent fellowship round the stove, when the meal is over. Every man sits down dull and languid; swallows his fare as if breakfasts, dinners, and suppers were necessities of nature never to be coupled with recreation or enjoyment; and, having bolted his food in a gloomy silence, bolts himself in the same state. But for these animal observances, you might suppose the whole male portion of the company to be the melancholy ghosts of departed book-keepers, and had fallen dead at the desk: such is their weary air of business and calculation. Undertakers on duty would be sprightly beside them; and a collation of funeral baked meats, in comparison with these meals, would be a sparkling festivity.

American Notes, 1842

Prison and Poverty

❦

Shah Jehan d. 1666
SHIVAJI RAO AND DEVI HOLKER

Aurangzeb, the last of the great Mughal rulers of Delhi, dethroned and imprisoned his father, Shah Jehan, in a crumbling fort in Agra. Shah Jehan's jewels, his women, and his food were gradually denied him by his son until, at last, he was forced to choose one single type of legume for his diet. This time the poor old emperor, who had little left to comfort him but a view of his beloved Taj Mahal, for once outwitted his cruel son. He chose as his legume the tiny chick-pea, the most versatile legume of all. Served as a vegetable, fresh or dried, or as a soup, simmered and puréed, the chick-pea is excellent fare. Powdered into flour, it will thicken or bind to make delicate breads and desserts.

Cooking of the Maharajas, 1975

Messes
WILLIAM SMITH C. 1776

It is little wonder that the prisoners in the hulks at Woolwich suffered from diarrhoea, few of them free of scorbutic blotches.

They eat in messes; each mess, which consists of six convicts, has an allowance of half a bullock's head, four pounds of biscuits, and broth thickened with bread and oat-meal, every twenty-four hours. Sometimes, though rarely, they have hearts and shins of beef. They calculate, but with what degree of exactness I cannot take upon me to say, that from three ounces to half a pound and upwards of meat come to each man's share daily . . . Their flesh-meat, as they inform me, is not at all times sweet, but even green with rottenness. The biscuit, which is the only bread they have, is made of the third or coarsest part of the flour and is very unwholesome.

State of the Gaols in London, 1776, quoted in *The Englishman's Food*,
1959

No Advocate for Luxury
JOHN HOWARD 1726–90

I have before said, that I am no advocate for luxury in prisons; for I would have no meat diet for criminals in houses of correction, or at most, only on Sundays. Yet I would plead that they should have, at least, a pound and a half of good household bread a day, and a quart of good beer; besides twice a day a quart of warm soup made from pease, rice, milk or barley. For a change they might sometimes have turnips, carrots, or potatoes. It may be said this diet will starve those who work in houses of correction; but I am persuaded of the contrary, by what I have seen abroad, in the galleys, in the houses of correction, and among the most robust labourers.

State of the Prisons in England and Wales, 1777, quoted in *The
Englishman's Food*, 1959

The Marquis de Sade
ISABELLE VISCHER d. 1963

À *propos* of cruelty, the Marquis de Sade had, we are told, 'a very sweet tooth'. When he was in prison, his wife took great pains to supply him with quince jelly, pots of raspberries and cherries, also marmalade of peaches and greengages. The Marquis was very exacting, and his wife was pleased when she could supply what he asked for to ease the burden of his captivity, but all too often he cursed and reviled the poor woman. In his correspondence and his papers he expressed his tastes in food. If they were complicated in matters of love, they were the opposite in questions of the table. He loved plain and very simple food, but it had to be cooked and served to perfection. He was very difficult to please on the question of eggs, and the meals served to him during his well-deserved prison sentence seem to have been remarkably good.

Now to the Banquet, 1953

Marie Antoinette in the Conciergerie

The Conciergerie was the famous prison in Paris where condemned prisoners were held during the Terror before being sent to the guillotine. This is a newspaper account of the Queen's imprisonment in the Conciergerie in 1793.

Antoinette rises every day at seven o'clock and goes to bed at ten. She calls her two gendarmes 'Messieurs', her servant-woman 'Madame Harel'. The police administrators and those who approach her officially call her 'Madame'. She eats with good appetite; in the morning, chocolate with a breadroll, at dinner, soup and a lot of meat – chicken, veal cutlets and mutton. She drinks only water, like her mother, she says, who never drank wine. She has finished reading *Les Révolutions d'Angleterre* and is at present reading *Le Voyage du jeune Anacharis*. She does her own toilet, but with the stylishness that a woman does not abandon until her dying breath. Her room looks out on to the women's prison; but the women prisoners seem not to heed the proximity of the former queen.

Last Letters: Prisons and Prisoners of the French Revolution 1793–4,
ED. Olivier Blanc, TRANS. Allan Sheridan, 1987

Condemned Men Send Out For Dinner
JEAN-PAUL ARON 1925–88

In the gaols, condemned men sent out for their dinners, and this paradoxical traffic is carried on without let or hindrance: 'The victims in the prisons worshipped their stomachs, and the most exquisite victuals were seen passing through the narrow wicket-gate, destined for men who were about to eat their last meal on earth and were fully aware of that fact. From the depths of a dungeon, arrangements were made with a restaurant and the contract signed by both parties with specific clauses as to the early seasonal vegetables and fresh fruits. It was unthinkable to visit a prisoner without bringing him, by way of consolation, a bottle of Bordeaux, liqueurs from the Indies and the most delicate patés. For his part, the pastrycook, who knows perfectly well that sweet things are always desirable, sent his price-lists down into the bowels of the prisons.'

The Art of Eating in France, TRANS. Nina Rootes, 1975

Bring a Lettuce

A great many letters between detainees and their families have survived. Whether they came from inside or outside the prison, all were seized by the keeper and handed over to Fouquier-Tinville [the Public Prosecutor].

To Citizeness Boilleau, Rue Révolutionnaire,
former Saint-Louis, at Paris, this 4 Floréal.

My dear friend,
I beg you to do your utmost to bring a well-seasoned lettuce salad or rather the materials for making one, we have bowls; but try to make sure that it is fresh and in good condition. If you have no money, try to get hold of some for this advance. As I am writing to you by the small post, I don't want to send it to you, but I shall get it to you later. Don't forget the oil and vinegar. If you cannot get money to do this, take the trouble to come and see me and I shall give you what you need to buy what is necessary. We have salt, but bring a little pepper. Try to do this for us today, if at all possible, I shall be very obliged to you, and bring as much oil as you can. I shall be very obliged to you and embrace you with all my heart.

Your husband Boilleau.

Last Letters: Prisons and Prisoners of the French Revolution 1793–4,
ED. Olivier Blanc, TRANS. Alan Sheridan, 1987

Prison Marmalade
ROGER COOPER

*When Iran freed Roger Cooper after five years' incarceration in
their jails, he confessed to a novel way of making marmalade.*

'In prison I used to make my own marmalade by chewing orange peel
and mixing it with syrup made from the sugar I was occasionally
allowed. It was the best available but it tasted nothing like this.' Mr
Cooper looked well but still slightly drawn from his ordeal, as he
breakfasted at the country cottage.

Evening Standard, 3 April, 1991

Less Serious Distractions
COMTE BEUGNOT d. 1794

Proximity to women provides us with less serious distractions of
which I was more jealous. We were often able to take luncheon with
them. Benches, more or less elbow-high, were improvised on either
side of the bars; amid all the confusion of the time and place, we laid
the table for luncheon and if a place still remained vacant on the
women's side, there was no lack of graces to fill it. In truth, they were
not of those women who spread themselves with abandon on a *chaise
longue* and besport themselves at some elegant tea party; they were
less pretentious and much more piquant. There, despatching sweetmeats, which one's appetite seasoned, despite the poor quality of the
produce, delicate observations, subtle allusions, brilliant witticisms
were exchanged from one side of the bars to the other. We would
speak pleasantly of all things while being tedious about nothing. We
treated misfortunes as one might a naughty but amusing child and
indeed we laughed very openly about the divinity of Marat, the
priestliness of Robespierre, the judiciousness of Fouquier. We seemed
to be saying to all those flunkeys: you will kill us when you will, but
you will not prevent us from being pleasant.

Last Letters: Prisons and Prisoners of the French Revolution 1793–4,
ED. Olivier Blanc, TRANS. Alan Sheridan, 1987

A Leg of Mutton and a Woman

EDMOND 1822–96 AND JULES 1830–70
GONCOURT

Sunday, 29 January [1860]
Saw Barrière who told us this striking anecdote. On the Place de Grève
he had seen a condemned man whose hair had visibly stood on end
when he had been turned to face the scaffold. Yet this was the man
who, when Dr. Pariset had asked him what he wanted before he died,
had answered: 'A leg of mutton and a woman.'

Pages from the Goncourt Journals, ED. TRANS. Robert Baldick, 1962

Skilly

ALEXANDER SOLZHENITSYN 1918–

There's a young lad at that table over there crossing himself before he
dips his spoon in. One of Bendera's* lot, must be. And a new boy at
that. The older ones give it up when they've been inside a bit.

The Russians don't even remember which hand you cross yourself
with.

It's cold sitting in the mess-hut. Most men eat with their caps on, but
they take their time, angling for gluey scraps of rotten little fish under
the leaves of frost-blackened cabbage, and spitting the bones onto the
table. When there's a mountain of them somebody will sweep them off
before the next gang sits down, and they will be crunched to powder
underfoot.

Spitting bones out on the floor is considered bad manners.

There were pillars or stanchions down the middle of the hut (two
rows of them). Fetyukov, a workmate of Shukhov's, sat by one looking
after his breakfast for him. Fetyukov was one of the lowliest members
of the gang – even Shukhov was a cut above him. Outwardly the gang
all looked the same, all wearing identical black jackets with identical
number patches, but underneath there were big differences. You'd

* Member of the Ukrainian nationalist underground.

never get Buynovsky to sit watching a bowl, and there were jobs that Shukhov left to those beneath him.

Fetyukov caught sight of him and gave up his seat with a sigh. 'It's all gone cold. I nearly ate it for you, I thought you were in the hole.'

He didn't wait around. He knew Shukhov would polish both bowls till they shone and leave nothing for him.

Shukhov drew his spoon from his boot. That spoon was precious, it had travelled all over the north with him. He'd cast it himself from aluminium wire in a sand mould and scratched on it 'Ust-Izhma, 1944'.

Next, he removed his cap from his shaven head – however cold it was he wouldn't let himself eat with his cap on – and stirred up his skilly, quickly checking what had found its way into his bowl. Could have been worse. Not ladled from the top of the cauldron, but not the dregs either. Fetyukov could have fished out the potato while he was guarding the bowl – be just like him!

The best you can ever say for skilly is that it's hot, but this time Shukhov's was cold. He started eating slowly, savouring it, just the same. If the roof burst into flames he still wouldn't hurry. Apart from sleep an old lag can call his life his own only for ten minutes at breakfast time, five at lunchtime, and five more at suppertime.

The skilly didn't change from day to day. What was in it depended on which vegetable was stockpiled for winter. Last year they'd laid in nothing but carrots in brine – so from September to June it was carrots all the way. This time round it was black cabbage. June is when the *zek* eats best: the vegetables run out, and there's meal instead. The leanest time is July, when chopped nettles go into the pot.

There was nothing much left of the little fish, only bones: the flesh had come away and dissolved, except for scraps of head and tail. Shukhov left neither flesh nor scales on the brittle skeletons. He champed and sucked them between his lips, then spat them out on the table. He ate every bit of every fish, gills, tails, even eyes if they were where they should be, but if they had boiled out of the head and were floating loose in the bowl – big fish-eyes goggling at him – he wouldn't eat them. The others laughed at him for it.

He'd been thrifty today. He hadn't gone to the hut for his ration and was eating without bread. He could scoff it by itself later on. More filling that way.

The second course was magara gruel. It had congealed into a solid bar. Shukhov broke bits off. Magara is bad enough hot – tastes of nothing, leaves you feeling empty. Yellowish like wheat, but just grass really. Somebody's bright idea, serving it instead of meal. Seemed they got it from the Chinese. Maybe three hundred grammes, boiled weight. So make the best of it: call it what you like, it was all you were getting.

One Day in the Life of Ivan Denisovich, 1962, TRANS. Harry Willetts

To the Editor of the *Daily Chronicle*
OSCAR WILDE 1854–1900

Oscar Wilde, sentenced to two years imprisonment with hard labour in 1895, was released in 1897. In 1898 The Ballad of Reading Gaol was published anonymously. In the same year on 24 March this letter appeared in the Daily Chronicle, *under the heading 'Don't read this if you want to be happy today.' The letter was signed: The author of 'The Ballad of Reading Gaol.' The letter was timed for the day the House of Commons began the debate on the second reading of the Prison Bill. This extract is taken from the middle of the letter and deals with hunger; the other two permanent punishments authorized by law, according to Wilde, were insomnia and disease.*

23 March [1898]   *[Paris]*
The food supplied to prisoners is entirely inadequate. Most of it is revolting in character. All of it is insufficient. Every prisoner suffers day and night from hunger. A certain amount of food is carefully weighed out ounce by ounce for each prisoner. It is just enough to sustain, not life exactly, but existence. But one is always racked by the pain and sickness of hunger.

The result of the food – which in most cases consists of weak gruel, badly-baked bread, suet, and water – is disease in the form of incessant diarrhoea. This malady, which ultimately with most prisoners becomes a permanent disease, is a recognised institution in every prison. At Wandsworth Prison, for instance – where I was confined for two months, till I had to be carried into hospital, where I remained for another two months – the warders go round twice or three times a day with astringent medicines, which they serve out to the prisoners as a matter of course. After about a week of such treatment it is unnecessary to say the medicine produces no effect at all. The wretched prisoner is then left a prey to the most weakening, depressing, and humiliating malady that can be conceived; and if, as often happens, he fails, from physical weakness, to complete his required revolutions at the crank or the mill he is reported for idleness, and punished with the greatest severity and brutality. Nor is this all.

Nothing can be worse than the sanitary arrangements of English prisons. In old days each cell was provided with a form of latrine. These latrines have now been suppressed. They exist no longer. A small tin vessel is supplied to each prisoner instead. Three times a day a prisoner is allowed to empty his slops. But he is not allowed to have access to the prison lavatories, except during the one hour when he is at exercise. And after five o'clock in the evening he is not allowed to leave his cell under any pretence, or for any reason. A man suffering from diarrhoea is consequently placed in a position so loathsome that it is unnecessary to dwell on it, that it would be unseemly to dwell on it. The misery and tortures that prisoners go through in consequence of the revolting sanitary arrangements are quite indescribable. And the foul air of the prison cells, increased by a system of ventilation that is utterly ineffective, is so sickening and unwholesome that it is no uncommon thing for warders, when they come in the morning out of the fresh air and open and inspect each cell, to be violently sick. I have seen this myself on more than three occasions, and several of the warders have mentioned it to me as one of the disgusting things that their office entails on them.

The food supplied to prisoners should be adequate and wholesome. It should not be of such a character as to produce the incessant diarrhoea that, at first a malady, becomes a permanent disease.

Selected Letters of Oscar Wilde, ED. Rupert Hart-Davis, 1962

Prison Food
JOHN BURNS 1858–1945

In 1898 John Burns spoke in the House of Commons on the Prison Bill. He had been imprisoned for 6 weeks after being arrested at a Labour demonstration in Trafalgar Square in 1887.

I have had No. 1 diet, bread and oatmeal . . . I went into prison with a strong constitution and I was there for six weeks. I never made any complaint. But what is 6 oz. of bread? It is as much as the Hon. gentlemen take with their chop and potatoes, and cabbage and spinach. I had the bread at 5.30 p.m. and nothing till 7.45 next morning. I am not ashamed to say that at 1 or 2 o'clock in the morning I have wetted my hands with my spittle and gone down on my hands and knees in the hope of picking up a stray crumb from the meal I had had ten hours before. By that diet you break down and enfeeble a man's constitution.

quoted in *The Englishman's Food*, 1959

How to Prepare a Large Quantity of Good Soup for the Poor
CHARLES ELMÉ FRANCATELLI 1805–73

It is customary with most large families, while living in the country, to kill at least some portion of the meat consumed in their households; and without supposing for a moment that any portion of this is ever wasted, I may be allowed to suggest that certain parts, such as sheep's heads, plucks, shanks, and scrag-ends, might very well be spared towards making a good mess of soup for the poor. The bones left from cooked joints, first baked in a brisk oven for a quarter of an hour, and afterwards boiled in a large copper of water for six hours, would readily prepare a gelatinized foundation broth for the soup; the bones, when sufficiently boiled, to be taken out. And thus, supposing that your copper is already part filled with the broth made from bones (all the grease having been removed from the surface), add any meat you may have, cut up in pieces of about four ounces weight, garnish plentifully with carrots, celery, onions, some thyme, and ground allspice, well-soaked split peas, barley, or rice; and, as the soup boils up, skim it well occasionally, season moderately with salt, and after about four hours' gentle and continuous boiling, the soup will be ready for distribution. It was the custom in families where I have lived as cook, to allow a pint of this soup, served out with the pieces of meat in it, to as many as the recipients' families numbered; and the soup was made for distribution twice every week during winter.

A Plain Cookery Book for the Working Classes, 1861

Of the Street Trade in Baked Potatoes
HENRY MAYHEW 1812–87

Henry Mayhew, playwright and journalist, is remembered today for his great sociological study London Labour and the London Poor, *which began as a series of articles in* The Morning Chronicle *1849–50. This is a record of Mayhew's investigations into the life and work of the poor and underprivileged. It is a remarkable document, giving a vivid and highly detailed portrait of the Victorian lower classes and their food.*

The baked potato trade, in the way it is at present carried on, has not been known more than fifteen years in the streets. Before that, potatoes were sometimes roasted as chestnuts are now, but only on a small scale. The trade is more profitable than that in fruit, but continues for but six months of the year.

The customers consist of all classes. Many gentlefolks buy them in the streets, and take them home for supper in their pockets; but the working classes are the greatest purchasers. Many boys and girls lay out a half-penny in a baked potato. Irishmen are particularly fond of them, but they are the worst customers, I am told, as they want the largest potatoes in the can. Women buy a great number of those sold. Some take them home, and some eat them in the street. Three baked potatoes are as much as will satisfy the stoutest appetite.

London Labour and the London Poor, 1851

Neapolitan Lazzaroni
ELISABETH VIGÉE-LE BRUN 1755–1842

The most curious section of Neopolitan society are the lazzaroni. These people have simplified the art of living, dispensing with houses and almost managing to do the same with food; their only lodging is the church porch, and their frugality is equal to their laziness, which is unbelievable. You may find them stretched out in the shade or by the seashore. They wear scarcely any clothing, and their children remain naked until the age of twelve. I was a little shocked at first, and frightened, to see them play on the quayside in Chiaia, where there was a continual stream of carriages; this same road was the main route for everyone in Naples, even princesses; all the same, I soon grew accustomed to the sight.

The poverty of the lazzaroni does not drive them to theft; perhaps they are simply too lazy, especially since their needs are so few. Most theft in Naples is committed by hired domestic servants, who generally seem to be very bad citizens and the dregs of many different foreign cities. I only ever heard of one lazzaroni stealing during my stay, but in the event the thief showed so much restraint that he might as well have been innocent. The Baron de Salis was giving a grand dinner and strolled along to the kitchen; as he quietly descended the stairway, he stopped at the sight of a man who, believing himself alone, went up to the fire, took a piece of beef and carried it off while the baron merely followed him with his eyes. All his silver ware was laid out on the table and the lazzaroni must have seen it but the poor man limited his theft to the piece of beef.

Memoirs, TRANS. Siân Evans, 1989

Shabby-genteel People
CHARLES DICKENS 1812–70

He first attracted our notice by sitting opposite to us in the reading-room at the British Museum; and what made the man more remarkable was, that he always had before him a couple of shabby-genteel books – two old dog's-eared folios; in mouldy, worm-eaten covers, which had once been smart. He was in his chair every morning just as the clock struck ten, he was always the last to leave the room in the afternoon; and, when he did, he quitted it with the air of a man who knew not where else to go for warmth and quiet. There he used to sit all day, as close to the table as possible, in order to conceal the lack of buttons on his coat; with his old hat carefully deposited at his feet, where he evidently flattered himself it escaped observation.

About two o'clock, you would see him munching a French roll or a penny loaf; not taking it boldly out of his pocket at once, like a man who knew he was only making a lunch; but breaking off little bits in his pocket, and eating them by stealth. He knew too well it was his dinner.

Sketches by 'Boz', 1836–7

Mushroom Catsup
FORD MADOX FORD 1873–1939

'Measter! Dun yo really want ketchup?'

I replied that I really did.

She said:

'Old Meary Spratt up by Hungry Hall wheer ye see me diggin' – she makes ketchup'.

I asked her why she had not told me before and she answered:

'Well, ye see the Quality do be asking foolish questions. I thought ye didn't really want to know.'

But indeed, as I learnt afterwards it wasn't only the dislike of being asked foolish questions. In Meary Walker's long, wise life she had experienced one thing – that no man with a collar and a tie is to be trusted. She had had it vaguely in her mind that, when I asked the question, I might be some sort of excise officer trying to find out where illicit distilling was carried on. She didn't know that the making of catsup was not illegal. She had heard that many of her poor neighbours had been fined heavily for selling bottles of home-made sloe-gin or mead. She had refused to answer, out of a sense of automatic caution for fear she should get poor old Meary Spratt into trouble.

But next morning she turned up at my cottage carrying two bottles of Meary Spratt's catsup in an old basket covered with a cloth. And after that, seeing her rather often at the shop on Saturday nights when all the world came to buy its Sunday provisions and, because she came in to heat the bake oven with faggots once a week, and to do the washing – in that isolated neighbourhood, among the deep woods of the Weald, I got to know her as well as I ever knew anybody. This is her biography:

She was the daughter of a day labourer among the hopfields of Paddock Wood. When she had been born, the youngest of five, her own mother had died. Her father had brought a stepmother into the house. I never discovered that the stepmother was notably cruel to Meary. But those were the Hungry Forties. The children never had enough to eat. Once, Meary cut off one of her big toes. She had jumped down into a ditch after a piece of turnip peel. She had of course had no shoes or stockings and there had been a broken bottle in the ditch.

Cultural Criticism, 1923

The Art of Using Leftovers: Paris, 1850–1900
JEAN-PAUL ARON 1925–88

In the morning, at dawn, a great basket was brought to the restaurant, a basket covered with a dark cloth that, in the jargon of pantries and kitchens, is called the *black flag*. In it were all the relics of fine banquets and suppers of the previous night, all the morsels that fine gentlemen and ladies with no appetite toyed with, in mansions or in night restaurants. Cooks and chefs sell for almost nothing the left-over salmon, the virtually intact filets of Normandy sole, the poultry carcasses, and the roebuck steaks . . . This is why you have a menu rivaling that of Rothschild when he hosts important figures, rivaling the menus that Lulu and Cuddles force their lovers to order for them during nocturnal love feasts. A little disinfectant over it all, a little decoration, and for seventeen sous you can eat the feast of Luculus – oh naive schoolboy, oh dreamy and tempestuous office boy – hypnotized by the ten-point stag hanging in the window, the stag who soon will go back home to its owner, the man who runs the big food store, when a week of aging has ripened it for actual sale. But do not weep! For this stag will return to you in pieces, under the black flag! . . .

Near the poultry building in the centrally located Halles, or market

– both before and after the construction of Baltard's cast-iron covered market complex in the 1850s – was a well-known section loved by customers and watched over by the police. Here every morning little zinc-lined carts would have their precious merchandise unloaded. This marked the end of a long journey through Paris, a tedious door-to-door trek from the major hotels to the famous restaurants, from government ministries to embassies, from fine dwellings to noble palaces. Their itineraries were not left to chance, for each cart went to specific addresses, often at a fixed time. The tradesman who accompanied them was known as the 'jeweler,' a title bestowed through either gratitude or derision. In a cellar reserved for him, the 'jeweler' would sort the foods. And, by nine o'clock, dishes had been set out and decorated, to be sold for prices ranging from three to five sous circa 1860 and four to twelve sous at the very end of the century. Pieces of meat, filet of game, fish heads and tails, cold cuts, desserts, cakes with only a few slices missing, and virtually intact bonbons were put on sale. And vegetables too. The cheapest platters had more vegetables than meat, which usually was stewed. More appealing were the six- to eight-sous mixed platters. But for ten to twelve sous one was better treated and could have attractively displayed poultry legs, a lobster claw, a filet of sole, a bit of pastry, and some pistachio custard. Or else a half a pig's foot, with truffles alongside a slice of galantine, a breaded cutlet, and a fish head, crowned by a chocolate eclair. Or even – for there was an admirable variety of jewels available – sauerkraut keeping company with crayfish in Bordeaux wine, sautéed rabbit, calf's head, roebuck filet, and apple charlotte. Imagine how exhausted the 'jeweler' would be after arranging these plates and distributing the leftovers equally, in terms of price and ingredients, with a mind to the combination of colors, odors, and dimensions. But he had to satisfy his faithful customers, who ranged all the way from people working for starvation wages to women trembling with fever to minor clerks and on to housewives from lower-class neighborhoods.

These neighborhoods of the city, it is true, had similar local resources. In the markets spread throughout the city were stalls specializing partially or entirely in this strange trade. Frédéric Le Play pointed out the role that leftovers played in the working-class diet. Take, for example, the family living near the Place Maubert – a ragpicker, his wife, and his daughter – with a total annual income of 631 francs 1 centime (roughly 4,500 francs, or $950, today), 457 of which went for food. Once a week during the four winter months his wife bought ready-cooked meat in the market of the quarter of Saint-

Honoré, and throughout the year she purchased fat made of a blend of butter, drippings, pork fat, and poultry fat, all leftover from middle-class kitchens. In order to purify this mixture and keep it for two weeks, her husband melted it down and added a little white salt.

Food and Drink in History, vol. 5, 1979

Double Suicide
FANNY TROLLOPE 1780–1863

It is not long since two young men – mere youths – entered a *restaurant*, and bespoke a dinner of unusual luxury and expense, and afterwards arrived punctually at the appointed hour to eat it. They did so, apparently with all the zest of youthful appetite and youthful glee. They called for champagne, and quaffed it hand in hand. No symptom of sadness, thought, or reflection of any kind was observed to mix with their mirth, which was loud, long, and unremitting. At last came the *café noir*, the cognac, and the bill: one of them was seen to point out the amount to the other, and then both burst out afresh into violent laughter. Having swallowed each his cup of coffee to the dregs, the *garçon* was ordered to request the company of the *restaurateur* for a few minutes. He came immediately, expecting perhaps to receive his bill, minus some extra charge which the jocund but economical youths might deem exorbitant.

Instead of this, however, the elder of the two informed him that the dinner had been excellent, which was the more fortunate as it was decidedly the last that either of them should ever eat: that for his bill, he must of necessity excuse the payment of it, as in fact they neither of them possessed a single sou: that upon no other occasion would they thus have violated the customary etiquette between guest and land-lord; but that finding this world, its toils and its troubles, unworthy of them, they had determined once more to enjoy a repast of which their poverty must for ever prevent the repetition, and then – take leave of existence for ever! For the first part of this resolution, he declared that it had, thanks to his cook and his cellar, been achieved nobly; and for the last, it would soon follow – for the *café noir*, besides the little glass of his admirable cognac, had been medicated with that which would speedily settle all their accounts for them.

The *restaurateur* was enraged. He believed no part of the rhodomontade but that which declared their inability to discharge the bill, and he talked loudly, in his turn, of putting them into the hands of the police. At length, however, upon their offering to give him their address, he was persuaded to let them depart.

On the following day, either the hope of obtaining his money, or some vague fear that they might have been in earnest in the wild tale that they had told him, induced this man to go to the address they had left with him; and he there heard that the two unhappy boys had been that morning found lying together hand in hand, on a bed hired a few weeks before by one of them. When they were discovered, they were already dead and quite cold.

On a small table in the room lay many written papers, all expressing aspirations after greatness that should cost neither labour nor care, a profound contempt for those who were satisfied to live by the sweat of their brow – sundry quotations from Victor Hugo, and a request that their names and the manner of their death might be transmitted to the newspapers.

Paris and the Parisians, 1835

The Fortunate Weaver
GEORGE BORROW 1803–81

We returned to the inn and dined. The duck was capital and I asked John Jones if he had ever tasted a better. 'Never, sir,' said he, 'for to tell you the truth, I never tasted a duck before.' 'Rather singular,' said I. 'What, that I should not have tasted duck? Oh, sir, the singularity is, that I should now be tasting duck. Duck in Wales, sir, is not fare for poor weavers. This is the first duck I ever tasted, and though I never taste another, as I probably never shall, I may consider myself a fortunate weaver, for I can now say I have tasted duck once in my life. Few weavers in Wales are ever able to say as much.'

Wild Wales, 1854

The Carter on 14/- a Week

DIANA COOPER 1892–1986

The carter told me about his early married life on 14/- a week. It sounds starvation at first, and then you find that he had all the butter he liked at 6d per lb. and all the whey-butter he liked for 4½d per lb., all the cheese he liked at 7d per lb. (N.B. the butter and cheese were made by Mr Osborne and would be better than what they have at Sandringham.) On Sundays they were given a bucketful of potatoes and very often one or two broccoli. They paid no rent; the corn they got gleaning supplied them with bread. And so on. The hours worked were long, but the food was much better than what they get now. I daresay 14/- didn't leave much for clothes, but they didn't have to pay £12 for a hat as you do.

Trumpets from the Steep, 1960

The Market at Juazeiro

GERMAINE GREER 1939–

In the market at Juazeiro, an old man is selling wild honey that he has collected in the *caatinga*, the dry scrubland that takes over beyond the narrow alluvial strip along the river. The volatile oils from the tough little shrubs that grow there make the air of the *caatinga* as heady as wine, if any wine could be so hot and so thin. The flowers of the *caatinga* are either short-lived or tiny and sparse, and the bees are an extremely select society. The old man has collected the honey in litre bottles which he has stopped with whittled wooden corks, round which the honey oozes in the heat, full of charred particles left from the murder of the bee community. Stupidly I ask if he can sell me just half a litre. The old man, who has tramped in from the back blocks lugging his six litre bottles, which must have grown heavier each step as the sun rose scorching from the first instant that it showed above the horizon, has stood all day hoping to find someone rich enough to buy his precious elixir. He looks wordlessly up at me and over his seamed face steals the look.

Newcomer that I was, I did not yet grasp how poor the poor of the

Nordeste are. The old man had no way of finding two half-litre bottles. He made no attempt to explain the situation, but simply shook his head and looked into the distance. I laid down my 5,000 cruzeiros and touched his sleeve. He did not smile as he folded up the bills and put them in the inside pocket of his tattered jacket. I carried that sticky bottle for thousands of miles before I finally gave it away.

River Journeys. From *The Madwoman's Underclothes*, 1986

A Miserable Inn

J. W. GOETHE 1749–1832

April 19. After Monreale . . . Under the shelter of an airy pergola attached to a miserable inn, we took a light midday meal. Dogs greedily gobbled up the discarded skins of our sausages; a beggar boy chased them away and hungrily consumed our apple parings until he, in his turn, was chased away by an old beggar. Professional jealousy is to be found everywhere. The old beggar ran up and down in his tattered toga, acting as both boots and waiter. I had observed on earlier occasions that if you order anything from an innkeeper which he hasn't got in the house at the moment, he calls a beggar to fetch it from the grocer's.

Italian Journey 1786–88, TRANS. W. H. Auden
and Elizabeth Mayer, 1962

English Working People Refuse Brown Bread

GEORGE ORWELL 1903–50

It is unfortunate that the English working class – the English nation generally, for that matter – are exceptionally ignorant about and wasteful of food. I have pointed out elsewhere how civilized is a French navvy's idea of a meal compared with an Englishman's, and I cannot believe that you would ever see such wastage in a French house as you habitually see in English ones. Of course, in the very poorest homes, where everybody is employed, you don't see much actual waste, but those who can afford to waste food often do so. I could give startling instances of this. Even the Northern habit of baking one's own bread is slightly wasteful in itself, because an overworked woman cannot bake more than once or, at most, twice a week and it is impossible to tell beforehand how much bread will be wasted, so that a certain amount generally has to be thrown away. The usual thing is to bake six large loaves and twelve small ones at a time. All this is part of the old, generous English attitude to life, and it is an amiable quality, but a disastrous one at the present moment.

English working people everywhere, so far as I know, refuse brown bread; it is usually impossible to buy wholemeal bread in a working-class district. They sometimes give the reason that brown bread is 'dirty'. I suspect the real reason is that in the past brown bread has been confused with black bread, which is traditionally associated with Popery and wooden shoes. (They have plenty of Popery and wooden shoes in Lancashire. A pity they haven't the black bread as well!) But the English palate, especially the working-class palate, now rejects good food almost automatically. The number of people who *prefer* tinned peas and tinned fish to real peas and real fish must be increasing every year, and plenty of people who could afford real milk in their tea would much sooner have tinned milk – even that dreadful tinned milk which is made of sugar and cornflour and has UNFIT FOR BABIES on the tin in huge letters. In some districts efforts are now being made to teach the unemployed more about food-values and more about the intelligent spending of money. When you hear of a thing like this you feel yourself torn both ways. I have heard a Communist speaker on the platform grow very angry about it. In London, he said, parties of Society dames now have the cheek to walk into East End houses and give shopping-lessons to the wives of the unemployed. He gave this as an instance of the mentality of the English governing class. First you condemn a family to live on thirty shillings a week, and then you have the damned impertinence to tell them how they are to spend their money. He was quite right – I agree heartily. Yet all the same it *is* a pity that, merely for the lack of a proper tradition, people should pour muck like tinned milk down their throats and not even know that it is inferior to the product of the cow.

The Road to Wigan Pier, 1937

Two Gallants
JAMES JOYCE 1882–1941

He walked listlessly round Stephen's Green and then down Grafton Street. Though his eyes took note of many elements of the crowd through which he passed, they did so morosely. He found trivial all that was meant to charm him and did not answer the glances which invited him to be bold. He knew that he would have to speak a great deal, to invent and to amuse, and his brain and throat were too dry for such a task. The problem of how he could pass the hours till he met Corley again troubled him a little. He could think of no way of passing them but to keep on walking. He turned to the left when he came to the corner of Rutland Square and felt more at ease in the dark quiet street, the sombre look of which suited his mood. He paused at last before the window of a poor-looking shop over which the words *Refreshment Bar* were printed in white letters. On the glass of the window were two flying inscriptions: *Ginger Beer* and *Ginger Ale*. A cut ham was exposed on a great blue dish while near it on a plate lay a segment of very light plum pudding. He eyed this food earnestly for some time, and then, after glancing warily up and down the street, went into the shop quickly.

He was hungry, for, except some biscuits which he had asked two grudging curates to bring him, he had eaten nothing since breakfast-time. He sat down at an uncovered wooden table opposite two work-girls and a mechanic. A slatternly girl waited on him.

'How much is a plate of peas?' he asked.

'Three halfpence, sir,' said the girl.

'Bring me a plate of peas,' he said, 'and a bottle of ginger beer.'

He spoke roughly in order to belie his air of gentility, for his entry had been followed by a pause of talk. His face was heated. To appear natural he pushed his cap back on his head and planted his elbows on the table. The mechanic and the two work-girls examined him point by point before resuming their conversation in a subdued voice. The girl brought him a plate of grocer's hot peas, seasoned with pepper and vinegar, a fork, and his ginger beer. He ate his food greedily and found it so good that he made a note of the shop mentally. When he had eaten all the peas he sipped his ginger beer and sat for some time thinking of Corley's adventure. In his imagination he beheld the pair of lovers walking along some dark road; he heard Corley's voice in deep energetic gallantries, and saw again the leer of the young woman's mouth. This vision made him feel keenly his own poverty of purse and spirit. He was tired of knocking about, of pulling the devil by the tail, of shifts and intrigues. He would be thirty-one in November. Would he never get a good job? Would he never have a home of his own? He thought how pleasant it would be to have a warm fire to sit by and a good dinner to sit down to. He had walked the streets long enough with friends and with girls. He knew what those friends were worth: he knew the girls too. Experience had embittered his heart against the world. But all hope had not left him. He felt better after having eaten than he had felt before, less weary of his life, less vanquished in spirit. He might yet be able to settle down in some snug corner and live happily if he could only come across some good simple-minded girl with a little of the ready.

Dubliners, 1914

Clean

GERMAINE GREER 1939–

Cleanliness was so high a value in our dusty community, that the dialect word for 'beautiful' when applied to objects was the Italian word for 'clean'. When Rosetta was given a crocheted dress to wear to the Assumption Day celebrations, she hardly dared to touch it. '*Quant'e p'lit*,' she kept saying.

The first time I went to eat with the shepherd's family in their windowless kitchen, I was appalled. A column of flies danced above the battered table, a thousand more crawled across it and over most other surfaces in the room. The women could barely squeeze past each other in the confined space, especially as two of them had to carry babies who couldn't be put down on the dirt floor. The meal consisted of a *piatto unico* of pasta flavoured with marrow flowers and plenty of olive oil and garlic. The home-made pasta tasted of dust and sweat. I had been invited to share this humble repast because it was considered a slap-up dinner. Another treat could be had if one of their hens laid an egg, a rare event in the summer heat; they would fry baby marrows and break the single egg into them, unless they sold the egg to me to get a little cash for some other necessity. The staple of their diet was bread, solid, grey bread which was all the men took to work with them, with an onion or a tomato to be sliced on top, a millimetre of tomato or onion on three centimetres of bread. And a thin, harsh wine that tasted of rusty nails.

The Madwoman's Underclothes, 1986

Hunger

SUSAN GEORGE

Hunger is not an unavoidable phenomenon like death and taxes. We are no longer living in the seventeenth century when Europe suffered shortages on an average of every three years and famine every ten. Today's world has all the physical resources and technical skills necessary to feed the present population of the planet or a much larger one. Unfortunately for the millions of people who go hungry, the problem is not a technical one – nor was it wholly so in the seventeenth century, for that matter. Whenever and wherever they live, rich people eat first, they eat a disproportionate amount of the food there is and poor ones rarely rise in revolt against this most basic of oppressions unless specifically told to 'eat cake'. Hunger is not a scourge but a scandal.

How the Other Half Dies, 1976

Markets

❧✿❧

Every Kind of Merchandise in New Spain
BERNAL DÍAZ 1498–1593

On reaching the market-place, escorted by the many *Caciques* whom
Montezuma had assigned to us, we were astounded at the great
number of people and the quantities of merchandise, and at the
orderliness and good arrangements that prevailed, for we had never
seen such a thing before. The chieftains who accompanied us pointed
everything out. Every kind of merchandise was kept separate and had
its fixed place marked for it.

Let us begin with the dealers in gold, silver, and precious stones,
feathers, cloaks, and embroidered goods, the male and female slaves
who are also sold there. They bring as many slaves to be sold in that
market as the Portuguese bring Negroes from Guinea. Some are
brought there attached to long poles by means of collars round their
necks to prevent them from escaping, but others are left loose. Next
there were those who sold coarser cloth, and cotton goods and fabrics
made of twisted thread, and there were chocolate merchants with their
chocolate. In this way you could see every kind of merchandise to be
found anywhere in New Spain, laid out in the same way as goods are
laid out in my own district of Medina del Campo, a centre for fairs,
where each line of stalls has its own particular sort. So it was in this
great market. There were those who sold sisal cloth and ropes and the
sandals they wear on their feet, which are made from the same plant.
All these were kept in one part of the market, in the place assigned to
them, and in another part were skins of tigers and lions, otters, jackals,
and deer, badgers, mountain cats, and other wild animals, some
tanned and some untanned, and other classes of merchandise.

There were sellers of kidney-beans and sage and other vegetables
and herbs in another place, and in yet another they were selling fowls,

and birds with great dewlaps,[1] also rabbits, hares, deer, young ducks, little dogs, and other such creatures. Then there were the fruiterers; and the women who sold cooked food, flour and honey cake, and tripe, had their part of the market. Then came pottery of all kinds, from big water-jars to little jugs, displayed in its own place, also honey, honey-paste, and other sweets like nougat. Elsewhere they sold timber too, boards, cradles, beams, blocks, and benches, all in a quarter of their own.

Then there were the sellers of pitch-pine for torches, and other things of that kind, and I must also mention, with all apologies, that they sold many canoe-loads of human excrement, which they kept in the creeks near the market. This was for the manufacture of salt and the curing of skins, which they say cannot be done without it. I know that many gentlemen will laugh at this, but I assure them it is true. I may add that on all the roads they have shelters made of reeds or straw or grass so that they can retire when they wish to do so, and purge their bowels unseen by passers-by, and also in order that their excrement shall not be lost.

But why waste so many words on the goods in their great market? If I describe everything in detail I shall never be done. Paper, which in Mexico they call *amal*, and some reeds that smell of liquid amber, and are full of tobacco, and yellow ointments and other such things, are sold in a separate part. Much cochineal is for sale too, under the arcades of that market, and there are many sellers of herbs and other such things. They have a building there also in which three judges sit, and there are officials like constables who examine the merchandise. I am forgetting the sellers of salt and the makers of flint knives, and how they split them off the stone itself, and the fisherwoman and the men who sell small cakes made from a sort of weed which they get out of the great lake, which curdles and forms a kind of bread which tastes rather like cheese. They sell axes too, made of bronze and copper and tin, and gourds and brightly painted wooden jars.

The Conquest of New Spain, TRANS. J. M. Cohen, 1963

---

[1] Turkeys.

Kin-Sai

MARCO POLO 1254–1324

When Marco Polo visited the city he called Kin-Sai, now known as
Hangchow or Hangzhou, it was at its height, with more than a
million inhabitants, and was known as a centre of artistic culture.
Its wealth came from the silk industry. It is still regarded as one of
the most beautiful cities in China, famous for its blossom in the
spring, carefully preserved 'Willow Pattern' scenic views, pleasure
gardens and ornamental lakes.

There are within the city ten principal squares or market-places,
besides innumerable shops along the streets. Each side of these squares
is half a mile in length, and in front of them is the main street, forty
paces in width, and running in a direct line from one extremity of the
city to the other. It is crossed by many low and convenient bridges.
These market-squares are at the distance of four miles from each other.
In a direction parallel to that of the main street, but on the opposite
side of the squares, runs a very large canal, on the nearer bank of which
capacious warehouses are built of stone, for the accommodation of the
merchants who arrive from India and other parts with their goods and
effects. They are thus conveniently situated with respect to the market-
places. In each of these, upon three days in every week, there is an
assemblage of from forty to fifty thousand persons, who attend the
markets and supply them with every article of provision that can be
desired.

There is an abundant quantity of game of all kinds, such as
roebucks, stags, fallow deer, hares, and rabbits, together with
partridges, pheasants, francolins, quails, common fowls, capons, and
such numbers of ducks and geese as can scarcely be expressed; for so
easily are they bred and reared on the lake, that, for the value of a
Venetian silver groat, you may purchase a couple of geese and two
couple of ducks.

There, also, are the shambles, where they slaughter cattle for food,
such as oxen, calves, kids, and lambs, to furnish the tables of rich
persons and of the great magistrates. As to the people of the lower
classes, they eat every kind of meat, without any discrimination.

At the seasons there is in the markets a great variety of herbs and fruits, and especially pears of an extraordinary size, weighing ten pounds each, that are white in the inside, like paste, and have a very fragrant smell. There are peaches also, in their season, both of the yellow and white kind, and of a delicious flavour. Grapes are not produced there, but are brought in a dried state, and very good, from other parts. This applies also to wine, which the natives do not hold in estimation, being accustomed to their own liquor prepared from rice and spices. From the sea, which is fifteen miles distant, there is daily brought up the river, to the city, a vast quantity of fish; and in the lake also there is abundance, which gives employment at all times to persons whose sole occupation it is to catch them. The sorts are various according to the season of the year. At the sight of such an importation of fish, you would think it impossible that it could be sold; and yet, in the course of a few hours, it is all taken off, so great is the number of inhabitants, even of those classes which can afford to indulge in such luxuries, for fish and flesh are eaten at the same meal.

The Travels of Marco Polo, TRANS. Manuel Komroff, 1953

Street Cries in Mexico
MME CALDERÓN DE LA BARCA 1804–82

There are an extraordinary number of street-cries in Mexico, which begin at dawn and continue till night, performed by hundreds of discordant voices, impossible to understand at first; but Señor – has been giving me an explanation of them, until I begin to have some distinct idea of their meaning. At dawn you are awakened by the shrill and desponding cry at the Carbonero, the coalmen, 'Carbon, Señor?' which, as he pronounces it, sounds like 'Carbosiu?' Then the grease-man takes up the song, 'Mantequilla! lard! lard! at one real and a half.' 'Salt beef! good salt beef!' ('Cecina buena!') interrupts the butcher in a hoarse voice. 'Hay cebo-o-o-o-o-o?' This is the prolonged and melancholy note of the woman who buys kitchen-stuff, and stops before the door. Then passes by the *cambista*, a sort of Indian she-trader or exchanger, who sings out, 'Tejocotes por venas de chile?' a small fruit which she proposes exchanging for hot peppers. No harm in that.

A kind of ambulating pedler drowns the shrill treble of the Indian cry. He calls aloud upon the public to buy needles, pins, thimbles, shirt-buttons, tape, cotton-balls, small mirrors, etc. He enters the house, and is quickly surrounded by the women, young and old, offering him the tenth part of what he asks, and which, after much haggling, he accepts. Behind him stands the Indian with his tempting baskets of fruit, of which he calls out all the names, till the cook or housekeeper can resist no longer, and putting her head over the balustrade, calls him up with his bananas, and oranges, and granadilas, etc.

A sharp note of interrogation is heard, indicating something that is hot, and must be snapped up quickly before it cools. 'Gorditas de horna caliente?' 'Little fat cakes from the oven, hot?' This is in a female key, sharp and shrill. Follows the mat-seller. 'Who wants mats from Pueblo? mats of five yards?' These are the most matinal cries.

At midday the beggars begin to be particularly importunate, and their cries, and prayers, and long recitations, form a running accompaniment to the other noises. Then above all rises the cry of 'Honey-cakes!' 'Cheese and honey?' 'Requeson and good honey?' (*Requeson* being a sort of hard curd, sold in cheeses.) Then come the dulce-men, the sellers of sweetmeats, of meringues, which are very good, and of all sorts of candy. 'Caramelos de esperma! bocadillo de coco!' Then the lottery-men, the messengers of Fortune, with their shouts of 'The last ticket yet unsold, for half a real!' a tempting announcement to the lazy beggar, who finds it easier to gamble than to work, and who may have that sum hid about his rags.

Towards evening rises the cry of 'Tortillas de cuajada?' 'Curd-cakes?' or, 'Do you take nuts?' succeeded by the night-cry of 'Chestnuts hot and roasted!' and by the affectionate vendors of ducks; 'Ducks, oh my soul, hot ducks!' 'Maize-cakes,' etc., etc. As the night wears away, the voices die off, to resume next morning in fresh vigour.

Tortillas, which are the common food of the people, and which are merely maize cakes mixed with a little lime, and of the form and size of what we call *scones*, I find rather good when very hot and fresh-baked, but insipid by themselves. They have been in use all through this country since the earliest ages of its history, without any change in the manner of baking them, excepting that, for the noble Mexicans in former days, they used to be kneaded with various medicinal plants, supposed to render them more wholesome. They are considered particularly palatable with *chile*, to endure which, in the quantities in which it is eaten here, it seems to me necessary to have a throat lined with tin.

Life in Mexico, 1843

The Feast of St Joseph
J. W. GOETHE 1749–1832

March 19. Naples 1787
Today is the Feast of St Joseph, the patron saint of all *frittaruoli*, or pastry cooks, using the word 'pastry' in its crudest sense. Since, under the black, boiling oil they use for frying, there is a constant flare of flame, all fiery torments are assigned to their mystery. Last night they decorated their house fronts with appropriate paintings: Soul in Purgatory and Last Judgements were blazing on all sides. In front of their doors, large frying plans stood on hastily erected stoves. One apprentice kneaded the dough, while a second shaped it into crullers and threw them into the boiling oil. A third stood beside the pan with a small skewer, picked out the crullers when they were cooked and put them on another skewer, held by a fourth apprentice, who then offered them to bystanders. The third and fourth apprentices were young boys wearing blond, elaborately curled wigs, which are regarded as the attribute of angels. To complete the group, there were some persons who handed wine to the cooks, drank themselves and cried their wares. Angels, cooks, everybody shouted at the top of their voices. They drew a great crowd because, on this night, all pastry goods are sold at greatly reduced prices and even a portion of this is given to the poor.

Italian Journey 1786–88, TRANS. W. H. Auden
and Elizabeth Mayer, 1962

Chinese Street Vendors
HSIANG JU LIN AND TSUIFENG LIN

The day could begin with sweet almond tea and it could end with dry hard biscuits; these were sold by street vendors until about four in the morning. Since the tea vendors went to work at about that time, there was really no interval between day and night when 'a little something' could not be had. Other vendors sold persimmons, frozen hard in the intense cold of winter. These are thawed in a bowl of water, and people enjoyed them just as much as the fresh turnips, carrots and water chestnuts which were eaten like fruit. It was a casual parade of vendors that passed through the alleys of Peking, each with his cry or sound at his particular hour. These sounds were made with wooden sticks or bells or small brass gongs, and each vendor making his precarious living formed a part of a now vanished way of life, unaware that decades later his particular sound or cry could evoke such nostalgia. It was a good time for many people, comfort and service were real and cheap. Vendors of steamed bread appeared at breakfast time, and in the afternoon the watermelon-seed vendor trotted by. One could easily spend a whole afternoon gossiping and cracking the seeds between the teeth. We were like squirrels cracking nuts. Our tongues and hands were kept busy.

The wonton and fried bean curd vendors passed by late at night, stoves suspended on the ends of poles, now and then hailed by a servant emerging from a rich man's home to get a snack for his master. More often, they were stopped by other night workers. The night labourers and rickshaw-pullers, whose gruelling efforts made them sweat and pant even in winter, paused in their work, ate silently, and continued their labour.

Chinese Gastronomy, 1969

Water Melons
FRANCES TROLLOPE 1780–1865

Many waggon-loads of enormous water-melons were brought to market every day, and I was sure to see groups of men, women, and children seated on the pavement round the spot where they were sold, sucking in prodigious quantities of this water fruit. Their manner of devouring them is extremely unpleasant; the huge fruit is cut into half a dozen sections, of about a foot long, and then, dripping as it is with water, applied to the mouth, from either side of which pour copious streams of the fluid, while, ever and anon, a mouthful of the hard black seeds are shot out in all directions, to the great annoyance of all within reach. When I first tasted this fruit I thought it very vile stuff indeed, but before the end of the season we all learned to like it. When taken with claret and sugar it makes delicious wine and water.

It is the custom for the gentlemen to go to market at Cincinnati; the smartest men in the place, and those of the 'highest standing' do not scruple to leave their beds with the sun, six days in the week, and, prepared with a mighty basket, to sally forth in search of meat, butter, eggs, and vegetables. I have continually seen them returning, with their weighty basket on one arm and an enormous ham depending from the other.

Domestic Manners of the Americans, 1832

Street Vendors of Palermo

MARY TAYLOR SIMETI

For the street vendors of old Palermo the heyday came in July with the Festino, the festival dedicated to Saint Rosalia, the city's patroness. For five days the city was (and still is) given over to processions, fireworks, concerts, horse races, and other celebrations, and with all this going on who ever would want to stay at home cooking! Moreover, the city was filled with people from the provinces – the *regnicoli*, as the Palermitani disdainfully called those who lived in the rest of the Regno – who flocked wide-eyed and open-mouthed to see the goings-on in the big city. A visit to the Festino was an event so tantalizing that it was often written into marriage contracts.

Those whose chefs had to cook willy-nilly ate *sarde a beccafico* for Saint Rosalia's feast day, but the special street food of the Festino has always been *babbaluci d'u festinu*, snails much smaller than escargots, sautéed in oil with lots of parsley and garlic. Sucking the *babbaluci* out of their shells is very laborious and time-consuming, so it seems you are getting a good deal of eating for your money.

The candy sellers did great business too, not only the ones with the stopwatches but the booths where *torrone* and *cubaita* were sold, together with crystallized almonds and a kind of nougat that is made in large loaves and cut into slices. Striped in bilious pink, white, and chartreuse, this colorful addition to the street scene resembles a serving of multiflavored ice cream, but since it doesn't need to be refrigerated, it is known as *gelato di campagna* ('country ice cream').

The *siminzari*, or seed sellers, did such good business for Saint Rosalia that they had special carts used only for the Festino, shaped like sailing ships and decorated with multicolored paper flags. The decks were spread with *semenza e càlia* – pumpkin seeds and toasted chickpeas – and with peanuts, hazelnuts, and dried chestnuts, which the vendors weighed out on a brass scale and poured into brown paper cones. Even today a Sicilian does not feel that he has taken a proper walk or watched a proper procession unless he has done so clutching a cone of *semenza e càlia* in one hand and leaving a trail of shells behind him.

But he who came to the Festino with only one penny in his pocket would neither spend it on *babbaluci* nor squander it on *semenza*. Shoving his way through the heat and the dust of the crowded streets, he would save it until he arrived at a booth belonging to one of those vendors who had elected Saint Rosalia as their patroness, the vendors who did more business than anyone else during the Festino, the vendors who satisfied the inordinate Sicilian craving for ice cream.

Sicilian Food, 1989

Verona
J. W. GOETHE 1749–1832

Verona. On market days the squares are piled high with garlic and most every sort of vegetable and fruit. The people shout, throw things, scuffle, laugh and sing all day long. The mild climate and cheap food make life easy for them.

Italian Journey 1786–88, TRANS. W. H. Auden and Elizabeth Mayer, 1962

Montpellier
ELIZABETH DAVID 1913–92

When we visited the big open-air retail market in the upper town at Montpellier, there was an ordinary enough little *charcuterie-épicerie* stall offering the ingredients of what might be called the small change of French cookery, but to our English eyes it looked particularly inviting and interesting.

The atmosphere helped, of course. The sun, the clear sky, the bright colours, the prosperous look of this lively, airy university town and wine-growing capital; the stalls massed with flowers; fresh fish shining pink and gold and silver in shallow baskets; cherries and apricots and peaches on the fruit barrows; one stall piled with about a ton of little bunches of soup or pot-au-feu vegetables – a couple of slim leeks, a carrot or two, a long thin turnip, celery leaves, and parsley, all cleaned and neatly bound with a rush, ready for the pot; another *charcuterie* stall, in the covered part of the market, displaying yards of fresh sausage festooned around a pyramid-shaped wire stand; a fishwife crying pussy's parcels of fish wrapped tidily in newspaper; an old woman at the market entrance selling winkles from a little cart shaped like a pram; a fastidiously dressed old gentleman choosing tomatoes and leaf artichokes, one by one, as if he were picking a bouquet of flowers, and taking them to the scales to be weighed (how extra-ordinary that we in England put up so docilely with not being permitted by greengrocers or even barrow boys to touch or smell the produce we are buying); a lorry with an old upright piano in the back threading round and round the market place trying to get out. These little scenes establish the character of Montpellier market in our memories, although by now we have spent many mornings in different southern markets and have become accustomed to the beauty and profusion of the produce for sale and to the heavy smell of fresh ripe fruit which everywhere hangs thick in the air at this time of year.

Well, plenty of tourists spend their mornings in museums and picture galleries and cathedrals, and nobody would quarrel with them for that. But the stomach of a city is also not without its importance. And then, I wouldn't be too sure that the food market of a big city shouldn't be counted as part of its artistic tradition.

Where do they get their astonishing gift for display, these French stall keepers? Why does a barrow boy selling bunched radishes and salad greens in the market at Chinon know by instinct so to arrange his produce that he has created a little spectacle as fresh and gay as a Dufy painting, and you are at once convinced that unless you taste some of his radishes you will be missing an experience which seems of more urgency than a visit to the Château of Chinon? How has a Montpellier fishwife so mastered the art of composition that with her basket of fish for the *bouillabaisse* she is presenting a picture of such splendour that instead of going to look at the famous collection of paintings in the Musée Fabre you drive off as fast as possible to the coast to order a dish cooked with just such fish? And what can there be about the arrangement of a few slices of sausage and a dozen black olives on a dish brought by the waitress in the seaside café to keep you occupied while your fish is cooking that makes you feel that this is the first time you have seen and tasted a black olive and a piece of sausage?

When one tries to analyse the real reasons for the respect which French cookery has so long exacted from the rest of the world, the French genius for presentation must be counted as a very relevant point, and its humble beginnings can be seen on the market stalls, in the small town *charcutiers'* and *pâtissiers'* shops, in the modest little restaurants where even if the cooking is not particularly distinguished, the most ordinary of little dishes will be brought to your table with respect, properly arranged on a serving dish, the vegetables separately served, the object of arousing your appetite will be achieved and the proprietors of the establishment will have made the most of their limited resources.

An Omelette and a Glass of Wine, 1960

Of the Character of the Street-stalls
HENRY MAYHEW 1812–87

The stalls occupied by costermongers for the sale of fish, fruit, vegetables, etc. are chiefly constructed of a double cross-trestle or moveable frame, or else of two trestles, each with three legs, upon which is laid a long deal board, or tray. Some of the stalls consist merely of a few boards resting upon two baskets, or upon two herring-barrels. The fish-stalls are mostly covered with paper – generally old newspapers or periodicals – but some of the street-fishmongers, instead of using paper to display their fish upon, have introduced a thin marble slab, which gives the stall a cleaner, and, what they consider a high attribute, a 'respectable' appearance.

Most of the fruit-stalls are, in the winter time, fitted up with an apparatus for roasting apples and chestnuts; this generally consists of an old saucepan with a fire inside; and the woman who vends them, huddled up in her old faded shawl or cloak, often presents a picturesque appearance, in the early evening, or in a fog, with the gleam of the fire lighting up her half somnolent figure. Within the last two or three years, however, there has been so large a business carried on in roasted chestnuts, that it has become a distinct street-trade, and the vendors have provided themselves with an iron apparatus, large enough to roast nearly half a bushel at a time. At the present time, however, the larger apparatus is less common in the streets, and more frequent in the shops, than in the previous winter.

There are, moreover, peculiar kinds of stalls – such as the hot eels and hot peas-soup stalls, having tin oval pots, with a small chafing-dish containing a charcoal fire underneath each, to keep the eels or soup hot. The early breakfast stall has two capacious tin cans filled with tea or coffee, kept hot by the means before described, and some are lighted up by two or three large oil-lamps; the majority of these stalls, in the winter time, are sheltered from the wind by a screen made out of an old clothes horse covered with tarpaulin. The cough-drop stand, with its distilling apparatus, the tin worm curling nearly the whole length of the tray, has but lately been introduced. The nut-stall is fitted up with a target at the back of it. The ginger-beer stand may be seen in almost every street, with its French-polished mahogany frame and bright polished taps, and its foot-bath-shaped reservoir of water, to cleanse the glasses. The hot elder wine stand, with its bright brass urns, is equally popular.

The sellers of plum-pudding, 'cake, a penny a slice', sweetmeats, cough-drops, pin-cushions, jewellery, chimney ornaments, tea and tablespoons, make use of a table covered over, some with old newspapers, or a piece of oil-cloth, upon which are exposed their articles for sale.

London Labour and the London Poor, 1851

Naples

J. W. GOETHE 1749–1832

There is no season when one is not surrounded on all sides by victuals. The Neapolitan not only enjoys his food, but insists that it be attractively displayed for sale. In Santa Lucia the fish are placed on a layer of green leaves, and each category – rock lobsters, oysters, clams and small mussels – has a clean, pretty basket to itself. But nothing is more carefully planned than the display of meat, which, since their appetite is stimulated by the periodic fast day, is particularly coveted by the common people.

In the butchers' stalls, quarters of beef, veal or mutton are never hung up without having the unfatty parts of the flanks and legs heavily gilded.

Several days in the year and especially the Christmas holidays are famous for their orgies of gluttony. At such times a general *cocagna* is celebrated, in which five hundred thousand people vow to outdo each other. The Toledo and other streets and squares are decorated most appetizingly; vegetables, raisins, melons and figs are piled high in their stalls; huge paternosters of gilded sausages, tied with red ribbons, and capons with little red flags stuck in their rumps are suspended in festoons across the streets overhead. I was assured that, not counting those which people had fattened in their own homes, thirty thousand of them had been sold. Crowds of donkeys with vegetables, capons and young lambs are driven to market, and never in my life have I seen so many eggs in one pile as I have seen here in several places.

Not only is all this eaten, but every year a policeman, accompanied by a trumpeter, rides through the city and announces in every square and at every crossroad how many thousand oxen, calves, lambs, pigs, etc., the Neapolitans have consumed. The crowd show tremendous joy at the high figures, and each of them recalls with pleasure his share in this consumption.

So far as flour-and-milk dishes are concerned, which our cooks prepare so excellently and in so many different ways, though people here lack our well-equipped kitchens and like to make short work of their cooking, they are catered for in two ways. The macaroni, the dough of which is made from a very fine flour, kneaded into various shapes and then boiled, can be bought everywhere and in all the shops for very little money. As a rule, it is simply cooked in water and seasoned with grated cheese. Then, at almost every corner of the main streets, there are pastry-cooks with their frying pans of sizzling oil, busy, especially on fast days, preparing pastry and fish on the spot for anyone who wants it. Their sales are fabulous, for thousands and thousands of people carry their lunch and supper home, wrapped in a little piece of paper.

Italian Journey 1786–88, TRANS. W. H. Auden
and Elizabeth Mayer, 1962

Quincy Market, Boston
ROBERT B. PARKER 19??–

Quincy Market is old and lovingly restored. It is vast and made of granite blocks. Along each side of the long centre aisle there were stalls selling yoghurt with fruit topping, kielbasy on a roll with sauerkraut, lobster rolls, submarine sandwiches, French bread, country pâté, Greek salad, sweet and sour chicken, baklava, cookies, bagels, oysters, cheese, fresh fruit on a stick, ice cream, cheese cake, barbecued chicken, pizza, doughnuts, cookies, galantine of duck, roast beef sandwiches with chutney on fresh baked bread, bean sprouts, dried peaches, jumbo cashews, and other nuts. There were also butcher-shops, cheese stores, a place that sells custom ground coffee, fruit stands, and a place that sells Korean ginseng root . . . We stopped and bought two skewers of fresh fruit and melon, and ate them as we walked.

Looking for Rachel Wallace, 1980

War and Rationing

❦

The Scots Invade England (1327)
JEAN DE FROISSART 1337–C. 1410

The Scots are a bold, hardy people, very experienced in war. When
they cross the border they advance sixty to seventy miles in a day and
night, which would seem astonishing to anyone ignorant of their
customs. The explanation is that, on their expeditions into England,
they all come on horseback, except the irregulars who follow on foot.
The knights and squires are mounted on fine, strong horses and the
commoners on small ponies. Because they have to pass over the wild
hills of Northumberland, they bring no baggage-carts and so carry no
supplies of bread or wine. So frugal are they that their practice in war is
to subsist for a long time on underdone meat, without bread, and to
drink river-water, without wine. This does away with the need for pots
and pans, for they cook their meat in the hides of the cattle it is taken
from, after skinning. Since they are sure to find plenty of cattle in the
country they pass through, the only things they take with them are a
large flat stone placed between the saddle and the saddle-cloth and a
bag of oatmeal strapped behind. When they have lived so long on half-
cooked meat that their stomachs feel weak and hollow, they lay these
stones on a fire and, mixing a little of their oatmeal with water, they
sprinkle the thin paste on the hot stone and make a small cake, rather
like a wafer, which they eat to help their digestion. Hence it is not
surprising that they can travel faster than other armies.

Froissart Chronicles, ED., TRANS. Geoffrey Brereton, 1968

The Siege of Paris
EDMOND 1822–96 AND JULES 1830–70
GONCOURT

Saturday, 31 December [1870]
In the streets of Paris, death passes death, the undertaker's waggon
drives past the hearse. Outside the Madeleine today I saw three coffins,
each covered with a soldier's greatcoat with a wreath of immortelles
on top.

Out of curiosity I went into Roos's, the English butcher's shop on
the Boulevard Haussmann, where I saw all sorts of weird remains. On
the wall, hung in a place of honour, was the skinned trunk of young
Pollux, the elephant at the Zoo; and in the midst of nameless meats
and unusual horns, a boy was offering some camel's kidneys for sale.

The master-butcher was perorating to a group of women: 'It's forty
francs a pound for the fillet and the trunk. . . . Yes, forty francs. . . .
You think that's dear? But I assure you I don't know how I'm going to
make anything out of it. I was counting on three thousand pounds of
meat and he has only yielded two thousand, three hundred. . . . The
feet, you want to know the price of the feet? It's twenty francs. . . . For
the other pieces, it ranges from eight francs to forty. . . . But let me
recommend the black pudding. As you know, the elephant's blood is
the richest there is. His heart weighed twenty-five pounds. . . . And
there's onion, ladies, in my black pudding.'

I fell back on a couple of larks which I carried off for my lunch
tomorrow.

Saturday, 7 January [1871]
The sufferings of Paris during the siege? A joke for two months. In the
third month the joke went sour. Now nobody finds it funny any more,
and we are moving fast towards starvation or, for the moment at least,
towards an epidemic of gastritis. Half a pound of horsemeat, including
the bones, which is two people's ration for three days, is lunch for an
ordinary appetite. The prices of edible chickens or pies put them out of
reach. Failing meat, you cannot fall back on vegetables; a little turnip
costs eight sous and you have to pay seven francs for a pound of
onions. Nobody talks about butter any more, and every other sort of
fat except candle-fat and axle-grease has disappeared too. As for the
two staple items of the diet of the poorer classes – potatoes and cheese

– cheese is just a memory, and you have to have friends in high places to obtain potatoes at twenty francs a bushel. The greater part of Paris is living on coffee, wine, and bread.

Pages from the Goncourt Journals, ED., TRANS. Robert Baldick, 1962

Russian Soldiers
ALEXANDRE DUMAS 1802–70

A Frenchman would be appalled by what a Russian soldier has to endure in this mountain warfare, living on sodden black bread, sleeping in the snow, dragging himself and his equipment over trackless wastes of granite crags. And what a war! A war with no quarter, no prisoners; where a wounded man is left for dead, and where his fiercest enemies collect human heads. (The mildest of them cut off their victims' hands.)

Our men have had something of the sort in Algeria, apart from the differences of the terrain, but they were well paid, well fed, well clad, and they had some hope of advancement, slight though it might be. In any case, that war was over in two or three years. With the Russians the war has been going on for forty years!

In the field, the Russian's daily ration is a bowl of cabbage soup, a pound and a half of bread, and a portion of dried meat, called *tchi*, which is prepared in advance. One speculator had a bright idea, and instead of making *tchi* from beef in the usual way he started making it from crows. Crows abound in Russia. They fly round in their hundreds, thousands, millions and are as tame as pigeons. In some districts of Little Russia, people use them to hatch out hen's eggs! No Russian will eat a pigeon, which he regards as sacred. He will not eat a crow, either, but for a different reason. Crows are considered unclean, unfit for human consumption.

As any hunter knows, the meat of crows makes excellent soup, and the *tchi* made from crows was probably much better than that made from beef, especially since, in Russia, 'beef' is the flesh of old cows. But the story had got around, and because of this prejudice, the Russian soldiers, throughout one campaign, threw away their *tchi* and lived as best they could on bread and cabbage soup.

The soldier is often cheated by his officers, too. One young soldier who had fought in the Crimea told me that his regiment was officially entitled to consume a bullock per day. For four or five hundred men, this was not excessive! So the captain bought a bullock in the province of Kaluga, and when the long march began, the animal brought up the rear. It was still in perfect health next day and for many days afterwards. Whenever an official came on a visit of inspection, there were the captain's accounts showing the purchase of one bullock per day, as instructed, and there was the bullock, large as life, 'ready for the men's supper tonight'.

So it went on until, two and a half months later, they reached Kherson. Perhaps you may think that at last the men had a chance to eat their beef? Not a bit of it! The captain sold the bullock, and since (unlike the men), it had been well fed every day, he made a handsome profit!

Adventures in the Caucasus, 1888

The Crimea

ALEXIS SOYER 1809–58

After we had examined this kitchen, Miss Nightingale prepared to leave us. I promised to call upon her the following day, to go round the wards, and see the dinners served.

At half-past six the next morning I was in the kitchen. The soldiers were at that hour making the coffee and tea for breakfast. I went with the serjeant on duty to inspect the quality of the meat, the quantity allowed, and the place of distribution. I found the meat of a very inferior quality, the method of distribution too complicated. When the weight of the quantity allowed was explained to me I found it correct. I was at first much puzzled at finding that some patients upon full diet received three quarters of a pound, some half a pound, and some a quarter of a pound of meat, accordingly as they were placed upon full, half, or quarter diet allowance – a system unavoidable in a hospital, but which would deceive the best cook. On some days, in providing for a hundred patients, this could make a difference of from ten to twenty pounds of meat, according to the number of half or quarter diets. Yet the same quantity of soup would nevertheless be required.

I made a note of this, and next perceived that every mess took their meat separately. Some messes numbered fifteen, twenty, or even thirty. The meat was spitted upon a rough piece of wood about two feet long, and then tied as tight as possible with a strong cord. Although this was a very bad method, I did not choose to interfere, as it was important for me to show them the evil effects of their system, and ensure a reform by pointing out a better. We then went to the store-rooms, and looked over what the contractor called the mixed vegetables, though they were principally of one kind, and half of these unfit for use. After having seen the rations weighed, I sent orders to the cooks not to commence operations until I arrived. We examined all kinds of preserved meats, soups, sweetmeats, &c. I next went to see the poultry, which I found of very inferior quality, consisting principally of old fowls, badly plucked and drawn. The gizzards, heads, and feet, which make such good broth, were thrown away. Mr. Bailey, whom I had not yet seen, then entered. When I had explained what we had already done, and the plan it would be most advisable to adopt for the future, he promised to bring the contractor, that we might talk the matter over. I examined the bread, which was very good indeed . . .

It was then noon, and about dinner-time. So I returned to the kitchen, where all was in the greatest confusion. Such a noise I never heard before. They were waiting for their soup and meat, and using coarse language, without making the least progress in the distribution. The market at old Billingsgate, during the first morning sale, was nothing compared to this military row. Each man had two tin cans for the soup. They kept running about and knocking against each other, in most admirable disorder. Such confusion, thought I, is enough to kill a dozen patients daily. As a natural consequence, several must go without anything; as, owing to the confusion, some of the orderly waiters get more and others less than their allowance. Any attempt to alter this at the time, would have been as wise as endeavouring to stop the current of the Bosphorus. As I did not wish to lose the chance of seeing the rations served out in the wards, I went for Dr. Macgregor, and we called for Mr. Milton – but the latter had not returned. I then fetched Miss Nightingale, and we went through the wards. The process of serving out the rations, though not quite such a noisy scene as that I had before witnessed, was far from being perfect. In the first place, the patients were allowed to eat the meat before the soup. As I was confident that this could not be by the doctor's order, I asked the reason. The reply was, 'we have only one plate.' (What they called a plate, was a round and deep tin dish, which held a pound of meat and a pint of soup.) I therefore recommended them to cut the meat as usual into small pieces, and pour the pint of boiling soup over it. This method had the advantage of keeping the meat hot.

'It will enable the patients,' I said, 'to eat both the soup and meat warm, instead of cold – the daily practice, in consequence of the slow process of carving.'

'Very true,' said Dr. Macgregor. 'Nay, more, the soup will comfort and dispose the stomach for the better digestion of the meat and potatoes. When the men are very hungry, they will often swallow their food without properly masticating it, and the meat is also probably tough.'

We then tasted both the soup and meat. The former was thin and without seasoning; the latter, mutton, tough and tasteless. The potatoes were watery. All these defects I promised to rectify the next day. We proceeded to a ward where they complained bitterly that the meat was never done; in fact, it was quite raw, and then of course the cook was blamed.

'Now,' said I to Miss Nightingale, 'I will wager anything that we shall find some parts very well done, and some, no doubt, too much done, though it is all cooked in the same caldron.'

'How do you account for that, Monsieur Soyer? is it owing to the bad quality of the meat?'

'Not at all; that may come from the same sheep, and yet vary.'

At another mess, the meat was well done; a small piece at the end only being over-cooked.

'I will explain this to you, madam,' said I. 'I remarked this morning that the man tied all the joints together very tight, after having put them upon a 'skewer,' as he calls it, almost as large as a wooden leg. The consequence is, that when the meat is thrown into boiling water, it is not properly done; the meat swells, and it is impossible for the heat or the water even to get at it.'

'Ah, I noticed that several of the men did exactly as you say this morning,' said Miss Nightingale. 'The parts which are well done were placed loose upon the stick; and this explains the mystery – but I shall alter that to-morrow.'

Culinary Campaign, 1857

Lord Berners
NANCY MITFORD 1904–73

There is something magic about all of Faringdon, and Lord Berners himself, in his skull cap, looks not unlike a magician, but perhaps the greatest, most amazing conjuring tricks are reserved for the dining room. In this pleasant sunny white room, scattered with large silver-gilt birds and wonderful Sèvres and Dresden china, a standard of culinary perfection has been maintained through the darkest days of war. Cook or no cook, raw materials or no raw materials, a succession of utterly delicious courses would somehow waft themselves to the sideboard, and the poor Londoner, starved, or sated with Spam, would see sights and taste tastes he had long ago forgotten to believe in.

A Talent to Annoy, 1986

Smoked Salmon in the Trenches
SIEGFRIED SASSOON 1886–1967

There was a continuous rumble and grumble of bombardment while we were going up with the rations on the day after I got back from leave. As we came over the hill beyond Bray the darkness toward Albert was lit with the glare of explosions that blinked and bumped. Dottrell remarked that there seemed to be a bit of a mix-up, which was his way of saying that he didn't altogether like the look of things that evening.

When we arrived at the ration dump the quartermaster-sergeant told us that the battalion had been standing to for the past two hours. It was possible that the Boches might be coming across. 'C' company was in the front line. The noise was subsiding, so I went up there, leaving Joe to pay his nightly call at battalion headquarters.

Stumbling and splashing up a communication trench known as Canterbury Avenue, with the parcel of smoked salmon stuffed into my haversack, I felt that smoked salmon wasn't much of an antidote for people who had been putting up with all that shell-fire. Still, it was something. . . . Round the next corner I had to flatten myself against the wall of that wet ditch, for someone was being carried down on a stretcher. An extra stretcher-bearer walking behind told me it was Corporal Price of 'C' company. 'A rifle-grenade got him . . . looks as if he's a goner. . . .' His face was only a blur of white in the gloom; then, with the drumming of their boots on the trench-boards, Corporal Price left the War behind him. I remembered him vaguely as a quiet little man in Durley's platoon. No use offering *him* smoked salmon, I thought, as I came to the top of Canterbury Avenue, and, as usual, lost my way in the maze of saps and small trenches behind the front line. Watling Street was the one I wanted. Finding one's way about the trenches in the dark was no easy job when one didn't live up there. I passed the dug-outs of the support company at Maple Redoubt. Candles and braziers glinted through the curtain-flaps and voices muttered gruffly from the little underground cabins (which would have been safer if they had been deeper down in the earth). Now and again there was the splitting crack of a rifle-shot from the other side, or a five-nine shell droned serenely across the upper air to burst with a hollow bang; voluminous reverberations rolled along the valley. The shallow blanching flare of a rocket gave me a glimpse of the mounds of bleached sandbags on the Redoubt. Its brief whiteness died downward, leaving a dark world; chilly gusts met me at corners, piping drearily through crannies of the parapet; very different was the voice of the wind that sang in the cedar tree in the garden at home. . . .

Pushing past the gas-blanket, I blundered down the stairs to the company headquarters' dug-out. There were twenty steps to that earthy smelling den, with its thick wooden props down the middle and its precarious yellow candlelight casting wobbling shadows. Barton was sitting on a box at the rough table, with a tin mug and a half-empty whisky bottle. His shoulders were hunched and the collar of his trench-coat was turned up to his ears. Dick was in deep shadow, lying on a bunk (made of wire-netting with empty sandbags on it). It was a morose cramped little scene, loathsome to live in as it is hateful to remember. The air was dank and musty; lumps of chalk fell from the 'ceiling' at intervals. There was a bad smell of burnt grease, and the frizzle of something frying in the adjoining kennel that was called the kitchen was the only evidence of ordinary civilization – that and Barton's shining pince-nez, and the maps and notebooks which were on the table. . . .

Smoked salmon from Piccadilly Circus was something after all. It cheered Barton immensely. He unpacked it; he sniffed it; and no doubt it brought the lights of London into his mind.

'Gosh, if only this war would stop!' he exclaimed. 'I'd be off to Scott's oyster-bar like a streak of light and you'd never get me away from it again!'

He held the smoked salmon under Dick's nose and told him what a lucky young devil he was to be going on leave in two or three days' time. Dick wasn't as bright as usual; he'd got a rotten headache, he said. Barton told him he'd better let Ormand go out with the wiring-party instead of him. But he said no, he'd be all right by then, and Ormand had been out last night. Barton told me they'd had a lively time with the C.O. lately: 'He gave orders for the whole of the front line to be re-wired; we've been at it every night, but he came up this morning with his big periscope, strafing like hell about the gaps along by the mine-craters. He says the wire isn't strong enough to stop a wheelbarrow – why a wheelbarrow God knows!' He laughed, rather hysterically; his nerves were on edge, and no wonder. . . . For, as he said, what with the muck everything was in since the snow melted, and being chivvied by Kinjack, and then being 'crumped' all the afternoon, life hadn't been worth living lately. The odd thing was that good old Barton seemed equally concerned because the snowy weather had prevented me from having any hunting while on leave. And Dick agreed that it had been very rough on me.

Mansfield and Ormand came in at that moment; these two were very good friends, and they always seemed to be cheering one another up. They had left Durley on duty in the front trench. They wanted to hear all about the 'shows' I had been to in London, but I couldn't tell them anything (though I wished I could) for I hadn't been to a theatre, and it was no use talking about the Symphony Concert at Queen's Hall, which now made me feel rather a prig.

Dick was still lying in this dark corner when I said goodnight and groped my way up the steps, leaving them to make the most of the smoked salmon. Going down Canterbury Avenue it was so pitch black that I couldn't see my own hand; once or twice a flare went up in the spectral region on the shoulder of the hill behind me; lit by that unearthly glare the darkness became desolation.

Memoirs of a Fox-Hunting Man, 1928

From the Plague Journal
IAN DUHIG 1954–

I have been asked to write about our food.
I remember nights spent hulling ration-rice,
soya beans pressed dry before they got to us,
boiling black-market sweetfish to hide their smell
from our Neighbourhood Monitor. We ate everything;
reed-root, pigweed, tugwort, bar-weed –
these may not be the scientific names.
We smuggled grated radish and bracken-sprouts
past our Neighbourhood Monitor once he started fainting,
propped beneath his Government banderoles:
    'There's Always Space to Plant a Pumpkin!'
    'The War is Only Just Beginning!'

Later our food became medicine:
dried fig-grubs for the incontinence;
ant-lions in saké for the headaches;
leek-leaves and cucumber for the burns.
I sold my son's thousand-stitch belt
for peaches and eggs which I mashed and strained,
mashed and strained. Still my children died,
the last little Tadashi setting his weasel-traps
of bamboo and abalone shells round the pond
he'd stocked with a few tiny carp fry.

That is all I remember about our food.

The Bradford Count, 1991

Eat The Weevils
J. G. BALLARD 1930–

When Jim and Mr Maxted returned with the rations to G Block the
prisoners were waiting silently with their plates and mess-tins. They
stood on the steps, the bare-chested men with knobbed shoulders and
birdcage ribs, their faded wives in shabby frocks, watching without

expression as if about to be presented with a corpse. At the head of the queue were Mrs Pearce and her son, followed by the missionary couples who spent all day hunting for food.

Hundreds of flies hovered in the steam that rose from the metal pails of cracked wheat and sweet potatoes. As he heaved on the wooden handles Jim winced with pain, not from the strain of pulling the cart, but from the heat of the stolen sweet potato inside his shirt. As long as he remained doubled up no one would see the potato, and he put on a pantomime of grimaces and groans.

'Oh, oh . . . oh, my God . . .'

'Worthy of the Lunghua Players, Jim.' Mr Maxted had watched him remove the potato from the pail as they left the kitchens, but he never objected. Crouching forward, Jim abandoned the cart to the missionaries. He ran up the steps, past the Vincents, who stood plates in hand – it never occurred to them, nor to Jim, that they should bring his plate with them. He dived through the curtain into his cubicle and dropped the steaming potato under his mat, hoping that the damp straw would smother the vapour. He seized his plate, and darted back to the foyer to take his place at the head of the queue. Mr Maxted had already served the Reverend and Mrs Pearce, but Jim shouldered aside their son. He held out his plate and received a ladle of boiled wheat and a second sweet potato which he had pointed out to Mr Maxted within moments of leaving the kitchens.

Returning to his bunk, Jim relaxed for the first time. He drew the curtain and lay back, the warm plate like a piece of the sun against his chest. He felt drowsy, but at the same time light-headed with hunger. He rallied himself with the thought that there might be an American air raid that afternoon – who did he want to win? The question was important.

Jim cupped his hands over the sweet potato. He was almost too hungry to enjoy the grey pith, but he gazed at the photograph of the man and woman outside Buckingham Palace, hoping that his parents, wherever they were, also had an extra potato.

When the Vincents returned with their rations Jim sat up and folded back the curtain so that he could examine their plates. He liked to watch Mrs Vincent eating her meals. Keeping a close eye on her, Jim studied the cracked wheat. The starchy grains were white and swollen, indistinguishable from the weevils that infested these warehouse sweepings. In the early years of the camp everyone pushed the weevils to one side, or flicked them through the nearest window, but now Jim carefully husbanded them. Often there were more than a hundred insects in three rows around the rim of Jim's plate, though recently even their number was in decline. 'Eat the weevils,' Dr Ransome had told him, and he did so, although everyone else washed them away. But there was protein in them, a fact that Mr Maxted seemed to find depressing when Jim informed him of it.

After counting the eighty-seven weevils – their numbers, Jim calculated, were falling less steeply than the ration – he stirred them into the cracked wheat, an animal feed grown in northern China, and swallowed the six spoonfuls. Giving himself a breather, he waited for Mrs Vincent to begin her sweet potato.

'Must you, Jim?' Mr Vincent asked. No taller than Jim, the stockbroker and former amateur jockey sat on his bunk beside his ailing son. With his black hair and lined yellow face like a squeezed lemon, he reminded Jim of Basie, but Mr Vincent had never come to terms with Lunghua. 'You'll miss this camp when the war's over. I wonder how you'll take to school in England.'

'It might be a bit strange,' Jim admitted, finishing the last of the weevils. He felt sensitive about his ragged clothes and his determined efforts to stay alive. He wiped his plate clean with his finger, and remembered a favourite phrase of Basie's. 'All the same, Mr Vincent, the best teacher is the university of life.'

Mrs Vincent lowered her spoon. 'Jim, could we finish our meal? We've heard your views on the university of life.'

'Right. But we should eat the weevils, Mrs Vincent.'

'I know, Jim. Dr Ransome told you so.'

'He said we need the protein.'

'Dr Ransome is right. We should all eat the weevils.'

Hoping to brighten the conversation, Jim asked: 'Mrs Vincent, do you believe in vitamins?'

Mrs Vincent stared at her plate. She spoke with true despair. 'Strange child . . .'

Empire of the Sun, 1984

How to Use Nature's Larder
VICOMTE DE MAUDUIT

The object of this book is to show where to seek and how to use Nature's larder, which in time of peace and plenty people overlook or ignore.

During the war it will serve to relieve some of the strain on the nations's food supply and will teach those of us who will turn to the country-side for immunity from direct war destruction how to maintain life in the case of difficulties with regard to the carriage and distribution of food.

And when Peace will again come on Earth, the people of Britain, already made conscious through food rationing that meals no longer consist of a hot and then cold 'joint with two veg.,' will find this book a practical and valuable guide to better things.

All those possessing a roof in the country together with the necessary sticks of furniture and apparels of clothing will be able, if armed with a copy of this book, to live in comfort, in plenty, and in health even if all banks, all shops, and all markets be closed for indefinite periods.

Country-dwellers, campers, caravanners, hikers, and the necessitous will find in each of the following pages something to stir their interest in what they see all around them, and will thus be led into the fascinating and satisfying secrets of self-sufficiency in the necessities of life.

They Can't Ration These, 1940

Savoury Rice
STELLA GIBBONS 1902–80

'It is Extremely Filling,' says Miss Gibbons. 'It's cheap, and men love it.'

METHOD: Fry a clove of garlic in margarine until it is brown. Then put into the pan a breakfast-cupful of cooked rice that has been washed before cooking (more rice can be used if you want more, of course) and keep on stirring it until it has absorbed the fat. Then put in curry

433

powder to taste, the pulp and seeds of three tomatoes, and a third of a cupful of currants and sultanas (well washed, of course). A dash of salt, pepper and lemon-juice improves it. (You need to be careful and choice with the seasoning, or there is a risk of the dish being merely rich and sticky.)

If the average housewife is scared of garlic she can use onion.

The dish goes well with a plain salad of lettuce leaves dressed sharply with vinegar and salt (but you might as well say a plain salad of gold leaf with the price lettuces can be during wartime).

A Kitchen Goes to War. A Ration-Time Cookery Book with 150
Recipes contributed by Famous People, 1940

Raiding The Officers' Galley
GEORGE MELLY 1926–

I had a sometime affair with a Corporal of the Marines who shared my watch on the Quarter Deck, but this was only in the middle watch and mostly, from his point of view anyway, to allay boredom. I think he really preferred our other pastime, which was to raid the officers' galley for bacon, eggs and sausages and fry-up on our electric fire laid dangerously on its back.

Rum, Bum and Concertina, 1977

Breakfast in the Dugout
BRIG. GEN. F. P. CROZIER 1879–1937

George and I have our breakfast together in the one and only dugout, now almost collapsed. Maguirty makes the eggs and bacon taste wonderful, while the jam and tea go down like one o'clock. George is a bit off his feed I notice, probably because eggs and bacon, as well as jam and tea, do not mix with unlimited whisky at 10 a.m. as a rule; but I make up for him!

A Brass Hat in No Man's Land, 1930

Soyer's Culinary Emblem of Peace
ALEXIS SOYER 1809–58

War having ceased, the camp bore the appearance of a monster banqueting-hall. 'We have done fighting,' said every one, 'so let us terminate the campaign by feasting, lay down our victorious but murderous weapons, and pick up those more useful and restorative arms – the knife and fork.'

'What can I do,' said I to myself, 'for an event of historical importance?' Neither Mr. Crockford nor the captain could assist me, when an idea struck me: – 'If you can't give me an idea,' said I to my friends, 'at any rate lend me a dish.'

'That I will,' said the captain.

'Recollect, I want a large one.'

'You had the largest for your salad yesterday.'

'That one will do; it will hold enough for twenty-five persons.'

'Then here goes,' said I, writing. 'To-day I shall dress in it the *Macedoine Lüdersienne à l'Alexandre II.*'

'A very good name in honour of the event,' said Mr. Crockford. 'But pray, of what is it to be composed?'

'Oh! for that,' said I, 'if I were to implore the Genius of Gastronomy, from Lucullus to Apicius and Vitellius, or Vatel to Ude and Carême, I could get nothing from them but inspiration; while what I require is something substantial, and not artificial. It strikes me that a word from you to your head man at Kadikoi (as you will not be there to-morrow) would do more for me in a few minutes than the whole of those defunct celebrities, whom I am not now inclined to trouble upon so material a subject. Pray give me *carte blanche* to get anything you may have and I require for the composition of this modern Babylon, which must be constructed upon a base sufficiently strong to resist the joint attack of the heads of three of the most powerful armies in the world, and only be destroyed after having conquered the conqueror's *place d'armes*, the stomach, so called in military parlance.'

The order was readily given by my friend Mr. Crockford, and we then lay down to sleep, being both completely exhausted with the fatigues of what was called a day of pleasure. We had hardly closed our eyelids, when morning caused them to be reopened; so up we got. My friend started for Constantinople, and I for headquarters. I started immediately – bought a few things in Balaklava market – called at

Crockford's store at Donnybrook, which I ransacked and despoiled of
condiments of every description. Instead of going direct to headquarters I changed my mind and went home to prepare, having
decided, as the time was so short, to produce one good dish only,
instead of several small and insignificant ones. This was, however, to
be worthy of the occasion. I was well aware that General Codrington's
cook, under the liberal management and command of Captain
Ponsonby, would turn out something worthy of the event. Upon
arriving at my hut, I sent two of my cooks to assist him, despatched my
groom on horseback to Kamiesch for various things, and then began
the construction of my *Lüdersienne* upon the lid of my new field-
stoves, the dish I had brought from the *Alar* being too small.

My novel dish was completed, and carried to headquarters by two
soldiers; and at a quarter to two I personally placed my culinary
wonder upon the table. It was called

SOYER'S CULINARY EMBLEM OF PEACE
The Macédoine Lüdersienne à l'Alexandre II.

This monster dish was composed of –

12 boxes of preserved lobsters	1 bottle Indian pickles
2 cases of preserved lampreys	1 bottle pickled French beans
2 cases of preserved sardines	2 bottles pickled mushrooms
2 bottles of preserved anchovies	½ bottle pickled mangoes
1 case of preserved caviar	2 bottles of pickled French
1 case of preserved sturgeon	truffles
1 case of preserved thunny	2 cases of preserved peas
2 cases of preserved oysters	2 cases of preserved mixed
1 pound of fresh prawns	vegetables
4 pounds of turbot clouté	4 dozen cabbage lettuces
12 Russian pickled cucumbers	100 eggs
4 bottles preserved olives	2 bottles of preserved
1 bottle mixed pickles	cockscombs.

The sauce was composed of six bottles of salad oil, one of Tarragon
vinegar, half a bottle of Chili Vinegar, two boxes of preserved cream
(whipped), four ounces of sugar, six eschalots, salt, cayenne pepper,
mustard, and a quarter of an ounce of Oriental herbs which are quite
unknown in England.

Culinary Campaign, 1857

Admiralty Regulations, 1757

And whereas some of the eldest pursers of the Royal Navy at some Time since presented a Memorial in behalf of themselves, and the rest of their Brethren, representing that it had been their constant Practice, as often as their respective Ships were victualled with Fresh Meat, to boil such a Quantity of Greens and Roots with it, as to give sufficient Satisfaction to the Men; and that, to give them no Room to murmur on Account of their Saving of Pease by boiling with Fresh Meat, to boil Pease for their Mondays Dinners, besides the allowed Oatmeal for Breakfasts; and proposing, if the Greens and Roots furnished by them should be judged sufficient for the Men, to increase the same to any Quantity that should be prescribed; all Commanders are to take Care, that their respective Pursers do comply with what is contained in the said Memorial, by furnishing a sufficient Quantity of Roots and Greens to Seamen, with their Fresh Meat; or to report to us, if they fail therein.

quoted in *The Englishman's Food*, 1959

The Flying Bum: 1944
WILLIAM PLOMER 1903–73

In the vegetarian guest-house
All was frolic, feast and fun,
Eager voices were enquiring
'Are the nettle cutlets done?'
Peals of vegetarian laughter,
Husky wholesome wholemeal bread,
Will the evening finish with a
Rush of cocoa to the head?

Yes, you've guessed; it's Minnie's birthday,
Hence the frolic, hence the feast.
Are there calories in custard?
There are vitamins in yeast.
Kate is here and Tom her hubby,
Ex-commissioner for oaths,

She is mad on Christian Science,
Parsnip flan he simply loathes.

And Mr Croaker, call him Arthur,
Such a keen philatelist,
Making sheep's-eyes at Louisa
(After dinner there'll be whist) –
Come, sit down, the soup is coming,
All of docks and darnels made,
Drinks a health to dear old Minnie
In synthetic lemonade.

Dentures champing juicy lettuce,
Champing macerated bran,
Oh the imitation rissoles!
Oh the food untouched by man!
Look, an imitation sausage
Made of monkey-nuts and spice,
Prunes tonight and semolina,
Wrinkled prunes, unpolished rice.

Yards of guts absorbing jellies,
Bellies filling up with nuts,
Carbohydrates jostling proteins
Out of intestinal ruts;
Peristalsis calls for roughage,
Haulms and fibres, husks and grit,
Nature's way to open bowels,
Maybe – let them practise it.

'Hark, I hear an air-raid warning!'
'Take no notice, let 'em come.'
'Who'll say grace?' 'Another walnut?'
'Listen, what's that distant hum?'
'Bomb or no bomb,' stated Minnie,
'Lips unsoiled by beef or beer
We shall use to greet our Maker
When he sounds the Great All-Clear.'

When the flying bomb exploded
Minnie's wig flew off her pate,
Half a curtain, like a tippet,
Wrapped itself round bony Kate,

Plaster landed on Louisa,
Tom fell headlong on the floor,
And a spurt of lukewarm custard
Lathered Mr Croaker's jaw.

All were spared by glass and splinters
But, the loud explosion past,
Greater was the shock impending
Even than the shock of blast –
Blast we veterans know as freakish
Gave this feast its final course,
Planted bang upon the table
A lightly roasted rump of horse.

Collected Poems, 1960

The Beginning of the Siege of Paris, 1870
EDMOND 1822–96 AND JULES 1830–70
GONCOURT

Saturday, 1 October
Horse-meat is sneaking slyly into the diet of the people of Paris. The day before yesterday, Pélagie brought home a piece of fillet which, on account of its suspicious appearance, I did not eat. Today, at Peters' restaurant, I was served some roast beef that was watery, devoid of fat, and streaked with white sinews; and my painter's eye noticed that it was a dark red colour very different from the pinky red of beef. The waiter could give me only a feeble assurance that this horse was beef.

Monday, 10 October
This morning I went to get a card for my meat ration. It seemed to me that I was looking at one of those queues in the great Revolution which my poor old cousin Cornélie used to describe to me, in that patient line of heterogeneous individuals, of ragged old women, of men in peaked caps, of small shopkeepers, cooped up in those improvised offices, those whitewashed rooms, where you recognized, sitting round a table, omnipotent in their uniforms of officers of the National Guard and supreme dispensers of your food, your far from honest tradesmen.

439

I came away with a piece of blue paper, a typographical curiosity for future Goncourts and times to come, which entitles me and my housekeeper to buy every day two rations of raw meat or two portions of food cooked in the municipal canteens. There are coupons up to 14 November: a good many things may happen between now and then.

24 September
In the capital of fresh food and early vegetables, it is really ironical to come across Parisians consulting one another in front of the displays of tinned goods in the windows of delicatessen shops or cosmopolitan groceries. Finally they go in, and come out carrying tins of *Boiled Mutton*, *Boiled Beef*, etc., every possible and impossible variety of preserved meat and vegetable, things that nobody would ever have thought might one day become the food of the rich city of Paris.

Pages from the Goncourt Journals, ED., TRANS. Robert Baldick, 1962

Snoek Piquante
SUSAN COOPER 1935–

In October 1947, with the butter and meat rations newly cut, the bacon ration halved, restaurants' food supplies dwindling, and potato rationing on the way, the hungry British first heard the word 'snoek'. Ten million tins of it from South Africa were to replace Portuguese sardines, whose import was restricted by exchange troubles; the new fish, said Mr Strachey, would go on points. 'I have never met a snoek,' he added, with the Ministerial waggishness that always holds a faint sense of doom, 'so I cannot tell you much about it. It is long and slender, weighing up to eighteen pounds.'

The name, of course, was a gift. Before it even arrived in the shops this unfortunate fish was seized with cries of delight by cartoonists, sub-editors, music-hall comedians, and Members of Parliament; not least when one early consignment was found to be packed in salt, and inedible except as fish paste. Research revealed that the snoek was a large, ferocious, tropical fish, like a barracuda; that it was dangerous to bathers, had rows of fearsome teeth, and when displeased hissed like a snake and barked like a dog. A Lieutenant-Colonel (retd) wrote a long letter to *The Times* about snoek fishing, ending: 'I have the greatest respect for this notable fighter as an article of diet. It tastes like a mackerel, only more so.' *The Times*, infected by the gentle delirium, headed his letter: 'Hunting the Snoek.'

Wholesalers did not welcome snoek; they had already imported a number of tins, off points, and these had not been a success. 'People didn't like it,' said one. 'Tasteless and unpalatable,' said another. 'Abominable stuff.' The Minister, however, had not only spent £857,000 on snoek, but had eaten it: at a picnic, in sandwiches. It was, he said with rash honesty, 'good, palatable, but rather dull.'

In May 1948, when the first large consignment arrived, Dr Edith Summerskill presided at a snoek-tasting party at the Ministry; the Government put up quantities of snoek posters (even, as an Opposition member pointed out, in fishing ports) and published eight remarkable recipes.

Snoek piquante: 4 spring onions, chopped; liquid from snoek; 4 tablespoons vinegar; ½ can snoek, mashed; 2 teaspoons syrup; salt to taste; ½ teaspoon pepper. Cook the onions in the fish liquor and vinegar for five minutes. Add the snoek, syrup, and seasoning and mix well; serve cold with salad . . .

It cost 1s.4½d. for a half-pound tin, and took only one point – thirteen points less than red salmon, five points less than household salmon, and much cheaper than either. But nobody seemed quite clear whether it was being eaten. The crescendo of music-hall jokes rose. 'We can sell every tin,' said Mr Strachey, in October 1948, and arranged to import some more. The *Daily Express* chose twenty-five Mrs Smiths from the telephone directory, rang them all up and asked if they had bought any snoek yet. 'The name frightened me,' said one Mrs Smith. 'Well, if I were *very* hard pushed,' said another. Only two, reported the *Express*, had actually bought a tin: one said it tasted terrible, and the other gave it to the cat. Grocers and distributors alike reported guardedly that snoek was 'not going well'.

The fact was that the housewife, conditioned by shortage, had learnt during the war years to regard any food publicized by the Ministry with fatalistic suspicion. She knew that its quality would probably be low, due to the austerity principle of selecting foods primarily for their capacity to 'go round', and, without the incentive of wartime effort, she was not now disposed to play ball. Also, she disliked the taste of snoek. By the summer of 1949 more than a third of the snoek imported since 1947 was still unsold: 3,270,000 half-pound tins, out of a total of 11,110,400 – with 1,209,000 still to come under existing contracts. The Ministry hopefully put out more recipes: snoek sandwich spread, snoek pasties, snoek with salad. Their leaflets were still going the rounds when in August 1949 two thousand more tons of tinned fish, in 8,960,000 half-pound tins, arrived from Australia to be sold at a shilling a tin. They called it barracuda, but it still tasted like snoek.

The ministry began to wilt. In September 1949 they reduced the price of their South African snoek from 1s. 4½d. to 1s. 3d. a tin. By December the Minister, on a note of affectionate farewell, was referring to it as 'dear old snoek', and claiming that every tin bought from South Africa had been sold without loss. His honest incredulity was even more apparent this time. 'It was eaten, believe it or not. I ate it myself. I must say, I thought it was one of the dullest fish I have ever eaten.'

Three weeks later snoek, with tinned tomatoes and various tinned meats, came off points. The worst privations of austerity were over by then, and decently obscure mists closed round the piles of tins; there were new jokes, this one wasn't needed any more. But eighteen months later, quiet among the junketings of the Festival of Britain, a mysterious quantity of tinned fish came on to the market, labelled: 'Selected fish food for cats and kittens.' It cost tenpence a tin, and its origins were left muffled in tact. One of the distributors admitted that it might be either snoek or barracuda. 'Cats,' he said, 'are very fond of both.'

Age of Austerity 1945–51, ED. Michael Sissons and Philip French, 1963

Recipes for Squirrel and Rooks
VICOMTE DE MAUDUIT

THE SQUIRREL

This is another great delicacy, the flesh of a squirrel being more tasty and tender than that of a chicken.

GRILLED SQUIRREL

Skin and clean the squirrel, then open it out as you would a chicken for grilling, and grill the squirrel in the same way.

SQUIRREL-TAIL SOUP

The tail, which is put aside after skinning, can be used with haricot beans, onions, and herbs in making a delicious soup.

ROAST SQUIRREL

Squirrel is also most tasty roasted, and this is done in the same way as for roast chicken.

STEWED ROOKS

Clean, draw, and skin the rooks. Make an incision half an inch thick on each side of the spine and remove the piece which is the bitter part of the rook. Put the birds in a casserole with equal parts of water and milk sufficient to cover the rooks, add salt, pepper, 1 sliced onion, 2 sliced turnips, 2 sliced carrots, some chopped mint, or preferably chopped fennel, and stew with the lid on the pan till tender.

They Can't Ration These, 1940

An Excellent Cake for the Troops
EVA TURNER 1892–1990

Eva Turner sends a cake that has had adventures.[1]
Dame Eva Turner was a famous soprano at the time.

IT NEEDS NO EGGS AND MAKES A GOOD-SIZED CAKE

6 oz. margarine	$\frac{3}{4}$ lb. mixed fruit.
6 oz. brown sugar, or	$\frac{3}{4}$ lb. flour.
granulated can be used	$1\frac{1}{2}$ teaspoonsful bi-carbonate of
2 oz. chopped peel (optional).	soda.
	Nearly $\frac{1}{2}$ pint milk.

METHOD: Cream the margarine and sugar. Warm the milk and pour on to the soda. Add the prepared fruit, the milk and the flour. Mix well. Bake in a moderate oven for about 2 hours in a 7-inch cake-tin, or in slabs, for about 1 hour.

A Kitchen Goes to War, 1940

---

[1] A slab of this cake was sent to the Front, travelled round France, chasing the owner, missed him and came back. Other things in the parcel were spoilt, but this cake was good after 10 weeks. It finally went out again and was much appreciated.

Butter

VICOMTE DE MAUDUIT

Goose, beef, and mutton drippings can take the place of butter as spreadings on toast or bread and in cooking, and cooking can entirely be done in fats and oils which after straining can be used over and over again.

They Can't Ration These, 1940

Ice-cream

NORMAN LONGMATE 1926–

Normal ice-cream was unobtainable for most of the war, though some strange concoctions were produced from substitute materials. One London girl munched her way through 'an appalling mess, yellow and lumpy like scrambled eggs, with gritty little lumps of ice embedded in it'. A woman holidaying in Kendal in 1941 recorded in her diary eating some 'very odd-looking ice-cream, with bits of wood-shaving in it'. Next day another entry was needed: 'Feeling seedy, developed biliousness.' When ice-cream did reappear, shortly before the end of the war, I can remember the army office where I was working emptying as scores of young soldiers poured down the road in a body to taste this almost forgotten delicacy.

How We Lived Then, 1971

Horse-meat in Chelsea Manor Street

THEODORA FITZGIBBON 1916–1991

A horse-meat shop opened in Chelsea Manor Street, called the Continental Butcher. At first it was hardly patronized, but later on when food was very scarce there were queues outside all the way past Jax's Stores, which didn't please Jack any . . . The search for food took more and more time, for with the many callers, some who stayed for hours, even days, meals had to be provided. I would make huge pots of onion soup, and when the horseflesh shop opened in Chelsea Manor Street not only the dogs profited, but also ourselves, for I had no scruples about making enormous horse-liver pâtés and jellied tongues. Would everyone's enjoyment have been so great had they known, I wonder? I even made a rook pie one day, which was eagerly devoured.

With Love, 1982

Onions

NORMAN LONGMATE 1926–

One of the first ways in which the war made itself felt to the ordinary housewife was in the sudden disappearance of onions, due to the loss of supplies from the Channel Islands and Britanny. This was, one Scottish journalist felt, 'the one real traumatic lack. Their absence was terribly noticeable.' The taste of this humble vegetable, so long taken for granted, seemed the peak of gastronomic pleasure, partly because with meat rationed by value, not weight, stews, which used the cheapest cuts, were in favour . . .

In February 1941 a one-and-a-half pound onion, raffled among the staff of *The Times*, raised £4 3s. 4d. and in March, when one woman remarked at a first aid lecture in Chelsea that she did not cry if she wore her gas mask when peeling onions, every woman present instantly shouted, 'Where did you get them?' Onions became popular prizes at socials and one wartime Girl Guide in Accrington can still recapture her pride at winning one in a treasure hunt, in honour of which her mother baked a special pie. A Cheshire doctor remembers 'taking home in triumph' the best gift he ever received from a grateful patient: a large Spanish onion. One 'aunt' on *Children's Hour*, wishing 'A Happy Birthday and lots of presents' to one small listener, added, 'I did hear of a lucky girl the other day who was given some onions, but we can't all expect a lovely present like that.' A Worcestershire woman used the same onion in cooking for a month before finally eating it, and in North Queensberry in Scotland one family 'tried putting an onion in a glass of water like a hyacinth bulb and, as the green shoots appeared . . . cut them off and used them for flavouring'. The Minister of Agriculture, announcing in February 1941 a fifteen-fold increase in the onion crop, expressed the hope that

'onions would then be eaten and not talked about', and by 1942 this
expectation was being fulfilled.

How We Lived Then, 1971

Caitlin's Tulip Bulbs
THEODORA FITZGIBBON 1916–1991

One-evening we were at Caitlin and Dylan's studio. The baby was
being fretful, and although the stew was richly going strong, I had got
some eggs from the country and we decided to have an enormous
omelette as well. It is difficult to realize now that we were *always*
hungry. There simply wasn't enough to eat. I whipped the eggs and
looked round for something to fill the omelette with. Our ration that
winter had been one pound of onions per person. I opened several
cupboards and drawers, and in one I found a whole heap of shallots.
Knowing that Caitlin and Dylan had been in Sussex, I thought they
must have brought them up with them. I peeled, sliced and cooked
them, made a magnificent dish and proudly bore it in. We all fell on it,
and then seconds later started to feel not only odd, but sick. Caitlin
questioned me as to where I had found the shallots: 'In that drawer.'
Her reply was terse and to the point. 'You've taken my bloody tulip
bulbs for the window-boxes.'

Never, never, no matter how hungry you are, eat a tulip-bulb
omelette.

With Love, 1982

Recipes for Sparrows, Starlings and Carlings
VICOMTE DE MAUDUIT

ROAST SPARROWS

Sparrows when roasted in this way are far from despicable. Pluck the
birds and cut off the head and neck and feet. Draw the birds from the
neck end, then truss them as you would pigeons, cover breasts with
slices of fat bacon, then (if available) wrap the birds in vine leaves and

tie round with string. Roast for 15 minutes, basting frequently. During this time chop finely the birds' livers, fry them in a little of the birds' gravy, season to taste, spread thickly over pieces of fried toast, place one bird on each piece of toast and pour the gravy over all.

STEWED STARLINGS

Clean, draw, and skin the starlings. Stew them till tender in water and milk, adding 1 sliced onion, 1 bruised shallot, mixed herbs, salt, and pepper.

ROAST STARLINGS

After skinning the birds, clean them and roast them as you would sparrows.

CARLINGS

Carlings are dried peas, which during a long famine kept the population of Yorkshire alive after a ship with a cargo of carlings was wrecked on the coast off Durham.

Carlings are still eaten in Yorkshire on the fourth Sunday in Lent – Carling Sunday – when in many village inns of North-East Yorkshire they are to this day traditionally served free.

To make carlings, soak the dried peas overnight, boil them till tender, strain well, rub them through a sieve, add salt, pepper, powdered mint, and shape into small rolls. Roll them in egged breadcrumbs, or dip them in melted butter and fry in deep fat until golden.

They Can't Ration These, 1940

Canned Grass

IT HAS ALL THE VITAMINS

Plain grass is the richest source of all the vitamins contained in all fruits and vegetables according to evidence given to the American Chemical Society by three Kansas City chemists.

They claim to have developed a powdered grass that can be canned and added to most foods in cooking.

They claim that 12 lb. of grass, dried, contains more vitamins than 340 lb. of fruits and vegetables, says the B.U.P. It contains all the vitamins except 'D.'

The grass must be dried quickly in a high temperature to preserve the vitamins. When sun-dried it loses its value.

Evening News, 25 April, 1940

Nourishing Food from Leaves
CAROL MARTIN 1928–89

The idea of making a nourishing food from leaves and grasses was first mentioned in the scientific press in 1920. It surfaced briefly again during the Second World War, when a simple processing method was developed at Rothamsted Experimental Station at Harpenden as part of Britain's arsenal of 'secret weapons'. Another forty years were to pass, however, before 'food from grass' received the UN accolade which at present is causing it to be promoted as a practical means of enriching poor diets in the Third World.

The extraction method consists of a simple pulping and pressing operation, known as 'fractionation', which separates the nutritious juice from the indigestible fibre in the green matter. It requires no more skill than cheese-making and is easily introduced at village level in needy areas. The extracted juice is heated to produce a curd containing high-grade protein, plus a significant amount of vitamins and minerals, and the residual fibre is used as cattle cake. There is no wastage of any part of the original leaf matter, and the simple technology gives a protein yield per acre several times that of any conventional farming system.

All Grass is Flesh, 1990

Vital Statistics

BARBARA GRIGGS

At the end of the war, the British were surprised to learn that they had never been healthier in their lives.

'The vital statistics during the war years,' reported the nation's Chief Medical Officer in 1946, 'have been phenomenally good.'

Particularly astonishing were the child mortality rates: they were lower than they had been for decades, even though the Blitz had claimed the lives of 7,000 children under fifteen, and there had been a sharp increase in accidental deaths due to the blackout. Fewer mothers had died in childbirth. Fewer babies had been stillborn.

The nation's children were sturdier and taller. Their teeth were better, too: in one Glasgow study, only 18 per cent of five-year-old children had had no decayed teeth in 1938; by 1944, nearly half the five-year-olds had perfect sets of teeth.

Tuberculosis was still a killer – but the deathrate had gone down steadily all through the war years, and this despite the fact that many patients had had to be sent home from sanatoria.

By the end of the war, too, there were fewer anaemic women and children, although the meat ration for years had been a few ounces a week at most.

The Food Factor, 1986

Food for All from the Fields

VICOMTE DE MAUDUIT

In conclusion for this chapter, here is a narrative which is in itself food for thought:

Early last year I was much interested after listening to a broadcast from the B.B.C. by Mr. J. R. B. Branson on the subject of Grass as a Food; and soon after that I sought this gentleman's acquaintance, and I shall now quote him:

'. . . By devoting attention to the careful drying of grass into hay, I have been able to so dry it artificially, that when I was eating my repast, consisting of hay with other ingredients, I appeared to myself to

449

be eating the most delightful meal, which was pervaded by the taste and aroma of new-mown hay. In like manner, by cutting up and mixing with freshly cut grass mowings, the petals of roses, lettuce leaves, and fruit, and adding sugar to suit my taste, I have been able to make myself most delicious salads. I have also been able by adding cut-up rose leaves to make a salad which consisted of fresh grass, rolled oats, sugar, and half an ounce of currants, to produce a meal which gave me the sense that I was enjoying a repast which had the taste and the aroma of fresh leechees, an Eastern fruit of the most delicate and delicious flavour. In addition to this, by mixing with my grass either fresh or dried rolled oats, grated cheese, and salt, with tomato and lettuce, I have given myself a salad repast which is both appetising and nourishing, and at the same time very inexpensive. In the winter, again, I have mixed with my dried grass rolled oats, grated carrot, and grated beetroot, both of them uncooked, adding either salt and cheese or sugar and currants or sultanas, according as I felt inclined, or apple or orange.'

Whereupon Mr. Branson voiced his twenty years' experienced theory thus:

'Eating beautiful fresh green grass, and beautiful fruit, and the petals of beautiful flowers, are merely incentives which I suggest towards the expression of that ego in terms of beauty, of delicacy, and of refinement. Fruit, flowers, and cereals. . . . At the age of sixty-six years my pulse is 75, and my blood-pressure 110; my respiration is absolutely free, and my "wind," when running, extremely good. All this on a diet which costs me less than 3s. 6d. a week! . . . A diet consisting mostly of grass!'

They Can't Ration These, 1940

In The Air-raid Shelter
AMBROSE HEATH 1891–1969

I think it would be a good thing to remind people of the useful things they can take to the shelter with them without having to cook them . . . Things that will help them through these rather . . . shall I say, up-and-down nights? Well, we've all been frightened at some time or another. We've been chased across a field by a bull, or, more likely, we've nearly been run over by something, and we've felt our hearts in our mouths, and by Golly, we've got a dry tongue after it! Well, one of the best things to have ready in an air-raid shelter is a drink. Water is a good thing, but perhaps something hot in a flask (I mean soft drink) is really excellent, because if there is anyone who feels a bit groggy, this is just the thing for them. I'm not decrying the brandy in the first-aid cabinet, but there's a state which doesn't need first-aid, but perhaps only, shall I say? half-first-aid, and here it is often the warmth of the drink itself that does the trick.

A block of chocolate is good to have to eat, if you're hungry, or some dried fruits like figs, sultanas or raisins. And figs, by the way, don't make you as thirsty as chocolate. Barley sugar and boiled sweets are a good stand-by, and so is chewing-gum, if you can get any. If you've looked at as many gangster films as I have, you'll have realised that chewing gum is more an occupation than a pastime. Or there are oranges. What could be more refreshing than an orange? It doesn't compete with chewing-gum in sucking-power, but it takes quite a long time to consume.

Here are just one or two other points, not about food, that may help you. Keep the children warm, especially their feet and legs. Put on their warmest stockings and shoes. If your child is nervous, and likely to be sick at excitement, wrap a warmed scarf firmly around its tummy, and see that it has a nice warm coat on top. Keep the children amused, if you can; if you can't get them to go to sleep, which is best, of course. And whatever you do, don't let them think that you are afraid. . . . I needn't tell you the thousand heroic ways of doing this. As for yourself, better keep your mouth open if bombs are near, because it will save your ears; or if you're really nervous, keep a piece of india-rubber or cork between your teeth.

Kitchen Front Recipes and Hints, 1941

Royalty at Table

❦

Bountiful Almoner
JEAN DE JOINVILLE 1224–1317

The saint loved truth to such a degree, that even with the Saracens he would not draw back from what he had promised them, as you will hear by-and-bye. As to his palate, he was so indifferent, that never in my life did I hear him ask for any particular dish, as many rich men do, but he eat contentedly of what his cooks served up to him.

The king was such a bountiful almoner that wherever he went through his kingdom, he made donations to poor, churches, lazaretti, town-halls, hospitals, and men and women of gentle blood reduced to poverty. Every day he fed a multitude of poor people, without reckoning those who dined in his chamber; and many a time I have seen him cut bread for them and pour them out drink.

From his very childhood the king took pity on the poor and afflicted; and the custom was that, wherever the king went, a hundred and twenty poor persons should every day have an abundant meal in his house of bread, wine, and meat, or fish. In Lent and Advent the number of the poor was increased; and several times it happened that the king waited upon them and placed food before them, and carved for them . . .

Particularly at the great vigils of solemn festivals he waited upon the poor, as above related, before he himself eat or drank anything. Besides all that, he had every day to dine and sup with him old men and cripples, to whom he gave of the same dishes that he himself partook of; and when they had eaten they carried away a certain sum in money.

Saint Louis of France, TRANS. James Hutton, 1910

The Count of Foix

JEAN DE FROISSART 1337–1410

Froissart visited the Count of Foix (a territory north of the Pyrenees) in the autumn of 1388.

The Count of Foix lived in the way that I am describing to you. When he came out of his room at midnight to sup in his hall, twelve lighted torches were carried before him by twelve serving-men, and these twelve torches were held up in front of his table, giving a bright light in the hall, which was full of knights and squires and always contained plenty of tables laid for supper for any who wanted it. No one spoke to him at his own table unless he first asked him to. He usually ate much poultry – but only the wings and the legs – and drank little. He took great pleasure in minstrelsy, of which he had an excellent knowledge. He liked his clerks to sing songs, rondeaux and virelays to him. He would remain at table for about two hours, and he also enjoyed having travelling entertainers to perform between the courses. After he had watched them, he sent them round the tables of the knights and squires.

Froissart Chronicles, ED., TRANS. Geoffrey Brereton, 1968

Bread and Salt

SIGMUND VON HERBERSTEIN 1486–1552

The author travelled to Russia in 1517–18 and again in 1526–27 on behalf of the Emperor Maximilian and then of King Ferdinand as ambassador of the Holy Roman Empire. His mission was to gain the support of the Grand Duke of Muscovy against the growing Turkish menace to Europe. The book was first published in 1549.

When we had taken our seats the stewards filed in through the door and stood before the Prince around the sideboard in their rich clothes. None made any obeisance to him; they walked with heads up as though they did not see him. After this the Grand-duke called his butler or cup-bearer, taking three slices of bread which had been specially cut and laid on top of a pile and giving them into his hand with the words: 'Give this to Count Leonhard, envoy of our brother, elected Roman Emperor and supreme monarch.' This butler summoned the interpreter on duty before the table and said: 'Leonhard, the great lord Basilius, King and Lord of all the Russians and Grandduke, does you the favour of sending bread from his own table.' Then he went a second time and said the same to me. These utterances are spoken loudly by the butler and interpreter. When such gifts and speeches were directed at us we stood up. As soon as we did so all those sitting near us stood up too, only the Prince and his brothers remaining seated. After receiving the bread we bowed our thanks to the Grandduke, then to the councillors nearest him, after which we bowed to the other side and in front of us. It is their custom that the Prince marks his favour by sending bread from his own table; if he sends salt this means affection, and it is reckoned a greater honour to receive salt. This fine white bread is baked in the shape of a horse-collar, and I reckon that those who commonly enjoy it have earned it by heavy toil and hard service.

Presently the stewards are sent to fetch the dishes. Meanwhile brandy is served, usually drunk before the meal. When there is meat they always bring in roast swans first, two or three of them being placed before the Grand-duke, who prods them with a knife to find out which is the most tender while the remaining stewards stand holding their dishes and their swans. Then the Prince orders the removal of the one selected, upon which they all move over to the door. Here stands the serving-table where the swans are carved, always four wings or four legs to a dish and then the rest as they think fit. Now the stewards bring out the dishes once more, placing four or five – for they are not large – before the Grand-duke and others before his brothers and the privy councillors, then the ambassador and finally the rest.

Meanwhile the Prince seeks out the tender cuts, calling a servant to take one on a dish to one of his brothers or privy councillors, or after them an ambassador. He to whom such is sent stands up and the others stand up to mark his honour; he thanks the Prince and the rest with a bow. All is dispatched with much ceremony. When the Prince bids his servant deliver something he cuts off a piece or takes a crumb of bread and gives it him to eat; he also carves something for the steward and gives it him for sampling.

All these tokens of favour sent hither and thither mean so much standing up that one is positively fatigued, especially when the next table is so close that one cannot stand up straight. On my first mission I noted that the Grand-duke's brothers were not highly esteemed, and since they did not stand up for me, an ambassador, I did not stand up for them. The man opposite addressed me and bade me, since the Grand-duke's brother was upstanding, to rise also. I chose the moment to speak to somebody as though not understanding what was taking place, then I finally looked about and raised myself a little for a few moments. When those opposite noticed this they tittered among themselves, and I asked them why they laughed. When none of them would make reply I said gravely: 'I pay fitting respect to him who does honour to my lord, but not to him who fails to do so.' And when the Prince was showing favour to some of the younger and less important and sent them something from his table, this was why I stood up before them although informed that I need not do so on account of their youth; none the less I stood up. The Prince saw that my neighbours were laughing and that I had been talking with them on the matter, and asked one of them what it was all about. No doubt he explained, and the Prince laughed too.

When we began to eat the swans they sprinkled them with pepper and poured vinegar and salt upon them. They have also soured milk and salted cucumbers, preserved for a year at least, standing upon the tables in various places. The other dishes are brought forward in the same way, although they are not taken out again like the swans. A variety of drink was set before us, malmsey, Greek wine and several sorts of mead. Often the Prince would request a drink, taste it and then summon the ambassador to come over to him, saying: 'Leonhard, you come from a great lord to a great lord on great affairs and have made a great journey. May you prosper now that you have felt my favour and looked me in the eyes. Drink and drain it, eat your fill, so that you can rest and return to your master.' The same was said to me. And on the same occasion the Prince asked me if I had clipped my beard, expressed in the single word: 'Bril?'. I said I had, using also this word. 'You followed my example,' he added, meaning he had done the same, unprecedented in a prince in such a country, for he had, when he took his second wife, had his beard clipped off.

All vessels upon the sideboard and the service from which we had eaten, drunk and taken pepper, vinegar and salt were of gold, as could be told from the weight apart from other evidence. Both previously and afterwards I was a guest of the Grand-duke when the sideboard and tables were laden with silver. Four servants stood by the sideboard each holding a vessel from which the Prince was wont to drink. At table he bore himself humanly enough, often addressing us, exhorting us to eat and drink, asking us questions. The first time I was at the Grand-duke's his servants and stewards were dressed almost like the assistant priests of our great churches, but not the second, when they wore something like a tabard which they call *terlik*, well garnished with pearls from the Prince's treasury.

Banquets last very long; some kept me until after one o'clock in the morning. All business is done before the meal. When transactions are afoot they eat nothing until night. In compensation they often spend the whole of one or several days in gluttony and drinking. At the end of a banquet the Prince tells the ambassadors when to leave; those who brought them are soon at hand to take them to their lodging. Here the members of the escort seat themselves and say they have orders to stay with us and cheer us up. They bring a cart with silver vessels and one or two with drink – the carts are small. With them arrive secretaries and other respected persons to help to fill the envoys' skins. For making people tipsy is here an honour and sign of esteem; the man who is not put under the table holds himself ill respected. The Muscovites are indeed masters at talking to others and persuading them to drink. If all else fails one of them stands up and proposes the health of the Grand-duke, upon which all present must not fail to drink and drain the cup. After this they try to provoke toasts to the health of the Emperor and others. There is much ceremony about this drinking. The man proposing the toast stands in the middle of the room, his head bared, states what he desires for the Grand-duke or other lord – happiness, victory, health – and wishes that as much blood may remain in the veins of his enemies as drink in his cup. When he has emptied it he reverses the cup upon his head and wishes the lord good health. Or he will take up a prominent position, have several cups filled, and distribute them with the motive for the toast. Then each goes into the middle of the room, drains his cup and claps it on his head. I disliked and still dislike tippling and could only get out of this by pretending to be drunk or saying I was too sleepy to go on and had had my fill.

When I took leave of the Grand-duke at the end of my first mission he was standing after the meal – for it is their custom to invite envoys to dine upon arrival and departure – by the table at which he had sat. He ordered a cup and said: 'Sigmund, we will drain this in honour of our brother Maximilian, elected Roman Emperor and supreme monarch; you shall drain it too and all the others afterwards in token of our affection for our brother Maximilian etc., and you shall tell him what you have seen.' Then he offered me the cup, saying: 'Drink it to the health of our brother Maximilian etc.', naming his titles. After which he gave a cup to each of the others, and addressed each in the same manner. Taking the cups we stepped back, keeping our heads inclined towards the Grand-duke, and drained them. After such a toast he would call me to him, give me his hand and say: 'Go now.' Upon which I withdrew to the lodging.

Description of Moscow and Muscovy, TRANS. J. B. C. Grundy, 1969

The Great Khan
MARCO POLO 1254–1324

Marco Polo met the Emperor Kublai Kahn (1215–94) in 1275.

In the middle of the hall, where the Great Khan sits at table, there is a magnificent piece of furniture, made in the form of a square coffer, each side of which is three paces in length, exquisitely carved in figures of animals, and gilt. It is hollow within, for the purpose of receiving a capacious vase, of pure gold, calculated to hold many gallons. On each of its four sides a smaller vessel, containing about a hogshead, one of which is filled with mare's milk, another with that of the camel, and so of the others, according to the kinds of beverage in use. Within this buffet are also the cups or flagons belonging to his Majesty, for serving the liquors. Some of them are of beautiful gilt plate. Their size is such that, when filled with wine or other liquor, the quantity would be sufficient for eight or ten men . . .

When the Great Khan sits at meals, in his hall of state – as shall be more particularly described in the following book – the table which is placed in the centre is elevated to the height of about eight cubits, and at a distance from it stands a large buffet, where all the drinking vessels are arranged. Now, by means of their supernatural art, they cause the flagons of wine, milk, or any other beverage, to fill the cups spontaneously, without being touched by the attendants, and the cups to move through the air the distance of ten paces until they reach the hand of the Great Khan. As he empties them, they return to the place from whence they came; and this is done in the presence of such persons as are invited by his Majesty to witness the performance . . .

The numerous persons who attend at the sideboard of his Majesty, and who serve him with victuals and drink, are all obliged to cover their noses and mouths with handsome veils or cloths of worked silk, in order that his victuals or his wine may not be affected by their breath. When drink is called for by him, and the page in waiting has presented it, he retires three paces and kneels down, upon which the courtiers, and all who are present, in like manner make their prostration. At the same moment all the musical instruments, of which there is a numerous band, begin to play, and continue to do so until he has ceased drinking, when all the company recover their posture. This reverential salutation is made as often as his Majesty drinks. It is unnecessary to say anything of the victuals, because it may well be imagined that their abundance is excessive.

The Travels of Marco Polo, TRANS. Manuel Komroff, 1953

Three Letters from the French Court
PRINCESS PALATINE 1652–1722

Charlotte-Elizabeth of Bavaria, who married Louis XIV's brother the Duke of Orleans, was known as the Princess Palatine. Her letters give a fascinating picture of life at the French court.

VERSAILLES, *March 3rd, 1707*.
'I lunch alone all the year round, but get it over as quickly as possible, for nothing is so annoying as to have twenty footmen round you who look at every mouthful that you swallow, and stare persistently at you. I do not spend half an hour at table. I dine with the King. We are five or six at table; no one speaks a word; all passes as though we were in a convent – perhaps two words said in a whisper to one's neighbour. We are rendered so serious here by the endless plots which one cannot discuss . . .'

TO THE PRINCESS OF WALES

PARIS, *Dec. 5th, 1718*.
'The King, Monsieur, the Dauphin, and the Duc de Berri were great eaters. I have often seen the King eat four platefuls of different kinds of

soup, a whole pheasant, a plateful of salad, two large slices of ham, mutton with garlic, a plateful of cakes, and then some fruit and hard-boiled eggs. Both the King and Monsieur were very fond of hard-boiled eggs.'

TO THE PRINCESS OF WALES

SAINT CLOUD, *Oct. 22nd, 1719.*

'Nobody seems surprised to see me eating black-pudding with pleasure. I have also brought raw ham into fashion. Everyone takes it now; and many of our other German dishes, such as sour-crout, sweetened cabbage, beans and bacon, have been adopted; they are rarely good here. But little game was eaten before I came. I also taught the King to like salted herrings. I have so accustomed myself to German dishes that I cannot bear any French concoction. I only take their roast beef, veal, and sometimes mutton, partridge, or chickens, never pheasants.'

Life and Letters, 1889

Fat Quails
JOHN HUSEE C. 1506–48

Husee was the agent for Lord Lisle, Governor of Calais which provided a regular supply of live quails to the court. Her Grace, the Queen, was Anne Boleyn.

TO LORD LISLE

23 May 1537

Pleaseth it your lordship to be advertised that this day, at my being at the Court, Sir John Russell called me unto him, and asked me when I heard from your lordship, saying further that he had these days past wrote unto your lordship ij sundry letters by the King's commandment expressly, and how the very effect of those letters was for fat quails for the Queen's Highness, which her Grace loveth very well, and longeth not a little for them; and he looked hourly for your lordship's answer with the said quails, in so much that he did further command me in the King's behalf to write your lordship with all haste expressly again for the said quails; so that his mind is that with most speed your lordship send ij or iij dozen, and cause them to be killed at Dover; and that in anywise that those same be very fat; and afterward, as shortly as your lordship may, to send xx or xxx dozen, as your lordship shall think best. Those that your lordship shall send by land, if they be delivered me, I will speedily see them conveyed unto Hampton Court, for so the said Mr Russell desired me: and further, in case your lordships can have none fat at Calais, that then you fail not to send with all speed into Flanders for them, for so the King's Majesty willeth, as his only trust is in your lordship. If your lordship may have them by ij or iij* dozens in Calais you may send them by every other passage. And I think there is none that will deny the carriage of them hither, and from hence I doubt not but I will use diligence to the Court with them. If your lordship send them by sundry times, and cause them to be killed at Dover, they shall come fat hither, which the Queen greatly desireth. Her Grace is great with child, and shall be open-laced with stomacher by Corpus Christi Day at the farthest. And your lordship send any by water, they must be well tended or else they will wax lean. Mr Russell caused me incontinent to depart from the Court to write your lordship this present . . .

By your lordship's own man bounden,
John Husee

The Lisle Letters, ED. Muriel St Clare Byrne, 1981–3

Portugal Broth, as It Was Made for the Queen
SIR KENELM DIGBY 1603–65

Sir Kenelm was a courtier in the reign of Charles I, and was also a philosopher, diplomat and scientist. He became a friend of the Queen, Henrietta Maria, and was also her chancellor. His book of receipts was published a few years after his death.

Make very good broth with some lean of Veal, Beef and Mutton, and with a brawny Hen or young Cock. After it is scummed, put in an Onion quartered, (and, if you like it, a Clove of Garlick,) a little

---

* the 'j' in the numeral is the final form of 'i', hence Husee is asking for two or three dozen quails.

Parsley, a sprig of Thyme, as much Minth, a little balm; some Coriander-seeds bruised, and a very little Saffron; a little Salt, Pepper and a Clove. When all the substance is boiled out of the meat, and the broth very good, you may drink it so, or, pour a little of it upon tosted sliced-bread, and stew it, till the bread have drunk up all that broth, then add a little more, and stew; so adding by little and little, that the bread may imbibe it and swell: whereas if you drown it at once, the bread will not swell, and grow like gelly: and thus you will have a good potage. You may add Parsley-roots or Leeks, Cabbage or Endive in the due time before the broth is ended boiling, and time enough for them to become tender. In the Summer you may put in Lettice, Sorrel, Purslane, Borage and Bugloss, or what other pot-herbs you like. But green herbs do rob the strength and vigor and Cream of the Potage.

The Queen's ordinary *Bouillon de santé* in a morning was thus. A Hen, a handful of Parsley, a sprig of Thyme, three of Spear-minth, a little balm, half a great Onion, a little Pepper and Salt, and a Clove, as much water as would cover the Hen; and this boiled to less than a pint, for one good Porrenger full.

The Closet Opened, 1669

Royal Manners

JEAN DE FROISSART 1337–1410

Henry Crystede tells Froissart how he taught manners to four Irish Kings: O'Neill, King of Meath, O'Brien of Thomond, Arthur McMorrough, King of Leinster and O'Connor, King of Connaught and Erp.

And because the Irish language comes as easily to my tongue as English – for I have always gone on speaking it with my wife and have started my grandchildren on learning it as well as I have been able – I was appointed by the King and the great nobles of England to persuade, direct and guide in the ways of reason and the customs of this country those four Irish kings who have made their submission to the English crown and have sworn to observe it for ever. But I must say that those four kings, whom I initiated and instructed to the best of my ability, did prove to be very uncouth and gross-minded people. I had the greatest difficulty in polishing them and moderating their language and characters. And even so, if they have made some progress, it is not very much. On many occasions they still slip back into their rough ways.

'The mission that was entrusted to me was based on the King's expressed wish that in behaviour, bearing and dress they should conform to the English pattern, because he wished to dub them knights. As a beginning, they were allotted a fine, big house in the city of Dublin, for themselves and their followers. I was instructed to live with them, never leaving them or going out, except in case of absolute necessity. I spent the first three or four days in their company, so as to get to know them, and they me, without contradicting anything they wished to do. I saw those kings behaving at table in a way which was not at all seemly, and I said to myself that I would change that. When they had sat down and were served with the first course, they would get their minstrels and their principal servants to sit with them and eat off their plates and drink from their goblets. They told me that such was the custom of the country. Except for their beds, they had everything in common. I allowed all this for three days, but on the fourth I had the tables in the hall arranged and laid in the correct manner. The four kings were seated at the high table, the minstrels at a table well away from theirs, and the servants at another. This appeared to make them very angry. They looked at each other and refused to eat, saying that it was a breach of the excellent custom in which they had been brought up. I answered, laughingly in order to placate them, that their previous arrangement was not a reasonable one and that they would have to abandon it and adopt the English usage, for those were my instructions and what the King and his council had appointed me to do.

Froissart Chronicles, ED., TRANS. Geoffrey Brereton, 1968

The Duc de Lauzun

DUC DE SAINT-SIMON 1675–1755

His health was of iron, with a misleading external appearance of delicacy. He dined and supped heavily every day; had very fine fare and very delicate, always with good company, morning and evening; he ate everything, feast and fast, with no sort of choice except his taste, and no caution; always took chocolate in the morning and kept near him on several tables fruits in their season and pastry at other times; with beer, cider, lemonade, and other such liquids iced; and going and coming, he ate and drank the whole afternoon and exhorted others to do likewise. He always left the table at night with the fruit, and went to bed directly. I remember once, among many other times, that he dined with me after his illness, and ate so much fish, vegetables, and all sorts of things, without our being able to prevent him, that we sent in the evening to inquire very gently if he did not feel the worse for it; the messenger found him at table eating his supper with a good appetite.

Memoirs of the Duc de Saint-Simon, TRANS. Katherine Wormeley, 1899

Montezuma
BERNAL DÍAZ 1498–1593

Díaz wrote his history at the age of seventy-six. It angrily refutes other chronicles, which he described as being without truth, 'neither in the beginning, nor the middle, nor the end'. Díaz was a member of the Spanish forces under Cortés who entered the city of Tenochtitlán in Mexico 8 November 1519. Here is his eye-witness account of Montezuma and how he dined.

The great Montezuma was about forty years old, of good height, well proportioned, spare and slight, and not very dark, though of the usual Indian complexion. He did not wear his hair long but just over his ears, and he had a short black beard, well-shaped and thin. His face was rather long and cheerful, he had fine eyes, and in his appearance and manner could express geniality or, when necessary, a serious composure. He was very neat and clean, and took a bath every afternoon. He had many women as his mistresses, the daughters of chieftains, but two legitimate wives who were *Caciques* in their own right, and when he had intercourse with any of them it was so secret that only some of his servants knew of it.

For each meal his servants prepared him more than thirty dishes cooked in their native style, which they put over small earthenware braziers to prevent them from getting cold. They cooked more than three hundred plates of the food the great Montezuma was going to eat, and more than a thousand more for the guard. I have heard that they used to cook him the flesh of young boys. But as he had such a variety of dishes, made of so many different ingredients, we could not tell whether a dish was of human flesh or anything else, since every day they cooked fowls, turkeys, pheasants, local partridges, quail, tame and wild duck, venison, wild boar, marsh birds, pigeons, hares and rabbits, also many other kinds of birds and beasts native to their country, so numerous that I cannot quickly name them all. I know for certain, however, that after our Captain spoke against the sacrifice of human beings and the eating of their flesh, Montezuma ordered that it should no longer be served to him.

Let us now turn to the way his meals were served, which was like this. If it was cold, they built a large fire of live coals made by burning the bark of a tree which gave off no smoke. The smell of the bark from which they made these coals was very sweet. In order that he should get no more heat than he wanted they placed a sort of screen in front of it adorned with the figures of idols worked in gold. He would sit on a soft low stool which was richly worked. His table, which was also low and decorated in the same way, was covered with white tablecloths and rather long napkins of the same material. Then four very clean and beautiful girls brought water for his hands in one of those deep basins that they call *xicales*.[1] They held others like plates beneath it to catch the water, and brought him towels. Two other women brought him maize-cakes.

When he began his meal they placed in front of him a sort of wooden screen, richly decorated with gold, so that no one should see him eat. Then the four women retired, and four great chieftains, all old men, stood beside him. He talked with them every now and then and asked them questions, and as a great favour he would sometimes offer one of them a dish of whatever tasted best. They say that these were his closest relations and advisers and judges of lawsuits, and if he gave them anything to eat they ate it standing, with deep reverence and without looking in his face.

Montezuma's food was served on Cholula ware, some red and some black. While he was dining, the guards in the adjoining rooms did not dare to speak or make a noise above a whisper. His servants brought him some of every kind of fruit that grew in the country, but he ate very little of it. Sometimes they brought him in cups of pure gold a

[1] gourds.

drink made from the cocoa-plant, which they said he took before visiting his wives. We did not take much notice of this at the time, though I saw them bring in a good fifty large jugs of this chocolate, all frothed up, of which he would drink a little. They always served it with great reverence. Sometimes some little humpbacked dwarfs would be present at his meals, whose bodies seemed almost to be broken in the middle. These were his jesters. There were other Indians who told him jokes and must have been his clowns, and others who sang and danced, for Montezuma was very fond of music and entertainment and would reward his entertainers with the leavings of the food and chocolate. The same four women removed the tablecloths and again most reverently brought him water for his hands. Then Montezuma would talk to these four old chieftains about matters that interested him, and they would take their leave with great ceremony. He stayed behind to rest.

As soon as the great Montezuma had dined, all the guards and many more of his household servants ate in their turn. I think more than a thousand plates of food must have been brought in for them, and more than two thousand jugs of chocolate frothed up in the Mexican style, and infinite quantities of fruit, so that with his women and serving-maids and breadmakers and chocolate-makers his expenses must have been considerable.

One thing I had forgotten to say is that two more very handsome women served Montezuma when he was at table with maize-cakes kneaded with eggs and other nourishing ingredients. These maize-cakes were very white, and were brought in on plates covered with clean napkins. They brought him a different kind of bread also, in a long ball kneaded with other kinds of nourishing food, and *pachol* cake, as they call it in that country, which is a kind of wafer. They also placed on the table three tubes, much painted and gilded, in which they put liquidamber mixed with some herbs which are called tobacco. When Montezuma had finished his dinner, and the singing and dancing were over and the cloths had been removed, he would inhale the smoke from one of these tubes. He took very little of it, and then fell asleep.

The Conquest of New Spain, TRANS. J. M. Cohen, 1963

The King's Pleasaunce

LOUIS SÉBASTIEN MERCIER 1740–1814

All the land reserved for the King's sport is called His Majesty's Pleasaunce. This land includes all the surroundings of Paris, and the gun is a weapon as strange to the inhabitants of our town as it is to those of Pekin. So you may perceive partridges in every field, perfectly tame, picking up the corn and not taking alarm at the passer-by. Hares are less timid than elsewhere, indeed, you might think they were aware that Parisians must respect them, for they will sit up on their tails and watch you pass.

Sometimes the King will allow three or four years to pass before he will honour with his presence land covered with game. He appears: and fifteen to eighteen thousand birds fall to the guns, but the partridges and hares which have escaped on this fatal day live on in safety and many die of old age.

The gamekeepers carry out their business very strictly; the smallest offence of that kind is vigorously punished. A burgher may not buy a hare that may have been shot in the fields, for fear of being thought an accomplice of its death. Should a wounded partridge come to die in your garden, you must restore it. The gamekeepers wage a bitter war against all dogs, even against lap-dogs, and shoot them down at the feet of their weeping and lamenting mistresses. So when we walk rather far afield we take care to shut our little lap-dog up at home, through fear of his falling a victim to the avenging lead in His Majesty's Pleasaunce. For the same reason there are paths you may not follow. At every step you come across incontestable laws, the laws of a chase which belongs entirely to princes; and the latter, on their own property, pursue the rulings that obtain in the environs of the city. You have to make a cast of thirty miles to avoid this thicket of prohibitions. I am not speaking of the inroads made by financiers, squires, and ecclesiastics on their own country properties; their shooting only drives all the game towards Paris, and the hare which was coursed over the vast plains of Picardy or the Beauce, is served up on some long silver dish which decorates a table in the Faubourg Saint-Honoré.

We eat a great many partridges shot by the King himself, or by the princes; so it is no vulgar lead that the burgher finds between his teeth. The spoils of the princes' shooting furnish the dinner tables.

The Picture of Paris, TRANS. Wilfred and Emilie Jackson, 1929

Not Enough Salt

CARYL BRAHMS 1901–82 AND S. J. SIMON
d. 1948

It was the sweet potato which returned with Raleigh to England and this was much enjoyed in dessert dishes with dried fruits and added sugar – not salt. But this should in no way spoil the mischief and delight of this extract.

The Flower of England was looking at its plates with a mixture of doubt tinged with awe. In front of each one of them lay a soggy island of white mush, shaped rather like a warped egg, only larger.

The potato!

This was it!

'Well, well, well,' said the Master of the Revels, in a resigned voice.

Sir Philip Sidney would not permit his doubts to show on his face. He was making up his mind not to let old Walter down. 'Delicious,' he was going to say, whatever it tasted like.

The Earl of Southampton picked his up and experimented. The potato turned over quite easily, and seemed to be the same on the other side.

In spite of the evidence of his eyes, Burghley showed no relaxation of his vigilance. He had picked up a knife, and was pricking delicately.

'I shall bite it most carefully,' he asserted stubbornly.

But Elizabeth of England showed no such daintiness. Forthright and purposeful, she dug her spoon into the potato, collected half of it, and carried it firmly to her mouth.

The Flower of England waited.

Sir Walter Raleigh gripped his seat under the table. He had sailed halfway round the world to find this root, he had faced great perils to bring it back, he had withstood the blandishments of the most expert cajolers at Court, and had not even hinted at the secret of its flavour, he had changed his chef six times, and now Elizabeth of England was tasting it.

He looked at her.

Elizabeth of England spat.

'Not enough salt,' she said.

No Bed for Bacon, 1941

Hiding from the Terror

MME DE LA TOUR DU PIN 1740–1853

Then there was Ferrari, who carried a paper, well hidden and sewn into the lining of his coat, which accredited him as a secret agent of the Regent, later Louis XVIII. He had been clever enough to scrape acquaintance even among the Representatives of the People. There he often mentioned how necessary it was for him to return to Italy with his daughter. For among all the ways we had considered of leaving France, was a plan that he and I should take a passport to Toulouse, with my husband as our servant. I was to pass as his widowed daughter, taking her children back to Italy to her husband's family. In the main cities along our route, such as Toulouse and Marseilles, we would have given concerts. I sang sufficiently well to pass as a singer without my ability being questioned. Every day, we practised different pieces which we planned to offer. Among them, I particularly remember the duet of Paesiello: *Nei giorni tuoi felici* which we were convinced would be a great success.

Our accompanist during these rehearsals was M. de Morin, a young man of considerable talent. He had played a leading part in the Bordeaux Association of Young Men,[1] which had achieved so little, but on account of it, he was heavily compromised. He never slept two nights in the same place. He went out after dark, carefully avoiding patrols, for he had no identity card. I suspect, though I never asked him, that he sometimes slept in our house. When he had been hidden during the day in a house where there was little food, he arrived to see me in the evening half-dead from hunger. I used to give him the remainder of my dinner and my white bread from Saintongue, often eggs as well, for I was kept plentifully supplied by the peasants from Le Bouilh. They used to be turned into excellent omelettes, with truffles which my cook had abstracted from the stores of the Representatives of the People. In our hiding place, this was a source of much amusement and laughter.

One really had to be young and French to remain so gay when the blade of the guillotine was posed to strike. For we were all in danger

---

[1] A group of royalist opponents of the Revolution. During the terror in Bordeaux they were all executed without trial, having been proclaimed, as a body, outside the law.

from it and when we bade one another goodnight, did not dare to add
'Until tomorrow'.

Memoirs, ED., TRANS. Felice Harcourt, 1969

Brighton Pavilion
THE COMTESSE DE BOIGNE 1781–1866

This pavilion was a masterpiece of bad taste. Heterogeneous treasures
from all parts of the world had been collected at enormous cost simply
to be placed under the eight or ten cupolas of this strange and ugly
palace which was largely composed of inlaid work and lacked any sort
of uniformity or architectural style. The interior was no better planned
than the exterior and certainly lacked any artistic taste.

But criticism must cease here. The comforts and refinements of
living had been studied to perfection within this royal residence, and,
after having condemned the extraordinary curiosities as lacking in
good taste, it was extremely amusing to spend one's time examining
them for their oddness and great value.

Guests staying at the Pavilion were usually invited for a certain
number of days, rarely exceeding a week. One arrived in time to dress
for dinner. Apartments were arranged with minute care in order to
satisfy the personal requirements of each guest. The royal host was
nearly always the first to enter the drawing-room. If by any chance he
happened to be late and the ladies had preceded him, he would make
apologies.

Guests at dinner were numerous. They consisted of the inmates of
the palace and specially invited residents of Brighton which was
frequented by brilliant society during the winter months. Mourning
prevented balls and concerts. The Prince, however, employed a private
band of musicians who blew horns and played other noisy instruments
in the vestibule during dinner and the rest of the evening. The distance
made it endurable, but to my mind it was not very pleasant. It
delighted the Prince, who often joined the band and beat time with a
gong.

Visitors used to call after dinner. Towards eleven o'clock the Prince
went into a drawing-room where a small cold supper had been
prepared. He was followed only by those whom he had especially
requested to do so, for instance the ladies living in the palace and two

or three gentlemen who were intimate friends. Here the Prince would be quite at his ease.

He would seat himself on a sofa between the Marchioness of Hertford and any other lady to whom he wished to show particular attention and begin a conversation. He had a marvellous knowledge of all the gallant adventures at the Court of Louis XVI as well as those at the English Court which he related at great length. His narratives were occasionally interrupted by short madrigals and more often by obscenities. The Marchioness put on a dignified air and the Prince made jokes which were not always in very good taste.

On the whole, these entertainments, lasting until two or three o'clock in the morning, would have been classed as boring if they had been given by a private individual. But the atmosphere of the Court kept all the company awake and sent it away delighted with the Prince's affability . . .

The guests at the Pavilion could choose between having lunch served in their apartments or being present at a meal presided over by Sir Benjamin and Lady Bloomfield.

Unless in the case of illness, the latter alternative was preferred, though some of the King's mistresses of long standing who endeavoured to conceal the irreparable ravages of time chose to appear only when candles were lit, a superfluous precaution and a badly rewarded sacrifice. Thus was the case with the Marchioness of Hertford.

I was much surprised on leaving my apartment to find the table set on the landing of the stairs. But what a landing! And such a table! All the carpets, the armchairs, the tables, and china, the plate, and all the refinements with which luxury and taste can embellish magnificence were displayed.

The Prince was most particular that this meal should be extremely well prepared although he himself was never present; nor did he wish any of the delicate attentions of a well-bred host towards his guest to be neglected.

He led pretty much the same life in Brighton as in London, remaining in his apartment until three o'clock in the afternoon and generally riding out alone. If by chance he met a newcomer to the Pavilion before setting out on his ride, he would take pleasure in leading his guest through his residence himself, and would take especial pride in showing off his kitchens which were heated by a steam system which was new at that time and delighted him.

Memoirs of the Comtesse de Boigne, ED. Sylvia de Morsier, 1956

The Death of Monsieur, 1701

DUC DE SAINT-SIMON 1675–1755

At this moment the king was informed that dinner was served. They left the room to sit down to table, – Monsieur a flaming scarlet, his eyes sparkling with anger. His burning face made several of the ladies at the table and the courtiers who stood behind them say that he ought to be bled. The dinner passed as usual. Monsieur ate enormously, as he always did at his two meals, not to speak of his abundant chocolate in the morning, and all that he managed to swallow of fruits, pastries, confectionery, and every sort of other dainty during the day. On leaving the table Monsieur, who had brought the Duchesse de Chartres to dine with the king, took her to Saint-Germain, and soon after returned with her to Saint-Cloud.

That evening, after supper, while the king was still in his cabinet with Monseigneur and the princesses, Saint-Pierre arrived from Saint-Cloud and asked to speak with the king on the part of the Duc de Chartres. He was brought to the cabinet and told the king that Monsieur had been seized with a faintness while supping; he was bled and felt better, but they had given him an emetic. The real truth was he was supping as usual with the ladies when, towards the last, as he was pouring out a glass of liqueur for Mme. de Bouillon, it was noticed that he stammered and pointed to something with his hand. As he sometimes talked Spanish some of the ladies asked him what he said, others cried out; it all happened in a moment, and then he fell over on the Duc de Chartres in a fit of apoplexy. They carried him to his room, shook him, walked him about, bled him, gave him an emetic, but without his showing more than a faint sign of life.

Memoirs of the Duc de Saint-Simon,
TRANS. Katharine Wormeley, 1899

Queen Victoria at Breakfast
GABRIEL TSCHUMI

Queen Victoria was always up for breakfast, I was told, and had it with one or two members of the Royal Family in the small oak dining-room in the centre of the corridor at Windsor Castle.

Towards the end of her life she was not a large eater. Rumours had it that her breakfast was usually a boiled egg, served in magnificent style. According to the upper servants, she used a gold egg-cup and a gold spoon, and two of her Indian servants, in their showy scarlet and gold uniforms, stood behind her chair in case she wanted anything. Most of the other members of the Royal Family took breakfast more seriously. They would begin with an egg dish, perhaps *Oeuf en cocotte*, followed by several rashers of streaky bacon, then grilled trout or turbot, cutlets, chops or steak, and finally a serving of roast woodcock, snipe or chicken.

Royal Chef, 1954

King Edward VII's Birthday
CHARLES NIELSON GATTEY 1921–

The most spectacular dinner party to be held at the Savoy took place on 30 June 1905 when George A. Kessler, the champagne millionaire at the head of Moët et Chandon in Europe and America, celebrated King Edward VII's birthday. The forecourt to the east entrance was enclosed and filled with water four feet deep and dyed blue, and was encircled by scenery depicting St Mark's, the Doge's Palace and its surroundings, lit by some 400 Venetian lamps. Into the water had been released salmon trout and whitebait, whilst on it floated swans, ducks, and a white, silk-lined gondola adorned with 31,000 carnations, roses and 5,000 yards of smilax. In the air above fluttered a hundred white doves.

Waiters costumed as gondoliers served twelve courses to twice that number of diners seated on gold chairs, who included Mme Réjane from Paris and the 'Belle of New York', Edna May. The *maître chef*, Thoraud, surpassed himself in the visual appeal and gastronomic excellence of the fare provided. Three impressive lions carved out of ice bore trays of peaches and glacé fruits; and at the finish a baby elephant carried a foot-tall, candle-lit birthday cake over a bridge from *terra firma* to the gondola. It was followed by a bevy of Gaiety girls drinking the health of the monarch in Moët et Chandon champagne.

Throughout the banquet an orchestra stationed in a smaller gondola played music. Then came a *coup de théâtre*. The lights dimmed as a melon-like moon, suspended overhead, was turned on and Caruso emerged through brocade curtains at the raised end of the gondola to sing – for a *douceur* of £450.

Foie Gras and Trumpets, 1984

Mangoes from the Aga Khan

GABRIEL TSCHUMI

Every June the Aga Khan sent Queen Mary a box of mangoes, and some of them were served as dessert, some given to friends, and the rest made into mango jelly, which was always popular at Marlborough House. Like many of the vast numbers of gifts of food Queen Mary received, these came down to the kitchens with a card attached, and early in June 1948 the card from the Aga Khan bore the two words, 'My Love'. It was only a few days before the Derby, and you didn't have to be a student of the Turf to know that in this particular Derby the Aga Khan had a horse called 'My Love'.

While we were unpacking the mangoes this particular year there was a lot of speculation at Marlborough House. Did the Aga Khan intend it as a tip? Was it a sufficiently safe bet for all of us to speculate pretty heavily on the 1948 Derby? We decided that it was, and probably the most excited five people in London when the Aga Khan's horse 'My Love' did come in to win were the kitchen staff at Marlborough House. We never found out whether Queen Mary followed the Aga Khan's tip as well, but to commemorate the occasion we each kept a mango seed on which we carved the words 'My Love, 8/6/48'.

Royal Chef, 1954

Coronation of George III
WILLIAM HICKEY 1749–1830

The coronation of His present Majesty being fixed for the month of September, my father determined that all his family should be present at the ceremony. He therefore engaged one of the nunneries, as they are called, in Westminster Abbey, for which he paid fifty guineas. They are situated at the head of the great columns that support the roof, and command an admirable view of the whole interior of the building. Upon this occasion they were divided off by wooden partitions, each having a separate entrance with lock and key to the door, with ease holding a dozen persons. Provisions, consisting of cold fowls, ham, tongues, different meat pies, wines, and liquors of various sorts were sent in to the apartment the day before, and two servants were allowed to attend. Our party consisted of my father, mother, brother Joseph, sister Mary, myself, Mr. and Miss Isaacs, Miss Thomas, her brother (all Irish), my uncle and aunt Boulton, and their eldest daughter. We all supped together in St. Albans Street on 21st September, and at midnight set off in my father's coach and my uncle's, and Miss Thomas's chariot. At the end of Pall Mall the different lines of carriages, nearly filling the street, our progress was consequently tedious; yet the time was beguiled by the grandeur of the scene; such a multitude of carriages, with servants behind carrying flambeauxs, made a blaze of light equal to day, and had a fine effect.

Opposite the Horse Guards we were stopped exactly an hour without moving onward a single inch. As we approached near the Abbey, the difficulties increased, from mistakes of the coachmen, some of whom were going to the Hall, others to the Abbey, and getting into the wrong ranks. This created much confusion and running against each other, whereby glasses and panels were demolished without number, the noise of which, accompanied by the screeches of the terrified ladies, was at times truly terrific. It was past seven in the morning before we reached the Abbey, which having once entered, we proceeded to our box without further impediment, Dr. Markham having given us tickets which allowed our passing by a private staircase, and avoiding the immense crowd that was within. We found a hot and comfortable breakfast ready, which I enjoyed, and proved highly refreshing to us all; after which some of our party determined to take a nap in their chairs, whilst I, who was well acquainted with every creek and corner of the Abbey, amused myself running about the long gallery until noon, when notice being given that the procession had began to move, I resumed my seat.

Exactly at one they entered the Abbey, and we had a capital view of the whole ceremony. Their Majesties, (the King having previously married), being crowned, the Archbishop of Canterbury mounted the pulpit to deliver the sermon; and, as many thousands were out of the possibility of hearing a single syllable, they took that opportunity to eat their meal when the general clattering of knives, forks, plates, and glasses that ensued, produced a most ridiculous effect, and a universal burst of laughter followed. The sermon being concluded, the anthem was sung by a numerous band of the first performers in the kingdom, and certainly was the finest thing I had ever heard.

Memoirs, ED. Peter Quennell, 1960

Dinner at Buckingham Palace, 1907

GABRIEL TSCHUMI

Both King Edward and Queen Alexandra were the most considerate of monarchs, and on all state occasions did everything within their power to make their guests feel at home. This was never illustrated so forcibly as at a dinner at Buckingham Palace in 1907, when a well-known Indian guest was in London for the first time and was entertained by their Majesties. As usual, there were no special Indian dishes, but the chef had provided a great many alternate courses so that the guest need not eat any meat forbidden by his religion. Quite high up on the menu was a dish of asparagus served as King Edward liked them best, plain with a little butter sauce, and the Indian visitor agreed to try a little. He was one of the first to begin eating and the King, looking up, saw a footman staring in horror as the visitor, with great unconcern, ate a piece of the delicacy and threw the less tasty part over his shoulder, where it landed with a tiny plop on the carpet. It was a difficult moment, but King Edward responded to it magnificently. He finished all but a small piece of his asparagus, and, following his guest, threw it over his shoulder. Within no time the rest of the party had followed suit, and when the dining-room staff came to clean up after the meal there were dozens of tiny messes of asparagus on the carpet behind the chairs.

Royal Chef, 1954

476

Coronation of George VI, 1937
DIANA COOPER 1892–1986

The Coronation! Nothing but the Coronation. Clothes, uniforms, robes, ermine, miniver, rabbit, velvet, velveteen. Where were the coronets? In the bank, at Carrington's, or in the attic? There were fears for bad places behind stone pillars, absurd fretting over starvation and retiring-rooms, alternative routes to the Abbey via Ealing or Purley. A Coronation still, in 1937, belonged to the Peers. The Ministers did not feel so certain of ringside seats. Still we would be there, and Molyneux embroidered me a gold dress and Eleanor Abbey's genius fashioned me a crown of golden flowers. I looked faded but not, thank God, overblown.

Our places we found to be behind the Viscounts, not all I hoped but good enough. The many hours of expectation were relieved by exquisitely funny comings and goings. Peers without pages in a crowded tribune cannot cope with their velvet robes. One hand holds the coronet, the other gathers up the heavy folds in the most impudic fashion. Retiring-rooms dotted all over the Abbey are magnets. Our Viscounts were dodging in and out like water-carriers. Hunger obsessed them. One, returning from retirement, brought from some first-aid booth an enormous box of mixed chocolate-creams. He naturally stumbled (his velvet brought him down) and the silver-papered chocolates went careering down the steeply built-up tribune. There was an ugly rush to catch them by any Viscount within reach of their rolling.

The Light of Common Day, 1959

Windsor Castle, 1937
DIANA COOPER 1892–1986

After a few minutes Lady Nunburnholme and Sir Hill Child knocked and came in for the smallest possible talk, and a minute or two later Alec Hardinge appeared. He warned me for my good that dinner was at 8.30, leave dining-room with gentlemen at 9.30, but gentlemen don't stop, they walk straight through us to the lu and talk and drinks.

Girls gossip until 10.15 when the men reappear flushed but relieved, and at 10.30 it's 'Good night.'

The Light of Common Day, 1959

Windsor Castle, 1973

JOYCE GRENFELL 1910-79

And in the White and Gold Dining-Room the whole length of the table at which all seventy of us sat was decorated with a repeat pattern of low bowls of yet more pastel-coloured flowers – roses, white, cream and pale yellow; white daisies; carnations, cream and white; and for a touch of colour, an occasional sharp coral-apricot rosebud. The visual pleasures, as they had been the only other time we had been to the castle, were endless. I was so busy looking at the pictures, the flowers, the other guests and finally, when they joined us in the Pink Drawing-Room, at the Queen and her party, that I have now forgotten the details of the procession into the Dining-Room. I know I enjoyed the journey, and remember feeling as if I were in a ballet. The table not only looked pretty with its many flowers, and at each place a five-piece setting of George III Waterford glass, but the food pleased the eye as well. It was just right for a summer occasion; it, too, was almost entirely pastel-coloured; cold avocado soup (pale green), hot salmon-trout (pale pink), veal in a delectable sauce with tiny new potatoes, baby carrots (cream, ivory and pale orange), and the exception to this delicate palette, leaf-spinach echoing the dark green of my dress and the silk damask curtains in the Green Drawing-Room. Then came pineapple ice-cream, piled up in hollow pineapple shells, with the kind of sponge fingers I most like – squidgy. I badly wanted to have a good tuck-in, but resolutely I took only sample-sized helpings and sacrificed greed to the performance ahead.

Towards the end of dinner there was the wailing sound of bagpipes tuning up. I looked across the table at Bill. He was wincing. In spite of having a great-great-grandfather from Dundee, I am not usually moved by the music of the pipes. But, as the party of at least a dozen Scots Guardsmen, in full dress, swung into the Dining-Room at a brisk tempo, their kilts swinging from side to side in perfect unison, I was both stirred and impressed. The volume was deafening. I was glad when they eventually swung out again. As Bill and I agreed later, we could only admire anything so brilliantly performed. We were also, as mere Sassenachs, amused at such goings-on.

When the ladies left the Dining-Room I couldn't join them for coffee because I had to race the long distance of the corridor and down the stairs to Sue's room to change my dress and get back to the White Drawing-Room, where Bill and I were to wait until the moment came for our entrance . . .

Reggie and I danced a little and stared a lot. We had never been inside the castle, and we were taken behind the scenes to see some of the pictures hanging in the curved corridor leading to the private apartments. I noticed an order form, on a table near the bedrooms, on which visiting royalty had written what they wanted for breakfast, and the hour it was to be brought to them. Most had specified nine o'clock and modestly asked for toast and coffee, but one healthy young European princess ordered cold meats – ham *and* beef – to come to her room at some unearthly hour the next morning. Back in the Waterloo Chamber the floor was too crowded for me to see all I wanted to see of the dresses, so we wandered through the drawing-rooms where other like-minded guests were also taking a good look, and what with the flowers, the splendour of the rooms and the people, we decided, as we drove back to London in the breaking light of an early spring dawn, that the evening had been a fair treat.

In Pleasant Places, 1979

The Windsors in Monte Carlo
NOËL COWARD 1899–1973

Monte Carlo
Saturday 6 April 1946.
In the evening the Windsors arrived. The hotel got itself into a fine frizz and Old General Politigor was round my neck like a laurel wreath. I gave them a delicious dinner: consommé, marrow on toast, grilled langouste, tournedos with sauce bearnaise, and chocolate soufflé. Poor starving France. After that we went to the Casino and Wallis and I gambled until 5 a.m. She was very gay and it was most enjoyable. The Duke sat rather dolefully at one of the smaller tables. At the end of the evening I was financially more or less where I started.

The Noël Coward Diaries, ED. Graham Payn and Sheridan Morley, 1982

479

The Windsors in Paris
LESLEY BLANCH 1907–

In Paris I sometimes dined with the Windsors, another house where the finer shades of gastronomy were perfectly expressed. The menus the Duchess composed were never banal; she boldly mixed simple and sophisticated food, thus tickling the most jaded palate. Countrified dishes and local fare such as a *cassoulet*, or a *navarin printanier* were found at her beautiful table, where she might mix rustic pottery with a service of vermeil. Subtle oriental sauces, Mexican black-eyed peas or the homely spud baked in its jacket were enjoyed there, as well as the classic French cuisine at its finest. The Duchess's knowledge was held in high respect by the critical circle of Paris chefs. 'She was the perfect *patron*' was their verdict. The Duke, who sometimes disturbed his chefs' Olympian calm by asking for a sandwich at some unlikely hour, used to speak fervently of typical English food, York ham, crumpets or Gentleman's Relish and once told me he had retained some aged servitor solely for the way in which he cooked the Duke's breakfast bacon.

From Wilder Shores, 1989

Two Wedding Breakfasts from Buckingham Palace
GABRIEL TSCHUMI

BUCKINGHAM PALACE,

Thursday, 26th April 1923.

WEDDING BREAKFAST.

Consommé à la Windsor.

Suprêmes de Saumon, Reine Mary.

Côtelettes d'Agneau, Prince Albert.

Chapons à la Strathmore.

Jambon et Langue découpés à l'Aspic.
Salade Royale.

Asperges, sauce Crême Mousseuse.

Fraises, Duchesse Elizabeth.
Paniers de Friandises.

Dessert.

Café.

Menu of Wedding Breakfast for the Duke and Duchess of York (Afterwards King George VI and Queen Elizabeth)

BUCKINGHAM PALACE

Thursday, 20th November, 1947

WEDDING BREAKFAST.

Filet de Sole Mountbatten

Perdreau en Casserole
Haricots Verts   Pommes Noisette
Salade Royale

Bombe Glacée, Princesse Elizabeth
Friandises

Déssert

Café

Menu of Wedding Breakfast for Princess Elizabeth (Now Queen Elizabeth II) and the Duke of Edinburgh

Royal Chef, 1954

Feast Days

❦

Chinese New Year
HSIANG JU LIN AND TSUIFENG LIN

The best time of all was the New Year festival, lasting two weeks. This was a general holiday for everyone. The servants, who had no days off, could take a few day's holiday to visit their relatives. Others stayed behind; collecting tips from the stream of courtesy callers, and from the guests who stayed to gamble and gave a share of their winnings *pour le personnel*. The joy of New Year came from many directions. Creditors looked forward to getting their debts paid, debtors to settling the accounts somehow. Madams of certain houses were paid at New Year. Children were given new clothes made specially for New Year's Day, and some entered in close alliance with the servants in their expectation of red packets of money, counting the number of visitors, shrewdly assessing their generosity. Housewives were not required to cook, and, in fact, were inviting bad luck if they did so. For this reason, the preparation for the holidays could begin a month ahead to supply the house with food for at least the first few days of the New Year. Great crocks of *chiaotse* were made and stored uncooked, frozen in the chill weather. Restaurants and butchers' shops cooked whole farmyards of chickens, ducks and pigs in tubs of soy sauce, and hung them up to drip, the juices half running out. Women were fond of gathering together in a circle, making little balls out of glutinous rice for dumplings, and discussing the coming holiday, taking care to say only the good and lucky things as they rolled balls of dough between their palms. The aura of the New Year extended a month afterwards if one still had sweet *nienkao* lying about the kitchen, and the chances were very good that this heavy, steamed cake, made from brown sugar and glutinous rice flour, would still be there. It had remarkable lasting and keeping qualities. Sweet *nienkao* came in various sizes, each stamped with a lucky word in red in top, and were exchanged in quantity during the holidays. Cut into slices and fried in oil, they became crusty and even palatable. Their somewhat elastic and rubbery texture was little altered by time, and they appeared indestructible, nor could they be thrown out without qualms. The other gifts, fresh fish, pig's knuckles and cold chickens, and tangerines, symbols of good luck, were received and rapidly disappeared down our throats, but we had to look at the *nienkao* for a long, long time before it went away.

On the morning of New Year's Day (about 5 February) one did not sweep, light fires or pour out water, these being unlucky. Fragrant candles were lit, everyone put on his best new clothes, still stiff from never having been washed, and with smiling faces received callers. Housewives settled down at the mahjong table, refusing to budge, telling people to help themselves to cold food. The clatter of mahjong chips mingled with the constant explosions of firecrackers, whose sulphurous fumes mingled with the light of the flickering candles. Children scampered about, for once freed from watchful mother's eyes, and went with their fathers to the fair. The devout chose to go to the temples, shaking out their fortunes for the next year by tipping out one stick from a large bundle. The sticks, each bearing a coded fortune, were tapered. The slight protrusion of one from the bundle caused the others to nudge it out even further with each shake of the cylinder, so that eventually it fell to the ground. The coded fortune was translated for a small fee by a gentleman sitting in a booth, to the side. The temple was permanent, but at New Year the fair would be set up close to it, so that the throngs going to each eventually milled about each other, and it was impossible to tell which was which.

The fortune-tellers were next to the physiognomists, and these were close to the main square where the jugglers and acrobats, sword-swallowers, magicians, boxers, animal trainers and story-tellers entertained the people. One listened to tales, told by the rhythm of the wooden fish, the *pipa* and the *huchin*. One goggled at the magician producing a steaming bowl of noodles from beneath a quilt, squinted into the Foreign Mirror, a kind of peepshow, and gazed at the pictures of magnified objects, more remote, it seemed, than the pictures of fairies and wise men. Farmers bought pictures of the farmer and the ox, and sugar animals for their children. Wineshops and teashops were jammed. Poor people, to make a few pennies, would fill waterpipes. About the lakes, people would throw pieces of steamed bread to the turtles and fish, or feed them pieces of orange. So it continued, with some marathon gambling games, until the sixteenth of the month, when the students went back to their books, and farmers and artisans went back to work. Then the housewife returned to her kitchen, and the chef to his cleaver and chopping board and his bottles of sauces. Now all things were back in their proper places.

Chinese Gastronomy, 1969

Sit and Be Hungry

RAYMOND SOKOLOV 1941–

Passover is a gastronomic holiday whose main point is to teach children about the privation of flight and exile. The protracted preprandial service forces the young to sit and be hungry, to experience directly the pangs their ancestors felt in the desert. During that service, they are from time to time allowed to consume small amounts of wine and symbolic anti-foods – salt water and horseradish and haroset (chopped fruits and nuts) – culinary eccentricities never eaten at any other time in quite this way, even during the Passover week. For an hour or so, the children wait and listen to an incomprehensibly scholastic and nonnarrative analysis of the historical events described in the book of Exodus. They grow hungry and then they are fed a very full meal, but a meal which is itself circumscribed by a set of prohibitions unique to the occasion.

So there are two systems of paradox at work. The first is that of the anti-meal of the service; the second is that of the special dietary restrictions of the Passover meal itself. The first paradox – the service of the Haggadah – is an object lesson in history taught through mortification of the flesh and a subversion of normal eating. This service is a fast in the form of a meal. The second paradox of the Seder embodies an even more fundamental paradox. It is the opposition between normal eating, whose most basic act is the consumption of bread, and the special festivities of the Seder, whose basic act is the consumption of unleavened anti-bread, matzo.

The Jewish American Kitchen, 1989

No-Ruz

O. A. MERRITT-HAWKES

No-Ruz, the great festival, begins at five in the morning on New Year's Day (21st March) and continues for thirteen days. It is a very ancient spring-festival; and is the only important annual, national holiday observed by the Persians. It is the historical equivalent of our Easter, but – whereas in the West, Christianity has so successfully domesticated the spring rejoicing that the majority of people would even be shocked to know its real origin – in Persia, the Moslem religion has not left the slightest impression upon this primitive rejoicing in the sun, fertility and re-awakening life.

On No-Ruz day the Shah sits on his Peacock Throne in Tehran, and receives all who are important enough to be received. Until a few years ago he used to give each one a golden coin. In the capital, the clubs, the restaurants, the hotels are gay, almost like an ordinary holiday in any part of the world. Little by little, slowly in remote places, quickly in large towns, No-Ruz is losing its old character and becoming merely a holiday with journeys to far friends and relations, local visits from house to house, as in Scotland and America, for there is a strong tendency to be ashamed of and despise these old habits. But perhaps some day in Persia, as has happened in England, the old symbols, after having been swept away, will be revived because of their picturesqueness and the satisfaction that comes to civilized people from feeling themselves in touch with the primitive.

Today, every shop, every house in England has its Easter eggs, but twenty years ago they were rare. What one European said is probably true, 'Today, Persia, in her struggle against the old ideas, which means a fight against ignorance, dirt and disease, cannot afford the luxury of the antique'.

Although I reached Bushire a fortnight before the festival it was already dominating the thoughts and plans of all classes. The bazaar showed its coming just as our European shops foretell the coming of Easter and Christmas. The sweetmeat shops were gay, almost too gay, with intense pink, green and orange colouring in the many sweets. Cakes were shaped, for luck, like crescents and hearts and decorated with bright orange icing and pistachios. Saffron, that favourite flavouring, was everywhere, making the bazaars smell strongly – call it a perfume or a stink, it depends upon your point of view. Bunches of wild pink gladioli and red poppies stood in vases among sweets, vegetables, meat and flies. Long strings of dried yellow dates were festooned across the shops, and there were especially large quantities of dried prawns and shrimps, which looked awful, smelt worse, but actually tasted very good. Everywhere there were pomegranates, symbols of fruitfulness throughout the East, on account of their red colour and many seeds. They were always decorated, and sometimes entirely covered, with bits of gold paper.

Beggars developed a special trade at this season; in one hand they held a little tray on which was a tiny dish of sprouting barley or wheat, and in the other hand a vase of rose-water which they sprinkled over passers-by, saying, 'Allah is one God, Mahomet is his prophet'. This salutation, together with the sprouting corn, brought good luck, so in return the pedestrian put money, dates, herbs, sweets, cakes upon the tray. I was nearly drenched by the time I reached the end of the bazaar and did not smell very nice, for rose-water is not always as sweet as roses.

In the smaller towns, No-Ruz is, as it has been for centuries, not resplendent with public happenings, but intense with primitive and domestic feeling. Eating is important in this as in all festivals throughout the world, so, for days before, the bazaar is full of buyers and sellers, cooks are working overtime and housewives are too busy to be visible.

Every house must, if it can afford it, have a representative collection of the produce of the country laid out on a table, a chicken plucked but not cooked, a fish uncooked, a little of every kind of vegetable and fruit, not only grown locally but from all parts of Persia. In the middle of the table is a mirror on which is placed an egg, which should, according to tradition, turn round in the night at the moment when the old year ends and the new begins. The old say it does, the young smile or are silent – that depends upon their degree of emancipation. The egg is the sun, the mirror the heavens. The old year does not end at the conventional midnight, but with the astronomical year. No-Ruz is the old Zoroastrian festival, celebrated in the famous friezes at Persepolis, hence a lamp is lit just when the year begins and should be kept alight for two hours. This lamp is, even to many Persians, merely a symbol of brightness and hope, but those who know realize that the lamp on the table today represents the fire on the sculptures at Naghshe Rostam and the spirit of the God of Good, Hormuzd.

The first duty of everyone is to pay their respects to the head of the family, who now generally sits upon a chair instead of on the floor. His hand is kissed by all the members of the family, and he, in return, kisses their face, and hands them a coin; the relations then kiss one another, saying, 'The best of good wishes to you', a greeting which is world-wide at the New Year. In Ispahan, I do not know in how many other towns, the guests, upon arrival, have rose-water poured over their hands, and sometimes their heads.

In a country where *purdah* is still general, there has to be a good deal of manoeuvring to allow both men and women to do their New Year duty and yet not permit the women to be seen by any men but their father, husband or brother. In the *anderoon*, where the women live, in the public room where the men receive their friends, one or more tables are laid with innumerable dishes of biscuits, sweets, nuts, fruit, a very large and Europeanized iced cake, hard-boiled eggs coloured red and yellow, stiff bunches of flowers, and a small dish of sprouting barley and wheat. In the more advanced houses the food is covered with a net, which may be plain or decorated with tinsel and embroideries, for everywhere there are multitudes of flies. The nuts are almonds, walnuts, salted toasted pistachios and filberts, and marrow and melon seeds.

On arrival the guests are given exceedingly strong tea in tiny glasses, without holders in the houses of the poor, with holders when people are better off; and in the homes of the rich there are heavy elaborate silver holders, each standing upon an elaborate silver tray. A great weight of silver and clever craftsmanship frequently takes the place of taste. In houses where Western influence is strong, the men have whiskies and sodas (when they can be obtained) as well as wine and the Persian spirit, *arak*. Everyone smokes cigarettes, and many the hubble-bubble, or *kalyon*, which is passed from mouth to mouth without fear of infection.

Persia, Romance & Reality, 1935

First Married Christmas
OSA JOHNSON 1894–1953

Osa Johnson was a sixteen-year-old schoolgirl when she met and married Martin Johnson, ten years her senior, in 1910. He had been one of the crew who sailed around the world with Jack London and his wife in 1907. This was their first Christmas together.

It took nearly everything we had for railroad fare, so when we arrived on Christmas Eve in Denver we pawned Martin's watch for five dollars, then hunted up a rooming house within walking distance of the theaters in the center of town where we hoped we might secure bookings.

'This will be fine, Martin,' I said, trying not to look at the torn places in the wallpaper. 'You go out and get some eggs and bread or something while I unpack, but don't spend more than fifty cents, because we might not get a booking right away.'

'Yes,' replied Martin in a kind of croak. 'Our first Christmas together and all I can do is go buy some eggs for my wife to fry over a gas flame.'

'Martin!' I ran to him. His face was hot and flushed. 'You've got a fever – you're sick!'

'I'm not sick, I'm just mad and disgusted with myself. I had no right to drag you into anything like this!' He was shouting by now. 'Look at that wallpaper! Layer on layer of it, dirty and peeling!' He seized a piece that was loose and ripped it from floor to ceiling. He began to laugh.

I wanted to cry, but instead I scolded and bossed him and got him into bed; then took fifty cents of our five dollars and ran out to get some lemons and quinine.

It was dusk now and sharply cold. In no time at all the tip of my nose was numb, and my feet pounded like stumps in the hard packed snow. I found a grocery store in the next block and bought some lemons. The nearest drugstore, I was told, was three blocks down and one block over.

Somehow I lost my way; I don't know how, and still strong upon me was the warning not to speak to strangers. I doubled back, I turned corner after corner in streets that were dark and alien. The tears ran unchecked from my eyes and nose, and with no sobs to dramatize them. My handkerchief was now a frozen ball that scratched my face.

I turned another corner and there, suddenly and miraculously, was a window edged in frosty lace like a valentine, and holding in its frame the great round crystal globes of green, blue and red liquid that said here was a drugstore. All terror dropped from the night as I stared at them, limpid-clear, glowing, warm. Here I would find the medicine I needed for Martin. To-morrow was Christmas – I'd nurse him out of his cold and, with care, our four dollars and fifty cents would see us through until he was better. Why, the very size of the city, which had been so frightening when I felt myself lost, assured me that somewhere there would be a theater that would want to put on Martin's fine lecture. It began to snow. Big, feathery, gentle flakes.

It was warm in the drugstore and bright, with a clean bitterish smell. I bought the quinine and had twenty-five cents left. The druggist, a kindly gentleman in a very white apron, directed me back to the shabby street where our rooming house stood and I set out on the run. Martin would be worried. Perhaps he would also be hungry. Most certainly I was.

I caught sight of a hand-lettered card in the window of a lunch room. 'Christmas dinner now being served,' it said. 'Twenty-five cents.'

Wonderful, I thought, and went in. The proprietor was a stout, energetic little woman who bounced as she walked. She listened sympathetically when I told her my husband was sick, and piled up a tray with some beef hash over which she poured a dark gravy. 'Genuine turkey flavor,' she said. Some mashed potatoes, pickled beets – 'exactly the color of cranberries,' – two thick slices of bread, a sad looking piece of apple pie and a cup of coffee completed the 'Christmas dinner.'

The tray was heavy and the snow now drove straight into my face. My footing on the ice-rutted sidewalk was precarious at best, and to see it at all I now lifted the tray to the top of my head. Added to my worries, of course, was the fear of breaking the dishes and having to pay for them out of our little bit of money.

Panting but relieved, I reached our rooming house with nothing spilled except the coffee. Hurrying up the stairs to our room on the second floor, I pushed the door open.

Cutting cleanly through the stale odors of cabbage, dust and grease, was the fresh, spicy smell of carnations. Then I saw them in the water pitcher – a great bouquet – all white, as I loved them best.

'Martin – the flowers – who – here in Denver? Who sent them to us? How did they find us?'

My husband lay shivering, the bedclothes pulled up around his head, his feet uncovered, out at the bottom. I set the tray down and fixed this, then shaking the snow from my coat put it over him. The bed quilts were thin and filled with wadded cotton. I looked around for something else and wished passionately for some of Grandma's good lamb's wool quilts. Martin's big overcoat. That would help. I picked it up from the chair over which he had thrown it and found it damp to my hand. And there on the shoulders I saw some flakes of only partly melted snow. I looked at the dressing table then where the four dollars and fifty cents had been. It was gone.

I Married Adventure, 1940

We Were Specially Poor
REBECCA WEST 1892–1983

We had a specially magnificent Christmas that year, though we were specially poor. For some reason that was left unstated Constance and Rosamund stayed with us all through the holidays: and they helped Mamma to make our dresses, which were the best we ever had; and Rosamund was beautiful to dress up. Richard was in good health by Christmas Day, and Papa had made for him an Arabian Nights Palace with looking-glass fountains in arcaded courtyards, and domes painted strange colours, very pale, very bright. When we saw it none of us could speak, and Mamma put her hand on his arm and said to us, 'No other father could do this for his children.' Several times, I remember, she came and sat on the floor with us when we were playing with it, and exclaimed every now and then, 'How does he think of such things? How does the idea come into his head?' Very soon I forgot the existence of Mrs. Phillips and Aunt Lily. But one morning all four of us, Cordelia and Mary and Rosamund and I, went into the best confectioner's at Lovegrove, to buy some meringues for Richard Quin's birthday tea; and because the assistant said there would be a batch of pink meringues coming up in a minute, we waited and watched the shop behind us reflected in the mirrored wall behind the counter. There was something called 'the confectioners' licence' which played its part in suburban society; and the place was a cave of well-being, crammed with tables at which well-dressed women, with cairns of parcels piled up on chairs beside them, leaned towards each other, their always large busts overhanging plates of tiny sandwiches and small glasses of port and sherry and madeira, and exchanged gossip that mounted to the low ceiling and was transformed to the twittering of birds in an aviary.

We had just time to get into our fancy dresses before dinner, which was wonderful. One of Papa's relatives in Ireland who never wanted to see us always sent us a turkey and a ham, and we had both sausage and chestnut stuffing with the turkey. Mamma had worried because the removal from Scotland had meant that she could not make her Christmas puddings before October, which was later than she had ever left it before, but really the one we had could not have been better. Each of us children got a charm out of the pudding, which we thought happened by chance. Afterwards we had tangerines, and almonds and raisins, and Carlsbad plums from the box with a picture of a plum on it which Papa's City friend, Mr. Langham, sent us every Christmas. We could not have crackers, none of us could bear the bang. On the sideboard there was one of the bottles of port which the margarine manufacturer had sent Papa, and he poured out two glasses for himself and Mamma, and then he asked Mamma if it were not true that Kate's mother, who was now a washerwoman at Wimbledon, and her brother, a blue-jacket on leave, were having their dinner with her in the kitchen. Since it was so, Cordelia was sent down to ask him to come up and drink a glass of port with Papa.

The Fountain Overflows, 1957

We Mean to Have a Large Turkey
SYDNEY SMITH 1771–1845

TO LADY GREY

Combe Florey, Taunton, Dec. 21st, 1843
So Mrs Sydney and I after a life of bustle and parturition are left alone. – We mean to have a large Turkey on Xmas day just the same as when there were people to eat it and we mean to have a twelfth Cake and draw King and Queen, a remarkable instance of the power of habit.

Selected Letters, ED. Nowell C. Smith, 1956

No Hams in Narayangunj
JON 1906–84 AND RUMER 1907– GODDEN

Christmas is usually marked by a feast of eating and drinking, but not for us: there were no traditional hams in Narayangunj, no turkeys; we had a goose which we children would not eat; it had been tethered near the cookhouse for weeks and we had fed it, unknowingly helping to fatten it. Mam and Aunt Mary made a Christmas cake which we all stirred – it was iced with home-made-looking icing; they made mince pies and we had a Christmas-pudding, tinned; but the only unusual treat, the one to which we looked forward, was the crystallised fruit put on the luncheon table as if for a dinner party; we were allowed six crystallised cherries each and one large fruit; it was agonising to choose between a candy pink pear, a dark greengage, or one of the deep gold globes of peaches.

After lunch it was time to dress for the Club party, the second highlight of the day . . .

On Christmas Day the Club was open not only to Europeans but to Eurasians and Anglo-Indians if they had children to bring. Long tables were set out on the lawn for tea; from bamboo poles enormous paper crackers were hung; when tea was over they would be burst open with a stick and a shower of parched rice and gimcrack presents would rain down on the children beneath. There was always a special cracker filled with pice, annas and four-anna bits for the ayahs, but Hannah was too dignified to join in the scramble; sometimes it turned into a fight with two ayahs fighting and tearing at each other's veils.

Two Under the Indian Sun, 1966

Meshed

ROBERT BYRON 1905–41

Meshed, Christmas Day   Hamber and I had lunch with Mr and Mrs Hart, also in the Consulate, and their little son Keith. I ate too much pudding, felt sick as one always does on Christmas afternoon, and was in form again for dinner. To this Hamber entertained the whole American mission, the Harts, and a German girl from Bolivia, governess to a family here, who was mondaine in a Teutonic cocktail-sniggering sort of way. Games followed. I won a fountain pen, the men's prize for trimming a lady's hat.

The Road to Oxiana, 1937

In the Lonely Cottage
D. H. LAWRENCE 1885–1930

It was Christmas time, and two friends came down to stay at the cottage with the Somers. Those were the days before America joined the Allies. The man friend arrived with a whole parcel of American dainties, buckwheat meal and sweet potatoes and maple sugar: the woman friend brought a good basket of fruit. They were to have a Christmas in the lonely cottage in spite of everything.

Kangaroo, 1923

Were There Any Sweets?
DYLAN THOMAS 1914–53

SELF: On Christmas Eve I hung at the foot of my bed Bessie Bunter's black stocking, and always, I said, I would stay awake all the moonlit, snowlit night to hear the roof-alighting reindeer and see the hollied boot descend through soot. But soon the sand of the snow drifted into my eyes, and, though I stared towards the fire-place and around the flickering room where the black sack-like stocking hung, I was asleep before the chimney trembled and the room was red and white with Christmas. But in the morning, though no snow melted on the bedroom floor, the stocking bulged and brimmed: press it, it squeaked like a mouse-in-a-box; it smelt of tangerine; a furry arm lolled over, like the arm of a kangaroo out of its mother's belly; squeeze it hard in the middle, and something squelched; squeeze it again – squelch again. Look out of the frost-scribbled window: on the great loneliness of the small hill, a blackbird was silent in the snow.

SMALL BOY: Were there any sweets?

SELF: Of course there were sweets. It was the marshmallows that squelched. Hardboileds, toffee, fudge and allsorts, crunches, cracknels, humbugs, glaciers, and marzipan and butterwelsh for the Welsh. And troops of bright tin soldiers who, if they would not fight, could always run. And Snakes-and-Families and Happy

Ladders. And Easy Hobbi-Games for Little Engineers, complete with Instructions. Oh, easy for Leonardo! And a whistle to make the dogs bark to wake up the old man next door to make him beat on the wall with his stick to shake our picture off the wall. And a packet of cigarettes: you put one in your mouth and you stood at the corner of the street and you waited for hours, in vain, for an old lady to scold you for smoking a cigarette and then, with a smirk, you ate it. And, last of all, in the toe of the stocking, sixpence like a silver corn. And then downstairs for breakfast under the balloons! . . .

SMALL BOY: Why didn't you go home for Christmas dinner?

SELF: Oh, but I did, I always did. I would be slap-dashing home, the gravy smell of the dinners of others, the bird smell, the brandy, the pudding and mince, weaving up my nostrils, when out of a snow-clogged side-lane would come a boy the spit of myself, with a pink-tipped cigarette and the violet past of a black eye, cocky as a bullfinch, leering all to himself. I hated him on sight and sound, and would be about to put my dog-whistle to my lips and blow him off the face of Christmas when suddenly he, with a violet wink, put *his* whistle to *his* lips and blew so stridently, so high, so exquisitely loud, that gobbling faces, their cheeks bulged with goose, would press against their tinselled windows, the whole length of the white echoing street.

SMALL BOY: What did you have for Dinner?

SELF: Turkey, and blazing pudding.

SMALL BOY: Was it nice?

SELF: It was not made on earth.

'Conversation About Christmas', Collected Stories, 1980

Ill-assorted People

M. F. K. FISHER 1908–92

It must not simply be taken for granted that a given set of ill-assorted people, for no other reason than because it is Christmas, will be joyful to be reunited and to break bread together. They must be jolted, even shocked, into excitement and surprise and subsequent delight. All the old routine patterns of food and flowers and cups must be redistributed, to break up the mortal ignominy of the family dinner, when what has too often been said and felt and thought is once more said, felt, and thought: slow poison in every mouthful, old grudges, new hateful boredom, nascent antagonism and resentment – why in God's name does Mother always put her arm *that* way on the chair, and why does Helen's girdle always pop as she lifts the denuded meat platter up and away from Father, and why does Sis always tap her fingers thus tinnily against the rim of her wine glass? Poison, indeed, and most deeply to be shunned!

An Alphabet for Gourmets, 1949

Glennie Nell's Roast Christmas Possum
ERNEST MATTHEW MICKLER 1940–88

1 live possum	5 or 6 slices of bacon
½ cup vinegar	Salt and pepper
Kitchen Bouquet	8 to 10 medium sweet potaters
Persimmon jam	

Now, Christmas possum is different from all other possum. It's got to be caught, not killed, two weeks to a month before the cookin day. That's right round late November. You can catch 'em in the hen house, or up a 'simmon tree or in a trap. It don't make no never mind, long as he's caught live, cause they got to be penned up so you can clean 'em out. Feed 'em nothin but corn bread and milk. That'll fix 'em up, fatten 'em out, and get rid of all them no-good flavors. This makes possum as good as corn-fed pig. Then, when the time comes, kill 'em quick, skin the rascal an git shed of all the insides.

Now you got a possum ready for cookin. Sink 'em in a 'namel dish pan or basin and make sure he's good an covered. Then add a half cup of vinegar and let it soak in the icebox overnight. In the morning drain off the water and cut up the possum into rabbit pieces. Thata way the city folk'll never know they eatin possum. An I'ma tellin ya it works. Boil the possum pieces in enough salted water until it's done, but not fallin off the bone. This timin depends on the age of the possum. Sometimes it's ready in a hour, other times it'll take two. When it's done, fish out the pieces and drain 'em. That'll git ridda just about all the possum grease. When it's cool, so you can handle it, rub the rabbit-size possum pieces with salt and black pepper. Plenty. Then make a mixture of Kitchen Bouquet and half a jar of persimmon jam. I always make my jam just after the first frost cause then it's sweeter, that is, if the possums ain't done et 'em all. Just a teaspoon or two of the Kitchen Bouquet and stir it into the jam. Now, if you ain't got persimmon jam, any light tastin one'll do. Smear the stuff all over the pieces until you've got 'em coated good. Lay on four or five slices of salt pork or bacon and surround it with ya greased sweet potaters. Put it in a hot oven at 350 degrees and roast, covered, for thirty minutes. Then uncover it and cook till it's sizzlin browned but never burned (about another thirty minutes). Spoon the juice up on it every few minutes while it's uncovered. I don't think I know a soul that don't surround their possum with sweet potaters, cause it takes just about a good hour for 'em to bake. Be extry shore ya possum is done. They ain't nothing in the world worst than bein accused of servin half-baked possum.

Sinkin Spells, Hot Flushes, Fits and Cravins, 1988

Real Old-fashioned Xmas
KATHERINE MANSFIELD 1888–1923

Katherine Mansfield went to Gurdjieff's Institute for the Harmonious Development of Man at Avon, Fontainebleau in October 1922. Her husband John Middleton Murry arrived for a visit on 9 January 1923 and she died that evening.

TO IDA BAKER

Le Prieuré. [24 December 1922]
We are going to fêter le Noel [celebrate Christmas] in tremendous style here. Every sort of lavish generous hospitable thing has been done by Mr Gurdjieff. He wants a real old fashioned *English* Xmas – an extraordinary idea here! – & we shall sit down to table 60 persons to turkeys, geese, a whole sheep, a pig, puddings, heaven knows what in the way of dessert, & wines by the barrel. Theres to be a tree, too & Father Xmas. I am doing all I can for the little children so that they will be roped in for once. Ive just sent them over coloured paper & asked them to help to make flowers. Its pathetic the interest they are taking – –

497

Our pudding was made in a babys bath, stirred by everybody & Mr
Gurdjieff put in a coin.

Selected Letters, 1989

A Whole Orange for Christmas
NORMAN LONGMATE 1926–

'I woke early . . . made sure the black-out curtains were over the
windows and . . . had a little peep at my presents . . . I had a pair
of slacks, Mummy made them out of a blanket . . . a bar of
chocolate, a whole orange.'
Diary of a ten-year-old schoolgirl, Christmas Day 1941

Christmas provided the greatest challenge of all. Turkeys were scarce
and expensive throughout the war and for an Oldham schoolgirl the
privations of wartime were summed up in her family's Christmas
dinner in 1944: mutton pie followed by 'wartime Christmas pudding',
made with grated carrots. (The official recipes also suggested grated
apples and chopped prunes and dried elderberries to replace the
missing dried fruit. The results were rarely very palatable to those old
enough to remember the real thing.) One Manchester woman had even
more reason than most to remember the great blitz of December 1940,
for 'my mother's house in Didsbury had had a direct hit *and* my
mother-in-law's house in Chorlton and they all descended on me in my
little flat. Our Christmas dinner consisted of corned beef hash and
wartime Christmas pudding, but we listened to the wireless, sang,
played cards and generally had a good time.' Alcohol of any kind was
hard to find. The Radio Doctor, as usual, struck the right note when,
broadcasting one wartime Christmas on the possible causes of a
hangover, he remarked incredulously: 'It may even be due to too much
drink, though if it was I'd like to know where you got it.'

How We Lived Then, 1971

Thirty-one Fruit Cakes
TRUMAN CAPOTE 1924–84

Imagine a morning in late November. A coming of winter morning more than twenty years ago. Consider the kitchen of a spreading old house in a country town. A great black stove is its main feature; but there is also a big round table and a fireplace with two rocking chairs placed in front of it. Just today the fireplace commenced its seasonable roar.

A woman with shorn white hair is standing at the kitchen window. She is wearing tennis shoes and a shapeless gray sweater over a summery calico dress. She is small and sprightly, like a bantam hen; but, due to a long youthful illness, her shoulders are pitifully hunched. Her face is remarkable – not unlike Lincoln's, craggy like that, and tinted by sun and wind; but it is delicate too, finely boned, and her eyes are sherry-colored and timid. 'Oh my,' she exclaims, her breath smoking the windowpane, 'it's fruitcake weather!'

The person to whom she is speaking is myself. I am seven; she is sixty-something. We are cousins, very distant ones, and we have lived together – well, as long as I can remember . . .

It's always the same: a morning arrives in November, and my friend, as though officially inaugurating the Christmas time of year that exhilarates her imagination and fuels the blaze of her heart, announces: 'It's fruitcake weather! Fetch our buggy. Help me find my hat.' . . .

We eat our supper (cold biscuits, bacon, blackberry jam) and discuss tomorrow. Tomorrow the kind of work I like best begins: buying. Cherries and citron, ginger and vanilla and canned Hawaiian pine-apple, rinds and raisins and walnuts and whiskey and oh, so much flour, butter, so many eggs, spices, flavorings: why, we'll need a pony to pull the buggy home . . .

The black stove, stoked with coal and firewood, glows like a lighted pumpkin. Eggbeaters whirl, spoons spin round in bowls of butter and sugar, vanilla sweetens the air, ginger spices it; melting, nose-tingling odors saturate the kitchen, suffuse the house, drift out to the world on puffs of chimney smoke. In four days our work is done. Thirty-one cakes, dampened with whiskey, bask on window sills and shelves . . .

Christmas Eve afternoon we scrape together a nickel and go to the butcher's to buy Queenie's traditional gift, a good gnawable beef bone. The bone, wrapped in funny paper, is placed high in the tree near

499

the silver star. Queenie knows it's there. She squats at the foot of the tree staring up in a trance of greed: when bedtime arrives she refuses to budge. Her excitement is equaled by my own. I kick the covers and turn my pillow as though it were a scorching summer's night. Somewhere a rooster crows: falsely, for the sun is still on the other side of the world.

'Buddy, are you awake?' It is my friend, calling from her room, which is next to mine; and an instant later she is sitting on my bed holding a candle. 'Well, I can't sleep a hoot,' she declares. 'My mind's jumping like a jack rabbit. Buddy, do you think Mrs. Roosevelt will serve our cake at dinner?' We huddle in the bed, and she squeezes my hand I-love-you. 'Seems like your hand used to be so much smaller. I guess I hate to see you grow up. When you're grown up, will we still be friends?' I say always. 'But I feel so bad, Buddy. I wanted so bad to give you a bike. I tried to sell my cameo Papa gave me. Buddy' – she hesitates, as though embarrassed – 'I made you another kite.' Then I confess that I made her one, too; and we laugh. The candle burns too short to hold. Out it goes, exposing the starlight, the stars spinning at the window like a visible caroling that slowly, slowly daybreak silences. Possibly we doze; but the beginnings of dawn splash us like cold water: we're up, wide-eyed and wandering while we wait for others to waken. Quite deliberately my friend drops a kettle on the kitchen floor. I tap-dance in front of closed doors. One by one the household emerges, looking as though they'd like to kill us both; but it's Christmas, so they can't. First, a gorgeous breakfast: just everything you can imagine – from flapjacks and fried squirrel to hominy grits and honey-in-the-comb. Which puts everyone in a good humor except my friend and me. Frankly, we're so impatient to get at the presents we can't eat a mouthful.

Well, I'm disappointed. Who wouldn't be? With socks, a Sunday school shirt, some handkerchiefs, a hand-me-down sweater and a year's subscription to a religious magazine for children. *The Little Shepherd*. It makes me boil. It really does.

My friend has a better haul. A sack of Satsumas, that's her best present. She is proudest, however, of a white wool shawl knitted by her married sister. But she *says* her favorite gift is the kite I built her. And it *is* very beautiful; though not as beautiful as the one she made me, which is blue and scattered with gold and green Good Conduct stars; moreover, my name is painted on it, 'Buddy.'

'Buddy, the wind is blowing.'

A Christmas Memory, 1956

First Cross Creek Christmas

MARJORIE KINNAN RAWLINGS 1896–1953

He introduced himself on my first Christmas Day at the Creek. He came out with a man named Whitey and it was a formal Christmas call. I was bustling about cooking Christmas dinner, some of the family were there, and Moe and Whitey sat on the back steps and visited with the men. It was long past the country noon dinner hour and I grew uneasy as the turkey browned and the squash and potatoes were done and the hard sauce finished for the plum pudding. I took my outdoor shower and dressed. I delayed, pushing the gravy to the back of the wood range. Moe and Whitey sat on. The turkey was beginning to dry out and the sauce had stood too long on the oyster cocktails in the ice-box.

In desperation, I said, 'Dinner is ready. Won't you men join us?'

According to my bringing up, that was the signal for uninvited guests to be on their way. I found that in rural Florida, to refuse an invitation to a meal, if one is there at the time it is ready or nearly so, is to insult hospitality so grievously that the damage can seldom be repaired. Moe and Whitey had of course had their dinner, but to my horror Moe said, 'Thank you, Ma'am,' led Whitey to the pump stand to wash up and came in. The family dinner was ruined for me. The intruders were as unhappy as I, but applied themselves with lowered heads and high-lifted elbows to their plates. Whitey was plainly only a follower and I stole a look at Moe. He was a great burly man with long arms and thick shoulders, slightly hunched from years of labor. His head was massive and beyond a full fine forehead the receding hair was shaggy and leonine. There was the look there of a man who might have been a statesman. He had one of the most beautiful speaking voices that I have ever heard. It had the deep resonance of a bass fiddle.

He plowed his way through the many-coursed dinner without comment. When I served the plum pudding that had taken so long to make and decorate, he looked briefly at the blanched almonds and sugared fruits on the top and scraped them to one side, as I should scrape unexpected insects. The dinner had been one of my best, and it seemed to me from the rough worn clothes and the backwoods speech that it must surely have been a little out of the ordinary for these men. My vanity about my cooking is known and pandered to, and it seemed incredible to me that uninvited guests like these should not only pay me no compliments, but should have put down the choice dishes like so much hay.

I said, 'You men have just eaten a typical Yankee Christmas dinner. Now tell me, what is the usual Cracker Christmas dinner?'

Moe lifted his big head and looked at me gravely.

'Whatever we can git, Ma'am,' he said. 'Whatever we can git.'

I should have given the dinner and all my work over it, not to have asked that question.

I heard later that in the village Moe described the meal dish by dish. He spoke even of the edible decorations on the plum pudding that he rejected.

'A meal like that,' I was told he said, 'a feller don't know what's cold-out rations and what's fancy fixin's. When I seed her face, I knowed I'd ought to of run the risk and et everything.'

Cross Creek, 1942

Two Christmases in Jamaica, 1949 and 1956
NOËL COWARD 1899–1973

1956 was the year Coward wrote: 'I have taken to cooking and listening to Wagner, both of which frighten me to death.'

Saturday 24 December 1949. Jamaica
A curious Christmas Eve. We lay in the broiling sun in the morning and floated over the reef on lilos. After that we went over to Port Maria, came home to a lunch of baked parrot-fish, packed and wrapped presents and gave them to the staff. Dined with Ian (Fleming), more presents, then canasta. All very enjoyable and full of charm.

31 December 1956. Jamaica
The Christmas dinner itself was fairly nasty because neither Coley nor I had time to oversee the preparations. The Turkey was passable, but there were no sausages with it, no rolls of bacon and no bread sauce, and the roast potatoes were beige and palely loitering.

The Noël Coward Diaries, ED. Graham Payn and Sheridan Morley,
1982

The Royal Household

GABRIEL TSCHUMI

We were particularly busy at Christmas, for Queen Victoria made presents of food to a great many people at this time. The workers on the estates would all be given a shoulder of lamb for their families, and a number of large raised pies were sent by her to friends. These pies were a great delicacy and took a lot of preparation. The birds used in them – turkey, chicken, pheasant and woodcock – had each to be boned and a stuffing of forcemeat, truffles and tongue prepared. The woodcock was put inside the pheasant, the pheasant inside the chicken, and the chicken inside the turkey, packed around with stuffing. A very rich pastry was used, and when the pie was sliced each piece had the different flavours of the birds from which it was made.

The staff had a particularly good Christmas dinner of turkeys, roast cygnet, plum puddings, mince-pies and roasted chestnuts. But sometimes after working so closely with food we had little appetite for Christmas dinner.

Royal Chef, 1954

Provence

SYBILLE BEDFORD 1911–

We went to the midnight mass at Les Baux – which was a touch for *les touristes,* and the lamb was led out alive – slept at Arles and walked next morning in the Cloister of St-Trophime, then on the Pont-du-Gard and to Le Nôtre's Garden and the arenas at Nîmes – the three of us happy in places we loved. On the third day we went down into the Rhône delta to Les-Saintes-Maries-de-la-Mer and Aigues-Mortes, and felt subdued by an eerie emptiness of winter. On our way to Sanary we were basking again, eating lunch on the Cours Mirabeau at Aix, sitting outside in the Café Les Deux Garçons in the mid-December sun. At Les Cyprès, Emilia had laid a fire of olive logs, which my mother lit. For kindling there were cypress cuttings, the chimney smoked a little but the smell was delicious.

Social life was in abeyance, the Kislings as well as the Desmirails had gone skiing. Sister Annette, the youngest Panigon, told me when I ran into her on the port, that Frédéric was away doing his *service militaire*. New Year's Eve we spent at home on our own, eating oysters from la *mère* Dédée, followed by *boudin blanc*, drinking Cassis which was then the liveliest, most aromatic dry white wine to be had in Provence. At midnight Emilia joined us, and my mother made us perform superstitious rituals recalled from her diverse origins, ending as the Romans do by breaking some glass. We each made a wish (undisclosed). My mother said, 'May we all live happily ever after.'

On New Year's Day – which in France was *the* day of the Christmas season for eating as well as presents – we were bidden to a large déjeuner the Panigons were giving for their cronies. The long menu was well composed and far less heavy and indigestible than what would have been unavoidably put before us in Britain. We began with a platter of *fruits de mer*: *palourdes*, *claires*, *écrevisses*, *oursins*, followed by *quenelles de brochet* as light as feathers, then some *dindonneaux*, small young turkeys, roasted unstuffed in butter, served with their own unthickened roasting juices and accompanied only by a creamy chestnut purée and a sharp salad of watercress; some carefully chosen cheeses and a *bombe à glace*. We drank Cassis with the shellfish, Pouilly-Fuissé with the *quenelles*, Bordeaux with the roast birds, burgundy with the cheese, and champagne (sec not brut) with the ice pudding. Brandy, *eaux-de-vie* and liqueurs – how not? – with the coffee.

Jigsaw, 1989

The Wilder Shores of Gastronomy

◄§§►

Barnacles That Are Born of the Fir-tree
GERALD OF WALES 1147–1223

There are many birds here that are called barnacles, which nature, acting against her own laws, produces in a wonderful way. They are like marsh geese, but smaller. At first they appear as excrescences on fir-logs carried down upon the waters. Then they hang by their beaks from what seems like sea-weed clinging to the log, while their bodies, to allow for their more unimpeded development, are enclosed in shells. And so in the course of time, having put on a stout covering of feathers, they either slip into the water, or take themselves in flight to the freedom of the air. They take their food and nourishment from the juice of wood and water during their mysterious and remarkable generation. I myself have seen many times and with my own eyes more than a thousand of these small bird-like creatures hanging from a single log upon the sea-shore. They were in their shells and already formed. No eggs are laid as is usual as a result of mating. No bird ever sits upon eggs to hatch them and in no corner of the land will you see them breeding or building nests. Accordingly in some parts of Ireland bishops and religious men eat them without sin during a fasting time, regarding them as not being flesh, since they were not born of flesh.

The History and Topography of Ireland, TRANS. John J. O'Meara,

1951

Native Bounty
GEORGE F. WILLISON 1896–1972

The gallants who founded Jamestown, too many of them being "gentlemen" who had never done a day's work and had no desire to begin, were among the worst frontiersmen the world has ever known. After the landing in May, 1607, things went steadily from bad to worse, leading to the terrible 'Starving Time' in the awful winter of 1609–10, when four out of five died.

'All was fish that came to net to satisfy crewell Hunger,' wrote a survivor, George Percy, recalling those harrowing days. With supplies exhausted, the starving were 'glad to make shift with vermin as doggs, catts, ratts, and myce . . . to feede upon Serpents and Snakes, and to digg for wylde and unknown Rootes.' One man, his mind unhinged by slow starvation, killed his wife, 'powdered [salted] her, and had eaten part of her before it was knowne,' for which he was hanged. 'Now whether shee was better roasted, boyled or carbonado'd, I know not,' quipped Captain John Smith, 'but such a dish as powdered wife I never heard of.'

The American Heritage Cookbook, 1964

Blood Sacrifice – Mexico
BERNAL DÍAZ 1498–1593

Moreover every day they sacrificed before our eyes, three, four, or five Indians, whose hearts were offered to those idols and whose blood was plastered on the walls. The feet, arms, and legs of their victims were cut off and eaten, just as we eat beef from the butcher's in our country. I even believe that they sold it in the *tianguez* or markets. Cortes told them that if they gave up these wicked practices, not only would we be their friends, but we would give them other provinces to rule. The *Caciques*, *papas*, and dignitaries all replied that it would be wrong for them to give up their idols and sacrifices, for these gods of theirs brought them health and good harvests and all that they needed; but as for sodomy, measures would be taken to see that the practice was stopped.

Let me go on to describe the great and splendid courts in front of Huichilobos, on the site where that church now stands, which was called at that time Tlatelolco. I have already said that there were two masonry walls before the entrance to the *cue*, and the court was paved with white stones like flagstones, and all was whitened, burnished and clean. A little apart from the *cue* stood another small tower which was also an idol-house or true hell for one of its doors was in the shape of a terrible mouth, such as they paint to depict the jaws of hell. This mouth was open and contained great fangs to devour souls. Beside this door were groups of devils and the shapes of serpents, and a little way off was a place of sacrifice, all blood-stained and black with smoke. There were many great pots and jars and pitchers in this house, full of water. For it was here that they cooked the flesh of the wretched Indians who were sacrificed and eaten by the *papas*. Near this place of sacrifice there were many large knives and chopping-blocks like those on which men cut up meat in slaughter-houses; and behind that dreadful house, some distance away, were great piles of brush-wood, beside which was a tank of water that was filled and emptied through a pipe from the covered channel that comes into the city from Chapultepec. I always called that building Hell.

The Conquest of New Spain, TRANS. J. M. Cohen, 1963

Quailing before Terrapin
RICHARDSON WRIGHT 1887–1961

When Arnold Bennett made his first visit to this country, his admirers in various literary centers turned themselves inside out to entertain him with the specialité of the section. Boston gave him cod delightfully served, New York superb beef, and in Philadelphia ardent citizens waited an hour for him to appear at a dinner of which the prize dish was terrapin well laced with ancient Madeira. He gave one glance at that dish, said it looked nasty and refused the stuff. Now terrapin can appear unappetizing and the stranger to it must really screw up courage to take the first plunge. Bennett lacked the courage.

His behavior shocked his hosts and revealed that he was no gentleman. All the pretensions and honors a man may accumulate can never offset cowardice and rudeness at table. He may have written

'The Old Wives Tale,' but to Philadelphians that could never mitigate his having quailed before terrapin.

The Bed-Book of Eating and Drinking, 1943

Turtle and Venison Feast at Richmond
WILLIAM HICKEY 1749–1830

By the time they had reached Richmond I had made myself of so much importance by my spirits and fun that one and all protested I must stay and eat turtle with them. I, who at no period of my life could resist a convivial party, very readily consented. By this time I had discovered that it was the Fishmongers' Company, going to a turtle and venison feast at the Castle Tavern at Richmond. The party in general were very civil and attentive to me, but more especially an elderly gentleman of the name of Grubb, an eminent attorney in the City, and Clerk to the Company. He desired me to set down next to him at table, and he would take care of me. At two o'clock we landed at the Castle, and by three the party, consisting of upwards of one hundred, set down to a magnificent dinner, consisting of three courses, in which every luxury in the eating way appeared. This was followed by a dessert equally splendid and costly with every hothouse fruit procurable.

Memoirs, ED. Peter Quennell, 1962

Turtle
A. L. TOMMIE BASS

I've never caught turtles, but Dad loved to eat them, and I've skinned several for old people. You take the turtle and first cut off the head. You can hardly kill them. They'll flop in the pan when you fry them! Anyways, put them on their back and take a good sharp knife and rip the underpart off and skin the legs out.

Folks says turtle got seven different kinds of meat – like chicken, beef, pork, lamb, and fish. Now, the young turtles you just fry, but the bigger ones you'd parboil first.

Plain Southern Eating, 1988

Many Species of Turtle
J. HECTOR ST JOHN DE CRÈVECOEUR
1735–1813

We have many species of turtles. Some creep through our woods and are harmless. The gold-spotted one is rather an ornament to our ditches. The snapping one is a hideous and very strong animal. Their bills would astonish you as to their size and strength. I have seen them that weighed forty pounds. Whatever goose or duck swims in their waters is soon pulled down and devoured. These [turtles] are good to eat, and as long as we feed on what would feed on us, that seems to be founded on a just retaliation. Traps of various kinds are laid to catch the otters, and their furs are the only reward they yield.

Letters from an American Farmer and Sketches of Eighteenth Century
America, 1963

Everybody's Stomach is Full of Green Fat
SYDNEY SMITH 1771–1845

TO LADY GREY

Lower College Green, Bristol,
Nov. 8th, (1828)
Heavenly Weather, and a very fine Climate at Bristol, a town remarkable for Burglary, and Turtle; Every body's Stomach is full of green fat, every bodies house is broken open; all this comes of not hanging people. It is seven years since any one was hung here. How can 100,000 people live together in peace upon such terms?

Selected Letters, ED. Nowell C. Smith, 1956

We are Beginning to Eat Blubber

CAPT. R. F. SCOTT 1868–1912

*The frozen bodies of Scott and his companions were found in their
tent on 12 November 1912.*

Thursday, March 9, [1911] A.M. – Yesterday and to-day very busy
about the hut and overcoming difficulties fast. The stove threatened to
exhaust our store of firewood. We have redesigned it so that it takes
only a few chips of wood to light it and then continues to give great
heat with blubber alone. To-day there are to be further improvements
to regulate the draught and increase the cooking range. We have
further housed-in the living quarters with our old *Discovery* winter
awning, and begin already to retain the heat which is generated inside.
We are beginning to eat blubber and find biscuits fried in it to be
delicious.

A SKETCH OF THE LIFE AT HUT POINT

We gather around the fire seated on packing-cases, with a hunk of
bread and butter and a steaming pannikin of tea, and life is well worth
living. After lunch we are out and about again; there is little to tempt a
long stay indoors, and exercise keeps us all the fitter.
  The failing light and approach of supper drives us home again with
good appetites about 5 or 6 o'clock, and then the cooks rival one
another in preparing succulent dishes of fried seal liver. A single dish
may not seem to offer much opportunity of variation, but a lot can be
done with a little flour, a handful of raisins, a spoonful of curry
powder, or the addition of a little boiled pea meal. Be this as it may, we
never tire of our dish and exclamations of satisfaction can be heard
every night – or nearly every night; for two nights ago [April 4]
Wilson, who has proved a genius in the invention of 'plats,' almost
ruined his reputation. He proposed to fry the seal liver in penguin
blubber, suggesting that the latter could be freed from all rankness.
The blubber was obtained and rendered down with great care, the
result appeared as delightfully pure fat free from smell; but appear-
ances were deceptive; the 'fry' proved redolent of penguin, a concentrated essence of that peculiar flavour which faintly lingers in the

meat and should not be emphasised. Three heroes got through their pannikins, but the rest of us decided to be contented with cocoa and biscuit after tasting the first mouthful. After supper we have an hour or so of smoking and conversation – a cheering, pleasant hour – in which reminiscences are exchanged by a company which has very literally had world-wide experience.

Sunday, March 18 [1912] – To-day, lunch, we are 21 miles from the depot. Ill fortune presses, but better may come . . . My right foot has gone, nearly all the toes – two days ago I was proud possessor of best feet. These are the steps of my downfall. Like an ass I mixed a small spoonful of curry powder with my melted pemmican – it gave me violent indigestion. I lay awake and in pain all night . . .

Monday, March 19 – Lunch. We camped with difficulty last night, and were dreadfully cold till after our supper of cold pemmican and biscuit and a half a pannikin of cocoa cooked over the spirit. Then, contrary to expectation, we got warm and all slept well . . .

Thursday, March 22 and 23 – Blizzard bad as ever – Wilson and Bowers unable to start – tomorrow last chance – no fuel and only one or two of food left – must be near the end. Have decided it shall be natural – we shall march for the depot with or without our effects and die in our tracks.

Thursday, March 29 – Since the 21st we have had a continuous gale from W.S.W. and S.W. We had fuel to make two cups of tea apiece and bare food for two days on the 20th. Every day we have been ready to start for our depot 11 miles away, but outside the door of the tent it remains a scene of whirling drift. I do not think we can hope for any better things now. We shall stick it out to the end, but we are getting weaker, of course, and the end cannot be far.

It seems a pity, but I do not think I can write more.

R. Scott

Last entry.
For God's sake look after our people.

Scott's Last Expedition, ED. L. Huxley, 1913

Bear Meat

MARJORIE KINNAN RAWLINGS 1896–1953

Bear meat is good according to the condition of the bear and the manner in which it is cooked. A male in the mating season is almost inedible, like a boar hog. If mast has been scarce and the late fall and winter have offered poor forage, bear meat is lean and inclined to stringiness in the early spring. But under proper conditions, a Florida bear may be fat and sweet at the end of winter. The Florida bear goes very late into hibernation, emerges early and the hibernation is never absolute. If acorn mast and palmetto berries have been plentiful and he has fed late, piling on layer after layer of fat; if the winter is warm and feed still abundant, he comes out often, lazily, feeds close to his den, sleeps again, rouses to stuff in a few mouthfuls of feed, and goes back to sleep. Under these already favorable conditions of established avoirdupois, sleep, continued feeding and no ranging, early spring may turn him out in plump condition.

The finest bear meat I have eaten was at a church meeting at Eureka. One of the village inhabitants had shot a bear along the Ocklawaha River a few days before and an enormous roast had been hung in the smokehouse just long enough to be tendered and aged in time for the church dinner. It had been cooked as a pot roast, browned in its own fat, simmered half a day in an iron pot on a wood range. It was served in cold slices and was the first dish on the long loaded plank tables to melt away. The flavor was that of the choicest prime beef, and an added rich gaminess. I gave thought to a second slice, but so many little Eurekans were holding up their plates for it that I retired.

I heard a mother say to a small overalled boy, 'Now son, you savor this good. This here's bear meat, and what with things changin' outen the old ways, and the bears goin', you're like not to never get to taste it again.'

Leonard's mother cooked it equally well. She also sometimes cut very thin slices from the rib steaks, dipped them in flour and fried them in deep hot bear fat. They were crisp and brown and tender. The steaks I ate came from a very large fat bear that Leonard's bride noticed lumbering down the scrub road. She called him casually to its despatching. The meat, some fried and put down in its own fat, some smoked lightly, lasted the family for many weeks. The golden liquid fat filled two lard tubs and provided a sweet nutty cooking fat for the whole summer.

Cross Creek, 1942

Across the Plains – Buffalo and Horse
GENERAL JOHN BIDWELL 1819–1900

As soon as we struck the buffalo country we found a new source of interest. Before reaching the Platte we had seen an abundance of antelopes and elk, prairie wolves and villages of prairie dogs, but only an occasional buffalo. We now began to kill buffaloes for food, and at the suggestion of John Gray, and following the practice of Rocky Mountain white hunters, our people began to kill them just to get the tongues and marrow bones, leaving all the rest of the meat on the plains for the wolves to eat. But the Cheyenne, who traveled ahead of us for two or three days, set us a better example. At their camps we noticed that when they killed buffaloes they took all the meat, everything but the bones. Indians were never wasteful of the buffalo except for the sake of the robes, and then only in order to get the whiskey which traders offered them in exchange. There is no better beef in the world than that of the buffalo; it is also very good jerked – cut into strings and thoroughly dried. It was an easy matter to kill buffaloes after we got to where they were numerous, by keeping out of sight and to the leeward of them. I think I can truthfully say that I saw in that region in one day more buffaloes than I have ever seen of cattle in all my life. I have seen the plains black with them for several days' journey as far as the eye could reach. They seemed to be coming northward continually from the distant plains to the Platte to get water, and would plunge in and swim across by thousands – so numerous that they changed not only the color of the water, but its taste, until it was unfit to drink – but we had to use it . . .

We found that these Indians were always at war with the Californians. They were known as the Horse Thief Indians, and lived chiefly on horse flesh; they had been in the habit of raiding the ranches even to the very coast, driving away horses by the hundreds into the mountains to eat. That night I overtook the party in camp.

A day or two later we came to a place where there was a great quantity of horse bones, and we did not know what it meant; we thought that an army must have perished there. They were, of course, horses that the Indians had driven in and slaughtered. A few nights later, fearing depredations, we concluded to stand guard – all but one man, who would not. So we let his two horses roam where they pleased. In the morning they could not be found. A few miles away we came to a village; the Indians had fled, but we found the horses killed and some of the meat roasting on a fire.

Echoes of the Past, 1942

Baby Fish – Sichang – 1930s
PETER GOULLART d. 1978

Each monastery was a self-contained unit built on a massive stone terrace with a breath-taking view of the sapphire lake below and the city beyond. In each there was a beautiful prayer hall with a Buddha or a Jade Emperor and a row of airy, clean and well-furnished guest-rooms with a kitchen behind. Each had a few monks in it, Buddhist or Taoist, as the case might be. We explored them all, gradually reaching the summit whence there was a glorious view all around, with the Taliangshan veiled in blue mist to the far east.

Many temples had already been occupied by other pleasure seekers from town, lolling on long chairs on the shady terraces in front or playing mah-jongg whilst cooking went on in the kitchens with the delicious smell of roasting chickens or stewing fish in the air, and jars of wine visible on the table. We put up at a Taoist monastery, which my companions always patronized, whose friendly monks at once made us feel at home filling our cups with *huangtsieu* (yellow wine), a famed product of Sichang tasting like sweet sherry. I spent the afternoon rambling all over the cool mountain in company with a Taoist monk while my hosts engaged in a game of poker.

In the evening we had a long feast on the lantern-lit terrace, featuring several kinds of lake fish.

'Talking about fish' one of my friends remarked as we plunged our chopsticks into a fat catfish, 'have you ever tried Baby Fish?' he asked me.

'No,' I replied in astonishment. 'What is it?' They all laughed at my ignorance.

'It's funny that you have not tried it, coming from Fulin, which is the place to eat it,' my neighbour continued. 'It is fairly big black fish, with two small hands and feet. It cries "Wa! Wa!" just like babies do; hence the name.'

'I'll be sure to try it when I get to Fulin,' I said, not to be outdone . . .

Madame Yang said she wanted to make a special feast. I protested long and vociferously according to etiquette but finally gave in. At dinner that night we talked again about fish.

'Madame,' I said. 'I was told so much in Sichang about a Baby Fish which, when caught, joins its little hands in supplication and kowtows crying 'Nanmu Amitabha'. They roared with laughter, but she said nothing. Then on the day of the farewell feast she beckoned me mysteriously to follow her into the kitchen. There in a big vat of water I saw a terrifying creature, black as coal, with a long fat tail and small, hand-like paws, and an enormous gape with cruel teeth, like a tyrannosaurus. The cook stirred the water and the creature tried to climb out crying 'Wa! Wa!' That was the Baby Fish, a kind of salamander, living in the underwater caverns of the Tatu. When stewed that evening, it tasted wonderful.

Princes of the Black Bone, 1959

Solving the Monkey Puzzle
PAUL LEVY 1941–

The southern Chinese, as any northerner will tell you with distaste, will eat almost anything. I have heard southerners themselves tell the story about the Indian and the Cantonese confronted by a creature from outer space: the Indian falls to his knees and begins to worship it, while the Chinese searches his memory for a suitable recipe.

Naturally, there are a lot of famous Chinese gastronomic atrocity stories. The most famous one features live monkey brains, and I have been told it fifty times – but always at second hand, by someone whose friend, husband or mother has absolutely, definitely witnessed it. It is claimed that decadent Chinese gourmands give banquets at which little boys are employed to shove shaven-headed monkeys up through a table with a hole in the centre, following which the host slices off the top of the animal's head with a machete, and the diners eat the still warm brains with long silver spoons.

I first began to think this might be monkey business only when an

American traveller told me that *he* had a friend who had been present at such a feast where unwanted girl babies were substituted for the simians. That was what made me class the tale with those of the disappearing hitch-hiker and the Swiss couple who ended up eating their own ginger and bamboo-shoot garnished poodle in a Hong Kong restaurant. (The truth of this last was sworn by a man sitting next to me at lunch one day at my Oxford college. He assured me that he had not only witnessed it, but was the author of the first newspaper report of this event of, I seem to remember, the summer of 1970.)

In fact, in *The Listener* for 1 March 1984, Derek Cooper gave an account of how Arthur Helliwell, a 'campaigning' journalist, was the original victim of the monkey brain hoax, a jape invented in Singapore in March 1952 by other British journalists seeking to deflate his pomposity. Arthur Helliwell reported the story, and his paper, *The People*, was promptly and successfully sued for defamation by the only Chinese millionaire living in Singapore's Queen Astrid Park. (The hapless Helliwell had begun his gastronomic horror story by writing, 'In his Arabian Nights palace out at Queen Astrid Park tonight, one of Singapore's many Chinese multimillionaires is giving a party to celebrate the birth of a son.') Cooper added that the table with the hole in it, which clinched the hoax for Helliwell, is used to hold the chafing dish or wok for *ke-tze* or steamboat, the local variation on hot-pot, in which the diners cook their own food in boiling broth heated by a flame placed beneath the table.

Thirty years later, Fred Thomas, controller of the Hong Kong RSPCA, claimed (in the Asian *Wall Street Journal* for 23 May 1983) that RSPCA personnel, four years earlier, rescued 'a monkey that escaped from a Kowloon restaurant, its body shaved in preparation for the table'. And that, a year before that, they had found, in a Kowloon dustbin, the carcass of a monkey with pate and brains removed. While this does not amount to an eye-witness account of live monkey brains actually being eaten (or rule out the possibility of the first primate escaping from a veterinary surgery), it is always possible that the currency of the story has led some people to imitate art. There are rumours amongst Hong Kong's large gastronomic community that someone had staged a monkey brain feast for a Japanese film crew, and the film *Mondo Cane* is often cited in this connection.

Willy Mark, the professional Hong Kong gastronome, assured me that he would have no compunction about telling me so if this practice was genuine. He had no experience of the dish, and his aged father, whom he consulted about it on my behalf, had never heard of it either.

Neither one of them expressed any horror at being asked the question – to them it was just another query about edible species of animals, of which they can count a great many more than you or I – but they knew nothing of it. It appears that the monkey brain feast is at bottom a *canard*.

Out to Lunch, 1986

Three Peeps and Monkey Brain

HSIANG JU LIN AND TSUIFENG LIN

The 'Three Peeps' is a coy reference by the Chinese writers to the Cantonese winter dish of dog, which according to Chinese medicine is very warming. Cantonese cookery writer Yan-kit So explains the complicated Cantonese pun. The three peeps are three luks *(looks) – three sixes. Three plus six is nine, or gau which sounds like the word for dog (also gau in another tone, of which the Cantonese dialect has roughly ten).*

There has been a story in circulation for a long time concerning live monkey brain of Kwangtung. We had almost dismissed it as pure fiction until by diligent questioning of the people who spread these stories, of which there were a number, we finally found one who had actually tasted it. The table did have a hole in the centre, and the monkey's head was shaved and cracked open. As there were a number of people at this table, each person had only a spoonful. After all, a monkey's brain is only so big. 'Any sauce?' we asked. He just shrugged. 'The usual soy sauce and ginger,' he replied. He went on to the description of another small horror called 'Three Peeps' – a descriptive name which requires no further elucidation. It was served with the same sauce.

Chinese Gastronomy, 1969

Dog in Macao
PAUL LEVY 1941–

From an alcove at the back came the whoosh of a butane gas jet, on which a large metal cauldron was boiling ferociously. In another alcove a clay stove, filled with charcoal and ignited, was placed in front of an electric fan to make the coals glow. The stove then was put in the centre of our table, and immediately made clear why one did not eat dog in the heat of the day. A clay pot was brought and balanced precariously on the stove. Little bowls of mustard and chilli sauce were placed on the table, as is the Cantonese habit, and the longhaired, death's head son used his asbestos fingers to lift the clay pot lid. Inside were chunks of brown meat with thin but substantial slices of ginger in a brown sauce. The meat had dark skin attached to it, was quite fatty and looked like pork. It was chewy, and had a very strong, though not disagreeable, flavour, like mutton, venison or goat. The matchstick-sized bones made it clear that it had come from a young animal.

The meal was completed by bringing plastic bowls of shredded Chinese leeks, yellow chives and a green spinach-like vegetable for adding to the clay pot. Those ingredients greatly improved the dish, and with the judicious application of mustard and chilli sauce, it was possible to eat enough to avoid disgracing oneself. Messrs. Lim and Tong seemed to relish the meal, and my young friend's appetite did not falter. The sight of the clay pot on our table attracted passers-by from the street, who knew that this meant dog was on tonight; and while we were there, two family parties came into the sleazy restaurant and ordered it.

(Willy Mark, the celebrated Hong Kong gastronome who had arranged for Mr Tong to take us to Macao, said later that this is a very provincial way to serve this admittedly rustic dish. While dog meat is not refined enough to serve in a first-class restaurant, gourmets occasionally serve it. If Mr Mark were to acquire a whole dog, he said, he would prepare it in four courses. First, the fillet shredded and stir-fried, with shredded bamboo shoots and black mushrooms, garnished with finely shredded lime leaves. Second, a double-boiled soup made of the bones and meat scraps, plus the penis and testicles, if the dog is not a bitch. Third, the paws and muzzle would be made into a braise, similar to the one I ate. Fourth, the ribs would be steamed, cut in thick slices, sandwiched with slices of ham and black mushrooms and served hot in their own juices. Exactly the same would apply if you had a whole muntjac, or barking deer, a protected species that is suitable for serving in an up-market eating establishment.)

When the patron joined us for a moment I asked him if the dog we were eating was farmed. He laughed at my foolishness, and Mr Tong explained that no one (except peasants on state farms in mainland China) raises dog for the table – 'you can't eat a dog that you have fed'. The old man grinned, revealing his need of a dentist's attentions, and made a pun to the effect that it was a 'hot' dog. He belongs to a buying syndicate with the other dog meat restaurants, and when one of them has a request, it is passed on to the supplier, who supplies the original requester with his few kilos and sells the surplus to the other members. Thus the restaurant owners all have clean hands, and it is no use for the police to interfere, though they know every bite of dog served in Macao is stolen.

The breed of preference is the black tongue chow. Straight-haired 'Chinese' dogs are always eaten in preference to curly-haired 'foreign' dogs. And only puppies are used for the pot.

'We do serve cat, as well,' the owner of the restaurant explained, 'but you did not give sufficient notice.' 'Dog must be young,' Tong explained, 'but old cat is better. Old cat is lazy and has some fat on it, like young dog.' Cat is scarce and expensive, as it's not easy to separate an older cat from its rightful owner. (In Hong Kong and southern China 'wild civet cat is in fact bred for the table, and with – perfectly legal – snake and chicken, goes to make up the famous dish of "tiger, dragon and phoenix".')

Out to Lunch, 1986

The Dog
ALEXIS SOYER 1809–58

We must beg pardon of the reader for informing him that the dog presented a very relishing dish to many nations advanced in culinary science. To them, one of these animals, young, plump, and delicately prepared, appeared excellent food.

The Greeks, that people so charming by their seductive folly, their love of the arts, their poetic civilization, and the intelligent spirit of research presiding over their dishes – the Greeks (we grieve to say it) ate dogs, and even dared to think them good; the grave Hippocrates himself – the most wise, the least gluttonous, and therefore the most impartial of their physicians – was convinced that this quadruped furnished a wholesome and, at the same time, a light food.

As to the Romans, they also liked it, and no doubt prepared it in the same manner as the hare, which they thought it resembled in taste.

However, it is but right to add, that this dish, which we will not even hear mentioned, was never favourably received by the fashionable portion of Roman society, and that the legislators of ancient gastrophagy even repulsed it with disdain.

There is every reason to believe that the people regaled themselves with a roast or boiled dog, especially once a year, at the period when they celebrated the deliverance of the Capitol from the siege of the Gauls. It is known that, at this solemnity, a goose, laid on a soft cushion, was carried in triumph, followed by an unhappy dog nailed to a cross, whose loud cries greatly amused the populace. In this manner they commemorated the signal service rendered by one animal, and the fatal negligence of the other. The Gauls scaled the Capitol while the dogs slept, and Rome had been lost if the deafening cries of the geese had not given an alarm to the garrison, who, it must be allowed, should have kept better watch.

The quadrupeds last mentioned are the only domestic animals of the kind used as food by the ancients. The case afforded them several others, which we shall mention, after having just glanced at the poultry – one of the most interesting divisions in natural history for the serious and reflective appreciator of gastronomic productions.

The Pantropheon, 1853

The Feast

GUSTAVE FLAUBERT 1821–80

It was at Megara, a suburb of Carthage, in Hamilcar's gardens.

The soldiers whom he had commanded in Sicily were treating themselves to a great feast to celebrate the anniversary of the battle of Eryx, and as their master was away and there were a large number of them, they ate and drank in complete freedom . . .

As Hamilcar's kitchens were not sufficient, the Council had sent them slaves, tableware, beds: and in the middle of the garden, as on a battlefield when the dead are being burned, appeared huge, bright fires where oxen roasted. Loaves dusted with aniseed alternated with great cheeses, weighing more than discuses, bowls full of wine, and pots full of water beside golden filigree baskets containing flowers. They were all wide-eyed with joy at being able to stuff to their heart's content at last: here and there singing began.   ·

First they were served birds in green sauce, on red earthenware plates decorated with black patterns, then all the kinds of shellfish found on the Punic shores, porridge of wheat, beans, and barley, and snails in cumin, on plates of golden amber.

Then the tables were covered with meat dishes; antelopes with their horns, peacocks with their feathers, whole sheep cooked in sweet wine, haunches of she-camels and buffaloes, hedgehogs in garum, fried grasshoppers and preserved dormice. In wooden bowls from Tamrapanni great lumps of fat floated in saffron. Everything over-flowed with brine, truffles, and assa foetida. Pyramids of fruit tumbled over honey-cakes, and they had not forgotten a few little dogs with big bellies and pink bristles, fattened on olive-pulp, that Carthaginian delicacy which other people found revolting. The unexpected sight of novel foods aroused their greed. Gauls, with long hair tied up on the top of their head, snatched watermelons and lemons, devouring them peel and all. Negroes who had never seen lobsters tore their faces on the red claws. But shaven Greeks, whiter than marble, threw behind them the peelings from their plate, while shepherds from Bruttium, dressed in wolf skins, munched in silence, heads bent over their food.

Salammbô, TRANS. A. J. Krailsheimer, 1977

Alligator Steaks – Florida

MARJORIE KINNAN RAWLINGS 1896–1953

It is the meats that I prepare at the Creek that are the most exotic of my dishes. I take no credit for some of them, for they are old in local culinary lore. Alligator steaks, for instance. It is no doubt absurd to balk at rattlesnake steaks and enthuse over alligator, for the saurians are not much removed from the reptiles. Drawing a line between dangerous rattlers and harmless alligators is as though a cannibal said he would eat a friend but would not eat an enemy. But surely we may all be allowed our prejudices, and I have none against steaks from the tail of an alligator. I can say dispassionately that properly cooked it is a great delicacy. The meat is pink and clean, like veal, and is similar in flavor. The first time I cooked it, I fried it too long, and it was tough and dry. I discovered that it is like veal cutlets or liver, in that it must be fried quickly, or simmered a long time. It is best, pounded, drenched with flour and fried rapidly in butter. Otherwise, it may be smother-fried, browned in the fat, hot water and lemon juice added, covered, and allowed to simmer until tender.

Cross Creek, 1942

Grasshoppers – Laos
ALAN DAVIDSON 1924–

'Try one of these,' said the beautiful princess. Having announced to her my interest in Lao foods and cookery, I had to suppress the suspicious expression with which I would otherwise have regarded the platter, and do as invited. 'Delicious.'

'Yes, they're deep-fried grasshoppers. And their nutritional value is quite high.'

'Oh, really? That's good.' So saying, I casually manœuvred myself in the direction of a platter of fried chicken. The piece I picked up was a gizzard, and it brought a foot with it, which I vainly tried to shake off with seemingly casual motions of the wrist. The kind Princess Marina had followed me. 'Ah,' said she, 'you know which are the best parts of the chicken.'

A Kipper with my Tea, 1988

Scorpions – Mexico 1840s
MME CALDERON DE LA BARCA 1804–82

Then there is a beautiful black and red spider, called the *chinclaquili*, whose sting sends a pain through all your bones; the only cure for which is to be shut up for several days in a room thick with smoke. There are also the *tarantula* and *casampulga* spiders. Of the first, which is a shocking-looking soft fat creature, covered with dark hair, it is said that the horse which treads on it instantly loses its hoof – but this wants confirmation. Of the scorpions, the small yellowish coloured ones are the most dangerous, and it is pretended that their bite is most to be apprehended at midday. The workmen occasionally eat them, after pulling out the sting. The flesh of the viper is also eaten roasted, as a remedy against eruptions of the skin. Methinks the remedy is worse than the disease . . .

Life in Mexico, 1843

Locusts – South America

ALFRED BOELDEKE

The Rio Uaupes is a peaceful river and we chugged along happily. There were huge sandbanks on either side of the black water, dazzling white against the deep green of the thick jungle, and the dawns and sunsets were as unusual and beautiful as any we had seen. From time to time we passed picturesque Indian huts decked with palm-leaves. Our only disappointment was the natives who were often dressed in a variety of ill-assorted town garments given them by the missionaries. Most of the Indians in this region belonged to the Tucano tribe and had seasonal homes by the river. During the dry season they collect turtle eggs, catch and smoke the fish which live in abundance in the warm waters of the river, and fatten themselves for the lean season when the rains come. They collect rubber and Brazil nuts, and the yellow fruits of the pupunha palm. This fruit is cooked to taste like potatoes or made into an alcoholic brew of considerable potency. The natives use the fibres of the tucuma palm-tree to make beautiful hammocks which they carry with them wherever they go, and also make beautifully carved stools and artistic baskets. The men hunt with blowpipes, the arrows of which are dipped in curare. A leaf from one of the plants used for this poison when dissolved in a little water can paralyse the tongue for several hours and the men, it is said, use it frequently when annoyed by a nagging wife.

Our Indian pilot had friends and relatives all along our route, so we spent many nights with the natives in their huts. The second night after our departure from São Gabriel we stayed in the hut of the pilot's brother-in-law while a thunderstorm raged outside. Aenne and Graciela caused a lot of amusement among the native women when they tried to cook the beans presented to us by the Bishop. However much they cooked and stirred them, they simply would not get soft. One of the women offered something to my wife. She was just going to put it into her mouth when Graciela said 'Mummy, always look first before you eat.' We all looked carefully in the dim light, and to our amazement we saw a crawling ball of locusts in Aenne's hand. To these natives, locusts are a delicacy. They tear the heads off the insects and swallow their fat little bodies with loud appreciative munching sounds. My wife and Graciela could not be tempted, but I sampled these insects later and found the flavour interesting. I am sure one could develop a liking for them in time. Quite a few white people in these regions do, in fact, eat them.

With Graciela to the Head-Hunters, 1958

Insects

PETER FARB 1929–80 AND GEORGE ARMELAGOS 1896–1972

The repugnance of modern North Americans and Europeans toward the eating of insects obscures the large proportion of protein they must have supplied for early humans, and still supply for some American Indians and groups in Africa and the Near East. Grasshoppers and other members of the locust family, for example, are an exceptionally nutritious food. Merely a handful provides the daily allowance of vitamin A, as well as protein, carbohydrate, and fat. In addition to locusts, early humans must also have consumed, as hunter-gatherers still do today, beetle grubs, caterpillars, bee larvae, termites, ants, cicadas, and aquatic insects. An analysis of the fried termites eaten in West Africa has shown that they contain about forty-five percent protein, a higher proportion even than in dried fish.

Consuming Passions: The Anthropology of Eating, 1980

Spiders and Caterpillars

VINCENT M. HOLT

Even Spiders have been relished as tid-bits, not only by uncivilized nations, but by Europeans of cultivation. For Reaumur tells of a young lady who was so fond of spiders that she never saw one without catching and eating it. Lalande, the French astronomer, had similar tastes; and Rosel speaks of a German who was in the habit of spreading spiders, like butter, upon his bread. This taste I do not in any way uphold, for the preying spider, which devours his fellow-insects, whether foul feeders or no, should be avoided, as are carnivorous beasts in our animal diet . . .

Caterpillars are well known to every one, whether Londoner or countryman, for they swarm, at the end of June, in town and country alike upon their favourite lime trees. Their yellow forms, striped and ringed with black, are often to be seen crawling across the arid desert of the London pavements in search of some congenial soil wherein they bury themselves for the term of insect purgatory. Looking up then at the tree from which these wanderers have descended, one may see branches, perhaps many, perhaps few, stripped of their foliage and down the stem other caterpillars hurriedly crawling, knowing that their time has come; that nature calls them to throw off their gay garments and humble themselves beneath the soil, before bursting out into rollicking Buff-tips. It never strikes the Londoner, as he hurries along beneath the shady trees, that these caterpillars are good to eat. He either stamps upon or carefully avoids them, according to his nature. The street boy picks up, plays with, and finally squashes them; but the extraordinary part of it is that it never strikes him to taste them. Boys taste almost everything. But this prejudice against insects seems rooted in them from the earliest age, for I have never seen a child experiment upon the unknown sweets of insect food. These Buff-tip caterpillars swarm upon the trees in such numbers, in favourable seasons, that many a dish can be obtained with a little trouble, which is amply repaid not only by their flavour, but also by the saving of the tender foliage of the limes. Most of the commoner moths which flit in thousands by night, around our fields and gardens, have nice fat carcases, and ought certainly to be used as food. Why, they are the very incarnescence of sweetness, beauty, and deliciousness; living store-houses of nectar gathered from the most fragrant flowers! They, too, voluntarily and suggestively sacrifice themselves upon the altar of our lamps, as we sit, with open windows, in the balmy summer nights. They fry and grill themselves before our eyes, saying, 'Does not the sweet scent of our cooked bodies tempt you? Fry us with butter; we are delicious. Boil us, grill us, stew us; we are good all ways!'

Why Not Eat Insects?, 1855

Bee Legs – Istanbul

DIANE ACKERMAN 1948–

When a vanilla bean lies like a Hindu rope on the counter, or sits in a cup of coffee, its aroma gives the room a kind of stature, the smell of an exotic crossroads where outlandish foods aren't the only mysteries. In Istanbul in the 1970s, my mother and I once ate Turkish pastries redolent with vanilla, glazed in caramel sugar with delicate filaments of syrup on top. It was only later that day, when we strolled through the bazaar with two handsome university students my mother had bumped into, that we realized what we had eaten with such relish. On a long brass platter sat the kind of pastries we had eaten, buzzed over by hundreds of sugar-delirious bees, whose feet stuck in the syrup; desperately, one by one, they flew away, leaving their legs behind. 'Bee legs!' my mother had screamed, as her face curdled. 'We ate *bee legs!*' Our companions spoke little English and we spoke no Turkish, so they probably thought it odd that American women became so excitable in the presence of pastry. They offered to buy us some, which upset my mother even more.

A Natural History of the Senses, 1990

Water Bug

ALAN DAVIDSON 1924–

The first official dinner which I attended in Laos was given by the (South) Vietnamese Ambassador for the Prime Minister, Prince Souvanna Phouma. When the main dish was served, I noticed that a Vietnamese girl of aristocratic appearance (no serving maid, evidently) knelt by the side of the Prime Minister and held up a medicine dropper for his approval. He nodded and she squeezed two drops of fluid from it on to his food. Goodness me, I thought, this must be some sort of oriental medicine intended to help his heart condition. But the girl then did the same for the Defence Minister. Could he suffer from the same trouble? And for the other notables, and eventually myself. By this time it had dawned on me that her mission was a culinary, not a medical one, so I too nodded and thus made my first acquaintance with this rarest South-East Asian 'sauce'.

I learned later what it is: a glandular secretion of which a few drops may be expressed from live specimens of the water bug *Lethocerus indicus*. I had it again, when I was feeling less bewildered and more analytical, in Hanoi in 1975. There is (or was) a restaurant there called simply 'The Fish Place', with one speciality, Cha Ca Lao Vong (literally, 'grilled, cut up fish meat of the old fisherman'). The Fish Place had managed to survive in Hanoi from the 1930s through the Second World War and the Vietnam war. The young women whose charms had attracted French officers there some forty years back were now quite elderly, but still beautiful and as expert as ever in their kitchen. They produced their speciality and proudly offered, as an 'extra', the medicine dropper whose significance I now knew. I had two drops, and afterwards sought words to convey the effect which they had. No word is quite right, since the flavour is unique. But 'musky' is quite a close approach. I wrote in my notebook that it was so potent, and such an exciting gastronomic experience, that it must be counted very good value at $10 a drop!

A Kipper with My Tea, 1988

Chili in Bimini

ERNEST HEMINGWAY 1898–1961

Johnny Goodner's cruiser, *Narwhal*, where they were waiting for Roger Davis, was headed into the ebbing tide and astern of her in the same slip, made fast so that the two cabin cruisers lay stern to stern, was the boat of the party that had been at Bobby's place all day. Johnny Goodner sat in a chair in the stern with his feet on another chair and a Tom Collins in his right hand and a long, green Mexican chile pepper in his left.

'It's wonderful,' he said. 'I bite just a little piece and it sets my mouth on fire and I cool it with this.'

He took the first bite, swallowed, blew out, 'thew!' through rolled tongue, and took a long swallow of the tall drink. His full lower lip licked his thin Irish upper lip and he smiled with his grey eyes. His mouth was sliced upwards at the corners so it always looked as though he were about to smile, or had just smiled, but his mouth told very little about him unless you noticed the thinness of the upper lip. His eyes were what you needed to watch. He was the size and build of a middleweight gone a little heavy; but he looked in good shape lying there relaxed and that is how a man looks bad who is really out of shape. His face was brown but peeling across the nose and the forehead that went back with his receding hairline. He had a scar on his chin that could have been taken for a dimple if it had been just a little closer to the centre and his nose had been just perceptibly flattened across the bridge. It wasn't a flat nose. It just looked as though it had been done by a modern sculptor who worked directly in the stone and had taken off just the shadow of a chip too many.

'Tom, you worthless character, what have you been doing?'

'Working pretty steadily.'

'You would,' he said, and took another bite of the chile. It was a very wrinkled and droopy chile about six inches long.

'Only the first one hurts,' he said. 'It's like love.'

'The hell it is. Chiles can hurt both ways.'

'And love?'

'The hell with love,' Thomas Hudson said.

'What a sentiment. What a way to talk. What are you getting to be? A victim of sheepherder's madness on this island?'

'No sheep here, Johnny.'

'Stone-crab herder's madness then,' Johnny said. 'We don't want to have you have to be netted or anything. Try one of these chiles.'

'I have,' Thomas Hudson said.

'Oh I know your past,' he said. 'Don't pull your illustrious past on me. You probably invented them. I know. Probably the man who introduced them into Patagonia on Yak-back. But I represent modern times. Listen Tommy. I have these chiles stuffed with salmon. Stuffed with bacalao. Stuffed with Chilean bonito. Stuffed with Mexican turtledoves' breasts. Stuffed with turkey meat and mole. They'll stuff them with anything and I buy them. Makes me feel like a damned potentate. But all that's a perversion. Just this long, drooping, uninspiring, unstuffed, unpromising old chile with the brown chupango sauce is the best. You bastard,' he blew out through his pursed tongue again, 'I got too much of you that time.'

Islands in the Stream, 1970

Rats in Chungking, 1940s

HSIANG JU LIN AND TSUIFENG LIN

During the war in the 1940's, the rats of Chungking grew so large that cats cowered before them, afraid to challenge them. At this time there appeared at certain tables dishes of red-cooked meat which people hesitated to identify, and some dared not eat. It is true that necessity and economy led people to explore all things. But this is only part of the story. The great cuisine, like a broad river, was constantly breaking up into side streams and eddies, each pool whirling about itself in ever smaller circles. These eccentric foci were occasionally drawn into the main stream, while others remained on the periphery. This would not be a world in itself, but for the fanatics and the lunatic fringe. The special character of the cuisine comes not from hunger or need, but from the cult of gastronomy. Were it not for the cult, such exotic experiments in search of taste would not have been made. One can see their point of view. Each thing is an entity, and its perfection of taste should be an end in itself. The more you taste it, the more tastes it has. The more closely you look, the finer the pattern; small differences loom as wide gaps. Were it not for the cult of gastronomy, the cuisine would not have its present depth and range.

Chinese Gastronomy, 1969

Rat in Canton, 1991

ANDREW HIGGINS 1958–

It is a sultry Saturday night in Canton, and business is booming at The Super Deer Restaurant, a fashionable new eatery on People's Road. I step inside, lured by a red sign outside promising "Western Food". More appropriate would perhaps be *Nouvelle Cuisine*: for here at The

Super Deer, proprietor Zhang Guoxun and his staff have entered a brave new world of culinary creation.

It's not just the clean, white table cloths and soft lighting that distinguish the enterprise from your grimy, run-of-the-mill Chinese restaurant. No rats scurrying across the floor here, Mr Zhang assures me. He takes pride in keeping his place clean. But, a glance at the pricy menu quickly reveals where I will find them: on my plate – beheaded, plucked of hair, steaming and ready to eat.

The menu is a tribute to the proprietor's imagination and his customers' courage: Crispy Fried Rat with Lemon, Braised Rat with Black Pepper, Traditional Style Salt-Roasted Rat, Satayed Rat Slices with Vermicelli. For the true gourmand there is Liquored Rat Flambé, followed by a bowl of Rat and Snake Soup to help clean the palate. Less extravagant diners can tuck into a bowl of Steamed Rat with Rice for under 50p.

Mr Zhang, talking between gulps of succulent rat fillet washed down with beer and Chinese tea, admits his speciality might not be to everyone's taste. His wife, for one, is not a fan. 'She doesn't eat much rat. She likes snake and dog, but only eats a bit of rat.'

He explains that his rats are not the ordinary sewer variety but 'field rats', free-range rodents caught in the wild by peasant rat-catchers who earn 50p per rodent: enough meat for a 4lb main course.

Though clearly a man with a mission, he is also practical. 'Why do you think I call my restaurant The Super Deer and not The Rat?' asks Mr Zhang. 'The word rat would have put some people off.' The menu is equally coy, referring to rat throughout as Super Deer, a euphemism borrowed from the lexicon of traditional Chinese medicine, which recommends drowning baby rats in rice wine as a health tonic.

The deceit continues in the cooking, with herbs and spices carefully masking the pungent gamey taste of raw rat meat. But Mr Zhang makes no apologies for trying to fool the tastebuds. Presentation also aims to allay fears of the squeamish. Mr Zhang's rodents are served minus the head, feet and tail, garnished with delicate slices of carrot and sprigs of Chinese coriander. The subterfuge doesn't always work. Braised Rat arrives at my table looking like nothing so much as a soggy dead rat – chopped into bite-size slices, its half-amputated legs splayed on an oval, rat-sized dish.

Proof of the rat, though, lies in the eating: a layer of rubbery flesh covering a core of mushy brown meat. A glue-like slime oozes into the mouth, fixing stray rat hairs to my gums. I gag, but avoid the ultimate insult to Mr Zhang's cooking with a gulp of warm beer.

Another dish, described alluringly on the menu as Gold Medal Beautiful Rat and strongly recommended by Mr Zhang, is crunchy instead of gooey – a texture achieved, he says, by leaving the rat's spindly rib-cage *in situ*. Fortunately, other creations are less revolting. Relief comes in the form of Steamed Rat with Fermented Bean Curd – boneless chunks of tasty rat meat wrapped in lotus leaves and cooked in a bamboo steamer. Also good is Rat Kebab, skewered cubes of rat fillet, onion and hot pepper, cooked on a hot plate at the table with soy and pepper sauces.

Independent on Sunday, 25 August 1991

Horsemeat

ALICE THOMAS ELLIS 1932–

Aunt Irene paid off her taxi in Leicester Square and went very secretively, like a woman on a dishonourable mission, down many mean streets, until she came to the shop of her friend the Maltese horse-butcher. She was very fond of horseflesh and cooked it well. Her mother's cook had always boiled it with a swatch of sweet hay and wild garlic leaves, but Aunt Irene had refined this method, using basil and a hint of cinnamon, white wine to soften any coarseness, and carrots to persuade her English guests that what they were eating was quite possibly boiled beef. Horse meat had been off the ration, and no one during the war had ever questioned her about the source of the unusual amount of meat they were enjoying. It would have been the height of tactlessness and ingratitude to suggest that your hostess might be dealing on the Black Market. People had sometimes thought it was venison. No one had ever dreamed it was horse. Unthinkable. What, mused Aunt Irene, did they imagine they were eating when they tucked into platelets of delicious Continental salami at a cold luncheon? Quite often sausage from the Balkan regions was made not only of horse, but of donkey. Sad, really, when you thought about it, she conceded. Donkeys were nice little things, but she'd never liked horses – with their barrel-like bodies stuck on those worryingly thin legs, biting at one end and kicking at the other. Thundering round race tracks with people bouncing about on top. No, the beauty of the living horse escaped Aunt Irene.

It was the Lord of the sea who was the horse-maker. He and a goddess in a rather childish competition to decide after whom the capital of Attica should be named invented, respectively, the horse and the olive in the interests of mankind. The gods (showing a bit of sense for once) judged unanimously that the olive was the more useful and beneficial and called the place Athens. And indeed, thought Aunt Irene warmly, the goddess truly deserved the honour; for the olive and its oil were among quite the best things in life. She popped into one of Soho's ubiquitous delicatessens and bought a bag of green ones.

When she got to the Maltese horse-butcher he greeted her ecstatically, wiping his hand on his apron, patting his hat and scuttling round the counter to welcome her. Most of his customers were hard-eyed restaurateurs or greyhound owners, and Aunt Irene was a pleasant change. They had a little joke – none of his beasts had ever stirred themselves to win the Derby or leap over Becher's Brook. All he offered were lazy also-rans, fresh from daisy-laden paddocks.

'About ten pounds of a really delicious cut,' said Aunt Irene. 'And will you cut it up in nice cubes – about *so* . . .' and she limned a little square on the air with her two forefingers.

'Is like *butter!*' exulted the knacker in a frenzy of self-congratulation.

'I *know*,' said Aunt Irene warmly and soothingly. 'I know how I can trust you.' But as he deftly cut and thrust among the piles of flesh, Aunt Irene's eyes were drawn unwittingly to the back premises where hung lean and melancholy eviscerated bodies as in Bluebeard's pantry; and she wondered for a moment what she was doing in a country where they wouldn't eat their horses but they hanged their women.

All the way back to Leicester Square, with her carrier bags full of forbidden flesh, Aunt Irene thought of the head of the horse Fallada, nailed above the gateway, speaking in pitying terms to its maiden. She took a taxi to the Ritz for a comforting tea, where as she ate tiny sandwiches and cakes she amused herself by wondering what the other ladies would say if she should leap on to one of the little tables brandishing her carrier bags, and do a sort of horse-eating dance. They would be surprised, she thought. They would find her very foreign. She felt about for half-a-crown to pay the waiter and hoped the man from the Inland Revenue wasn't watching as she emerged from the Ritz and climbed into yet another taxi.

The 27th Kingdom, 1982

Jellyfish et al.

CALVIN W. SCHWABE 1927–

JELLYFISH

Particularly in China and Japan jellyfish are dried and prized as food. In the Gilbert Islands even highly venomous jellyfish called sea wasps are considered a delicacy. Their ovaries are dried and deep-fried and are said to taste rather like tripe.

PICKLED JELLYFISH (*Alu alu*) / SAMOA
Fresh jellyfish are cut into pieces, marinated briefly in lemon juice or vinegar, and then eaten raw.

BEETLES

Beetles, both adults and grubs (larvae) of various types, are probably eaten as commonly as locusts. One favorite in several countries is the palmworm, which is the grub of *Rhynchophorus palmarum*. Other species of snout beetles occur in the United States, where they are costly pests. Their grubs are certainly worth a try, too.

The culinary adaptability of the French is world-renowned. Here they have imaginatively combined two local ingredients.

Roasted Palmworms with Orange Juice / French West Indies
Skewer the palmworms and roast over charcoal. Roll in a mixture of fine bread crumbs, salt, pepper, and nutmeg and sprinkle with orange juice. Return to the fire to brown.

ANNELIDS

I include only one recipe for earthworms, invertebrate animals which are nationally abundant and which are now raised on many worm farms, chiefly as fish bait. However, Gaddie's North American Bait Farms, of Ontario, Calif., have for several years sponsored earthworm recipe contests that annually produce about 500 recipes! Gaddie says, 'Worms [presumably dried] taste like shredded wheat. I like them best in oatmeal cookies, but I've eaten them with rice, sprinkled on top of salads . . . , with scrambled eggs and with steak and gravy.' Another devotee describes the taste of salted earthworms as like jerky; they are said to be 72 percent protein and less than 1 percent fat.

The Chinese discovered this cheap, nutritious meat long ago. In China earthworm broth is said to be a good treatment for fever, but it probably would not be a bad first course for any meal, if one is sick or not.

Earthworm Broth (*Tio in tin tan*) / China
Slit open some earthworms and wash them well to remove particles of soil. Simmer them in water until the broth is reduced by half.

Unmentionable Cuisine, 1979

Preparation of Human Pie
JENI COUZYN 1942–

1   Always use fresh humans.
It is best to buy them alive
and keep them in a bucket
in a cool place until use.
They should move around a good deal
emitting various squeaks and growls.
This shows that they're in good condition
and likely to be tender.

2   When you come to use them
there may be a few dead
at the bottom of the bucket.
These should be discarded.
If any of those alive are rotting
throw them away.
Sort away those excessively large or small.
It is attention to fine details like these
that gives your home cooking
a professional quality.

3   Using a small sharp knife
remove heads hands and feet.
These contain only bone and waste matter.
Slit the garments carefully
and peel them clean.

About half will have genitals.
These consist of a small projection
at the base of the trunk
which will come away quite easily.
Prepared separately
they can be used in the sauce if desired.

4 Some recipes recommend
the removal of innards.
Although it can be done
with a pointed knife slitting the back
I would not advise it.
It is time consuming and quite unnecessary
from a health point of view.
In fact it is innards
that gives human pie its sophisticated
slightly exotic flavour. Furthermore
it's an extremely delicate operation
and if badly done
the humans will start breaking up
which quite spoils the look of the dish.

5 Rinse in a sieve and lay out on a board.
You are now ready to prepare the rolls.
Sprinkle with hemlock and thyme.
Lay the humans in a row along the board
necks towards you.
Fold the arms across the chest.

6 Using the third finger of your right hand
tuck in the neck and begin to roll
between your thumb and forefinger
pressing down gently to snap the bones.
As you gain practice
you will find that four or five breakages
are quite enough to make
a perfect roll.
Secure the legs in position with a sharp squeeze.

7 Fry briskly in their own fat until delicate brown.
If using the brown kind test for crispness with a fork.

8 Sprinkle with raw fruit and tip into casserole carefully, so as not to damage them.

Life by Drowning, 1985

Cannibals

WILLIAM BUEHLER SEABROOK 1886–1945

Seabrook began his writing career as a reporter on the Augusta, Georgia, Chronicle *and became City Editor at 22. He was encouraged to write by H. L. Mencken, and began his travelling life with a hobo tour of Europe. His trips to Arabia, Kurdistan, Turkestan, Africa, and Haiti were all described in his books: his sensational accounts of devil worship, voodoo and cannibalism and his book* An Analysis of Magic and Witchcraft *prompted one writer to accuse him of 'deliberate reversion to primitive paganism'. After his suicide in 1945 one obituary remarked that his 'fame rests on bizarre tales of the supernatural'.*
This is an edited account of the highlight of the author's stay with the Gueré tribe on the French Ivory Coast in the early 1930s.

It will be better, I think, to have this clear at the start before launching on the general tale of my adventure in the Gueré country. One of my chief purposes in going to Africa was to see and meet and live with cannibals . . .

I present the issue here fairly at the outset, because in what will follow somewhat later, I honestly do not want to shock or distress any one. I made up my mind before leaving New York that when it came to the subject of cannibals I would either write nothing whatever about them, or I would know what I was writing about. It is really too dull to sit through a long book or film about cannibals only to learn at the end that the guests after all did not remain for dinner . . .

For the fact is that I have brought back, among other things, a number of recipes of which I can speak with substantial authority . . .

When I said to them, 'How is it that you are cannibal while neighboring tribes are not?' their first useless answer, of course, was, 'The Gueré have always been cannibal.' It was like asking a Georgia farmer why he ate cornbread or a New Englander why he ate white .

But presently in the course of general talk an old counselor hushed the others and said: 'We have attacked and fought a certain village. We have slain some men there with our spears. We have marched a long way, we have fought well, we are hungry, and we want to feast. Perhaps there are sheep and goats and chickens in the conquered village, perhaps not, but why slay them when there is already slain provision of good meat? Is it reasonable to let it spoil and wastefully kill other which is no better? You have asked *us* many questions and we have answered.'

They waited now to hear what I had to say. Decidedly this black old Socrates had passed the buck. As he had framed his query, no criminal element of murder was involved. True, they had killed some human neighbors in a fight. But who was I, or any white man, in the name of Julius Caesar, Charlemagne, Saint Louis and the Crusaders of the Lord, U. S. Grant and Sherman, Ludendorff and Papa Joffre and Sergeant York, to tell black Socrates that it was all right for us to do it with machine guns, poison gas, and bombs, but naughty-naughty and uncivilized for him to do it with a spear?

'The reason, my dear unenlightened friends, why you shouldn't eat your neighbors is because you shouldn't have killed them in the first place!'

If one isn't a Methodist missionary, one must preserve a shred of intellectual decency at least, even in a discussion with cannibals. Decidedly, that answer was out. And being out, just what did it leave for our further philosophic and moral consideration? It left the flesh of the mammal *homo sapiens*, not criminally murdered, no longer *sapiens* since he was dead, freshly, cleanly killed, and according to their statement, yet to be verified, excellent meat. To my asking why they ate it, they had turned the question back against me, saying, 'Why shouldn't we eat it?' . . .

I asked what parts of the meat were considered the best. He replied that for solid meat the loin cuts, the ribs, and rump steak were the best. The liver, heart, and brains were tidbits, but tasted identically the same as those of all other animals. Fire Helmet interpolated that as a matter of personal choice, the palm of the hand was the most tender and delicious morsel of all.

There was one point in these recipes which seemed to me somewhat strange, to wit, the unusual length of time they took for cooking. They were all in agreement on the explanation. They said that the meat was the best you could imagine when sufficiently well cooked, but that it was tougher than most and therefore must be cooked longer and more slowly.

'But what about young tender meat?' I asked. 'For instance, a fine plump young girl roasted with bananas. That ought to be tender as any lamb.'

They looked at me in some surprise. They all began talking at once, some of them laughing and others indignant. 'But we don't eat children and babies,' they said. 'We are Guéré warriors. Such things have certainly happened, but if you want to know about things like that, go find some woman who was starving, or go and ask some Panther Man in the French prisons.' One of the old counselors looked at me gravely and added a simple saying, full of self-respect, and which might stand, I thought, as a motto for their tribe: 'We are men, and eaters of men.'

These Guéré, then, as nearly as I could understand, were in the traditional anthropological and ethnological sense true cannibals . . .

The occasion was one which would probably never be repeated, so that I felt in duty bound to make the most of it. In addition, therefore, to a portion of stew with rice, sure to be so highly seasoned with red pepper that fine shades of flavor might be lost to an unaccustomed palate, I had requested and been given a sizable rump steak, also a small loin roast to cook or have cooked in whatever manner I pleased.

It was the meat of a freshly killed man, who seemed to be about thirty years old – and who had not been murdered . . .

No matter what phrases I choose, whether I write well or awkwardly, the authenticity will take care of itself, for I propose to set down details as full, objective, and complete as if I were recounting a first experience with reindeer meat, shark meat, or any other unfamiliar meat experimented with for the first time . . .

The raw meat, in appearance, was firm, slightly coarse-textured rather than smooth. In raw texture, both to the eye and to the touch, it resembled good beef. In color, however, it was slightly less red than beef. But it was reddish. It was not pinkish or grayish like mutton or pork. Through the red lean ran fine whitish fibers, interlacing, seeming to be stringy rather than fatty, suggesting that it might be tough. The solid fat was faintly yellow, as the fat of beef and mutton is. This yellow tinge was very faint, but it was not clear white as pork fat is.

In smell it had what I can only describe as the familiar, characteristic smell of any good fresh meat of the larger domestic animals . . .

I had determined to prepare the steak and roast in the simplest manner, as nearly as possible as we prepare meat at home. The small roast was spitted, since an oven was out of the question, and after it had been cooking for a while I set about grilling the steak. I tried to do it exactly as we do at home. It took longer, but that may have been partly because of the difference between gas flame and wood coals.

When the roast began to brown and the steak to turn blackish on the outside, I cut into them to have a look at the partially cooked interior. It had turned quite definitely paler than beef would turn. It was turning grayish as veal or lamb would, rather than dark reddish as a beef-steak turns. The fat was sizzling, becoming tender and yellower. Beyond what I have told, there was nothing special or unusual. It was nearly done and it looked and smelled good to eat.

I sat down to it with my bottle of wine, a bowl of rice, salt and pepper at hand. I had thought about this and planned it for a long time, and now I was going to do it. I was going to do it, furthermore – I had promised and told myself – with a completely casual, open, and objective mind. But I was soon to discover that I had bluffed and deceived myself a little in pretending so detached an attitude. It was with, or rather after, the first mouthful, that I discovered there had been unconscious bravado in me, a small bluff-hidden unconscious dread. For my first despicable reaction – so strong that it took complete precedence over any satisfaction or any fine points of gastronomic shading – was simply a feeling of thankful and immense relief. At any rate, it was perfectly good to eat! At any rate, it had no weird, startling, or unholy special flavor. It was good to eat, and despite all the intelligent, academic detachment with which I had thought I was approaching the experience, my poor little, cowardly and prejudiced subconscious real self sighed with relief and patted itself on the back.

I took a good big swallow of wine, a helping of rice, and thoughtfully ate half the steak. And as I ate, I knew with increasing conviction and certainty what it was like. It was like good, fully developed veal, not young, but not yet beef. It was very definitely like that, and it was not like any other meat I had ever tasted. It was so nearly like good, fully developed veal that I think no person with a palate of ordinary, normal sensitiveness could distinguish it from veal. It was a mild, good meat with no other sharply defined or highly characteristic taste such as for instance goat, high game, and pork have. The steak was slightly tougher than prime veal, a little stringy, but not too tough or stringy to be agreeably edible. The roast, from which I cut and ate a central slice, was tender, and in color, texture, smell as well as taste, strengthened my certainty that of all the meats we habitually know, veal is the one meat to which this meat is accurately comparable. As for any other special taste or odor of a sort which would be surprising and make a person who had tasted it not knowing exclaim, 'What is this?' it had absolutely none. And as for the 'long pig' legend, repeated in a thousand stories and recopied in a hundred books, it was totally, completely false. It gives me great comfort here to be able to write thus categorically. A small helping of the stew might likewise have been veal stew, but the overabundance of red pepper was such that it conveyed no fine shading to a white palate; so I was glad I had tried it first in the simpler ways.

If I had begun, despite my objective intentions, with a certain unconscious trepidation, I finished well enough, able after the first sensation of relief had passed to consider the meat as meat, and to be absolutely sure of the correctness of my impressions. And I felt a great satisfaction in having learned the empiric truth on a subject concerning which far too many books and pieces have been written and rewritten, filled with almost nothing but speculation, hearsay, legend, and hot air. A sense of pride also in having carried something through to its finish. And a long-standing personal curiosity satisfied at last.

Jungle Ways, 1931

Index of Authors

General Index

❦

Abbas, Shah 310
Aga Khan 474
alligator steaks 521–2
America 30, 68–9, 76–7, 92–7, 208–9,
    235–8, 299–302, 320–1, 373, 380–1,
    501–2, 506, 507–8, 509; Native
    Americans 513–14; water melons
    413–14
annelids (earthworms) 533–4
aphrodisiacs 138–9
Apollona 349–50
apples 42–3; apple butter 30; custard
    apple 44
Arab hospitality 291–2
artichokes 46, 47
asparagus 45–6
Australia 71–2, 327–9; Aborigines 70–1
avocado pear 160–2

Babylonian toothache remedy 167–8
bacon 183; white 76–7
Balmoral (Scotland) 123–4
Balzac, Honoré de 336
banquets 273–4; Chinese 281–4; in
    Ethiopia 322–3; Lord Mayor's 318–19
bear meat 512–13
bee legs 526
beetles 533
Berners, Lord 427
Bimini 527–9
birds: barnacles 505; crows 423; fig-
    peckers 278–9; ortolans 152–3; pie
    disaster 315–16; raized pie 503; rooks
    443, 445; sparrows 446–7; starlings
    447; wheatears 152–3; see also
    navettes
biscuits 83–4; ship's 365–6; see also
    navettes
black pudding 52–3
Boston, USA 419–20
bread 184, 454–8; Cossack 110–11
breakfast 13–14, 20, 81–3, 89, 275–6,
    434
Brighton Pavilion (England) 470–1
Bristol (England) 509

Britons 66
broth 250; Portugal 461–2
buffalo 513; milk 104
bunni 377–8
butter: apple butter 30; melted 88–9;
    substitutes for 444; western-style 250–1

cake 197, 443; fruit cakes 499–500;
    Scottish 76; 'triumph of gluttony'
    338–40; see also weddings
Calcutta 321–2
California (USA) 142, 313
Calvary 168–9
Cambridge (England), dinner parties
    147–9
cannibalism 506–7, 534–40
Canton (China) 302–3, 343–4, 529–31
Carême, chef 216, 224–6
carlings 447
Castiles (Spain) 104
caterpillars 525–6
catsup 395–6
Central Asia 304–6
cheese 51; Chester 379–80
chicken 230, 304–6, 358–9
chickpea 383
childhood 1–23
chili 527–9
China 151–2, 181–3, 281–4, 515–17,
    533, 534; markets 409–10; street
    vendors 412–13
Chinese food and cooks 67, 75, 219–20
Chinese New Year 483–5
Chong Sung, cook 210, 219–20
Christmas 5–6, 488–503
Chungking (China) 529
cinnamon rolls 57–9
Compiègne (France) 106–7
convents see nuns
cookery books 189–90
cookies see biscuits; navettes
cooks 207–65, 366–7; see also Carême;
    Chong Sung; Soyer, Alexis; Ude, Louis
    Eustache; Vatel

545